Muhammad Messenger of Allah

Ash-Shifa of Qadi 'Iyad

Qadi 'Iyad ibn Musa al-Yahsubi

Translated by Aisha Abdurrahman Bewley

Madinah Press

First edition 1991, Madinah Press, Granada
Revised edition 2011
Reprinted 2018
© Aisha Bewley

Published by: Diwan Press Ltd.
                         Norwich
                         UK
Website: www.diwanpress.com
E-mail: info@diwanpress.com

By: Qadi 'Iyad ibn Musa al-Yahsubi
Translated by: Aisha Abdarrahman Bewley
Edited by: Abdalhaqq Bewley and Idris Mears
Typeset by: Abdussabur Kirke
Cover by: Abdussabur Kirke & Abdassamad Clarke

A catalogue record of this book is available from the British Library.

ISBN13:   978-1-908892-26-3 (Paperback)
                         978-1-908892-27-0 (Hardback)
                         978-1-908892-28-7 (ePub)
                         978-1-908892-29-4 (Kindle)

Printed by: Mega Basim

IN THE NAME OF ALLAH, THE MERCIFUL, THE COMPASSIONATE

AUTHOR'S PREFACE

O Allah, bless Muhammad and his family and grant them peace.

Thus speaks the *faqih* and *qadi*, Imam and Hafiz, Abu'l-Fadl 'Iyad ibn Musa ibn 'Iyad al-Yahsubi, may Allah have mercy on him:

Praise be to Allah who is unique in possessing His most splendid Name and alone possesses invincible might. There is no final end falling short of Him and no target to aim at beyond Him. He is the Outwardly Manifest without need for the use of imagination and without illusion, and the Inwardly Hidden, absolutely pure without that bringing about non-existence. He encompasses everything by His mercy and knowledge. He pours out universal blessings on His Friends. He sent a Messenger from among themselves to both Arabs and non-Arabs, who was the most noble of them, the purest of them in nature and upbringing, the greatest of them in intelligence and forbearance, the most abundant in knowledge and understanding, the strongest in certainty and resolution, the one with the greatest compassion and mercy for them.

Allah purified him both in spirit and body and kept him free from all faults and blemishes and bestowed wisdom and judgement on him. By means of him Allah opened eyes that were blind, hearts that were covered and ears that were deaf, and He made people believe in Him. Those to whom Allah had allotted a portion of the booty of happiness honoured and helped him. Those for whom Allah had written wretchedness rejected him and turned away from His signs. **"Whoever is blind in this world is blind in the Next World."** (17:73) May Allah bless him with a blessing that grows and flourishes, and his Family and Companions, and grant them peace.

May Allah illuminate my heart and your heart with the lights of certainty! May He show you and me the kindness which He bestows on His Friends, those who fear Him, those whom He has honoured with the hospitality of His absolute purity and whom He has alienated from other creatures through intimacy with Him. He has singled them out for gnosis of Him and for the vision of some of the marvels of His *Malakut* and the traces of His power and this fills their hearts with delight and leads their intellects into utter confusion, lost in His immensity. They make Him their sole concern and witness only Him in this world and the Next. They are blessed by beholding His beauty and majesty, and they go backwards and forwards between the traces of His power and the wonders of His immensity. They glory in their exclusive devotion to Him and their reliance on Him. They are dedicated to the application of His words, **"Say, 'Allah,' and then leave them playing in their plunging."** (6:91)

You have repeatedly asked me to write something which gathers together all that is necessary to acquaint the reader with the true stature of the Prophet, peace and blessings be upon him, with the esteem and respect which is due to him, and with the verdict regarding anyone who does not fulfill what his stature demands or who attempts to denigrate his supreme status – even by as much as a nail-paring. I have been asked to compile what our forebears and Imams have said on this subject and I will amplify it with *ayats* from the Qur'an and other examples.

Know, may Allah ennoble you! that you have burdened me with a very difficult task. You have confronted me with a momentous undertaking which fills my heart with trepidation.

Writing about this calls for evaluation of the primary sources, examination of secondary sources and investigation of the depths and details of the science of what is necessary for the Prophet, what should be attributed to him, and what is forbidden or permissible in respect of him; and deep knowledge of messengership and prophethood and of the love, intimate friendship and the special qualities of this sublime rank.

Here we find vast desert wastes in which even the sand-grouse becomes bewildered and which cannot be traversed, and unknown places in which dreams go astray if they are not guided by a waymark of knowledge and a clear eye, and slippery slopes where feet falter if they do not rely on success and support from Allah alone. However, I have great hopes of gaining reward and repayment for both me and you in the matter of answering this question by making known the great value and sublime character of the Prophet and clarifying his special qualities. No other creature has ever possessed all these qualities. I will mention the duty that Allah gave him which is the highest of duties, **"So that those who have been given the Book would know for certain and those who believe would be increased in their belief."** (74:31)

Allah has made it an obligation on those who have been given the Book to make it clear to people and not to conceal it, as in the hadith related to me by Abu'l-Walid Hisham ibn Ahmad, the *faqih*, when I studied with him. He said: We were told by al-Husayn ibn Muhammad from Abu 'Umar an-Numayri from Abu Muhammad ibn 'Abdu'l-Mu'min from Abu Bakr Muhammad ibn Bakr from Sulayman ibn al-Ash'ath from Musa ibn Isma'il from Hammad from 'Ali ibn al-Hakam from 'Ata' that Abu Hurayra, may Allah be pleased with him, said, "The Messenger of Allah, may Allah bless him and grant him peace, said, 'Anyone who is asked about knowledge and conceals it, Allah will bridle him with a bridle of fire on the Day of Rising.' "

For this reason I have hastened to find some clear anecdotes with the object of achieving my goal and fulfilling the prescribed duty. I seized upon them quickly because in his life a man's body and mind are occupied with the trials and tribulations of affliction by which he is tested and which very nearly distract him from both obligatory and superogatory actions and cause him, after having the best of forms, to revert to the lowest of the low.

If Allah desires the best for man, He makes him totally concerned with what will be praised tomorrow, in the Next World, and not censured. On that day there will be only the radiance of Bliss or the punishment of *Jahim*. Therefore a man must mind his own business, look to the salvation of his own soul, seek to increase the number of his right actions and acquire useful knowledge for his own and other people's benefit.

Allah is the One who mends our broken hearts, forgives the immensity of our wrong actions, lets us make all our preparations for our return to Him, gives us many reasons for doing things that will save us and bring us near to Him and bestows His favour and mercy on us.

So having made the intention to proceed with the task, I planned out the chapters and organised the material and set about putting it together. I have called it *Ash-Shifa' bi-ta'rif huquq Mustafa*. ("Healing by the Recognition of the Rights of the Chosen One")

CONTENTS

PART ONE

Allah's great estimation of the worth of His Prophet expressed in both word and action

CHAPTER TWO: ALLAH'S PERFECTING HIS GOOD QUALITIES
OF CHARACTER AND CONSTITUTION, AND
GIVING HIM ALL THE VIRTUES OF THE *DEEN*
AND THIS WORLD 31

PART TWO

Concerning the rights which people owe the Prophet, peace be upon him

PART THREE

On what is necessary for the Prophet and what is impossible for him, what is permitted for him and what is forbidden for him and what is valid in those human matters which can be ascribed to him

This part is the secret of the book and the core of its fruit. What comes before it lays the foundation and provides the proofs for the clear anecdotes we will relate in it. It governs what follows it and accomplishes the goal of this book. When its promise is put to the test and its duty fulfilled, the breast of the accursed enemy will be constricted and the heart of the believer will shine with certainty and its lights will fill his breast. The man of intellect will then value the Prophet as he should be valued.

CHAPTER TWO: THE STATES OF THE PROPHET IN RESPECT OF THIS WORLD AND WHAT NON-ESSENTIAL HUMAN QUALITIES HE COULD HAVE   345

PART FOUR

The Judgements concerning those who think the Prophet imperfect or curse him, may Allah bless him and grant him peace

Thus the book ends: a bright light on the brow of belief, a priceless pearl in the crown of clarification, removing every confusion and clarifying every conjecture, a healing for the breasts of the believers. It brings the truth out into the open and confronts the ignorant with it.

I seek help with Allah - there is no god but Him.

APPENDICES

PART ONE

**Allah's great estimation
of the worth of His Prophet
expressed in both
word and action**

Introduction

It cannot be hidden from anyone who applies himself to the least study or who has been given the smallest gleam of understanding that Allah greatly esteems our Prophet, may Allah bless him and grant him peace, and has endowed him with virtues, excellent qualities and fine traits too numerous to be counted. Doing any kind of justice to his immense worth would wear out both tongues and pens.

Allah's high estimation of His Messenger can be partly seen from what is clearly stated in His Book about his exalted position. He has praised him in it for his character and his conduct. He has encouraged the slaves of Allah to hold fast to him and obey what he imposed on them. Allah is the One who bestowed honour and preference on him and then praised him and rewarded him for it with the fullest reward. Allah is overwhelmingly bountiful in the beginning and in the return, and to Him belongs all praise in this world and the Next.

Further instances of Allah's high estimation of him can be seen in His presenting him before the eyes of His creatures in the most complete form of perfection and sublimity, and His distinguishing him with beautiful qualities, praiseworthy characteristics, noble opinions and numerous virtues. He supported him with dazzling miracles, clear proofs and manifest signs of honour. These were witnessed by his contemporaries and Companions, and those who came after him knew about them with certain knowledge so that the knowledge of the reality of them has reached us and their light has overflowed on us. May Allah bless him and grant him peace abundantly.

Anas said that the *Buraq*[1] was brought bridled and saddled to the Prophet, may Allah bless him and grant him peace, on the evening of his Night Journey. It shied away from the Prophet, so Jibril said to it, "Do you do this to Muhammad? No-one more honoured by Allah than he has ever ridden you." Anas related that upon this the *Buraq* broke out into a sweat.[2]

1.The mount on which the Prophet made his Night Journey, from Makka to Jerusalem and then up through the seven heavens to the Divine Presence.
2. At-Tirmidhi.

Chapter One

ALLAH'S PRAISE OF HIM AND HIS GREAT ESTEEM FOR HIM

This chapter is an exposition of some of the clearest *ayats* in the Book of Allah which speak well of the Prophet, may Allah bless him and grant him peace, enumerate his good qualities and Allah's esteem of him, and praise him.

SECTION 1
Concerning praise of him and his numerous excellent qualities

Allah says: **"A Messenger has come to you from among yourselves."** (9:128)[1]

Allah informs the believers, or the Arabs, or the people of Makka, or all people (according to different commentaries on the meaning of these words) that He has sent to them from among themselves a Messenger whom they know, whose position they are sure of and whose truthfulness and trustworthiness they cannot but recognise. Therefore, since he is one of them, they should not suspect him of lying or of not giving them good counsel. There is no Arab tribe without descent from, or kinship with, the Messenger of Allah, may Allah bless him and grant him peace. This, according to Ibn 'Abbas and others, is the meaning of His words, **"except love for kin"** (42:23). He is from the noblest, highest and most excellent of them. How much further in the *ayat* can praise go?

Then Allah continues the *ayat* by attributing to him all kinds of praiseworthy qualities and greatly praises his eagerness to guide people to Islam, his deep concern for the intensity of what afflicts and harms them in this world and the Next, and his compassion and mercy for the believers.

One of the men of knowledge, Al-Husayn ibn al-Fadl, said, "He honoured him with two of His own names: the "compassionate" and the "merciful" (*ra'uf, rahim*)". The same point is made in another *ayat*: **"Allah was kind to the believers when He sent among them a Messenger from among themselves."** (3:164) Another *ayat* says: **"He is the One who sent a Messenger from you among the unlettered people."** (62:2) Allah also

---

1. As-Samarqandi said that some people read it (a *shadhdh* reading from 'A'isha and Fatima) as *min anfasikum* (from the most precious among you) rather than *min anfusikum* (from among yourselves) but the latter is the more common reading.

says: **"As We sent among you a Messenger from you."** (2:151)

It is related that 'Ali said that the words of Allah, **"from among yourselves"** mean "...by lineage, relationship by marriage and descent. There was no fornicator among his forefathers from the time of Adam. All of them were properly married."

Ibn al-Kalbi said, "I wrote down five hundred female ancestors of the Prophet, may Allah bless him and grant him peace, and I did not find any fornication among them nor any of the evils which were prevalent in the *Jahiliyya* period."

Ibn 'Abbas said that the words of Allah, **"when you turn about among those who prostrate,"** (26:219) mean "from Prophet to Prophet until I brought you out as a Prophet."[1]

Ja'far ibn Muhammad [as-Sadiq] said, "Allah knew that His creatures would not be capable of pure obedience to Him, so He told them this in order that they would realise that they would never be able to achieve absolute purity in serving Him. Between Himself and them He placed one of their own species, clothing him in His own attributes of compassion and mercy. He brought him out as a truthful ambassador to creation and made it such that when someone obeys him, they are obeying Allah, and when someone agrees with him, they are agreeing with Allah. Allah says: **'Whoever obeys the Messenger has obeyed Allah.'** (4:80)"

Allah says, **"We did not send you except as a mercy to all the worlds."** (21:107) Abu Bakr Muhammad ibn Tahir said in explanation of this *ayat*, "Allah imbued Muhammad with mercy, so that his very being was mercy and all his qualities and attributes were mercy to all creatures. Whoever is touched by any aspect of his mercy is saved in both worlds from every hateful thing and obtains everything he loves. Do you not see that Allah says, **'We did not send you except as a mercy to all the worlds.'**? His life was mercy and his death was mercy. As the Prophet himself said, 'My life is a blessing for you and my death is a blessing for you.'[2] The Prophet also said, 'When Allah desires mercy for a community, He takes its Prophet to Him before them and He makes him one who goes ahead to prepare the way for them.' "[3]

As-Samarqandi explains that the words **"a mercy to all the worlds"** mean for both the *jinn* and mankind. It is also said that it means for all creation. He is a mercy to the believers by guiding them, a mercy to the hypocrites by granting them security from being killed, and a mercy to the unbelievers by deferring their punishment. Ibn 'Abbas said, "He is a mercy to the believers and also to

---

1. As in Ibn Sa'd, al-Bazzar and Abu Nu'aym.
2. From al-Harith ibn Abi Usama in al-Bazzar with a sound *isnad*.
3. Muslim.

the unbelievers since they are saved from what befell the other communities who cried lies."

It is related that the Prophet said to Jibril, "Has any of this mercy touched you?" He replied, "Yes, I used to have fear about what would happen to me, but now I feel safe because of the way Allah praised me when He said, **'Securely placed with the Lord of the Throne, obeyed there, trustworthy..' "** (81:21)[1]

It is related that Ja'far as-Sadiq said that the words of Allah, **"'Peace be upon you!' from the Companions of the Right"** (56:91) mean "because of you, Muhammad." The cause of their peace is the high honour bestowed upon Muhammad, may Allah bless him and grant him peace.

Allah says, **"Allah is the Light of the heavens and the earth. The likeness of His Light is that of a niche in which there is a lamp, the lamp inside a glass, the glass like a brilliant star, lit from a blessed tree, an olive, neither of the east nor of the west, its oil all but giving off light even if no fire touches it. Light upon Light. Allah guides to His Light anyone He wills and Allah makes likenesses for mankind and Allah has knowledge of everything."** (24:35)

Ka'b al-Ahbar and Ibn Jubayr said, "By the second light He means Muhammad. Allah says, **'the likeness of his light...'** meaning the light of Muhammad."

Sahl ibn 'Abdullah at-Tustari said that it means that Allah is the Guide of the people of the heavens and the earth. Then Sahl said, "...like the light of Muhammad when it is lodged in the loins like a niche. By the lamp He means his heart. The glass is his breast. It is as if it were a brilliant star because of the belief and wisdom it contains, lit from a blessed tree, i.e. from the light of Ibrahim. He makes a comparison with the blessed tree and He says, **'Its oil all but giving off light,'** i.e. Muhammad's prophethood is almost evident to the people before he speaks, just like this oil."

A lot more is said about this *ayat*, and Allah knows best what it means.

Elsewhere in the Qur'an, Allah calls his Prophet a light and a light-giving lamp. He says, **"A light and a Clear Book have come to you from Allah."** (5:15) Allah also says, **"We sent you as a witness, a bringer of good news and a warner, one who calls to Allah with His permission and a light-giving lamp."** (33:46)

This is why He says: **"Did We not expand your breast for you?"** (94:1) To expand, *'sharaha'*, is to make wide, vast. By the word "breast", Allah here means the heart. Ibn 'Abbas said, "He expanded it with the light of Islam." Sahl at-Tustari said, "With the light of the message." Hasan al-Basri said, "He filled it with judgement and knowledge." It is also said that it means, "Did We not

---

1. This tradition is not found in the books of *hadith*.

purify your heart so that it does not allow in any whispering from Shaytan?"

The *sura* continues: **"And We lifted your burden from you, the burden that weighed down your back."** (94:2-3) It is said that this means his wrong actions, i.e. from the time before he was a Prophet. It is said that it means the burden of the days of the *Jahiliyya*. It is said that the meaning is the message which weighed down his back before he conveyed it, and this is the opinion of al-Mawardi and as-Sulami. It is also said that it means, "We protected you and if it had not been for that, wrong actions would have burdened your back," and this is what as-Samarqandi relates

The *sura* continues: **"Did We not raise high your renown?"** (94:4) Yahya ibn Adam said that this meant by being given prophethood. It is said that the meaning of these words is explained by the *hadith qudsi*, "When I am mentioned, you are mentioned with Me in the statement, 'There is no god but Allah and Muhammad is the Messenger of Allah.' " It is also said that the same is done by means of the *adhan*.

What is clear is that by these words Allah confirms the immensity of the favour He has bestowed on His Prophet, his noble station with Him and the honour in which He holds him. He expanded his breast to belief and guidance and made it wide enough to contain knowledge and bear wisdom. He removed from him the burdens of all the things of the *Jahiliyya* and made their pursuance hateful to him by giving victory to His *deen* over all other *deens*. He lightened for him the weighty responsibility of the message and prophethood so he could convey to people what was sent down to him. He re-emphasised the sublime position, majestic rank, high renown of His Prophet and joined his name to His own name.

Qatada said, "Allah exalted his fame in this world and the Next. There is no speaker, witness nor anyone doing the prayer who fails to say, 'There is no god but Allah and Muhammad is the Messenger of Allah.'"

Abu Sa'id al-Khudri related that the Prophet said, "Jibril, peace be upon him, came to me and said, 'My Lord and your Lord says, "Do you know how I have exalted your fame?" ' I said, 'Allah and His Messenger know best.' He said, 'When I am mentioned, you are mentioned with Me.'"[1]

Ibn 'Ata' quoted a *hadith qudsi* saying, "I completed belief with your being mentioned with Me." And another one which says, "I have made your mention part of My mention so whoever mentions Me, mentions you."

Ja'far ibn Muhammad as-Sadiq said, "No-one mentions you as the Messenger but that he mentions Me as the Lord."

Some of the people of knowledge, such as al-Mawardi, suggested that the Station of Intercession was being referred to by this.

---

1. In the *Sahih* of Ibn Hibban and the *Musnad* of Abu Ya'la.

The fact that mention of the Prophet is directly connected to mention of Allah also shows that obedience to the Prophet is connected to obedience to Allah and his name to Allah's name. Allah says, **"Obey Allah and His Messenger"** (2:32) and **"Believe in Allah and His Messenger."** (4:136) Allah joins them together using the conjunction *wa* which is the conjunction of partnership. It is not permitted to use this conjunction in connection with Allah in the case of anyone except the Prophet.

Hudhayfa said that the Prophet said, "None of you should say, 'What Allah wills and (*wa*) so-and-so wills.' Rather say, 'What Allah wills.' Then stop and say, 'So-and-so wills.'"[1]

Al-Khattabi said, "The Prophet has guided you to correct behaviour in putting the will of Allah before the will of others. He chose 'then' (*thumma*) which implies sequence and deference as opposed to 'and' (*wa*) which implies partnership."

Something similar is mentioned in another *hadith*. Someone[2] was speaking in the presence of the Prophet, may Allah bless him and grant him peace, and said, "Whoever obeys Allah and His Messenger has been rightly guided, and whoever rebels against them both (joining them together by using the dual form)..." The Prophet said to him, "What a bad speaker you are! Get up! [Or he said: Get out!]"[3]

Abu Sulayman said, "He disliked the two names being joined together in that way because it implies equality." Someone else thought that what he disliked was stopping at "whoever rebels against them". Abu Sulayman's statement is sounder since it is related in another sound recension of the *hadith* that he said, "Whoever rebels against them has erred," without stopping after "...whoever rebels against them."

The commentators and etymologists disagree regarding the words of Allah, **"Allah and His angels pray blessings on the Prophet."** (33:56) about whether the word "pray (masc. pl.)" refers to both Allah and the angels or not. Some of them allow it to refer to both while others forbid this because of the idea of partnership. They make the pronoun refer to the angels alone and understand the *ayat* as "Allah prays and His angels pray."

It is related that 'Umar, may Allah be pleased with him, said to the Prophet, "Part of your excellence with Allah is that He has made obedience to you obedience to Him. Allah says, **'Whoever obeys the Messenger has obeyed Allah'** (4:80) and **'If you love Allah, then follow me and Allah will love you.'**" (3:31) It is related that when this *ayat* was sent down, people said, "Muhammad wants us to take him as a mercy in the way the Christians did

1. From Abu Dawud; also related by an-Nasa'i and Ibn Abi Shayba.
2. Said to be Thabit ibn Qays.
3. Related by Abu Dawud, an-Nasa'i and Muslim.

with 'Isa, so Allah revealed, **'Say: Obey Allah, and the Messenger.'** " (3:32)[1] Allah connected obedience to Muhammad with obedience to Himself in spite of what the people said.

The commentators disagree about the meaning of the words of Allah in the *Fatiha*, **"Guide us on the Straight Path, the path of those You have blessed."** Abu'l-'Aliyya and al-Hasan al-Basri said, "The Straight Path is the Messenger of Allah, may Allah bless him and grant him peace, the best of the People of his House and his Companions." Al-Hasan al-Mawardi related from Abu'l-'Aliyya and al-Hasan al-Basri, "The Straight Path is the Messenger of Allah and the best of the people of his House and his Companions." Makki related something similar, "This refers to the Messenger of Allah, may Allah bless him and grant him peace, and his two Companions, Abu Bakr and 'Umar, may Allah be pleased with them both."

Abu'l-Layth as-Samarqandi related almost the same from Abu'l-'Aliyya regarding the words of Allah, **"The path of those whom You have blessed."** Al-Hasan al-Basri heard it and said, "It is true, by Allah, and it is good counsel." Al-Mawardi relates this in his commentary on the words **"The path of those whom You have blessed,"** from 'Abdu'r-Rahman ibn Zayd.

Abu 'Abdu'r-Rahman as-Sulami related that one of the commentators said that in the words of Allah, **"He has taken hold of the firmest handle,"** (2:256) "the firmest handle" is Muhammad, may Allah bless him and grant him peace. It is also said that it means Islam. It is said that it means the testimony of *tawhid* (that there is no god but Allah).

Sahl at-Tustari said that the words of Allah, **"If you were to count the blessings of Allah, you will not be able to number them,"** (14:34) refer particularly to the blessing of Muhammad, may Allah bless him and grant him peace.

Allah says, **"He who brings the truth and he who confirms it – such are the godfearing."** (39:33) Most of the commentators say that the one who brought the truth is Muhammad, may Allah bless him and grant him peace. One of them said, "He is the one who confirmed it." Sometimes this word is read as *sadaqa* (spoke the truth) and sometimes *saddaqa* (confirmed it) i.e. referring to the believers. It is said that Abu Bakr is meant and it is said that it refers to 'Ali, and other things are said as well.

Mujahid said that the words of Allah, **"Hearts are stilled by the remembrance of Allah,"** (13:28) refer to Muhammad, may Allah bless him and grant him peace, and his Companions.

---

1. This was related by Ibn al-Jawzi.

SECTION 2
Allah's describing him as a witness, and the praise and honour entailed by that

Allah says: **"O Prophet! We have sent you as a witness, and a bringer of good news and a warner, and a caller to Allah by His permission and a light-giving lamp."** (33:45) In this *ayat*, Allah endows his Prophet with all the ranks of nobility and every praiseworthy quality. He made him a witness over his community by the fact that he has conveyed the message to them. That is one of his special qualities. He is a bringer of good news to the people who obey him, a warner to the people who rebel against him. He calls to the oneness of Allah and to worship of Him, and he is a light-giving lamp by which people are guided to the Truth.

'Ata' ibn Yasar said, "I met 'Abdullah ibn 'Amr ibn al-'As and said, 'Describe the Messenger of Allah to me.' He replied, 'Certainly! By Allah, some of the characteristics by which he is described in the Qur'an can also be found in the Torah. It says: "O Prophet, We have sent you as a witness, a bringer of good news and a warner and a refuge for the unlettered. You are My slave and My Messenger. I have called you the one on whom people rely, one who is neither coarse nor vulgar and who neither shouts in the markets nor repays evil with evil, but rather pardons and forgives. Allah will not take him back to Himself until the crooked community has been straightened out by him and they say, 'There is no god but Allah.' Through him, blind eyes, deaf ears and covered hearts will be opened.'"" Something similar is reported from 'Abdullah ibn Salam and Ka'b al-Ahbar.

One path of transmission from Ibn Ishaq has, "Who does not shout in the markets nor use obscene language nor indecent words. I open him to every excellent quality and I give him every noble trait. I make tranquillity his garment, devotion his motto, fear of Allah his conscience, wisdom his understanding, truthfulness and loyalty his nature, pardon and correct behaviour his character, justice his behaviour, the truth his *shari'a*, guidance his leader, Islam his religion and Ahmad his name. I will guide him after misguidance and I will teach him after ignorance. I will elevate him after obscurity. I will make his name known after non-recognition. I will give him much after scarcity. I will enrich him after poverty. I will gather him after separation. I will bring together separated hearts and scattered passions and separate communities through him. I will make his community the best community that has come forth to people."

In another *hadith*, the Messenger of Allah told us about the way he was described in the Torah: "My slave, Ahmad, the Chosen, born in Makka, who will emigrate to Madina (or he said *Tayyiba*), his community will be those who praise Allah in every state."[1]

Allah says: **"Those who follow the Messenger, the Unlettered Prophet, whom they find written down with them in the Torah and the Gospel, commanding them to do right and forbidding them to do wrong, making good things lawful for them and bad things unlawful for them, releasing them from their heavy loads and the chains which were around them. Those who believe in him and honour him and help him, and follow the Light that has been sent down with him, they are the successful."** (7:157)

Allah says: **"It is a mercy from Allah that you were gentle with them. If you had been rough or hard of heart, they would have scattered from around you. So pardon them and ask forgiveness for them, and consult with them in the affair. Then when you have reached a firm decision, put your trust in Allah. Allah loves those who put their trust in Him."** (3:159)

As-Samarqandi said, "Allah is reminding them that He made His Messenger merciful to the believers, compassionate and lenient. If he had been harsh and severe in speech, they would have left him. However, Allah made him magnanimous, easy-going, cheerful, kind and gentle." Ad-Dahhak said something similar to this.

Allah says: **"Thus We made you a middlemost nation so that you would be witnesses against people and so that the Messenger would be a witness against you."** (2:143) Abu'l-Hasan al-Qabisi said, "In this *ayat* Allah makes clear the excellence of our Prophet and the excellence of his community."

Allah says in another *ayat*: **"In this the Messenger is a witness against you and you are witnesses against people."** (22:78) He also says: **"How will it be when We bring a witness from every community and bring you to witness against those?"** (4:41)

When Allah talks about a "middlemost nation", He means balanced and good. The meaning of the *ayat* is: As We guided you, so We chose you and preferred you by making you an excellent balanced community to allow you to be witnesses on behalf of the prophets against their communities. The Messenger will witness for you with truthfulness.

It is said that when Allah asks the Prophets, "Have you conveyed it?" they will reply, "Yes." Then their communities will say, **"Neither any bringer of good news nor any warner came to us."** (5:19) Then the community of Muhammad will testify on behalf of the Prophets, and the Prophet will vouch for them.[2] It is also said that this *ayat* means: You are an argument against anyone who opposes you, and the Messenger is an argument against you.

Allah says: **"Give good news to those who believe that they are on a sure**

---

1. Related by ad-Darimi from Ka'b; and by at-Tabarani and Abu Nu'aym from Ibn Mas'ud.
2. Found in al-Bukhari and elsewhere.

footing with their Lord." (10:2) Qatada, Hasan al-Basri and Zayd ibn Aslam said, "The 'sure footing' is Muhammad, may Allah bless him and grant him peace, who intercedes for them." Hasan al-Basri also said, "It is their being given their Prophet." Abu Sa'id al-Khudri said, "It is the intercession of Muhammad. He is the sure intercessor with their Lord." Sahl at-Tustari said, "It is the pre-ordained mercy which Allah placed in Muhammad."

Muhammad ibn 'Ali at-Tirmidhi said, "He is the Imam of the Truthful and the True, the Accepted Intercessor, the Answered Asker: Muhammad, may Allah bless him and grant him peace." As-Sulami related it from him.

SECTION 3
Concerning Allah's kindness and gentleness to him

Included in this are the words of Allah, **"Allah pardon you! Why did you excuse them until it was clear to you which of them were telling the truth and until you knew the liars?"** (9:43)

'Awn ibn 'Abdullah commented about this *ayat*, "Allah informs the Prophet how He has pardoned him before He tells him about his mistake."

As-Samarqandi related that one of the people of knowledge said that this means, "Allah has protected you, and you are sound of heart. Why did you then excuse them?" If the Prophet had first been addressed with the words, "Why did you excuse them?" his heart might have burst out of terror at those words. However, Allah informed him first of pardon by His mercy so that the Prophet's heart would remain calm and only then said to him, "Why did you excuse them before it was clear to you who was telling the truth in his excuse and who was lying?"

This shows his high station with Allah – which is not hidden from anyone with the least intelligence. It shows the honour in which He holds the Prophet and His kindness to him, and if the whole of it were to be known, the heart would burst.

Niftawayh said, "Some people think that the Prophet was rebuked by this *ayat*. Far from it! In fact he was preferred by it. When he excused them, Allah informed him that if he had not excused them, they would in any case have remained sitting because of their hypocrisy, so no objection can be made to his having excused them."

Any Muslim who strives with himself and holds fast to the *Shari'a* in his character must take on the *adab* of the Qur'an in his words, actions, pursuits and conversation. This is the basis of true knowledge and the arena of correct behaviour both as far as the *deen* and this world are concerned. This extraordinary kindness should be taken into consideration when asking from the Lord of all lords, the One who blesses all, the One who has no need of anything. The benefits this *ayat* contains should be taken to heart – the fact that Allah begins with honour before censure and takes pleasure in granting pardon before mentioning the error, if indeed there was any error.

Allah says: **"If We had not made you firm, you would have leaned towards them the tiniest bit."** (17:74) One of the *mutakallimun* said, "Allah chided the other Prophets after their slips. He chided our Prophet before anything occurred so that the chiding would be more effective and a greater indication of love. This shows the greatest possible concern."

Observe how Allah begins by talking of his firmness and security before He mentions what He wants to rebuke him for, fearing that His Prophet might fix on that. His innocence was maintained during the rebuke. The warning in no way jeopardises his security and honour.

The same applies to the words of Allah: **"We know that what they say distresses you. It is not that they are calling you a liar. The wrongdoers are just refuting Allah's Signs."** (6:33)

'Ali said that Abu Jahl told the Prophet, "We do not call you a liar. We say that what you have brought is a lie." So Allah revealed this *ayat*.

It is also related that the Prophet was distressed when his people denied him. So Jibril came to him and said, "Why are you distressed?" He replied, "My people have called me a liar." Jibril said, "They know that you are telling the truth." Then Allah sent down this *ayat*.

This *ayat* aims in a gentle way to console the Prophet and speak kindly to him, affirming that he is considered a truthful man among his people and that they are not denying him personally. They admit that he is truthful in both word and belief. Before he became a prophet, they called him 'the trustworthy.' His grief at being branded a liar was removed by this affirmation.

Then Allah censures his people by calling them deniers and evil-doers. He says: **"The wrongdoers are just refuting Allah's Signs."**

Allah removes any disgrace from His Prophet and then brands his people with pigheadedness when they epitomised wrongdoing by denying his signs. Denial can only come from someone who knows something and then denies it. As Allah says: **"And they refuted them wrongly and haughtily, in spite of their own certainty about them."** (27:14)

Then Allah consoles him and makes him rejoice by what He says about those before and the promise of His help to come when He continues by saying: **"Messengers before you were also denied but they were steadfast in the face of the denial and injury they suffered until Our help arrived."** (6:34)

Among the things that are mentioned about his special qualities and Allah's kindness to Muhammad is that Allah addressed all of the other prophets directly by their names, saying: "O Adam (2:23), O Nuh (11:48), O Ibrahim (37:104-105), O Musa (20:14), O Da'ud (38:26), O 'Isa (3:55), O Zakariyya (19:7) and O Yahya (19:12,)" whereas He only addressed him as "O Messenger (5:67), O Prophet (33:45), O Enwrapped (73:1), O Enshrouded (74:1)."

SECTION 4
Concerning Allah's swearing by his immense worth

Allah says: **"By your life, they are wandering about in their drunkenness."** (15:72) The commentators agree that this is an oath from Allah sworn on the length of Muhammad's life. It means, "By your continuing, O Muhammad." It is also said that it means, "By your life." And also, "By your living." This indicates the greatest respect and extreme honour.

Ibn 'Abbas said, "Allah did not create, originate or make any soul that He honoured more than Muhammad. I have not heard that Allah made an oath by the life of any other person." Abu'l-Jawza' said, "Allah did not make an oath by the life of anyone except Muhammad because he is the noblest of creation in His eyes."

Allah says: **"Yasin. By the Wise Qur'an."** (36:1-2) The commentators disagree about the meaning of *Yasin*, saying different things about it. Abu Muhammad Makki related that the Prophet said, "I have ten names with my Lord." He mentioned *Taha* and *Yasin* as two of these names. Abu 'Abdu'r-Rahman as-Sulami related that Ja'far as-Sadiq said that the meaning of *Yasin* is, "O master!" (*Ya Sayyid*) addressing the Prophet. Ibn 'Abbas said that *Yasin* means "O man" (*Ya Insan*), i.e. Muhammad. He also said that it is an oath and one of the names of Allah. Az-Zajjaj said that it means, "O Muhammad." It is said that it means, "O man" or "O human".

Muhammad ibn al-Hanafiyya said that *Yasin* means "O Muhammad." Ka'b said that *Yasin* is an oath by which Allah swore a thousand years before He created heaven and earth, meaning: "O Muhammad, you are one of the Messengers."

Then Allah continues, **"By the Wise Qur'an, you are truly one of the Messengers."** If it is confirmed that *Yasin* is one of the names of the Prophet, and it is a valid oath, then it certainly involves respect and the first oath is further strengthened by being joined to the second oath. Although it is in the vocative case, Allah invokes another oath after it to verify the Prophet's messengership and to attest to the truth of his guidance. Allah swears by the Prophet's name and His Book that he is one of the Messengers bearing His revelation to His slaves and that he is on a straight path by his belief, i.e. a path without any crookedness or deviation from the truth.

An-Naqqash said, "In His Book, Allah did not swear by any of His Prophets that they were Messengers except for Muhammad."

In the case of those who interpret it as meaning, "O master," the use of *Yasin* definitely shows Allah's high esteem for him. And indeed the Prophet himself said, "I am the master of the children of Adam, and it is no boast."[1]

Allah says: **"No, I swear by this land, and you are a lodger (or lawful) (*hill*) in this land."** (90:1-2) Makki said that the correct reading is "I do not swear"[2] by it when you are no longer in it after your departure. It is also said that the word "No" is extra, i.e. I swear by it when you, O Muhammad, are staying (*halal*) in it, or whatever you do in it is lawful (*hill*), according to two commentaries. They say that the word "land" refers to Makka.

Al-Wasiti said, "Allah means: 'We swear to you by this land which He honoured by the fact that you lived there and by the blessing of your grave when you are dead (i.e. Madina).' "

The first interpretation is sounder because the *sura* is a Makkan one. What follows confirms this when He says, **"a lodger in this land."** Ibn 'Ata' said something similar to this in his commentary on the words: **"By this secure land."** (95:2) He said, "Allah made it safe to be in because the Prophet was there. His existence brings security wherever he is."

Then Allah says: **"By the begetter and what he begot."** (90:3) Some say that Adam is meant and therefore it is a universal statement. Some say that it means Ibrahim and what he begot, thereby indicating Muhammad, may Allah bless him and grant him peace, in which case the *sura* swears by Muhammad in two places.

Allah says: **"Alif-Lam-Mim. That Book. No doubt in it."** (2:1-2) Ibn 'Abbas said that these letters are oaths by which Allah swears. He and other people have said various things about them.

Sahl at-Tustari said, "The *Alif* is Allah, the *Lam* is Jibril, and the *Mim* is Muhammad, may Allah bless him and grant him peace." As-Samarqandi also said this, but did not attribute it to Sahl. He said that it means that Allah sent down Jibril to Muhammad with this Book in which there is no doubt. According to the first interpretation, the import of the oath is that this Book is true without doubt and it involves the direct connection of the two names – a matter whose excellence has previously been stated.

Ibn 'Ata' said that when Allah says: **"Qaf, by the Glorious Qur'an,"** (50:1-2) He is swearing by the strength (*quwwa*) of the heart of His beloved Muhammad since it was able to bear the impact of His speech and witnessing. Doing that

---

1. Muslim and at-Tirmidhi from Abu Hurayra.
2. Reading "*ma*" as making the verb negative rather than simply as "No".

did not affect him because of his exalted state. It is also said that *Qaf* is one of the names of the Qur'an. It is said that it is one of the names of Allah. It is said that it is a mountain.

Ja'far ibn Muhammad said that the *ayat* ,**"By the star when it plunges,"** (53:1) refers to Muhammad. He said, "The star is the heart of Muhammad. When it plunges, it is expanded by lights." He said, "He is cut off from other-than-Allah."

Ibn 'Ata' said about the words of Allah, **"By the dawn and the ten nights,"** (89:1) that the dawn is Muhammad, may Allah bless him and grant him peace, because belief dawns from him.

SECTION 5
Concerning Allah's oath to confirm his place with Him

Allah says: **"By the brightness of the morning and the night when it is still, your Lord has not abandoned you nor does He hate you. The Last will be better for you than the First. Your Lord will soon give to you and you will be satisfied. Did He not find you orphaned and shelter you? Did He not find you wandering and guide you? Did He not find you impoverished and enrich you? So as for orphans, do not oppress them. And as for beggars, do not berate them. And as for the blessing of your Lord, speak out!"** (93:1-11) There is some disagreement about the reason for the revelation of this *sura*. Some say that it came down at a time when the Prophet had stopped staying up at night to pray on account of something which was afflicting him and a certain woman started saying things about this.[1] It is also said that the idolworshippers started talking during a period of lapse in the revelation and that this was why this *sura* was sent down.[2]

But in any case it is clear the this *sura* is an absolute warranty of the honour in which Allah holds His Prophet, His praise of him and His great respect for him, and it demonstrates this in six ways.

Firstly, by swearing by something to indicate his state, Allah says: **"By the brightness of the morning and the night when it is still,"** i.e. by the Lord of the morning. This is one of the highest forms of esteem.

Secondly by clarifying his station with Allah and his position of favour with Him when He says: **'Your Lord has not abandoned you nor does He hate you,'** i.e. He has not forsaken you and He does not hate you. It is said that it means: He has not neglected you after He chose you and He does not despise you.

---

1. Related from Jundub in Muslim and al-Bukhari. Al-Hakam says that the woman was the wife of Abu Lahab.
2. Indicated by a *hadith* in Muslim and at-Tirmidhi.

Thirdly by the use of the words: **"The Last will be better for you than the First."** Ibn Ishaq said, "It means that your end when you return to Allah will be better than the honour He has given you in this world." Sahl at-Tustari said that it means that the Intercession and the Praiseworthy Station which He has stored up for him is better for him than what He gave him in this world.

Fourthly when He says: **"Your Lord will soon give to you and you will be satisfied."** This *ayat* combines honour with happiness and blessings in both the worlds. Ibn Ishaq said, "He will satisfy him by relief in this world and reward in the Next World." It is said that He will give him the Basin (*Hawd*) and Intercession. It is related that one of the family of the Prophet said, "There is no *ayat* in the Qur'an which contains more hope than this one. The Messenger of Allah will not be satisfied if any of his community enter the Fire."[1]

Fifthly the blessings which He enumerated for him and the favours which He confirmed in the rest of the *sura* including his guidance, or guidance of people by him, depending on the commentary; the fact that he had no property and Allah enriched him by what He gave him, or by the contentment and wealth He placed in his heart; that he was an orphan and his uncle cared for him and he found shelter with him – it is also said about this that he found shelter with Allah and that the meaning of his being an orphan was that there was no-one like him, so he was given shelter with Allah. It is also said that these *ayats* mean, "Did We not find you and guide the misguided by you, enrich the poor by you and give the orphan shelter by you?" Allah is reminding him of these blessings. It is well-known that Allah did not neglect him when he was young, poor, an orphan and before he recognised Him. He did not abandon him nor hate him. How then could He do so after He had chosen him?

Sixthly by Allah's command to his Prophet to display the blessings He had given him and to be thankful for His honour to him by broadcasting it and praising it when He says, **"And as for the blessing of your Lord, speak out!"** This is addressed both specifically to him and generally to his community.

Allah says: **"By the star when it descends, your companion is not misguided or misled; nor does he speak from whim. It is nothing but Revelation revealed, taught him by one immensely strong, possessing power and splendour. He stood there stationary – there on the highest horizon. Then he drew near and hung suspended. He was two bows'-lengths away or even closer. Then He revealed to His slave what He revealed. His heart did not lie about what he saw. What! Do you dispute with him about what he saw? He saw him again another time by the Lote-tree of the Final Limit, beside which is the Garden of Refuge, when that which covered the Lote-tree covered it. His eye did not waver nor did he look away. He saw some of the Greatest Signs of his Lord."** (53:1-18)

---

1. Related by Abu Nu'aym (*mawquf*), and ad-Daylami in the *Musnad al-Firdaws* (*marfu'*).

The commentators disagree about the word "Star", saying various things. Some say it is a star as in the normal understanding of the word. Some say that it is the Qur'an. Ja'far ibn Muhammad said that it is Muhammad, and that it is the heart of Muhammad. People say similarly that in the verses: **"By heaven and the night-star! What will teach you what is the night-star! The piercing star!"** (86:1-3) the star is Muhammad.

These *ayats* abundantly demonstrate his excellence and honour. Allah affirms by oath the guidance of the Prophet, his lack of caprice and his truthfulness in what he recited. It is a revelation revealed which came to him from Allah by means of Jibril who is strong and powerful. Then Allah confirms his excellence by the story of the Night-Journey and his reaching the Lote-tree of the Boundary and the soundness of his sight in what he saw, telling us that what he saw was one of the greatest signs of his Lord. Allah also tells us of this incident at the beginning of the *sura* entitled the Night-Journey.

What Allah disclosed to him of His unseen dominion (*jabarut*) and what he saw of the wonders of the angelic worlds (*malakut*) cannot be expressed in words and the human intellect would not be able to withstand hearing even the least part of it. Allah indicates it by indirect allusion and reference which shows the esteem in which the Prophet is held. Allah says: **"Then He revealed to his slave what he revealed."** This sort of address is called insinuation and subtle indication by the scholars of criticism and rhetoric. According to them it is the most eloquent form of expression.

Allah says: **"He saw some of the Greatest Signs of his Lord"** Ordinary understanding is not able to grasp the details of what was revealed and becomes lost in the attempt to define what that great sign really was.

In this *ayat* Allah alludes to the Prophet's state of total purity and his protection from harm during this journey. He affirmed the purity of his heart, his tongue, and his eye: his heart by the words, **"His heart did not lie about what he saw.";** his tongue by the words, **"He does not speak from whim";** and his eye by the words, **"His eye did not waver nor did he look away."**

Allah says: **"No! I swear by the planets with their retrograde motion, swiftly moving, self-concealing, and by the night when it draws in, and by the dawn when it exhales, it truly is the speech of a noble Messenger, possessing great strength, securely placed with the Lord of the Throne, obeyed there, trustworthy. Your companion is not mad. He saw him on the clear horizon. Nor is he miserly with the Unseen. Nor is it the word of an accursed Shaytan."** (81:15-25)

The meaning of this is: I swear that it is the speech of a noble Messenger – noble with the One who sent him – having power to convey the revelation with which he was charged, secure and firm in his station and position with his Lord, obeyed in the heavens and trusted with the revelation.

'Ali ibn 'Isa ar-Rumani and others said that the noble Messenger is Muhammad, so all these attributes are his. Others said that it is Jibril, so these qualities are his. He truly saw him, means that he, Jibril, saw Muhammad. It is said that it means that he, Muhammad, saw his Lord. It is said that it means he saw Jibril in his true form. One variant says that the use of the word "miserly" means that the Prophet does not doubt the Unseen; another says that it means that he is not niggardly with his supplication to Allah and with his mentioning Allah's wisdom and knowledge. However, by general consensus, the whole passage refers to Muhammad, may Allah bless him and grant him peace.

Allah says: **"Nun. By the Pen and what they write down! By the blessing of your Lord, you are not mad. You will have a never-failing wage. Indeed you are truly vast in character."** (68:1-4)

Allah swears by this great oath that His Chosen Prophet was free of what the unbelievers ascribe to him in their disdain and rejection of him. He brings joy to him and increases him in hope when He addresses him gently, saying: **"By the blessing of your Lord, you are not mad."** This shows the greatest respect and is an example of the highest degree of *adab* in conversation.

Then He tells him that he will have eternal blessings and an immeasurable reward with Him – one that can be counted and will not make him in any way indebted – using the words: **"You will have an unfailing wage."** Then He praises him for the gifts that He has given him. He guides him to Himself and confirms that to emphasise his praiseworthiness. He says, **"Indeed you are truly vast in character."** It is said that these words refer to the Qur'an;[1] it is said that they refer to Islam;[2] and it is said that they simply mean noble nature. It is also said that the meaning of them is that the Prophet has no aspiration except Allah.

Al-Wasiti said, "He was praised for his complete acceptance of the blessings Allah had endowed him with and so Allah preferred him above others by forming him on that character."

Glory be to the Subtle, the Generous, the Praiseworthy who made doing good easy and guided people to it, and Who praises the one who does it and rewards him for it. Glory be to Him! How abundant His blessing is! How vast His favours are!

Then Allah continues the *sura* by consoling him for what they said about him by promising him that they will be punished. He threatens them by His words: **"So you will see and they will see which of you is mad. Your Lord knows best who is misguided from His Way and He knows best those who are guided."** (68:5-7)

---

1. When 'A'isha was asked to describe the character of the Prophet she said, "His character was the Qur'an."
2. By Ibn 'Abbas.

Then, after praising him, Allah censures his enemies, makes known their bad character and enumerates their faults. Then He follows this with His bounty and His helping the Prophet. He mentions some ten censured qualities with the words: **"So do not obey those who deny. They wish that you would conciliate them, then they too would be conciliating. But do not obey any vile swearer of oaths, any backbiter, slandermonger, impeder of good, evil aggressor, gross, coarse and furthermore, despicable, simply because he possesses wealth and sons. When Our Signs are recited to him, he says, 'Myths of the earlier peoples!'"** (68:8-15)

Allah concludes these words with the real threat that their misery will be complete and their ruin total by saying: **"We will brand him upon the snout."** (68:16) Allah's helping of him is more effective than his own self-help. Allah's confounding of his enemies is more effective than his own confounding of them.

SECTION 6
Concerning Allah's addressing the Prophet with compassion and generosity

Allah says: **"Ta Ha. We did not send down the Qur'an to you to make you miserable."** (20:1-2)

It is said that *Taha* is one of the names of the Prophet. It is said that it is a name of Allah. It is said that it means, "O man". And it is said that it refers to separate letters with different meanings. Al-Wasiti said that it means, "O Pure (*Tahir*), O Guide (*Hadi*)!"

It is also said that it is the imperative of the verb to tread and that the *ha* indicates the earth, i.e. stand on the earth with both feet and do not tire yourself by standing on one foot. That is why Allah says, **"We did not send down the Qur'an to you to make you miserable."** He sent down the *ayat* when the Prophet used to make himself stay awake and exhaust himself standing in prayer through the night. Ar-Rabi' ibn Anas said that when the Prophet prayed, he used to stand on one leg and then the other, and so Allah revealed to him, "*Taha*," i.e. "Stand with both feet on the earth, O Muhammad. We have not sent down the Qur'an upon you for you to be wretched." In any case it is clear that all this indicates honour and excellent behaviour.

Whether we say that *Taha* is one of his names or that it is an oath, it is still a demonstration of compassion and respect.

Allah says: **"Perhaps you may destroy yourself with grief, chasing after them, if they do not believe in these words,"** (18:6) i.e. kill yourself out of sorrow, anger or exasperation, which is similar to His words: **"Perhaps you will destroy yourself with grief because they will not become believers."** (26:3) which are followed by: **"If We willed We could send down a Sign to them from heaven, before which their heads would be bowed low in subjection."** (26:4)

In this same vein, Allah says: **"Openly proclaim what you have been ordered to and turn away from the idolaters. We are enough for you against the mockers, those who set up another god beside Allah. They will soon know! We know that your breast is constricted by what they say."** (15:94-97) And again: **"Messengers before you were mocked. I gave those who rejected a little more time and then I seized them. And how terrible was My retribution!"** (13:32)

Makki said, "Allah consoled him by speaking of this and made what he had to endure from the idolaters easy for him. He told him that if people persisted in this kind of behaviour, what befell those before them would happen to them as well."

Similar consolation is contained in the words: **"If they deny you, Messengers before you were denied,"** (35:4) and: **"Equally, no Messenger came to those before them without their saying, 'A magician or a madman!'"** (51:54)

Allah consoles him by telling him about previous communities, what they had said to their prophets and the affliction the prophets had had to endure from them. He comforts him by the fact that what he was having to endure at the hands of the unbelievers of Makka was a similar phenomenon. He was not the first to encounter that kind of treatment.

Then Allah set his mind at rest and excused him, saying: **"So turn away from them for you are not to blame,"** i.e. turn aside from them, you will not be held responsible for their not carrying out what you have conveyed and nor will you be blamed for conveying what you have been charged with.

Similarly Allah says: **"So wait steadfastly for the judgement of your Lord – you are certainly before Our eyes."** (52:48) This means be steadfast in the face of the harm they inflict on you. You are constantly in Our sight and under Our protection. Allah consoles him about this in many similar *ayats*.

SECTION 7

Concerning Allah's praise of him and his numerous excellent qualities

Allah says: **"When Allah made a covenant with the Prophets: 'Now that I have given you a share of the Book and Wisdom, when a messenger comes to you confirming what is with you, you must believe in him and help him.' He asked, 'Do you agree and undertake my charge on that condition?' They replied, 'We agree!' He said, 'Bear witness! I am with you as one of the witnesses.'"** (3:81)

Abu'l-Hasan al-Qabisi said about this, "Allah singled out Muhammad for an excellence which He did not give to anyone else. He clearly states this in this *ayat*."

The commentators say that Allah made this pact by means of revelation. He did not send any prophet without mentioning and describing Muhammad to him. The pact stipulated that if he met him, he must believe in him. It is said that the pact entailed them telling their people about him and that it stipulated that they must explain this and describe him to those coming after them. Allah's words: **"when a Messenger comes to you,"** is in fact addressed to the People of the Book contemporary with Muhammad.

'Ali ibn Abi Talib said, "Allah did not send any prophet from the time of Adam onwards without making a pact with him about Muhammad. If

Muhammad were sent while that prophet was still alive, then he would have to believe in him and help him. He had to make a contract to that effect against his own people." As-Suddi and Qatada said something similar about some other *ayats* which refer to the excellence of the Prophet in more ways than one.

Allah says: **"When We made a covenant with all the Prophets, with you, and with Nuh, and Ibrahim, Musa and 'Isa son of Maryam."** (33:7)

And again: **"We have revealed to you as We revealed to Nuh and the Prophets who came after him. And We revealed to Ibrahim and Isma'il and Ishaq and Ya'qub and the Tribes, and 'Isa and Ayyub and Yunus and Harun and Sulayman. And We gave Da'ud the Zabur. Messengers We have already told you about and Messengers We have not told you about. And Allah spoke directly to Musa. Messengers bringing good news and giving warning, so that people will have no argument against Allah after the coming of the Messengers. Allah is Almighty, All-Wise. But Allah bears witness to what He has sent down to you."** (4:163-166)

It is related that while 'Umar ibn al-Khattab was lamenting the death of the Prophet, he said, "My father and mother be your ransom, O Messenger of Allah! It has come down that part of your excellence with Allah is that He sent you as the last of the Prophets while mentioning you among the first of them: **"When We made a covenant with the Prophets, with you and with Nuh."** My mother and father be your ransom, O Messenger of Allah! It has come down that part of your excellence with Him is that the people of the Fire will wish they had obeyed you even while they are being punished in its depths. They will say, **"If only we had obeyed Allah and obeyed the Messenger!"** (33:66)

Qatada said that the Prophet said, "I was the first of the Prophets to be created and the last of them to be sent." That is why he was mentioned before Nuh and the others.

As-Samarqandi said, "Our Prophet is singled out by being mentioned before them even though he was the last of them to be sent. It means that Allah made a pact with them when He brought them out from the back of Adam like small ants."

Allah says: **"These Messengers: We favoured some of them over others. Allah spoke directly to some of them and raised up some of them in rank."** (2:252)

The commentators say that His words, **"He raised up some of them in rank,"** refer to Muhammad because he was sent to all mankind. He also made booty lawful for him and gave him special miracles. No other Prophet was given a virtue or mark of honour without Muhammad being given its equivalent. One said that part of his excellence is that in His Book, Allah addresses the other prophets by their names while He addresses him as "Prophet" and "Messenger".

As-Samarqandi related that al-Kalbi said about Allah's words, **"Of his party was also Ibrahim,"** (37:83) that the pronoun "his" refers to Muhammad, may Allah bless him and grant him peace, meaning that Ibrahim was from the party of Muhammad, from his *deen* and path. Al-Farra' allowed this interpretation and Makki related it from him. It is also said that Nuh is meant.[1]

SECTION 8
Concerning Allah instructing His creation to say the prayer on the Prophet, His protecting him and removing the punishment because of him

Allah says: **"Allah would never punish them while you are among them,"** (8:33) meaning as long as you are in Makka. When the Prophet left Makka and some of the believers were still there, Allah sent down, **"Allah would not punish them as long as they were asking for forgiveness."** This is like His words, **"Had those among them who reject been clearly distinguishable, We would have punished them with a painful punishment."** (48:25) He also says in the same *ayat*: **"If it had not been for certain men and women believers whom you did not know."**

When the believers emigrated, it was revealed, **"But what is there to stop Allah from punishing them now?"** (8:34) These *ayats* present one of the clearest demonstrations of the Prophet's exalted position. The punishment was averted from the people of Makka firstly because of his presence there, and then because of the presence of his Companions after him. When none of them were left in Makka, Allah punished the Makkans by giving the believers power and victory over them. He made their swords rule them and the Muslims inherited their land, homes and property.

The *ayat* is also interpreted another way by Abu Musa who said, "The Messenger of Allah said, 'Allah sent down on me two sureties for my community: the *ayat*, **"Allah would never punish them while you are among them,"** (8:33) and the *ayat*, **"Allah would not punish them as long as they were asking for forgiveness."'"**[2] (8:33) This harks back to the words of Allah, **"We only sent you as a mercy to the worlds."** (21:107)

The Prophet said, "I am a surety for my companions."[3] Some say that this means against innovations and others say it means against disagreement and disorder. One of the men of knowledge said, "The Messenger was the greatest surety while he was alive and he is present as long as his *sunna* is present. When

---

1. This latter statement is the opinion of most of the commentators.
2. From at-Tirmidhi alone (*gharib*).
3. Muslim from Abu Musa.

his *sunna* dies out, then expect affliction and disorder."

Allah says, "**Allah and His angels call down blessings on the Prophet. O believers, call down blessing on him and and ask for complete peace and safety for him.**" (33:56)

Allah makes the merit of His Prophet clear by first praying blessing on him Himself, and then by the prayer of the angels, and then by commanding His slaves to pray blessing and peace on him as well.

Abu Bakr ibn Furak related that one of the *'ulama* interpreted the words of the Prophet, "The coolness of my eye is in the prayer," as meaning Allah's prayer, that of the angels and that of his community in response to Allah's command until the Day of Rising. The prayer of the angels and men is supplication for him and that of Allah is mercy.

It is said that "they pray" means they invoke blessing (*baraka*). However, when the Prophet taught people the prayer on himself, he made a distinction between the word *salat* (prayer) and *baraka* (blessing). We will return to the meaning of the prayer on him later.

One of the commentators said that the interpretation of the letters *Kaf-Ha-Ya-'Ayn-Sad* (19:1) is that the *kaf* refers to Allah being enough (*kifaya*) for His Prophet from His words: **"Is not Allah enough for His slave?"** (39:36) The *ha* refers to His guidance (*hidaya*) as in His words: **"He will guide you to a straight path."** (48:2) The *ya* refers to His support (*tayyid*) as in His words: **"He will support you with His help."** (8:26) The *'ayn* refers to His protection (*'isma*) as in His words: **"Allah will protect you from the people."** (5:67) And the *sad* refers to His prayer (*salat*) on him as in His words: **"Allah and His angels pray blessing on the Prophet."** (33:56) Allah says, "**If you support one another against him, Allah is His *mawla*, and Jibril and the righteous believers.**" (66:4) *Mawla* here means protector. The right-acting believers are said to be the prophets. It is also said that it should be taken literally as meaning all the believers.

SECTION 9
Concerning the marks of honour given to the Prophet in *Sura al-Fath*

Allah says: "**Truly We have granted you a manifest victory, so that Allah may forgive you your earlier errors and any later ones and complete His blessing upon you, and guide you on a Straight Path, and so that Allah may help you with a mighty help (*fath*). It is He who sent down Serenity into the believers' hearts thus increasing their belief with more belief – the legions of the heavens and the earth belong to Allah. Allah is All-Knowing, All-Wise – so that He might admit the believing men and**

women into Gardens with rivers flowing under them, remaining in them timelessly, forever, and erase their bad actions from them. And in Allah's sight that is a mighty victory. And so that He might punish the men and women of the hypocrites and the men and women of the idolaters – those who think bad thoughts about Allah. They will suffer an evil turn of fate. Allah is angry with them, and has cursed them and prepared Hell for them. What an evil destination! The legions of the heavens and the earth belong to Allah. Allah is Almighty, All-Wise. We have sent you bearing witness, bringing good news and giving warning so that you may all believe in Allah and His Messenger and honour Him and respect Him and glorify Him morning and evening. Those who pledge you their allegiance pledge allegiance to Allah. Allah's hand is over their hands." (48:1-10)

These *ayats* are charged with aspects of the favour and praise of Allah for His Messenger and the nobility of his position and blessing with Allah, which cannot all be adequately described. Allah begins by telling him about the clear decision He has given him regarding his victory over his enemy and how Allah's word and *Shari'a* will become dominant, and how he has been forgiven and will not be taken to task for any action either past or future. One of the people of knowledge said that Allah meant forgiveness for what had occurred and what had not occurred. Makki said, "Allah made favour a cause for forgiveness. Everything comes from Him. There is no god but Him. Favour upon favour and bounty upon bounty."

Then Allah says: **"...and complete His blessing upon you..."** It is said that this is by abasing those who show arrogance towards him and it is said that He means the conquest of Makka and Ta'if. It is said that He means "by elevating your renown in this world, helping you and forgiving you." Allah is telling him that the completion of His blessing upon him lies in the abasement of his haughty enemies, opening up the most important and best beloved of towns, elevating his renown and guiding him to the Straight Path which leads to the Garden and Happiness. His victory is the mighty victory. Allah shows favour to the community of the believers by His gift of the *Sakina* (tranquillity of heart) and peace which He places in their hearts, by the good news He gives them regarding the overwhelming success and forgiveness their Lord has in store for them, by His covering over of their wrong actions, and by the destruction of His enemies in this world and the Next, their accursedness, their distance from His mercy and their evil destiny.

Then He says: **"We have sent you bearing witness, bringing good news and giving warning..."** Here Allah enumerates some of the Prophet's good qualities and special characteristics. He is a witness on his own behalf against his community that he has indeed conveyed the message to them. It is said that this also means that he will bear witness to Allah's oneness on their behalf. He gives good news to his community either about their reward or about forgiveness. He warns his enemies about their punishment and also warns about going astray in such a way that those who have been predestined with good from Allah will believe in Allah and himself.

Then they will **"honour him and respect him"**. It is also said that they will go to great lengths to esteem him. The most common and clear statement about this is that it refers to Muhammad, may Allah bless him and grant him peace.

Then He says: "...**and glorify Him morning and evening"**, referring to glorifying Allah.

Ibn 'Ata' said, "This *sura* contains various blessings for the Prophet – the "clear victory," which is a sign of being answered; "forgiveness," which is a sign of love; "completed" blessing, which is a sign of election; and "guidance," which is a sign of friendship (*wilaya*). Forgiveness consists in being freed from faults. The completed blessing is to attain to the degree of perfection. Guidance is a summons to witnessing."

Ja'far ibn Muhammad said, "Part of Allah's completed blessing to him is that He made him His beloved, swore by his life, abrogated other *shari'as* by him, raised him to the Highest Place, protected him in the *Mi'raj* so that his eye "did not swerve nor sweep aside", sent him to all mankind and made booty lawful for his community. He also made him an accepted intercessor and the master of the descendants of Adam. He coupled his name with His own name, and his pleasure with His pleasure. He made him one of the two pillars of *tawhid*."

Allah then continues: **'Those who pledge you their allegiance pledge allegiance to Allah,'** meaning in the Pledge of ar-Ridwan.[1] They pledge allegiance to Allah when they pledge allegiance to you.

"Allah's hand is over their hands" in the pledge. This metaphorically refers to the power of Allah, His reward, His favour or His contract, and strengthens the act of their pledging allegiance to him and exalts the one to whom the allegiance is given.

These words of Allah are similar to: **"You did not kill them, but Allah killed them. You did not throw when you threw, but Allah threw."** (8:17)[2]

However, whereas the former is metaphorical the latter is the literal truth since in the latter case the Killer and the Thrower was in reality Allah. He was the Creator of the Prophet's action, his throwing, his power to do it and his decision to do it. No man has the power to throw in such a way that every single man in the enemy ranks has his eyes filled with dust. The act of the angels killing was also real.

---

1. At al-Hudaybiya.
2. Referring to an incident during the Battle of Badr.

It is also said that this latter *ayat* is based on a certain kind of Arabic metaphor, meaning you did not kill them and you yourself did not throw at them when you threw stones and earth at their faces. It was Allah who threw terror into their hearts. This means that the benefit of the action comes from Allah's action. Allah is the Killer and Thrower in meaning, and you are it in name.

SECTION 10
How Allah, in His Mighty Book, demonstrates the honour in which He holds him and his position with Him and other things which Allah gave him

Some of this is contained in what Allah says about the Night Journey in the *sura* of the same name[1] and the *sura* entitled *The Star*[2] which refer directly to his incomparable station and nearness to Allah and the wonders he witnessed.

A further demonstration is the fact that he is protected from people. Allah says: **"Allah will protect you from people,"** (5:67) and: **"When those who reject were plotting against you to imprison you or kill you or expel you: they were plotting and Allah was plotting,"** (8:30) and: **"If you do not help him, Allah did help him."** (9:40)

Allah averted the harm of his enemies from him when they conferred secretly about him and plotted to kill him. He took their sight away when the Prophet went out past them and He caused them not to look for him in the cave. The signs connected with that, the *sakina* (tranquillity) which was sent down on him and the story of Suraqa ibn Malik are all mentioned by the people of *hadith* and *sira* in connection with the story of the cave and the *Hijra* of the Prophet to Madina.

Allah also says: **"We have given you *Kawthar*, so pray to your Lord and sacrifice. The one who hates you, he is the one who is cut off."** (108: 1-3)

Allah told him about what He had given him. *Kawthar* is said to refer to his Basin. It is also said that it is a river in the Garden, abundant blessing, intercession, his numerous miracles, his prophethood, or gnosis. Then Allah replied to his enemies for him and refuted what they had said by His words: **"The one who hates you, he is the one who is cut off,"** meaning your enemy

---

1. Qur'an 17:1 **"Glory be to Him who took His slave on a journey one night from the Sacred Mosque to the Furthest Mosque, whose surroundings We have blessed, in order to show him some of Our Signs. He is the All-Hearing, the All-Seeing."**
2. Quran 53:13-18 **"He saw him again another time by the Lote-tree of the Final Limit, beside which is the Garden of Refuge, when that which covered the Lote-tree covered it. His eye did not waver nor did he look away. He saw some of the Greatest Signs of his Lord."**

and the one who despises you. "Cut off" means poor and abased or left all alone or one with no good in him at all.

Allah says: **"Truly We have given you the Great Abundance (*Kawthar*). So pray to your Lord and sacrifice. It is the one who hates you who is cut off without an heir."** (108:1-3)

It is said that the Seven *Mathani* are the first long *suras* and that the Immense Qur'an refers to the Mother of the Qur'an. [*Umm al-Qur'an, Suratu'l-Fatiha*] It is also said that the Seven *Mathani* are themselves the Mother of the Qur'an and that the Immense Qur'an means the rest of the Qur'an. It is also said that the Seven *Mathani* refers to the commands and prohibitions, the good news and warnings, the metaphors and the enumerations of blessings in the Qur'an. In other words, "We have given you news of the Immense Qur'an." It is said that the Mother of the Qur'an is called "*mathani*" because it is said at least twice in every prayer. It is said that Allah set it aside for Muhammad and stored it up for him rather than other prophets. He called the Qur'an "*mathani*" because the stories are repeated in it. It is said that the "Seven *Mathani*" means, "We have honoured you with seven marks of honour: guidance, prophecy, mercy, intercession, friendship, esteem and tranquillity."

Allah says: **"We sent down the Remembrance to you that you might make things clear to mankind,"** (16:44) and **"We only sent you to all people as a bringer of good news and a warner,"** (34:28) and **"Say: O people! I am the Messenger of Allah to you all."** (7:158)

This is one of the special favours he was granted. Allah says: **"We only send a messenger with the language of his people to make things clear to them."** (14:4) Allah specifies their peoples, but He sent Muhammad, may Allah bless him and grant him peace, to all people. As he said of himself, "I was sent to all mankind."

Allah says: **"The Prophet is nearer to the believers than their selves; his wives are their mothers."** (33:6)

The commentators say that "nearer to the believers than their selves" means that they must do whatever he commands just as the slave must carry out what his master commands. It is said that it is better to follow his command than to follow one's own opinion. "His wives are their mothers" means that they enjoy the same respect as mothers. They cannot be married to anyone after him. This is a mark of honour to him and a special favour. It is also because they are his wives in the Garden. An unusual reading of the Qur'an includes, "He is a father to them," but it is no longer recited since it is at variance with the version of 'Uthman.[1]

---

1. This refers to the final standardisation of the Qur'an during the khalifate of 'Uthman ibn 'Affan.

Allah says: **"Allah has sent down the Book and Wisdom to you ,"** and **"Allah's favour to you is indeed immense."**(4:113) It is said that His "immense favour" refers to prophethood or to what he already had in Pre-eternity. Al-Wasiti said that it indicates his ability to bear the vision which Musa could not bear.

Chapter Two

ALLAH'S PERFECTING HIS GOOD QUALITIES OF CHARACTER AND CONSTITUTION, AND GIVING HIM ALL THE VIRTUES OF THE *DEEN* AND THIS WORLD

Introduction

Whoever loves the noble Prophet and is searching out the complete details of the inestimable treasure of his being should know that man's beautiful and perfect qualities can be placed in one of two categories:

1. Characteristics which are innate and a necessary part of the life of this world – such as natural form and things connected to the necessary acts of daily life.
2. Characteristics which are acquired as part of the *deen* – these are things for which one is praised and which bring one near to Allah.

These qualities can be further divided into two categories:

1. Qualities which are either purely innate or acquired.
2. Qualities which combine both elements.

Man has no choice in or ability to acquire innate qualities. These include things like perfection of physique, physical beauty, strength of intellect, soundness of understanding, eloquence of tongue, acuteness of the senses, strength of limb, balance, nobility of lineage, the might of one's people and the honour of one's land.

Also connected to this are the things that are the necessities of daily life, such as food, sleep, clothes, dwelling place, marriage, property and rank. These things, however, can be connected to the Next World if the intention in them is related to fear of Allah and teaching the body to follow the path of Allah, in spite of the fact that they are all defined as necessities and governed by the rules of the *Shari'a*.

As for the acquired things which pertain to the Next World, they include all virtues and the *adab* of the *Shari'a* – things such as practice of the *deen*, knowledge, forbearance, patience, thankfulness, justice, doing-without, humility, pardon, chastity, generosity, courage, modesty, manliness, silence, deliberation, gravity, mercy, good manners, comradeship and other similar qualities. They can be summed up as 'good character'.

Some of these qualities can be part of natural instinct and basic disposition in some people. Others do not have them and have to acquire them. However, some basic rudiments of them must exist in a person's natural disposition as, Allah willing, we will make clear.

Even when the face of Allah and the Next World is not what is intended by these worldly qualities, they are still considered good character and virtues according to the consensus held by men of sound intellect. However, there is disagreement as to the reason for people having these qualities.

SECTION 1
Preface

If someone has been blessed with even one or two of these qualities of perfection and nobility – whether of lineage, beauty, power, knowledge, forbearance, courage or generosity – he is considered noteworthy and people use him as an example. People's heart-felt esteem of these qualities makes people who have them honoured long after their bones have turned to dust.

So what then can be said of the inestimable worth of someone who possesses all of these qualities in such abundance that they cannot be counted or expressed in words? It would be impossible for him to have gained them either by graft or guile. Such a thing is only possible by the gift of Allah the Almighty. They include prophethood, bearing the message, close friendship with Allah, His love, being chosen, the Night Journey, vision of Him, nearness, proximity, revelation, intercession, mediation, all the virtues, high degree, the Praiseworthy Station, *Buraq*, the Ascension, being sent to all mankind, leading the prophets in prayer, the witnessing for him of the prophets and their communities, mastery over the descendants of Adam, his being the bearer of the Banner of Praise, bringing good news and warning, his place with the One with the Throne, obedience, bearing the trust, guidance, being a mercy for the worlds, Allah's being pleased with him so that he is allowed to ask of Him, *Kawthar*, being listened to, the perfection of blessing on him, pardon for past and future wrong actions, the expanding of his breast, the removing of his burden, the elevation of his renown, his being helped by a mighty victory, the sending down of the *Sakina*, support by the angels, his bringing the Book and Wisdom and the Seven *Mathani* and the Immense Qur'an, his community being purified, his calling to Allah, the prayer of Allah and the angels on him, his judging between people by what Allah showed him, his removing the chains and burden from them, Allah's swearing by his name, his supplication being answered, inanimate objects and animals speaking to him, the dead being brought to life for his sake, the deaf hearing, water gushing from between his fingers, his turning a little into a lot, the splitting of the moon, the sun going back, his changing of the essence of things,[1] his being helped by terror, his knowing the Unseen, the clouds shading him, the glorification of the pebbles, his removing pain, his protection from people and so on. And this is just some of what Allah gave him. There is much more. Knowledge of his qualities can only be contained by someone who is given it and only Allah can bestow it. There is no god but Him.

Add to all this the stations of honour, degrees of purity, ranks of happiness, excellence and increase which Allah has prepared for him in the domain of the Next World, which cannot be numbered, which intellects are unable to grasp and which confound the imagination.

SECTION 2
His physical attributes

There is absolutely no way to conceal the fact that the Prophet is the worthiest of all mankind, the greatest of them in position and most perfect of them in good qualities and virtue. I am setting out to detail his qualities of perfection in the best way I can, which has filled me with longing to call attention to some of his attributes, may Allah bless him and grant him peace.

Know, may Allah illuminate my heart and yours and increase my love and your love for this noble Prophet! – that if you were to look into all those qualities of perfection which cannot be acquired and which are part of one's constitution, you will find that the Prophet has every one of them – all of the various good qualities without there being any dispute about it among the transmitters of the traditions.

The beauty of his form and the perfect proportion of his limbs are related in numerous sound and famous traditions from 'Ali, Anas ibn Malik, Abu Hurayra, Al-Bara' ibn 'Azib, 'A'isha, Ibn Abi Hala, Abu Juhayfa, Jabir ibn Samura, Umm Ma'bad, Ibn 'Abbas, Mu'arrid ibn Mu'ayqib, Abu't-Tufayl, Al-'Ida' ibn Khalid, Khuraym ibn Fatik, Hakim ibn Hizam and others.

He had the most radiant colouring, deep black eyes which were wide-set and had a sort of red tint to them, long eyelashes, a bright complexion, an aquiline nose, and a gap between his front teeth. His face was round with a

---

1. For instance, the stick of 'Ukasha being turned into a sword in his hands.

wide brow and he had a thick beard which reached his chest. His chest and abdomen were of equal size. He was broad-chested with broad shoulders. He had large bones, large arms, thick palms and soles, long fingers, fair skin and fine hair from the chest to the navel. He was neither tall nor short, but between the two. In spite of that, no tall person who walked with the Prophet seemed taller than him. His hair was neither curly nor straight. When he laughed and his teeth showed, it was like a flash of lightning or they seemed as white as hailstones. When he spoke, it was like light issuing from between his teeth. He had a well-formed neck, neither broad nor fat. He had a compact body which was not fleshy.

Al-Bara' said, "I did not see anyone with a more beautiful lock of hair resting on a red robe than the Messenger of Allah."

Abu Hurayra said, "I have not seen anything more beautiful than the Messenger of Allah. It was as if the sun was shining in his face. When he laughed, it reflected from the wall."

Jabir ibn Samura was asked, "Was his face like a sword?" He replied, "No, it was like the sun and the moon. It was round."[1]

In her description, Umm Ma'bad said, "From afar, he was the most beautiful of people, and close up he was the most handsome."[2]

Ibn Abi Hala said, "His face shone like the full moon."

At the end of his description, 'Ali said, "Anyone who saw him suddenly was filled with awe of him. Those who kept his company loved him."

All who described him said they had not see anyone like him either before or since.

There are many famous *hadith* which describe him. We will not take the time here to give them all. We have restricted ourselves to some aspects of his description and given a summary of them which is enough to serve our purpose.

You will find, Allah willing, that we have concluded these sections with a *hadith* which combines all these things.

SECTION 3
His cleanliness

The complete cleanliness of his body, the sweetness of his smell and perspiration, and his freedom from uncleanliness and bodily defects comprise a special quality given to him by Allah which no-one else enjoys and these were

---

1. In al-Bukhari and Muslim and elsewhere.
2. Al-Bayhaqi.

made yet more complete by the cleanliness dictated by the *Shari'a* and the ten practices of natural behaviour (*fitra*).[1]

The Messenger of Allah said, "The *deen* is based on cleanliness."[2]

Anas said, "I have not smelled amber, musk or anything more fragrant than the smell of the Messenger of Allah, may Allah bless him and grant him peace."[3]

Jabir ibn Samura said that the Messenger of Allah touched his cheek. He said, "I felt a cool sensation and his hand was scented. It was as if he had taken it from a bag of perfume."[4]

Someone else said, "No matter whether he had put scent on his hand or not, if he shook a man's hand, the fragrance would remain for the whole day. If the Prophet placed his hand on the head of a child, that child could be recognised among the other children by the fragrance."

The Messenger of Allah slept on a rug in the house of Anas and perspired. Anas's mother brought a long-necked bottle in which to put his sweat. The Messenger of Allah asked her about this. She said, "We put it in our perfume and it is the most fragrant of scents."[5]

In his *Great History*, al-Bukhari mentioned that Jabir said, "When the Prophet went down a road, anyone who followed him knew that he had passed that way because of his scent."

Ishaq ibn Rahawayh mentioned that the Prophet's fragrance occurred without the use of perfume.

Al-Muzani and al-Harbi related that Jabir said, "The Prophet, may Allah bless him and grant him peace, let me ride behind him, so I put my mouth on the seal of prophethood and it spread over me like musk."

One of the scholars concerned with reports about the Prophet and his qualities related that when he wanted to defecate, the earth split open and swallowed up his faeces and urine, and it gave off a fragrant smell.

Muhammad ibn Sa'd, al-Waqidi's scribe, related that 'A'isha said to the Prophet, "When you come from relieving yourself, we do not see anything noxious from you." He said, "'A'isha, don't you know that the earth swallows up what comes out of the prophets so that none of it is seen?"[6]

Although this tradition is not famous, the people of knowledge still mention

---

1. From the *hadith* in Muslim from 'A'isha: they are clipping the moustache, letting the beard grow, using the toothpick, snuffing water up the nose, cutting the nails, washing the knuckles, plucking the hair of the armpit, shaving the pubes, cleansing oneself with water (in the lavatory). The narrator forgot the tenth, but thought it could be rinsing the mouth. One version has circumcision rather than letting the beard grow.

2. Ibn Hibban from 'A'isha, a weak *hadith*.

3. In Muslim and at-Tirmidhi.

4. Muslim.

5. Muslim and al-Bukhari.

6. Although it has firm *isnad*, this *hadith* is not well-known. It is related by ad-Daraqutni.

the purity of his faeces and urine. One of the companions of ash-Shafi'i stated that and Imam Abu Nasr as-Sabbagh related it in his Collection. The *'ulama'* relate both of the preceding statements. Abu Bakr ibn Sabiq al-Makki included them in his book, *Al-Badi'*, about the branches of Maliki *fiqh,* which outlines those things which are not part of their school and come from the secondary judgements of the Shafi'is. The point is that nothing objectionable or unpleasant came from the Prophet, may Allah bless him and grant him peace.

Connected to this we have the *hadith* of 'Ali: "I washed the Prophet, may Allah bless him and grant him peace, and I began to look for what is normally found in a corpse, but I did not find anything. I said, 'You were pure in life and pure in death.'" He added, "A sweet smell came from him whose like I have never experienced."[1]

When Abu Bakr kissed the Prophet after his death, he said something to the same effect.[2]

There was also the time when Malik ibn Sinan drank his blood on the Day of Uhud and licked it up. The Prophet allowed him to do that and then said, "The Fire will not touch you."[3]

Something similar occurred when 'Abdullah ibn az-Zubayr drank his cupped blood. The Prophet said, "Woe to you from the people and woe to the people from you," but he did not object to what he had done.[4]

Something similar is related about when a woman drank some of his urine. He told her, "You will never complain of a stomach-ache."[5]

He did not order any of them to wash their mouths out nor did he forbid them to do it again.

The *hadith* of the woman drinking the urine is sound. Ad-Daraqutni follows Muslim and al-Bukhari who relate it in the *Sahih.* The name of this woman was Baraka, but they disagree about her lineage. Some say that it was Umm Ayman, who used to serve the Prophet. She said that the Messenger of Allah had a wooden cup which he placed under his bed in which he would urinate during the night. One night he urinated in it and when he examined it in the morning, there was nothing in it. He asked Baraka about that. She said, "I got up and felt thirsty, so I drank it without knowing." The *hadith* is related by Ibn Jurayj and others.

The Prophet was born circumcised with his umbilical cord cut. It is related that his mother Amina said, "He was born clean. There was no impurity on him."

---

1. Reported by Ibn Majah, Abu Dawud, al-Hakim and al-Bayhaqi.
2. In al-Bazzar from 'Umar with a sound *isnad.*
3. At-Tabarani from Abu Sa'id al-Khudri; al-Bayhaqi from 'Umar ibn as-Sa'ib.
4. Related by al-Hakam, al-Bazzar, ad-Daraqutni, al-Bayhaqi, al-Baghawi and at-Tabarani with a good *isnad.*
5. Related by al-Hakim, and confirmed by adh-Dhahabi and ad-Daraqutni.

'A'isha said, "I never ever saw the private parts of the Messenger of Allah, may Allah bless him and grant him peace."[1]

'Ali said, "The Prophet, may Allah bless him and grant him peace, asked me to make sure that no-one except me washed him. He said, 'No-one has seen me naked without going blind.'"[2]

In the *hadith* of 'Ikrima ibn 'Abdullah from Ibn 'Abbas, it says that the Prophet slept until he could be heard breathing deeply. Then he got up to pray without doing *wudu*'.[3] 'Ikrima said, "That was because he, may Allah bless him and grant him peace, was protected."

SECTION 4
His intellect, eloquence and the acuteness of his faculties

As for his ample intellect, intelligence, the acuteness of his senses, his eloquence, the grace of his movements and the excellence of his faculties, there is no doubt that he was the most intelligent and astute of people.

Anyone who reflects on how he managed the inward and outward affairs of people and the politics of the common people and the elite and his amazing qualities and wonderful life, not to mention the knowledge which flowed from him and the way he confirmed the *Shari'a* without any previous instruction, experience or reading any books, will have no doubts about the superiority of his intellect and the firmness of his understanding. None of this requires confirmation because it has already been amply verified.

Wahb ibn Munabbih said, "I have read seventy-one books, and in all of them I found that the Prophet had the most superior intellect and best opinion." In another version, "I found from all of these books that all of the intelligence which Allah had given to people, from the beginning of this world to its end, is like a grain of sand in comparison with his intellect, may Allah bless him and grant him peace."

Mujahid said, "When the Messenger of Allah got up for the prayer, he could see all those behind him as if they were in front of him."[4] This affords one commentary on the words of Allah, **"Your turning about among those who prostrate."** (26:219)

The *Muwatta'* contains the words of the Prophet, "I can see you behind me." There is something similar from Anas in the two *Sahih* Collections. 'A'isha said the same thing, adding from herself, "It is something extra which Allah gave

---

1. Al-Bazzar and al-Bayhaqi.
2. Ibid.
3. In al-Bukhari and Muslim.
4. As related from Ibn al-Mundhir and al-Bayhaqi (*mursal*).

him as an additional proof." One of the variants has, "I can see whoever is behind me as I see whoever is in front of me." Another has, "I see the one behind my neck as I see the one before me."

Baqi ibn Mukhallad related that 'A'isha said, "The Prophet, may Allah bless him and grant him peace, could see as well in the dark as he saw in the light."[1]

There are many sound traditions about the Prophet seeing the angels[2] and the *shaytans*.[3] He was able to see the Negus (in Abyssinia)[4] so he could pray for him. In the same way, he saw Jerusalem (after his Night Journey) and described it to the Quraysh.[5] He also saw the Ka'ba when he was building the mosque in Madina.

Ahmad ibn Hanbal and others related that the Prophet could see eleven stars in the Pleaides. This, according to Ahmad ibn Hanbal and others, refers to the total which it is physically possible to see with the naked eye. One of them[6] believed that this referred to his knowing about it. However, the clear meaning contradicts this and there is no impossibility of his having done this. Clear-sightedness is one of the special traits of the Prophets and one of their qualities.

Abu Hurayra said that the Prophet said, "When Allah the Mighty manifested Himself to Musa, he was able to see an ant on a stone in the darkness of the night at a distance of ten leagues."[7]

Therefore it is in no way impossible for our Prophet to have been able to do what we have mentioned in this chapter after his Night Journey and the favour he received in seeing one of the greatest signs of his Lord.

Traditions have come down to the effect that he threw down Rukana, the strongest of the people of his time, and called him to Islam. He wrestled with Abu Rukana, renowned for his incredible strength in the *Jahiliyya*, three times. The Messenger of Allah threw him every time.

Abu Hurayra said, "I did not see anyone who walked more swiftly than the Messenger of Allah, may Allah bless him and grant him peace. It was as if the earth rolled up for him. We would exhaust ourselves and yet he was not tired at all."[8]

Another of his qualities was that his laugh was only a smile. When he turned

---

1. Reported by Ibn 'Adi and al-Bayhaqi with a weak *isnad*.
2. As in al-Bukhari and elsewhere: "He saw Jibril in his form with six hundred wings on a throne between the heaven and the earth, and he blocked the horizon."
3. Al-Bukhari: "An *'ifrit* came to me last night in the *Maghrib* prayer holding a brand of fire with which to burn my face. Allah gave me power over him."
4. Muslim and al-Bukhari: "The Prophet said, 'Your brother, the Negus, has died, so get up and pray over him.'"
5. Muslim and al-Bukhari.
6. An-Nawawi.
7. In *as-Saghir* of at-Tabarani.
8. At-Tirmidhi and al-Bayhaqi.

to face someone, he would turn to face them directly. When he walked, he walked as if he were coming down a slope.

SECTION 5
His eloquence and sound Arabic

The Prophet's pre-eminence in eloquence and fluency of speech is well-known. He was fluent, skillful in debate, very concise, clear in expression, lucid, used sound meanings and was free from affectation.

He was given mastery of language (lit. all the words) and was distinguished by producing marvellous maxims. He learned the dialects of the Arabs, and would speak to each of their communities in their own dialect and converse with them in their own idiom. He answered their arguments using their own style of rhetoric so that, more than once, a large number of his Companions had to ask him to explain what he had said. Whoever studies his *hadiths* and biography will know and verify that. The way he spoke to the Quraysh, the Ansar and the people of the Hijaz and Najd was not the same as the way he spoke to Dhu'l-Mish'ar al-Hamdhani, Tihfa al-Handi, Qatan ibn Haritha al-'Ulaymi, al-Ash'ath ibn Qays, Wa'il ibn Hujr al-Kindi and others from among the chiefs of Hadramawt and the kings of Yemen.[1]

Look at his letter to the tribe of Hamdhan: "You have the highlands and the lowlands and the wild lands. You eat its fodder and graze on its range. You have, from their produce and fruit and livestock, what they surrender by treaty and trust. In the *zakat*, they have the three year old camel, the old she-camel, the weaned camel, the one kept in the houses and the young unweaned male camels. They owe in the *zakat* for the six year old livestock and the five year old."[2]

He said to the tribe of Najd, "O Allah, bless them in their milk, butter and yoghurt. Send their herdsman to great wealth and let scarcity depart from them. Bless them in their property and children. Whoever performs the prayer is a Muslim. Whoever brings the *zakat* is a *muhsin*. Whoever testifies that there is no god but Allah is sincere (*mukhlis*).

"Banu Najd, you still have your contracts and property deposits. Do not withhold the *zakat* nor deviate while you are alive. Do not consider the prayer burdensome and so abandon it."

He wrote to them, "You pay the minimum amount in *zakat*. You have the camel who has been ill, the camel after giving birth, the one who is tamed for

---

1. The point of the these examples is that they represent different Arabic dialects quite different to the language of Quraysh.
2. The language of this letter is very different from the Arabic spoken in the Hijaz.

riding and the wild colt. Your livestock are not to be withheld nor your palm-spathes cut. Your milk-cows will not be taken as long as you do not conceal hypocrisy or break the contract. Whoever agrees to something must fulfill the contract and the pledge of protection (*dhimma*) Whoever refuses has an increased obligation [as a penalty]."[1]

Part of what he wrote to Wa'il ibn Hujr was: "To the Qayls, the Kings of Yemen, the Fair-faced Ones, the Elders." He further said, "There is a sheep from the minimum amount of forty, neither lean nor fat. Give what is in the middle. There is a fifth on treasure. Whoever is unmarried and commits fornication, give him a hundred lashes and then banish him for a year. Whoever has been married and commits fornication should be stoned by groups of men. Do not be lax in the *deen* nor waver in the obligations due to Allah. Every intoxicant is forbidden. Wa'il ibn Hujr is appointed over the Qayls."

Compare how different this letter is compared to the famous one to Anas about *zakat*! He used the vocabulary of these particular people as well as their stylistic metaphors and common expressions, employing this language with them so that he could make what had been revealed for them clear to the people and in order to speak to people in a way that they would recognise.

This is similar to how he spoke in the *hadith* of 'Atiyya as-Sa'di. He said, "The upper hand is the giving one and the lower hand is the receiving," using their dialect.[2]

In the *hadith* when al-'Amiri asked him for something, the Prophet used the dialect of the Banu 'Amir.

As for his everyday speech, famous oratory and his comprehensive statements and maxims which have been related, people have written volumes about them, and books have been compiled containing their words and meanings. His speech comprises unequalled eloquence and incomparable fluency. This is shown by such expressions as:

"The blood of the Muslims is the same. The least of them can offer their protection. They are a single hand against other people."[3]

"People are like the teeth of a comb."[4]

"A man is with the one he loves."[5]

"There is no good in company which does not show you what you show them."[6]

"People are like mines of gold and silver. The best of you in the *Jahiliyya* is

1. These passages are more examples of the Prophet's mastery of different dialects.
2. In al-Hakim confirmed by al-Bayhaqi.
3. Abu Dawud and an-Nasa'i.
4. Ibn Lal.
5. Muslim and al-Bukhari.
6. Ibn 'Adi with a weak *isnad*.

the best of you in Islam if they have understanding."[1]

"A man who knows his own worth is not destroyed."[2]

"The person who is being asked advice is in a position of trust, and he has the choice about what he is going to say as long as he has not spoken."[3]

"Allah shows mercy to His slave who speaks well and gains, or who keeps silent and safe."[4]

"Become Muslim and you will be safe. Become Muslim and Allah will give you your wage twice over."[5]

"Those I love most among you and those who will sit nearest to me on the Day of Rising are the best of you in character – those who give shelter, those who protect and bring together."[6]

"Perhaps he used to speak about what did not concern him and was miserly with what did not enrich him."[7]

"The two-faced person has no standing with Allah."[8]

He forbade, "Gossiping, asking a lot of questions, squandering property, forbidding gifts, disobedience to mothers and burying girls alive."

He said, "Fear Allah wherever you are. Follow up a bad action with a good one which will wipe it out. He created people with good character."[9]

"The best of affairs is the middle way."[10]

"Answer the one you love gently lest one day he becomes one who hates you."[11]

"Injustice will appear as darkness on the Day of Rising."[12]

He said in one of his supplications, "O Allah, I ask You for mercy from You by which my heart will be guided, my scattered affairs joined together, my affairs put straight, my unseen part put right and the part of me that is visible elevated, my actions purified, by which I will be inspired to right guidance, my intimacy will be returned and by which I will be protected from every evil. O Allah! I ask you for a good outcome in the Decree, the food of martyrs, the life of the blissful and victory over my enemies."[13]

There is much more besides this that various groups of people have related

1. Muslim and al-Bukhari.
2. Ibn as-Sam'ani.
3. Related by the four and al-Hakim and at-Tirmidhi.
4. Muslim and al-Bukhari.
5. Ibid.
6. At-Tirmidhi.
7. Al-Bayhaqi.
8. Muslim and al-Bukhari.
9. Ahmad, at-Tirmidhi, al-Hakim and al-Bayhaqi from Abu Dharr.
10. Ibn as-Sam'ani.
11. At-Tirmidhi and al-Bayhaqi from Abu Hurayra.
12. Muslim and al-Bukhari.
13. At-Tirmidhi and others from Ibn 'Abbas. All these statements are remarkable not only for their meaning but also for the beauty of the Arabic.

about his words, conversations, speeches, supplications, comments and contracts. There is no disagreement about the fact that in these things he occupied a station beyond compare. He obtained a pre-eminence in them which cannot be properly estimated.

His unique sayings that no mouth had ever uttered before have also been compiled. No-one can ever do justice to them.

Such as his saying, "The fight is fierce (lit. The oven is hot)."

"He breathed his last."

"A believer is not harmed from under the same stone twice."

"Happy is the one who accepts someone else's warning."

There are many more like these. Anyone examining them cannot cease to marvel at their contents and reflect on the wisdom they contain.

His companions said to him, "We do not find anyone more eloquent than you." He said, "How could it be otherwise? The Qur'an was revealed on my tongue, a clear Arabic tongue!"[1]

Another time, he said, "I am the most eloquent of the Arabs since I am from Quraysh and was brought up among the Banu Sa'd." This gave him the strength and purity of the desert along with the eloquence of the expressions of the city and the beauty of its words. This was all combined with the divine support which accompanies revelation and which no mortal can comprehend.

When Umm Ma'bad[2] described him, she said, "Sweet in speech, distinct, without using too few or too many words. It was as if his speech consisted of threaded pearls. He had a loud voice which was very melodious, may Allah bless him and grant him peace."

SECTION 6
The nobility of his lineage, the honour of his birthplace and the place where he was brought up

His noble lineage and the honour of his land and the place where he was brought up do not require any proof or clarification. They are not concealed.

He was from the best of the Banu Hashim, and the stock and core of the Quraysh. He was from the noblest and mightiest of the Arabs, both on his paternal and maternal side. He was from the people of Makka, from the noblest of lands in the reckoning of Allah and of His slaves.

Abu Hurayra said that the Messenger of Allah said, "I was sent from the best

---

1. Al-Bayhaqi.
2. A bedouin woman who gave hospitality to the Messenger and his companion, Abu Bakr, on their *hijra* to Madina.

of each generation of the children of Adam, generation after generation, until I was in the generation from which I came."[1]

Al-'Abbas said that the Prophet said, "Allah created Creation and He placed me among the best of them from the best of their generations. Then He selected the tribes and He put me among the best tribe. Then He selected the families, and He put me among the best of their families. I am the best of them in person and the best of them in family."[2]

Wa'ila ibn al-Asqa' said that the Messenger of Allah said, "Allah chose Isma'il from the children of Ibrahim and He chose the Banu Kinana from the children of Isma'il. He chose the Quraysh from the Banu Kinana and He chose the Banu Hashim from the Quraysh. He chose me from the Banu Hashim."[3]

In a *hadith* narrated by Ibn 'Umar which at-Tabarani has related, the Prophet says, "Allah, the Mighty and Majestic sifted through His creation and chose the Banu Adam from them. Then He sifted through Banu Adam and chose the Arabs from them. Then He sifted through the Arabs and chose the Quraysh from them. Then He sifted through the Quraysh and chose the Banu Hashim from them. Then He sifted through the Banu Hashim and chose me from them. I am the best of the best. Whoever loves the Arabs, loves them through love for me. Whoever hates the Arabs, hates them through hatred of me."

Ibn 'Abbas said that the spirit of the Prophet was a light in the hands of Allah two thousand years before He created Adam. That light glorified Him and the angels glorified by his glorification. When Allah created Adam, He cast that light into his loins.

The Messenger of Allah said, "Allah brought me down to earth in the loins of Adam, placed me in the loins of Nuh and then cast me into the loins of Ibrahim. Allah continued to move me from noble loins and pure wombs until He brought me out of my parents. None of them were ever joined together in fornication."

The famous poem of al-'Abbas in praise of the Prophet, may Allah bless him and grant him peace, testifies to the soundness of this tradition.

---

1. Al-Bukhari.
2. Al-Bayhaqi and at-Tirmidhi.
3. At-Tirmidhi said that this *hadith* is sound. Muslim also has it in the *Sahih*.

SECTION 7
His state regarding the necessary actions of daily life

The things necessary for daily life can be of three kinds:

1) There is the kind which is excellent when it is little in quantity.
2) There is the kind which is excellent when it is large in quantity.
3) There is the kind which varies according to the situation.

The sort of thing agreed to be more perfect and praiseworthy when it is little in quanity in any situation, both according to custom and the *Shari'a*, consists of such things as food and drink. Both the Arabs and the men of wisdom continue to praise making do with little of them and censure having too much of them, because indulging in a lot of food and drink indicates greed, avarice, avidity and being dominated by appetite. That results in harm in this world and the Next. It brings about physical illnesses, coarseness in the self and dullness in the brain. A little of it indicates contentment and self-control. Restraint of the appetite produces health, clear thought and a sharp mind.

The same applies to excess of sleep. It is an indication of feebleness and weakness, and lack of intelligence and astuteness. This produces laziness, the habit of failure, frittering away one's life in what is not useful, hardness of heart and the neglect and death of the heart. The proof of this is well-known, observed and transmitted in what previous communities and wise men of the past have said, particularly in the poems of the Arabs and their stories. It is also to be found in sound *hadiths* and the traditions of the *Salaf* and those who came after them which do not need to be quoted. We will not mention them in full here, giving only a summary, since the knowledge they contain is quite well-known.

Regarding both of the above-mentioned things, the Prophet was the most abstemious of men, a fact which can be gleaned from his well-known biography. He commanded and encouraged people to make do with little of them, connecting them together.

Al-Miqdam ibn Ma'dikarib said that the Messenger of Allah said, "The son of Adam does not fill any container worse than his belly. Sufficient for the son of Adam are some morsels to keep his back straight. If there must be [more], then it is a third for his food, a third for his drink and a third for breath,"[1] because the result of a lot of food and drink is a lot of sleep.

Sufyan ath-Thawri said, "By having only a little food, one is able to stay awake at night."

---

1. At-Tirmidhi, an-Nasa'i and Ibn Hibban.

One of the *Salaf* said, "Do not eat a lot so that you drink a lot and then sleep a lot and lose a lot."

It is related that the Prophet said, "The kind of food which I prefer is that with many hands in it."[1]

'A'isha said, "The Prophet, may Allah bless him and grant him peace, never filled his stomach completely. When he was with his family, he did not ask them for food nor desire it. If they fed it to him, he ate. He accepted whatever they served him and he drank whatever they gave him to drink."

This is not contradicted by the *hadith* of Barira when the Prophet said, "Didn't I see a pot with meat in it?"[2]

It is possible that the Prophet asked in this instance since he realised that they thought it was not lawful for him and he wanted to make the *sunna* clear. Seeing that they did not offer him any of it, even though he knew that they did not prefer themselves to him, he ascertained whether what he thought was true and made the matter clear for them by saying, "It is *sadaqa* for her and a gift for us."

One of Luqman's aphorisms was, "My son, when the intestines are full, reflection sleeps, wisdom is dumb and the limbs falter in worship."

Sahnun said, "Knowledge is not fitting for someone who eats until he is full."

In a sound *hadith*, the Prophet said, "As for myself, I do not eat sitting in a settled posture."[3]

Sitting in a settled posture is sitting firmly settled or reclining in order to eat, for instance cross-legged or in some other such comfortable manner of sitting. Someone who sits in this manner demands food and seeks a lot of it. When the Prophet sat down to eat, he sat squatting, as someone ready to get up.[4]

He said, "I am a slave. I eat as a slave eats and I sit as a slave sits."[5]

The import of this *hadith* is not merely reclining on one's side as some people say.

It was the same with his sleep, may Allah bless him and grant him peace. He slept but little. Sound traditions testify to that. Furthermore, the Prophet said, "My eyes sleep, but my heart does not sleep."[6]

He used to sleep on his right side in order to be able to sleep less (heavily) because sleeping on the left side is easier for the heart and the internal organs since they incline to the left side. Sleeping on the left side leads to a deep, long

---

1. Related by all from Anas and Jabir.
2. Muslim and al-Bukhari. The point of which was to prove the lawfulness of the meat Barira was cooking.
3. Al-Bukhari.
4. Muslim.
5. Al-Bazzar from Ibn 'Umar with a weak *isnad*.
6. Muslim and al-Bukhari.

sleep. When someone sleeps on his right side, the heart is suspended and agitated, and the sleeper tends to wake up quickly and is not overpowered by deep sleep.

SECTION 8
Marriage and things connected with it

The second category of necessities of daily life is praised and boasted of when it is abundant and includes such things as marriage and rank.

The necessity for marriage is agreed upon in the *Shari'a* and in custom. It is a proof of perfection and sound masculinity. It has always been customary to boast of and praise a lot of it and, as far as the *Shari'a* is concerned, it is a transmitted *sunna*.

Ibn 'Abbas said, "The best of this community is the one with the most wives," indicating the Prophet.[1]

The Prophet said, "Marry and procreate. I want to increase communities by you."[2]

He forbade celibacy. This is because marriage brings with it restraint of the appetites and lowering the eye as the Prophet pointed out. He said, "Whoever has the capacity should marry. It lowers the eyes and protects the private parts."[3]

For this reason the *'ulama'* do not consider it something that detracts from the virtue of abstinence. Sahl at-Tustari said, "Women were loved by the Master of the Messengers, so how could we abstain from them?" Ibn 'Uyayna says something to the same effect.

The most ascetic of the Companions had a lot of wives and slave-girls and had much sexual intercourse with them. More than one of them disliked the idea of meeting Allah unmarried.

It might be asked, "How can it be that marriage has so many virtues when Allah praised Yahya, son of Zakariyya, for being chaste? How could Allah praise him for not doing something considered to be a virtue? Furthermore, 'Isa ibn Maryam remained celibate. If things were as you claim, would he not have married?"

The answer is this. It is clear that Allah did praise Yahya for being chaste. It was not, as someone has said, that he was timid or without masculinity. Astute commentators and critical scholars reject this assertion, saying that it would

---

1. Al-Bukhari.
2. Ibn Mardawayh in his *Tafsir* from Ibn 'Umar, *marfu'* with a weak isnad. At-Tabarani also has something similar in *al-Awsat*.
3. At-Tabarani, and Muslim and al-Bukhari.

imply an imperfection and a fault and that is not fitting for one the prophets. It means that he was protected from wrong actions, i.e. it was as if he were kept from them. Some say that he was kept from all his bodily appetites, and some say that he did not have any desire for women.

It is clear from this that the lack of the ability to marry is an imperfection. Virtue lies in its taking place. Therefore the absence of it can only be through the existence of a counter virtue, either striving as in the case of 'Isa, or by having sufficiency from Allah as Yahya did, since marriage frequently distracts from Allah and brings a person down into this world.

Someone able to marry and carry out the obligations incurred by marriage without being distracted from his Lord has a lofty degree. Such is the degree of our Prophet, may Allah bless him and grant him peace. Having many wives did not distract him from worshipping his Lord. Indeed, it increased him in worship in that he protected his wives, gave them their rights, earned for them and guided them. He clearly stated that such things were not part of the portion of his earthly life but that they are part of the portion of the earthly life of others.

He said, "He made me love, in this world of yours, women and scent, and the coolness of my eye (i.e. my delight) is in the prayer,"[1] and then he indicated that his love was for women and scent which are worldly things for other people whereas his occupation with them was not for his worldly life, but rather for the life of the Next World because of the otherworldly benefits of marriage already mentioned and his desire to come out to the angels wearing scent. Scent also encourages intercourse, assists it and stimulates it. He loved these two qualities for the sake of others and for the restraint of his appetite. His true love, particular to him, lay in witnessing the *Jabarut* of his Lord and intimate conversation with Him. That is why he made a distinction between the two loves and separated the two conditions, saying, "and the delight of my eye is in the prayer."

Yahya and 'Isa were on the same level regarding the trial of women. However, there is an extra virtue in satisfying women's needs. The Prophet was among those who have been given the ability to do so and he was given it in abundance. This is why he was allowed a greater number of wives than anyone else.

It is related from Anas, "The Prophet, may Allah bless him and grant him peace, used to visit his wives in one hour of the day or night, and there were eleven of them."[2]

Anas said, "We used to say that he had been given the power of thirty

---

1. Al-Hakim and an-Nasa'i.
2. Al-Bukhari and an-Nasa'i.

men."[1] Something similar was related from Abu Rafi'. Tawus said, "The Prophet was given the power of forty men in intercourse." A similar statement came from Safwan ibn Sulaym.

Salama, the female client of the Prophet, said, "The Prophet would go around in the night to his nine wives and then purify himself from each of them before going to the next. He said, 'This is better and purer.'"[2]

The Prophet Sulayman said,[3] "I went around in the night to a hundred or ninety-nine women." So he had that capacity as well. Ibn 'Abbas said, "There was the semen of a hundred men in the loins of Sulayman, and he had three hundred wives and three hundred slave-girls." An-Naqqash and others related that he had seven hundred wives and three hundred slavegirls.

While the Prophet Da'ud was being ascetic and eating from the work of his own hands, he had ninety-nine wives and he completed the hundred by marrying Uriya'. Allah mentions that in His Mighty Book when He says, **"This brother of ours had ninety-nine ewes."** (38:23)

In the *hadith* of Anas, the Prophet said, "I have been preferred over people in four things: generosity, courage, much intercourse and great power."[4]

As for rank, it is normally praised by intelligent men. There is esteem in the hearts according to rank. When He described 'Isa, Allah said, **"He is noble in this world and the Next."** (2:45)

However, it also is the cause of much misfortune and is harmful for some people in relation to the Next World. That is why people have censured it and praised its opposite. The *Shari'a* also praises obscurity and censures exaltedness in the earth.

The Prophet, may Allah bless him and grant him peace, possessed modesty, position in the hearts of men and their esteem both before his prophethood, during the *Jahiliyya,* and after it. Then they rejected him, injured him, injured his Companions and tried to harm him secretly. But whenever he encountered them face to face, they showed him respect and gave him what he needed. The traditions about this are well-known and we will give some of them.

Anyone who had not seen the Prophet before would become perplexed and terrified when he saw him. This was related about Qayla. When she saw the Prophet she trembled with terror. He said, "Poor girl, you must be calm."[5]

In the *hadith* of Abu Mas'ud, it tells of a man who stood before the Prophet and trembled. He said to him, "Relax, I am not a king."[6]

As for his inestimable worth by reason of his being a Prophet, the honour of

---

1. An-Nasa'i related that. It is also in al-Bukhari.
2. Sound *hadith* related by Abu Dawud.
3. Ibid.
4. At-Tabarani.
5. In *ash-Shama'il* of at-Tirmidhi and the *Sunan* of Abu Dawud. Ibn Sa'd transmitted it.
6. *Mursal hadith* from Qays in al-Bayhaqi. Al-Hakim has it and says that it is sound.

his position by being a Messenger, his exalted rank by being chosen by Allah and his honour in this world, it is as great as it is possible to be. And in the Next World, he will be the master of the Children of Adam.[1] The implication to be drawn from this section forms the basis of this entire chapter.

SECTION 9
Things connected to money and goods

The third category of necessities whose praiseworthiness and excellence vary according to the situation, includes things like having a lot of wealth.

Generally someone with wealth is esteemed by the common people because they believe that he can get what he needs with it and his goals can be attained by it. It is not a virtue in itself. When someone has money and spends it on meeting his own needs and the needs of those who come to him with the intention of helping them, using it correctly, it brings him nobility, praise, excellence and a good station in the hearts of other people. It is a virtue for him in the eyes of the people of this world.

If he uses it in the paths of piety and spends it in the way of charity, intending Allah and the Next World, then it is a virtue in the eyes of everyone in every instance.

When the one who has it withholds it and does not use it properly and is avid to amass it, then, even if there is a lot of it, it is as if it did not exist. It is an imperfection in the one who has it. It does not take him to safe ground but throws him into the ditch of the vice of miserliness and meanness.

Praise of wealth and its virtue, when it is considered a virtue, does not lie in the wealth itself. It is elevated through its connection to something else and its being used in the proper way. If the one who amasses wealth does not use it properly, he is not really wealthy and not rich in the true sense of the word. None of the men of intellect praise him. He is always poor and does not obtain any of his objectives since he possesses the wealth to realise them but does not have real control over it. He is like a treasurer in charge of someone else's property who has no property himself. It is as if he had nothing.

The one who spends it is really rich and wealthy. He has obtained the benefits of money, even if none of the wealth remains in his possession.

Examine the biography of our Prophet and his character in dealing with wealth. You will find that he was given the treasures of the earth and the keys to the lands. Booty, which had not been lawful for any prophet before him, was allowed to him. During his lifetime, he conquered the Hijaz, the Yemen and all

---

1. As in the *hadith* in al-Bukhari.

of the Arabian Peninsula, as well as the areas bordering Syria and Iraq. He was brought a fifth of the booty as well as the *jizya*-tax and *zakat*-tax of which earlier kings had only obtained a fraction. He was given gifts by several foreign kings. He did not keep any of this for himself nor withhold a single dirham of it. He spent it all in its proper channels, enriched others with it and strengthened the Muslims by it.

He said, "I do not feel easy if any gold dinar remains with me overnight, except for a dinar which I have set aside to pay a debt."[1]

Sometimes he was given dinars and divided them and perhaps six would be left over. Then he would give them to some of his wives. He would not sleep until he had divided them out. Then he would say, "Now I can rest." When he died, his armour was in pawn to feed his family.

As far as his maintenance, clothes and dwelling were concerned, he was content with the demands of necessity and abstained from anything more than that. He used to wear whatever he had available. Generally, he would wear a cloak, a coarse garment, or a thick outer garment. He would distribute outer garments made of brocade and embroidered with gold to those who were there and send them to people who were not there. That is because, with the people of Allah, pride in dress and adornment is not one of the qualities of nobility and honour. It is one of the qualities of women.

The garments which are most praised are those which are clean and of medium quality. Wearing clothes of this kind does not detract from manliness and does not lead to aggrandisement in other people's eyes. The *Shari'a* censures that. The most frequent cause of boasting for people is the vaunting of many clothes and much wealth.

The same applies to pride in a sumptuous dwelling place, a spacious house or having a lot of goods, servants and animals. Anyone who has some land and harvests it and then gives the produce away out of asceticism and disattachment obtains the virtue of his property and has the right to boast of this quality, if boasting can indeed ever be said to be a virtue. There is firm praise for turning away from wealth, making do with little when it is no longer there and spending it properly.

SECTION 10
Praiseworthy qualities

There are some praiseworthy qualities and noble *adab* which are acquired. All the men of intelligence agree that the one who has them is virtuous and someone who has even one of them is highly esteemed. The *Shari'a* praises them all, commands to them and promises perpetual happiness to those who

---

1. Muslim and al-Bukhari.

have them. Some of them are described as being part of prophethood. As a whole, they are called good character. Good character consists of balance in the faculties and the qualities of the self, and following moderation rather than inclining towards extremes.

Our Prophet was completely perfect in all of them and completely balanced so that Allah praises him for that, saying, **"Indeed you are truly vast in character."** (68:4)

'A'isha said, "His character was the Qur'an. He was pleased by what it finds pleasing and angry according to what it finds hateful."[1]

He said, "I was sent to perfect noble character."[2]

Anas said, "The Messenger, may Allah bless him and grant him peace, was the best of people in character."[3] 'Ali ibn Abi Talib said something similar.

In the Prophet's case, according to the people of knowledge, these qualities were possessed by him from the time he was created, from the beginning of his natural constitution. He did not acquire them or learn them through education. He received them by divine generosity and the special gift of his Lord.

That is how it was with all the prophets. Reading their life stories from the time that they were children until the time they were sent as prophets makes one realise this, as is evident in the cases of 'Isa, Musa, Yahya, Sulayman and others. They were naturally disposed to these qualities and they were given knowledge and wisdom when they were created.

Allah says, **"We gave him judgement while still a child."** (19:12)

The commentators say that Allah gave Yahya knowledge of the Book of Allah while he was still a child. Ma'mar said that he was only two or three years old.[4] The children asked him, "Why don't you play with us?" He replied, "Was I created for playing games?"

Allah says: **"Confirming a word from Allah."** (3:39)

Yahya confirmed 'Isa when he was three years old. He testified that he was the word of Allah and His spirit. It is said that he confirmed him when he was in his mother's womb. Yahya's mother said to Maryam, "I feel what is in my womb bowing to what is in your womb to greet him."

Allah quotes what 'Isa said to his mother when he was born, saying: **"A voice called out to her from under her, 'Do not grieve!'"** (19:24)

Some say that the one who called out was 'Isa. His words when he was in the cradle are quoted in the Qur'an: **"I am the slave of Allah. He has given me the Book and He made me a prophet."** (19:30)

---

1. Al-Bayhaqi.
2. Ibn Hanbal and al-Bazzar. Malik has it in the *Muwatta'* in a somewhat different form as does al-Baghawi.
3. Muslim and al-Bukhari.
4. According to what is related by Ibn Hanbal in *Zuhd*, Ibn Abi Hatim in his *Tafsir*, ad-Daylami and al-Hakim.

Allah says: **"We gave Sulayman understanding of it. We gave each of them judgement and knowledge."** (21:79)

The judgement of Sulayman when he was a child is mentioned – in the case of the woman about to be stoned and in the story about the child, in which Da'ud followed his judgement. At-Tabari says, 'When he was given the kingdom, he was twelve years old.'

The story of Musa grabbing Pharaoh's beard when he was a child is similar.

The commentators say that the words of Allah, **"We gave Ibrahim right guidance before,"** (21:51) have the meaning, "We guided him when he was young." Mujahid and others said this. Ibn 'Ata' said, "He chose him before He created him." Someone else said, "When Ibrahim was born, Allah sent an angel to him with a command from Allah to recognise Him with his heart and to remember Him with his tongue. He replied, 'I have done it.' He did not say, 'I will do it.' That was his right guidance."

It is said that when Ibrahim was thrown into the fire and tested, he was sixteen years old. When Ishaq was tested by the sacrifice, he was seven years old. When Ibrahim sought a proof in the star, the moon and the sun, he was fifteen months old.

It is said that Allah gave revelation to Yusuf when he was a child at the time his brothers threw him in the well. Allah says, **"We revealed to him to tell him about what they were doing."** (12:15) There are more traditions like these about the Prophets.

Amina bint Wahb[1] said that when the Prophet Muhammad was born, he spread his hands out to the earth and lifted his head to heaven.[2]

He said about himself, may Allah bless him and grant him peace, "As I was growing up, idols were made loathsome to me and poetry was made loathsome to me. I was not tempted by anything done in the *Jahiliyya* except on two occasions. Allah protected me from them and I did not repeat that."[3]

The Prophets had complete mastery of the affair and the breezes of Allah wafted over them one after the other and the light of gnoses shone in their hearts until they reached the goal. They reached the goal because Allah chose them to be prophets and to obtain the noble qualities without education or discipline. Allah says: **"When he came of age, and was straight, We gave him judgement and knowledge."** (28:14)

We find that other people have been formed with some of these qualities but not all of them. A person is born with some of them and it is made easy for him to complete them with Allah's favour. We can see this by the fact that He creates some children with excellent manners, cleverness, truthfulness or generosity

---

1. The Prophet's mother.
2. Ibn al-Jawzi in *Wafa'* from Abu'l-Husayn. *Mursal hadith.*
3. Abu'n-Nu'aym in *ad-Dala'il.*

and some with the opposite of that.

Then by acquisition people can complete what is lacking. It is by discipline and striving that they acquire what they lack and balance what is in disequilibrium. People differ according to these two states. Everyone is eased to that for which he has been created. This is why the *Salaf* had some disagreement about whether qualities of character are innate or acquired. At-Tabari related that one of the *Salaf* said, "Good character is innate and a natural instinct in the servant of Allah." He related this from 'Abdullah ibn Mas'ud and al-Hasan al-Basri. We have found it to be sound.

Sa'd ibn Abi Waqqas related that the Prophet said, "The believer may naturally have every imperfection of character except for treachery and lying."[1]

'Umar ibn al-Khattab said, "Boldness and cowardice are natural qualities which Allah places wherever He wills."

These praiseworthy qualities and beautiful noble attributes are numerous, but we will mention their fundamentals and indicate them all. We will verify and establish, Allah willing, that he, may Allah bless him and grant him peace, had all of them.

SECTION 11
His intellect

The intellect is the root of all the branches of knowledge, the fountainhead and nucleus from which knowledge and gnosis spring forth. From it comes keen understanding, clear perception, accuracy of observation, sound opinion, knowing what is best for the self, striving against appetite, judicious policy and management and the acquisition of virtues and avoidance of vices.

We have already indicated the position of the Prophet in respect of this and his attainment in respect of the intellect and in plumbing depths of knowledge which no mortal but him has reached. The majesty of his state comes from this and is one of its manifestations which can be verified by anyone who studies the development of his states, the course of his life, the wisdom of his *hadith*, his knowledge of what was in the Torah, the *Injil*, the revealed books, the wisdom of the sages and the history of past nations and their battles, making metaphors, managing people, establishing the laws of the *Shari'a*, laying the foundation of his incomparable *adab* and praiseworthy habits.

It is clearly visible in every branch of knowledge where people use his words as a model and his examples as a proof – in dream interpretation, medicine, shares of inheritance, lineage, and other such things as we will make clear when discussing his miracles, Allah willing. This was all without any

---

1. Ibn 'Adi, a sound *hadith* related by Ibn Hanbal.

teaching or instruction or reading earlier scriptures or sitting with their scholars. He was an unlettered prophet who did not know any of these things until Allah expanded his breast, clarified his affair, taught him and made him recite the Qur'an.

All this can be ascertained without even the least doubt by reading and investigating what he was like and by examining the decisive proofs of his prophethood. We will not make this too long by giving stories and individual cases in detail since it would be impossible to enumerate them in total or cover them completely.

Commensurate with his intellect was his acknowledgement of what Allah had taught him and acquainted him with regarding the knowledge of what was to come and what had passed, and of the wonders of His power and the immensity of His *Malakut*.

Allah says: **"He taught you what you did not know before. Allah's favour to you is indeed immense"** (4:113)

Intellects are bewildered in their attempt to assess the overflowing favour of Allah. Tongues are rendered speechless, lacking any description that could possibly reach it, let alone encompass it.

SECTION 12
His forbearance, long-suffering and pardon

Forbearance, long-suffering, pardoning in spite of having the power to punish and patient endurance in affliction are distinct from each other. Forbearance (*hilm*) is a state of dignified bearing and constancy despite provocation. Long-suffering (*ihtimal*) is self-restraint and resignation in the face of pains and injuries. Patience (*sabr*) is similar to it, but its meaning is slightly different. As for pardoning (*'afw*), it is refusing to hold something against someone else.

All of these qualities are part of the *adab* with which Allah endowed His Prophet. Allah says: **"Make allowances for people, command what is right, and turn away from the ignorant."** (7:199) It is related[1] that when this was revealed to the Prophet, he asked Jibril to interpret it for him. Jibril told him, "Wait until I ask the One who Knows." He left and came back to him and said, "O Muhammad, Allah commands you to unite yourself with those who cut you off and to give to those who refuse to give to you and to pardon those who are unjust to you."

Allah told him: **"Be steadfast in the face of all that happens to you."** (31:17) and **"So be steadfast as the Messengers with firm resolve were also**

---

1. In the *tafsir* of Ibn Jarir and Ibn Abi Hatim and elsewhere.

steadfast," (46:35) and **"They should rather pardon and overlook."** (24:22) He says: **"But if someone is steadfast and forgives, that is the most resolute course to follow."** (42:43)

The results of his forbearance and long-suffering are quite evident. Every man with forbearance is known to have occasional lapses. The Prophet, however, was only increased in steadfastness when the injury to him was great, and was only increased in forbearance when faced with an excess of importunate people.

'A'isha said, "The Messenger of Allah, may Allah bless him and grant him peace, was not given a choice between two matters but that he chose the easier of the two as long as it was not a wrong action. If it was a wrong action, he was the furthest of people from it. The Messenger of Allah did not take revenge for himself unless the honour (*hurma*) of Allah was violated. Then he would take revenge for the sake of Allah."[1]

It is related that when the Prophet had his tooth broken and his face cut on the day of the Battle of Uhud, it was practically unbearable for his Companions. They said, "If only you would invoke a curse against them." He replied, "I was not sent to curse, but I was sent as a summoner and as a mercy. O Allah, guide my people for they do not know."

It is related that 'Umar said to him, "My mother and father be your ransom, O Messenger of Allah! Nuh invoked a curse against his people when he said, **'My Lord, do not leave even one of the rejectors upon the earth.'** (71:26) Had you invoked a curse like that against us, we would have been destroyed to the last man. Your back has been trodden on, your face has been bloodied and your tooth has been broken, and yet you have refused to utter anything but good. You have said, 'O Allah, forgive my people for they do not know.'"

Look at the perfection of bounteousness, degree of virtue (*ihsan*), excellent character, generosity and extreme patience and forbearance exemplified by this statement. The Prophet did not restrict himself to silence regarding them, but pardoned them, was compassionate to them, merciful towards them, supplicated and interceded for them. He said, 'Forgive' or 'Guide', then apologised for their ignorance and said, 'They do not know.'

When a man[2] said to the Prophet, "Act fairly. This is a division by which the face of Allah is not desired," the Prophet did not go further than making it clear to him how ignorant he was, admonishing and reminding him of what he had said to him. He said, "Confound you! Who will be fair if I am not fair? I would fail and be lost if I did not act fairly."[3] He restrained one of his Companions who wanted to kill him.

---

1. In Muslim and al-Bukhari, and Abu Dawud.
2. A hypocrite called Dhu'l-Huwaysira, later killed as a Kharijite. The incident referred to is the distribution of booty following the Battle of Hunayn.
3. In Muslim from Jabir, also in al-Bukhari and al-Bayhaqi.

Ghawrath ibn al-Harith, whilst he and some other people were talking about the raid of Dhatu'r-Riqa', undertook to assassinate the Messenger of Allah. He found him sitting alone under a tree. The Messenger of Allah did not stop him until he was standing over him with an unsheathed sword in his hand. He said, "Who will protect you from me?" The Prophet replied, "Allah." The sword fell from his hand and the Prophet grabbed it and said, "Who will protect you from me?" He said, "Punish in the best manner," so he left him and pardoned him. He came to his people and said, "I have come to you from the best of people."[1]

One of the major reports about his pardoning was his pardoning the Jewess who had poisoned him with the sheep after she had confessed to the poisoning.[2]

He did not punish Labid ibn al-A'zam when he used magic against him although he was informed about it and it was revealed to him with an explanation of what had happened. He did not even chide him, let alone punish him. Nor did he punish 'Abdullah ibn Ubayy and other hypocrites in spite of the seriousness of what they had done and said about him. On the contrary, he said to the person who indicated that one of them should be killed, "No, let it not be said that Muhammad kills his companions."[3]

Anas said, "I was with the Prophet, may Allah bless him and grant him peace, when he was wearing a thick cloak. A bedouin pulled him so violently by his cloak that the edge of the cloak made a mark on the side of his neck. Then he said, 'Muhammad! Let me load up these two camels of mine with the property of Allah that you have in your possession! You will not let me load up from your property or your father's property.' The Prophet was silent and then he said, 'The property is the property of Allah and I am His slave.' Then he said, 'Shall I take retaliation from you, bedouin, for what you have done to me?' He replied, 'No.' The Prophet asked, 'Why not?' The bedouin replied, 'Because you do not pay back a bad action with a bad action.' The Prophet laughed and ordered that one camel be loaded up with barley and the other camel with dates."[4]

'A'isha said, "I never the saw the Messenger of Allah, may Allah bless him and grant him peace, ever take revenge for an injustice done to him as long as it was not regarding one of the orders of Allah which must be respected. He never struck anyone with his hand at all except when doing *jihad* in the way of Allah. He never hit a servant or a woman."[5]

A man was brought to him and he was told, "This man wanted to kill you."

1. Muslim and al-Bukhari.
2. Ibid.
3. Ibid.
4. Ibid.
5. Ibid.

The Prophet said, "Have no fear! Have no fear! Even though you wanted to do that, you would not have been given power over me."[1]

Before he was a Muslim, Zayd ibn Sa'na came to him demanding that he repay a debt to him. He pulled his garment from his shoulder, seized hold of him and behaved coarsely to the Prophet, saying, "Banu 'Abdu'l-Muttalib, you are procrastinating." 'Umar chased him off and spoke harshly to him while the Prophet merely smiled. The Messenger of Allah said, "'Umar, he and I need something else from you. Command me to repay well and command him to ask for his debt well." Then he said, "I still owe him three." 'Umar commanded that he be paid and he added twenty *sa'* more since he had alarmed him. That, according to Zayd's explanation, was the reason for him becoming Muslim. He said, "There were only two remaining signs of prophethood which I had not yet recognised in Muhammad or noticed: forbearance overcoming quick-temperedness and extreme ignorance only increasing him in forbearance. I tested him for these and I found him as described."[2]

The *hadiths* about his forbearance, patience, and pardon in spite of having power to punish are too many to present. Those we have mentioned should be sufficient. They can be found in the *Sahih* collections and other reliable books transmitted by many paths of transmission. They deal with his patience in the face of Quraysh's harshness and the injury done to him in the *Jahiliyya* and his endurance of great hardships at the hands of Quraysh until Allah let him conquer them and gave him power over them. They did not doubt that they would be wiped out and their wealthy men killed, but he kept on pardoning and overlooking. He said, "What do you say I have done to you?" They replied, "Good – a generous brother and a generous nephew." He said, "I say as my brother Yusuf said, **'No reproach will be upon you.'** (12:92) Go, you are free."

Anas said, "Eight men from Tan'im came to the Dawn Prayer with the intention of killing the Messenger of Allah, may Allah bless him and grant him peace. They were seized and the Messenger of Allah set them free. Allah revealed, **'He is the one who restrained their hands from you.'** " (48:24)[3]

When Abu Sufyan was brought to him after he had brought the Confederates against him, killed his uncle and Companions, and made a punitive example of them, the Prophet forgave him and was gentle to him. He said, "Confound you, Abu Sufyan! Isn't it high time that you knew that there is no god but Allah?" He said, "My father and mother be your ransom! How forbearing and generous you are, maintaining ties of kinship!"[4]

The Messenger of Allah was the slowest person to anger and the easiest to please, may Allah bless him and grant him peace.

---

1. Ibn at-Tabarani and Ahmad ibn Hanbal with a sound *isnad*.
2. Al-Bayhaqi, Ibn Hibban, at-Tabarani and Abu Nu'aym. Its *isnad* is sound.
3. *Hadith* in Muslim, Abu Dawud, at-Tirmidhi and an-Nasa'i.
4. At-Tabarani and al-Bayhaqi.

SECTION 13
His generosity and liberality

As for generosity, benevolence, magnanimity and liberality, they too have different meanings. Some people divide them into different branches. They say that benevolence (*karam*) is to spend cheerfully in what is important and useful. They also call it courage and the opposite of baseness. Liberality is to forgo what one is owed by others cheerfully. It is the opposite of ill-nature. Magnanimity is to spend easily and to avoid the acquisition of what is not praised. It is the opposite of tightfistedness.

The Prophet had no equal in these noble qualities and no-one exceeded him in them. All who knew him would describe him so.

Ibn al-Munkadir heard Jabir ibn 'Abdullah say, "The Messenger of Allah, may Allah bless him and grant him peace, was not asked for anything to which he said, 'No.'"[1] Anas and Sahl ibn Sa'd made similar reports.

Ibn 'Abbas said, "The Prophet, may Allah bless him and grant him peace, was the most generous of people in giving gifts and most generous of all in the month of Ramadan. When he met with Jibril, he was more generous than even the wind which is sent forth."[2]

Anas said, "A man asked him for something and he gave him all the sheep between two mountains. The man returned to his people and said, 'Become Muslim. Muhammad gives the gift of a man who does not fear poverty.'"[3]

He gave a hundred camels to more than one person. He gave Safwan a hundred, then a hundred, and then a hundred. This had been his character since before he was entrusted with the message. Waraqa ibn Nawfal told him, "You bear all and attain to what others are denied."[4]

He returned the captives of Hawazim who numbered six thousand. He gave al-'Abbas so much gold that he could not carry it. 90,000 dirhams were brought to him and he placed them on a mat and then got up and distributed them. He did not turn away anyone who asked until he had given them all away.

A man came and asked him for something. The Prophet said, "I do not have anything, but buy something on my account and when I get some money, I will pay for it." 'Umar said to him, "Allah has not obliged you to do what you are not able to do!" The Prophet disliked that, so a man of the Ansar said, "Messenger of Allah! Spend and do not fear diminution from the Master of the Throne!" The Prophet smiled and the pleasure could be seen in his face. He said, "I am commanded to this."[5]

---

1. Al-Bukhari.
2. Muslim and al-Bukhari.
3. Muslim.
4. Al-Bukhari and Muslim.
5. At-Tirmidhi related this.

It is mentioned that Mu'awwidh ibn 'Afra' said, "I brought the Prophet, may Allah bless him and grant him peace, a plate of fresh dates and cucumber, and he gave me a handful of jewelry and gold."

Anas said, "The Messenger of Allah, may Allah bless him and grant him peace, did not store up anything for the next day."

There are many such reports about his generosity and liberality.

Abu Hurayra said that a man came to the Prophet, may Allah bless him and grant him peace, to ask him about a certain thing. The Messenger of Allah, may Allah bless him and grant him peace, had borrowed half a *wasq* from him and the man had come to collect it. The Prophet gave him a *wasq*. He said, "Half of it is repayment and half is a gift."[1]

SECTION 14
His courage and bravery

As for courage and bravery, courage is the virtue which consists of the force of anger when it is made to obey the intellect. Bravery is the valour of the self when it is sent out to its death where bravery rather than fear is praiseworthy.

It was far from unknown for the Prophet to be found in dangerous situations. He went more than once into difficult places from which the valiant and heroic fled. He was firm and did not leave. He advanced and did not retreat or waver. There is not a single courageous person who has not fled or turned at some point – except for him.

Abu Ishaq al-Hamdani said that a man asked al-Bara', "Did you desert the Messenger of Allah in the Battle of Hunayn?" Al-Bara' said, "But the Messenger of Allah did not flee." Then he added, "I saw him on his white mule. Abu Sufyan was holding its reins. The Prophet was saying, 'I am the Prophet and it is no lie.'" Another added that he said, "I am Ibn 'Abdu'l-Muttalib." It is said that it has not been related that there was anyone fiercer than him on that day. Someone else said, "The Prophet got down from his mule." Muslim mentioned that al-'Abbas said, "When the Muslims and the unbelievers met and the Muslims turned to retreat, the Messenger of Allah began to gallop his mule towards the unbelievers while I was holding onto the rein. I was holding the mule back, not wanting it to rush. Abu Sufyan was beside his saddle. Then he called out, 'O Muslims!'"

It is said that when the Messenger of Allah was angry – and he was only angry for Allah – nothing could withstand his anger.

Ibn 'Umar said, "I never saw anyone more courageous, intrepid, generous or pleasing than the Messenger of Allah."[2]

---

1. It is not known who related this.
2. Ad-Darimi.

'Ali said, "When the situation was hot, fear intense and the fighting fierce, we were concerned for the Messenger of Allah, may Allah bless him and grant him peace. None was closer to the enemy than he. I saw him on the Day of Badr when we were keeping close to him and he was the closest one to the enemy. He was the bravest person on that day."[1]

It is said that the brave man was the one who stayed near the Prophet when the enemy drew near, simply by virtue of the fact that he was near the Prophet [who was in a forward position].

Anas said, "The Prophet, may Allah bless him and grant him peace, was the most excellent, most generous and bravest of people."[2]

One night, the people of Makka were alarmed and people made for the source of the disturbance. The Messenger of Allah met them on his way back for he had got to the source of the noise before them. He told them that a horse of Abu Talha had got loose. His sword was hanging from his neck. He said, "Do not be alarmed."

'Imran ibn Husayn said, "The Messenger of Allah did not meet a regiment without being the first to strike."

Ubayy ibn Khalaf caught sight of the Prophet in the Battle of Uhud and Ubayy had been shouting, "Where is Muhammad? May I not survive if he survives!" Previously when Ubayy had been ransomed on the Day of Badr, he had said, "I have a horse which I feed several measures of wheat every day. I will kill you if I am riding him." The Prophet told him, "I will kill you if Allah wills." So when he saw the Prophet on the Day of Uhud, Ubayy urged his horse on after him. Some of the Muslim men blocked his way. The Prophet said, "Leave him alone." He took a spear from al-Harith ibn Simma and shook it in such a way that all the men flew away from him as the flies fly off the back of a camel when it shakes itself. Then the Prophet, may Allah bless him and grant him peace, turned to face him and pierced him in the neck so that he swayed and fell from his horse. People said, "He's broken a rib." He returned to Quraysh and said, "Muhammad has killed me." They said, "There's nothing wrong with you!" He said, "Anyone would have been killed by what I have received. Did he not say, 'I will kill you.' By Allah! If he had spat on me, it would have killed me." He died at Sarif on the return journey to Makka.[3]

SECTION 15
Modesty and lowering the glance

As for modesty and lowering the glance, modesty is a fine quality which makes a man turn his face away when something he dislikes happens or when

---

1. Ibn Hanbal, an-Nasa'i, at-Tabarani and al-Bayhaqi. Muslim has part of it.
2. Muslim and al-Bukhari.
3. Ibn Sa'd, al-Bayhaqi and 'Abdu'r-Razzaq. Al-Waqidi has it as well.

it is something that would have been better left undone. Lowering the eye is to restrain the glance from what human beings naturally find disagreeable.

The Prophet was of all people the most modest and the most assiduous in restraining his eyes from looking at people's private parts. Allah says: **"Doing that causes annoyance to the Prophet though he is too reticent to tell you so."** (33:53)

Abu Sa'id al-Khudri said, "The Messenger of Allah was more modest than a secluded virgin. When he disliked something, we recognised it in his face."[1]

The Prophet was extremely sensitive in his character. He did not say anything to a person which that person would dislike out of his modesty and generosity. 'A'isha said, "When the Prophet heard something which he disliked about anyone, he would not say, 'What do you think about so-and-so doing or saying this?' He would say, 'What do you think about a people who do or say this?' so he could forbid it without actually naming the one who had done it."[2]

Anas related that a man came to the Prophet with a trace of saffron on him. The Prophet did not say anything since he never confronted anyone with something they would dislike. When he left, he said, "Could you tell him to wash it off?" It is also related that he said, "Tell him to remove it."[3]

'A'isha said in the *Sahih*, "The Prophet, may Allah bless him and grant him peace, was not lewd nor did he use bad language. He did not shout in the marketplace and he did not pay back evil with evil. He forgave and overlooked." Something similar is mentioned as being in the Torah in a transmission from Ibn Salam and 'Abdullah ibn al-'Abbas.

Part of his modesty was that he would not stare into anyone's face and he would use a *kunya* for someone who pressed him importunately regarding something he disliked.

'A'isha said, "I never ever saw the private parts of the Messenger of Allah, may Allah bless him and grant him peace"[4]

SECTION 16
Good companionship, good manners, and good nature

His good companionship, good manners and cheerfulness with all types of people is demonstrated by many sound reports. When 'Ali described him, he said, "He was the most generous of people, the most truthful, the most naturally lenient and the most generous with his company."[5]

---

1. Abu Dawud.
2. Muslim and al-Bukhari, at-Tirmidhi and Ibn Majah.
3. Abu Dawud.
4. At-Tirmidhi.
5. At-Tirmidhi, sound *hadith*.

Qays ibn Sa'd said, "The Messenger of Allah visited us. When he wanted to leave, my father Sa'd brought him a donkey with a saddle-cloth. The Messenger of Allah, may Allah bless him and grant him peace, mounted. Then Sa'd said, 'Qays, accompany the Messenger of Allah.' The Messenger of Allah told me to get on with him. I refused. He said, 'Either get up with me or go.' So I left." Another variant has, "Ride in front of me – the owner is more entitled to be at the front."[1]

The Messenger of Allah used to bring people close. He did not drive them away. He honoured those of high rank among any group of people and appointed them over their fellows. He was cautious and careful about people without abandoning his cheerfulness or good character with them. He paid proper attention to his Companions and gave each of those in his company his due. The one who was in his company thought that no-one had been shown more honour than he.

He was patient with anyone who sat with him or came near him wanting something, so that it was that person would be the first to leave. When anyone asked him for something, he would either give it to him or say something kind to him. His good character and good nature embraced everyone so that he seemed like a father to them. They were equal in respect of what they were apportioned by him.

Ibn Abi Hala described him saying, "He was always joyful with an easy disposition. He was gentle, neither gruff nor rude nor clamorous nor obscene nor carping nor excessively complimentary. He left food which he did not want without complaining about it."[2]

Allah says: **"It is a mercy from Allah that you were gentle with them. If you had been rough or hard of heart, they would have scattered from around you."** (3:159)

Allah says: **"Repel the bad with what is better and, if there is enmity between you and someone else, he will be like a bosom friend."** (41:34)

He would reply to the one who invited him and accepted a gift even if it was only a sheep's trotter, and he would reward it equally.

Anas said, "I served the Messenger of Allah, may Allah bless him and grant him peace for ten years and he never said 'Uff!' to me. He did not say about anything I had done, 'Why did you do it?' or about anything I had not done, 'Why didn't you do it?'"[3]

'A'isha said, "There was no-one with a better character than the Messenger of Allah, may Allah bless him and grant him peace. Whenever any of his Companions or the people of his household called him, he would reply, 'At

1. Abu Dawud and an-Nasa'i.
2. *Ash-Shama'il* of at-Tirmidhi.
3. Muslim and al-Bukhari.

your service!' "[1]

Jabir ibn 'Abdullah said, "The Messenger of Allah, may Allah bless him and grant him peace, never kept himself apart from me from the time I became a Muslim and whenever he saw me, he smiled."[2]

He used to joke with his Companions and mix with them and converse with them and play with their children. He let them sit in his room and he answered the invitation of the free man, the slave, the slavegirl and the very poor. He visited the sick in the furthest part of the city and he accepted the excuse of anyone who offered an excuse.

Anas said, "When anyone spoke in the ear of the Messenger of Allah, he would not move his head away until the man had first moved his. When anyone took his hand, he would not let go his hand until the one who had taken it let go. He was not seen to put his knees in front of anyone who was sitting beside him."[3]

He was the first to give the greeting when he met someone. He was the first to shake hands with his Companions. He was never seen stretching his feet out among his Companions so as to constrict any of them. He honoured whoever came to him. Sometimes he would spread out his garment for him and offer him the cushion he was sitting on, preferring the other person to himself. He would persist in making him sit on it if that person refused. He gave his companions *kunyas* and called them by the best of their names in order to honour them. He did not stop a conversation with anyone until it petered out and then he would break it by stopping it or getting up. It is related that no-one came into his company while he was praying but that he shortened his prayer to ask what they needed. When they finished, he returned to his prayer.

He was the most smiling and the most cheerful of people – except when the Qur'an was being revealed, when he was admonishing someone, or giving a speech. 'Abdullah ibn al-Harith said, "I did not see anyone who smiled more than the Messenger of Allah."[4]

Anas said, "The servants of Madina used to bring the Messenger of Allah, may Allah bless him and grant him peace, their vessels of water in the morning when he was praying. Whenever he was brought a vessel, he would dip his hand in it and sometimes the mornings were cold. They sought blessing through that."[5]

---

1. Abu Nu'aym.
2. Muslim and al-Bukhari.
3. Abu Dawud, at-Tirmidhi and al-Bayhaqi. Ibn al-Bazzar has it from Abu Hurayra and Ibn 'Umar.
4. Ibn Hanbal and at-Tirmidhi.
5. Muslim.

SECTION 17
Compassion and mercy

As for compassion, tenderness and mercy to all creation, Allah said about him: **"Your suffering is distressful to him. He is deeply concerned for you, gentle and merciful to the believers."** (10:128) Allah says: **"We only sent you as a mercy to all the worlds."** (21:107)

Part of his excellence is that Allah gave him two of His names, saying: *"merciful, compassionate* to the believers."

Ibn Shihab said, "The Messenger of Allah, may Allah bless him and grant him peace, went on a raid [and he mentioned Hunayn]. The Messenger of Allah gave Safwan ibn Umayya a hundred camels, then a hundred, then a hundred." Ibn Shihab said, "Sa'id ibn al-Musayyab related that Safwan said, 'By Allah, he gave me what he gave me. He was the most hated of people to me and he continued to give to me until he was the most beloved of people to me.'"

It is related that a bedouin came asking for something from him. He gave the man something and said, "Have I been good to you?" The bedouin said, "No, you have not and you have not done well." The Muslims became angry and went for him. The Prophet indicated that they should hold off. Then the Prophet got up and went into his house. Then the Prophet sent for him and added something to his gift and said, "Have I been good to you?" The bedouin replied, "Yes, may Allah repay you well in family and tribe." The Prophet said, "You said what you said and that angered my Companions. If you like, say what you said in my presence in their presence so as to remove what they harbour in their breasts against you." He said, "Yes." He came back later and the Prophet said, "This bedouin said what he said and then we gave him more. He claims that he is content. Isn't that so?" He said, "Yes, may Allah repay you well in your family and tribe." The Prophet said, "The example of this man and me is like a man who has a she-camel who bolts from him. People chase it and they only make it shy away more. The owner calls to them to stay clear of him and his she-camel, saying, 'I am more compassionate and better to it than you.' He goes in front of it and takes some clods of dirt and drives it back until it comes and kneels. He saddles and mounts it. If I had given you your heads when the man said what he said, you would have killed him and he would have entered the Fire."[1]

It is related that the Prophet said, "None of you should come to me with anything about any of my Companions for I do not want to go out to you except with a clear heart."[2]

---

1. Al-Bazzar from Abu Hurayra.
2. Abu Dawud and at-Tirmidhi from Ibn Mas'ud.

Part of his compassion towards his community was that he made things easy for them. The Prophet disliked doing certain things out of the fear that they would become obligatory for them. He said, "If I had not been compassionate to my community, I would have commanded them to use the *siwak* every time they did *wudu'*."[1]

There is also the tradition about the night prayer and the one forbidding them to fast continuously and the one about his dislike of entering the Ka'ba lest it became incumbent on his community and his desire that his Lord should make his curse against them a mercy to them. When he heard a child weeping, he would shorten the prayer.

An instance of his compassion was that he called on his Lord and made a compact with Him saying, "If ever I curse a man or make an invocation against him, make it *zakat* for him and mercy, prayer, purification and an act of drawing-near by which he will draw near to you on the Day of Rising."[2]

When his people rejected him, Jibril came to him and said, "Allah has heard what your people say to you and how they reject you. He has ordered the angels of the mountains to obey whatever you tell them to do." The angel of the mountains called him, greeted him and said, "Send me to do what you wish. If you wish, I will crush them between the two mountains of Makka." The Prophet said, "Rather, I hope that Allah will bring forth from their loins those who will worship Allah alone and not associate anything with Him."[3]

Ibn al-Munkadir related that Jibril told the Prophet, "Allah has ordered heaven, earth and mountains to obey you." He said, "Reprieve my community. Perhaps Allah will turn to them."[4]

'A'isha said, "The Messenger of Allah, may Allah bless him and grant him peace, was never given a choice between two things but that he chose the easier of the two."

Ibn Mas'ud said, "The Messenger of Allah, may Allah bless him and grant him peace, was careful when he admonished us, fearing he would tire us."[5]

'A'isha was riding an unruly camel which was recalcitrant and started to hit it repeatedly. The Messenger of Allah, may Allah bless him and grant him peace, said, "You must have compassion."[6]

---

1. Muslim and al-Bukhari.
2. Muslim and al-Bukhari and Abu Hurayra.
3. Muslim and al-Bukhari and the Six Books.
4. *Mursal hadith*.
5. Muslim and al-Bukhari.
6. Al-Bayhaqi.

SECTION 18
Integrity, probity in contracts and maintaining ties of kinship

'Abdullah ibn al-Hamsa' said, "I made a sales-agreement with the Prophet to sell something before it was actually despatched. I still had some of it to bring to him, so I promised him that I would bring it to him where he was. Then I forgot about it and only remembered three hours later. I brought it and he was still there. He said, 'Lad, you have been hard on me. I have been here for three hours waiting for you.'"[1]

Anas said, "Once when a gift was brought to the Prophet, he said, 'Take it to the house of such-and-such a woman. She was a friend of Khadija. She loved Khadija.'" 'A'isha said, "I was never jealous of any woman the way I was jealous of Khadija when I heard him mention her. If he sacrificed a sheep, he would send it to her friends. Her sister (i.e. Hala bint Khuwaylid) asked for permission to enter and he was happy to see her. A woman came to him and he received her with kindliness and asked after her very considerately. When she left, he said, 'She used to come to us when Khadija was with us. Maintaining ties is part of belief.'"[2]

One of the people of knowledge described him, saying, "He used to maintain contact with kinsfolk without preferring them over those who were better than them." The Prophet said, "The people of the Banu so-and-so are not my friends. However, they have kinship with me, so we will treat them with kindness because of their kinship."[3]

The Prophet used to carry Umama, his grand-daughter by Zaynab, on his shoulders. When he prostrated, he would put her down. When he stood up, he picked her up.

Abu Qatada said, "A delegation from the Negus arrived and the Prophet got up to serve them. His Companions said to him, 'Let us do it for you.' He said, 'They were generous and honoured our Companions, so I want to do the same for them.'"[4]

When his milk-sister, ash-Shayma', was brought among the captives of Hawazin, and made herself known to him, he spread out his cloak for her and offered her a choice, "If you like, you can stay with me in honour and love, or I will give you supplies and you can return to your people." She chose her people and he gave her supplies.[5]

Abu't-Tufayl said, "I saw the Prophet, may Allah bless him and grant him peace, when I was a boy. A woman came towards him. When she was near him,

---

1. Abu Dawud.
2. Al-Bukhari.
3. Muslim and al-Bukhari.
4. Al-Bayhaqi.
5. Ibn Ishaq and al-Bayhaqi.

he spread out his cloak for her and she sat on it. I asked, 'Who is this?' They replied, 'His foster-mother who suckled him.'"[1]

'Amr ibn as-Sa'ib related that one day the Messenger of Allah, may Allah bless him and grant him peace, was sitting when his father by suckling came up to him. He put out part of his garment for him and the man sat on it. Then his mother by suckling came up and he put out half of his garment on the other side for her and she sat on it. Then his brother by suckling came up and the Prophet, may Allah bless him and grant him peace, got up and made him sit in front of him.[2]

He used to send gifts and clothes to Thuwayba, the client of Abu Lahab, who had been his wet-nurse. When she died, he asked, "Which of her relatives are still alive?" He was told, "No-one."

In the *hadith* from Khadija, she told him, may Allah bless him and grant him peace, "Rejoice! By Allah, Allah will never bring you to grief. You maintain connections with kinsfolk, you bear all, you give help to those who are in need, you give hospitality to the guest and you help people to get what is due to them."[3]

SECTION 19
His humility

In spite of his high position and exalted rank, the Prophet was extremely humble and not in the least proud. There is proof enough of that in the fact that he was given a choice between being a king-prophet or a slave-prophet, and he chose to be a slave-prophet. When he did that, Israfil said to him, "Allah has been generous to you because of your humility to Him. You are the master of the children of Adam on the Day of Rising and the first for whom the earth will open on the Day of Rising and the first to intercede."[4]

Abu Umama said, "The Messenger of Allah, may Allah bless him and grant him peace, came out to us leaning on a staff and we got up for him. He said, 'Do not get up as the Persians do to show esteem for one another.'"[5]

He said, "I am a slave. I eat as a slave eats and I sit as a slave sits."

The Prophet used to ride a donkey and would have someone ride behind him on it. He used to visit the very poor and sit with the poor. He accepted the invitation of the slave and sat among his Companions, mixing with them. He would sit down among whichever part of the company he came to.

In a *hadith* related by 'Umar, the Prophet said, "Do not lavish praise on me

---

1. Abu Dawud.
2. Abu Dawud.
3. Muslim and al-Bukhari.
4. Abu Nu'aym.
5. Abu Dawud and Ibn Majah.

as the Christians lavish praise on the son of Maryam. I am a slave, so say, 'The slave of Allah and His Messenger.'"[1]

Anas said that a woman who had something wrong with her mind came to him and said, "I need something from you." He said, "Sit down, Umm so-and-so, in any of the roads of Madina you choose and I will sit with you until I get you what you need." Anas said that she sat down and the Prophet followed suit until she had got what she needed.[2]

Anas said that the Messenger of Allah used to ride a donkey and answer the invitation of the slave. In the battle against the Banu Qurayza, he rode a donkey with a saddle-cloth which was haltered with with a rope made of palm-fibre. He said that the Prophet would be invited to eat barley bread and rancid butter and he would accept such an invitation. He said that the Prophet went on *hajj* on a shabby saddle on which was a fringed cloth worth four dirhams. He said, "O Allah, make it an accepted *hajj* without any showing-off or desire for reputation in it." This was after the lands had been opened up for him. In that *hajj* he sacrificed a hundred camels.[3]

When he conquered Makka and entered it with the armies of the Muslims, he bowed his head while on his mount so that he nearly touched the front part of the saddle out of humility to Allah.

One of the signs of his humility is that he said, "Do not prefer me over Yunus ibn Matta (the Prophet) and do not create any rivalry between the Prophets and do not prefer me over Musa. We are more entitled to doubt than Ibrahim. If I had remained in prison like Yusuf, I might have answered the summons." When someone said to him, "O best of creation!" he said, "That is Ibrahim."[4] These *hadith* will be discussed later, Allah willing.

'A'isha, al-Hasan ibn 'Ali, Abu Sa'id al-Khudri and others described him. They said that he would work in the house with his family. He would delouse his clothes, mend his sandals, serve himself, sweep the house and hobble the camel. He would take the camels to graze and eat with the servants. He would knead bread with them and carry his own goods from the market.

Anas remarked, "Any of the female slaves in Madina could take the hand of the Messenger of Allah, may Allah bless him and grant him peace, and lead him wherever she wished until what she needed was taken care of."[5]

A man came to him and began to tremble out of awe of him. The Prophet told him, "Relax. I am not a king. I am the son of a Qurayshi woman who eats dried meat."

Abu Hurayra said, "I entered the market with the Prophet, may Allah bless

1. Al-Bukhari.
2. Muslim.
3. Ibid.
4. Ibn Ishaq and al-Bayhaqi.
5. Al-Bukhari.

him and grant him peace, and he bought some trousers. He told the weigher, 'Weigh and then add some.' The man leapt up to kiss the hand of the Prophet who pulled his hand back and said, 'This is what the Persians do with their kings. I am not a king. I am one of your men.' Then he took his trousers and started to carry them, saying, 'The owner is more entitled to carry his property.'"[1]

SECTION 20
His justice, trustworthiness, decency and truthfulness

The Prophet was the most trustworthy, just, decent and truthful of people. Even his opponents and enemies admitted that. He was called "the Trustworthy" before he became a prophet. Ibn Ishaq said, "He was called 'the Trustworthy' because of the sound qualities which Allah had concentrated in him."

Allah said: **"Obeyed, then trustworthy."** (81:21)

Most of the commentators say that this refers to Muhammad, may Allah bless him and grant him peace.

When Quraysh disagreed and formed into factions in the dispute about who should put the Black Stone in its place when the Ka'ba was being rebuilt, they decided that the first man who came would be their judge. It was the Prophet who came, and that was before he was a Prophet. They said, "This is Muhammad. This is the Trustworthy one. We are satisfied with him."

Ar-Rabi' ibn Khuthaym said, "In the *Jahiliyya* they would stand by a judgement between two parties if it came from the Messenger of Allah.[2]

He said, "By Allah, I am the trustworthy one in the heavens and the trustworthy one in the earth."[3]

'Ali said that Abu Jahl said to the Prophet, "We are not calling you a liar. We are saying that what you have brought is a lie." Then Allah revealed, **"They do not call you a liar."** (6:33)

Another person related that Abu Jahl said, "We do not call you a liar and you are not someone who is called a liar among us."

It is said that al-Akhnas ibn Shurayq met Abu Jahl on the day of the Battle of Badr and said to him, "Abu'l-Hakam! There is no-one here to hear what we say. Tell me about Muhammad. Does he tell the truth or is he is a liar?" Abu Jahl said, "By Allah, Muhammad is a truthful man and does not ever lie."

Heraclius asked Abu Sufyan about him, saying, "Did you suspect him of being a liar before he said what he said?" He replied, "No."

An-Nadr ibn al-Harith told Quraysh, "When Muhammad was a young man

---

1. At-Tabarani.
2. Ibn Abi Shayba.
3. At-Tirmidhi.

among you, he was the most pleasing, truthful and trustworthy of you until he had white hairs at his temples and brought you what he brought you. Then you said, 'A magician!' No, by Allah, he is not a magician!"[1]

One *hadith* says that his hand never touched a woman over whom he did not have rights.[2]

In the *hadith* where 'Ali describes him, he says that he was the most truthful of people.[3]

The Prophet said in the *Sahih*, "Woe to you! Who will be just if I am not just? I will lose and be disappointed if I am not just."

'A'isha stated, "Whenever the Messenger of Allah was given a choice between two matters, he chose the easier of the two as long as it was not a wrong action. If it was a wrong action, he was the furthest of people from it."[4]

Abu'l-'Abbas al-Mubarrad said that Chosroes divided up his days allocating them as follows: a windy day was for sleep; a cloudy day was for hunting; a rainy day was for drinking and play; and a sunny day was for attending to people's needs. Ibn Khalawayh said, "Chosroes was not the most knowledgeable of them about the organization of this world, for **'They know the outward of the life of this world while they are heedless of the Next World.'**" (30:7)

"However, our Prophet divided his day into three parts: one part for Allah, one part for his family and one part for himself. Then he divided his own part between himself and his people. He asked the elite to help the common people, telling them to convey to him the needs of those unable to convey it themselves. If someone conveys the needs of someone who is unable to convey it, Allah will give him security on the Day of the Greatest Terror."

Al-Hasan al-Basri said that the Messenger of Allah did not admonish anyone because of someone else's wrong action and he did not accept something that someone said against someone else as true.[5]

Abu Ja'far at-Tabari reported from 'Ali that the Prophet said, "I was never attracted to anything that the people of the *Jahiliyya* used to do except on two occasions. Both times Allah came between me and what I wanted to do. Ever since Allah has honoured me with His message, I have never even considered doing anything evil. One night I asked a slave boy who was herding with me if he would watch the sheep for me while I went into Makka to spend a night as young men spend the night. I went out to do so. When I came to the first house of Makka, I heard the flutes and drums playing for someone's marriage and sat down to watch. I was overcome with sleep and only woke up after sunrise. I

---

1. Ibn Ishaq and al-Bayhaqi from Ibn 'Abbas.
2. Al-Bukhari and Muslim from 'A'isha.
3. At-Tirmidhi.
4. Ibid.
5. Abu Dawud in his *mursal hadith*.

went back without having done anything. The same thing happened another time. I have not considered any evil since then."

SECTION 21
His sedateness, silence, deliberation, manly virtue and excellent conduct

'Umar ibn 'Abdu'l-'Aziz ibn Wuhayb heard Kharija ibn Zayd say that the Prophet was the most sedate of people in any assembly. He almost never moved his limbs.

Abu Sa'id al-Khudri related that when the Messenger of Allah sat in an assembly, he sat with his legs pulled up against his stomach by his hands. This is how he sat most of the time. Jabir ibn Samura said that he sat cross-legged, but sometimes sat squatting. This is also mentioned in the *hadith* of Qayla.

He was often silent and did not speak except when necessary, avoiding people who did not speak well.

His laughter was a smile and his statements were incisive, neither too long nor too short. His companions smiled rather than laughed in his presence out of respect for him and to imitate him. His assembly was one of forbearance, modesty, good-feeling and trust. Voices were not raised in it and disrespect to sacred things did not arise in it. When he spoke, his companions bowed their heads in silence as if there were birds sitting on them.

One of the things that is said about him is that he walked inclining forward, walking as if he were going down a slope. It says in another *hadith*, "When he walked, he walked with concentration. He was known neither to press forward nor falter in his gait, i.e. he was neither impatient nor feeble."

'Abdullah ibn Mas'ud said, "The best conduct is that of Muhammad, may Allah bless him and grant him peace."[1]

Jabir ibn 'Abdullah said, "The words of the Messenger of Allah contained both elegant phrasing and easy flow."[2]

Ibn Abi Hala said, "He was silent for four reasons: forbearance, caution, appraisal and reflection."

'A'isha said that the Messenger of Allah would say something in such a way that someone would have been able to count his words if he had so wished.[3]

The Prophet liked scent and perfume, and he used them often. He encouraged their use and said, "I have been made to love three things in this world of yours: women, scent, and the coolness of my eye is in the prayer."[4]

1. Al-Bukhari.
2. Abu Dawud.
3. Muslim and al-Bukhari.
4. An-Nasa'i and al-Hakim from Anas.

Part of his manliness[1] was that he forbade people to blow on food and drink. He told people to eat the food that was near. He commended the use of the *siwak*, cleaning between the fingers and the toes, and observing the practices of the *fitra*.[2]

SECTION 22
His abstinence regarding the things of this world

More than enough traditions have already been mentioned on the subject of his asceticism in the course of this account. It is sufficient to say that he was content with little of this world and turned away from its fruits. This world was handed to him, lock, stock and barrel, and piled up in heaps in front of him during the course of the conquests, yet when he died, his armour was still in pawn with a Jew in order to provide for his family. He made supplication, saying, "O Allah! Make the provision of the family of Muhammad consist of nourishment."[3]

'A'isha said, "The Messenger of Allah, may Allah bless him and grant him peace, never had his fill of bread for three consecutive days until he passed away." In another variant, "...barley bread for two consecutive days. If he had wanted, Allah would have given him such things that you cannot even imagine." In another version it says, "The family of the Messenger of Allah never had their fill of bread until he met Allah, the Mighty and Majestic."[4]

'A'isha stated, "The Messenger of Allah did not leave a single dinar nor dirham nor a sheep nor a camel."[5]

In the *hadith* of 'Amr ibn al-Harith we find it reported that: "The Messenger of Allah, may Allah bless him and grant him peace, left only his armour, his mule, and some land which he made a gift of charity (*sadaqa*)."[6]

"When he died," 'A'isha said, "there was nothing in his house that a living creature could eat except for some barley on one of my shelves. He told me, 'I was offered the valley of Makka filled with gold and I said, "O Lord, I prefer to be hungry one day and full one day. On the day when I am hungry, I will supplicate and plead with You. On the day when I am full, I will praise You."'"[7]

In another *hadith* it is mentioned that Jibril came down to him, saying, "Allah

---

1. *Muru'a*: manly virtue or moral probity, behaving in a manner which comprises all the virtues: manliness, courage, generosity, honour, refraining from doing secretly what one would be ashamed to do publicly, etc.
2. See page 35.
3. Al-Bukhari and Muslim.
4. Ibid.
5. Muslim.
6. Al-Bukhari.
7. Muslim and al-Bukhari.

greets you and asks you: Would you like Me to give you this mountain in gold to accompany you wherever you want to go?" He bowed his head for an hour and then said, "Jibril, this world is the abode of someone who has no abode and the property of someone who has no property. It is amassed only by those with no intellect." Jibril said to him, "Allah has made you firm, Muhammad, confirming you with the firm word."[1]

'A'isha said, "Sometimes we, the family of Muhammad, went for a month without lighting a fire. There was nothing but dates and water."

'Abdu'r-Rahman ibn 'Awf said, "When the Messenger of Allah, may Allah bless him and grant him peace, died, he and his family did not even have their fill of barley bread."[2] 'A'isha, Abu Umama al-Ansari and Ibn 'Abbas reported something similar. Ibn 'Abbas stated that the Messenger of Allah and his family would go through several consecutive nights without finding anything for their evening meal.

Anas said, "The Messenger of Allah, may Allah bless him and grant him peace, did not eat off a table or off a platter. Fine bread was not prepared for him and boiled sheep was never to be seen."[3]

'A'isha reported that the Prophet's bed consisted of a skin stuffed with palm fibre. Hafsa reported that his bed consisted of a doubled-up hair-cloth on which he slept. She said, "One night, we doubled it four times for him. In the morning, he asked, 'What kind of bed did you make for me last night?' We told him and he said, 'Put it back the way it was. Its softness kept me from praying in the night.' Sometimes he slept on a bed of palm-rope which left marks on his side."[4]

"The Prophet's stomach was never full," 'A'isha said, "but he did not complain to anyone. He preferred poverty to wealth. If he remained doubled-up from hunger for the entire night, that did not prevent him from fasting the next day. If he had wanted, he could have asked his Lord for all the treasures and fruits of the earth and a life of plenty. I used to weep for him because of the state in which I saw him and I rubbed his stomach with my hand because of his hunger. I said, 'May I be your ransom! If only you had enough of this world to feed you!' He replied, ' 'A'isha, what do I have to do with this world? My brothers among the resolute Messengers were patient and steadfast in the face of worse than this. They died as they were and went on to their Lord and how honoured they were! Allah was very generous in rewarding them. Therefore I am too shy to enjoy a life of ease if it means that tomorrow I will fall short in comparison to them. There is nothing I want more than to be joined to my

---

1. Muslim and al-Bukhari.
2. At-Tirmidhi and al-Bazzar.
3. Al-Bukhari.
4. At-Tirmidhi.

brothers and bosom friends.'" She said that he died before a month had passed.[1]

SECTION 23
His fear of Allah, obedience to Him and intensity of worship

His fear of Allah, obedience to Him and the intensity of his worship was based on his knowledge of his Lord. Abu Hurayra said that the Messenger of Allah used to say, "If you knew what I know, you would laugh little and weep much."[2] There is a variant from Abu Dharr, which adds, "I see what you do not see and I hear what you do not hear. The heaven cries out and it has the right to cry out. There is no place in it of four fingers' width but that it contains an angel who is on his forehead in prostration to Allah. By Allah, if you knew what I know, you would laugh little and weep much, and you would not have enjoyed women in your beds and you would have gone out to the mountains crying in order to draw near Allah. Would that I were a tree standing."[3] It is also said that it was Abu Dharr himself who said this. That is the sounder view.

There is the *hadith* of al-Mughira ibn Shu'ba in which he states that the Prophet prayed until his feet became swollen. Another variant says, "until his feet puffed up." The Prophet was asked, "Why do you burden yourself in this way when Allah has forgiven you your past and future wrong actions?" He said, "Should I not be a grateful slave?" The same is related by Abu Salama and Abu Hurayra.[4]

'A'isha said, "The Messenger of Allah, may Allah bless him and grant him peace, was constant in his actions. Which of you can do what he did?" She added, "He would fast until we said, 'He will not break it.' He would not fast until we said, 'He does not fast.'" Something similar is related by Ibn 'Abbas, Umm Salama and Anas.[5]

Anas said, "When you did not want to see him praying at night, you would only see him praying. When you did not wish to see him sleeping, you only saw him sleeping."

'Awf ibn Malik said, "I was with the Messenger of Allah, may Allah bless him and grant him peace, one night. He used the *siwak*, did *wudu'*, and then stood up and prayed. I stood with him. He began with *Surat al-Baqara*. Whenever he passed a verse of mercy, he stopped and made supplication to Allah. Whenever he passed a verse of punishment, he stopped and sought

---

1. There is something approximately the same in Ibn Abi Hatim.
2. Al-Bukhari in *ad-Daqa'iq*.
3. Abu 'Isa at-Tirmidhi.
4. Al-Bukhari and others.
5. Muslim and al-Bukhari.

refuge with Allah. Then he bowed and remained bowing as long as he had stood, saying, 'Glory be to the Master of the *Jabarut*, the *Malakut*, of Greatness and Might.' Then he prostrated and said something similar. Then he recited *Surat Al 'Imran*, and so on, *sura* by *sura*. That is how he did it."[1] Hudhayfa says something similar to this and states that he prostrated for as long as he stood and he sat for a similar length of time between the two prostrations. He then stood up until he had recited *Surat al-Baqara*, *Al 'Imran*, *an-Nisa'*, and *al-Ma'ida*.

'A'isha said that the Messenger of Allah would stand reciting a single verse of the Qur'an for the entire night.

'Abdullah ibn ash-Shankhir said, "I came to the Messenger of Allah, may Allah bless him and grant him peace, while he was praying, and a sound of weeping came from his breast which sounded like a cauldron boiling."[2]

Ibn Abi Hala said, "The Messenger of Allah, may Allah bless him and grant him peace, was always sorrowful and reflective. He never had any rest."[3]

The Prophet said, "I ask forgiveness of Allah a hundred times every day." It is also related that he said it was seventy times.[4]

'Ali reported that he asked the Messenger of Allah about his *sunna*, and he said in reply: "Gnosis is my capital. Intellect is the basis of my *deen*. Love is my foundation. Yearning is my mount. Remembrance of Allah is my intimate companion. Reliance is my treasure. Sorrow is my companion. Knowledge is my armour. Patience is my cloak. Satisfaction is my booty. Incapacity is my boast. Doing-without is my profession. Certainty is my food. Truthfulness is my intercessor. Obedience is enough for me. *Jihad* is my character, and the coolness of my eye is in the prayer."[5]

In another *hadith* the Prophet said: "The fruits of my heart lie in His remembrance. My sorrow is for the sake of my community. My yearning is for my Lord, the Mighty."

SECTION 24
The qualities of the Prophets

The qualities of all the Prophets and Messengers include perfect constitution, handsome form, noble lineage, good character and good traits. This is so because they possess the attributes of perfection, the fulfilment of humanness and all virtue since their rank is the noblest and their degree the highest.

---

1. Abu Dawud and an-Nasa'i.
2. Abu Dawud, at-Tirmidhi and an-Nasa'i.
3. At-Tabarani.
4. Muslim.
5. Mentioned in the *Ihya' of* al-Ghazzali. As-Suyuti says that it is forged. Qadi 'Iyad is reliable and his good opinion of it is based on clear proof.

However, Allah preferred some of them over others.

Allah says: **"Those Messengers, We preferred some of them over others."** (2:252) And He says: **"We selected them with knowledge above all beings."** (44:32)

The Prophet said, "The first company to enter the Garden will be like the full moon..."[1] At the end of the *hadith*, he said, "Every man will have the form of their father, Adam – sixty cubits tall."

He said in a *hadith* transmitted by Abu Hurayra: "I saw Musa. He was a tall, curly-haired man, resembling the men of Shanu'a.[2] I saw 'Isa. He was of medium height, and very red in the face as if he had just come out of a hot bath."[3] In another *hadith* he said that 'Isa was as slender as a sword.

The Prophet said, "Among the descendants of Ibrahim, I am the one who most resembles him."

He said in another *hadith* describing Musa, "He is like the best of the men of dark complexion you have ever seen."[4]

In the *hadith* of Abu Hurayra he also says, "Allah did not send a prophet after Lut who was not from the most noble class of his people."[5] It is also related, "among the wealthy and powerful."

At-Tirmidhi related from Qatada, and ad-Daraqutni from Qatada from Anas, "Allah did not send a prophet without making his face beautiful and his voice beautiful. Your Prophet was the most handsome of them in face and the best of them in voice, may Allah bless him and grant him peace."

In the *hadith* recounting the meeting with Heraclius, Heraclius said, "I questioned you about his lineage and you said that he was of good lineage among you. That is how all the Messengers have been sent – from among the noble families of their people."[6]

Allah says about the Prophet Ayyub: **"We found him steadfast. What an excellent slave! He truly turned to his Lord."** (38:44)

Allah says: **"'O Yahya, take hold of the Book with vigour.' We gave him judgement while still a child, and tenderness and purity from Us – he was godfearing – and devotion to his parents – he was not insolent or disobedient. Peace be upon him on the day he was born, and the day he dies, and the day he is raised up again alive."** (19:12-15)

And He says: **"Allah gives you the good news of Yahya, who will come to confirm a Word from Allah, and will be a leader and a celibate, a Prophet and one of the righteous."** (3:39)

He says: **"Allah chose Adam, Nuh, the family of Ibrahim and the family of Imran."** (3:33-34)

---

1. Muslim and al-Bukhari.
2. A place in Yemen.
3. Muslim and al-Bukhari.
4. Al-Bukhari.
5. Abu Ya'la and Ibn Jarir.
6. Muslim and al-Bukhari.

He says about Nuh: **"He was a thankful servant."** (17:3)

He says about 'Isa: **"Your Lord gives you the good news of a Word from Him. His name is the Messiah, 'Isa, son of Maryam, of high esteem in this world and the Next World, one of those brought near. He will speak to people in the cradle, and also when fully grown, and will be one of the righteous."** (3:45)

He also says quoting 'Isa: **"I am the slave of Allah, He has given me the Book and made me a Prophet. He has made me blessed wherever I am and directed me to pray and give zakat as long as I live"** (19:30-31)

Allah says: **"O you who believe, do not be like those who abused Musa."** (33:69)

The Prophet said, "Musa was a modest man who kept himself covered. Part of his body was never seen due to his modesty."[1] Allah says that Musa said: **"My Lord gave me judgement."** (26:21)

Allah says when mentioning several prophets that every one of them said: **"I am a trusty messenger to you."** (26:108)

He says in reference to Musa: **"The best man you can hire is the one who is strong and trusty."** (28:26)

He says: **"So be steadfast as the Messengers with firm resolve were also steadfast."** (46:35)

He says referring to Ibrahim: **"We gave him Ishaq and Ya'qub, each of whom We guided. And before him We had guided Nuh. And among his descendants were Da'ud and Sulayman, and Ayyub, Yusuf, Musa and Harun. That is how We recompense good-doers. And Zakariyya, Yahya, 'Isa and Ilyas. All of them were among the righteous. And Isma'il, Alyasa', Yunus and Lut. All of them We favoured over all beings. And some of their forebears, descendants and brothers – We chose them and guided them to a straight path. That is Allah's guidance. He guides by it any of His slaves He wills. If they had attributed partners to Him, nothing they did would have been of any use. They are the ones to whom We gave the Book, Judgement and Prophethood. If these people reject it, We already entrusted it to a people who did not. They are the ones Allah guided, so be guided by their guidance."** (6:84-90)

He described them as possessing many qualities – right action, being chosen, judgement and prophethood.

Allah says: **"We gave him the good news of a son imbued with knowledge,"** (51:28) and **"forbearing."** (37:101)

He says: **"Before them We put the Pharaoh's people to the test when a noble Messenger came to them. 'Hand over to me the slaves of Allah. I am a trustworthy Messenger to you.'"** (44:17-18)

He says: **"Allah willing, you will find me among the steadfast."** (37:102)

---

1. Muslim and al-Bukhari.

He says about Isma'il: **"He was true to his promise."** (19:54)

About Musa: **"He was sincere."** (19:51)

About Sulayman: **"What an excellent slave! He truly turned to his Lord."** (38:30)

He further says: **"And remember Our slaves Ibrahim, Is'haq and Ya'qub, men of true strength and inner sight. We purified their sincerity through sincere remembrance of the Abode. In Our eyes they are among the best of chosen men."** (38:45-47)

About Da'ud He says: **"He truly turned to his Lord."** (38:17)

And: **"We made his kingdom strong and gave him wisdom and decisive speech."** (38:20)

He says that Yusuf said: **"Entrust to me the country's stores. Truly I am a knowing guardian."** (12:55)

Regarding Musa: **"Allah willing, you will find me steadfast."** (18:69)

Allah says that Shu'ayb said: **"You will find me, Allah willing, among the right-acting."** (28:27)

And Allah also relates his words, **"I would clearly not want to go behind your backs and do something I have forbidden you to do. I only want to put things right as far as I can."** (11:88)

He says: **"We gave right judgement and knowledge to Lut."** (21:74)

He says: **"They outdid each other in good actions."** (21:90)

Sufyan ath-Thawri said, "Constant sorrow is among many of the qualities and character traits which are mentioned, indicating their perfection. There are many *hadith* about this.

The Prophet said: 'The noble son of a noble son of a noble son of a noble son of a noble man was Yusuf, son of Ya'qub, son of Ishaq, son of Ibrahim, the prophet son of a prophet, son of a prophet, son of a prophet.'"[1]

There is a *hadith* from Anas which says, "Thus the eyes of the prophets slept and their hearts did not sleep."[2]

It is related that in spite of the great kingdom Sulayman was given, he did not lift his eyes towards heaven out of fear and humility towards Allah. He would feed people delicious foods while he ate barley bread. It was revealed to him: "O leader of the worshippers and goal of the ascetics." Once when he was riding on the wind among his armies, an old woman protested to him and he commanded the wind to stop so he could see what she needed before he went on.

Yusuf was asked, "Why are you hungry when you are in charge of the treasures of the earth?" He replied, "I fear that I will become full and so forget the hungry person!"

Abu Hurayra related that the Prophet said,[3] "Recitation was made easy for

---

1. Al-Bukhari and Ibn Hibban.
2. Al-Bukhari.
3. Ibid.

Da'ud. He would give a command to his riding beast and let it loose and could finish his recitation before his animal went off. He only ate from the work of his own hands. Allah says, **"And We made iron malleable for him. 'Make full-length coats of mail, measuring the links with care.'"** (34:11) He used to ask his Lord to provide for him from the work of his own hands so that he would not need to take anything from the treasury.

The Prophet said, "The prayer which Allah loves most is that of Da'ud. The fast which Allah loves most is that of Da'ud. He used to sleep for half of the night, stand up for a third and sleep for a sixth. He would fast every other day. He wore wool and slept on hair. He ate barley bread with salt and ashes. He mixed his drink with tears. He was never seen to laugh after his error nor to look directly at the sky because of his shyness before his Lord and he continued to weep for the rest of his life. It is said that he wept until the plants sprang up from his tears and until the tears formed ridges in his cheeks. It is said that he went out in disguise to learn what people thought of him, and hearing himself praised only made him more humble."[1]

'Isa was asked, "Why do you not ride a donkey?" He replied, "I exalt Allah too much to be occupied with looking after a donkey." He used to wear hair and to eat from the trees. He did not even have a house. He slept wherever sleep overtook him. The name he liked to be called by the most was "the very poor."

It is said that when Musa reached the water of Midian, green vegetables could be seen in his stomach due to his emaciated state.

The Prophet said, "Some of the prophets before me were tested with poverty and lice. They preferred that trial to gifts."[2]

'Isa greeted a pig he met with, "Go in peace." He was asked about it and said, "I do not like to make my tongue move with evil speech."

Mujahid said, "Yahya's food was herbs. He used to weep out of fear of Allah until the tears made ridges in his cheeks. He used to eat with the wild animals to avoid mixing with people."[3]

At-Tabari related from Wahb ibn Munabbih that Musa sought shelter in a shack and ate from a depression in a stone and sipped from it. He drank like an animal out of his humility to Allah because of the honour He had shown him by speaking to him.

All of these reports about them are recorded. Their attributes of perfection, good character, handsome forms and qualities are famous and well-known. We will not dwell at length on them. Do not pay any attention to anything you find in the books of certain ignorant historians and commentators which contradicts this.

---

1. Muslim and al-Bukhari, Ibn Hanbal, Abu Dawud, an-Nasa'i, and Ibn Majah from Ibn 'Umar.
2. Al-Hakim.
3. Ibn Abi Hatim and Ibn Hanbal in *Zuhd*.

SECTION 25
The hadith of al-Hasan from Ibn Abi Hala on the Prophet's qualities

We have told you about some of his praiseworthy qualities, glorious virtues and attributes of perfection. We have shown you that he truly had them, and we have presented ample traditions to support this. The matter itself is far more extensive, so although this chapter about him ranges wide, we have hardly even begun to exhaust all the proofs. The ocean of the knowledge of his qualities is overflowing. Bucket-fulls drawn from it have a negligible effect upon it.

However, we think that we should finish these sections with al-Hasan's *hadith* from Ibn Abi Hala since it covers so many of his qualities and includes quite a lot of his biographical detail.

Al-Hasan ibn 'Ali said, "I asked my uncle Hind ibn Abi Hala about the features of the Messenger of Allah since he was wont to describe them. I wanted him to describe them to me so that I could retain them in my mind. He said:

'The Messenger of Allah, may Allah bless him and grant him peace, was imposing and majestic. His face shone like the full moon. He was somewhat taller than medium height and a little shorter than what could be described as tall. His head was large and he had hair that was neither curly nor straight. It was parted, and did not go beyond the lobes of his ears. He was very fair-skinned with a wide brow, and had thick eyebrows with a narrow space between them. He had a vein there which throbbed when he was angry. He had a long nose with a line of light over it which someone might unthinkingly take to be his nose.

'His beard was thick. He had black eyes, firm cheeks, a wide mouth and white teeth with gaps. The hair of his chest formed a fine line. His neck was like that of a statue made of pure silver.

'His physique was finely-balanced. His body was firm and full. His belly and chest were equal in size. His chest was broad and the space between his shoulders wide. He had full calves. He was luminous.

'Between his neck and his navel there was a line of hair, but the rest of his torso was free of it. He had hair on his forearms and shoulders and the upper part of his chest. He had thick wrists, wide palms, rough hands and feet. His fingers were long. He was fine sinewed. He had high insteps and his feet were so smooth that water ran off of them.

'When he walked, he walked as though he were going down a hill. He walked in a dignified manner and walked easily. He walked swiftly. When he walked, it was as though he were heading down a slope. When he turned to address somebody, he turned his whole body completely. He lowered his glance, glancing downwards more than upwards. He restrained his glance. He spoke first to his Companions and was the first to greet any person he met.'

Al-Hasan said, "Tell me how he spoke."

Ibn Abi Hala replied, 'The Messenger of Allah, may Allah bless him and grant him peace, was always subject to grief and was always reflective. He had no rest and he only spoke when it was necessary. He spent long periods in silence. He began and ended what he said correctly. His words were comprehensive without being either superfluous or wordy or inadequate.

'He had a mild temperament, being neither harsh nor cruel. He valued a gift, even if it was small. He did not censure anything nor criticise or praise the taste of food. He did not get angry because of it. He did not attend to securing his own due nor did he get angry for himself nor help himself.

'When he pointed, he did so with his whole hand. When he was surprised about something, he turned his palm upside down. When he talked, he held his right thumb in his left palm. When he was angry, he turned away and averted his face. When he was happy, he looked downwards. Generally his laughter consisted of a smile and he showed his teeth which were as white as hailstones.'"

Al-Hasan said, "I refrained from mentioning this to al-Husayn ibn 'Ali for a time. Then I spoke to him and found that he had beaten me to it. He had asked our father about how the Messenger of Allah behaved at home and when he was out, and about his features. He had not omitted anything."

Al-Husayn said, "I asked my father about how the Messenger of Allah was at home.

He said, 'It was allowed him to enter his house for his own comfort. When he retired to his house, he divided his time into three parts – one part for Allah, one for his family and one for himself. Then he divided his part between his people and himself. He used the time for the people more for the common people than for the elite. He did not reserve anything for himself to their exclusion. Of his conduct in the part reserved for himself was that he would show preference to the people of merit, and would divide the time according to their excellence in the *deen*. Some people needed one thing, some needed two, and some had many needs. He concerned himself with them and kept them busy doing things that were good for them and the community. He always asked about them and what was happening to them. He used to say, "Those who are present should convey things to those who are absent and you should let me know about what is needed by people who cannot convey their needs to me. On the Day of Rising, Allah will make firm the feet of a person who conveys to a ruler the need of someone who cannot convey it himself." This was all that was mentioned in his presence and he would only accept this from people.""

The *hadith* of Sufyan ibn Waki' says, "They entered as seekers and only parted after having tasted something, leaving as guides," i.e. as men of *fiqh*.

Al-Husayn said, "Tell me about when he went out and how he behaved then?"

His father replied, "The Messenger of Allah, may Allah bless him and grant him peace, held his tongue except regarding what concerned people. He brought people together and did not split them. He honoured the nobles of every group of people and appointed them over their people. He was cautious about people and on his guard against them, but he did that without averting his face from them or being discourteous. He asked about his Companions and he asked people how other people were. He praised what was good and encouraged it, and disliked what was ugly and discouraged it. He took a balanced course, without making changes. He was not negligent, fearing that people would become negligent or weary. He was prepared for any eventuality. He did not neglect a right nor did he let his debts reach the point where others had to help him. The best and most preferred people in his eyes were those who had good counsel for all. Those he most esteemed were those who supported and helped him."

Al-Husayn then asked him about his assembly and how he behaved in it.

He said, "The Messenger of Allah, may Allah bless him and grant him peace, did not sit down or stand up without mentioning Allah. He did not reserve a special place for himself and forbade other people to do so. When he came to people, he sat down at the edge of the assembly and told other people to do the same. He gave everyone who sat with him his share so that no-one who sat with him thought that anyone was honoured more than he was. If anyone sat with him or stood near him to ask for something, he put up with that person until the person turned away. When someone asked him for something he needed, he either departed with it or with some consoling words. He had the kindest and best behaviour of all people, being like a father to them. They were all equal in respect of their rights with him.

"His assembly was one of forbearance, modesty, patience and trust. Voices were not raised in it nor were shortcomings made public nor lapses exposed. Its members were attached to each other by fear of Allah and were humble. The old were respected and mercy was shown to the young. They helped those with needs and showed mercy to strangers."

Al-Husayn then asked about how the Messenger of Allah behaved with his companions.

'Ali said, "The Messenger of Allah, may Allah bless him and grant him peace, was always cheerful, easy-tempered, mild. He was neither rough nor coarse. He did not shout nor utter obscenities. He did not find fault with nor over-praise people. He ignored what was superfluous and left it. He abandoned three things in himself: hypocrisy, storing things up and what did not concern him. He also abandoned three things in respect of other people: he did not censure anyone, he did not scold them, nor try to find out their secrets.

"He only spoke about things for which he expected a reward from Allah. When he spoke, the people sitting with him were as still as if there were birds on their heads. When he was silent, they talked, but did not quarrel in his presence. When someone talked in front of him, they kept quiet until he had finished. Their conversation was about the first topic broached. He laughed at what they laughed at and was surprised at what surprised them. He was patient with a stranger who had coarse language. He said, 'When you find someone asking for something he needs, then give it to him.' He did not look for praise except to counterbalance something. He did not interrupt anyone speaking until that person had himself come to an end by either speaking or getting up from where he was sitting."

This is the end of the *hadith* of Sufyan ibn Waki'.

Someone else asked 'Ali what the silence of the Messenger of Allah was like.

He said, "He was silent for four reasons: forbearance, caution, appraisal, and reflection. His appraisal lay in constantly observing and listening to the people. His reflection was upon what would endure and what would vanish. He had forbearance in his patience. Nothing provocative angered him.

"He was cautious about four things: in adopting something good which would be followed, in abandoning something bad which would be abandoned, in striving to determine what would be beneficial for his community and in establishing for them what would combine the business of this world and the next."

This, with Allah's praise and help, brings to a close our description of him.

Chapter Three

ON THE SOUND AND WELL-KNOWN TRADITIONS RELATED ABOUT THE IMMENSE VALUE PLACED ON HIM BY HIS LORD, HIS EXALTED POSITION AND HIS NOBILITY IN THIS WORLD AND THE NEXT

There is no disputing that he was the noblest of mankind, the Master of the Children of Adam, the person with the highest position in the eyes of Allah, the highest in rank, and the nearest to Him. Know that the *hadiths* which have been reported regarding this are very numerous indeed. We have confined ourselves to those which are sound and well-known, and we have devoted twelve sections to discussing them and their meaning.

SECTION 1
What has come concerning his place with his Lord, the Mighty and Majestic, his being chosen, his high renown, his being preferred, his mastery over the children of Adam, the prerogative of the ranks he was given in this world and the blessing of his excellent name.

Ibn 'Abbas said that the Messenger of Allah said, "Allah divided people into two groups, and He put me in the best group. Allah talks of **'the Companions of the Right'** and **'the Companions of the Left.'** I am among the Companions of the Right and I am the best of the Companions of the Right. Then He divided the two groups into three and put me in the best of the three. He says, **'The Companions of the Right and the Companions of the Left and the Outstrippers, the Outstrippers.'** (56:9) I am among the Outstrippers and I am the best of the Outstrippers. Then He divided the three into tribes and He put me in the best tribe. Allah says, **'We have appointed you races and tribes that you may know one another. Indeed the noblest among you is the most godfearing. Allah is All-Knowing, All-Aware.'** (49:13) I am the most godfearing of the sons of Adam and the noblest in the sight of Allah, and it is no boast. Then He divided the tribes and put me in the best house. He says, **'Allah only desires to remove impurity from you, People of the House, and to purify you.'** " (33:33)[1]

---

1. *Hadith* from at-Tabarani and al-Bayhaqi.

Abu Salama said that Abu Hurayra said, "They asked, 'Messenger of Allah, when was prophethood decreed for you?' He replied, 'When Adam was between the body and the spirit.'"[1]

Wa'ila ibn al-Asqa' reported that the Messenger of Allah said, "Allah chose Isma'il from the children of Ibrahim. He chose the Banu Kinana from the children of Isma'il. He chose the Quraysh from the Banu Kinana. He chose the Banu Hashim from the Quraysh. He chose me from the Banu Hashim."[2]

In the *hadith* of Anas, the Prophet said, "I am the most honoured of the Children of Adam with my Lord and it is no boast."[3]

Then there is what is reported in the *hadith* of Ibn 'Abbas, "I am the noblest of the first and the last and it is no boast."[4]

'A'isha reported that the Prophet said, "Jibril, peace be upon him, came to me and said, 'I have searched the East and West of the earth and I saw no man better than Muhammad and I saw no clan better than the Banu Hashim.'"[5]

Anas said that the *Buraq* was brought to the Prophet on the night of his Night Journey. It shied away from him and Jibril said to it, "Would you do this to Muhammad? No-one has ever ridden you who is more honoured with Allah than he." At that the *Buraq* broke into a sweat.[6]

Ibn 'Abbas reported that the Prophet said, "When Allah created Adam, He made me descend to the earth in his loins. He put me in the loins of Nuh in the Ark and cast me into the fire in the loins of Ibrahim. Then he continued to move me from noble loins to pure wombs until He brought me out from my parents. None of them ever met in fornication."[7]

This is what al-'Abbas ibn 'Abdu'l-Muttalib was indicating when he said:

> Before you came to this world,
>> you were excellent in the shadows and in the repository
> in the time (of Adam)
>> when they covered themselves with leaves.
> Then you fell through the ages –
>> not as a mortal nor a lump of flesh nor as a clot.
> Rather as a drop which rode the ships -
>> and put a bridle on the idol
> Nasr while its people were drowned
>> (in the time of Nuh).

---

1. At-Tirmidhi, sound *hadith.*
2. Muslim.
3. At-Tirmidhi.
4. Ibid.
5. Al-Bayhaqi, Abu Nu'aym and at-Tabarani.
6. Muslim and al-Bukhari.
7. Related by Ibn Abi 'Umar al-'Adani in his *Musnad.*

The drop was transferred from loin to womb.
    As the world proceeded, the next era appeared.
Then your guardian house contained loftiness from Khindif
    underneath which were mountain ranges.
When you were born, the earth shone
    and the horizon was illuminated by your light.
We travel in that illumination
    and in the light and the paths of right guidance.
O coolness of the fire of Ibrahim!
    O cause of the protection in the blazing fire!

Abu Dharr, Ibn 'Umar, Ibn 'Abbas, Abu Hurayra and Jabir ibn 'Abdullah related that he said, "I have been given five things[1] which no Prophet before me was given. I was helped by terror being cast in the hearts of my enemies a month in advance of my arrival. The earth has been made a mosque for me and a place of purity so that when the time of the prayer comes, any man of my community can pray. Spoils, which were not made lawful for any Prophet before me, have been made lawful for me. I have been sent to all people. I have been given intercession."

Another version includes, "Ask and you will be given it." In yet another version, "My community will be presented before me and I will have no fear about what can come to the followed from the follower."

One version has, "I was sent to the red and the black." It is said that the black are the Arabs and the red are the foreigners. It is said that the red are men and the black are the *jinn*.

In another *hadith* reported from Abu Hurayra the Prophet said, "I have been helped by terror being cast into the hearts and I have been given all the words. While I was asleep, I dreamt that the keys of the treasures of the earth were brought and placed in my hands." One variant has, "The Prophets were sealed by me."[2]

'Uqba ibn 'Amir reported that the Prophet said, "I will go ahead on your behalf and I will be a witness for you. By Allah, I am looking at the Water-Basin even now. I have been given the keys to the treasures of the earth. By Allah, I do not fear that you will associate (with Allah) after me, but I fear that you will contend with each other for this world."[3]

'Abdullah ibn 'Amr said that the Messenger of Allah said, "I am Muhammad, the unlettered Prophet. There is no prophet after me. I was given all the words and their seals. I was made to recognise the guardians of the Fire and the bearers of the Throne."[4]

1. Some of them say six. Muslim from Abu Hurayra.
2. Al-Bukhari and Muslim.
3. Ibid.
4. Ahmad ibn Hanbal with a good *isnad*.

Ibn 'Umar said, "I was sent not long before the Final Hour."[1]

Ibn Wahb reported that the Prophet said, "Allah said, 'Ask, O Muhammad!' I said, 'What shall I ask for, my Lord? You took Ibrahim as a friend; You spoke directly to Musa; You chose Nuh; and You gave Sulayman a kingdom which no-one after him can have.' Allah said, 'What I have given you is better than that. I have given you *Kawthar*, and I have placed your name alongside My name which is called out in the heavens. I have made the earth a place of purity for you and for your community. I have forgiven you your past and future wrong actions. You walk among people who are forgiven because of you. I have not done this for anyone before you. I have made the hearts of your community their Qur'ans. I have stored up your intercession for you and I have not stored it up for any prophet but you.'"[2]

The Prophet said in a *hadith* which Hudhayfa related, "My Lord has given me the good news that the first people to enter the Garden will be seventy thousand of my community along with me. With each seventy thousand there will be another seventy thousand and they will not be subjected to any reckoning. He has granted me that my community will not go hungry and that they will not be overcome. He has given me victory, might and terror which runs a month ahead of me. Booty has been allowed for me and my community. He made lawful for me much of what he barred to those before me. He has not put any constriction in the *deen* for us."[3]

Abu Hurayra said that the Prophet said, "Every Prophet has been given signs by which people will believe in him, and what I have been given is the revelation which Allah has revealed to me, and I hope that I will have the greatest number of followers on the Day of Rising."[4]

According to scholars, this means that his miracle will continue as long as this world remains. All the miracles of the Prophets vanished after a time and were only seen by those who were present during their time. The Qur'an will remain generation after generation as something that can be seen by the eye, not just as information, and it will remain until the Day of Rising. This is a simplified discussion of a vast subject. It is also mentioned in the final chapter on miracles.

'Ali said, "Every Prophet was given seven noble companion helpers from among his community. Our Prophet, may Allah bless him and grant him peace, was given fourteen. They included Abu Bakr, 'Umar, Ibn Mas'ud and 'Ammar."[5]

The Prophet said, "Allah protected Makka from the Elephant and He gave

---

1. Ahmad ibn Hanbal with a good *isnad*, also Muslim, al-Bukhari and at-Tirmidhi from Anas.
2. Al-Bayhaqi from Asma'.
3. In the History of Ibn 'Asakir, *marfu'*.
4. Al-Bukhari and Muslim.
5. Ibn Majah and at-Tirmidhi.

His Messenger and the believers power over it. That will not be allowed for anyone after me. It was only made lawful for me for one hour of one day."[1]

Al-'Irbad ibn Sariyya reported that he heard the Messenger of Allah say, "I am the slave of Allah and the Seal of the Prophets. I was cast into the clay of Adam and was the promise of my father Ibrahim and the good news of 'Isa ibn Maryam."[2]

Ibn 'Abbas said, "Allah preferred Muhammad over the angels of the heavens and over all the prophets, may the blessings of Allah be upon them." The people asked, "What is his excellence over the inhabitants of the heavens?" He replied, "Allah says to the inhabitants of the heavens, **'Were any of them to say, "I am a god apart from Him," We would repay him with Hell. That is how We repay wrongdoers,** (21:29) while He said to Muhammad, **'Truly We have granted you a manifest victory, so that Allah may forgive you your earlier errors and any later ones and complete His blessing upon you, and guide you on a Straight Path.'** (48:2)

"They asked, 'What is his excellence over the Prophets?' He replied, 'Allah says, **"We have not sent any Messenger except with the language of his people so he can make things clear to them. Allah misguides anyone He wills and guides anyone He wills. He is the Almighty, the All-Wise"** (14:4) while He said to Muhammad, **"We sent you to all people."'"** (34:28)[3]

Khalid ibn Ma'dan reported[4] that a group of the Companions of the Messenger of Allah said, "Messenger of Allah! Tell us about yourself!" He replied, "Yes, I will. I am the answer to the supplication of my father, Ibrahim, when He said, **'Our Lord, send among them a Messenger from among them.'** (2:129) 'Isa gave good news of me. When my mother was pregnant with me, she dreamt that a light came from her that illuminated the castles of Bosra in Syria. I was suckled among the Banu Sa'd ibn Bakr. While I was out with one of my foster-brothers behind our tents herding some animals of ours, two men wearing white garments came up to me.[5] They held me fast and split open my chest from my throat to my lower belly. Then they took out my heart and split it open. Then they extracted a black drop from it and threw it away. Then they washed my heart and chest with that snow until they had cleaned it."

He said in another *hadith*, "Then one of them reached for something and there was a ring made of light in his hand which would dazzle anyone who looked at it. He sealed my heart with it and my heart was filled with belief and wisdom. Then he put it back. Then the other one passed his hand over that part

---

1. Al-Bukhari and Muslim.
2. Ibn Hanbal, al-Bayhaqi and al-Hakam, *sahih isnad.*
3. *Hadith* al-Bayhaqi, ad-Darimi and Ibn Abi Hatim.
4. The same thing is related from Abu Dharr, Shaddad ibn Aws and Anas ibn Malik.
5. One variant has 'three men with a golden basin filled with snow.'

of my chest and it was healed.[1]

"Then one of them said to his fellow. 'Weigh him against ten of his community,' so they weighed me against them and I outweighed them. Then he said, 'Weigh him against a hundred of his community,' so they weighed me against them and I outweighed them. Then he said, 'Weigh him against a thousand of his community,' so they weighed me against them and I outweighed them. Then he said, 'Leave him. If you were to weigh him against all of his community, he would still outweigh them all.'

"Then they embraced me and kissed my head and kissed me between my eyes. Then they said, 'O beloved, do not fear! If you only knew the blessing that this meant for you, you would be delighted!' Then they said, 'How honoured you are with Allah! Allah and His angels are with you.'" In Abu Dharr's version of the *hadith*, he said, "They left me, and I can almost see them still."

Abu Muhammad al-Makki, Abu'l-Layth as-Samarqandi and others related that when Adam rebelled, he said, "O Allah, forgive me my error by the right of Muhammad!" Allah said to him, "How do you know Muhammad?" He said, "I saw written in every place in the Garden, 'There is no god but Allah, Muhammad is the Messenger of Allah.' So I knew that he was the most honoured of creation in Your eyes." So Allah turned to him and forgave him. It is said that this is the interpretation of the words of Allah, **"Adam learned some words from his Lord."** (2:27)

Another variant has that Adam said, "When you created me, I lifted my gaze to Your Throne and written on it was: "There is no god but Allah, Muhammad is the Messenger of Allah," so I knew there would be no-one held in greater esteem by You than the one whose name You placed alongside Your own name." Allah then revealed to him, "By My might and majesty, he is the last of the prophets among your descendants. If it had not been for him, I would not have created you." It is said that Adam was given the *kunya*, Abu Muhammad. Some people say that it was Abu'l-Bashar (father of mankind).

It is related that Surayj ibn Yunus[2] said, "Allah has angels who, as part of their worship, visit every house which has an Ahmad or Muhammad in it because of the honour in which they hold Muhammad."

Ibn Qani', the Qadi, related from Abu'l-Hamra' that the Messenger of Allah said, "When I was taken on my Night Journey to the heavens, written on the Throne was: 'There is no god but Allah; Muhammad is the Messenger of Allah; I have supported him with 'Ali.'"[3]

Ibn 'Abbas said in explanation of the words of Allah, **"Under it was a treasure for them,"** (18:82) "It is a tablet of gold on which has been written:

---

1. In one variant, from Ad-Darimi and Abu Nu'aym, Jibril said, "It is a sturdy heart which has two eyes in it which see and two ears which hear."
2. Surayj ibn Yunus al-Baghdadi was one of the Imams of *hadith* from whom Muslim, al-Baghawi and Abu Hatim transmitted.
3. At-Tabarani.

How extraordinary for the one who is certain about the decree! – How can he begin? How extraordinary for the one who is certain of the Fire! – How can he laugh? How extraordinary for the one who sees this world and its vicissitudes in respect of people! – How can he be at peace there? I am Allah. There is no god but Me. Muhammad is My slave and My Messenger."[1]

Ibn 'Abbas said, "Written on the door of the Garden is: I am Allah. There is no god but Me. Muhammad is the Messenger of Allah. I will not punish anyone who says that."[2]

It is related that writing was found on an ancient stone which said, "Muhammad is a godfearing, right-acting man and a trusty master." As-Simintari mentioned that he saw a child in one of the cities of Khorasan who had, "There is no god but Allah" written on one side of him and "Muhammad is the Messenger of Allah" on the other. Historians say that a red rose was found in India which had written on it in white, "There is no god but Allah. Muhammad is the Messenger of Allah."

Ja'far ibn Muhammad related that his father said, "A call will be given on the Day of Rising: Let whoever is named Muhammad stand up and enter the Garden by virtue of the honour of his name, may Allah bless him and grant him peace."

Ibn al-Qasim and Ibn Wahb reported that Malik said, "I heard the people of Makka say that there is no house in which there is the name Muhammad which does not prosper and the people of that house are provided for as are their neighbours."

The Prophet said, "None of you will be harmed if he has one, two, or three Muhammads in his house."[3]

'Abdullah ibn Mas'ud said, "Allah looked into the hearts of the slaves and He chose the heart of Muhammad from among them. He chose him for Himself and sent him with His Message."[4]

An-Naqqash related that when the *ayat* was revealed, **"It is not right for you to cause annoyance to the Messenger of Allah or ever to marry his wives after him. To do that would be dreadful in Allah's sight,"** (33:54) the Prophet got up and addressed the people, saying, "Company of the people of belief! Allah the Immense has preferred me over you greatly and He has preferred my wives over you greatly."

---

1. Al-Bazzar.
2. It is not known who related it from him.
3. Ibn Sa'd.
4. Ibn Hanbal, al-Bazzar and at-Tabarani.

SECTION 2
The miracle of the Night Journey

This concerns his intimate conversation with Allah, his vision, his being *imam* of all the prophets and his ascent to the Lote-Tree of the Furthest Limit and what he saw of the greatest signs of his Lord during his Night Journey.

One of his special qualities is revealed by the story of the Night Journey and the exalted degrees that were conferred on him by it. It is mentioned in the Mighty Book and there are commentaries on it in sound *hadith*.

Allah says: **"Glory be to Him who took His slave on a journey one night from the Sacred Mosque to the Furthest Mosque, whose surroundings We have blessed, in order to show him some of Our Signs. He is the All-Hearing, the All-Seeing."** (17:1)

And: **"By the star when it descends, your companion is not misguided or misled; nor does he speak from whim. It is nothing but Revelation revealed, taught him by one immensely strong, possessing power and splendour. He stood there stationary – there on the highest horizon. Then he drew near and hung suspended. He was two bows'-lengths away or even closer. Then He revealed to His slave what He revealed. His heart did not lie about what he saw. What! Do you dispute with him about what he saw? He saw him again another time by the Lote-tree of the Final Limit, beside which is the Garden of Refuge, when that which covered the Lote-tree covered it. His eye did not waver nor did he look away. He saw some of the Greatest Signs of his Lord."** (53:1)

The Muslims do not doubt that his Night Journey is true since it is written in the Qur'an and many and widespread *hadiths* have reported its details and commented on its marvels and the special qualities of our Prophet, Muhammad, it demonstrates. We think that the most complete version of it has already been given but we will indicate a little more about it.

Anas ibn Malik reported that the Messenger of Allah said, "The *Buraq* was brought to me. It was a white animal somewhat taller than a donkey, but smaller than a mule. Its step covered a distance equal to the range of its vision. I mounted it and rode until I was brought to Jerusalem. Then I tied it to the ring which the Prophets use. Then I entered the mosque and prayed two *rak'ats* there. I came out and Jibril brought me a vessel of milk and a vessel of wine. I chose the milk and Jibril said, 'You have chosen the *fitra*.'

"Then he went up with me to the first heaven. Jibril asked for it to be opened and a voice said, 'Who is it?' He replied, 'Jibril.' The voice said, 'Who is with you?' He replied, 'Muhammad.' It said, 'Was he sent for?' He replied, 'He was sent for,' and the door opened for us. I found Adam who welcomed me and prayed for me. Then we went up to the second heaven and Jibril asked for it to be opened. A voice said, 'Who is it?' He replied, "Jibril." It said, "Who is with you?" He replied, "Muhammad." It said, 'Was he sent for?' He replied, 'He was,' and the door was opened for us. There I found my cousins, 'Isa ibn Maryam and Yahya ibn Zakariyya. They welcomed me and prayed for me. Then we went up to the third heaven and the same thing happened. It was opened for me and there was Yusuf. He had been given half of all beauty. He welcomed me and prayed for me. Then we went up to the fourth heaven and the same thing happened. I found Idris, and he welcomed me and prayed for me. Allah has said, **'We raised him up to a high place.'** (19:56) Then we went up to the fifth heaven and the same thing happened. There was Harun who welcomed me and prayed for me. Then we went up to the sixth heaven and the same thing happened. There I found Musa who welcomed me and prayed for me. Then we went up to the seventh heaven and the same thing happened. There I found Ibrahim leaning against the Frequented House (*Al-Bayt al-Ma'mur*). Every day, seventy thousand angels enter into it and do not emerge.

"Then he took me to the Lote-tree of the Furthest Limit whose leaves are like the ears of elephants and whose fruits are like earthernware vessels. When a command from Allah covers it, what is covered undergoes a change which no creature is capable of describing due to its sublime beauty. Then Allah revealed to me what He revealed and He made fifty prayers every day and night obligatory for me. I came down to Musa and he asked, 'What did your Lord make obligatory for your people?' I replied, 'Fifty prayers.' He said, 'Go back to your Lord and ask Him to lighten it. Your community will never be able to do that. I have tested the Banu Isra'il and know by experience.' So I went back to my Lord and said, 'My Lord, lighten it for my community!' so he deducted five prayers. I went back to Musa and said, 'He deducted five for me.' He said, 'Your community will not be able to do that, so go back and ask Him to lighten it.'

"I kept going back and forth between my Lord and Musa until Allah said, 'Muhammad, they are five prayers every day and night. Each prayer counts as ten, so that makes fifty prayers. Whoever intends to do something good, and then does not do it, a good action will be written for him. If he does it, then ten will be written for him. Whoever intends to do something bad and does not do it, nothing will be written against him. If he does it, then one bad action will be recorded.' Then I went down to Musa and told him about that. He said, 'Go back to your Lord and ask Him to lighten it.' The Messenger of Allah said, 'I have gone back to my Lord so often that I am ashamed before Him.'"[1]

1. Muslim. Thabit considers this *hadith* to be excellent (*jayyid*) from Anas. No-one has transmitted it in a more correct form than him. Other people mixed a lot with it from Anas, especially the transmission of Sharik ibn Abi Namir. In the beginning, he mentions the angel coming to him and splitting open his abdomen and washing it with the water of Zamzam which took place before the revelation while he was a child. Sharik says in his *hadith*, "That was before he received revelation," and then he mentions the story of the Night Journey, but there is no disagreement about the fact that it took place after the revelation. More than one person has said that it took place a year before

Yunus ibn Yazid al-Ayli related from Ibn Shihab from Anas that Abu Dharr said that the Messenger of Allah said, "The roof of my house was split open and Jibril descended and opened my breast. Then he washed it with water from Zamzam. Then he brought a gold dish filled with wisdom and belief and he poured it into my breast and then closed it up. He took me by the hand and ascended with me to heaven."[1]

Qatada related a similar *hadith* from Anas from Malik ibn Sa'sa'a which puts things in a different order and has different details and a different order of the Prophets in the heavens. Thabit's *hadith* is better and more precise. There are some additions to the Night-Journey and I will mention some of the useful points in them.

In the *hadith* of Ibn Shihab we find, "Every Prophet said to me, 'Welcome to the right-acting Prophet and right-acting brother,' except for Adam and Ibrahim who said 'a right-acting son.'"

Ibn 'Abbas has, "Then he went up with me until I came to a level plain where I heard the squeaking of pens." Anas has, "Then he went up with me until I came to the Lote-Tree of the Furthest Limit. It was covered in colours that I did not recognise. Then I was brought into the Garden."

In the *hadith* of Malik ibn Sa'sa'a we find, "When I passed Musa, he wept. He was asked, 'Why are you weeping?' He replied, 'Lord, this is a young man who was sent after me and more of his community will enter the Garden than those of my community.'"[2]

In the *hadith* of Abu Hurayra we find, "I saw myself in a group of the Prophets. When the time for the prayer came, I was their *imam*. Someone said, 'Muhammad! This is Malik, the guardian of the Fire, so greet him' I turned around and he greeted me first."[3]

In the *hadith* of Abu Hurayra we find, "Then he travelled until he came to Jerusalem and dismounted. He tied his horse to the Rock and prayed with the angels. When the prayer was over, they asked, 'Jibril, who is this with you?' He said, 'This is Muhammad, the Messenger of Allah and the Seal of the Prophets.' They asked, 'Has he been sent already?' He said, 'Yes.' They said, 'May Allah give him long life as a brother and a khalif! An excellent brother! An excellent khalif!' Then he met the spirits of the Prophets who praised their Lord and he

---

the Hijra. Some say that it was even earlier. Thabit related from Anas from the transmission of Hammad ibn Salama how Jibril came to the Prophet while he was playing with some children at his wet-nurse's place and split open his heart. That story is separate from the *hadith* of the Night Journey as people relate it. The Night Journey to Jerusalem and to the Lote-tree of the Furthest Limit are the same story and the fact that he reached Jerusalem and ascended from there has been proved beyond any doubt.

1. Muslim and al-Bukhari.
2. Ibid.
3. Al-Bayhaqi.

mentioned what each of them said. They were: Ibrahim, Musa, 'Isa, Da'ud, and Sulayman."

He continued, "Muhammad praised his Lord, the Mighty and Majestic, saying, 'All of you have praised your Lord, so I will praise Him. Praise be to Allah who has sent me as a mercy to the worlds and as a bringer of good news and a warner for all people. He has sent down the *Furqan* (Discrimination) on me which makes all things clear. He has made my community the best community and He has made my community a middle community. They are the first and they are the last. He opened my breast for me and removed my burden from me and elevated my renown and made me an opener and a seal.' Ibrahim said, 'This is why Muhammad is better than you.'"

In the *hadith* of Ibn Mas'ud[1] we find, "He brought me to the Lote-Tree of the Furthest Limit which is in the sixth heaven. What rises from the earth to it reaches it and touches part of it. What falls from above it reaches it and touches part of it. Allah says, **'that which covered the Lote-tree covered it.'"** (53:15)

In the version of Abu Hurayra through ar-Rabi' ibn Anas we find, "I was told, 'This is the Lote-Tree of the Furthest Limit. Each member of your community who travels your path will reach it. It is the Furthest Lote-Tree. From its roots issue rivers of sweet water, rivers of unaltered milk, rivers of wine to delight the drinkers, and rivers of pure honey. This tree is so immense that it would take a rider seventy years to ride across its shadow. A single leaf from it would shade creation. Light covers it and angels cover it.'" Abu Hurayra said that this refers to His words, **"that which covered the Lote-tree covered it."**

Allah said to him, "Ask!"

Muhammad said, "You took Ibrahim for a close friend and You gave him an immense kingdom. You spoke directly to Musa. You gave Da'ud an immense kingdom and made iron malleable for him and subjected the mountains to him. You gave Sulayman an immense kingdom and You subjugated to him men, *jinn, shaytans,* and the winds and gave him a kingdom that no-one after him would have. You taught 'Isa the Torah and the Evangel and You let him heal the blind and the leper and You protected him and his mother from the accursed Shaytan so that he would find no way against them."

Allah said to him, "I have taken you as a close friend and a beloved. Written in the Torah is: 'Muhammad is the Beloved of the Merciful.' I have sent you to all people and I made your community such that none will be permitted to speak until they have testified that you are My slave and My Messenger. I made you the first of the prophets to be created and the last of them to be sent. I gave you the seven *Mathani* and I did not give them to any prophet before you. I gave

---

1. Abu Nu'aym.

you the seals of the *Surat al-Baqara* from a treasure under My Throne, and I did not give them to any prophet before you. I made you an opener and a seal."

Another version has: "The Messenger of Allah was given three things: he was given the five prayers; he was given the seals of *Surat al-Baqara*; and he was given pardon for the major wrong actions of everyone of his community who did not associate anything with Allah."[1] Allah says: **"His heart did not lie about what he saw."** Ibn Mas'ud says that he saw Jibril in his true form which had six hundred wings.

The *hadith* of Sharik ibn Abi Namr says that he saw Musa in the seventh heaven. He was taken higher than that to what only Allah knows. Musa said, "I did not think that anyone would ever be raised above me."

Anas said that the Prophet prayed with the Prophets in Jerusalem.

Anas reported that the Messenger of Allah said, "One day while I was sitting, Jibril came and struck me between my shoulders. I got up and went up to a tree in which there was something which resembled two birds' nests. He sat in one and I sat in the other. It grew until it filled the east and west. Had I so wished, I could have touched the sky. Looking around, I glanced at Jibril and it seemed as if he was a piece of transparent cloth. I recognised the superiority of his knowledge of Allah over mine. The gate of heaven was opened and I saw a blinding light and the veil dropped below me. The pearl and the ruby split open, and then Allah revealed to me what He wished to reveal."[2]

Al-Bazzar mentioned that 'Ali ibn Abi Talib said, "When Allah wanted to teach His Messenger the *adhan*, Jibril came to him with a riding beast called the *Buraq*. He went to mount it and it shied away from him. Jibril said, 'Be still. By Allah, no slave more honoured with Allah than Muhammad has ever ridden you.' So he mounted it and rode until it brought him to the veil just below the Merciful. Then an angel came out of the veil and the Messenger of Allah asked, 'Jibril! Who is this?' He said, 'By the One who sent you with the truth, I have the closest station of all creatures to Allah, but I have not seen this angel from the time I was created until this very minute.' The angel said, 'Allah is greater! Allah is greater!' A voice came from behind the veil, 'My slave has spoken the truth. I am greater! I am greater!' The angel said, 'I testify that there is no god but Allah.' A voice from behind the veil said, 'My slave has spoken the truth. There is no god but Me,' and the rest of the *adhan* is mentioned, although he did not mention the response to the words, 'Come to the prayer, come to success.'"

He said, "Then the angel took Muhammad by the hand and advanced him so that he was the *imam* of the inhabitants of the heavens, including Adam and Nuh."

---

1. Muslim.
2. Al-Bazzar and al-Bayhaqi.

Abu Ja'far Muhammad ibn 'Ali ibn al-Husayn said, "Allah honoured Muhammad above the inhabitants of the heavens and the earth."[1]

The veil is for creatures, not for the Creator. They are veiled. The Creator – may He be magnified! – is disconnected from anything that could veil Him since veils are defined by the senses. He veils the eyes, the inner eyes, and the perception of His creatures how and when He wills as He has said, **"No indeed! Rather what they have earned has rusted up their hearts."** (83:14)

In this *hadith*, it says, "Then an angel came out of the veil," so it must be that it is a veil which veils what is beyond it so that the angels cannot perceive His power, immensity, and the marvels of His *Malakut* and *Jabarut* beyond that point. This indicates that this veil is not particular to the Essence. What Ka'b ibn Mati' said in his commentary on the Lote-Tree of the Furthest Limit indicates this: "The knowledge of the angels ends there. There they find the command of Allah and their knowledge does not pass beyond that point."

As for, "below the Merciful," it can be considered that what is connected to it has been omitted, i.e. below the Throne of the Merciful, or one of His immense signs or the bases of the realities of His gnoses, as He knows best. It is similar to the words of Allah, **"Ask the village,"** (12:82) meaning its people.

It says, "A voice came from behind the veil, 'My slave has spoken the truth. I am greater! I am greater!'" The literal meaning of this is that he does not hear Allah's words here, but from behind a veil as Allah says, **"It is not proper for Allah to address any human being except by inspiration, or from behind a veil, or He sends a messenger who then reveals by His permission whatever He wills. He is indeed Most High, All-Wise."** (42:51) This means he does not see Him. His eye is veiled from seeing Him.

If the statement, "Muhammad, may Allah bless him and grant him peace, saw his Lord, the Mighty and Majestic" is true, it is possible that that occurred in another place before or after this and at that time the veil was lifted from his eye so that he saw Him. Allah knows best.

SECTION 3
The reality of the Night Journey

There is disagreement among the early Community and the *'ulama'* about whether the Prophet went on his Night Journey in body or only in spirit. There are three positions.

One group maintain that he went in spirit and that it was a dream, while acknowledging that the dreams of the prophets are true and revelationary. This is what Mu'awiya believed. It is also attributed to al-Hasan al-Basri, although he is also known to have held the opposite position as indicated by Muhammad

---

1. Al-Bazaar.

ibn Ishaq. As evidence for their position they cite Allah's words, **"We did not appoint the vision We showed you, except as a trial and temptation for the people, nor the Accursed Tree in the Qur'an."** (17:60) There is also what is related from 'A'isha, "I did not miss the body of the Messenger of Allah, may Allah bless him and grant him peace." Furthermore, the Prophet said, "While I was asleep", and Anas said, "He was asleep in the *Masjid al-Haram*." The Prophet said, "I woke up and I was in the *Masjid al-Haram*."

Most of the *Salaf* and the Muslims believe that he went on the Night Journey in his physical body while he was awake. This is the truth and has been stated by Ibn 'Abbas, Jabir, Anas, Hudhayfa, Abu Hurayra, Malik ibn Sa'sa'a, Abu Habba al-Badri, Ibn Mas'ud, ad-Dahhak, Sa'id ibn Jubayr, Qatada, Ibn al-Musayyab, Ibn Shihab, Ibn Zayd, al-Hasan al-Basri, Ibrahim, Masruq, Mujahid, 'Ikrima, and Ibn Jurayj. It is proof of what 'A'isha said and it is what is stated by at-Tabari, Ibn Hanbal and many Muslims. It is also what has been said by most of the later *fuqaha'*, men of *hadith*, *kalam*, and Qur'anic commentary.

Another group say that the Night Journey was taken in body while awake from the *Masjid al-Haram* to Jerusalem, and then he went in spirit through the heavens. As evidence for their position they cite the words of Allah, **"Glory be to Him who took His slave on a journey one night from the Sacred Mosque to the Furthest Mosque..."** (17:1) making "the Furthest Mosque" the end of the journey. This event in itself is sufficiently awe-inspiring by reason of the immense honour shown to the Prophet Muhammad by it and the miraculous nature of such a night journey. These people say that if the Night Journey in his physical body had been further than the Furthest Mosque, Allah would have mentioned it so that it would have become even more praiseworthy.

Then these two latter groups disagree about whether he actually prayed at Jerusalem or not. In the *hadith* of Anas and others it says that he prayed there, but Hudhayfa ibn al-Yaman disagrees with that. He said, "By Allah, they did not leave the back of the *Buraq* until they came back."

The true, sound position in this, Allah willing, is that the Night Journey was both in spirit and in body throughout the entire event. The Qur'anic verses, sound traditions and considered opinion all indicate this. One does not abandon the truth of the literal meaning for interpretation except when nothing else is possible. That he went on the Night Journey in body while awake is not impossible. If it had been a dream, Allah would have said, "with the spirit of His slave". Allah also says, **"His eye did not waver nor did he look away."** (53:16)

If it had only been a dream, then it would not have involved either a sign or a miracle. The unbelievers would not have thought it impossible and rejected it and the weak Muslims would not have been doubtful about it and found it a test since things like this are not unknown in dreams. This doubt only arose because they knew that his report indicated it being in his physical body while awake, including what he mentioned about praying with the Prophets in Jerusalem or in the heavens, Jibril bringing him the *Buraq*, the ascension, asking for the heavens to open and it being said, "Who is it?" and the answer "Muhammad" being given, his meeting the Prophets there and what happened with them and their welcome to him, the obligation of the prayer being confirmed and his going back and forth to Musa. Ibn 'Abbas said, "It was direct vision which he saw with his own eyes. It was not a dream."

Al-Hasan al-Basri reported that the Prophet said, "While was I sleeping in the *Hijr*, Jibril came to me and prodded me with his foot. I sat up but I did not see anything so I lay back down again." That happened three times. He said, "The third time, he grabbed me by the arm and pulled me to the door of the mosque. There was the riding animal, the *Buraq*."

Umm Hani' said, "The Messenger of Allah was taken on the Night Journey the night he was in my house. He had prayed the final night prayer and slept with us. At the time of *Fajr*, the Messenger of Allah woke us up. Then he prayed *Subh* with us. He said, 'Umm Hani'! I prayed the final night prayer with you, as you saw, in this valley, then I went to Jerusalem and prayed there. Then I prayed the morning prayer with you as you see.'"[1] This makes it clear that he went in his physical body.

Abu Bakr mentioned[2] that he said to the Prophet about the night of the Night Journey, "Messenger of Allah, I looked for you in your place but I did not find you." The Prophet replied, "Jibril carried me to the Furthest Mosque."

'Umar said that the Messenger of Allah said, "I prayed in the front of the mosque on the evening of the Night Journey and then came to the Rock in Jerusalem. An angel was standing there with three vessels."[3]

These are explicit statements which are clear and not impossible, so the literal meaning is taken.

Abu Dharr reported that the Prophet said, "The roof of my house was split open while I was in Makka. Jibril came down and opened my breast and washed it with Zamzam water. ... Then he took me by the hand and ascended with me."[4]

Anas said, "I was fetched and they took me to Zamzam and opened my breast."

Abu Hurayra reported that the Prophet said, "I saw myself in the *Hijr* when Quraysh were asking me about my Night Journey. They asked me about things about which I was not sure, so I was more distressed than I have ever been. Then Allah made it appear before me so that I could look at it."[5]

1. Ibn Ishaq, at-Tabarani and Ibn Jarir.
2. From Shaddad ibn Aws; in al-Bayhaqi and Ibn Mardawayh.
3. Ibn Mardawayh.
4. Al-Bukhari and Muslim.
5. Muslim.

The same is related from Jabir.[1]

'Umar ibn Al-Khattab related in the *hadith* of the Night Journey that the Prophet said, "I returned to Khadija and she had not yet turned over."

SECTION 4
Refutation of those who say it was a dream

Those who say it was a dream use this *ayat* as proof, **"We did not appoint the vision (ru'ya) We showed you, except as a trial and temptation for the people,"** (17:59) He called it a vision (*ru'ya*).[2] We counter this by saying that Allah said, **"Glory be to Him who took His slave on a journey one night..."** (17:1) This refutes it because you cannot say about someone who is asleep that he went on a journey. Allah also said that **"it is a trial for people."** This confirms that it is vision with the naked eye and a physical journey in the body since a dream would not constitute a "trial". No-one would reject it because anyone can dream something like that and see himself in different places at the same time.

However, the commentators do disagree about this *ayat*. Some of them believe that it was revealed regarding the decision made at Hudaybiya and what the people felt about that.[3] However this is not generally believed to be the case.

As for their statement that he said, "in sleep (*manam*)" in the *hadith* and in another *hadith*, "Between being asleep and awake", and "I was asleep and then woke up", there is no proof in that since it is probable that when the angel first came to him, he was asleep, thus he was asleep at the beginning of his being taken and conveyed at night. There is nothing in the *hadith* that says he was asleep during the entire event, unless you infer that from his words, "I woke up and I was in the *Masjid al-Haram*." His words, "I woke up" could mean "In the morning I found myself..." or he could have woken up from another sleep after he had been returned to his house. It merely indicates that his Night Journey did not last the entire night.

His words, "I woke up and I was in the *Masjid al-Haram*," may be indicative of his immersion in the marvels he perceived in the Unseen Realms (*Malakut*) of the heavens and the earth, and his witnessing of the Highest Assembly which had an inward effect, as well as his vision of the greatest signs of his Lord so that he only recovered and returned to the state of normal humanity when he was back in the *Masjid al-Haram*.

---

1. Al-Bukhari and Muslim.
2. This word is also used for a dream.
3. This refers to the treaty that the Prophet made with Quraysh when he went with some of the Companions from Madina to perform *'umra*. The treaty was an apparent set-back, seemingly prejudicial to the interests of the Muslims, and some were unhappy about it. In the end it showed itself to be an extremely wise decision and a major contributory factor to the final Muslim victory.

A third possibility is that both his sleep and wakefulness were real as the words suggest in that he travelled at night with his body asleep while his heart was conscious. The dreams of Prophets are true. Their eyes sleep and their hearts do not sleep. One of the people of spiritual indication (*isharat*) inclined to something like this opinion, saying that the Prophet closed his eyes so that nothing sensory would distract him from Allah. It would not be sound to say this of the time he was praying with the Prophets. Perhaps there were different states during the course of the Night Journey.

A fourth possibility is that "sleep" here might refer to the physical position of the sleeper lying down. It is strengthened by what is said in the version of 'Abdallah ibn Humayd from Hammam, "While I was asleep – or perhaps he said lying down..." Another version has "...between being asleep and being awake." It is said this expresses the usual position assumed by someone sleeping.

These extra references to sleep, and mention of the splitting of his chest and his drawing near to his Lord occur in the version of this *hadith* through Sharik from Anas in a rare recension. In sound *hadiths*, the splitting of his belly occurred when he was young, before his prophethood, since the *hadith* states, "before he was sent." By general consensus, the Night Journey occurred after he was sent. All of this weakens what is related in the version of Anas, and Anas clearly stated that he was relating from someone else and did not hear it directly from the Prophet.[1]

As for 'A'isha saying, "I did not miss his body", 'A'isha could not have spoken about it from actual witnessing because she was not his wife then nor was she at an age where she could be precise. It could be that she was not even born until after the event. There is some disagreement about exactly when the Night Journey took place. According to the statement of az-Zuhri and those who agree with him, it was at the beginning of Islam, about a year and a half after he became a prophet. 'A'isha was about eight years old at the time of the *hijra*.[2]

Others say that the Night Journey was five years before the *hijra*. It is also said that it was a year before it. Since 'A'isha was not an *actual* witness to it, this indicates that she was relating from someone else. Therefore her report does not supersede other reports which are firmer. Her statement indicates that she would not acknowledge that he saw his Lord with his naked eye. If it had been a dream, she would not have disavowed it.

If it is said that Allah says, **"The heart did not lie about what it saw,"** (53:10) specifying that it was the heart that saw, thus indicating that it was a dream and

---

1. In one place he said, "From Malik ibn Sa'sa'a. In Muslim's book we find, 'Perhaps it was Malik ibn Sa'sa'a with some doubt." Once he said that Abu Dharr related it.
2. The *hijra* took place thirteen years after the commencement of prophethood.

revelation, and not the witnessing of the eye and the senses, we say that this is countered by His words, **"His eye did not waver nor did he look away,"** (53:16) in which the vision is clearly ascribed to the eye. The Qur'anic commentators say that His words, **"His heart did not lie about what he saw,"** means that the heart did not imagine the eye to have been other than truthful. It confirmed what was seen. In other words his heart did not reject what his eye saw.

SECTION 5
His vision of his Lord

The Early Community disagreed about this. 'A'isha rejected it out of hand, and when Masruq asked her, "*Umm al-Mu'minin*! Did Muhammad see his Lord?" she replied, "My hair is standing on end at what you have said," and she repeated it three times. "Whoever told you that has lied. Whoever told you that Muhammad saw his Lord has lied." Then she recited, **"The eyes do not reach to Him, but He reaches to the eyes. He is the All-Penetrating, the All-Aware."** (6:103)[1] Some people agree with what 'A'isha said, and it is well-known that Ibn Mas'ud and Abu Hurayra said similar things, stating that it was Jibril he saw. However, this is disputed.

Certain *hadith* scholars, theologians and the *fuqaha'* reject this statement and the prohibition on the Prophet seeing Allah in this world. Ibn 'Abbas said, "He saw Him with his eyes," while 'Ata' related from him that he saw Him with his heart. Abu'l-'Aliyya said that he saw Him with his heart twice. Ibn Ishaq mentioned that Ibn 'Umar sent to Ibn 'Abbas to ask him whether Muhammad had seen his Lord. He replied, "Yes." The best known opinion is that he saw his Lord with his eye. This is related from him by various paths of transmission. He said that Allah singled out Musa for direct speech, Ibrahim for close friendship and Muhammad for the vision. The proof of it lies in the words of Allah, **"His heart did not lie about what he saw. What! Do you dispute with him about what he saw? He saw Him again another time..."** (53:12-13)

Al-Mawardi said, "It is said that Allah divided His vision and His speech between Musa and Muhammad. Muhammad saw Him twice and He spoke directly to Musa twice."

Abu'l-Fath ar-Razi and Abu'l-Layth as-Samarqandi relate this from Ka'b al-Ahbar, and 'Abdullah ibn al-Harith said that Ibn 'Abbas and Ka'b agreed on this point. Ibn 'Abbas stated, "As for us, the Banu Hashim, we say that Muhammad saw his Lord twice." Ka'b said, "Allah is greater!" until the mountains echoed him. He further said, "Allah divided His vision and His

---

1. The *hadith* is recorded by al-Bukhari, Muslim, at-Tirmidhi and an-Nasa'i.

speech between Muhammad and Musa. He spoke directly to Musa twice and Muhammad saw Him with his heart."

Sharik relates that when Abu Dharr commented on this *ayat*, he said, "The Prophet, may Allah bless him and grant him peace, saw his Lord." As-Samarqandi relates from Muhammad ibn Ka'b al-Qurdhi and Rabi' ibn Anas that the Prophet was asked, "Have you seen your Lord?" He said, "I saw Him with my heart, but I did not see Him with my eye." Malik ibn Yukhamir related from Mu'adh ibn Jabal that the Prophet said, "I saw my Lord and He asked me, 'Muhammad, about what did the Higher Assembly[1] disagree?'"[2]

'Abdu'r-Razzaq ibn Hammam related that Hasan al-Basri used to swear by Allah that Muhammad saw his Lord. Abu 'Umar at-Talamanki related this from 'Ikrima. One of the theologians related this position from Ibn Mas'ud. Ibn Ishaq related that Marwan ibn al-Hakam asked Abu Hurayra, "Did Muhammad see his Lord?" and he replied, "Yes."

An-Naqqash related that Ahmad ibn Hanbal said, "I say that the *hadith* of Ibn 'Abbas means that he saw Him with his eye. He saw Him. He saw Him." He kept repeating that until he ran out of breath.

Abu 'Umar at-Talamanki said that Ahmad ibn Hanbal said that he saw Him with his heart. He shrank from saying that he saw Him with his eyes in this world.

Sa'id ibn Jubayr said, "I do not say that he saw Him nor that he did not see Him."

There is some disagreement between Ibn 'Abbas, 'Ikrima, al-Hasan al-Basri and Ibn Mas'ud in their interpretations of the *ayat*. It is related from Ibn 'Abbas and 'Ikrima, "He saw Him with his heart." Al-Hasan al-Basri and Ibn Mas'ud said, "He saw Jibril." 'Abdullah ibn Ahmad ibn Hanbal related that his father said, "He saw Him."

Ibn 'Ata' relates that Allah's words, **"Did We not expand your breast for you?"** (94:1) mean that He expanded his breast for the vision while He expanded Musa's breast for direct speech.

Abu'l-Hasan 'Ali ibn Isma'il al-Ash'ari and a group of his companions said that he saw Allah with his physical eyes. They said, "Every Prophet is given a sign. Our Prophet was also given one. He was singled out among them by being given the vision." One of the shaykhs hesitated about this and said, "There is no clear proof for it, although it is permitted for it to be so."

The undoubted truth is that it is conceivable for him to have seen Him in this world. There is nothing which makes it logically impossible. The proof that it is permitted in this world lies in the fact that Musa asked for it. It is impossible for a prophet not to know what is permitted for Allah and what is permitted for

1. The angels.
2. Ibn Hanbal and at-Tirmidhi.

himself. He would only ask for something permitted not something impossible. However, the actual event and his witnessing is from the realm of the Unseen about which none has any knowledge except someone who is taught it by Allah.

Allah says, **"You will not see Me, but look at the mountain. If it remains firm in its place, then you will see Me,"** (7:143) meaning you will not be able to bear My vision. Then He made an example for Musa of something stronger and even firmer than his own physical form – the mountain. This does not mean that it is impossible to see Him in this world. In principle, it is feasible. There is no decisive proof in the *Shari'a* that it is impossible or forbidden since it is feasible to see any existent thing, not impossible. There is no proof for the one who says that it is forbidden by the words of Allah, **"The eyes do not reach to Him,"** (6:103) since there are different interpretations of this *ayat* and since, as has already been said, the qualification of the one who says "in this world" does not necessitate the vision of Allah being impossible.

Certain people have used this *ayat* itself as a proof that it is permitted to see Him, and that, in principle, it is not impossible. Some say that it is the eyes of the unbelievers which do not reach to Him. Some say that **"the eyes do not reach to Him"** means they do not encompass Him, as Ibn 'Abbas has said. Others say that the eyes do not perceive Him, but those with inner sight do perceive him. None of these interpretations mean that vision is forbidden or impossible.

Equally, there is no real proof in the words of Allah, **"You will not see Me,"** and **"I have turned to You, and I am the first of the believers,"** (7:143)[1] because, as we have already stated, such statements as these do not constitute a general prohibition. The first of the statements is further said to mean, "You will not see Me *in this world*." This is an interpretation. Furthermore, there is no text forbidding the vision and the *ayat* refers specifically to Musa. Since there are various interpretations and mere probabilities dominate the case, no definitive statement can be reached. His words, "I have turned to You in repentance," mean from asking for what I cannot have.

Abu Bakr al-Hudhali said that **"You will not see Me"** means "It is not for a mortal to be able to look at Me in this world. Whoever looks at Me dies."

I have seen that some of the Early Community and later people thought that it meant that seeing Him in this world is forbidden due to the weakness of people's bodily structure and faculties in this world. These faculties are liable to mishap and destruction. Therefore, they do not have the capacity for the vision of Allah. However, in the Next World, people will have a different structure and will be given more durable faculties and the lights of their inner

---

1. Musa was turning to Allah in repentance because of his request to see Allah.

eyes and hearts will be illuminated. They will then have the strength to bear the vision. Malik ibn Anas said something similar to this: "He is not seen in this world because He is Enduring. The Enduring cannot be seen by the passing. In the Next World they will be provided with enduring eyes, so the Enduring will be seen by the enduring."

These are excellent words, but they do not contain any proof that vision is impossible except in respect of the weakness of the faculties. If Allah strengthens whomever He wills among His slaves and gives him the power to bear the vision, then it is not forbidden for him. The power of the sight of Musa and Muhammad has already been mentioned and their perception was accomplished by a divine power which they had been given so that they could perceive what they perceived and see what they saw. Allah knows best.

Qadi Abu Bakr al-Baqillani mentions in the course of his answers about this *ayat* that it means that Musa saw Allah and that is why he fell down in a swoon. The mountain saw its Lord and became dust as the result of a special perception Allah created for it.

He derives that – and Allah knows best – from His words, **"But look at the mountain. If it remains, then you will see Me."** (7:143) Then He says, **"But when His Lord manifested Himself to the mountain, He crushed it flat and Musa fell unconscious to the ground."** His manifestation to the mountain was His appearance to Musa so that, according to this statement, he actually saw Him.

Ja'far ibn Muhammad said that He distracted him with the mountain so that He could manifest Himself. If it had not been for that, he would have died in his swoon without recovering. He says that this indicates that Musa saw Him. One of the commentators said he saw the mountain. Seeing the mountain is used as a proof by those who say that Muhammad, our Prophet, saw Allah since it is a proof that it is permissible. It is undoubtedly permissible since there is nothing in the *ayat* to forbid it.

As for the vision being necessary for our Prophet and the statement that he saw Him with his eyes, there is nothing to forbid this. One must rely on the these two *ayats* of the *Sura* of the *Star*: **"His heart did not lie about what he saw. What! Do you dispute with him about what he saw?"** (53:11-12) along with the discussion about them which has already been mentioned earlier. It is possible to say what they probably mean, but there is no definitive tradition transmitted from the Prophet regarding this matter.

The report of Ibn 'Abbas concerns his own belief and does not have an *isnad* going back to the Prophet so it is not necessary to act on what he believes the *ayat* contains. It is the same with the *hadith* of Abu Dharr giving his commentary on the *ayat*. The *hadith* of Mu'adh is open to interpretation and both its *isnad* and text are inadequate.

The other *hadith* of Abu Dharr has various versions and is obscure. One recension has, "A light which I saw." One of our shaykhs related that he said, "I saw Him luminous." Another version has, "I asked him and he said, 'I saw a light.'" It is not possible to use any of these versions as a proof for the validity of the vision. If the sound version is, "I saw a light," then he is reporting that he did **not** see Allah. He saw a light and was therefore prevented from seeing Allah. This is what his words, "A light which I saw," refer to – how he saw Him with the veil of light which obscures the sight. This is similar to another *hadith*, "His veil of light." Another *hadith* has, "I did not see Him with my eye, I saw Him with my heart." Then he recited, **"Then he drew near and hung suspended."** (58:8)

Allah is able to create in the heart the perception which normally belongs to the eye or however else He wishes. There is no god but Him. If a *hadith* with a clear text had been related about the subject, it would be believed and relied on since there is no absolute impossibility that it could occur. Allah gives success to what is correct.

SECTION 6
His conversing intimately with Allah

As regards his conversing intimately with Allah during the Night Journey as is indicated by His words, **"Then He revealed to His slave what He revealed,"** (53:1) and the contents of various *hadiths*, most of the commentators say that the One who revealed was Allah to Jibril, and then Jibril revealed it to Muhammad.

There are some who differ from this opinion. Ja'far ibn Muhammad as-Sadiq said, "He revealed to him without any intermediary." Something similar is stated by al-Wasiti. Some of the *mutakallimun*, including al-Ash'ari, believe that Muhammad spoke to his Lord during the Night Journey. They relate this from Ibn Mas'ud and Ibn 'Abbas. Others reject this. An-Naqqash mentioned a narration from Ibn 'Abbas that the Prophet said about the words of Allah, **"He drew near and hung suspended,"** (58:8) "Jibril raised me up and sounds were cut off from me so that I could not hear them. Then I heard my Lord say, 'Calm your terror, Muhammad. Draw near, draw near.'"

The discussion centres on the words of Allah: **"It is not proper for Allah to address any human being except by inspiration, or from behind a veil, or He sends a messenger who then reveals by His permission whatever He wills."** (42:51)

They say that this consists of three categories:

1) From behind a veil, as when He spoke to Musa.

2) By sending angels, as is the case with all the Prophets and most of the time with our Prophet.

3) The third category lies in His words, **"...revealed to His slave what He revealed."** The only form of speech which remains is direct speech with witnessing. It is said that this "revelation" is what He casts into the heart of the Prophet without any intermediary.

Abu Bakr al-Bazzar mentions that 'Ali said something about the *hadith* of the Night Journey which clarifies the way in which the Prophet listened to the words of Allah in the *ayat*. He said, "The angel said, 'Allah is greater! Allah is greater!' and I was told from behind the veil, 'My slave has spoken the truth. I am greater! I am greater!'"

The problems that this *hadith* and the *hadith* mentioned previously by an-Naqqash bring up will be later discussed in detail.

It is permissible for Allah to speak to Muhammad, may Allah bless him and grant him peace, and whichever of His Prophets He singles out, and it is not beyond the bounds of reason. There is nothing in the *Shari'a* which definitively forbids that. If there was a sound tradition about this, it would be relied on.

That Allah spoke to Musa is true. There is a definitive text concerning it in the Qur'an and it is grammatically emphasized. According to what has been related in *hadith*, Allah elevated Musa's position to the seventh heaven because He spoke to him. He raised Muhammad up above this until he reached a level plain where he heard the scratching of pens. How then can it be said to be impossible or unlikely for him to have heard speech in this way? Glory be to the One who singles out whom He chooses for what He wills and raises some above others in degree.

SECTION 7
His proximity and nearness

As for what is related in the *hadith* of the Night Journey and the literal statement of the *ayat* about drawing near and proximity, **"He drew near and hung suspended and was two bows' lengths away or nearer,"** (53:9) most commentators say that the 'drawing near' and 'hanging suspended' either refer to Muhammad and Jibril, or are particular to one of them rather than the other, or refer to the Lote-Tree of the Furthest Limit. Ar-Razi and Ibn 'Abbas say that it is Muhammad who drew near and hung suspended near his Lord. Makki and al-Mawardi relate from Ibn 'Abbas that it is the Lord who drew near to Muhammad and lowered Himself to him, i.e. His command and judgement did.

An-Naqqash relates that al-Hasan said, "He drew near to His slave, Muhammad, and hung there and came close to him. Then He showed him what He wished to show him of His power and immensity."

Ibn 'Abbas said, "It is both forward and back. The Carpet drew near to Muhammad on the evening of the Night Journey and he sat on it. Then it went up and he drew near to his Lord. He said, 'Jibril raised me up and sounds were cut off from me and I heard the words of my Lord, the Mighty and Majestic.'"

We find from Anas in the *Sahih*, "Jibril ascended with him to the Lote-Tree of the Furthest Limit and the Majestic Lord of Might drew near and hung suspended until He was the distance of two bows'-lengths from him or nearer." Then He revealed to him what He wished and He revealed the fifty prayers to him.

Muhammad ibn Ka'b said, "Muhammad drew near his Lord, and the distance was two bows'-lengths." Ja'far ibn Muhammad as-Sadiq said, "His Lord brought him near Him, something like two bows'-lengths."

Ja'far ibn Muhammad said, "Allah's 'drawing-near' has no definition or limit. The slaves' 'drawing-near' is limited."

He also said, "'Howness' cannot be applied to 'drawing near'. Don't you see how Jibril was veiled from His 'drawing-near'? Muhammad, may Allah bless him and grant him peace, drew near to the gnosis and belief in his own heart. He was suspended near by his heart's tranquillity with what drew him near. Doubt and hesitation were removed from his heart."

Know that what is said about drawing near and nearness to or from Allah has nothing to do with nearness of place or proximity in space. As we mentioned from Ja'far as-Sadiq, "'Howness' cannot be applied to 'drawing near.'" The Prophet's drawing near to his Lord and his nearness to Him is made clear by his position, the honour of his rank, the splendour of the lights of his gnosis, and his witnessing the secrets of Allah's unseen world and His power. From Allah to him came kindness, intimacy, expansion and generosity.

Interpretation has to be employed here as with his words, "Our Lord descends to the nearest heaven" since one of the aspects of descent (*nuzul*) is the granting of favours, kind behaviour, acceptance and kindliness. Al-Wasiti said, "Whoever speculates that the Prophet himself drew near sees this in terms of distance. All that draws near to the Real hangs in the distance, i.e. far from the perception of its reality since the Real has neither nearness nor distance."

He said, "Two bows'-lengths or nearer." Whoever makes the pronoun refer to Allah and not to Jibril in this *ayat*, makes it a statement about the limit of nearness, the subtleness of the place, clarification of gnosis, and honour for Muhammad, may Allah bless him and grant him peace. It refers to the fulfilling of his desire, the granting of his request, and the extending to him of a warm welcome and the increase of his position and rank from Allah.

It can be interpreted in the same way as His words, "When he draws near Me by a hand-span, I draw near him an arm-span. Whoever comes to Me walking, I come to him running."[1] Nearness takes place by answering, acceptance, bringing good and hastening what is hoped for.

SECTION 8
His preceding people on the Day of Rising

Anas reported that the Messenger of Allah said, "I will be the first to emerge when men are brought back to life and I will be their spokesman when they arrive [at the Gathering]. I will give them the good news when they despair. The Banner of Praise will be in my hand. I am the noblest of the children of Adam with my Lord, and it is no boast."[2]

In the version of Ibn Zahr from Rabi' ibn Anas, the Prophet stated, "I will be the first of people to emerge when they are brought back and I will be their leader when they arrive and I will be their spokesman when they are silent. I will be their intercessor when they are constrained. I will give them good news when they despair. The Banner of Praise will be in my hand. I am the noblest of the children of Adam with my Lord, and it is no boast. A thousand servants will go around me as if they were hidden pearls."[3]

Abu Hurayra related that the Prophet said, "I will be clothed in one of the robes of the Garden. Then I will stand on the right of the Throne where no created being except me will stand."[4]

Abu Sa'id al-Khudri said that the Messenger of Allah, may Allah bless him and grant him peace, said, "I will be the Master of the Children of Adam on the Day of Rising. The Banner of Praise will be in my hand, and it is no boast. All the Prophets from Adam onwards will be under my banner and I will be the first for whom the earth splits open, and it is no boast."[5]

Abu Hurayra reported that the Prophet stated, "I will be the Master of the Children of Adam on the Day of Rising and the first one for whom the grave splits open, the first to intercede and the first whose intercession is accepted."[6]

Ibn 'Abbas reported that the Prophet said, "I will be the bearer of the Banner of Praise on the Day of Rising and it is no boast. I will be the first to intercede and the first whose intercession is accepted, and it is no boast. I will be the first

1. *Hadith qudsi* in al-Bukhari.
2. At-Tirmidhi.
3. Al-Bukhari in *Al-Adab al-Mufrad*.
4. At-Tirmidhi.
5. Ibn Hanbal and at-Tirmidhi.
6. Muslim and Abu Dawud.

to knock at the gates of the Garden and they will open for me and I will enter with the poor believers, and it is no boast. I will be the most honoured of the first and the last, and it is no boast."[1]

Anas reported from him, "I will be the first of people to intercede in the Garden and I will be the one with the most followers."[2]

Anas reported that the Prophet, peace and blessings be upon him, said, "I will be the master of people on the Day of Rising. Do you know why that is? Allah will gather the first and last ..."[3]

Abu Hurayra reported that the Prophet said, "I hope that I will be the Prophet with the greatest wage on the Day of Rising."[4]

In another *hadith* the Prophet, may Allah bless him and grant him peace, said, "Are you not content that Ibrahim and 'Isa will be among you on the Day of Rising?" Then he added, "They will be among my community on the Day of Rising. Ibrahim will say, 'You are the answer to my prayer and my descendant, so place me among your community.' As for 'Isa, the Prophets are brothers with one father and different mothers. 'Isa is my brother and there is no Prophet between him and me, so I am the closest person to him."[5]

The Prophet said, "I will be the master of the people on the Day of Rising." He will be their master in this world and on the Day of Rising.

However, the Prophet indicated that he alone will have mastery and intercession on that day since people will take refuge with him and will not find anyone but him. A master is that one to whom people go when seeking what they need. On that day he will be the only master among mankind. No-one will compete with him about it or lay claim to it, as Allah says, **"'To whom does sovereignty belong today?' To Allah, the One, the Conqueror!"** (40:16) The Kingdom is His in this world and the Next World. However, in the Next World the claims of those who made them in this world will be cut off. Furthermore, all people will seek refuge with Muhammad to intercede for them. He will be their master in the Next World without any pretension.

Anas reported that the Messenger of Allah said, "On the Day of Rising, I will come to the Gate of the Garden and ask it to open. The Guardian will say, 'Who are you?' I will reply, 'Muhammad.' He will say, 'Because of you I was commanded not to open the door to anyone before you.'"[6]

'Abdullah ibn 'Amr reported that the Messenger of Allah said, "My Basin (*hawd*) is a month's journey across. Its water is whiter than silver and its odour is sweeter than musk. Its jugs are like the stars of heaven. Whoever drinks from

---

1. At-Tirmidhi and ad-Darimi.
2. Muslim.
3. Rest of the *hadith* of intercession. Al-Bukhari and Muslim.
4. Muslim.
5. Ibid.
6. Ibid.

it will never be thirsty again."[1]

Abu Dharr said something similar, mentioning that its length is the distance between Aden and Aila. Rivulets from the Garden flow into it.[2]

The *hadith* about the Basin is also related by Anas, Jabir ibn Samura, Ibn 'Umar, 'Utba ibn 'Amir, Haritha ibn Wahb al-Khuza'i, al-Mustawrid, Abu Barza al-Aslami, Hudhayfa ibn al-Yaman, Abu Umama, Zayd ibn Arqam, Ibn Mas'ud, 'Abdullah ibn Zayd, Sahl ibn Sa'd, Suwayd ibn Jabala, Abu Bakr, 'Umar ibn al-Khattab, Ibn Burayda, Abu Sa'id al-Khudri, 'Abdullah as-Sunabihi, Abu Hurayra, al-Bara', Jundub, 'A'isha, Asma' bint Abi Bakr, Abu Bakra, Khawla bint Qays and others, may Allah be pleased with all of them.

SECTION 9
On his being singled out for Allah's love and close friendship

There are sound traditions concerning this matter. He is called the "Beloved of Allah" by the Muslims.

Abu Sa'id al-Khudri said that the Prophet said, "If I had taken a close friend other than my Lord, I would have taken Abu Bakr."[3]

Another *hadith* states, "Your companion is the close friend of Allah." And from 'Abdullah ibn Mas'ud, "Allah took your companion as a close friend."[4]

Ibn 'Abbas said, "Some of the Companions of the Prophet sat down to wait for him. He came out and stood near them and heard what they were saying to one another. One of them said, 'How extraordinary! Allah took Ibrahim from among His creation as His close friend.' Another said, 'Even more extraordinary was when Allah spoke directly to Musa!' Another said, ''Isa is the word of Allah and His spirit!' Another said, 'Allah chose Adam!'

"Then the Prophet, may Allah bless him and grant him peace, came and greeted them and said, 'I have heard what you were saying and noticed your amazement at the fact that Allah chose Ibrahim as a close friend, and it is the case; that Musa is the intimate of Allah, and it is the case; that 'Isa is the spirit of Allah, and it is the case; and that Adam was chosen, and it is the case. I am the beloved of Allah and it is no boast. I will bear the Banner of Praise on the Day of Rising, and it is no boast. I will be the first to intercede and the first whose intercession is accepted, and it is no boast. I am the first who will knock at the gate of the Garden and Allah will open it for me and let me enter it along with the poor among the believers, and it is no boast. I am the most honoured of the first and the last, and it is no boast.'"[5]

---

1. Muslim and al-Bukhari.
2. Muslim.
3. Al-Bukhari.
4. Muslim, at-Tirmidhi and an-Nasa'i.
5. Ad-Darimi and at-Tirmidhi.

In the *hadith* of Abu Hurayra, part of what Allah said to His Prophet, may Allah bless him and grant him peace, is, "I have taken you for a close friend. It is written in the Torah, 'the Beloved of the Merciful'."[1]

Most disputation in this matter concerns the term "close friendship" and the root from which it is derived. Some say that "close friend (*khalil*)" means "devoted to Allah" since there is no gap (*ikhtilal*) in such a person's devotion to Him and his love for Him. It is also said that *khalil* means "chosen", and He chose this word rather than any other. Another of the scholars has said that the root of the word comes from "considering something to be pure". Ibrahim was called the *khalilu'llah* because he devoted himself constantly to Allah and took his devotion to its limits. The friendship (*khulla*) of Allah was his victory and He made him an Imam for those who have come after him. Others have said that the root of *khalil* is "needy poor person". It is derived from *khulla* meaning need. Ibrahim is called that because he confined his need to his Lord and devoted himself to Him for his needs. He did not place them in front of anyone else. When Jibril came to him when he was in the catapult about to be thrown into the flames and asked, "Do you have any need?" He replied, "Nothing from you, no."

Abu Bakr ibn Furak said, "*Khulla* is the pure love which demands that one be singled out for being permeated (*takhallull*) by the secrets."

Someone else has said that the root of *khulla* is love. It means assistance, kindness, elevation and intercession. This is made clear in the Book of Allah when He says, **"The Jews and the Christians say, 'We are Allah's sons and those He loves.' Say: 'Why, then, does He punish you for your wrong actions?'"** (5:18) It is not conceivable for someone who is beloved to be punished for his wrong actions.

It is thus said that *khulla* is stronger than prophethood because prophethood can contain enmity as Allah said, **"Some of your wives and children are an enemy to you, so be wary of them."** (64:14) But there cannot be any enmity connected with *khulla*.

Ibrahim and Muhammad, peace be upon them, were both called "close friends" because of their devotion to Allah, their looking to Him for their needs and their cutting themselves off from other-than-Him, forsaking other means and causes, or because their election and His hidden kindness to them was greater, and the divine secrets and hidden things of the unseen worlds and gnosis which penetrated (*khalala*) their inward parts. Or it could be because they purified their hearts from other-than-Him so that love for anything else could not penetrate them. This is why one scholar said, "The *khalil* is the one whose heart has no room for other-than-Him." According to them, this is what the Prophet meant when he said, "If I were to take a close friend, I would have

---

1. Al-Bayhaqi.

taken Abu Bakr, but there is the brotherhood of Islam."[1]

Those *'ulama'* who are masters of the matters of the heart disagree about which is higher – the degree of close friendship or the degree of love. Some consider them equal so that the beloved is a close friend and the close friend is a beloved. However, Ibrahim was given close friendship and Muhammad was given love.

One of the scholars said, "The degree of friendship is higher." For proof, he took the words of the Prophet, "If I had taken a close friend other than my Lord, the Mighty...", but he did not do so. The word love was applied to his feelings towards Fatima, her sons, Usama, and others.

Most of them, however, consider "love" higher than "friendship" because the degree of the "Beloved", our Prophet, is higher than that of the *Khalil*, Ibrahim.

The basis of love is inclination to what the beloved finds agreeable. However, this refers to what one can validly incline to and is approved by general consensus. This is the rank of the creature. As for the Creator, He is disconnected from non-essential things. His love for His slave consists in his happiness, protection, success, what will bring him near and the overflowing of His mercy on him. Its furthest extent consists in the removal of the veils from his heart so that he sees Him with his heart and looks at Him with his inner eye. Then, as it says in the *hadith*, "When I love him, I am his hearing by which he hears, his sight by which he sees, and his tongue by which he speaks."[2]

What should be understood by it is that this means nothing other than isolation for the sake of Allah, devotion to Allah, turning from other-than-Allah, the purity of the heart for Allah and the sincerity of actions for Allah.

'A'isha said, "His character was the Qur'an. His pleasure was its pleasure and his anger its anger."

This is why one of those who dealt with the meaning of *khulla* said:

> You penetrated (*khallala*) the path of my spirit.
>> That is why the *khalil* is called *khalil*.
> When I speak, You are my speech.
>> When I am silent, You are the One who stops my tongue.

The fact that our Prophet received the quality of close friendship and the special quality of love is verified by what is indicated in sound traditions which are accepted by the community.

There is enough proof in the words of Allah, **"Say: if you love Allah, follow me, and Allah will love you and forgive you your wrong actions."** (3:30)

The commentators relate that when this *ayat* was revealed, the unbelievers

---

1. Al-Bukhari.
2. *Hadith qudsi* related by al-Bukhari.

said, "Muhammad means that we should love him as the Christians love 'Isa son of Maryam." Angry with them, Allah Almighty revealed this *ayat*, **"Say: Obey Allah and the Messenger. If they turn their backs, Allah does not love the unbelievers."** (3:32) So He increased his honour by commanding them to obey him and connected that to obedience to Himself. He threatened them if they turned away from him by saying, **"If they turn their backs, Allah does not love the unbelievers."** (3:32)

Imam Abu Bakr ibn Furak related that one of the *mutakallimun* spoke about the difference between love and close friendship saying that the *khalil* reaches Allah via an intermediary as indicated by the words of Allah, **"That is how We showed Ibrahim the Kingdom of the heavens and the earth,"** (6:75) whereas the beloved reaches Him by Him as indicated by His words, **"He was two bows'-lengths or nearer."** (53:9)

It is said that the *khalil* is the one the limit of whose desire is forgiveness, as in Allah's words about Ibrahim, **"He who I sincerely hope will forgive my mistakes."** (26:82)

The "beloved" is the one who is absolutely certain of forgiveness as in His words about the Prophet, **"...so that Allah might forgive your past and future wrong actions and complete His blessing on you and guide you to the straight path."** (48:2)

The *Khalil*, Ibrahim, said, **"Do not disgrace me on the day they are raised up,"** (26:82) while it was said to the "Beloved", **"The day when Allah will not disgrace the Prophet and those who believe with him, their light running before them, and at their right hands."** (66:8) The good news comes before the questioning.

In affliction, the *Khalil* said, **"Allah is enough for me,"** but the Beloved was told, **"O Prophet, Allah is enough for you and those of the believers who follow you."** (8:64)

The *Khalil* said, **"Give me a tongue of truthfulness among the last,"** (26:84) whereas the Beloved was told, **"We have elevated your mention."** (94:4) He was given that honour without asking for it.

The *Khalil* said, **"Keep me and my sons from worshipping idols."** (14:35)

The Beloved was told, **"Allah only wishes to remove filth[1] from you, People of the House and purify you."** (33:33)

There is ample information in what we have mentioned to clarify what the people of understanding in this matter have meant concerning the superiority of his stations and states. **"Everyone works according to his form, and your Lord knows best the one who is guided to the path."** (17:70)

---

1. Filth here refers to idol-worship.

SECTION 10
On his being given Intercession and
"the Praiseworthy Station" (al-Maqam al-Mahmud)

Allah says to the Prophet: **"Perhaps your Lord will raise you up to a praiseworthy station."** (17:79)

Adam ibn 'Ali heard Ibn 'Umar say, "People will arrive kneeling on the Day of Rising. Every community will follow their Prophet, saying, 'O so-and-so! Intercede for us!' until intercession comes to the Prophet. That is the day when Allah will raise him to the Praiseworthy Station."[1]

Abu Hurayra said that the Messenger of Allah was asked about the words of Allah: **"Perhaps your Lord will raise you up to a praiseworthy station."** He said, "It means intercession."[2]

Ka'b ibn Malik related that the Prophet said, "People will be gathered on the Day of Rising, and my community and I will be on a hill and my Lord will clothe me in a green robe and give me permission. Then I will say what Allah wills I say. That is the Praiseworthy Station."[3]

Ibn 'Umar mentioned the *hadith* about intercession and said, "He will advance until he knocks at the gates of the Garden. On that day, Allah will grant him the Praiseworthy Station He promised him."

Ibn Mas'ud said, "The Prophet will stand on the right of the Throne in a station where none but he will stand. The first and the last will envy it."[4]

Ibn Mas'ud said that the Messenger of Allah said, "I will stand in the Praiseworthy Station." He was asked, "What is it?" He said, "On that day, Allah will descend on His Throne..."[5]

Abu Musa al-Ash'ari reported that the Prophet said, "I was given a choice between having half of my community enter the Garden or being granted intercession. I chose intercession because it is more encompassing. Do you think that it is on behalf of those who fear Allah? It is for those who err and commit wrong actions."[6]

Abu Hurayra said, "I asked, 'Messenger of Allah! What has come to you about intercession?' He replied, 'My intercession is for the one who testifies that there is no god but Allah sincerely, his tongue confirming what is in his heart.'"[7]

Umm Habiba reported that the Messenger of Allah said, "I was shown what would happen to my community after me and that they would shed each

---

1. Al-Bukhari.
2. Ibn Hanbal and al-Bayhaqi.
3. Ahmad ibn Hanbal.
4. Ibn Hanbal. Ka'b and al-Hasan also related it. One version has, "It is the station in which I will intercede for my community."
5. *Hadith* in Ibn Hanbal.
6. Ibn Majah.
7. Al-Bayhaqi.

other's blood and that what had happened to previous communities from Allah would also happen to them. Therefore I asked Allah to grant me intercession on their behalf on the Day of Rising, and He did that."[1]

Hudhayfa said, "Allah will gather people together on one vast plain where, after hearing the summoner, they will all appear. They will be barefoot and naked as when they were created. They will be silent and no-one will speak except by His permission. There will be a call, 'Muhammad!' He will reply, 'At Your service! Good is in Your hands and evil is not (attributed) to You! The one You guide is guided and Your slave is in Your presence, Yours, to You. There is no place of safety or refuge from You except with You. You are Blessed and Exalted. Glory be to You, the Lord of the House.'" Hudhayfa continued, "That is the Praiseworthy Station which Allah has spoken of."[2]

Ibn 'Abbas said, "As the people of the Fire enter the Fire and the people of the Garden enter the Garden, and only the last company of the Garden and the last company of the Fire are left, the company of the Fire will say to the company of the Garden, 'Your belief has not helped you.' They will call on their Lord, bellowing, and the people of the Garden will hear them, and they will ask Adam and the Prophets after him to intercede on their behalf. Each of the Prophets will make some excuse until they come to Muhammad. He will intercede for them. That is the Praiseworthy Station."[3]

Jabir ibn 'Abdullah said to Yazid al-Faqir,[4] "Have you heard of 'the station of Muhammad'?" (i.e. the station which Allah will grant him.) He replied that he had and said, "It is the Praiseworthy Station of Muhammad by means of which Allah will bring out of the Fire whoever comes out of it," and he mentioned the *hadith* of intercession about bringing the people out of *Jahannam*.[5] Anas said that this refers to the Praiseworthy Station which the Prophet was promised.

In the version of Anas, Abu Hurayra and others, the Prophet said, "Allah will join the first and the last on the Day of Rising and they will be anxious – or consumed. They will say, 'If only we could seek intercession with our Lord!' (One variant has, 'People will surge against each other.')"[6]

Abu Hurayra said, "The sun will draw close and people will feel such intense distress that they will not be able to bear it. They will say, 'Is there no-one to intercede for us?' They will come to Adam and say, 'You are Adam, the father of mankind. Allah created you with His hand and breathed some of His

---

1. Al-Hakim and al-Bayhaqi.
2 Al-Bayhaqi and an-Nasa'i.
3. We find the same as this from Ibn Mas'ud and Mujahid, and 'Ali ibn al-Husayn relates this, attributing it to the Prophet.
4. Yazid ibn Suhayb.
5. Muslim.
6. Muslim and al-Bukhari.

spirit into you and let you dwell in His garden and made the angels prostrate to you and taught you the names of everything. Intercede for us with your Lord so that He will rescue us from the position we are in. Don't you see what we are going through?' He will say, 'My Lord is angry today with such an anger that has never been before and which will never be again. He forbade me the Tree and I rebelled. O my soul! My soul! Go to someone else. Go to Nuh.'

"They will come to Nuh and say, 'You are the first of the Messengers to be sent to the people of the earth and Allah called you a thankful slave. Don't you see what we are going through? Would you intercede for us with your Lord?' He will say, 'My Lord is angry today with such an anger that has never been before and will never be again. O my soul! My soul! (In Anas' version, he mentioned the error which he had committed when he asked his Lord without knowledge. In Abu Hurayra's version, he said, 'I made a supplication on behalf of my family.') Go to someone else. Go to Ibrahim. He is the close friend of Allah.'

"They will come to Ibrahim and say, 'You are the Prophet of Allah and His close friend from among the people of the earth. Intercede with your Lord for us! Don't you see what we are going through?' He will say, 'My Lord is angry today with such an anger that has never been before and will never be again (and he mentioned the lies that he told).[1] O my soul! My soul! I cannot do it. You must go to Musa. He is the *Kalim* of Allah. (One version has, 'He is a slave to whom Allah gave the Torah and spoke directly and whom He made a near confidant.')

"They will come to Musa and he will say, 'I cannot do it and he will mention the error he committed by killing a person. O my soul! My soul! You must go to 'Isa. He is the Spirit of Allah and His Word.'

"They will come to 'Isa and he will say, 'I cannot do it. You must go to Muhammad, a slave whose past and future wrong actions have been forgiven.'

"They will come to me and I will say, 'I will do it. I will go and ask permission from my Lord and He will give me permission. When I see Him, I will fall down in prostration.' (One version has, 'I will come under the Throne and fall down in prostration,' and in another, 'I will stand before Him and praise Him with praises such as I could not articulate if Allah had not inspired me.' In yet another, 'Allah will open up His praises to me, praises of an excellence not granted to anyone before me.')"[2]

In the version of Abu Hurayra we find, "It will be said, 'Muhammad, lift up your head. Ask and it will be given to you. Intercede and your intercession will be granted.' The Prophet will say, 'I will raise my head and say, 'O Lord, my

---

1. When he said, "I am ill" when summoned to the idols; when he said that his wife was his sister to the king; and when he said that the biggest of the idols had done the deed. However, all these are true when interpreted properly.
2. Muslim and al-Bukhari.

community! O Lord, my community!' He will say, 'Bring in by the right-hand gate those of your community who will not be subjected to reckoning, and the rest of your community can share with people in the other gates.'"

This section is not mentioned in Anas' version. Instead he says, "Then I will fall down in prostration and I will be told, 'Muhammad, lift up your head! Speak and you will be heard. Intercede and it will be granted. Ask and you will be given!' I will say, 'O Lord, my community! O Lord, my community!' It will be said, 'Go and bring out whoever has as much as a barley-grain of belief in his heart.' I will go and do that. Then I will return to my Lord and praise him with those praises. Allah will tell me to bring out whoever has the smallest mustard-seed of belief and I will do that."

Then he mentioned the fourth time and said, "I will be told, 'Lift up your head! Speak and you will be heard. Intercede and it will be granted. Ask and you will be given!' I will say, 'O Lord, give me permission for the one who says, "There is no god but Allah".' He will say, "That is not your affair, but by My might, My pride, My immensity and My greatness, I will bring out of the Fire those who say, "There is no god but Allah." (In the version of Qatada, he said, "I do not know if it was the third or fourth time.") I will say, 'O Lord, let the only ones who remain in it be those whom the Qur'an has barred,'" i.e. those obliged to remain in it endlessly.[1]

Similar *hadiths* are related from Abu Bakr, 'Uqba ibn 'Amir, Abu Sa'id al-Khudri and Hudhayfa. Hudhayfa said, "They will come to Muhammad and permission will be granted to him. Then trust (*amana*) and kinship will come and stand on both sides of the *Sirat*."

In the version of Abu Malik from Hudhayfa it says, "They will come to Muhammad and he will intercede. The *Sirat* will be set up and the first of them will pass over like lightning, the next like the wind, the next like a bird and the next running, while our Prophet, may Allah bless him and grant him peace, is on the *Sirat* saying, "O Allah! Grant safety! Grant safety!" until all the people have gone across."[2]

In Abu Hurayra's version, he said, "I will be the first to pass over."

Ibn 'Abbas said that the Prophet said, "*Minbars* will be set up for the Prophets on which they will sit. My *minbar* will remain, but I will not sit on it and will remain standing before my Lord. Allah will ask, 'What do you want Me to do with your community?' I will reply, 'O Lord, make their reckoning quick.' He will call for them and they will be judged. Some of them will enter the Garden by His mercy and some of them will enter the Garden by my intercession. I will continue to intercede until He gives a paper of good deeds to men who have been commanded to the Fire. The Guardian of the Fire will

---

1. See Qur'an 4:116, 4:14.
2. Ibn Abi Da'ud on *Ba'th*.

say, 'Muhammad! You haven't left any scope for the anger of your Lord against your community!'"[1]

From a path of transmission through Ziyad an-Numayri, Anas said that the Messenger of Allah said, "I am the first from whose skull the earth will part, and it is no boast. I am the master of the people on the Day of Rising, and it is no boast. The Banner of Praise will be with me on the Day of Rising and I will be the first for whom the Garden will open, and it is no boast. I will knock at the gate of the Garden and it will be said, 'Who is this?' and I will say, 'Muhammad.' It will open for me and the Majestic will receive me and I will fall down in prostration."[2]

The version of Unays al-Ashhali has in it, "I heard the Messenger of Allah, may Allah bless him and grant him peace, say, 'I will intercede on the Day of Rising for most of the stones and trees on the earth.'"[3]

The general import of these different traditions is that the intercession of the Prophet and his Praiseworthy Station extends from the first intercession to the last. When the people are gathered for the Gathering, and their throats are constricted and they are sweating in the sun, standing all the while before the final Reckoning, he intercedes to allow people relief from the Standing. Then when the *Sirat* is set up and people are judged, he intercedes to hasten to the Garden those among his community who have no reckoning, then he intercedes for those who are to be punished and go to the Fire, and then he intercedes for those who say, "There is no god but Allah". None except the Prophet, may Allah bless him and grant him peace, can do this.

In a sound and famous *hadith* it says, "Every Prophet has a supplication which he makes. I have reserved my supplication for intercession for my community on the Day of Rising."[4]

The people of knowledge say that this means that it is a supplication which he knows will be answered for them and that what they desire from it will be obtained. Every Prophet has a supplication which is answered. Our Prophet, may Allah bless him and grant him peace, has one whose worth cannot be reckoned. However, when the Prophets make a supplication, they waver between hope and fear. The answer of a supplication is guaranteed for them in what they wish to ask for so long as they are sure it will be answered.

Muhammad ibn Ziyad and Abu Salih al-Basri related from Abu Hurayra, "Every Prophet has a supplication which he uses for his community and which is answered. I want to delay my supplication to use as intercession for my community on the Day of Rising." In Abu Salih's version, "Every Prophet has

1. Al-Hakim and al-Bayhaqi.
2. Al-Bayhaqi and Abu Nu'aym.
3. Ibn 'Abdu'l-Barr.
4. Muslim and al-Bukhari.

a supplication which is answered, but every Prophet has already used his supplication."[1]

This supplication is particular to this community and its answer is guaranteed. The Prophet said that he asked for certain things in the *deen* and this world for his community and that some of them were granted and some of them were withheld. He has stored up this supplication for them for the Day of Poverty, the Seal of all Afflictions, the Time of Unanswerable Questions and Unquenchable Desires.[2] May Allah repay him with the best that a prophet can be repaid with from his community! May Allah bless him and grant him peace abundantly!

SECTION 11
On Allah giving mediation, high degree, and *Kawthar* to him in the Garden

'Abdullah ibn 'Amr ibn al-'As said that he heard the Prophet say, "When you hear the *mu'adhdhan*, then say the same as he says and ask for blessings on me. Whoever blesses me once, Allah will bless him ten times. Then ask Allah to give me mediation (*wasila*),[3] for that is a station in the Garden which is designated for only one of the slaves of Allah and I hope that I will be that one. Whoever asks Allah for this mediation will receive intercession."[4]

In another *hadith* from Abu Hurayra, "The 'mediation' is the highest degree in the Garden."[5]

Anas said that the Messenger of Allah, may Allah bless him and grant him peace, said, "While I was travelling in the Garden, a river appeared before me whose banks were domes of pearls. I asked Jibril, 'What is this?' He replied, 'This is *Kawthar* which Allah has given you.' Then he struck the earth with his hand and brought out musk."[6]

'A'isha and 'Abdullah ibn 'Amr relate a similar *hadith* in which the Prophet said, "It flows over pearls and rubies and its water is sweeter than honey and whiter than snow." One version has, "When it flows, it does not cut a ravine. There is a basin to which my community will come."

There is a similar *hadith* from Ibn 'Abbas and he also said, "*Kawthar* is the abundant good which Allah gave him."[7] Sa'id ibn Jubayr said, "It is the river which is in the Garden from the good which Allah gave him."

Hudhayfa said regarding what the Prophet, may Allah bless him and grant

---

1. We find something similar to this is in the transmission of Abu Zur'a from Abu Hurayra and from Anas something similar to the transmission of Ibn Ziyad from Abu Hurayra.
2. The Day of Reckoning.
3. *Wasila* is something which makes something else take place, like a gift or affection. See Qur'an 5:25. What is meant is a high station in the Garden, said to be the nearest to the Throne.
4. Abu Dawud.
5. At-Tirmidhi.
6. Muslim and al-Bukhari.
7. Al-Bukhari.

him peace, mentioned that he had received from his Lord, "He has given me *Kawthar*, a river in the Garden which flows into my Basin."

Ibn 'Abbas said about the words of Allah, **"Your Lord will give to you and you will be satisfied,"** (95:5) that there are a thousand castles of pearl whose earth is musk and which contain what is appropriate for them to contain. A variant version states that they contain the wives and servants which are appropriate for him.

SECTION 12
The *hadiths* related about the prohibition of disparity between the Prophets

Since it is established by the proof of the Qur'an, sound tradition and the consensus of the community that Muhammad is the noblest of mankind and the best of the Prophets, what is the meaning of those *hadiths* which speak of the prohibition against stating any preference between them? For instance, Ibn 'Abbas said that the Prophet said, "No slave should say that I am better than Yunus ibn Matta."[1]

There is also the *hadith* of Abu Hurayra about a Jew who said, "By the One who chose Musa over mankind." One of the Ansar hit him, saying, "How dare you say that when the Messenger of Allah, may Allah bless him and grant him peace, is among us!" The Prophet heard that and said, "Do not make disparity between the Prophets."[2]

One version has, "Do not make me better than Musa." And he says in it, "I do not say that any is better than Yunus ibn Matta."[3]

From Abu Hurayra we have the Prophet's words, "Whoever says that I am better than Yunus ibn Matta has lied,"[4] and Ibn Mas'ud reported that he said, "Do not let any of you say that I am better than Yunus ibn Matta."

In another *hadith* we find: "A man came to him and said, 'O best of mankind!' 'That is Ibrahim,' he retorted."[5]

Know then that the *'ulama'* give different interpretations of these *hadiths*. One interpretation is that the prohibition occurred before he knew that he was the Master of the Children of Adam, so he forbade disparity since he was not yet aware of that. Whoever makes disparity without knowledge has lied. Similarly the statement, 'I do not say that any is better than him,' does not necessarily mean that he is better. It simply prohibits disparity.

The second possibility is that the Prophet said what he said out of humility and to forbid pride and arrogance. This is debatable.

---

1. Al-Bukhari and Muslim, at-Tirmidhi.
2. Al-Bukhari and Muslim, Abu Dawud, an-Nasa'i.
3. Al-Bukhari and Muslim.
4. Al-Bukhari.
5. Muslim, Abu Dawud and at-Tirmidhi.

The third possibility is that making disparity between them would lead to lessening or detracting from the stature of one of them, especially in respect of Yunus, since Allah has told us what He has told us about him. This is to prevent someone with no knowledge from diminishing or detracting from his high rank because of the fact that Allah says, **"When he ran away to the laden ship,"** (37:140) and **"And Dhu'n-Nun when he left in anger and thought We would not punish him."** (21:87) Someone with no knowledge might imagine that he is diminished by this.

The fourth possibility is the prohibition of making disparity in respect to prophethood and the delivery of the message. The Prophets are on the same level in that respect since it is the same in every case and there is no disparity in it. There is disparity regarding increase in the states, election, miracles, rank and kindness which they have received. But as for prophethood itself, there is no disparity in that. Disparity occurs only in matters beyond that. That is why there are the Messengers who simply have a message, those Messengers who possess resolution,[1] the one who has been raised to a high position,[2] and the one who was given judgment as a child.[3] One of them was given the Zabur[4] and another was given the Clear Signs.[5] Allah spoke to one of them[6] and He elevated some of them in degree. He said, **"We favoured some of the Prophets over others."** (17:55) He said, **"These Messengers: We favoured some of them over others."** (2:253)

One of the people of knowledge said, "In this case 'preferring' has to do with preference between them in this world. There are three aspects to it:

1. The greatness and fame of their signs and miracles.
2. The purity and size of their communities.
3. The quality and conspicuousness of their own essential being.

"The last of these refers to the generous gifts for which they were singled out by Allah as particular marks of honour, such as being singled out for direct speech, close friendship, the vision, or whatever other subtle kindnesses or gifts of friendship and election Allah wished to bestow on them."

It is related that the Prophet said, "Prophethood has burdens and Yunus was unable to bear them just as a weak young camel is unable to bear a heavy load."[7]

The Prophet was concerned to guard against anything which might prove a

---

1. Nuh, Ibrahim, Musa, 'Isa and Muhammad.
2. Idris.
3. Yahya.
4. Da'ud.
5. Miracles which no-one could deny, i.e. 'Isa.
6. Musa.
7. *Tafsir* of Ibn Abi Hatim and the *Mustadrak* of al-Hakim from Wahb ibn Munabbih.

source of dissension (*fitna*) because of the illusions of those who would hasten to denigrate the prophethood of Yunus or the fact that he was chosen, lower his rank and diminish his being protected from wrong actions (*'isma*). It is an act of compassion from the Prophet for his community.

There is also a fifth possibility. It is that the "I" refers to the speaker himself, i.e. no-one should think, no matter how great his intelligence, immunity and purity, that he is better than Yunus because of what Allah has related about him. The degree of prophethood is better and higher and its value cannot be reduced by a single atom.

In Part Three we will clarify this matter further if Allah wills. We have made our objective clear and the doubts of the recalcitrant are eliminated by what we have put forward.

Success is by Allah and He is the Helper. There is no god but Him.

SECTION 13
On his names and their excellence

Jubayr ibn Mut'im reported that his father said that the Messenger of Allah, may Allah bless him and grant him peace, said, "I have five names. I am Muhammad. I am Ahmad. I am *al-Mahi* (the Obliterator) by whom Allah will wipe out disbelief. I am *al-Hashir* (the Gatherer) at whose feet people will gather. I am *al-'Aqib* (the Last in Succession)."[1]

Allah calls him Ahmad and Muhammad in His Book.

One of the special gifts of Allah to him lies in the fact that He made his names contain praise of him[2] so the immensity of his gratitude is contained in his mention.

The Prophet, may Allah bless him and grant him peace, is the most sublime of all who give praise and the best of those who are praised and the person who deserves the most praise. He is the most praised (Ahmad) of the praised and the one who praises the most. He will have the Banner of Praise on the Day of Rising as the completion of the perfection of praise for him. He will be known in that place by the attribute of praise. His Lord will give him the Praiseworthy Station there as He has promised him. The first and the last generations will praise him at that time and place for his intercession on their behalf. On that day the Prophet will begin with praises which, as he said, "no-one else has been given." In the books of the Prophets, his community are called "the praisers", therefore it is only fitting that he be called Muhammad and Ahmad.

These two names have other special qualities and signs. Allah, in his wisdom, kept anyone from being called by them before his time. Allah kept

---

1. *Al-Muwatta'*, al-Bukhari, Muslim, Abu Dawud, an-Nasa'i and at-Tirmidhi.
2. Muhammad and Ahmad are both derived from the Arabic root meaning praise.

anyone from being called Ahmad, and even though it was a name which had appeared in the Books and the Prophets had given good news about the bearer of that name, no-one had laid claim to it before him so that there would be no doubt or confusion for the weak of heart.

It is the same with the name Muhammad. None of the Arabs or anyone else had been called that until it became known shortly before his birth that a Prophet would be sent whose name was Muhammad. Thereupon a few Arabs named their sons that hoping that one of them would be him, but Allah knows best where He puts His message. They were: Muhammad ibn Uhayha ibn al-Julah al-Awsi, Muhammad ibn Maslama al-Ansari, Muhammad ibn Barra' al-Bakri, Muhammad ibn Sufyan ibn Mujashi, Muhammad ibn Humran al-Ju'fi and Muhammad ibn Khuza'i as-Sulami. There are only six.

It is said that the first of them to be named Muhammad was Muhammad ibn Sufyan. In Yemen they say that it was Muhammad ibn al-Yuhmid from the tribe of Azd. Then Allah kept everyone named that from claiming the prophethood. No-one could lay claim to it or show any reason to make anyone doubt the Prophet's claim until the two names were established as properly his. Then there was no dispute about it.

As for his saying, "I am *al-Mahi* (the Obliterator) by whom Allah will wipe out disbelief," this can be explained as possibly referring to the obliteration of disbelief from Makka and the lands of the Arabs although he was not alive to witness it, which he was promised that his community would reach; or it could be that the obliteration referred to is general, meaning victory and overcoming as in Allah's words, **"...to exalt it over every other deen."** (9:33) This is explained in this *hadith* as meaning that the Prophet is the one by whom the evil qualities of his followers will be obliterated.

He is called *al-'Aqib*, the Last in Succession, because he follows the other Prophets. As it says in the *Sahih*, "I am *al-'Aqib* and there is no Prophet after me."

The Prophet said, "I am *al-Hashir* (the Gatherer) at whose feet people will be gathered," i.e. in my time and according to my contract, i.e. there is no Prophet after me as confirmed by his being described by Allah as **"the Seal of the Prophets."** (33:40)

It has also been said that the meaning of "at whose feet" is that people will be gathered about him as Allah says, **"so that you could be witnesses against mankind and the Messenger could be a witness against you."** (2:143) It is said that "at whose feet" indicates his precedence. Allah says, **"...they are on a sure footing with their Lord."** (10:2) It is also said that "at whose feet" means in front of him and around him, i.e. they will be gathered to him on the Day of Rising. It is said that "at whose feet" means following his *Sunna*.

"I have five names" is said to mean that they existed in the ancient books and those with knowledge among previous communities knew them.

It is also related that he said, "I have ten names,"[1] mentioning Taha and Yasin among them. Makki is also among those who have related this.

It is said in one of the commentaries that *Taha* means "O Pure! (*Tahir*) O Guide! (*Hadi*)" and that *Yasin* is "O Master! (*Ya Sayyid*)."

Another has mentioned it as, "I have ten names," and he listed the five in the first *hadith* and then added, "I am the Messenger of Mercy, the Messenger of Rest, the Messenger of Fierce Battles, and I am the Tracker. I followed in the tracks of the Prophets. I am *al-Qayyim* (Straight), and *al-Qayyim* is the Complete Unifier."[2]

It is also found in the books of the Prophets that the Prophet Da'ud said, "O Allah, send Muhammad to us to make the *sunna* straight (*muqim*) after the gap." This can be said to have the same meaning as *Qayyim*.

An-Naqqash related that the Prophet said, "I have seven names in the Qur'an: Muhammad, Ahmad, Yasin, Taha, *al-Mudhath-thar* (Enshrouded). *al-Muzzammil* (Enwrapped), and 'Abdullah."

A *hadith* from Jubayr ibn Mut'im mentioned his names as being six: "Muhammad, Ahmad, Khatim, 'Aqib, Hashir and Mahi."

In the *hadith* of Abu Musa al-Ash'ari, the Prophet gives his names, saying, "I am Muhammad, Ahmad, the Tracker, the Gatherer, the Prophet of Repentance, the Prophet of Fierce Battles, the Prophet of Mercy (and one version has the Prophet of Mercy and Rest)."[3]

They are all correct, Allah willing.

As for being the Prophet of Mercy, Repentance, Compassion and Rest, Allah says, **"We only sent you as a mercy to the worlds."** (21:107) He also describes him as having been sent **"to purify them and teach them the Book and the Wisdom"** (62:2) and **"to guide them to the Straight Path"** (5:16) and as **"compassionate, merciful to the believers."** (9:128)

The Prophet said, describing his community, "It is a community which has been shown mercy." Allah Almighty has said about them, **"and they bid each other to steadfastness and bid each other to compassion,"** (90:17) i.e. they are merciful to one another.

Allah sent him as a mercy to his community, a mercy to all the worlds, and one who asks for mercy and forgiveness for them. He made his community one which is shown mercy and attributed mercy to it. The Prophet commanded them to show mercy to each other and praised it, saying, "Allah loves those of His slaves who are merciful."[4]

The Prophet, may Allah bles him and grant him peace, also said, "The

---

1. Al-Bayhaqi and Abu Nu'aym who report it from Ibn Jubayr.
2. Al-Bayhaqi and Abu Nu'aym from ibn Jubayr.
3. Muslim.
4. Muslim and al-Bukhari from Usama.

Merciful loves those who are merciful. Show mercy to whoever is in the earth and whoever is in the heaven will show mercy to you."[1]

As for the term "the Prophet of Fierce Battles", it indicates the fighting and the sword with which he was sent. It is sound.

Hudhayfa related a *hadith* similar to Abu Musa's, "The Prophet of Mercy, the Prophet of Repentance and the Prophet of Fierce Battles."[2]

Al-Harbi related that the Prophet said, "An angel came to me and said, 'You are *al-Quthum* (the Gathered).'"[3]

Al-Harbi added that *al-Quthum* means someone who gathers good. This is known to have been in use as a name among the people of his house, may Allah bless him and grant him peace.

A large number of titles and names for him, may Allah bless him and grant him peace, other than those we have already mentioned are found in the Qur'an, such as: Light, Luminous Lamp, Warner, Giver of Good News, Witnesser, Witnesser, Clear Truth, Seal of the Prophets, the Compassionate, the Merciful, the Trusty, the Foot of Truthfulness, Mercy to the Worlds, the Blessing of Allah, the Firm Handle, the Straight Path, the Piercing Star, Generous, the Unlettered Prophet, and the Caller to Allah.

He has many other attributes and majestic names. Some of them are in the ancient Books and the books of the Prophets, the *hadiths* of the Messenger and the general usage of the community like: the Chosen, the Selected, Abu'l-Qasim, the Beloved, the Messenger of the Lord of the Worlds, the Accepted Intercessor, the Fearfully Aware, the One who Puts Things Right, the Outward, the Guardian, the Truthful, the Confirmer, the Guide, the Master of the Children of Adam, the Master of the Messengers, the Imam of the Fearfully Aware, the Leader of the Glorious Radiant Ones, the Beloved of Allah, the Friend of the Merciful, the Possessor of the Visited Basin, Intercession and the Praiseworthy Station, the Possessor of the Means, Excellence and the High Degree, the Possessor of the Crown, the Ascension, the Banner and the Staff, the Rider of the *Buraq,* the She-Camel and the Fine Camel, the Possessor of the Proof, Power, the Seal, the Sign and the Evidence, the Possessor of the Stick and the Two Sandals.

Among his names in the previous Books are: the Relied-on, the Chosen, the Establisher of the *Sunna*, the Pure, the Spirit of Purity, the Spirit of the Real. That is the meaning of Paraclete in the Gospel. Tha'lab said that the Paraclete is the one who distinguishes between the true and the false.

One of his names in earlier books is "Madh Madh" meaning "Excellent, excellent", and Hamtaya and al-Khatim and al-Hatim according to what Ka'b

---

1. Abu Dawud and at-Tirmidhi from Ibn 'Umar.
2. Ibn Hanbal and at-Tirmidhi.
3. Abu Nu'aym.

al-Ahbar related.

Tha'lab said that *al-Khatim* is the one who seals the line of Prophets. *Al-Hatim* is the best of the Prophets in character and physical form. In Syriac, he is called *Mushaffah* and *al-Munhaminna* (meaning Spirit of Purity). His name is also in the Torah as *Ahid* which Ibn Sirin relates.

The meaning of staff in the phrase "Possessor of the Staff" is the sword. This is explained in the Gospel: "He will have a staff of iron with which he will fight as will his community." It is probable that it is the long staff which the Prophet, may Allah bless him and grant him peace, would hold, and which the Khalifs of this time also have. As for the stick which he is described as having, it is also a staff. Allah knows best, but I think that it is the staff mentioned in the *hadith* of the Basin, "I will drive people from it with my staff for the sake of the People of the Right."

As for "Crown", the turban is meant. At that time, it was particular to the Arabs. The turban is the crown of the Arabs.

His qualities, titles and names are numerous in the books. Those we have mentioned are sufficient, Allah willing.

It is related from Anas that when Ibrahim was born to the Prophet, Jibril came to him and said, "Peace be upon you, Abu Ibrahim."

SECTION 14
On Allah honouring the Prophet with some of His own Beautiful Names and describing him with some of His own Sublime Qualities

It would have been more suitable to include this section in the first chapter because it covers the same subject matter. However, Allah only expanded my breast and guided me to discovery of it by illuminating my thinking, to enable me to extract its jewel, after examining the previous section. We therefore thought that we should include it here to be more complete.

Know that Allah has bestowed a mark of honour on many of the Prophets by investing them with some of His names – for instance, as when He calls Ishaq and Isma'il 'knowing' (*'alim*) and 'forbearing' (*halim*), Ibrahim 'forbearing', Nuh 'thankful' (*shakur*), 'Isa and Yahya 'devoted' (*barr*), Musa 'noble' (*karim*) and 'strong' (*qawwi*), Yusuf a 'knowing guardian' (*hafidh, 'alim*), Ayyub 'patient' (*sabur*) and Isma'il 'truthful to the promise' (*sadiq al-wa'd*). The Mighty Book has referred to them as such in various places where they are mentioned.

Yet He has preferred our Prophet Muhammad, may Allah bless him and grant him peace, since He has adorned him with a wealth of His names in His Mighty Book and on the tongues of His Prophets. We have collected them together after reflecting on the subject and searching our memory since we were unable to locate anyone who had compiled more than two names nor anyone who had dealt with it to any great extent before. We have recorded some of these names in this section. There are about thirty of them. Perhaps Allah, as He inspired what He has already taught us of them and verified this, will now complete the blessing by clarifying what He has not showed us on the subject and unlock it for us.

One of His names is the Praiseworthy (*al-Hamid*). This means the One who is praised because He praises Himself and His slaves praise Him. It also means the One who praises Himself and praises acts of obedience. The Prophet is called Muhammad and Ahmad. Muhammad means praised, and that is how his name occurs in the Zabur of Da'ud. Ahmad means the greatest of those who give praise and the most sublime of those who are praised. Hassan ibn Thabit indicated this when he said:

> It is taken for him from His own name in order to exalt him.
> The One with the Throne is praised (*Mahmud*) and he is Muhammad.

Two of Allah's names are the Compassionate, the Merciful (*ar-Ra'uf, ar-Rahim*). They are similar in meaning. He calls him by them in His Book when He says, "**Compassionate, merciful to the believers.**" (9:128)

One of His names is the Clear Truth (*al-Haqq al-Mubin*). The Truth (*al-Haqq*) means that which exists and is indisputably real. Similarly the Clear (*al-Mubin*) is the One whose divinity is clear. *Bana* and *Abana* mean the same – to make clear to His slaves the matter of their *deen* and their return to Him. He calls the Prophet by this name in His Book when He says, "**Until the Truth comes to you and a *clear* Messenger.**" (43:29) He says, "**Say: I am the *Clear* Warner.**" (15:89) He says, "**The *Truth* has come to you from your Lord.**" (4:170) He says, "**They rejected the *truth* that came to them.**" (6:5)

It is said that this means Muhammad, may Allah bless him and grant him peace. It is said that it means the Qur'an. The meaning here is that it is the opposite of the false. His truthfulness and everything about him is indisputably real. "The clear" is the one whose business and message is clear or the one who clarifies from Allah what he was sent with, as Allah says, "**to make clear to people what was sent down to them.**" (16:44)

Another of Allah's names is the Light (*an-Nur*). It means Possessor of Light, i.e. its Creator or the Illuminator of the heavens and the earth with lights, and the One who illuminates the hearts of the believers with guidance. Allah calls the Prophet "light" when He says, "**A light and a clear book has come to you from Allah.**" (5:15) It is said that this refers to Muhammad. It is also said that it refers to the Qur'an. Allah also calls him "**a luminous lamp.**" (33:46) He called him that to make his position clear, to clarify his prophethood and to illumine the hearts of the believers and the gnostics by what he had brought.

Another of His names is the Witness (*ash-Shahid*). Its meaning is the One who Knows. It is said that He is the Witness of His slaves on the Day of Rising. He calls the Prophet a witness when He says, **"We sent you as a witness,"** (33:46) and **"The Messenger is a witness over you."** (2:143)

One of His names is the Generous/Noble (*al-Karim*). It means the One with Much Good. It is said that it means the Overflower. It is said that it means the Forgiving. It is said it means the High. In the *hadith* related about his names we find, "He is the most generous." Allah calls the Prophet "noble" when He says, **"It is the word of a noble messenger."** (81:19) It is said that this refers to Muhammad and it is also said that it refers to Jibril. The Prophet said, "I am the noblest of the children of Adam." All the meanings of the name can be validly applied to him, may Allah bless him and grant him peace.

Among His names is the Mighty (*al-'Adhim*). It means the One Whose nature is majestic. Everything is under Him. He says about the Prophet, **"Indeed you are truly vast ('adhim) in character."** (68:4) In the beginning of one of the books of the Torah it quotes Isma'il, as saying, "A mighty one will be born for a mighty community and he is mighty with a mighty character."

One of His names is the Compeller (*al-Jabbar*). It means the One who puts things right. It is said that it means the Conqueror. It is said that it means the One with the Mighty Affair. It is said that it means the Proud. The Prophet was called *Jabbar* in the Book of Da'ud. He says, "O *Jabbar*, gird on your sword! Your law and your *shari'a* are accompanied by the awe of your right hand." It means that the Prophet is either putting his community to rights through guidance and instruction or through his power against his enemies or through the height of his station over mankind and his inestimable importance. Allah denied that he had the compelling force (*jabriyya*) of pride which would be inappropriate for him. He says, **"You are not a tyrant over them."** (50:45)

Another of Allah's names is the All-Aware (*al-Khabir*). It means the One who is acquainted with the essence of a thing and knows what its reality is. It is said that it means the One who informs. Allah says, **"The Merciful, ask one aware about Him."** (25:59) Qadi Bakr ibn al-'Ala' said, in this instance, that the one who is commanded to ask is not the Prophet and the one who is to be asked is the one who is aware, namely the Prophet, may Allah bless him and grant him peace. The Prophet is "aware" in both the above-mentioned ways. It is said that he is called this because what he knows is at the limits of the knowledge of what Allah has taught him about His hidden knowledge and immense gnosis. Allah is informing his community about the permission given him to teach.

One of His names is the Opener (*al-Fattah*). It means the One who judges between His slaves, or the Opener of the doors of provision, mercy and of those aspects of their affairs which are shut off from them, or the Opener of their hearts and eyes by gnosis of the Truth.

It can also mean the Helper as in His words, **"If you are seeking victory, victory has come to you,"** (8:19). It is said that it means the one who initiates opening and victory. Allah called the Prophet Muhammad "the Opener" in the long *hadith* of the Night Journey. It says, "I have made you an opener and a seal." In it are the words of the Prophet in praise of His Lord and the enumeration of his ranks: "He elevated my mention for me and made me an opener and a seal."

The Opener here means the judge, or the Opener of the doors of mercy for his community, and the one who opened their inner eyes to the recognition of the Truth and faith in Allah, or the one who helped the truth or began the guidance of the community or the first set forward among the Prophets and their seal as he, may Allah bless him and grant him peace, said, "I was the first of the Prophets to be created and the last of them to be sent."

One of His names is the Thankful (*ash-Shakur*). It means the One who rewards for little action. It is also said that it means the One who praises those who obey. He describes His Prophet Nuh with it, saying, **"He was a thankful slave."** (17:3) The Prophet described himself as such, saying, "Am I not a thankful slave?"[1] acknowledging the blessing of his Lord and recognising its worth, praising Him and striving for increase since He says, **"If you are thankful, I will increase you. If you are ungrateful, My punishment is severe."** (14:7)

One of Allah's names is the Knower (*al-'Alim*), the Knowing (*al-'Allam*), the Knower of the Unseen and the Visible. He described His Prophet as having knowledge and bestowed it on him as a virtue for him from Him. He says, **"He taught you what you did not know, and the bounty of Allah to you was immense."** (4:113) He said, **"He will teach you what you do not know."** (2:151)

Allah's names include the First and the Last. They mean what precedes things before their existence and what remains after they have disappeared. To be exact, He, in Himself, does not have a first or a last. The Prophet said, "I was the first of the Prophets to be created and the last of them to be sent." With that, he explained the words of Allah, **"When We made a covenant with the Prophets and with you and with Nuh."** (33:7) He put Muhammad first.

The Prophet said, "We are the last who goes ahead."[2] He also said, "I am the first for whom the earth will open up, the first to enter the Garden, the first intercessor and the first whose intercession will be accepted." He was the Seal of the Prophets and the last of the Messengers, may Allah bless him and grant him peace.

One of Allah's names is the Strong (*al-Qawi*), the One with Strength, and the Firm. It means the Powerful. Allah describes him with that, saying, **"possessing**

---

1. At-Tirmidhi.
2. Muslim.

great strength, securely placed with the Lord of the Throne." (81:20) It is said that this refers to Muhammad and it is also said that it means Jibril.

One of His names is the Truthful (*as-Sadiq*), and there are *hadiths* which also report that one of the Prophet's names is the Truthful.

Allah's names include the Guardian (*al-Wali*) and the Master (*al-Mawla*). They mean the Helper. Allah says, **"Your Guardian is Allah and His Messenger."** (5:55) The Prophet said, "I am the guardian of every believer."[1]

Allah Almighty says, **"The Messenger is more entitled (*awla*) to the believers."** (33:6) The Prophet said, "As for the one whose master I am, he has an exalted master."[2]

One of His names is the Pardoning (*'Afw*). It means the One who overlooks. Allah describes the Prophet with this attribute in the Qur'an and the Torah and He commands him to pardon. He says, **"Make allowances for people."** (7:199) He also says, **"Pardon them and overlook."** (5:13)

When the Prophet asked about His words, **"Make allowances for people,"** Jibril said, "You should pardon the one who wrongs you." In the Torah and the Gospel, it says, describing his qualities, "He is neither coarse nor harsh, but pardons and overlooks."

One of His names is the Guide (*al-Hadi*). It means that Allah Almighty gives success to whomever He wants among His slaves. It means to indicate the way and to call them to it. Allah says, **"Allah calls to the Abode of Peace and guides whomever He wills to a straight path."** (10:25) Its root comes from 'inclination'. In the commentary on *Taha* it is said to mean, "O Pure! O Guide!" referring to the Prophet. Allah Almighty says to him, **"You guide on a straight path."** (42:52) And He says of the Prophet, **"calling to Allah by His permission."** (33:46) Allah in particular possesses the first meaning (giving success in guidance). He says, **"You do not guide the one you want, but Allah guides whomever He will."** (28:56) The meaning here indicates the way that this attribute can be applied to other-than-Allah.

Allah's names include the Guardian of Faith (*al-Mu'min*), the Protector (*al-Muhaymin*). It is said that these names have the same meaning. The meaning of *Mu'min*, in respect of Allah, is the One who confirms His promise to His slaves. He confirms His true word and confirms His believing slaves and His Messengers. It is said that it means the One who affirms His own unity to Himself. It is said that it means the One who protects His slaves in this world from His injustice and the believers in the Next World from His punishment. It is also said that *Muhaymin* means the Trustworthy (*Amin*). It is said that the word used at the end of supplications, *Amin*, is one of the names of Allah and that it means *Mu'min*. It is said that *Muhaymin* means the

---

1. Al-Bukhari.
2. At-Tirmidhi.

Witness and the Protector.

The Prophet, may Allah bless him and grant him peace, is called *amin* (trustworthy) by Allah Almighty. He says, **"Obeyed, then trusty."** (81:21) The Prophet was known as *al-Amin*, the trustworthy, and was famous for it before and after his prophethood began. In his poem, al-'Abbas called him "protector" when he said:

> Then your protecting house contained loftiness
> from Khindif under which there are mountains.

It is said that *al-Amin* means "protector".

Allah says, **"He believes in Allah and believes the believers"** (99:61) i.e. confirms. The Prophet said, "I am the trustworthy one of my companions."[1] This means the believer (*mu'min*).

Another of Allah's names is the Pure (*al-Quddus*). It means the One disconnected from imperfections and pure of traces of in-timeness. It is said that the *Bayt al-Muqaddis* (Jerusalem) is called so because in it the Prophet was purified from wrong actions. From this root comes the Pure Valley (*Wadi Muqaddis*) and the Spirit of Purity (*Ruh al-Quddus*). It has come down from the books of the Prophets that one of the Prophet's names is *Muqaddas*"(Pure). That is, he is purified of wrong actions as Allah Almighty says, **"That Allah might forgive you your wrong actions,"** (48:2) or that he is the one by whom people are purified of wrong actions and that following him frees people of wrong actions as Allah says, **"...to purify you."** (62:2) Allah Almighty further says, **"He will bring you out of the darkness into the light."** (5:16) Or it can mean purified of blameworthy qualities and base attributes.

One of the names of Allah is the Mighty (*al-'Aziz*). It means the difficult of access, victor, or the one who has no like, or the self-exalted. Allah says, **"Might belongs to Allah and His Messenger"** (63:8) i.e. by inapproachability and majestic value.

Allah describes Himself as bringing good news and warning. He says, **"Their Lord will give them good news of a mercy from Him and satisfaction."** (9:21) He says, **"Allah gives you good news of Yahya,"** (3:39) and **"...a word from Him."** (3:45) Allah calls him a bringer of good news, a warner and a herald, i.e. one who gives good news to the people who obey Him and a warner to the people who rebel against Him.

According to one of the commentaries already referred to, Allah's names include *Taha* and *Yasin*. One of the commentators has also mentioned that they are also among the names of Muhammad, may Allah bless him and grant him peace and bless his family and ennoble them!

---

1. Muslim.

SECTION 15
Recapitulation of the qualities of the Creator and the creature

Here I will mention a point with which I will conclude this section. It will remove any obscurity in what has preceded for those of weak imagination and poor understanding. It will purify such people from the traps of ambiguity and rescue them from subtle distortions.

The point is that all should believe that Allah, in His immensity, greatness and *Malakut*, His beautiful names and sublime attributes, does not resemble any of His creatures and none resembles Him. What the *Shari'a* applies to both the Creator and the creature cannot in reality be considered as similar since the attributes of the Out-of-Time are different from the attributes of created beings. Just as His essence is not like other essences, so His attributes are not like the attributes of created beings since their attributes are not free of non-essential qualities and desires. Allah is far above that. He subsists everlastingly as do His attributes and names. An adequate statement of that is His words, **"There is nothing like Him."** (42:11)

By Allah, how excellent is the statement made by the *'ulama'* of realisation and the gnostics who say: "*Tawhid* is the affirmation of an essence which is not like other essences nor separate from His attributes."

Al-Wasiti went on to clarify this point, and this is also our purpose. He said: "There is no essence like His essence. There is no name like His name. There is no action like His action. There is no attribute like His attribute – except inasmuch as the expressions are similar."

His essence which is out-of-time is too majestic to have a quality which is in-time, just as it is impossible for an essence which is in-time to have an out-of-time attribute. This is what is held by the people of the truth, the *sunna*, and the community as a whole.

Imam Abu'l-Qasim al-Qushayri, commenting on this point to make things clear, said, "This contains all of the points of *tawhid*. How can His essence be like the essence of things which are in-time when It is independent by Its very existence? How can His action resemble the action of a creature when It is not attracted nor is It repelling an acquired imperfection, nor does It come by thoughts or desires. It does not come about by any physical cause or endeavour. The action of the creature only emerges from these factors."

Another of our shaykhs has said, "What they imagine with their imagination or perceive with their intellect is in-time just as they are."

Imam Abu'l-Mu'ali al-Juwayni said, "Whoever stops at something which exists and which he is capable of conceiving is an anthropomorphist. Whoever stops at pure negation is an atheist. If he states that something exists, he admits that it is impossible to perceive His reality and thus he is a unifier. How excellent is the statement of Dhu'n-Nun al-Misri! He said, 'The reality of *tawhid* is that you know that the power of Allah is in things without stating the means and that this occurs without His being mixed with them, and that His action is the cause of everything, but this action has no cause. Whatever you formulate in your imagination, Allah is not that.' These are precious, wonderful, precise words."

The last part of Dhu'n-Nun's statement is an explanation of His words, **"There is nothing like Him."** (42:11) Another part explains His words, **"He will not be questioned about what He does, but they will be questioned."** (21:23) It also explains His words, **"Our word to a thing when We desire it is that We say to it, 'Be!' and it is."** (36:82)

May Allah make you and us firm in *tawhid* and affirmation and disconnection and make us avoid the areas of misguidance and errors which lead to atheism and anthropomorphism by His favour and mercy!

Chapter Four

ON THE MIRACLES WHICH ALLAH MANIFESTED AT HIS HANDS AND THE SPECIAL QUALITIES AND MARKS OF HONOUR (KARAMAT) WITH WHICH HE HONOURED HIM

SECTION 1
Preface

Anyone who reflects will have gathered that this book was not compiled for those who deny the prophethood of our Prophet nor for those who contest his miracles. This would require us to establish proofs for these miracles and to defend them so that any opponent would find no way to contest them. We will, however, mention the preconditions of the miracles, the Challenge (*tahaddi*) and its definition, and the invalidity of the statement of those who disclaim the abrogation of other *shari'as* and how they are refuted. We have written this book for the people of the *deen* of the Prophet who answer his call and confirm his prophethood so that it will intensify their love for him and increase their actions and so that **"they might increase their belief with more belief "** (48:5)

Our intention in this chapter is to affirm the bases of his miracles and famous signs in order to demonstrate the immense value placed on him by his Lord. We will present those miracles and signs which have been verified and have sound *isnads* and so are largely certain or nearly so. We have added some of what is found in the famous books of the Imams.

When the fair-minded reader reflects on what we have already presented regarding the beautiful things that have come down about the Prophet, his praiseworthy life, all his qualities, the evidence of his exalted state and his exact words, he will be left in no doubt regarding the validity of his prophethood and the truth of his claim.

This has been enough to cause more than one person to become Muslim and believe in him. We related from at-Tirmidhi, Ibn Qani' and others that 'Abdullah ibn Salam said, "When the Messenger of Allah, may Allah bless him and grant him peace, came to Madina I came to look at him. When I saw his face, I recognised that his face was not the face of a liar."[1]

Abu Rimtha at-Taymi said, "I came to the Prophet with one of my sons. The

---

1. At-Tirmidhi

Prophet was shown to me. When I saw him, I exclaimed, 'This is indeed the Prophet of Allah'."[1]

Muslim and others related that when Dimad came to him, the Prophet said to him, "Praise be to Allah! We praise Him and We seek His help. None can misguide whoever Allah guides. Whoever He misguides has no guide. I testify that there is no god but Allah alone without any associate and that Muhammad is His slave and His Messenger." Dimad said to him, "Repeat your words to me. They have reached a depth like that of the ocean. Give me your hand, I will give you my allegiance."

Jami' ibn Shaddad said, "One of our men was called Tariq. He related that he had seen the Prophet at Madina and the Prophet had asked, 'Do you have anything with you to sell?' We replied, 'This camel.' The Prophet said, 'How much?' We said, 'So many *wasqs* of dates.' He took its rein and went to Madina. Tariq and his companion said, 'We have sold to a man and we do not even know who he is!' One of the women with us said, 'I will guarantee the price of the camel. I saw the face of a man like the full moon. He will not cheat you.' In the morning, a man brought us the dates and said, 'I am the messenger of the Messenger of Allah. He bids you eat of these dates and weigh until you have full weight.' We did so."[2]

When al-Julanda, the King of Oman, heard that Muhammad had called him to Islam, he said, "By Allah Who has guided me to this unlettered Prophet. If he commands something good, he is the first to do it. If he forbids something, he is the first to leave it. He conquers and is not proud. He is defeated and is not grieved. He fulfills the contract and carries out the promise. I testify that he is a Prophet."

Niftawayh said regarding the words of Allah, **"Its oil almost gives light when no fire has touched it,"** (24:35) "This is the likeness that Allah has made of His Prophet. He said that the meaning of the *ayat* was that his face almost indicated his prophethood even before he had received the Qur'an, as 'Abdullah ibn Rawaha said:

> Even if there had not been clear signs among us,
> His face would have told you the news."

SECTION 2
Prophethood and the Messengership

Know that Allah has the power to bring about direct knowledge of Himself in the hearts of His slaves and knowledge of His essence, His names, His

---

1. Ibn Sa'd.
2. Al-Bayhaqi.

attributes and all His commands all at once without any intermediary, if He so wills, as has been related about His transaction with certain of the Prophets. One of the commentators mentioned it in connection with Allah's words, **"It is not proper for Allah to address any human being except by inspiration."** (42:51)

It is permitted then that such knowledge should all reach them by means of an intermediary who brings His words to them. The intermediary can be non-human, as in the case of the angels with the Prophets, or one of their own kind as in the case of the Prophets with their communities. This is not forbidden by intellectual proof since it is permissible and not impossible.

The Messengers brought miracles which indicate their truthfulness and necessitate their being confirmed in all that they brought since the miracle is generally accompanied by a challenge from the Prophet concerned, based on the words of Allah, "My slave has spoken the truth, so obey him and follow him." Here Allah is testifying to the Prophet's truthfulness, and this is enough. To say more would be to go beyond our purpose. Whoever wants to pursue this matter further will find it fully dealt with in the books of our Imams.

The word prophet in linguistic terms comes from the verbal root with the *hamza*, "*naba'a*", which means to give news, to report. The meaning is that Allah acquainted them with His unseen and taught them that they were His Prophet, so they were informed Prophets, or could inform others about what Allah had sent them with and proclaim what Allah had taught them. Those who say it is without a *hamza* take it as coming from a root meaning what rises from the earth, indicating that Prophets had a noble rank and a high position with their Lord. Both meanings apply to the Prophets.

As for the word Messenger (*ar-rasul*), he is someone who is sent. His being sent is Allah's command to him to convey the message he has been sent with to those to whom he was sent. It is also derived from succession. "The people came one after another (*arsal*) when they succeeded each other." Linguistically, it is as if the verbal root *r-s-l* obliges the repetition of conveying or that the community must keep following him.

The *'ulama'* disagree about whether Prophet and Messenger mean the same thing or have different meanings. It is said that they are the same, and their root comes from news and means to inform. For proof, the people of this opinion use the words of Allah, **"We did not send any Messenger or Prophet before you,"** (22:52) in which He affirms that they are both sent. The Prophet said, "The Prophet is a Messenger and the Messenger is a Prophet."

It is said that they are different in one respect. They are the same in that both entail prophethood which means informing others about the unseen and teaching people what the special properties of prophethood and elevation are so that their prophethood and rank can be acknowledged. They differ in that a Messenger is given a message which is the command to warn and teach as we have said. The proof for this opinion is taken from the same *ayat* by reason of the fact that the two names are kept separate. If they meant the same thing, what would be the point of repeating them?

The people of this opinion say that the meaning of the *ayat* is, "We did not send any Messenger to a community nor a Prophet."[1] Some believe that Messengers were those who brought a new *shari'a*. Those who did not bring a *shari'a* were Prophets and not Messengers.

The sound position which most people take is that every Messenger is a Prophet but not every Prophet is a Messenger. The first Messenger was Adam and the last was Muhammad, may Allah bless him and grant him peace.

In the *hadith* of Abu Dharr, it says that there were 124,000 Prophets of whom 313 were Messengers. The first of them was Adam.[2]

So the meaning of prophethood and messengership should now be clear. According to the people of verification, Prophets do not have any special essence or quality of essence, with the exception of the position held by the Karramiyya,[3] a sect which is not to be relied on.

As for revelation (*wahy*), its root means to hasten. When a Prophet learns what comes to him from his Lord quickly, that is called revelation. Other varieties of inspiration are also called revelation since they are comparable to the revelation given to a Prophet. Handwriting is called *wahy* to denote the swiftness of the movement of the writer's hand. The *wahy* of the eyebrow and the glance refers to the speed with which they convey a message.

Allah said, **"He gestured (awha) to them to glorify Allah in the morning and the evening,"** (19:11) i.e. He indicated and alluded. It is also said that it means He wrote. From the same root come the words, *"al-Waha al-Waha,"* meaning quickly, quickly! It is said that the root means secrecy and concealment. Because of this, simple inspiration is sometimes called revelation. Allah says, **"The shaytans inspire their friends,"** (6:121) i.e. whisper in their breasts. He says, **"We revealed to the mother of Musa,"** (28:7) i.e. cast into her heart. On that note, He also says, **"It is not proper for Allah to address any human being except by inspiration,"** (42:52) i.e. by what He casts into his heart without any intermediary.

SECTION 3
The meaning of miracles (*mu'jizat*)

Know that the reason we call what the Prophets have brought a "miracle" (*mu'jiza*) is that creatures are incapable (*'ijaz*) of doing the like of it. There are

---

1. As a Prophet who is not a messenger is not sent with a message.
2. Ibn Hanbal, Ibn Hibban and al-Hakim.
3. A group who derive from Muhammad ibn Karram.

two sorts of miracle. One sort is something that human beings are potentially able to do, but which they are prevented from doing by an act of Allah in order that the truthfulness of His Prophet should be confirmed. These include such things as their turning away from seeking death (when they were asked to do so) and their incapacity to bring the like of the Qur'an and similar things.

The other sort is things that are beyond their power and which they cannot do – such as bringing the dead to life, turning a staff into a snake, bringing the she-camel out of the rock, the tree speaking, water flowing from between the fingers, and splitting the moon. Only Allah can do these things. They are things that Allah does at the hand of one of His Prophets. The Prophet's challenge to those who denied him to produce something similar was in order to show their incapacity.

Know that the miracles which appeared at the hand of our Prophet, the proofs of his prophethood and the indications of his truthfulness are made up of both types. He is the Messenger with the most miracles, the one with the clearest sign and most manifest proof as we will make clear. Due to their great quantity, his miracles cannot be numbered. The number of subsidiary miracles contained by just one of them – the Qur'an – cannot be counted. There are literally thousands of them which is shown by the fact that the Prophet issued the challenge to bring a *sura* like it and none of the people of knowledge was able to do so, not even to the extent of the shortest *sura, al-Kawthar* (108). Every single *ayat* is therefore a miracle. And it also has other miraculous properties as we will explain further on.

The miracles of the Prophet fall into two categories. One category is of those that are well-known and have been transmitted to us through many channels – like the Qur'an. There is no doubt or dispute that the Prophet brought it and it appeared from him and that he used it as a proof. If some pig-headed denier rejects this, it is like denying the fact that Muhammad existed in this world. The deniers themselves are refuted by the very existence of the Qur'an itself. It in itself and all the miracles that it contains are, therefore, indisputable. The fact of its inimitability is also both indisputable and verified by investigation as we will demonstrate.

One of our Imams stated: "This principle applies generally to the signs and the breaking of norms that occurred at the hands of the Prophet, for if no single one of them on its own is absolutely fixed and decisive, all of them together reach the level of indisputability. There is no doubt these extraordinary things occurred at his hands and neither believer nor unbeliever dispute their occurrence. What the obstinate do dispute is that they were from Allah." We have already stated that they were from Allah Almighty and that this is the confirmation of His words, "You have been truthful."

It is well known that these sort of things happened in the case of our Prophet just as it indisputably follows that Hatim was generous, 'Antara was brave and al-Ahnaf[1] was forbearing since the reports transmitted about them all agree that the first was generous, the second brave, and the third forbearing. However, each separate report would not in itself necessitate coming to that conclusion nor would it constitute decisive validation.

The second category consists of those things that do not reach the level of certainty and this category is divided in two. There are those things that are famous and widely known – a number of people relate them and they are well-known to the people of *hadith* and the relators and transmitters of the *sira*. These include things like water flowing from his fingers and a little food becoming copious. There are also things that were only known to one or two people. A small number relate them and they are not as famous as the other category. But when they are joined to others, they are compatible with them and together they confirm the miracles as a whole as we have already stated.

Many of the signs related from him are definitely known. There is the splitting of the moon whose occurrence is confirmed by the Qur'an and about which there are subsidiary reports. One should never depart from the literal meaning unless a definite proof is produced. Its probability is increased by sound reports from many places, so our resolution to uphold it should not be weakened by the opposition of some stupid weakling devoid of religion nor should one pay any attention to the stupidity of an innovator who casts doubts into the hearts of weak believers. Nay, rather we throw this in his face and turn our back on his stupidity.

It is the same with the story of the water flowing and the small amount of food becoming larger. Reliable people and numerous individuals related these things from a great number of the Companions. Among them are the things that have been universally related directly from a group of the greatest Companions such as when many of them were gathered together on the Day of the Ditch,[2] the Battle of Buwat,[3] the 'Umra of Hudaybiya,[4] the raid on Tabuk,[5] and other times when the armies of the Muslims were assembled together. It is not related that any of these Companions contradicted any transmitter in what he said, nor did they object to any of the statements attributed to them, and in

---

1. Pre-Islamic Arabs famous for these particular qualities.
2. When the idol-worshippers and Jews besieged Madina, the Prophet, following the suggestion of Salman al-Farisi, commanded that a ditch be dug to protect the city. It was something unknown among the Arabs, although common for the Persians. This happened in 4 or 5 AH.
3. Buwat is one of the mountains of Juhayna in the territory of Radwa about fifty miles from Madina. The Prophet intercepted a caravan of Quraysh there. This event took place thirteen months after the *Hijra*.
4. A place near Makka. The Prophet and his companions had set out to perform *'umra* and were prevented from doing so by Quraysh. The Treaty of Ridwan was signed under a tree there in 6 AH.
5. Tabuk was the last of the expeditions of the Prophet and took place in 9 AH. It is a place near Syria, fourteen travel stages from Madina.

their case the silence of those who remained silent is the same as the words of those who spoke since they were not silent about anything that was untrue and they were not given to lying sycophancy. Neither desire nor fear stopped them. If they heard something that was not generally acknowledged as true and not known to them, they would reject it, as some of them did reject things which others among them related regarding the *sunna*, the *sira* and the readings of the Qur'an. Some of them are known to have said that others had erred or misconstrued something. All of this is connected to his indisputable miracles as we have already made clear.

Also, any examples of traditions which have no basis and which are founded on falsehood must necessarily be discovered to be weak or obscure with the passage of time and the number of people who investigate them as is seen in the case of many untrue traditions and false rumours. These signs of our Prophet related through different individuals are only made more manifest by the passage of time. In spite of a succession of sects, frequent attacks by the enemy with the purpose of undermining and weakening the reports of such signs and the efforts of the unbelievers to suppress them, the strength and acceptance of them is only increased. All who attack these signs are only increased in grief and rancour. It is the same regarding his reports about the unseen worlds and his foretelling what was to come. This in itself is known to be one of his signs, which is true and cannot be covered up.

This has all been stated by our Imams, Qadi Abu Bakr al-Baqillani, Abu Bakr ibn Furak and others. And everything I know verifies that if anyone states that these famous stories have only reached us by the report of a single person, it is due to their lack of reading the reports and their transmission and their occupation with other sciences. Whoever studies the paths of transmission and reads the *hadith* and the *sira* will not be able to doubt the validity of these famous stories as we have mentioned. It is by no means unlikely for one person to acquire knowledge of something by many paths of transmission while another does not. Most people know that Baghdad exists and that it is a large city and the place of the Imamate and Khalifate, yet there are people who do not even know its name, let alone what it is like.

It is because of this that the *fuqaha'* among Malik's companions know by necessity and multiple transmission from him that his school requires recitation of the *Fatiha* in the prayer by the Imam and the person praying on his own and permits making the intention on the first night of Ramadan for the rest of it, while ash-Shafi'i thought that the intention had to be renewed each night and that it was enough to wipe only part of the head in *wudu*. It is likewise the reason for the Maliki *fuqaha's* position regarding retaliation for killing with a blade and other such things, the obligation to make the intention for *wudu*, and the precondition of there being a *wali* for a marriage to take place, whereas Abu

Hanifa disagreed with them concerning these matters. Other people are not concerned with their own schools and do not even relate what their schools say, not knowing what is in their own school, let alone the schools of others.

In mentioning some of these miracles, we will also add something to clarify them, Allah willing.

SECTION 4
On the inimitability of the Qur'an

There are many aspects of the Mighty Book of Allah which cannot be imitated. In order to deal with them properly, they have been put into four categories.

This section deals with the first of these which is the excellence of its composition, the cohesion of its word-structure and the purity of its Arabic. This is part of its inimitability because the eloquence of its language is far beyond the norm of the Arabs.

The Arabs were the masters of linguistic expression, having been given eloquence and aphorisms not given to any other nation. They were given a sharpness of tongue not possessed by other peoples and an incisiveness of speech penetrating right to the heart of the meaning. Allah gave them that as part of their nature and character. It is natural to them and comes easily. They use it spontaneously to evoke amazement and it enables them to deal with any situation, speaking extemporaneously. They compose *rajaz* poems using powerful language between thrust and riposte, in praise and defamation, when making requests and entreaties, to raise up and bring low. By use of language they work permissible magic, and are able to string together adjectives more beautiful than a string of pearls. With it they can deceive the intelligent, make what is difficult easy, heal ancient feuds, bring ancient ruins to life, make cowards brave, open up clenched hands, make the imperfect perfect and reduce the highborn to obscurity.

Among the Arabs the bedouin is renowned for lucid expression, decisive words, superbly clear speech, a pure nature and a strong manner. The city man has skilful eloquence, clear expression, comprehensive words, an easy nature and the ability to put much splendour of manner into few and courteous words. They both have an eloquence containing effective arguments and a driving force which wins the day and opens the way. They do not doubt that words obey their will and that eloquence is the property of their leadership. They possess the arts of language and have discovered its springs. They have entered through all its doors and built palaces with it. They have spoken on all subjects, both the weighty and the insignificant. They were the masters of both sparing and substantial argumentation. They can converse with concision and prolixity. They contend in prose and poetry.

No-one but a noble Messenger could have amazed them with a book about which is said: **"Falsehood cannot reach it from before it or behind it – a revelation from One who is All-Wise, Praiseworthy."** (41:42) Its *ayats* are exact and its words distinguished. Its eloquence dazzles the intellect. Its pure Arabic overcomes every other speech. Its terseness and inimitability conquer all. The real and metaphorical in it are clearly articulated. Its verses and divisions vie in beauty. Its concise passages and brilliant new expressions make all clear. Its excellent composition is balanced by its concision. The expressions chosen convey a multitude of meanings.

The Arabs are the people with the greatest capacity in this field and had the most illustrious orators, the most contests in rhymed prose and poetry, the greatest usage of rare words and expressions in their everyday language and the most unique way of arguing with each other.

These are the people whom the Prophet was challenging and rebuking for more than twenty years:

"Do they say, 'He has fabricated it'? Say: 'Then produce a sura like it and call on anyone you can besides Allah if you speak the truth.'" (10:38)

"If you have doubts about what We have sent down to Our slave, produce another sura the same as it, and call your witnesses, besides Allah, if you speak the truth. If you do not do that – and you will not do it ..." (2:23-24)

" Say: 'If both men and jinn banded together to produce the like of this Qur'an, they could never produce anything like it, even if they backed each other up.'" (17:88) and **"Say: 'Then produce ten invented suras like it.'"** (11:13)

It is easier to plagiarize than to originate. Writing something false and fabricated is far easier. The phrase which is striving after a sound meaning is more difficult to compose. That is why it is said, "So-and-so writes as he is told and so-and-so writes as he wants." The first is better than the second, and there is a vast chasm between them.

The Prophet continued to rebuke them with the harshest rebukes and reprimand them in the strongest possible terms. He called their dreams foolish and abased their nobles. Their social structures were shattered. He censured their gods and their own selves as well. Their houses and property were taken as booty. Despite all of this, they shrank from confronting his challenge and proved themselves unable to produce anything like it. They deceived themselves by making trouble through rejection, self-delusion, and forgery.

They said, **"This is nothing but magic from the past. This is nothing but the words of a human being,"** (74:24-25) or a **"continuing forgery."** (54:24) It is **"a lie which he forged,"** (25:4) and **"the myths of the ancients."** (25:5) They lied and were satisfied with baseness.

As Allah says, it is as if they said, **"Our hearts are uncircumcised."** (2:88) **"Our hearts are covered up against what you call us to and there is a heaviness in our ears. There is a screen between us and you."** (41:5) **"Do not listen to this Qur'an. Drown it out so that perhaps you may gain the upper hand."** (41:26)

Their presumption of capacity is illustrated by their saying, **"If we had liked, we would have said the like of it."** (8:31) Allah says to them, **"You will not do it."** (2:24) And surely enough, they did not do it and were powerless to. Any foolish person, such as Musaylima,[1] who tried to do it had his faults exposed to everyone and was stripped by Allah of the fine words he had written. If that had not been the case, the people of intelligence among them would not have realised that the Qur'an was something more than their own form of pure speech or eloquence. When such people heard the Qur'an they came away submitting to it, either guided or at least enraptured.

This is why when al-Walid ibn al-Mughira[2] heard the Prophet say, **"Allah commands justice and acting in the best way,"** (16:90) he said, "By Allah, it has sweetness and it has grace. The least of it is abundant and the highest of it is fruitful. No mortal could have said this."

Abu 'Ubayd al-Qasim ibn Salam mentioned that a Bedouin heard a man recite, **"Shout what you are commanded."** (15:94) He prostrated and said, "I have prostrated because of its fine Arabic." Another Bedouin heard a man recite, **"When they despaired of moving him, they conferred privately apart."** (12:80) He said, "I testify that no creature is capable of these words."

It is related that one day 'Umar ibn al-Khattab was sleeping in the mosque when someone suddenly stood at his head testifying to the truth. He asked him who he was and the man told him that he was one of the Byzantine generals who knew Arabic and other languages well. He had heard a Muslim captive reciting the Book. He said, "I reflected on it and it contained the same as Allah sent down on 'Isa ibn Maryam regarding the states of this world and the Next." What he had heard recited were Allah's words: **"All who obey Allah and His Messenger and have awe of Allah and show fear of Him, it is they who are the victorious."** (24:52)

Al-Asma'i related that he heard a slavegirl say something and said to her, "Confound it! What has made you so eloquent?" She said, "Is this to be considered eloquence after the words of Allah, **'We revealed to the mother of Musa: Suckle him...'**? (28:7) In a single *ayat* two commands, two prohibitions, two pieces of information and two pieces of good news are joined together."

This type of inimitability we are citing is unique and bears no relationship

---

1. A false prophet who arose during the last part of the Prophet's life and was the most prominent leader in the *Ridda* (Wars of Apostasy).
2. A man of standing among the Quraysh who was asked to make a statement about what he had heard of the Qur'an. This is part of his statement. See Ibn Ishaq trans., p. 121.

to anything else. It is sound on two counts. The Qur'an came through the Prophet and he brought it – this is definitely known. It is also known that the Prophet made it a challenge and the Arabs were unable to respond to it. It is known without doubt by those who know eloquence and the techniques of rhetoric that its eloquence is a miracle. The way that someone who is not one of the people of this art knows that it is a miracle is by the incapacity of the skilled people of that art to respond to its challenge and the fact that they have confirmed the inimitability of its eloquence.

All you need do is reflect on the words of Allah, **"There is life for you in retaliation,"** (2:179) and, **"If you could see when they are terrified and there is no escape, and they are seized from a near place,"** (34:51) and His saying, **"Respond with that which is better and if there is enmity between you and him, he will be as if he were a warm friend,"** (41:34) and, **"It was said: Earth, swallow your waters and heaven, stop,"** (11:44) and His words, **"Each We seized for his wrong action. Against some of them We sent pebbles."** (29:40) There are many other *ayats* such as these – indeed much of the Qur'an.

You have seen what we have clarified concerning the concision of its phrases, the abundance of its meanings, its finely woven expressions, the excellent formation of its letters and the harmony of its words. Each phrase contains many degrees of meaning and overflowing oceans of knowledge. Volumes could be filled with just some of its benefits, and numerous treatises have been written about what has been discovered in it. There is discussion about how the long stories and histories of the previous generations flow into one another, which would normally be considered weak and lacking in clarity by the people of eloquence. In fact it is a sign for the one who reflects on it with regard to the cohesion of its words and presentation, and how all the different facets are put in balance – like the story of Yusuf in its entirety. When these stories are repeated in different places of the Qur'an, the expressions used in them vary so much that it is as if each instance where the story occurs is totally unique in the way it is elucidated. This aspect of counterpoise is part of its beauty. The self never feels averse to repeating these stories nor is it hostile to hearing them again and again.

SECTION 5
The inimitability of the Qur'an's composition and style

The second aspect of its inimitability lies in the form of its marvellous composition and rare style which is so different from the style of the Arabs and their methods of composition and prose writing. The divisions of its *ayats* stop and finish while the words continue through. This sort of thing did not exist before or after it. No-one was able to do anything like it. Peoples' intellects became bewildered by it and their intelligence abandoned them. They were not guided to the composition of any language like it whether in prose, verse, rhymed prose, *rajaz* or poetry.

When al-Walid ibn al-Mughira heard the ordinary speech of the Prophet and then the Qur'an was recited to him, he softened and Abu Jahl went to him to rebuke him. He said, "By Allah, there is none of you who knows poetry better than I, and by Allah, his ordinary speech does not resemble this (Qur'an) in any way."

Another tradition reports the Quraysh gathering together at the time of their annual fair and saying, "The delegations of the Arabs are coming, so let us agree on one opinion about him so that we will not contradict each other." They said, "We say he is a soothsayer." Al-Walid said, "By Allah, he is not a soothsayer. He does not mutter nor speak in rhymed prose." They said, "He is mad, possessed by a *jinn*." He said, "He is not mad nor *jinn*-possessed. There is no choking nor whispering." They said, "We say he is a poet." He said, "He is not a poet. We know poetry in all its forms and metres and he is not a poet." They said, "We say he is a sorcerer." He said, "He is not a sorcerer – there is no spitting and no knots." They said, "Then what will we say?" He said, "You have not said anything about this matter which I do not recognise to be false. The closest you have come is the statement that he is a sorcerer, for magic is something that can come between a man and his son, a man and his brother, a man and his wife, and a man and his tribe." Then they separated and sat down in the road to warn people. Allah revealed about al-Walid, **"Leave him to Me whom I created alone."** (74:11)[1]

When 'Utba ibn Rabi'a heard the Qur'an, he said, "O people! You know that I have not left anything without learning it, reading it and saying it. By Allah, I have heard a type of speech, and by Allah, I have never heard anything like it. It is not poetry and it is not spells nor soothsaying." Al-Nadr ibn al-Harith said something similar.

In the *hadith* of Abu Dharr becoming Muslim, he describes his brother Unays and says, "By Allah, I have not heard of anyone who knows more poetry than my brother Unays. He contested with twelve poets in the *Jahiliyya* and I was one of them." This brother went to Makka and on his return told Abu Dharr about the Prophet. Abu Dharr asked, "What do people say?" He replied, "They say: he is a poet, a soothsayer and a sorcerer. I have heard the words of the soothsayers and this is not like their words. I compared him with the reciters of poetry and it was not like them. No-one after me should err and say he was a poet. He is truthful and they are liars."[2]

The traditions about the inimitability of the Qur'an's composition and style

---

1. Al-Bayhaqi from Ibn 'Abbas.
2. Muslim.

are sound and numerous. Its inimitability lies in both things – the concision and eloquence itself and its extraordinary style. Properly speaking, each of them constitute a different type of inimitability and the Arabs could not duplicate either of them since each was beyond their power. It was different in its pure Arabic and the words it used. More than one of the Imams has held this view.

One of their followers believed that the Qur'an's inimitability consists merely in the sum of its eloquence and style put together and made a statement to that effect which both ears and hearts reject. The sound position is the one we have presented and knowledge of all these matters is definitive and clear. We have only stated what is well-known to the masters of the science of eloquence and the *adab* of this craft who are penetrating in thought and tongue.

The Imams of the people of the *Sunna* have disagreed about the *way* in which people were incapable of imitating it. Most of them have said that what is not within the capacity of a human being is the force of its lucidity and clear expressions, its beautiful composition, its terseness and its wonderful structure and style. These things are part of its miraculous nature which are beyond the power of created beings to imitate, in the same way that miracles such as bringing the dead to life, transforming the staff and the glorification of the pebbles[1] are beyond them.

Shaykh Abu'l-Hasan al-Ash'ari, on the other hand, believed that its imitation is something which is within the capacity of human beings and that Allah could give them the power to achieve it, but this did not and will not happen. Allah has prevented them from achieving it and has made them incapable of doing so. A number of scholars hold this opinion and it is based on two arguments.

The first is the already established fact that the Arabs were incapable of it. It would not be valid to have held this against them if it had not been within the power of a human being to achieve it.

The second is the known fact that they were challenged to try and imitate it. This proves their impotence more effectively and makes them more worthy of rebuke. A justification could be found for their incapacity if they were being challenged to do something which was not within the capacity of a human being. This is an overwhelming proof and definitive argument.

In any case, the Arabs were not able to imitate the Qur'an but suffered instead many casualties and the evacuation of their city, Makka. They drank the cup of humility and abasement having been previously among the haughty and disdainful. They most certainly did not voluntarily choose to suffer this and were not pleased when they were forcibly compelled to do so. If it had been within their power it would have been far easier for them to have risen to the challenge which would have brought quick success, a definitive victory and

---

1. In the hand of the Prophet which the Companions heard.

would have finally silenced their adversary.

The Arabs were among those who had a great power of speech and were in fact exemplars of that science for all people. Each of them tried his best and summoned all his powers in the attempt to eclipse the Qur'an's appearance and extinguish its light. They could not come up with any hidden depths nor produce a drop from the springs of the water of their being, despite the length of time they spent trying, their great number and the fact that they were aiding and abetting one another. On the contrary they remained speechless, unable to utter a single word. They were cut off and their way was blocked.

SECTION 6
Information about unseen things

The third type of Qur'anic inimitability lies in the reports it contains about the things of the unseen and things that did not yet exist and had not yet occurred and then did come into existence as has been reported. This includes such things as Allah's words, **"You will enter the Masjid al-Haram in safety, Allah willing,"** (48:27) **"They will be overcome after their victory,"** (30:3) **"Allah has promised those who believe among you and act rightly that He will make them khalifs in the earth,"** (24:55) and **"When comes the help of Allah and victory."** (110:1)

All these things happened just as Allah said they would. The Greeks defeated the Persians within a few years. People entered Islam in droves. At the time of the Prophet's death there was not one place in all the Arab lands which Islam had not entered. Allah made the believers khalifs in the earth and made their *deen* firm in it. He gave them power over it from the furthest east to the furthest west, as the Prophet said, "The earth was collected together for me so that I was shown its easts and wests. The kingdom of my community will reach to the extent that it was brought together for me."[1]

Allah says, **"We sent down the *dhikr* and We will guard it."** (15:9) This has indeed been the case. Innumerable heretics and atheists, especially the Qarmatians,[2] have tried to alter it and change what it says. They have been gathering together and joining forces in the attempt right up to the present time, which is about five hundred years, but they still have not been able to extinguish any of its light nor to alter a single word nor to make the Muslims doubt a single letter. Praise be to Allah![3]

The same applies to the words of Allah Almighty, **"The host will be routed**

---

1. Muslim.
2. An heretical sect which originated in Iraq.
3. This, of course, remains the case today after more than fourteen hundred years.

and turn their backs," (54:45) and "**Fight them. Allah will punish them at your hands,**" (9:14) and "**He is the One who sent the Messenger with the guidance.**" (9:33) Allah also says, "**They will not harm you, except a little, and if they fight you, they will turn their backs on you.**" (3:111) These things happened as He said they would.

Another aspect of this information about unseen things is the unveiling of the secrets of the hypocrites and the Jews and what they said and their lies in their private circles and His rebuking them for that. Allah says, "**They say in themselves: Why does not Allah punish us for what we say?**" (58:8) He says, "**They are concealing in themselves what they do not show you.**" (3:154) Allah also says, "**Those of the Jews who listen to lies, listen to other people who have not come to you, twisting words from their meanings,**" (5:42) and He says "**Some of the Jews twist words from their meanings saying, 'We hear and disobey' and 'Hear, and do not be given to hear,' twisting with their tongues and traducing the *deen*.**" (4:46)

Allah Almighty says, showing what He had given to His Prophet and what the believers believed on the Day of the Batle of Badr, "**When Allah promised you that one of the two parties would be yours and you were wishing that the one unarmed would be yours.**" (8:7) On another occasion Allah Almighty says, "**We are enough for you against the mockers.**" (15:90) When this was revealed, the Prophet gave his Companions the good news that Allah was enough for him and for them.

The "mockers" in this *ayat* were a group of people in Makka who were causing people to turn away from the Prophet and causing him harm. They were destroyed. Allah says, "**Allah will protect you from the people.**" (5:67) This was indeed the case regarding those who wanted to harm him and kill him. The traditions confirming this are sound and well-known.

SECTION 7
The reports of past generations and departed nations

The fourth aspect of the Qur'an's inimitability is that it tells about previous generations, past nations and vanished *shari'as* of which only a single story was known to only one individual among the scholars of the People of the Book whose life had been devoted to its study.

The Prophet brought these reports in the proper way with proper texts, so that all men of knowledge were forced to admit their soundness and truthfulness and that they could not have been gained through study. They knew that the Prophet was illiterate and could not read or write and was not occupied with study or constant research. He did not travel away from his people and people were not unaware of his situation. The People of the Book used to question him a lot about these things, so he recited to them the part of the Qur'an that was revealed to him which dealt with such things as the accounts of the Prophets' dealings with their peoples, the story of Musa and al-Khidr, Yusuf and his brothers, the people of the Cave, Dhu'l-Qarnayn, Luqman and his son, and other similar reports about the various Prophets, and the account of the beginning of creation and what was in the Torah and the Injil (Evangel) and the Zabur (Psalms) and the Scrolls of Ibrahim and Musa. The men of knowledge confirmed him in this, not being able to deny it but rather affirming it. Those who were destined for ultimate success in the Hereafter believed in the good that came to him while those whose lot in the Hereafter was wretchedness remained stubborn and envious.

Furthermore, there is no evidence of denial of these things on the part of any of the Christians or the Jews, in spite of their intense enmity towards the Prophet and the fact that they urged people to deny him and argued against him by what was in their books and rebuked him by what their books contained. They did not deny what had come in the Qur'an despite the abundance of their questions to him and the fact that they pressured him with difficult questions about their prophets, the secrets of their knowledges, the contents of their biographies and information about what was hidden inside their *shari'as* and the contents of their books – like their asking about the spirit, Dhu'l-Qarnayn, the People of the Cave, 'Isa, the judgement of the strong and what Isra'il made *haram* for himself and what had become *haram* for them of beasts and good things which had previously been lawful for them and was then made forbidden for them because of their outrageous behaviour. Allah says, **"That is their likeness in the Torah and their likeness in the Injil."** (48:29)

Other such matters were revealed in the Qur'an, and he answered them and acquainted them with what had been revealed to him about them. It is not known that any of them rejected or denied any of this. Most of them declared the validity of his prophecy and the truthfulness of what he said and admitted their stubbornness and envy of the Prophet – like the people of Najran[1] and Ibn Suriya[2] and the sons of Akhtab[3] and others.

Anyone who invented lies about any of these things and claimed that what they had about a particular matter was different from what he had told the Muslim community was called to provide his proof and his claim was shown to be false. As the Qur'an says, it was said to such a person, **"Say: then bring the Torah and recite it if you are speaking the truth. Whoever forges falsehood against Allah after that, they are the wrongdoers."** (3:93) He was rebuked and reprimanded and asked for something possible, not impossible. Whoever admitted his denial and behaved insolently had his ignominy

---

1. A group of Christians who argued with him about 'Isa.
2. One of the Jewish rabbis in Madina who tried to cover up the verse of stoning in the Torah.
3. Huyayy and Abu Yasir, prominent Jews in Madina.

demonstrated from his own book in his own hand. It is not related that any of the Jews or Christians managed to produce in evidence anything, either sound or weak, from the pages of their books.

Allah says, **"O People of the Book! Our Messenger has come to you to make clear to you much of what you were hiding of the Book and erasing much."** (5:15-16)

SECTION 8
The challenge to the Arabs and their incapacity to respond and informing them that they would not be able to do so

These four ways in which the Qur'an is inimitable are clear. There is no dispute or doubt about them. Another clear facet of its inimitability are the *ayats* related about people's incapacity in certain cases to respond to a particular challenge whilst informing them that they would not meet it. Then they were indeed unable to do so. This is illustrated by what Allah says to the Jews: **"Say: If you have the Abode of the Next World exclusively, then long for death if you are speaking the truth."** (2:94)

Abu Ishaq az-Zajjaj said, "This *ayat* provides the greatest proof and clearest indication of the soundness of His Message because He told them, 'Long for death,' and informed the Jews that they would never long for it and subsequently none of them longed for it. The Prophet said, 'By the One in whose hand my soul is, not a man of them could say that without choking on his spit,' i.e. dying where he stood.[1] So Allah turned the Jews away from longing for death and terrified them in order to manifest the truthfulness of His Messenger and the soundness of what had been revealed to him since none of them really wished for death although they would have been eager to reject him if they had been able to do so. But Allah does what He wills. By this *ayat* his miracles were evident and his proof was clear."

Abu Muhammad al-Usayli said, "An amazing thing about this business is that there was not a single group or individual among the Jews from the day that Allah commanded His Prophet to say this who came forward against him or answered him. It remained available as a pretext for anyone among them who wanted to put him to the test."

It was the same with the *ayat* of the mutual curse. When the bishops of Najran came to him and refused Islam, Allah sent down the *ayat* of the mutual curse on them saying, **"Whoever disputes with you about him[2] after the knowledge that has come to you, say: 'Come now, let us call on our sons and your sons, our wives and your wives, our selves and your selves, then let us**

---

1. Al-Bayhaqi.
2. i.e. 'Isa.

humbly pray and lay the curse of Allah on those who lie.'" (3:61) They were stopped from doing that and were content to pay the *jizya* tax. That is because al-'Aqib, their leader, told them, "You know that he is a Prophet. A Prophet never lays a curse on a people but that neither their small or great survive."

It is the same when Allah says, **"If you are in doubt about what We have sent down on Our slave then bring a** *sura* **like it and call upon your witnesses, apart from Allah, if you are truthful. If you do not, and you will not, then fear the Fire whose fuel is men and stones, prepared for the unbelievers."** (2:24) Allah told the Arabs that they would not do it and indeed they did not. This *ayat* is one of the reports about the unseen, but it still contains their incapacity to respond to the challenge at the beginning of the *ayat*.

SECTION 9
The terror aroused by hearing the Qur'an and the awe it inspires in people's hearts

Another aspect of its inimitability is the terror which clutches at the hearts of those who listen to it and which affects their ears when they hear it and the awe which seizes them when it is recited because of its power and grave sublimity.

It has an even greater effect on those who reject it so that, as Allah says, **"And We put coverings over their hearts lest they should understand (the Qur'an) and deafness in their ears. When you remember your Lord in the Qur'an and Him alone, they turn their backs in flight."** (17:46) Hearing it is heavy for them and they are increased in aversion. They desire to stop it because of their dislike of it. This is why the Prophet said, "The Qur'an is hard and difficult for the one who hates it. It is the arbiter."

The believer continues to be terrified and in awe of it when he recites it, and it attracts him and it brings him joy by his heart's inclination to it and confirmation of it. Allah says, **"The skins of those who fear their Lord tremble at it. Then their skins and hearts soften to the remembrance of Allah."** (39:23)

He also says, **"Had We sent down this Qur'an on a mountain, you would have seen it humbled, split in two, out of fear of Allah."** (59:21) This indicates that this is something unique to it. It can even seize someone who has no understanding of its meanings and does not know its explanation. This was related about a Christian who passed by someone reciting and he stopped and wept. He was asked, "Why are you weeping?" He said, "Because it has broken my heart and because of the beauty of its arrangement." This awe has seized many before Islam and after it. Some of them became Muslim the first moment they heard it, believing in it, while some of them rejected it.

It is related in the *Sahih* that Jubayr ibn Mut'im said, "I heard the Prophet recite *Sura at-Tur* in the *Maghrib* prayer. When he reached the words, 'Or were they created out of nothing? Or were they the creators? Or did they create the heavens and the earth? No, but they do not have sure belief. Or are your Lord's treasuries in their keeping? Or are they the registrars?' (52:35-37) my heart practically flew to Islam." One version has, "That was the first time that Islam had importance in my heart."

'Utba ibn Rabi'a said that when he spoke to the Prophet about the revelation he had brought which was against his people's beliefs, he recited *Sura Ha-Mim* (41). 'Utba put his hand over the Prophet's mouth and begged him to stop. One version has that the Prophet began to recite and 'Utba listened carefully, putting his hands behind his back and leaning on them until he reached the *ayat* of prostration and the Prophet prostrated. 'Utba got up and did not know how to retort. He went back to his family and did not go out to his people until they came to him. He apologised to them and said, "By Allah, he spoke some words to me and by Allah, I have never heard the like of them. I did not know what to say to him."[1]

It is related that more than one person wanted to answer the Prophet's challenge, but then terror and awe seized them and they were prevented from doing so. It is related that Ibn al-Muqaffa' sought to do that and set out to achieve his purpose. Then he passed by a lad who was reciting, **"Say: O earth, swallow your water,"** (11:44) and went back and wiped out what he had written down, saying, "I testify that this is not to be opposed and these are not the words of a mortal." He was the most eloquent of the people of his time.

Yahya ibn Hakam al-Ghazzal was the foremost man in eloquence in Andalusia in his time. It is related that he wanted to create something similar to the Qur'an, so he looked at *Sura al-Ikhlas* in order to follow its example. He actually began to carry that out but then he said, "Fear stopped me and weakness moved me to repentance and regret."

SECTION 10
The Qur'an's remaining throughout time

One of the recognised aspects of the Qur'an's inimitability is that it is an enduring sign which will not cease to exist, remaining as long as this world remains since Allah has undertaken to preserve it. He says, **"We sent down the Remembrance and We will preserve it,"** (15:9) and **"Falsehood does not come to it from in front of it nor from behind it."** (41:42)

All the miracles of the Prophets pass when their time passes and only reports about them remain. The Mighty Qur'an has clear *ayats* and manifest miracles which are still there today in spite of the five hundred and thirty-five years

---

1. Al-Baghawi.

which have passed from the first revelation to our time.[1] This is a decisive proof and there is no effective refutation of it. Every age overflows with people of clarification and bearers of the science of language and Imams of eloquence and craftsmen of words and brilliant men of skill. There are many such people who deviate and such opponents of the *Shari'a* are obdurate. None of them, however, has been able to bring any effective opposition to it nor to compose even two words to diminish it. Not one of them has been able to mount a sound attack. Any criticism of it by some dim-witted person is totally ineffectual. What is transmitted about everyone who has desired to oppose the Qur'an is that he has fallen into incapacity by his own hand and turned on his heels, retreating.

SECTION 11
Other aspects of the Qur'an's inimitability

Some of the Imams and those who follow them in the Muslim community have enumerated other aspects of the Qur'an's inimitability. One of them is that reciters and listeners never get bored by it. Continual recitation of it increases its sweetness and repetition of it makes one love it. It remains fresh and sweet. Other words, even if they are very eloquent and beautiful, pall with repetition and this results in antipathy. Our Book is delightful to recite in times of retreat and it proves itself, through recitation, an excellent companion in times of crisis. Other books do not possess this quality. Thus people have developed different cadences and recitational methods for it and by that brought animation into its recitation.

The Messenger of Allah described the Qur'an with the words, "It does not wear out when it is recited a lot. Its lessons do not end and its wonders do not fade. It is the Discrimination. It is not a jest. The *'ulama'* do not become sated with it and the passions are not misguided by it and the tongues do not mistake it. It is that which the *jinn* did not leave once they had heard it. They said, **'We heard a wonderful Qur'an which guides to right guidance.'** (72:1-2)"[2]

Another aspect of its inimitabilty is that it gathers together knowledges and gnoses with which the Arabs in general, and Muhammad before his prophethood in particular, were unfamiliar. They neither knew of them nor paid any attention to them. Nor had any of the *'ulama'* of other nations mastered them. Nor did any of their books contain them. Gathered in it is the clarification of the science of the *Shari'a,* and information about the methods of educing intellectual proofs, and refutation by strong arguments of the deviant sects of other communities using simple, succinct expressions. Those who wanted to show how clever they were later wanted to establish comparable

---

1. This, of course, remains the case today after fourteen hundred years.
2. At-Tirmidhi.

proofs to those in the Qur'an but were not able to accomplish that.

For instance Allah says, **"Is not the One who created the heavens and the earth powerful enough to create the like of them? Yes, indeed!"** (36:81) and **"Say: He will bring it back to life who originated it the first time,"** (36:79) and **"Had there been any gods in them except Allah, they would have come to ruin."** (21:22)

The Qur'an also contains much of the science of *sira*, the histories of former nations, warnings, wise maxims and the news of the Next World as well as defining good behaviour and virtues.

Allah says, **"We have not neglected anything in the Book."** (6:38) **"We sent down the Book on you to make everything clear."** (27:89) **"We struck every likeness for people in this Qur'an."** (30:58)

The Prophet said, "Allah sent down this Qur'an to command and prevent, and as a *sunna* to be followed and a parable. It contains your history, information about what came before you, news about what will come after you and correct judgement between you. Repetition does not wear it out and its wonders do not end. It is the Truth. It is not a jest. Whoever recites it speaks the truth. Whoever judges by it is just. Whoever argues by it wins. Whoever divides by it is equitable. Whoever acts by it is rewarded. Whoever clings to it is guided to a straight path. Allah will misguide whoever seeks guidance from other than it. Allah will destroy whoever judges by other than it. It is the Wise Remembrance, the Clear Light, the Straight Path, the Firm Rope of Allah and the Useful Healing. It is a protection for the one who clings to it and a rescue for the one who follows it. It is not crooked and so puts things straight. It does not deviate so as to be blamed. Its wonders do not cease. It does not wear out with much repetition."[1]

Ibn Mas'ud related something similar to this, adding, "It does not differ nor lose its freshness, and it contains the news of the first and the last."[2]

In the *hadith*, Allah said to Muhammad, may Allah bless him and grant him peace, "I am sending down a new Torah on you which will open blind eyes, deaf ears and closed hearts. It contains the springs of knowledge and the understanding of wisdom and the meadow of the hearts."[3]

Ka'b al-Ahbar said, "There is no substitute for the Qur'an. It is the understanding of the intellects and the light of wisdom."

Allah says, **" Indeed this Qur'an recounts to the Tribe of Israel most of the things about which they differ."** (27:86) He says, **"This is clarification for people and guidance."** (3:138) Gathered in it, despite the succinctness of its phrases and the concentration of its words, is much more than what is

---

1. At-Tirmidhi.
2. Al-Hakim.
3. Ibn Abi Shayba and Ibn ad-Daris.

contained in the books before it which are much more verbose.

Another aspect of the Qur'an's inimitability lies in the fact that it is at one and the same time, the proof and what is proven. That is because the composition of the Qur'an, the beauty of its description, its inimitability and eloquence is used as a proof. In this eloquence lies His command and prohibition, and His promise and threat. The one who recites it simultaneously grasps both the proof and the obligation in a single word and single *sura*.

Another aspect of the Qur'an is that He has placed it within the realm of verse composition, but of a kind which is unknown elsewhere. It is not in prose form because verse is easier for the souls, easier on the ears and sweeter for the understanding. People incline to it more easily and passions go quicker to it.

Another aspect is that Allah has made it easy to memorize for those who study it. Allah says, **"We made the Qur'an easy for remembrance."** (54:17) Not one of the other communities could memorize their books, even if they were to spend years doing it, yet the Qur'an is easy for boys to memorize in a short time.

A final aspect of the Qur'an's inimitability is the resemblance of some of its parts to others, the excellence of the harmony of its different parts, the harmony of its divisions, the beauty of finishing one story and going on to another, going from one subject to another with their different meanings, and the inclusion within the same *sura* of command and prohibition, information and inquiry, promise and threat, affirmation of prophethood, *tawhid* and confirmation, stimulating desire and fear, and other benefits in a seamless fashion. If good Arabic like this is found elsewhere, its force is weak, its purity of style is soft, its beauty is lesser and its phrases are unsettled.

So reflect on the beginning of *Sura Sad* (38) and the information it contains about the unbelievers, their schism, and their being rebuked by the destruction of the generations before them. It mentions their denial of Muhammad, their astonishment at what he brought, information about their council agreeing in disbelief, the envy that appeared in their words, their incapacity, their weakening and the threat to disgrace them in this world and the Next, the rejection by the communities before them and Allah's destruction of those communities and the threat that a similar disaster would befall them, the patience of the Prophet when they injured him and his consolation on account of all that has already been mentioned. Then Allah begins to talk of Da'ud and the stories of the Prophets. All of this is in the most succinct words and the best composition. Also included in the style of the Qur'an is the great number of sentences which contain only a few words.

All of this and much more must be taken into consideration when looking at the inimitability of the Qur'an. There are many more aspects about its inimitability which the Imams have mentioned. We have not covered all of them since many of them appear in the section on eloquence. We were only concerned at this juncture with its inimitability. In the section which concerns the art of eloquence, much of what has already been mentioned is considered in respect of its special qualities and virtues of eloquence rather than of its inimitability.

The reality of the inimitability of the Qur'an is contained in the first four aspects we mentioned, so rely on them. The Qur'an has special properties and wonders which do not come to an end. Allah is the granter of success.

SECTION 12
The splitting of the moon and holding back the sun

Allah says, **"The Hour has drawn near and the moon has been split. Yet if they see a sign, they turn away and then say, 'A continuing sorcery.'"** (54:1-2) Allah informs people about the splitting of the moon using the past participle and refers to the unbelievers turning away from his signs. The commentators and people of the *sunna* agree that it took place.

Ibn Mas'ud reported, "The moon was split into two parts during the time of the Messenger of Allah. One part was above the mountain and the other part below it. The Messenger of Allah, peace be upon him, said, 'Witness!'"[1] It is also related that Ibn Mas'ud al-Aswad said, "When I saw the mountains between the two halves of the moon..."[2]

Masruq said that this was at Makka and added that the unbelievers of Quraysh said, "The son of Abu Kabsha has bewitched you." One of them said, "If Muhammad has bewitched the moon, his magic is not such that it would extend to the entire earth. Ask those who have come from other cities whether they saw it." They came and were questioned and told them that they too had seen it.

As-Samarqandi related something similar from ad-Dahhak in which Abu Jahl said, "This is magic, so send to the people of the remote areas to see whether or not they saw it." The people of the remote areas continued that they too had seen it split in two. The unbelievers said, "This is a continuous magic." 'Alqama also related it from Ibn Mas'ud, and these four had it from 'Abdullah.

Other people than Ibn Mas'ud related it, including Anas, Ibn 'Abbas, Ibn 'Umar, Hudhayfa, 'Ali and Jubayr ibn Mut'im.

'Ali related from the version of Abu Hudhayfa al-Arhabi, "The moon was split when we were with the Prophet, may Allah bless him and grant him peace."

---

1. Al-Bukhari. Mujahid's version said, "We were with the Prophet." In one of the paths of transmission from al-A'mash we find something similar.
2. Ibn Hanbal.

Anas said, "The people of Makka asked the Prophet to show them a sign and he showed them the splitting of the moon in two so that they saw Mount Hira between the two halves."

In the version of Ma'mar and others from Qatada it says that he showed them the splitting of the moon in two, and Allah revealed, **"The Hour has drawn near and the moon has been split."** (54:1)

It is also related from Jubayr ibn Mut'im by his son, Muhammad, and in turn his son, Jubayr. It is also related from Ibn 'Abbas by 'Ubaydullah ibn 'Abdullah ibn 'Utba. Mujahid relates it from Ibn 'Umar and Abu 'Abdu'r-Rahman as-Sulami and Muslim ibn Abi 'Imran al-Azdi relate it from Hudhayfa. Most of the paths of transmission of these *hadith* are sound.

The sign was clearly evident. One does not pay any attention to the objection of the disaffected that if this had taken place, it would not have been hidden from any of the people of the earth since it is something that would have been evident to all, and yet it has not been transmitted to us that any other people of the earth watched that night and saw the moon split. Even if it had been related to us [that they did not see the moon split] from those whom, in any case, one does not consult since they frequently lie, there still would not be any proof in that since the moon is not in the same state for all the people of the earth. It might rise for some people before it rises for others. The moon is in a different state for people who are on the opposite side of the earth. Mountains and clouds can come between it and people. This is why we find eclipses in certain lands rather than others, and a partial eclipse in some places when it is total in others. In some places, only those who claim to have astronomical knowledge know this. **"That is the determination of the Mighty, the All-Knowing."** (36:38)

Apart from all this, the sign of the moon splitting occurred at night. The custom of people at night is to be calm and still, close their doors, and not go out. What happens in the sky is hardly ever known except by those who watch and wait for it. That is why lunar eclipses occur frequently in every land but most people do not know about them unless they are told. Much of what reliable sources report about wonderous lights and luminous stars rising takes place in the sky at night but very few people have any knowledge of them.

At-Tahawi related in an obscure *hadith* from Asma' bint 'Umaysh that the Prophet received a revelation while resting in 'Ali's tent, and he did not pray 'Asr until after the sun had set. The Messenger of Allah said, "Did I pray, 'Ali?" He replied, "No." The Prophet said, "O Allah, if it is in Your obedience and the obedience of Your Messenger, return the sun to him!" Asma' said, "I had seen it set and then I saw it rise after it had set and it stopped between the mountain and the earth." That was at as-Sabha' in Khaybar.

At-Tahawi related that Ahmad ibn Salih used to say, "The one who is on the path of knowledge must not miss out learning the *hadith* of Asma' because it is one of the signs of prophethood."

Yunus ibn Bukayr related from Ibn Ishaq, "When the Messenger of Allah went on his Night Journey and informed his people about the approaching caravan and its company as a sign, they asked, 'When will it arrive?' He replied, 'Wednesday.' That day Quraysh began to look and the day passed and it did not come. The Messenger of Allah asked Allah to add an hour to the day for him, and the sun was kept back."

SECTION 13
On water flowing from the Prophet's fingers and increasing by his *baraka*

There are numerous *hadiths* about this. Some of the Companions, including Anas, Jabir and Ibn Mas'ud, related the *hadith* about water flowing from his fingers.

Anas ibn Malik said, "I saw the Messenger of Allah, may Allah bless him and grant him peace, at the time of the 'Asr prayer. People looked for water for *wudu'* and could not find any, so the Messenger of Allah was brought some *wudu'* water. He then placed his hand in the vessel and commanded the people to do *wudu'* from it." He added, "I saw the water flowing from his fingers, and everyone, down to the last man, did *wudu'* from it."[1]

Qatada also relates this from Anas, mentioning, "a vessel in which water overflowed from between his fingers." Qatada asked Anas, "How many were you?" He replied, "About three hundred." Humayd said that there were eighty men. Thabit said that there were about seventy men.

There is a *hadith* in the *Sahih* collection from Ibn Mas'ud from the variant of 'Alqama in which 'Alqama said, "Once when we were with the Messenger of Allah, may Allah bless him and grant him peace, and were without water, the Messenger of Allah told us, 'Find someone who has some extra water with him.' Water was brought and he poured it in a vessel and then placed his hand in it. The water then began to flow from between the fingers of the Messenger of Allah, may Allah bless him and grant him peace."

In the *Sahih* from Salim ibn Abi'l-Ja'd, Jabir ibn 'Abdullah reported, "People were thirsty on the Day of Hudaybiyya and the Messenger of Allah, may Allah bless him and grant him peace, had a water-vessel in front of him. He did *wudu'* from it. The people went to him and said, 'We have no water except what is in your vessel.' The Prophet placed his hand in the vessel and water flowed from between his fingers like springs." Jabir was asked how many were there and he

---

1. Muslim and al-Bukhari.

said, "There would have been enough if we had been a hundred thousand. We were fifteen thousand." Similar to this is related from Anas from Jabir with the words, "He was at al-Hudaybiya."

In the version of al-Walid ibn 'Ubada ibn as-Samit in the long *hadith* in Muslim concerning the raid of Buwat, Jabir said, "The Messenger of Allah said to me, 'Jabir, call for *wudu'* water.' Only a drop in a dry skin could be found which was brought to the Prophet. He pressed it, saying something unintelligible. Then he said, 'Call for the bowls of the caravan.' They were brought and set before him. The Prophet, may Allah bless him and grant him peace, spread his hand out in a bowl, parting his fingers, and Jabir poured the water on them. He said, 'In the name of Allah' and saw the water flowing from between his fingers. Then the water gushed up in the bowl and went around until it was full and he commanded people to use the water and they did so until they had all finished. He asked, 'Is there anyone who still needs water?' Then the Messenger of Allah took his hand from the bowl and it was still full."

Ash-Sha'bi said that on one of his journeys the Prophet was brought a small water-vessel. He was told "This is all the water we have with us, Messenger of Allah." So he poured it in a bowl and placed his fingers in the middle of it, dipping them in the water. People came to him, did *wudu'* and got up.

At-Tirmidhi said that these events took place in gatherings where there were many people, so it does not arouse any suspicion in the mind of the *hadith* scholar because the Companions were the quickest of people to deny something if it was not true and were the sort of people who were not silent in the presence of falsehood. They related this and circulated it, and it was ascribed to the Prophet, may Allah bless him and grant him peace, in the presence of all of them. No-one objected to what anyone said about this. They experienced this and saw it so it was like a confirmation by every one of them.

SECTION 14
His causing water to flow by his *baraka*

Another miracle he performed similar to this was causing water to flow by his *baraka* and increasing it by his touch and his supplication.

Malik has related the story of Tabuk in the *Muwatta'* on the authority of Mu'adh ibn Jabal who said that they came to a spring which was dripping with a little water. They scooped the water from the spring with their hands and gathered it into something. The Messenger of Allah washed his face with it, letting it drip back into the bowl which then began to overflow with water so that the people were able to drink. In the *hadith* of Ibn Ishaq it says, "It welled up from the water that was already there as quick as lightning." Then the

Prophet said, "Mu'adh, if you were to live a long time, you would see what is here fill gardens."

In the *hadith* of al-Bara' and Salama ibn al-Akwa' recording the story of al-Hudaybiyya, there were 14,000 men and the well could not provide water for fifty sheep. He said, "We crowded around it and did not leave a drop in it. The Messenger of Allah sat down beside it." Al-Bara' said, "We brought him a bucket and he spat and supplicated." Salama said, "Either he supplicated or spat in it and the water burst out. We had enough water for ourselves and our containers." In another version via Ibn Shihab it says, "He brought out an arrow from his quiver and placed it in the bottom of the waterless well and the people got water to the extent that they turned it into a regular water-hole for animals."

Abu Qatada mentioned that people were complaining to the Messenger of Allah, may Allah bless him and grant him peace, about thirst on a certain journey. He called for a *wudu'*-pot and put it under his arm and then covered its mouth. Allah knows best whether he spat in it or not. People drank until they had had enough and they even filled every water-skin they had with them. There were seventy-two men.[1]

At-Tabarani mentions the *hadith* of Abu Qatada differently to the way it is in the *Sahih*: "The Prophet, may Allah bless him and grant him peace, went out with them to help the people of Mu'ta when he heard about the killing of the expedition leaders..."[2] He goes on to mention a long *hadith* containing various marvels and signs of the Prophet, amongst which he says that one day they were without water and then he proceeds to tell the story of the *wudu'*-pot. He says that there were about three hundred people. In the collection of Muslim, the Prophet, may Allah bless him and grant him peace, is reported as saying to Abu Qatada, "Keep your *wudu'*-pot for news of this will spread."

Another example of this occurs in the *hadith* of 'Imran ibn Husayn when the Prophet and his Companions were afflicted by thirst during one of his journeys. He turned to two of his companions and told them that they would find a woman in a certain place with a camel that would have two water-skins on it. They found her and brought her to the Prophet. He put the water from the skins in a vessel and said what Allah wished him to say over it and then put the water back into the skins. Then the skins were opened and he told people to fill up their water containers until every last one of them was filled. 'Imran said, "It seemed to me that after that, the skins were even fuller." Then he gave a command and some provisions were gathered for the woman which filled her garment. He said, "Go. We did not take any of your water. Allah gave us water."[3]

Salama ibn al-Akwa' said that the Prophet of Allah, may Allah bless him and

---

1. Al-Bayhaqi.
2. The expedition to Mu'ta took place in 8 AH, and in it three leaders were killed holding the standard - Zayd ibn Arqam, Ja'far ibn Abi Talib and 'Abdullah ibn Rawaha.
3. Muslim and al-Bukhari.

grant him peace, asked, "Is there any *wudu'*-water?" A man brought a skin which had some water in it and we all did *wudu'*. It flowed out so that there was enough for 14,000 men."

In his *hadith* about the army of 'Usra,[1] 'Umar mentioned that they were afflicted by thirst so that a man was ready to kill his camel, squeeze its stomach and drink its contents. Abu Bakr asked the Prophet to make supplication, so he raised his hands and had not put them back before the sky clouded over and it poured with rain. They filled the vessels they had. The cloud-burst did not extend beyond the army.[2]

'Amr ibn Shu'ayb said that one time when he was riding behind the Prophet at Dhu'l-Majaz,[3] Abu Talib said to him, "I am thirsty and do not have any water with me." The Prophet got down and struck the earth with his feet and water came forth. He said, "Drink."

There are many *hadiths* to this effect, including the answer of the prayer for rain and what it caused.[4]

SECTION 15
Making food abundant by his *baraka* and supplication

Jabir ibn 'Abdullah said that a man came to the Prophet to ask him for food, and he gave him half a *wasq* of barley. He and his wife and guests continued to eat from it until he weighed it. The Prophet came and he told him that and he said, "If you had not weighed it, you would have continued to eat from it and it would have remained with you."[5]

Another example is the famous *hadith* of Abu Talha in Muslim and al-Bukhari where the Prophet fed seventy or eighty men from some barley loaves which Anas brought under his arm. He commanded the loaves to be broken up and said whatever Allah wished him to say over them.

There is also the *hadith* of Jabir in al-Bukhari about when the Prophet fed a thousand men on the Day of the Ditch from a *sa'* of barley and a lamb. Jabir said, "I swear by Allah that they ate and when they left our pot was just as full as it had been. Our dough was being made into bread and the Messenger of Allah spat in the dough and the pot and blessed it." Sa'id ibn Mina' and Ayman transmitted it from Jabir.

Thabit reported something similar from a man of the Ansar and his wife whom he did not name. He said, "He brought about a handful and the Messenger of Allah began to spread it in the vessel and say what Allah wished.

---

1. The expedition to Tabuk in 9 AH.
2. Ibn Khuzayma, al-Bayhaqi and al-Bazzar.
3. A market at 'Arafat.
4. After the Prophet made the rain prayer, it rained for a full week and the people complained about the effect on the houses, roads and flocks. (See *al-Muwatta'*. 13.2.3.)
5. Muslim.

Everyone in the house, the room and the building ate from it and it satisfied whoever came with him and afterwards there remained the same amount there had originally been in the vessel."

There is the *hadith* of Abu Ayyub in which he prepared enough food for the Messenger of Allah and Abu Bakr. The Prophet told him, "Invite thirty of the Ansar nobles." He invited them and they ate and then left. Then he said, "Invite sixty more," and the same thing happened. Then he said, "Invite seventy more," and they ate their fill and still left some. None of them left without becoming a Muslim and giving homage. Abu Ayyub said that, in all, one hundred and eighty men ate from his food.[1]

Samura ibn Jundub said that the Prophet, peace be upon him, was brought a bowl in which there was some meat and people came to eat from it in successive groups from morning to night. Some people would get up and then others would sit down.[2]

'Abdu'r-Rahman ibn Abi Bakr said, "There were one hundred and thirty of us with the Prophet," and he mentioned that a *sa'* of flour was kneaded, a sheep was prepared and its offal was roasted. He said, "By Allah, there was not one of the hundred and thirty who did not have a piece of the offal. Then two plates were made from it and we all ate together and there were two plates left over which I carried to the camel."[3]

'Abdu'r-Rahman ibn Abi 'Amr al-Ansari, Salama ibn al-Akwa', Abu Hurayra and 'Umar ibn al-Khattab mentioned that on one of his raids the people with the Prophet were hungry. He called for all the remaining provisions, and each man brought a handful of food or a bit more. The most any of them brought was a *sa'* of dates. He gathered it all on a mat and Salama said, "I reckoned it to be the amount of a goat. Then he called the people with their vessels and not a single vessel remained in the army that was not full. What remained was more than the amount with which we had started. If all the people of the earth had come to him, it still would have been enough for them."[4]

Abu Hurayra said that the Prophet told him to invite the people of the Suffa on his behalf. He gathered them and a plate was put before them and they ate what they wished and then left. It remained as it had been when it was laid out except that there were finger marks in it.

'Ali ibn Abi Talib said that the Messenger of Allah gathered together the Banu 'Abdu'l-Muttalib. There were forty of them. Some of the people were eating a young sheep and drinking from a large vessel. He put down a *mudd* of food for them and they ate until they were full and what was left was the same amount of food as there had been in the first place. Then he called for a cup and

1. At-Tabarani and al-Bayhaqi.
2. At-Tirmidhi and al-Bayhaqi.
3. Muslim and al-Bukhari.
4. Ibn Sa'd and al-Bayhaqi.

they drank until they were quenched and it remained as if they had not drunk from it.[1]

Anas said that when the Prophet had a house built for Zaynab, he told Anas to invite certain people he named as well as everyone he met until the house was full. A vessel was brought to him with some dates made into *hays*. He put it in front of him and dipped three fingers into it. People began to eat and then leave. The vessel remained as it had been to start with. The people numbered seventy-one or seventy-two.[2]

In another version of this story, there were about three hundred. He was told to take the bowl away and he said, "I did not know whether it was more full when I put it down or when I picked it up."

In the *hadith* of Ja'far ibn Muhammad from his father from 'Ali, it mentions that Fatima cooked a pot of food for their supper and sent 'Ali to fetch the Prophet so he could eat with them. The Prophet told her to serve out a plate for each of his wives one by one, and then one for himself and 'Ali and then one for herself. When she lifted the pot, it was overflowing. She said, "We ate what Allah willed from it."[3]

The Prophet commanded 'Umar ibn al-Khattab to make provision for four hundred riders from the Ahmas, a subtribe of the Hanifa, and he said, "Messenger of Allah, there are only a few *sa's*." He said, "Go." So he went and provisioned them from it. There was the amount of dates of a small kneeling camel and it remained like that. This is transmitted by Dukayn al-Ahmasi and Jarir ibn 'Abdullah. It is also related from an-Nu'man ibn Muqarrin except that he mentioned it as being "four hundred riders from Muzayna."

There is the *hadith* of Jabir ibn 'Abdullah about the debt his father died leaving. He offered his capital to his father's creditors. They would not accept that offer and there were not enough dates in the harvest to pay two years' debts. The Prophet came to him having commanded him to divide the creditors into groups and he began with the basic debts. He went in among the creditors and called and Jabir paid his father's creditors from it in full. Left over from it was the usual amount of the crop that was found every year. One version has, "The same amount as he had given them." He added, "The creditors, who were Jews, were amazed at that."[4]

Abu Hurayra said, "The people were afflicted by hunger and the Messenger of Allah asked me, 'Is there anything to eat?' I replied, 'Yes, some dates in the provisions.' He said, 'Bring them to me.' He put his hand in the bag and brought out a handful. He made supplication for *baraka* and then said, 'Call ten.' They ate until they were full. Then another ten came, and so it went until

---

1. Ibn Hanbal and al-Bayhaqi.
2. Muslim and al-Bukhari.
3. Ibn Sa'd.
4. Al-Bukhari.

all the army was satisfied, He said, 'Take what you brought and put your hand in the bag and do not turn it upside down.' I took out more than I had brought and ate from it. I ate from it during the life of the Messenger of Allah, Abu Bakr and 'Umar until the murder of 'Uthman. Then it was taken from me."[1]

One version has, "I carried such-and-such number of *wasqs* of those dates in the way of Allah." A similar story was mentioned about the Tabuk raid in which there were about ten dates.[2]

Another example of this occurs in the *hadith* of Abu Hurayra in al-Bukhari when he is hungry and the Prophet asks him to follow him. He finds some milk in a cup which has been given to him and he orders the people of the *Suffa* to be called. Abu Hurayra says, "I said, 'What! Is this milk for them? I am more entitled to take a drink from it so that I might be strengthened by it.' I called them and remembered the command of the Prophet to let them drink, so I began to give to a man and he drank until he was quenched. Then the other took it until he was quenched and so it went on until they were all quenched. The Prophet took the cup and said, 'You and I remain. Sit and drink.' I drank and then he said, 'Drink.' He kept saying, 'Drink' until I said, 'No! By the One who sent you with the truth, I cannot find any room for it.' He took the cup and praised Allah, said 'In the name of Allah' and drank the rest."[3]

In the *hadith* of Khalid ibn 'Abdu'l-'Uzza, it mentions that the Prophet slaughtered a sheep. Khalid's family was large. Whenever he slaughtered a sheep for himself, it would not be enough for his family. The Prophet ate from this sheep and put the rest of it in Khalid's pot and asked for *baraka* for him and distributed it to his family and they ate and there was some left over. Ad-Dulabi mentioned the report.[4]

In the *hadith* of al-Ajurri about the Prophet giving Fatima in marriage to 'Ali, it mentions that the Prophet commanded Bilal to bring a pot of four or five *mudds* and sacrifice a sheep for the feast. He said, "I brought the sheep and he slaughtered it. Then the people came group by group to eat from the sheep until they had finished. There were some leftovers. He blessed them and commanded they be carried to his wives, saying, 'Eat and have your supper.'"

In the *hadith* of Anas about the Messenger of Allah, may Allah bless him and grant him peace, getting married, he says, "My mother, Umm Sulaym, prepared *hays* and I put it in a pot and took it to the Messenger of Allah and he said, 'Put it down and invite so-and-so and so-and-so for me and whoever you meet.' I invited them and did not omit anyone I met (he mentioned that there were about three hundred) until they filled the *Suffa* and the room. The Prophet told them, 'Sit in circles of ten.' The Prophet placed his hand on the food and

---

1. Al-Bayhaqi.
2. At-Tirmidhi.
3. Also in at-Tirmidhi and Ibn Majah from Abu Qatada.
4. Al-Bayhaqi.

supplicated and said what Allah wished him to say, so they ate until they were full. He said, 'Take it away.' I did not know whether there was more when I put it down or picked it up."[1]

There are many *hadiths* on these three subjects in the *Sahih*. Some ten Companions agree on the import of these *hadith*. Many more among the Followers and innumerable people after them have related it from them. Most of them are to be found in famous stories and well-known collections. It is not possible to say anything but the truth about it nor to think that anyone present would have been silent about anything not recognised in it.

SECTION 16
On the tree speaking and testifying to his prophethood and its answering his call

Ibn 'Umar reported: "We were with the Messenger of Allah, may Allah bless him and grant him peace, on a journey and a bedouin came up to him and he asked, 'Bedouin, where are you going?' He replied, 'To my family.' He said, 'Do you want something good?' The man asked, 'What is it?' The Prophet said, 'That you testify that there is no god but Allah alone without partner and that Muhammad is His slave and Messenger.' The Bedouin asked, 'Who will testify to what you say?' He replied, 'This mimosa tree.' It advanced from the edge of the wadi, furrowing the earth until it stood before him and he asked it to testify three times and it did so and then returned to its place."[2]

Burayda reported: "A bedouin asked the Prophet for a sign and he said to him, 'Tell that tree that the Messenger of Allah calls it.' The tree leaned to the right and left, in front and behind, pulled up its roots and came splitting the earth, dragging its dusty roots until it stood before the Messenger of Allah. It said, 'Peace be upon you, Messenger of Allah.' The Bedouin said, 'Command it to return to its place.' It returned, dropped its roots and was still. The bedouin said, 'Give me permission to prostrate to you.' The Prophet said, 'If I had commanded anyone to prostrate to anyone, I would have commanded the woman to prostrate to her husband.' The bedouin then said, 'Give me permission to kiss your hands and feet.' He gave him permission."[3]

In the *Sahih* in the long *hadith* of Jabir ibn 'Abdullah, it is reported that the Messenger of Allah went to relieve himself and did not see anything with which to shield himself. There were two trees at the edge of the wadi. The Messenger of Allah went to one of them and took one of its branches, saying, "Let me lead you by the permission of Allah," and he led it like a camel on a halter whose leader cajoles it. Jabir mentioned that he did the same with the

1. Muslim and al-Bukhari.
2. Ad-Darimi, al-Bayhaqi and al-Bazzar.
3. Al-Bazzar.

other one until they were level. Then he said, "Join together for me by the permission of Allah," and they joined.[1]

In another version, Jabir said to the tree, "The Messenger of Allah asks you to join your companion so he can sit behind you." It pushed ahead until it joined its companion and he sat between them. Jabir said, "I quickly went away and sat down, talking to myself, and I turned and the Messenger of Allah was coming. The two trees parted and each of them stood on its own as it had been. The Messenger of Allah stopped a moment and indicated right and left by the movement of his head."[2]

Usama ibn Zayd reported, "The Messenger of Allah said during one of his raids, 'Is there anywhere?' meaning a place to relieve himself. I said, 'The wadi does not have any place in it for people.' He said, 'Did you see a palm tree or a stone?' I replied, 'I saw some scattered palms.' He said, 'Go and tell them that the Messenger of Allah commands them to come to his aid.' He told me to say the same to the stones and I did so. By the One who sent him with the truth, I saw the palm-trees coming near each other until they joined. The stones came together until they became a heap behind the Prophet. When he finished, he told me, 'Tell them to part.' By the One who has myself in His hand, I saw the trees and stones part and return to their places."[3]

Ya'la ibn Siyyaba said, "I was on a journey with the Prophet, may Allah bless him and grant him peace..." and he mentioned something similar to these two *hadiths,* saying, "He commanded two small palms and they joined together."[4] Ghaylan ibn Salama ath-Thaqafi has something similar about the two trees. Ibn Mas'ud has something similar about the Prophet on the raid to Hunayn.

Ya'la ibn Murra, who is also called Ibn as-Siyyaba, mentioned some things that he saw happen with the Messenger of Allah, may Allah bless him and grant him peace. He mentioned that a palm or mimosa tree came and circled them and then returned to its place. The Messenger of Allah said, "It asked for permission to greet me."

In the *hadith* of 'Abdullah ibn Mas'ud it says: "A tree announced the presence of the *jinn* to the Prophet one night when they were listening to him." From Mujahid from Ibn Mas'ud concerning this is the *hadith* that the *jinn* said, "Who will testify for you?" He replied, "This tree. Come, tree!" It came dragging its roots and clattering.[5]

Ibn 'Umar, Burayda, Jabir ibn 'Abdullah, Ibn Mas'ud, Ya'la ibn Murra, Usama ibn Zayd, Anas ibn Malik, 'Ali ibn Abi Talib, Ibn 'Abbas and others are

---

1. Muslim.
2. Muslim and elsewhere.
3. Al-Bayhaqi and Abu Ya'la.
4. Ibn Hanbal, al-Bayhaqi and at-Tabarani with a sound *isnad*.
5. Muslim and al-Bukhari.

all agreed on this same story. Many more Followers related it from them, so it is further strengthened.

Ibn Furak mentioned that the Prophet was travelling by night during the Ta'if raid and became sleepy. A lote-tree in his way split into two halves for him and he passed between the two halves. They remained with their trunks until this day and are well known.

Another example is the *hadith* of Anas which records that Jibril, seeing the Prophet in sorrow, asked, "Shall I show you a sign?" He replied, "Yes." The Messenger of Allah looked at a tree beyond the wadi and said, "Call that tree." It came walking until it stood in front of him. The Prophet said, "Command it to go back," and it went back to its place.[1]

There is a similar account from 'Ali, but it does not mention Jibril. In it, the Prophet says, "O Allah, show me a sign so that I will not ever be concerned about those who envy me." He summoned a tree and the rest of the story is similar. The sorrow of the Prophet was on account of his people rejecting him and he wanted a sign for them, not for himself.[2]

Ibn Ishaq mentions that the Prophet showed Rukana[3] a similar sign in respect of a tree. He called it, and it came until it stood in front of him. Then he said, "Return," so it returned.

From al-Hasan ibn 'Ali there is a report that the Prophet complained to his Lord about his people who were causing him concern. He asked for a sign by which he would know that he had nothing to fear. It was revealed to him, "Go to this wadi which has a certain tree in it and call a branch of it. It will come to you." He did so and it came splitting the earth in a furrow until it stood in front of him. He detained it as long as Allah willed and then told it, "Go back as you came," and it returned. He said, "O Lord, now I know that I have nothing to fear."[4]

'Umar said something similar which mentions the Prophet as saying, "Show me a sign so that I will never worry about anyone denying me." Then he mentioned a similar story.[5]

Ibn 'Abbas said that the Prophet said to a bedouin, "Tell me whether I should summon this trunk of the palm tree to testify that I am the Messenger of Allah." He said, "Yes, do so." He called it and it began to furrow a path until it reached him. Then he said, "Go back," and it did so.[6] At-Tirmidhi says this is a sound *hadith*.

---

1. Ibn Majah, ad-Darimi and al-Bayhaqi.
2. As-Suyuti said he could not find it from 'Ali, but from Jabir.
3. Rukana al-Muttalibi, the strongest man among the Quraysh. The Prophet wrestled with him and threw the previously undefeated wrestler two times. Rukana thought this extraordinary and so the Prophet offered to show him something even more extraordinary.
4. Al-Bayhaqi, *mursal hadith*.
5. Al-Bazzar, Abu Ya'la and al-Bayhaqi.
6. Al-Bukhari's *History*, al-Bayhaqi and ad-Darimi.

SECTION 17
The story of the yearning of the palm-trunk

The *hadith* about the stump corroborates these reports. It is famous in itself and well known. It is related by many parallel paths of transmission. The *Sahih* collections relate it. It is related by about ten of the Companions, including Ubayy ibn Kalb, Jarir ibn 'Abdullah, Anas ibn Malik, 'Abdullah ibn 'Umar, 'Abdullah ibn 'Abbas, Sahl ibn Sa'd, Abu Sa'id al-Khudri, Burayda, Umm Salama, and al-Muttalib ibn Abi Wada'a. All of them have related a version of this *hadith*. At-Tirmidhi said that the *hadith* of Anas is sound.

Jabir ibn 'Abdullah said in the *Sahih* of al-Bukhari, "The mosque was constructed of the trunks of palm-trees with a roof laid on top of them. When the Prophet addressed the people, he would lean against one of the trunks. When the minbar was built for him, we heard that trunk make a sound like a camel."

In Anas' version, "Until the mosque was shaken by its moaning."

In Sahl's version, "People wept a lot when they saw that."

In the version of al-Muttalib and Ubayy, "Until it nearly split and burst apart, at which the Prophet came to it and placed his hand on it. Then it was still."

Another added that the Prophet said, "This trunk is weeping at the remembrance of what it has lost."

Another added, "By the One who has my soul in His hand, if he had not taken care of it, it would have remained moaning like that until the Day of Rising out of grief for the Messenger of Allah."

The Messenger of Allah commanded that it be buried under the minbar. This is related in the *hadiths* according to al-Muttalib, Sahl ibn Sa'd, and Ishaq who have it from Anas. One of the transmissions from Sahl says, "It was buried under the minbar or placed in the roof."

In the *hadith* of Ubayy, it mentions that when the Prophet prayed, the trunk would lean towards him. When the mosque was demolished, Ubayy took it and it remained in his possession until termites consumed it and it turned to dust.

Al-Isfira'ini said, "The Prophet called it to him and it came furrowing the earth, and clung to him. Then he commanded it and it returned to its place."

In the *hadith* of Burayda, the Prophet said, "If you like, I will put you back in the garden where you were so your roots can grow and your form will be complete and you will have fruit and leaves again. Or, if you like, I will plant you in the Garden so that the friends of Allah can eat from your fruit." The Prophet listened to hear what it would say. It said, "Yes, plant me in the Garden so that the friends of Allah can eat from me and I will be in a place where I will not decay." Those who were near it heard what it said. The Prophet said, "I have done it." The Prophet said, "It has chosen the Lasting Abode over the Passing Abode."

When al-Hasan ibn 'Ali told the story, he wept and said, "Slaves of Allah, the wood yearned for the Messenger of Allah, may Allah bless him and grant him peace, longing for him because of his position. You are the ones who should yearn to meet him."

This story was related from Jabir by Hafs ibn 'Ubaydullah – and it is also said 'Abdullah ibn Hafs – Ayman, Abu Nadra, Ibn al-Musayyab, Sa'id ibn Abi Karb, Kurayb ibn Abi Muslim and Abu Salih Dhakwan az-Zayyat. It is also related from Anas ibn Malik by al-Hasan, Thabit, and Ishaq ibn Abi Talha. It is related from Ibn 'Umar by Nafi' and Abu Hayya. Abu Nadra and Abu'l-Waddak related it from Abu Sa'id; 'Ammar ibn Abi 'Ammar from Ibn 'Abbas; Abu Hazim and 'Abbas ibn Sahl from Sahl ibn Sa'd; Kathir ibn Zayd from al-Muttalib; 'Abdullah ibn Burayda from his father, Burayda; and at-Tufayl ibn Ubayy from his father, Ubayy.

So, as you can see, this *hadith* is transmitted from people who are sound. Those we have mentioned and many other Followers related it from the Companions to others we have not mentioned. Knowledge of an incident is established by less witnesses than this in the kind of matter under discussion here.

Allah gives firmness in the right way.

SECTION 18
Similar incidents with inanimate things

Ibn Mas'ud said, "We used to hear the food glorifying its Lord while it was being eaten."[1]

In another version he it is reported that he said, "We were eating with the Messenger of Allah, may Allah bless him and grant him peace, and could hear the food glorifying its Lord."

Anas said, "The Prophet, may Allah bless him and grant him peace, took a handful of pebbles and they glorified Allah in the hand of the Messenger of Allah so that we could hear their glorification. Then he poured them into the hand of Abu Bakr and they continued to glorify Allah, and then into our hands, and they went on glorifying Allah there."[2]

Abu Dharr related something similar to this and added that they glorified Allah in the hands of 'Umar and 'Uthman.[3]

'Ali said, "We were in Makka with the Messenger of Allah, may Allah bless

---

1. Al-Bukhari and at-Tirmidhi.
2. Ibn 'Asakir.
3. At-Tabarani, al-Bayhaqi and al-Bazzar.

him and grant him peace, and he went to one of its districts and every single tree and mountain he passed said to him, 'Peace be upon you, Messenger of Allah.'"[1]

Jabir ibn Samura related that the Prophet said, "I know a stone in Makka which used to greet me."[2] It is said that this was the Black Stone.

'A'isha related that the Prophet said, "When Jibril came to me with the message, it came about that every stone or tree I passed said to me, 'Peace be upon you, Messenger of Allah.'"[3]

Jabir ibn 'Abdullah said, "Every stone or tree that the Prophet passed prostrated to him."[4]

Ibn 'Abbas said that when the Prophet wrapped him and his sons in a cloak and prayed that they would be veiled from the Fire just as he had veiled them with his cloak, the walls of the house said, "Amen, Amen."[5]

Ja'far ibn Muhammad related from his father, "The Prophet was ill and Jibril brought him a plate which had pomegranates and grapes on it. The Prophet ate from it, and it glorified Allah."

Anas said, "The Prophet, Abu Bakr, 'Umar and 'Uthman climbed Uhud. It shook under them. He said, 'Be firm, Uhud. A prophet, a true man and two martyrs are on you.'"[6]

There is something similar about Hira' from Abu Hurayra, but he added that 'Ali, Talha and az-Zubayr ibn al-'Awwam were the ones who were with the Prophet. In this version, the Prophet said, "There is only a prophet or a true man or a martyr on you."[7]

'Uthman stated in this story, "Ten Companions were with him and I was one of them." He added 'Abdu'r-Rahman and Sa'd to the names, saying, "I have forgotten two."

Sa'id ibn Zayd said something similar. He mentioned ten, and added himself.[8]

It is related that when Quraysh were pursuing the Prophet, Thabir (a mountain at Muzdalifa) said to him, "Get down, Messenger of Allah. I fear that they will kill you on my back and so Allah will punish me." Hira' (another mountain) said, "To me, Messenger of Allah!"

Ibn 'Umar said, "The Prophet recited on the minbar, **'They do not value Him with His true value.'** (6:9) Then he said, 'The Compeller glorifies Himself, saying, "I am the Compeller, I am the Compeller, I am the Great, the Self-Exalted."' The minbar shook until we said, 'He will fall off it.'"[9]

---

1. Ad-Darimi and at-Tirmidhi.
2. Muslim.
3. Al-Bazzar.
4. Al-Bayhaqi.
5. Ibid.
6. Al-Bukhari and Ibn Majah.
7. Muslim.
8. Abu Dawud and at-Tirmidhi.
9. Muslim, an-Nasa'i and Ibn Hanbal.

From Ibn 'Abbas we are told, "There were three hundred and sixty idols around the house. The feet of the idols were reinforced with lead in stone. When the Messenger of Allah, may Allah bless him and grant him peace, entered the mosque in the Year of the Victory, he began to point with the staff in his hand at them, but did not touch them. He said, **"The truth has come and falsehood vanishes."** (17:81) Whenever he pointed at the face of an idol, it fell on its back. When he pointed at its back, it fell on its face. Finally not a single idol remained standing."[1]

There is a similar report in the *hadith* of Ibn Mas'ud which says, "He began to attack them, saying, **'The truth has come. Falsehood cannot originate nor regenerate.'**" (34:49)

Another example of this kind of thing is contained in the *hadith* which mentions the monk he met when he was young and travelling as a merchant with his uncle. The monk never came out for anyone, but on this occasion he came out and began to mingle with them until he took the hand of the Messenger of Allah. He said, "This is the master of the worlds. Allah will send him as a mercy to the worlds." The shaykhs of Quraysh asked him, "How do you know?" He said, "There was no stone or tree that did not prostrate to him. They only prostrate to a Prophet." He said, "He came with a cloud shading him. When he drew near to the people, he found that they had got to the shade of the tree first. When he sat down, it moved to shade him."[2]

SECTION 19
Signs in connection with various animals

'A'isha said, "We used to have a pet animal. When the Messenger of Allah was with us, it stayed in its place without moving. When the Messenger of Allah went out, it would move about."[3]

'Umar said that the Messenger of Allah was with a group of his Companions when a bedouin came who had caught a lizard. The bedouin asked, "Who is this?" They replied, "The Prophet of Allah." He said, "By al-Lat and al-'Uzza, I do not believe in you nor does this lizard believe in you." He threw it in front of the Prophet who said, "Lizard!" It answered in a clear tongue which everyone heard, "At your service, O adornment of the One who will bring the Rising!" He asked, "Who do you worship?" It said, "The One Whose throne is in the heaven and Whose power is in the earth, Whose path is in the sea, Whose mercy is in the Garden and Whose punishment is in the Fire." He asked, "Who am I?" It replied, "The Messenger of the Lord of the Worlds and the Seal of the

---

1. Al-Bukhari and Muslim, al-Bazzar, and others.
2. At-Tirmidhi and al-Bayhaqi.
3. Ibn Hanbal, al-Bazzar, Abu Ya'la, at-Tabarani, al-Bayhaqi and ad-Daraqutni. It is sound.

Prophets. Whoever confirms you is successful and whoever denies you is lost."
The bedouin became Muslim.[1]

Another example is the famous story from Abu Sa'id al-Khudri about what
was said by the wolf: "While a herdsman was herding his sheep, a wolf made
for one of the sheep, but the herdsman took it from him. The wolf sat down on
its haunches and said, 'Don't you fear Allah? You have come between me and
my provision.' The herdsman exclaimed, 'A marvel! A wolf who speaks like a
human!' The wolf retorted, 'Shall I tell you something even more
extraordinary? The Messenger of Allah between the two mounds tells people
the news of what has happened.' The herdsman went to the Prophet and told
him what had happened. The Prophet told him, 'Get up and tell the people.'
The Prophet said, 'He spoke the truth.'" The *hadith* containing the story is very
long.[2]

In the version from Abu Hurayra, the wolf said, "You are more
extraordinary – standing here with your sheep and abandoning a Prophet when
Allah has never sent a Prophet whom He values more than him. The doors of
the Garden have been opened for him and its people look at his Companions to
see their actions. Nothing stands between you and him except this ravine, so go
and join the armies of Allah." The herdsman said, "Who will care for my
sheep?" The wolf replied, "I will guard them until you return," so the man
turned over his sheep to the wolf and left. When he found the Prophet, the
Prophet, peace be upon him, told him, "Return to your sheep. You will find
them all there." He found them all there and he slaughtered one of the sheep
for the wolf. It is related from Ihban ibn Aws, who was the one to whom the
wolf spoke. It is also related from Salma ibn 'Amr ibn al-Akwa'. The reason he
became Muslim is the same as in the *hadith* of Abu Sa'id al-Khudri.[3]

Another story, related by Ibn Wahb, says that Abu Sufyan ibn Harb and
Safwan ibn Umayya found a wolf who had taken a gazelle. The gazelle entered
the Haram and the wolf left it. They were amazed at that. The wolf said, "More
extraordinary than this is Muhammad ibn 'Abdullah who calls you to the
Garden while you call him to the Fire." Abu Sufyan said, "By al-Lat and al-
'Uzza, if you had mentioned this in Makka, it would have been left deserted."
Something similar occurred to Abu Jahl and his companions.

'Abbas ibn Mirdas was amazed at the words of Damari, his idol,[4] and its
composing poetry in which the Prophet was mentioned. A bird swooped down

1. This *hadith* is weak in *isnad* and *matn*, although many quote it, disagreeing about whether it is
weak or forged.
2. Ibn Hanbal, al-Bazzar and al-Bayhaqi. It is considered sound.
3. Ibn Hanbal, al-Bazzar, and al-Bayhaqi consider it sound. Al-Baghawi and Abu Nu'aym say its
isnad is sound.
4. After being told by his father to worship a stone idol called Damari, he heard a voice from within
it reciting a poem which begins, "Say to all the tribes of Sulaym, Damari is dead and the people of
the mosque do live." Ibn Ishaq, p. 776.

and said, "'Abbas, do you marvel at what Damari says and yet do not wonder at yourself when the Messenger of Allah calls you to Islam while you are sitting here!" That was the reason he became Muslim.[1]

Jabir ibn 'Abdullah said that a man came to the Prophet and accepted him while he was besieging one of the fortresses of Khaybar. The man was herding some sheep for the people of Khaybar and said, "Messenger of Allah, what about the sheep?" He said, "Throw pebbles in their faces. Allah will take care of your trust for you and return them to their owners." He did and all the sheep went back to their own people.[2]

Anas said, "The Prophet went with Abu Bakr, 'Umar and an Ansari into a garden belonging to one of the Ansar. There were some sheep in the garden and they prostrated to him. Abu Bakr said, 'We are more duty-bound to prostrate to you than they.'"[3]

Abu Hurayra said, "The Prophet entered a garden and some camels prostrated to him."[4]

There is a similar story about a camel related by Tha'laba ibn Malik, Jabir ibn 'Abdullah, Ya'la ibn Murra, and 'Abdullah ibn Ja'far. Tha'laba ibn Malik said, "No-one entered the garden without the camel attacking him. When the Prophet entered the garden, he called it and the camel put its mouth on the ground and knelt before him. He put a halter on it. He said, 'There is nothing between the heavens and the earth which does not know that I am the Messenger of Allah except for the rebels among the *jinn* and men.'"[5] The same thing is related from 'Abdullah ibn Abi Awfa.

Another tradition about a camel relates that, "The Prophet asked some people about a certain camel and they told him that they wanted to slaughter it." In one version he said, "It has complained of too much work and too little fodder," and in another, "It complained to me that you want to slaughter it after you have made it toil in hard labour since it was small."[6]

In the above story of the split-eared camel which told the Prophet about itself, it was put out to pasture and the wild beasts avoided it, calling out to it, "You belong to Muhammad!" After the Prophet died, it would neither eat nor drink until it died. Al-Isfira'ini mentioned this.

Ibn Wahb related, "The doves of Makka shaded the Prophet, may Allah bless him and grant him peace, on the day he conquered Makka. He made supplication to Allah to bless them."

1. As-Suyuti says that he did not find the words of the bird in the form of the *hadith* which he found in at-Tabarani.
2. Al-Bayhaqi.
3. Ibn Hanbal and al-Bazzar with a sound *isnad*.
4. Al-Bazzar with a good *isnad*.
5. Abu Nu'aym.
6. At-Tabarani and Ibn Majah in his *Sunan* regarding the expedition of Dhat ar-Riqa'.

Anas, Zayd ibn Arqam and al-Mughira ibn Shu'ba related that the Prophet said, "On the Night of the Cave,[1] Allah commanded a tree to grow in front of the Prophet and shield him. He commanded two doves to stop at the mouth of the cave."[2]

Another *hadith* about the cave says that a spider spun a web at its entrance. When the seekers came for him and saw that, they said, "If there had been anyone in there, these two doves would not be at its mouth." The Prophet heard what they said. Then they went off.[3]

'Abdullah ibn Qurt said that five, six or seven sacrificial camels came up to the Prophet on their own to allow him to sacrifice them on the 'Id.[4]

Umm Salama said that the Prophet was in the desert when a gazelle called out to him, "Messenger of Allah!" He replied, "What do you need?" It said, "This bedouin has captured me and I have two fawns in the mountains, so release me so that I can go and suckle them. Then I will return." He asked the man, "Will you do that?" He replied, "Yes." Then he let it go and it went and returned and he tied it up. The bedouin came back and said, "Messenger of Allah, is there anything you want?" He said, "Let this gazelle go." He let it go and it went running off into the desert, saying, "I testify that there is no god but Allah and that you are the Messenger of Allah."[5]

There is also what is related about the lion being subjected to Safina, the client of the Messenger of Allah, when the Prophet, may Allah bless him and grant peace, sent him to Mu'adh ibn Jabal in the Yemen. He met a lion and told him that he was the client of the Messenger of Allah and that he was carrying his letter. The lion snarled and moved from the road.[6]

Another version has it that Safina was misrouted and went to an island where he found a lion. Safina said, "I am the client of the Messenger of Allah, may Allah bless him and grant him peace." The lion began to push him with its shoulder until it put him straight on the road.[7]

The Prophet took hold of the ear of a sheep which belonged to some people from the clan 'Abdu'l-Qays and then let go. There was a mark on it which remained on it and its offspring afterwards.

There is also what Ibrahim ibn Hammad related about what was said by the donkey which was given to the Prophet at Khaybar. The Prophet said to it,

---

1. When the Prophet and Abu Bakr made *hijra* from Makka, they first hid in a cave while the idol-worshippers of Makka were looking for them.
2. Ibn Sa'd, al-Bazzar, at-Tabarani and Abu Nu'aym.
3. Ibid.
4. Al-Hakim and at-Tabarani.
5. Al-Bayhaqi.
6. As-Suyuti was not able to find this story. Al-Bayhaqi says that it happened to Safina when he strayed from the army in Greek territory. However, al-Bukhari relates it in his *History*.
7. Al-Bazzar and al-Bayhaqi. As-Suyuti considers it sound.

"What is your name?" It said, "My name is Yazid ibn Shihab." The Prophet, may Allah bless him and grant peace, named it Ya'fur. The donkey would take him to the houses of his companions and knock on the door for him with its head and call them. When the Prophet died, it fell into a well out of grief and died.[1]

There is the *hadith* which mentions the she-camel which testified for its owner in the presence of the Prophet that it was not stolen and was his property.[2]

There is the *hadith* about a goat coming to the Messenger of Allah, may Allah bless him and grant peace, while he was with his army and they were thirsty and had pitched camp at a place without water. There were about three hundred men. The Messenger of Allah milked the goat and all the army were able to drink. Then the Prophet said to Abu Rafi', "I think you own it." The Messenger of Allah added, "The one who brought it is the one to take it away." Ibn Qani' and others related it.

He once said to his horse when he had stopped for the prayer on one of his journeys, "Do not move, may Allah bless you, until we finish our prayer." He turned it towards *qibla* and it did not move a muscle until he had finished the prayer.

Al-Waqidi related that when the Prophet, may Allah bless him and grant him peace, sent his messengers to the kings, six of them left on the same day and each found he could speak the language of the people to whom he was sent.

There are many *hadiths* on this topic. We have presented the most famous of them.

SECTION 20
Bringing the dead to life, their speaking, infants and suckling children speaking and testifying to his prophethood

Abu Hurayra said, "A Jewess at Khaybar gave the Prophet a roasted sheep which she had poisoned. The Messenger of Allah and some other people ate some of it. He said, 'Take your hands away. It tells me that it is poisoned.' Bishr ibn al-Bara' died. The Prophet, may Allah bless him and grant peace, asked the Jewess, 'What made you do it?' She replied, 'If you are a Prophet, what I did would not harm you. If you are just a king, I would have freed people from you.' He commanded that she be killed."[3]

In the version of Anas, she said, "I wanted to kill you," and he replied, "Allah would not give you the power to do that." The people said, "We will kill her," but he said, "No." It is related like that from Abu Hurayra by another transmission which does not have Wahb ibn Munabbih in it. He said, "She had

---

1. Ibn Hibban relates it in weak *hadith*.
2. At-Tabarani.
3. In Sa'id from Ibn al-A'rabi from Abu Dawud.

no power." Jabir ibn 'Abdullah also related it. It says in his version, "This shoulder told me," and, "He did not punish her." In the version of al-Hasan al-Basri, the Prophet, may Allah bless him and grant peace, said, "Its thigh tells me that it is poisoned." Ibn Ishaq says that he pardoned her.[1]

Anas said, "I used to recognise its effects in the lower lip of the Messenger of Allah." When the Prophet had his final illness, he said, "The food of Khaybar comes back to me. At times it makes me choke."[2]

Ibn Ishaq related that the Muslims say that the Messenger of Allah, may Allah bless him and grant him peace, died a martyr thus adding to the honour of prophethood which Allah had given him.

Ibn Sahnun said, "The people of *hadith* agree that the Messenger of Allah killed the Jewess who poisoned him." We have mentioned the different transmissions regarding this incident from Abu Hurayra, Anas and Jabir. In the version of Ibn 'Abbas, the Prophet handed her over to the relatives of Bishr ibn al-Bara' and they killed her.

They also disagree about the Prophet killing the man who bewitched him. Al-Waqidi says that he forgave him and we think that that is the most likely. It is also related that he killed him.

Al-Bazzar has also related the *hadith* from Abu Sa'id, saying at the end of it, "He stretched out his hand and said, 'Eat in the name of Allah.' We ate. He mentioned the name of Allah and it did not harm any of us."

The compilers of the *Sahih* have related the speech of the poisoned sheep which the Imams related. It is famous. The Imams of the people of speculation disagree about such speech. Some say that it is speech which Allah created in the dead sheep, the stone or the tree, and they state that Allah originates the letters and sounds which are heard from them without altering their form or changing their shape. That is the position of Shaykh Abu'l-Hasan al-Ash'ari and Qadi Abu Bakr al-Baqillani. Others believe that He puts life into them first and then brings speech out of them, and this is also related from Shaykh Abu'l-Hasan al-Ash'ari. Both are possible and Allah knows best.

If life is not a precondition for the existence of the letters and voices, then it is not impossible that these things exist on their own without life being present. If it is physical speech that is being talked about, then the existence of life is a precondition since the physical speech can only exist in something that has life. This is contrary to what al-Jubba'i says, in opposition to the rest of the *mutakallimun* of the different sects, about articulate speech, letters and voices issuing only from a living being with the necessary capacity to actually articulate the letters and sounds. This would be necessary in the case of the pebbles, the palm-trunk and the foreleg.

---

1. Al-Bukhari and Muslim.
2. Ibn Sa'd.

He said, "Allah created life in them and gave them a mouth and a tongue and the necessary instruments to make it possible for them to speak." If this had been the case, it would have been transmitted. It is more suspect than any suspicion about the transmission of the glorification of the pebbles or sighing of the stump itself. None of the people of the *sira* or transmission has transmitted anything indicating that this happened, which suggests that al-Jubba'i's claim is unfounded. Furthermore, there is no need to consider it. Allah is the One who gives success.

Waki' ibn al-Jarrah relates from Fahd ibn 'Atiyya that the Prophet was brought a child who had grown up without ever speaking. He asked, "Who am I?" The child said, "The Messenger of Allah."[1]

It is related from Mu'arrid ibn Mu'ayqib, "I saw an amazing thing from the Prophet, may Allah bless him and grant him peace. A child was brought to him the day it was born and it spoke. The Prophet said to it, 'You have spoken the truth, may Allah bless you.' Then the child never spoke after that until it grew up. He was called Mubarak al-Yamana. This took place at Makka during the Farewell Hajj." This *hadith* is known by the *hadith* of Shasuna who is in its chain of transmission.[2]

Al-Hasan al-Basri said, "A man came to the Prophet, may Allah bless him and grant him peace, and told him that he had left a small daughter of his to die in a certain wadi. The Prophet went with him to the wadi and called her by her name, 'So-and-so! Answer me by Allah's permission.' She came out and said, 'At your service!' He told her, 'Your parents have become Muslim. If you like, I will return you to them.' She said, 'I have no need of them. I have found that Allah is better for me than them.'"[3]

Anas said that a young man of the Ansar, whose mother was old, died and they shrouded him and tried to comfort her. She cried, "My son is dead?" They said that he was. The old woman said, "O Allah! If you know that I emigrated for You and Your Messenger, hoping that You would help me in every affliction, do not burden me with this affliction!" They took the cloth from his face and he ate with them.[4]

'Abdullah ibn 'Ubaydullah al-Ansari said, "I was one of those who buried Thabit ibn Qays ibn Shammas, who was killed at Yamama. When we put him in the grave we heard him say, 'Muhammad is the Messenger of Allah, Abu Bakr is the Siddiq, 'Umar is the martyr and 'Uthman is the merciful and good.' We looked and he was dead."[5]

An-Nu'man ibn Bashir said that Zayd ibn Kharija fell down dead in one of the alleys of Madina. He was lifted up and shrouded. Between the two evening prayers while the women were wailing around him, they heard him say, "Be

1. Al-Bayhaqi.
2. Al-Bayhaqi and Ibn 'Asakir.
3. Al-Bayhaqi.
4. Ibn 'Adi, al-Bayhaqi, Ibn Abi Dunya and Abu Nu'aym.
5. Al-Bayhaqi.

silent! Be silent!" His face was uncovered and he said, "Muhammad is the Messenger of Allah, the Unlettered Prophet and the Seal of the Prophets. It is like that in the First Book." Then he said, "It is true. It is true." He mentioned Abu Bakr, 'Umar and 'Uthman, and then said, "Peace be upon you, Messenger of Allah, and the mercy of Allah and His blessing." Then he became dead as he had been before.[1]

SECTION 21
On healing the sick and those with infirmities

Ibn Shihab, 'Asim ibn 'Umar ibn Qatada and others mention the story of Uhud. Sa'd ibn Abi Waqqas reported: "The Messenger of Allah, may Allah bless him and grant him peace, gave me an arrow without an arrowhead and said, 'Shoot it.' That day, the Messenger of Allah shot from his bow until it broke. Qatada's eye was injured that day by an-Nu'man so that the eye fell out onto one of his cheeks. The Messenger of Allah put it back and it became his best eye." Qatada's story is related by 'Asim ibn 'Umar ibn Qatada and Yazid ibn 'Iyad ibn 'Umar ibn Qatada.

Abu Sa'id al-Khudri said that the Prophet spat on the mark left by the arrow on Abu Qatada's face on the day of Dhu Qarad. Abu Qatada said, "It did not throb nor was there any pus."[2]

An-Nasa'i related from 'Uthman ibn Hunayf that a blind man said, "Messenger of Allah, ask Allah to unveil my eyes for me." He said, "Go and do *wudu'* and then pray two *rak'ats* and say, 'O Allah, I ask You and I turn to You by the Prophet Muhammad, the Prophet of Mercy. O Muhammad, I turn by you to your Lord to unveil my eyes. O Allah, let him intercede for me!'" He returned and Allah had restored his sight.

It is related that Ibn Mula'ib al-Asinna was afflicted by dropsy. He sent to the Prophet who took some dust from the ground, spat on it and gave it to the messenger. The messenger took it in wonder thinking that he would be laughed at. When he returned with it, Ibn Mula'ib was on the brink of death. He drank it and Allah healed him.

Al-'Uqayli has mentioned from Habib ibn Fudayk (or Furayk) that his father's eyes went white so that he could not see anything. The Messenger of Allah, may Allah bless him and grant him peace, spat in his eyes and he saw. They saw him threading a needle when he was eighty.

Kulthum ibn al-Husayn was shot in the throat in the battle of Uhud. The Messenger of Allah spat on his wound and it was healed. He spat on the head-wound of 'Abdullah ibn Unays and it did not go septic.[3]

1. At-Tabarani.
2. Al-Bayhaqi.
3. At-Tabarani.

He spat in 'Ali's eyes in the Battle of Khaybar when he had a pain in them and they were healed.[1]

He spat on the the thigh-wound of Salama ibn al-Akwa' during the Battle of Khaybar and he was healed.[2]

He spat on the foot of Zayd ibn Mu'adh when the sword meant for Ka'b struck him when Ka'b ibn al-Ashraf was killed, and it healed.[3]

He spat on the broken thigh of 'Ali ibn al-Hakam during the Battle of the Ditch and it healed immediately without 'Ali even dismounting.[4]

'Ali ibn Abi Talib once complained and began to call on Allah. The Prophet said, "O Allah, heal him!" Then he struck him with his foot and he did not complain of the pain again.[5]

In the Battle of Badr, Abu Jahl cut off the hand of Mu'awwidh ibn 'Afra'. He came carrying his hand and the Messenger of Allah spat on it and replaced it and it remained. Ibn Wahb related this. Ibn Wahb also related that Khubayb ibn Yasaf was injured in the Battle of Badr by a blow to his neck so that half of it was hanging loose. The Messenger of Allah, may Allah bless him and grant him peace, put it back and spat on it and it healed up.[6]

A woman of Khuth'am brought to the Prophet a child who had an affliction and was unable to speak. Some water was brought and he rinsed out his mouth and washed his hands in it. Then he gave it to her and told her to wash the child and wipe him with it. The child was healed and had an intellect superior to most people.[7]

Ibn 'Abbas said, "A woman brought her son who was possessed. The Prophet, may Allah bless him and grant him peace, stroked his breast and the child vomited up something like a black puppy and was healed. A boiling pot overturned on the arm of Muhammad ibn Hatib when he was a child. The Prophet stroked it and made supplication for him and spat on it and it healed immediately.[8]

Shurahbil had a wen on his hand which kept him from gripping a sword and holding the reins of his animal. He complained about that to the Prophet who kept pressing it with his hand until he had removed it and not a trace of it remained.[9]

A slave-girl asked the Prophet, may Allah bless him and grant him peace, for some food while he was eating and he gave her some from in front of him. She was not very modest and said, "I want the food in your mouth." He gave

1. Al-Bukhari and Muslim.
2. Al-Bukhari.
3. Ibn Ishaq and al-Waqidi.
4. Al-Baghawi.
5. Al-Bayhaqi.
6. Al-Bayhaqi from Ibn Ishaq.
7. Ibn Abi Shayba.
8. An-Nasa'i, at-Tayalisi and al-Bayhaqi.
9. Al-Bayhaqi.

her what was in his mouth. When he was asked for something, he never refused it. When it settled in her stomach, some modesty was put into her so that, after that, there was no woman in Madina more modest than she.[1]

SECTION 22
On the Prophet's supplication being answered

It is well-known by many paths of transmission that when the Prophet made supplication or cursed any group of people, it was answered. Hudhayfa said that when the Prophet made a supplication for a man, that supplication reached as far as his sons and grandsons.[2]

Anas said, "My mother said, 'Messenger of Allah, Anas serves you. Make supplication to Allah for him.' He said, 'O Allah, give him many children and much wealth and bless him in what You bring him!'"[3]

'Ikrima said that Anas said, "By Allah, I have great wealth and my children and grandchildren today number about a hundred."[4] One version has, "I do not know anyone who has had more wealth than me. I have buried a hundred children with these hands – without a miscarriage or grandson among them."

There was the Prophet's supplication for 'Abdu'r-Rahman ibn 'Awf. 'Abdu'r-Rahman said, "If I were to lift a stone, I would expect to find gold under it which Allah would show me."[5]

When 'Abdu'r-Rahman died, the gold he left had shovels taken to it until hands were blistered from the effort of shifting it. Each of his four wives took eighty thousand dinars. It is also said that it was a hundred thousand. It is said that one of them was given a settlement of about eighty thousand because he had divorced her in his final illness. He bequeathed fifty thousand dinars to add to all the famous *sadaqa* he had given away during his lifetime and his habit of freeing thirty slaves on a single day. Once he gave as *sadaqa* a caravan which had seven hundred camels in it. It came to him bearing all kinds of goods and he gave it away with everything in it, including its saddles and saddle-cloths.

The Prophet made supplication for Mu'awiya to be firm in the land and he became Khalif.[6]

He asked Allah to answer the supplication of Sa'd ibn Abi Waqqas. Whenever Sa'd made supplication for anyone it was answered.

He asked Allah to make Islam strong through either 'Umar ibn al-Khattab or Abu Jahl. The supplication was answered in favour of 'Umar.[7]

---

1. At-Tabarani.
2. Ibn Hanbal.
3. Al-Bukhari and Muslim.
4. Muslim.
5. Al-Bayhaqi.
6. Ibn Sa'd.
7. Ibn Hanbal and at-Tirmidhi.

Ibn Mas'ud said, "We began to be powerful from the time 'Umar became Muslim."[1]

On one of the raids the people became very thirsty. 'Umar asked the Prophet to supplicate, so he did so and a cloud came, gave them the water they needed, and then went away. Another time the Prophet made supplication in the Rain Prayer and it rained. Then they complained to him about the rain, so he made supplication and it cleared away.[2]

The Messenger of Allah said to Abu Qatada, "May your face prosper! O Allah! Bless him in his hair and his skin."[3] He died when he was seventy but looked no older than fifteen.

He said to an-Nabigha, "May Allah not break your teeth!"[4] None of his teeth fell out. One version states that he had the most handsome front teeth. When one of his teeth fell out, another grew for him. He lived to be 120.

He made supplication for Ibn 'Abbas, "O Allah, give him understanding in the *deen* and teach him its interpretation."[5] After this, he was called *al-Habr* (scholar) and the Translator of the Qur'an.

He made supplication for 'Abdullah ibn Ja'far for his hands to be blessed in business transactions. Everything he ever bought realised a profit.[6]

He made a supplication for blessing for al-Miqdad ibn 'Amr and he had sacks of money.[7]

He made a similar supplication for 'Urwa ibn Abi'l-Ja'd who said, "I used to live at Kinasa (in Kufa). I came back with a profit of forty thousand."[8] Al-Bukhari said about this *hadith*, "If 'Urwa had purchased dust, he would have made a profit on it."

There is a similar *hadith* about Gharqada. One of his she-camels bolted. He called it and a strong wind forced it back to him.

He made a supplication for the mother of Abu Hurayra and she became a Muslim.[9]

He made supplication for 'Ali that he be protected from heat and bitter cold. He could wear summer clothes in the winter and winter clothes in the summer. Neither heat nor cold bothered him.[10]

He asked Allah that Fatima, his daughter, should never be hungry. She said,

---

1. Al-Bukhari.
2. Al-Bukhari and Muslim.
3. Al-Bayhaqi.
4. Al-Bayhaqi and Ibn Majah.
5. Muslim and al-Bukhari.
6. Al-Bayhaqi.
7. Ibid.
8. Al-Bukhari.
9. Muslim.
10. Ibn Majah and al-Bayhaqi.

"I was never hungry after that."[1]

At-Tufayl ibn 'Amr asked him for a sign for his people. The Prophet said, "O Allah! Illuminate him!" and a light shone between his eyes. At-Tufayl said, "I fear they will say that it is a punishment," so he moved the light to the tip of his whip and it used to give light on a dark night. He was called *Dhu'n-Nur* (Possessor of Light) because of that.[2]

The Prophet made a supplication against Mudar and they went without rain until Quraysh had to conciliate him. Then he made supplication for them and it rained.[3]

He made supplication against Chosroes, when he tore up his letter, asking Allah to tear up his kingdom. None of it remained and Persia retained no leadership at all anywhere in the world.[4]

He made supplication against a youth who had stopped praying that Allah would stop him in his tracks, and he went lame.[5]

When he saw a man eating with his left hand, he told him, "Eat with your right hand." The man replied, "I am not able to." The Prophet said, "You are not able to," and he never again lifted it to his mouth.[6]

He said about 'Utba ibn Abi Lahab, "O Allah! Give one of your beasts of prey power over him." A lion ate him.[7]

He told a woman, "May a lion eat you," and she was eaten by a lion.[8]

There is also the famous *hadith* from Ibn Mas'ud about when the Prophet cursed Quraysh for putting a placenta filled with fluid and blood on his neck while he was in prostration. He named each of them by name. Ibn Mas'ud said, "I saw all of them killed at Badr."[9]

When al-Hakam ibn Abi'l-'As was twitching his face and winking in the presence of the Prophet, the Prophet said, "Be like that." He continued to twitch until the day he died.[10]

He cursed Muhallim ibn Jaththama and he was killed by a wild beast and the earth threw him up. After they had tried several times to bury him and each time the earth had thrown him up, they threw him between two sides of a gulley and covered him over with stones.[11]

A man once denied that he had sold a horse. He gave up the horse after the

1. Al-Bayhaqi.
2. Ibn Ishaq and al-Bayhaqi.
3. An-Nasa'i.
4. Al-Bukhari.
5. Abu Dawud and al-Bayhaqi.
6. Muslim from Salma ibn al-Akwa'.
7. Ibn Ishaq.
8. Ibn Sa'd.
9. Muslim and al-Bukhari.
10. Al-Bayhaqi.
11. Ibid.

Prophet had spoken against him, saying, "O Allah! If he is lying, do not give him any blessing in it," and it became stiff in its feet.

This chapter could go on for ever.

SECTION 23
On his *karamat* and *barakat* and things being transformed for him when he touched them

Anas ibn Malik said that on one occasion the people of Madina were alarmed and the Messenger of Allah rode out on a horse belonging to Abu Talha which was known to be a slow animal. When he returned, he said, "We found your horse very fast," but it was never fleet again after that.

He prodded a camel of Jabir ibn 'Abdullah which was tired and it became so lively that he could not rein it in.[1]

He did the same thing with a horse belonging to Ju'ayl al-Ashja'i. He gave it a flick with a whisk that he had with him and blessed it. Then Ju'ayl could not hold it back due to its friskiness. Twelve thousand foals from it were sold.[2]

He rode a slow donkey of Sa'd ibn 'Ubada, and it returned going at a fast pace which no-one could keep up with.[3]

Khalid ibn al-Walid kept some of the hairs from this animal in a cap of his and he never fought a battle with that cap on without gaining a victory.[4]

In the *Sahih* it says that Asma' bint Abi Bakr brought out a black shirt. She said, "The Messenger of Allah used to wear it. We would wash it when people were sick so that they could be cured by the water from it."

Qadi Abu 'Ali related that his shaykh, Abu'l-Qasim ibn al-Ma'mun said, "We had one of the dishes of the Prophet in our possession. We used to put water in it for the sick and they would be healed by it."

Jihjah al-Ghifari snatched the Prophet's staff from 'Uthman's hand in order to break it across his knee. The people shouted at him not to. The itch[5] seized him in his knee and in spite of it being amputated, he died before the year was out.

He poured his left-over *wudu'* water into the well of Quba and it never diminished afterwards.

He spat in a well that was in Anas' house and there was no water in Madina sweeter than it.[6]

---

1. Muslim and al-Bukhari.
2. Al-Bayhaqi.
3. Ibn Sa'd.
4. Al-Bayhaqi.
5. A disease characterised by itching and the dropping off of parts of the body.
6. Al-Bayhaqi.

Once the Prophet was passing by some water and he asked about it. He was told that its name was Balsan (black elder) and that its water was salty. He said, "It is Nu'man (anemone) and its water is good." It became good.[1]

He brought a bucket of water from Zamzam and spat into it. It became sweeter than musk.[2]

He gave al-Hasan and al-Husayn his tongue to suck. They had been weeping from thirst and upon this they became quiet.[3]

Umm Malik al-Ansariyya had a skin with some ghee in it which she gave to the Prophet. The Prophet handed it back to her telling her not to squeeze it and it was filled with ghee. Her sons would come to her to ask for some seasoning because they had none and she would go to it and find there was ghee in it. It continued to be their seasoning until she squeezed it.[4]

He used to spit into the mouths of suckling children and his saliva would satisfy them until nightfall.

There was also the blessing in the hand of the Prophet when he touched and planted the trees for Salman al-Farisi when his masters wrote that he would be set free for three hundred small palm-trees, planted, tied and bearing fruit in addition to forty *awqiya* of gold. The Prophet got up and planted them for him with his own hand except for one tree which someone else planted. All took root except that one. The Prophet pulled it up, put it back and it took root. Al-Bazzar says, "The trees gave fruit from that very year, except for that one tree. The Messenger of Allah pulled it up and planted it and it gave fruit from that year on. He gave him an amount of gold equal to a chicken's egg which he had rolled on his tongue. Forty *awqiya* of gold were weighed out from it for his masters and he still had the same amount left that he had given them."

In the *hadith* of Hanash ibn 'Uqayl, we find, "The Messenger of Allah would give me a drink of *sawiq* (a kind of mash). He would drink first and I would drink last. I always found that it filled me up when I was hungry and quenched me when I was thirsty and was cool when I was parched."

Qatada ibn an-Nu'man prayed the evening prayer with the Prophet on a dark rainy night. He gave him a palm bough and said, "Take it with you. It will light up an arm's length before you and behind you. When you enter your house, you will see something dark. Strike it until it goes away, for it is *shaytan*." He left and the bough lit his way to his house where he found the darkness. He beat it until it left.[5]

When 'Ukasha's sword broke in the Battle of Badr, the Prophet gave him a

1. Abu Nu'aym.
2. Ibn Majah and al-Bayhaqi.
3. At-Tabarani.
4. Muslim.
5. Ibn Hanbal.

stick of wood and said, "Strike with it!" It became a sharp, gleaming sword of great length and strength. He fought with it and kept it. He went to all his battles with it until he was martyred fighting the people of the *Ridda*.[1] The sword was called *al-'Awn* (help).[2]

'Abdullah ibn Jahsh lost his sword in the Battle of Uhud and the Prophet handed him a palm stick which turned into a sword.[3]

There is the *baraka* he possessed in making dry sheep have abundant milk as shown in the story of the sheep of Umm Ma'bad, the goat of Mu'awiya ibn Thawr, Anas' sheep, Halima's sheep, the sheep of 'Abdullah ibn Mas'ud which had never been mated, and the sheep of al-Miqdad.

He provisioned his Companions with a skin of water which he tied up and made a supplication over. When the prayer-time came, they alighted and untied it. There was sweet milk in it with cream on the top.[4]

He wiped the head of 'Umayr ibn Sa'd and blessed him. When he died at the age of eighty, his hair had not gone white. This is related about several people, including as-Sa'ib ibn Yazid and Madluk.

'Utba ibn Farqad had a scent which overpowered his women's perfumes because the Messenger of Allah had wiped his hand on his belly and back.

He wiped the blood from the face of 'A'idh ibn 'Amr when he was wounded in the Battle of Hunayn and made supplication for him, and 'A'idh had a blaze like that of a horse.

He wiped the head of Qays ibn Zayd al-Judhami and made supplication for him. Qays died at the age of a hundred and all his hair was white except for the place that the Messenger of Allah had touched which was black. He was called *al-Agharr* (the one with a blaze). This is also told about 'Amr ibn Tha'laba al-Juhani.

He wiped the face of someone else and a light remained in his face.

He stroked the face of Qatada ibn Milhan and his face had a shine in it so that looking into his face was like looking into a mirror.

He placed his hand on the head of Hanzala ibn Hidhaym and blessed him. A man was brought to Hanzala whose face was swollen and a sheep whose udders were swollen. They were placed on the spot that the Prophet's hand had touched and the swelling vanished.[5]

He splashed the face of Zaynab bint Salama with water and afterwards she possessed a beauty in her face previously unknown among the women.[6]

He wiped the head of a child who had a defect. He was healed and his hair

---

1. *Ridda*, the apostasy of bedouin tribes after the death of the Prophet.
2. Al-Bayhaqi.
3. Ibid.
4. Ibn Sa'd.
5. Al-Bayhaqi.
6. Ibn 'Abdu'l-Barr.

remained straight. Something similar is related about al-Muhallab ibn Qubala and there are other similar traditions about children, the sick and the insane.

A man with a scrotal hernia came to the Prophet who commanded that it be sprinkled with water from a spring in which he had spat. That was done and the man was healed.

Tawus said that whenever the Prophet was brought someone touched with insanity, he would stroke their chests and the madness would leave them.

He spat in a bucket from a well and then poured it into the well and the smell of musk issued from it.

During the Battle of Hunayn, he took a handful of dust and threw it into the faces of the unbelievers, saying, "May their faces be ugly!" They turned away wiping the filth from their eyes.[1]

Abu Hurayra complained to the Prophet about being forgetful. The Prophet told him to spread out his garment and he scooped his hands into it. Then he told him to draw it up. He did so and did not forget anything after that. Much is related on these lines.[2]

He struck the breast of Jarir ibn 'Abdullah and made supplication for him. He had not been firm on a horse and then he became the best and firmest of Arab horsemen.[3]

He wiped the head of 'Abdu'r-Rahman ibn Zayd ibn al-Khattab when he was a small, ugly, short child and prayed for blessing for him. After that he attained near average height.

SECTION 24
The Prophet's knowledge of the unseen and future events

The *hadiths* on this subject are like a vast ocean whose depths cannot be plumbed and which does not cease to overflow. This is one aspect of his miracles which is definitely known. We have many *hadiths* which have reached us by multiple paths of transmission regarding his familiarity with the Unseen.

Hudhayfa said, "The Messenger of Allah, may Allah bless him and grant him peace, gave us an address in which he did not leave out anything that would happen until the Last Hour came. Whoever remembered it remembered it and whoever forgot it forgot it. Many companions of mine have known it. When any of it came to pass, I would recognise it and remember it as a man remembers the face of a man who has gone away and which he recognises when he sees him again." Then Hudhayfa said, "I do not know whether my companions may have forgotten or pretended to forget, but the Messenger of Allah did not leave out the instigator of a single disaster that was going to

1. Ibn Hanbal.
2. Al-Bukhari.
3. Muslim and al-Bukhari.

happen until the end of the world. There were more than three hundred of them. He named them for us, each with his own name, the name of his father and his tribe."[1]

Abu Dharr said, "When the Messenger of Allah, may Allah bless him and grant him peace, left us there was not a bird that flies in the sky but that he had given us some knowledge about it."[2]

The compilers of the *Sahih* and the Imams have related what he taught his Companions and family about regarding his promises to them of victory over his enemies, the conquest of Makka, Jerusalem, the Yemen, Syria and Iraq, and the establishment of security so that a woman could go from Hira in Iraq to Makka fearing none but Allah.

He said that Madina would be raided and Khaybar would be conquered by 'Ali the next day. He foretold those parts of the world that Allah was going to open up to his community and what they would be given of its flowers and fruits – such as the treasures of Chosroes and Caesar. He told about what would happen among them with regard to sedition, disputes and sectarianism, acting as those before them had done, their splitting into seventy-three sects, only one of which would be saved, that they would spread out in the earth, that people would come who would wear one fine garment in the morning and another in the evening, and dish after dish would be placed before them. They would embellish their houses as the Ka'ba is embellished. Then he said at the end of the *hadith*, "Today you are better than you will be on that day."[3]

He said that they would strut about on the earth and that the girls of Persia and Byzantium would serve them. Allah would withdraw their strength from them and the evil ones would overcome the good. They would fight the Turks and the Khazars and Byzantium. Chosroes and Persia would be obliterated so that there would be no Chosroes or Persia afterwards. Caesar would pass away and there would be no Caesar after him. He mentioned that Byzantium would continue generation after generation until the end of time. The noblest and best people would be taken away. When the time grew near, knowledge would be taken away, and sedition and bloodshed would appear. He said, "Alas for the Arabs for an evil that draws near!"[4]

The earth was rolled up for him so that he could see its eastern and western extremities and the dominion of his community was to reach what was rolled up for him. That is why it has extended from the east to the west, from the Indies in the east to the sea of Tangier, beyond which is no civilization. That was not given to any of the nations. Islam did not extend to the north and south in the same way.

---

1. Abu Dawud, al-Bukhari and Muslim.
2. Ibn Hanbal and at-Tabarani.
3. At-Tirmidhi.
4. Muslim and al-Bukhari.

He said, "The people of the west (*al-gharb*) will know the truth until the Hour comes."[1]

Ibn al-Madini believed that this refers to the Arabs because they are distinguished by drinking from a certain kind of leather bucket (*al-gharb*). Another believed that it refers to the people of the Maghrib.

In a *hadith* from Abu Umama, the Prophet, may Allah bless him and grant him peace, said, "A group of my community will remain constant to the truth, conquering their enemy until the command of Allah comes to them while they are still in that condition." He was asked, "Messenger of Allah, where are they?" He replied, "In Jerusalem."

He foretold the kingdom of the Umayyads and the rule of Mu'awiya and counselled him and said that the Umayyads would make the kingdom of Allah a dynasty. He said that the descendants of al-'Abbas would emerge with black banners and would rule a far larger area than they now ruled.

He said that the Mahdi would appear and told about what the *Ahl al-Bayt*, the People of his House, would experience and about their slaughter and exile.

He foretold the murder of 'Ali and said that the most wretched of people would be his killer and that 'Ali would be the apportioner of the Fire – his friends would enter the Garden and his enemies the Fire. Among those who would oppose him would be the Kharijites[2] and the *Nasibiyya*[3] and a group who claimed to follow him among the Rafidites[4] would reject him.

The Messenger of Allah said, "'Uthman will be killed while reciting the Qur'an. Perhaps Allah will have him wearing a shirt. They will want to remove it and his blood will fall on the words of Allah, **'Allah will be enough for you against them.'** (2:137)"[5]

He said that sedition would not appear as long as 'Umar was alive, az-Zubayr would fight against 'Ali, the dogs of Haw'ab would bark at one of his wives and many would be killed around her and she would barely escape. They barked at 'A'isha when she went to Basra.

He said that 'Ammar would be killed by an unjust group and the companions of Mu'awiya killed him. He said to 'Abdullah ibn az-Zubayr, "Woe to the people from you and woe to you from the people!"

The Prophet said about Quzman,[6] "He will be tested together with the Muslims although he is one of the people of the Fire," and Quzman later committed suicide.

He said about a group which included Abu Hurayra, Samura ibn Jundub

---

1. Muslim.
2. Kharijites: those who came out against 'Ali and the Umayyads.
3. Those who violently hated 'Ali.
4. Those who curse the Companions and declare the people of the *Sunna* to be unbelievers.
5. Al-Bukhari and Muslim.
6. A hypocrite.

and Hudhayfa, "The last of you will die in a fire." They kept asking about each other, and Samura was the last of them to die when he was old and senile. He tried to warm himself over a fire and burned himself in it.

He said about Hanzala al-Ghasil (the Washed), "Ask his wife about him. I saw the angels washing him." They asked her and she said, "He left in *janaba* and died before he could do *ghusl*." Abu Sa'id said, "We found his head dripping with water."[1]

He said, "The khalifate is with Quraysh. This business will remain with Quraysh as long as they establish the *deen*."[2]

He said, "There will be a liar and a destroyer from Thaqif."[3] It was thought that this referred to al-Hajjaj ibn Yusuf and al-Mukhtar ibn 'Ubayd.

He said that Musaylima would be destroyed by Allah and that Fatima would be the first of his family to follow him to the grave.

He warned about the *Ridda* and said that the khalifate after him would last for thirty years and that it would then become a kingdom. This happened in the period of al-Hasan ibn 'Ali.

He said, "This business began as prophethood and mercy, then mercy and a khalifate, then a voracious kingdom and then arrogance and tyranny and corruption will enter the community."[4]

He told of the existence of Uways al-Qarni[5] and that there would be Amirs who would delay the prayer beyond its time.

In one *hadith*, he says that there would be thirty deceiving liars in his community and four of them would be women. Another *hadith* says thirty deceiving liars, one of whom would be the *Dajjal*. They would all deny Allah and His Messenger.

He said, "The time is near when there will be a lot of non-Arabs among you who will consume your property and strike your necks. The Last Hour will not come until a man from Qahtan drives the people with his staff."[6]

He also said, "The best of you are my generation, then those after them and then those after them. After that, people will come who give testimony without being asked to do so, who will be treacherous and are not trustworthy, who promise and do not fulfill. There will be corpulence among them."

He said, "A time is only followed by one worse than it."[7]

The Messenger of Allah also said, "My community will be destroyed at the hands of young men from Quraysh."[8] In one version from Abu Hurayra the

---

1. Ibn Ishaq.
2. Ibn Hanbal and at-Tirmidhi.
3. Muslim and al-Bukhari.
4. Al-Bazzar.
5. A hermit of great spirituality who did not become known to the Muslims until after the death of the Prophet.
6. Al-Bazzar and at-Tabarani.
7. Al-Bukhari from Anas.
8. Muslim and al-Bukhari.

Prophet is reported as saying, "If I had wanted to, I could have named them for you – the Banu so-and-so and the Banu so-and-so."

He told about the appearance of the *Qadariyya*[1] and the Rafidites,[2] and said that the last of this community would curse the first of it. He said that the Ansar would diminish until they became like the salt in food. Their position would continue to dissipate until not a group of them remained. He said they would meet with despotism after him.

He told about the Kharijites, describing them down to the malformed one among them, and said that their mark would be shaved heads.

He said that shepherds would become the leaders of the people and the naked barefoot ones would vie in building high buildings. Mothers would give birth to their mistresses.

He said that Quraysh and their confederates would not conquer him, but that he would conquer them.

He foretold "the Death"[3] which would come after the conquest of Jerusalem and described what the houses of Basra would be like.

The Prophet also said that they would raid in the sea like kings on thrones. He said that if the *deen* had been hung in the Pleaides, men from Persia would have obtained it.

A wind blew up during one of his raids and the Prophet stated, "It blows for the death of a hypocrite." When they returned to Madina, they discovered it was true.[4]

He told some people sitting with him, "The tooth of one of you in the Fire will be greater in size than the mountain of Uhud." Abu Hurayra said, "The people eventually were all dead except for me and one other man. Then he was killed as an heretic during the *Ridda* in the Battle of Yamama."[5]

He told about the man who stole some pearls from a Jew and the jewels were found in that man's saddle-bag, and about the man who stole a cloak and it was found where he said it would be. He told about his she-camel when she had strayed and how she was tied to a tree with her halter. He told about the letter of Hatib to the people of Makka.

He told about the case where Safwan ibn Umayya persuaded 'Umayr ibn Wahb to go to the Prophet and kill him. When 'Umayr arrived where the Prophet was, intending to kill him, the Messenger of Allah told him about his business and secret, and 'Umayr became Muslim.

---

1. *Qadariyya*: a sect who said that all things are not by the decree of Allah but that man is the creator of his actions and has the power (*qudra*) to do them - hence their name.
2. See page 188.
3. A plague which occurred in the time of 'Umar in which seventy thousand people perished. Abu 'Ubayda ibn al-Jarrah died in it.
4. Rifa'a ibn Zayd.
5. At-Tabarani.

He informed them about the money which his uncle, al-'Abbas, had left concealed with Umm al-Fadl. Al-'Abbas said, "No-one except she and I knew where it was." So he became Muslim.

He informed them that he would kill Ubayy ibn Khalaf and that 'Utba ibn Abi Lahab would be eaten by one of Allah's beasts of prey. He knew about the deaths of the people of Badr and it happened as he had said it would.

He said about al-Hasan, "This son of mine is a master and Allah will make peace between two groups through him."[1]

He said to Sa'd, "Perhaps you will survive until some people profit by you and others seek to harm you."[2]

He told about the killing of the people of Mu'ta on the very day they were slain, even though there was more than a month's distance between he and them.

The Negus died and he told them about it the very day he died although he was in his own land.[3]

He informed Fayruz[4] of the death of Chosroes on the very day that a messenger came to him bearing the news of his death. When Fayruz verified the story, he became Muslim.

One time when the Prophet found Abu Dharr sleeping in the mosque in Madina he told him how he would be exiled. The Prophet said to him, "How will it be with you when you are driven from it?" He said, "I will dwell in the *Masjid al-Haram*." He asked, "And when you are driven from there?" The Prophet told him of his life alone and his death alone.[5]

He said that the first of his wives to join him would be the one with the longest hand. It was Zaynab bint Jahsh because of the length of her hand in giving *sadaqa*.

He foretold the killing of al-Husayn at Taff.[6] He took some dirt from his hand and said, "His grave is in it."

He said about Zayd ibn Suhan, "One of his limbs will precede him to the Garden." His hand was cut off in *jihad*.

He said about those who were with him on Mount Hira, "Be firm. On you is a prophet, a true man and a martyr." 'Ali, 'Umar, 'Uthman, Talha and az-Zubayr were killed and Sa'd was attacked.

He said to Suraqa, "How will it be with you when you wear the trousers of Chosroes?" When they were brought to 'Umar, Suraqa put them on and said, "Praise be to Allah who stripped Chosroes of them and put them on Suraqa!"[7]

1. Muslim and al-Bukhari.
2. Ibid.
3. The Negus was the king of Abyssinia.
4. The Persian minister.
5. Ibn Hanbal.
6. An old name for Karbala'.
7. Al-Bayhaqi.

The Prophet said, "A city will be built between the Tigris and Dujayl and Qutrubull and as-Sara. The treasures of the earth will be brought to it which the earth will swallow up," clearly indicating Baghdad.[1]

He said, "There will be a man called al-Walid[2] in this community and he will be worse for this community than Pharaoh was for his community."[3]

He also said, "The hour will not come until two parties fight each other with the same claim."[4]

The Messenger of Allah said to 'Umar about Suhayl ibn 'Amr, "Perhaps he will be in a position where he will delight you, 'Umar."[5] That happened. He stood up in Makka in a similar way to Abu Bakr on the day when they heard about the Prophet's death. He addressed them with a similar speech and strengthened their insight.

When he sent Khalid to Ukaydir, he said, "You will find him hunting for wild cows," and he did.

All these matters took place during his lifetime, and after his death, just as he had said they would.

He also informed his Companions about their secrets and inward thoughts. He told them about the secrets of the hypocrites and their rejection and what they said about him and the believers, so that one of the hypocrites would say to his friend, "Be quiet! By Allah, if he does not have someone to tell him, the very stones of the plain would inform him."

He described the magic which Labid ibn al-'Asim used against him and how it was in the comb, the combings and the spathe of the male palm and that he had thrown them into the well of Dharwan. It was found to be just as he had described it.

The Prophet informed Quraysh that the termites would eat what was in the paper which they issued against the Banu Hashim by which they cut off relations with them. He said that every mention of Allah would remain. It was found to be as he had said.

He described Jerusalem to the unbelievers when they did not believe what he had said as is related in the *hadith* of the Night Journey, describing it to them as someone who really knows it. He told them about their caravan which he had passed on his way and told them when it would arrive.

All of these things happened as he had said, including all that he told them regarding events which would take place and things whose beginnings had not yet even appeared, such as his words, "The flourishing of Jerusalem will prove

1. Abu Nu'aym.
2. Thought to be al-Walid ibn 'Abdu'l-Malik or his nephew, al-Walid ibn Yazid in whose time civil unrest began.
3. Ahmad ibn Hanbal and al-Bayhaqi.
4. As occurred at Siffin. Muslim and al-Bukhari.
5. Al-Bayhaqi.

the ruin of Yathrib. The ruin of Yathrib will result in the emergence of fierce fighting. The emergence of fierce fighting will encompass the conquest of Constantinople."

He mentioned the preconditions of the Hour, the signs of its arrival, the Rising and the Gathering, and told about what would happen to the good and those who deviated, the Garden and the Fire and the events of the Rising.

A whole volume could be devoted to this subject, but there is enough for you in what we have indicated. Most of the *hadiths* are in the *Sahih* volumes and have been mentioned by the Imams.

SECTION 25
Allah's protecting the Prophet from people and his being enough for him against those who injured him

Allah says, **"Allah will protect you from people."** (4:70) He says, **"Be steadfast under the judgement of your Lord. You are in Our eyes."** (52:48) He says, **"Is not Allah enough for His slave?"** (39:36) It is said that this means He is enough for Muhammad against his enemies, the idolaters. It is said that it means something else. Allah says, **"We are enough for you against the mockers,"** (15:95) and **"When those who reject were plotting against you to imprison you or kill you or expel you: they were plotting and Allah was plotting."** (8:30)

'A'isha said, "The Prophet was guarded until this *ayat* was revealed: "**Allah will protect you from people**." The Messenger of Allah, may Allah bless him and grant him peace, put his head from out of the tent and told them, 'Go away, people. My Lord has given me protection.'"[1]

It is related that once when the Prophet, may Allah bless him and grant him peace, alighted in a place, his Companions chose a tree for him under which he could rest from the midday heat. A bedouin came to him and drew his sword. He said, "Who will protect you from me?" The Prophet said, "Allah the Mighty." The hand of the bedouin trembled and the sword fell from it and he struck his head on the tree so hard that his brain was exposed, and the *ayat* was revealed. This story is related in the *Sahih*. The Prophet forgave the man whose name was Ghawrath ibn al-Harith and he returned to his people, saying, "I have come to you from the best of people."

Something similar happened to him at Badr. He went apart from his Companions to relieve himself and one of the hypocrites followed him and a similar thing occurred.

It is related that a similar thing also happened to him during the raid of

---

1. At-Tirmidhi.

Ghatafan at Dhu Amar with a man called Du'thur ibn al-Harith. The man became Muslim and went to his people who had encouraged him in his attempt to kill the Prophet. He was their master and the bravest of them. They said to him, "What has happened regarding what you said you would do when you had the opportunity to do it?" He replied, "I saw a tall white man who pushed me in the chest, and I fell backwards. My sword fell and I was sure it was an angel. Therefore I became a Muslim." It is said that it was about this that this *ayat* was revealed, **"O you who believe! Remember Allah's blessing to you when certain people were on the verge of raising their hands against you."** (5:12)

According to al-Khattabi, Ghawrath ibn al-Harith al-Muharibi wanted to assassinate the Prophet, a fact of which only he was aware. Ghawrath was standing at the Prophet's head with his sword unsheathed and the Prophet said, "O Allah, you are enough for me against him if that is Your will." Ghawrath fell on his face because of a pain that struck him between his shoulders. His sword fell from his hand.

It is said that the Messenger of Allah had feared Quraysh. When this *ayat* was revealed, he lay down and said, "Whoever wants to harm me, will suffer a disappointment."

'Abd ibn Humayd mentioned that the "bearer of firewood"[1] put down thorns (like embers) in the path of the Messenger of Allah, but it was as though he were walking on soft sand.[2] Ibn Ishaq mentioned that when Umm Jamil heard about the revelation of the *sura*, **"Perish the hands of Abu Lahab,"** (111:1) and how Allah had censured her and her husband, she went to the Messenger of Allah while he was sitting in the mosque with Abu Bakr. She had a stone pestle in her hand. When she stopped before them, she could only see Abu Bakr. Allah had made the Prophet invisible to her. She asked, "Where is your companion, Abu Bakr? I have heard that he has satirised me. By Allah, if I had found him, I would have smashed his mouth in with this pestle!"

Al-Hakam ibn Abi'l-'As said, "We conspired to kill the Prophet when we came across him. When we saw him, we suddenly heard a terrible sound behind us that we thought would not leave anyone in Tihama alive. We fainted and did not recover until after he had finished his prayer and returned to his family. Then we agreed to try another night and waited until we saw him, but Safwa and Marwa[3] came and stood between him and us."[4]

'Umar said, "Abu Jahm ibn Hudhayfa and I agreed to kill the Messenger of Allah, may Allah bless him and grant him peace, one night. We came up to his home and listened out for him. He began to recite, **'The Undeniable! What is**

---

1. Umm Jamil, the wife of Abu Lahab, mentioned in the Qur'an, *Sura* 111.
2. Ibn Jarir related this in a *mursal* form in his *Tafsir*.
3. Two small hills in Makka that pilgrims go between as one of the rites of *hajj* and *'umra*.
4. Abu Nu'aym and at-Tabarani.

the Undeniable? What will convey to you what the Undeniable is? Thamud and 'Ad denied the Crushing Blow. Thamud were destroyed by the Deafening Blast. 'Ad were destroyed by a savage howling wind. Allah subjected them to it for seven whole nights and eight whole days without a break. You could see the people flattened in their homes just like the hollow stumps of uprooted palms. Do you see any remnant of them left?' (69:1-8) Abu Jahm struck 'Umar's arm and said, 'Save yourself!' and they ran away in flight. It was one of the things that led to 'Umar becoming Muslim.[1]

There is the famous example of when the Quraysh made the Prophet afraid, having agreed to kill him, and spent the night waiting for him. He came out of his house and stood in front of them, Allah having taken away their sight. He put dust on their heads and left them.

He was protected from being seen by them in the cave by the signs that Allah prepared for him and by the spider which spun a web for him so that when they said, "Let's look inside the cave," Umayya ibn Ubayy said, "He can't be here with this spider's web in front of it which must have been there since before Muhammad was born." One of the other Qurayshis said, "If there had been anyone in it, these doves would not be there either."[2]

There is the story of Suraqa ibn Malik ibn Ju'shum during his *hijra*.[3] The Quraysh put a reward on the Prophet and Abu Bakr, and Suraqa heard about it. He followed them on his horse and almost caught them up. The Prophet made a supplication against him and the feet of his horse sank into the earth and he was thrown off. Suraqa threw his divining arrows and got an unfavorable reading which he disliked.[4] He then rode on and drew near enough to be able to hear the Prophet reciting. The Prophet did not turn round, but Abu Bakr did and said, "He is coming up to us." The Prophet replied, **"Do not grieve. Allah is with us."** (9:40) Suraqa's horse once more sank up to its knees in the earth and Suraqa was thrown off again. He reined it in and the horse got up with something like smoke coming from its feet. Suraqa called out, asking for a safe-conduct and the Prophet gave it to him. Abu Fuhayra wrote one down for him, or some people say that it was Abu Bakr himself. Suraqa gave them the news of what had been happening and the Prophet told him not to let anyone follow them. Suraqa then went off telling people, "You don't need to look. He isn't here."[5] It is also said that Suraqa said to the Prophet, "I saw you make supplication against me, so make supplication for me," and he was saved.

---

1. A similar *hadith* is recorded by Ibn Hanbal.
2. Ibn Ishaq and al-Bayhaqi.
3. The Prophet's emigration with Abu Bakr from Makka to Madina. The incident of the cave mentioned above also took place on this journey.
4. Arrows without feathers. On some of them is written, "I will do it" and on others, "I will not do it." These are placed in a bag and one of them is pulled out to give an answer.
5. Al-Bukhari and Muslim.

In another tradition it says that a herdsman recognised them and went rushing off to notify Quraysh. When he reached Makka, his heart was struck and he did not know what he was doing and forgot what had brought him until he had returned home.

Ibn Ishaq and others have mentioned that once when the Prophet, may Allah bless him and grant him peace, was in prostration Abu Jahl got hold of a stone and Quraysh were encouraging him to throw it at him. It stuck to his hand and his hands went to his neck and he began to retreat. Then he asked the Prophet to pray for him which he did and Abu Jahl's hands were released. Abu Jahl had made an agreement with Quraysh to throw the stone. He had sworn that if he saw him, he would smash his brains out. They questioned him about what had happened and he said, "A stallion such as I have never seen before appeared behind him. It looked at me as if it would eat me." The Prophet said, "That was Jibril. If he had come near, it would have seized him."

As-Samarqandi mentioned that a man from the Banu'l-Mughira came to kill the Prophet, but Allah blinded him so that he could not see the Prophet although he could hear what he said. He went back to his people who could not see him until they called to him. The *ayat* which is mentioned as referring to these two stories is: **"We have put iron collars round their necks reaching up to the chin, so that their heads are forced back. We have placed a barrier in front of them and a barrier behind them, blindfolding them so that they cannot see."** (36:8-9)

Ibn Ishaq mentioned a story about when the Prophet, may Allah bless him and grant him peace, went out to the Banu Qurayza with his companions and sat against the wall of one of their fortresses. 'Amr ibn Jihash sent one of his people to throw a millstone down on him. The Prophet got up before they could do it, went back to Madina, and told them the story. It is said that the *ayats*, **"O you who believe, remember the blessing of Allah to you..."** (5:12) was revealed in reference to this story.

As-Samarqandi related that the Prophet went out to the Banu'n-Nadir to seek help in paying the blood money for the people of Kalb who had been killed by 'Amr ibn Umayya. Huyayy ibn Akhtab said, "Sit down, Abu'l-Qasim, so we can feed you and give you what you ask." The Prophet sat down with Abu Bakr and 'Umar. Huyayy was in fact plotting to kill him. Jibril told the Prophet that, so he got up as if he wanted to go to the lavatory and went out and kept going until he reached Madina.

The commentators mention another *hadith* from Abu Hurayra. Abu Jahl had promised Quraysh that he would tread on Muhammad's neck if he saw him. They told him when the Prophet was praying and he came. When he drew near him, he turned away in flight, retreating, protecting himself with his hands. He was asked about that and said, "When I came near him, I looked down and saw a ditch full of fire. I almost fell into it. I saw a terrifying sight and the fluttering of wings filled the earth." The Prophet, may Allah bless him and grant him peace, said that that was the angels. He said, "If he had come near, they would have torn him limb from limb." Then the following *ayat* from *Sura al-'Alaq* (96:6) was revealed : **"But, no. Indeed man is excessive."**[1]

It is related that Shayba ibn 'Uthman al-Juhani came up to him during the Battle of Hunayn. Hamza[2] had killed his father and uncle. He cried, "Today my revenge will be wreaked on Muhammad." In the melée, he came up behind the Prophet and raised his sword to strike him. "When I came near," he said, "a fiery flame rose before me swifter than lightning, so I turned to flee. The Prophet was aware of me and summoned me. He placed his hand on my breast. He had been the most hated of people to me and when he lifted his hand, he was the most beloved of people to me. He said to me, 'Draw near and fight!' I went ahead of him to defend him with my sword. If I had met my father, I would have fallen on my own father rather than the Prophet."[3]

Fadala ibn 'Amr said, "I wanted to kill the Prophet in the year of the Conquest when he was going around the Ka'ba. When I came near him, he asked, 'Is it Fadala?' I replied, 'Yes.' He asked, 'What were you telling yourself?' I said, 'Nothing.' He laughed and asked for forgiveness for me, placed his hand on my breast and stilled my heart. By Allah, as soon as he lifted it, Allah had not created anyone more beloved to me than him."[4]

There is the famous tradition of 'Amir ibn at-Tufayl and Arbad ibn Qays when they came upon the Prophet, may Allah bless him and grant him peace. 'Amir said to the other, "I will distract Muhammad for you so that you can strike him." But Arbad could not see anything. When Arbad spoke later to 'Amir about that, he said, "By Allah, whenever I intended to strike him, I found you between him and me, so how could I strike you?"[5]

Part of Allah's protection of him is that many of the Jews and soothsayers warned Quraysh about him and told them about his power over them and urged them to kill him. Allah protected him so His command could be effected. He was, as he himself said, helped by terror entering the hearts of his enemies up to a month's journey away from him.

SECTION 26
His knowledges and sciences

His radiant miracles include the knowledges and sciences which Allah concentrated in him, the familiarity he was given with all the affairs of this

---

1. Muslim and an-Nasa'i.
2. The favourite uncle of the Prophet and a great Muslim warrior.
3. Abu Nu'aym.
4. Ibn Ishaq.
5. Ibn Ishaq and al-Bayhaqi

world and this *deen*, his knowledge of the commands of the *Shari'a*, the laws of his *deen*, politics and the best interests of his community. He had knowledge of what existed in earlier communities, the stories of the Prophets and Messengers, tyrants, and earlier generations from Adam until his time and their laws and books. He knew about their lives, events and battles, the description of their notable men and their different opinions. He knew about the length of their lives and the wise maxims of their sages. He could argue with every group of the unbelievers and answer every sect of the People of the Book according to what was contained in their own books. He informed them of the secrets of their Books and their hidden sciences and told them what they had concealed of them or altered in them.

He knew the dialects of the Arabs and the odd words of various tribes. He grasped the various styles of eloquence that exist in pure Arabic. He knew their battle accounts, similes, wisdoms and what their poems meant. He possessed all their words, knowing how to make up clear parables and maxims to facilitate the understanding of profound matters and clarify what was obscure. He made the rules of the *Shari'a* easy – they are neither lax nor contradictory.

His *Shari'a* contains good character, praiseworthy behaviour-models (*adab*) and every kind of desirable excellent trait. Not even an atheist of sound intellect can object to anything in it except perhaps out of sheer frustration. All those who opposed and rejected him in the Time of Ignorance, and then heard what it was that the Prophet called them to, would say that it was correct and excellent without trying to disprove him.

Then there are the good things he made lawful for them and the foul things he forbade them. By this, he protected their lives, honour and property from immediate detriment and made them fearful of the Fire to come.

The knowledge he possessed can only be known, and even then only in part, by someone who has dedicated himself to study and uninterrupted preoccupation with books. It requires a great deal of research to encompass even some of his various sciences and knowledges – such as medicine, dream interpretation, the shares of inheritance, arithmetic, lineage and other sciences whose practitioners derive their knowledge from what the Prophet said, taking him as a model and basis for their knowledge.

The Prophet said, "Dreams should only be interpreted by people who really know the science of interpretation and they flutter above a man's head (until they are interpreted)."[1]

The Prophet also said, "There are three types of dreams: the true dream, the dream in which a man talks to himself, and the dream which causes grief from Shaytan."[2]

---

1. Ibn Majah from Anas.
2. Al-Bukhari and Muslim.

He said, "When the end of time is near, even the dreams of a believer will nearly lie."[1]

He said, "The root of every illness is indigestion."[2]

There are his words related by Abu Hurayra that, "The intestines are the drain of the body and the veins reach it."[3]

He spoke about medicines to be used in the ear and the side of the mouth and about cupping and laxatives. The best time for cupping is on the seventeenth, nineteenth and twenty-first of the month.

He mentioned that aloes-wood contains seven cures, one of which is for pleurisy.

He said, "The son of Adam has not filled any container worse than his belly. If it has to be, then a third of it is for food, a third for drink and a third for the breath."[4]

When he was asked whether Sabi' was a man, woman or a land, he said, "He was a father who fathered ten – six in Yemen and four in Syria."[5]

He gave similar answers about the lineage of Qada'a and other things which arose from people's preoccupation with genealogy.

He said, "Himyar is the head of the Arabs and their tooth. Madh-hij is their head and throat. Azd is the base of their neck and skull. Hamdhan is their withers and top."[6]

He said, "Time revolves in a circle which was its form on the day that Allah created the heavens and the earth."[7]

He said about the Basin (*al-Hawd*), "Its corners form a square."[8]

He said in the *hadith* on *dhikr*, "The good deed has ten like it. So one hundred and fifty on the tongue is fifteen hundred in the Balance."[9]

When he was in a certain place, he said, "This is the best place for a *hamam* (public bath)."

He said, "Everywhere between the east and the west is a *qibla*."[10]

He told 'Uyayna ibn Hisn or al-Aqra' ibn Habis, "I have a better eye for horses than you."

He told his scribe, "Put your pen behind your ear. It is easier to remember where it is." This is in spite of that fact that the Prophet could not write himself. However, he was given the knowledge of everything so that there are traditions

---

1. Al-Bukhari and Muslim.
2. Ad-Daraqutni.
3. At-Tabarani.
4. Ibn Hanbal, at-Tirmidhi and Ibn Majah.
5. At-Tirmidhi and Ibn Hanbal.
6. Al-Bazzar.
7. Muslim and al-Bukhari.
8. Ibid.
9. Abu Dawud and Ibn Majah.
10. In other words anywhere can be a place of prayer.

which report about his knowledge of how letters are properly written such as when he said, "Do not extend the letter *sin* in the *Basmala*."

Once Mu'awiya was writing in the presence of the Prophet who said to him, "Put cotton in the inkwell, cut the quill obliquely, make the *ba'* straight, make the *sin* distinct and do not deform the *mim*. Write '*Allah*' well, extend the *Rahman* and make *Rahim* good." Even if the *riwaya* does not confirm that he wrote, it is not improbable that he was provided with such knowledge, even without being able to read or write.

His knowledge of the dialects of the Arabs and recall of their poems is very well-known indeed, and we have already mentioned it.

It is the same with his knowledge of many other languages. He used words in Ethiopian and Persian. Even someone who has studied a lot and devoted himself constantly to books throughout his life can accomplish only some of this. As Allah has said, the Prophet was "illiterate", neither able to read nor write. He had no familiarity with the company of literate people. He did not grow up among people who had knowledge nor did he read about any of these subjects. It was not known that he had any particular flair for such things.

Allah says, **"You never recited any Book before it nor did you write one down with your right hand."** (29:48-49)

The most widespread sciences among the Arabs were genealogy, reports of ancient poetry and rhetoric. They became proficient by devoting themselves to their science, researching it and discussing it. This science is but a single drop in the sea of the Prophet's knowledge.

There is no way for an atheist to reject any of what we have mentioned nor for the rejecter to find a device to repudiate what we have said beyond saying, **"The myths of the ancients,"** (25:5) or **"a mortal taught him."** (16:103) Allah refuted them when He said, **"The tongue of him they allude to is a foreign one whereas this is in a clear and lucid Arabic tongue."** (16:103) Then there is what the notables said when they ascribed his instruction either to Salman or the Greek slave.

The Prophet met Salman after the *hijra* when much of the Qur'an had already been revealed and many *ayats* had already appeared. The Greek became Muslim and used to study under the Prophet. They disagree about his name. It is said that the Prophet used to sit with him at Marwa. Both of these men spoke a foreign language while the Quraysh spoke clear Arabic, were fierce disputants and fluent speakers. Yet even they were incapable of refuting what the Prophet brought them or producing anything like it.

Indeed the Arabs were incapable of fully grasping the quality and the form of the Qur'an's composition, so how could it have been produced by a non-Arab with ungrammatical language – Salman, Bul'am the Greek, or Ya'ish, Jabr or Yassar or whatever this non-Arab's name was. He lived among them and they spoke with him throughout their lives. Nothing like what Muhammad brought was ever attributed to any of them. In spite of their number, the diligence of their pursuit of it and the intensity of their envy, the Prophet's enemies were prevented from sitting down to accomplish this with this non-Arab and acquiring from him what could be used to refute the Qur'an or learning things which could be used to argue against the Muslims, although this was tried by an-Nadr ibn al-Harith who told superstitious tales culled from reports in books he had read.

The Prophet, may Allah bless him and grant him peace, never left his people and he scarcely visited the lands of the People of the Book. His enemies said that he had sought the help of the People of the Book, but he had remained with the Arabs throughout his youth, herding sheep as was the custom of the Prophets. He only left Arab territory on one or two journeys and even then he did not stay long enough to learn even a little of their languages. During the course of his journeys, he was always in the company of his people, companions and tribe, and was never away from them. Nor did this state of affairs change during the time he was in Makka nor did he ever visit a rabbi, priest, astronomer or soothsayer. Even if all this had happened, the miraculous contents of the Qur'an itself, which he brought, would cut off any pretext, invalidate any argument and make everything clear.

SECTION 27
Reports of the Prophet's dealings with the angels and *jinn*

There are many reports about the Prophet's dealings with the angels and *jinn* which is one of his gifts, miracles and radiant signs. Allah Almighty helped him by means of the angels and *jinn* who obeyed him. Many of his Companions saw them.

Allah says, **"If you support one another against him. Allah is His Protector and Jibril."** (66:4) He says, **"When your Lord revealed to the angels, 'I am with you, so confirm those who believe,'"** (8:12) and **"When you called on your Lord for help and He responded to you: 'I will reinforce you with a thousand angels riding in your rear.'"** (8:9-10) Allah also says, **"And We diverted a group of jinn towards you to listen to the Qur'an."** (46:29)

About the words, **"He saw one of the greatest signs of his Lord."** (53:18) 'Abdullah ibn Mas'ud said, "He saw Jibril in his true form and it has six hundred wings." There is the famous tradition about his conversation with Jibril, Israfil and other angels and how he witnessed their great number and the immensity of some of their forms on the Night Journey.

Among his Companions, there were those who saw them in his presence at different times and places. His Companions saw Jibril in the form of a man who asked questions about Islam and Belief. Ibn 'Abbas, Usama ibn Zayd and others saw Jibril in the form of Dihya.[1] Sa'd saw Jibril on his right and Mika'il on his left as two men wearing white garments. One of them saw the unbelievers' heads flying off but could not see those who struck them. On that day, Abu Sufyan ibn al-Harith saw white men on piebald horses suspended between the heaven and the earth.

The angels used to shake hands with 'Imran ibn Husayn. The Prophet showed Jibril to Hamza in the Ka'ba and he fainted. 'Abdullah ibn Mas'ud saw the *jinn* on the Night of the Jinn[2] and heard them speak. They resembled the men of Zutt.[3]

Ibn Sa'd mentioned that when Mus'ab was killed in the Battle of Uhud, an angel in his form took up the banner. The Prophet told him, "Advance, Mus'ab!" The angel told him, "I am not Mus'ab," and he realised it was an angel.

More than one source has mentioned that 'Umar ibn al-Khattab said, "While we were sitting with the Prophet, an old man with a staff in his hand came and greeted the Prophet. He returned the greeting and said, 'You have the voice of the *jinn*. Who are you?' He replied, 'I am Hama ibn al-Haym ibn Laqis ibn Iblis.'" He mentioned that he had met Nuh and those after him. The Prophet taught him some *suras* of the Qur'an.

Al-Waqidi mentioned that when Khalid destroyed al-'Uzza, he killed a black woman who came out to him naked with her hair flying, cutting her down with his sword. The Prophet was informed of that and said, "That was al-'Uzza."

The Prophet said, "Yesterday Shaytan rushed up suddenly to interrupt my prayer. Allah gave me power over him and I seized him. I wanted to tie him to one of the pillars of the mosque so that all of you could look at him, but then I remembered the supplication of my brother Sulayman, **'O Lord, forgive me and give me a dominion that no-one after me will have.'** (38:35) Allah turned him away in humiliation."[4]

This too is a vast subject.

SECTION 28
Reports about his attributes and the signs of his messengership

The proofs of his prophethood and the signs of his messengership include mutually complementary traditions from the monks, rabbis and scholars of the

---

1. Dihya al-Kalbi, a Companion who died during the khalifate of Mu'awiya. He was one of the most beautiful of people and that is why Jibril came in his form.
2. The night on which the Messenger of Allah saw the jinn and was commanded to warn them and call them to Islam.
3. Tall men of Sudani or Indian extraction.
4. Al-Bukhari and Muslim.

People of the Book regarding his description, his community, his names and his signs. The seal between his shoulder-blades was mentioned. There is the contents of the poems of earlier unitarians – the poetry of Tubba',[1] al-Aws ibn Haritha,[2] Ka'b ibn Lu'ayy,[3] Sufyan ibn Mujashi',[4] and Quss ibn Sa'ida,[5] and what is mentioned about Sayf ibn Dhi Yazin[6] and others.

There is also Zayd ibn 'Amr ibn Nufayl,[7] Waraqa ibn Nawfal, 'Athkalan al-Himyari and the Jewish scholar Shamul.

There is what the Torah and Evangel say about him, which has been compiled and clarified by the '*ulama*' and transmitted by reliable people who became Muslim – like 'Abdullah Ibn Salam, the sons of Sa'ya, Ibn Yamim, Mukharyria, Ka'b and other Jewish scholars who converted, and Christians such as Buhayra' and Nestor from among the Ethiopians, the chief of Bosra, Daghatir the Bishop of Syria, al-Jarud, Salman, the Negus, the Christians of Ethiopia, the bishops of Najran and other Christian scholars who converted to Islam.

These reports were recognised by Heraclius and the Pope of Rome, the leaders of the Christians, Muqawqi[8] and his venerable companion,[9] Ibn Suriya,[10] Ibn Akhtab and his brother, Ka'b ibn Asad, az-Zubayr ibn Batiya and other Jewish scholars who were moved by envy and rivalry to remain in misery.

There are numerous reports about this. The Jews and Christians were forced to admit the existence of these things he said could be found in their books describing him and his Companions. He used the things that their own scrolls contained as an argument against them. He censured them for altering their books, concealing what the books said and twisting those words in them which made his affair clear and he invited them to pray that the liars should be cursed. All of them avoided opposing him and thus having to present what he claimed that their books showed. If they had found that they contained other than what he had said, it would have been far easier for them to present that than to give up their lives and property, have their houses destroyed and give up the fight.

---

1. The King of Yemen who wanted to destroy Yathrib and the Jews there and was told by the most learned of them, Shamul, that a Prophet would migrate there. He gave a long description of him and Tubba' left.
2. A poet born in the time between Prophets who naturally inclined to belief in one God and not worshipping idols. He knew what the scriptures contained relating to the Prophet.
3. The first to institute a gathering on Fridays. He foretold of the coming of the Prophet.
4. A man from Tamim who foretold that there would be an Arab Prophet named Muhammad.
5. Bishop of Najran.
6. A king of Himyar who conquered Yemen and defeated the Abyssinians. He told 'Abdu'l-Muttalib that he had read in a book, which was kept hidden, that a Prophet would be born in Tihama.
7. Who gave a description of a Prophet from the Banu 'Abdu'l-Muttalib who was to come.
8. The leader of the Copts in Egypt.
9. See *Kitab al-'Aja'ib* by Al-Mas'udi.
10. The main scholar of the Torah at that time.

He told them, **"Say: Bring the Torah and recite it if you are speaking the truth."** (2:94)

There is the warning given about the Prophet Muhammad by soothsayers like Shafi' ibn Kulayb, Shiqq, Sath, Sawad ibn Qarib, Khanafir, Af'a of Najran, Jidhl ibn Jidhl al-Kindi, Ibn Khalsa ad-Dawsi, Sa'd ibn bint Kurayz, Fatima bint an-Nu'man and many others.

There is what was heard from idols about his prophethood and the advent of his messengership. There are the unseen voices of the *jinn* that were heard and what was heard from the sacrifices made to the idols and from inside the statues.[1]

There is the name of the Prophet and testimony to his message which was found written in ancient writing on stones and graves. This is quite famous. It is known that certain people became Muslims for that reason.

SECTION 29
What is related about his birth

There are the signs which appeared when he was born and the wonders related by his mother and those present.

He lifted his head when he was born, looking skywards. A light issued with him when he was born. Umm 'Uthman ibn Abi'l-'As saw the stars lowering themselves and a light appeared when he was born so that she could see nothing but light.

The midwife, ash-Shifa' Umm 'Abdu'r-Rahman ibn 'Awf said, "When he dropped into my hands and sneezed, I heard someone say, 'May Allah have mercy on you!' and the entire horizon was illuminated for me so that I could see the castles of the Greeks."[2]

Halima, his wet-nurse, and her husband recognised the blessings that came with him and the abundance of her milk for him and of the milk of her old she-camel and the fertility of their sheep, the vigour of his youth and the excellence of his growth.

There are the wonders that took place the night he was born when the arcade of Chosroes shook and its balconies fell down, the waters of Lake Tiberias ebbed, and the flame of Persia, which had not been put out for a thousand years, was extinguished.

When he ate with his uncle Abu Talib and his family as a child, they always had their fill of food and drink. When he was absent, they ate and were not satisfied. All the sons of Abu Talib got up in the morning disheveled whereas

---

1. Testifying to his prophethood.
2. Abu Nu'aym.

the Prophet, may Allah bless him and grant him peace, was invariably neat, oiled and wearing kohl.

His nurse, Umm Ayman, said, "I never saw him complain of hunger or thirst either as a child or as an adult."[1]

Another example of what happened is that the heaven was guarded by meteors thus cutting off the spying of the *shaytans* and preventing them from listening. Hatred for idols grew naturally in him, and he abstained from the things done in the Time of Ignorance. Allah protected him, even in keeping his modesty as in the famous tradition about when the Ka'ba was rebuilt and he took off his wrapper and put it round his neck to use for carrying stones making himself naked. He kept on falling down until he put his wrapper back on. His uncle asked him, "What is wrong with you?" He replied, "I was stopped from being naked."[2]

Another example is that he was shaded by clouds when he travelled. Khadija said, "When he was approaching, they would see that two angels were shading him."[3] She mentioned that to Maysara and he told her that he had seen that happening from the time they set out with him on their journey. It is related that Halima also saw a cloud shade him when he was with her.

Before he was a Prophet, on one of his journeys, he alighted under a dry tree. All around it became green and the tree itself became full grown, spread out and lowered its branches for him for all to see. In some traditions, the shade of the tree inclined towards him to shade him. It is mentioned that he had no shadow in the sun or moon because he was a light. Flies did not alight on his clothes or body.

He was made to love withdrawing from the world until the time he was given revelation. He told people about his coming death and its nearness and where his grave would be in Madina and that it would be in his house. What is between his house and the minbar is one of the Meadows of the Garden.

Allah gave him a choice regarding his death. There are marks of honour and nobility contained in the story of his death. The angels prayed over his body. The Angel of Death asked his permission which he had never done with anyone before him. There was a call they heard, "Do not remove the shirt from him when he is washed." It is related that al-Khidr and the angels consoled the People of his House when he died. There were the miracles and blessings of his Companions during his life and after his death – like 'Umar asking for water for his uncle and the blessings at the hands of more than one of his descendants.

---

1. Ibn Sa'd and Abu Nu'aym.
2. Al-Bukhari and Muslim.
3. Ibn Sa'd.

SECTION 30
Conclusion and Appendix

In this chapter we have presented some points about his evidentiary miracles and a summary of the signs of his prophethood, although mentioning just one of them would have been sufficient. We omitted many others and we condensed some long *hadiths* to achieve our purpose. We mostly used sound and famous *hadiths*, although there are a few which were only mentioned by the famous Imams. We shortened *isnads* in order to be concise. This subject would require many volumes for a complete register.

The miracles of our Prophet are more manifest than the miracles of all the other Messengers in two ways. One is their abundance and the fact that no Prophet brought a miracle without our Prophet having something like it or better. Many people have pointed this out. If you wish, you can study the sections of this chapter and the miracles of the previous Prophets and you will discover this to be true, Allah willing.

As for their being numerous, every bit of the Qur'an is a miracle. According to certain Imams, the least amount in which a miracle occurs is the *sura,* **"We have given you Kawthar,"** (108) or an *ayat* of the same length. Some of them believe that every *ayat* of it, no matter what its size, is a miracle. Others added that every sentence is a miracle, even if it consists of only one or two words.

The truth is in the words of Allah we have already quoted, **"Bring a sura like it."** (10:28) The *sura* is His minimum challenge, including its composition and precision which is too long to discuss here. If this is so, the Qur'an contains about seventy-seven thousand words. **"We have given you Kawthar"** consists of ten words. The Qur'an is therefore divided into more than seven thousand parts, each of which is a miracle in itself.

Its miraculous nature, as has already been stated, has two aspects: the manner of its eloquence, and the method of its composition. Each of these parts therefore contains two miracles and in this way the number is doubled.

Then it has aspects of a miraculous nature which involve reports about the knowledge of the unseen. A single *sura* will report about many things of the unseen and each report is a miracle in itself. So the number is multiplied yet again. Then there are the other miraculous aspects which we mentioned which multiply the total yet again. This is only in respect of the Qur'an, and therefore the number of its miracles alone cannot really be fixed and its proofs cannot be encompassed.

The *hadiths* and traditions from the Prophet about these matters which we have pointed out can do no more than give an indication about the miraculous aspects of his life.

The second aspect is the clarity of his miracles. The Messengers are given miracles in accordance with the interests of their people at that time and the science in which their generation excelled. At the time of Musa, magic was the greatest science of the people. Musa was sent to them with a miracle which resembled their own claim to power. What he brought broke their normal patterns and was beyond their power, so their magic was rendered powerless. It was the same in the time of 'Isa. The fullest science of his people was medicine. Therefore something was presented to them which they could not do and he confronted them with what was beyond the normal bounds of medicine – like bringing the dead to life and curing the blind and the leper without any treatment or medicine. It was the same with the miracles of all the Prophets.

When Allah sent Muhammad, the pinnacle of the sciences and knowledge of the Arabs consisted in four things: rhetoric, poetry, traditions of their forebears and divination. Then Allah sent down the Qur'an on him to go beyond the bounds of these four categories with pure Arabic, impossibility of imitation, and eloquence beyond their linguistic norms. It has a strange composition and extraordinary style whose method of composition they were unaware of. They were unable to recognise it among the styles of the different metres.

It contained reports about beings, events, secrets, hidden things and inner thoughts, and these were found to be the case and were reported to be sound and true, no matter how hostile the critic. He invalidated divination which was only true one time out of ten. Then he cut it off at its root by the stoning with meteors and guarding the stars. He brought reports about past generations, news of the previous Prophets, vanished nations and events which were beyond the scope even of those who devoted themselves exclusively to the study of this knowledge. We have already made the miraculous aspects of these things clear.

This miracle of the Qur'an, combining as it does all the miraculous aspects we have already mentioned, will remain firm until the Day of Rising, providing a clear proof for every future community. The ramifications of this cannot be kept from anyone who investigates it and reflects on its incomparability and what it reports concerning unseen things. No age or time has passed without its truthfulness being made abundantly manifest by what it says. Faith is renewed and the proof is clearly displayed. Hearing is not the same as seeing with one's eyes. Witnessing further increases certainty. The soul's trust is raised from the knowledge of certainty to the vision of certainty. All of it is true.

All the miracles of the other Messengers have passed away with them when they died, ceasing to exist when their source no longer existed, but the great miracle of our Prophet will never cease nor come to an end. Its signs are continually renewed and do not vanish. This is what the Prophet indicated in the words related by Abu Hurayra, "Every Prophet was given signs of a kind that other people believe. I have been given revelation which Allah revealed to me. I hope that I will be the one with the most followers on the Day of Rising." This is the meaning of the *hadith* according to some scholars, and it is evident and strong, Allah willing.

Certain *'ulama'* believe that the interpretation of this particular *hadith* and the manifestation of the miracle of our Prophet has a deeper meaning than its mere manifestation as revelation and speech in which imagination, trickery and false deduction are not possible. In the miracles of other Messengers, the recalcitrant try to seek out things which they can use to make weak people doubtful about them – like when the sorcerers cast their ropes and staffs and they seemed to change into snakes and other things which sorcerers use to bedazzle people.

The Qur'an consists of words without any tricks, magic or illusion in any part of it. For this reason, people find it clearer than other miracles, just as a poet or orator is not properly a poet or orator simply by devising some trick or pretence.

The first interpretation is clearer and more satisfying. This second interpretation is somewhat abstruse and is disregarded.

There is a third aspect based on the school of the *Sarfa* [1] who said that people were diverted from bringing something like it. They said that man has the capacity to respond to the challenge but was diverted from doing so.

According to one of the two positions accepted by the *sunna*, bringing something like the Qur'an is something that lies within human capacity, but no-one has brought its like either before or since because Allah did not give them the power nor make them capable of doing it.

There is a clear difference between the two positions, but in both cases, the Arabs abandoned what it was in their power to bring, or what lay within their capacity to do, even though that meant enduring affliction, evacuation, capture, abasement, a changed situation, loss of life and property, rebuke, reproach, being rendered incapable, intimidation and threat. It is this that constitutes the clearest sign of their incapacity to bring something like it and their inability to rise to the challenge. They were prevented from it even though it was within their capacity to do it.

This is what Imam Abu'l-Ma'ali al-Juwayni and others believe. He said, "This, in our opinion, is a more conclusive form of the breaking of norms than actions which are marvelous in themselves – like a staff turning into a snake. Anyone who sees such a thing immediately thinks that it is one of the gifts of a master of magic because of his greater knowledge of that art and superior knowledge. This is what he thinks until sound investigation refutes that it is by his own power.

---

1. A school of certain Mu'tazilites and Shi'a who say that Allah diverted (*sarafa*) them from bringing a *sura* even though they were capable of it.

"As for the challenge that has been made to people over hundreds of years to bring something like the Qur'an, they have not done so. Even though the pretenders have gone to every length to answer the challenge, they have been unsuccessful because Allah has prevented creatures from doing this. It is as if a Prophet were to say, 'My sign is that Allah will stop people from standing up although it is in their power to do so, and they are not ill.' If that had happened, and Allah had made them incapable of standing up, that would have been one of the most radiant signs and clearest proofs. Success is by Allah."

One of the 'ulama' did not grasp the superiority of the Prophet's sign over the signs of all the other Prophets and had to posit an excuse for it in the fineness of the Arabs' understanding, their mental acumen and intellect making them able to perceive the miracle in the Qur'an through their perspicacity. From his point of view, the Prophet brought them the Qur'an because of their fine perception. Other people, like the Copts, the Banu Isra'il and others, did not have this quality. They were dense and stupid, having been rendered thus by Pharaoh who made them accept that he was their Lord, so that the Samiri was able to make them accept what he foisted on them about the Calf after they had believed in Allah.

Others of them worshipped the Messiah in spite of agreeing that he had been crucified, although in fact **"They did not kill him nor crucify him. It was only a likeness they were shown."** (4:157) Musa brought these people clear signs which were evident to them and which they could not doubt even though their understanding was coarse. In spite of this, they still said, **"We will not believe you until we see Allah openly."** (2:55) They were not content with the manna and quail and exchanged that which was better for that which was base.

The Arabs, in spite of their ignorance, were more prone to recognise their Maker. They sought nearness to Allah through idols. Some of them believed in Allah alone before the Messenger came by following their intellects and by the purity of their hearts. When the Messenger brought them the Book of Allah, they grasped its wisdom, and its miraculous nature was clear to them immediately by virtue of their superior perception. They believed him and they were increased every day in belief. They abandoned this world entirely in his company and emigrated from their houses and property. They killed their fathers and sons in order to help him. Things of a similar meaning have come whose truth shines through and whose beauty astonishes when it is proven and verified. But we have already clarified our Prophet's miracle and its manifestation in a way which spares us from having to embark on its inner and outward paths.

I seek help with Allah. He is enough and the best guardian.

PART TWO

Concerning the rights which people
owe the Prophet

Chapter One

THE OBLIGATION TO BELIEVE IN HIM, OBEY HIM AND FOLLOW HIS SUNNA

SECTION 1
The obligation to believe in him

The previous pages provide conclusive evidence of his prophethood and the soundness of his message. It is, therefore, necessary to believe in him and confirm what he brought.

Allah says, **"Believe in Allah and His Messenger and the light which We have sent down."** (64:8) He says, **"We have sent you bearing witness, bringing good news and giving warning so that you may all believe in Allah and His Messenger."** (48:8-9) He says, **"Believe in Allah and His Messenger, the unlettered Prophet."** (7:158) Belief in the Prophet Muhammad is therefore a necessary obligation for every individual. Belief is not complete without it and Islam is only valid with it.

Allah says, **"Whoever does not believe in Allah and His Messenger – We have prepared a Blazing Fire for the rejectors."** (48:13)

Abu Hurayra said that the Messenger of Allah said, "I was commanded to fight people until they testify that there is no god but Allah and believe in me and what I have brought. When they do that, their blood and property are protected from me except for a right (they owe). Their reckoning is with Allah."[1]

To believe in the Prophet is to confirm his prophethood and Allah's message to him and to support him in all that he brought and said. Corresponding to the confirmation of the heart is testimony with the tongue – that he is the Messenger of Allah. The combination of confirmation in the heart with the articulation of that testimony on the tongue constitutes belief in him and confirmation of him as has been related in a version of the *hadith* above from 'Abdullah ibn 'Umar, "I was commanded to fight people until they testify that there is no god but Allah and that Muhammad is the Messenger of Allah."[2]

It is clearer in another *hadith* in which Jibril is reported as saying, "Tell me about Islam." The Prophet said, "It is that you testify that there is no god but

---

1. Muslim and al-Bukhari.
2. Ibid.

Allah and that Muhammad is the Messenger of Allah," and he went on to mention the pillars of Islam. Then he asked him about belief and he said, "It is that you believe in Allah, His angels, His Books and His Messengers."[1]

He confirmed that belief in the Prophet implies acceptance in the heart while Islam demands articulation by the tongue. Together they lead to the complete praiseworthy state. The blameworthy state consists of testimony on the tongue without confirmation by the heart. That is hypocrisy.

Allah says, **"When the hypocrites come to you they say, 'We bear witness that you are indeed the Messenger of Allah.' Allah knows that you are indeed His Messenger and Allah bears witness that the hypocrites are certainly liars."** (63:1) i.e. they lie in respect of what they say regarding what they believe and confirm. They do not really believe it. If their consciousness does not confirm their words, it will not benefit them to say with their tongues what is not in their hearts. They fall short of belief. They will not benefit by its jurisdiction in the Next World since they do not possess faith. They will join the unbelievers in the lowest level of the Fire. However, because they give verbal testimony, they are still judged as Muslims as far as the jurisdiction of this world is concerned, by Muslim Imams and judges who can only give judgment according to people's outward display of Islam since there is no way one human being can uncover the secrets of another. They are not commanded to investigate such people and the Prophet forbade passing judgement on them as unbelievers and censured doing so, saying, "Why did you not split open his heart?"[2] The difference between what is affirmed with the tongue and true belief is clarified by the *hadith* of Jibril – verbal testimony is part of Islam and confirmation with the heart is part of belief.

There are other states which lie between these two. One such state is when someone confirms with his heart and then dies before he has had time to testify with his tongue. There is some disagreement about the states of such a person. Some make it a precondition that he should have completed his faith by verbal testimony. Others think that he is a believer who will necessarily go to the Garden according to the words of the Prophet, "Whoever has an atom's weight of belief in his heart must come out of the Fire."[3] The Prophet only mentioned what was in the heart. A person who believes in his heart is neither a rebel nor negligent by not pronouncing it. This is the sound opinion regarding this matter.

The second case concerns someone who believes in his heart and then waits a long time to testify to it even though he knows that it is necessary to do so. He does not speak of it or testify to it even once in his entire life. There are similar disagreements about such a person. It is said that he is a believer because he

---

1. Muslim.
2. Muslim and al-Bukhari.
3. Ibid.

confirmed it inwardly. However, because testimony is part of required action, he is a rebel for not doing so but will not be in the Fire forever. It is also said that he is not really a believer until he accompanies his belief with verbal testimony since testimony is entering into a contract and a requirement of belief. It is directly connected to belief. Delayed confirmation is only completed by verbal testimony. This is the sounder opinion.

This is a small matter which, however, has been the source of extensive discussion on the nature of Islam and Belief and related subjects, and increase and decrease in them. Is the reward for simple confirmation denied when there is no valid statement? Is it dependant on having action added to it? Or might it appear solely through its different qualities and various states – strong certainty, resolute belief, clear recognition, a constant state and the presence of the heart?

To say more on this is beyond the goal of this book. We have said enough for our purposes here, Allah willing.

SECTION 2
The obligation to obey him

As for the obligation to obey the Prophet, may Allah bless him and grant him peace, belief in him demands it. Confirmation of what he brought requires obedience to him because that is part of what he brought. Allah says, **"O you who believe, obey Allah and His Messenger..."** (8:20) **"Say: obey Allah and obey the Messenger..."** (24:54) He says, **"Obey Allah and the Messenger so that perhaps you will gain mercy."** (3:132) **"If you obey him, you will be guided..."** (24:54) **"Whoever obeys the Messenger has obeyed Allah..."** (4:79) **"Whatever the Messenger gives you you should accept and whatever He forbids you you should forgo..."** (59:7) **"Whoever obeys Allah and the Messenger will be with those whom Allah has blessed."** (4:68) **"We did not send any Messenger but for him to be obeyed by the permission of Allah."** (4:63)

He made obeying His Messenger tantamount to obeying Himself, and He placed obedience to Himself alongside obedience to His Messenger. Allah promises that doing this will result in an abundant reward and threatens a severe punishment for opposing it. He made it obligatory to obey the things that the Prophet commanded and to avoid those he prohibited.

The commentators and Imams have said that obeying the Messenger means to cling to his *sunna* and submit to what he brought. They said that Allah did not send a Messenger without obliging those to whom he was sent to obey him and that obeying the Messenger in his *sunna* is equivalent to obeying Allah in His obligations. Sahl at-Tustari was asked about the *Shari'a* of Islam and he quoted, **"Whatever the Messenger gives you you should accept."** (59:7)

As-Samarqandi said that it was said: obey Allah in His obligations and the Messenger in his *sunna*. It is also said: obey Allah regarding what He makes forbidden for you and obey the Messenger regarding what he conveys to you. It is said that it means to obey Allah by testifying that He is the Lord and to obey the Prophet by testifying to his prophethood.

Abu Salama ibn 'Abdu'r-Rahman heard Abu Hurayra say that the Messenger of Allah said, "Whoever obeys me has obeyed Allah. Whoever rebels against me has rebelled against Allah. Whoever obeys my Amir has obeyed me. Whoever rebels against my Amir has disobeyed me."[1]

Obeying the Messenger is part of obeying Allah since Allah commands that he be obeyed. True obedience is obedience to Allah's command and therefore obedience to His Prophet.

Allah talks about the unbelievers in the depths of the Fire saying, **"They will say on the Day their faces are rolled over in the Fire, 'If only we had obeyed Allah and obeyed the Messenger!'"** (33:66) They will wish they had obeyed when the wish will not profit them.

The Prophet said, "When I forbid you to do something, avoid it. When I command you to do something, then do it as much as you are able."[2]

In the *hadith* of Abu Hurayra we find that the Prophet said, "All of my community will enter the Garden except for those who refuse to." They asked, "Messenger of Allah, who will refuse?" He replied, "Whoever obeys me will enter the Garden. Whoever rebels against me has refused."[3]

In another sound *hadith* the Prophet said, "My likeness and the likeness of what Allah has sent me with is like a man who comes to a people and says, 'O people, I have seen the army with my own eyes and I am a sincere warner, so save yourselves!' One group of his people obey him and they travel at the beginning of the night, go at their leisure and are saved. Another group reject him and remain where they are and the army arrives in the morning and wipes them out. Such is the likeness of those who obey me and follow what I bring and the likeness of those who rebel against me and deny what I bring."[4]

In a similar *hadith* we find, "It is like someone who builds a house and lays out a fine feast in it and sends out a summoner. Whoever answers the summoner enters the house and eats from the feast. Whoever does not answer the summoner does not enter the house and eat from the feast."[5]

The house is the Garden and the summoner is Muhammad, may Allah bless him and grant him peace. Whoever obeys Muhammad has obeyed Allah.

---

1. Muslim and al-Bukhari.
2. Ibid.
3. Al-Hakim.
4. Al-Bukhari.
5. Muslim and al-Bukhari

Whoever rebels against the Messenger of Allah has rebelled against Allah. Muhammad distinguishes between people.

SECTION 3
The obligation to follow him and obey his *Sunna*

As for the obligation to follow him and obey his *sunna* and follow his guidance, Allah says, **"Say: if you love Allah, follow me and He will love you and forgive you for your wrong actions."** (3:31) **"Believe in Allah and His Messenger, the unlettered Prophet who believes in Allah and His words. Follow him, perhaps you may be guided."** (7:157) **"No, by your Lord, they are not believers until they make you their judge in the disputes that break out between them, and then find no resistance within themselves to what you decide and submit themselves completely,"** (4:64) i.e. obey your judgement.

Allah also says, **"You have an excellent model in the Messenger of Allah, for all who put their hope in Allah and the Last Day."** (33:21) Muhammad ibn 'Ali at-Tirmidhi said, "To take the Messenger as a model means to emulate him, follow his *sunna* and abandon opposition to him in either word or action." Several commentators said words to that effect.

It is said that this was intended as a criticism of those who fail to follow him. Sahl said that the *ayat* from the *Fatiha* (*Sura* 1), **"The path of those whom You have blessed"**, means to follow the *sunna*. Allah commands this and promises they will be guided by following him by reason of the fact that Allah has sent him with the guidance and the *deen* of the truth to purify them, teach them the Book and the Wisdom, and guide them to a straight path.

In the first *ayat* mentioned, Allah promises His love and forgiveness to those who follow the Prophet and prefer him to their own passions and inclinations. Soundness of belief is based on submission to the Prophet and satisfaction with his judgement and abandoning opposition to him.

It is related from al-Hasan al-Basri that some people said, "Messenger of Allah, we love Allah," so Allah revealed, **"Say: if you love Allah, follow me and Allah will love you."** (3:31) It is related that this verse was revealed about Ka'b ibn Ashraf and others. They said, **"We are the sons of Allah and His beloveds,"** (5:20) and **"We are stronger in love for Allah,"** (2:165) so Allah revealed the *ayat*.

Az-Zajjaj says that the meaning of, **"Say: if you love Allah"** is if you desire to obey Him, then do what He has commanded you to do since the love of the slave for Allah and the Messenger lies in obeying both of them and being happy with what they command. Allah's love for them is His pardon to them and His blessing them with His mercy. It is said that love from Allah manifests itself in protection and success. Love on the part of the slaves manifests itself in obedience.

A poet[1] has said:

> Do you rebel against God when you claim to love Him?
>   By my life, this is an extraordinary example!
> If your love had been true, then you would have obeyed Him.
>   The lover obeys the one he loves.

It is said that the slave's love for Allah is to exalt Him and be in awe of Him, and the love of Allah for him is His mercy to him and His beautiful concern for him. It can also mean praise. Al-Qushayri said, "When love means mercy, desire and praise, it is one of the attributes of Allah's essence." More will be said concerning the slave loving something else by the power of Allah.

Al-'Irbad ibn Sariyya relayed the warning of the Prophet, "You must follow my *sunna* and the *sunna* of the Rightly-Guided Khalifs. Cling to it fiercely and beware of new things. These new things are innovations, and every innovation is misguidance." Jabir added, "Every misguidance is in the Fire."[2]

Abu Rafi' reported that the Prophet said, "Do not let any of you be found reclining on his bed when he hears an injunction from me which is from among those things which I myself commanded or forbade so that he says, 'I do not know. We only follow what we find in the Book of Allah.'"[3]

'A'isha said, "The Messenger of Allah, may Allah bless him and grant him peace, did something as an example in order to make things easier for people but some people still refrained from doing it. When the Prophet heard about that, he praised Allah and said, 'What do you think of people who refrain from anything that I myself do? By Allah, I am the greatest of them in knowledge of Allah and the strongest of them in fear of Allah.'"[4]

It is related that the Prophet said, may Allah bless him and grant him peace, "The Qur'an is hard and difficult for anyone who hates it. It is judgement. Whoever clings to what I say and understands it and retains it, then it will be like the Qur'an for him. Whoever considers the Qur'an and what I say unimportant and neglects it loses this world and the Next. My community is commanded to take my words and obey my command and follow my *sunna*. Whoever is pleased with my words is pleased with the Qur'an. Allah says, **'Whatever the Messenger gives you you should accept.'"** (59:7)[5]

The Prophet said, "Whoever follows me is of me and whoever wants to

1. Al-Mahmud ibn al-Hasan al-Warraq.
2. Muslim.
3. Ash-Shafi'i in *al-Umm,* Abu Dawud, at-Tirmidhi and Ibn Majah. A sound *hadith.*
4. Muslim and al-Bukhari.
5. Abu'sh-Shaykh, ad-Daylami and Abu Nu'aym from al-Hakam ibn 'Umayr.

abandon my *sunna* is not of me."

Abu Hurayra said that the Prophet said, "The best speech is the Book of Allah and the best guidance is the guidance of Muhammad. The worst matters are innovations."

It is related from 'Abdullah ibn 'Amr ibn al-'As that the Prophet said, "There are three types of knowledge – any other knowledge is superfluous – a precise *ayat*, an established *sunna* or a just share (of inheritance)."[1]

Al-Hasan ibn al-Hasan said that the Prophet said, "Doing a little of something which is a *sunna* is better than doing a lot of something which is an innovation."[2]

The Prophet said, "Allah will bring a man into the Garden by the fact that he clings to my *sunna*."

Abu Hurayra said that the Prophet said, "The one who clings to my *sunna* when the community is corrupt will have the reward of a hundred martyrs."[3]

The Prophet said, "The Banu Isra'il split into about seventy-two sects. My community will split into seventy-three. All of them will be in the Fire except for one." They asked, "Who are they, Messenger of Allah?" He replied, "Those who base themselves on what I and my Companions are doing today."[4]

Anas reported that the Prophet, may Allah bless him and grant him peace, said, "Whoever brings the *sunna* to life has brought me to life. Whoever brings me to life will be with me in the Garden."[5]

'Amr ibn 'Awf al-Muzani said that the Prophet told Bilal ibn al-Harith, "Whoever brings to life any of my *sunna* which has died after me will have the reward of all those who act by it without decreasing their reward in any way. Whoever introduces a misguiding innovation which does not please Allah and His Messenger will have the like of all those who act by it without that decreasing their burden."[6]

SECTION 4
What is related from the *Salaf* and the Imams about following his *Sunna*, taking his guidance and the *Sira*

A man from Khalid ibn Asid's family asked 'Abdullah ibn 'Umar, "Abu 'Abdu'r-Rahman! We find the Fear Prayer and the prayer at home in the Qur'an, but we do not find the travelling prayer." Ibn 'Umar said, "My nephew, Allah sent Muhammad to us when we did not know anything. We do as we saw him doing."

1. Abu Dawud and Ibn Majah.
2. Ad-Darimi.
3. At-Tabarani.
4. At-Tirmidhi.
5. Al-Isbahani.
6. At-Tirmidhi. Ibn Majah considers it *hasan*.

'Umar ibn 'Abdu'l-'Aziz said, "The Messenger of Allah made a *Sunna* and the people in command after him made *sunnas*. To adopt them is to confirm the Book of Allah and to act on them is to obey Allah and strengthen the *deen* of Allah. It is not for anyone to change the *Sunna* or alter it or to look into the opinion of those who oppose it. Whoever follows it is guided. Whoever seeks help by it will have victory. Whoever opposes it and follows other than the path of the believers, Allah will entrust him to what he turns to and will roast him in *Jahannam*, which is a bad ending."[1]

Al-Hasan ibn Abi'l-Hasan said, "A little action following a *sunna* is better than a lot of action following an innovation."

Ibn Shihab said, "It has reached us that some of the people of knowledge said, 'Holding fast to the *sunna* is salvation.' "

'Umar ibn al-Khattab wrote to his governors telling them to learn the *Sunna*, the shares of inheritance and the dialects, saying, "People will try to argue with you (i.e. by using the Qur'an), so overcome them with the *Sunna*. The people of the *Sunna* have the greatest knowledge of the Book of Allah."

When 'Umar prayed two *rak'ats* at Dhu'l-Hulayfa,[2] he said, "I do as I saw the Messenger of Allah doing."

When 'Ali joined the *hajj* and *'umra* together, 'Uthman said to him, "Why do you do this, when you know that I have forbidden the people to do it?" He replied, "I do not abandon a *sunna* of the Messenger of Allah, may Allah bless him and grant him peace, for the statement of anyone."

'Ali said, "I am not a Prophet nor have I received revelation, but I act according to the Book of Allah and the *Sunna* of the Prophet Muhammad as much as I can."

Ibn Mas'ud used to say, "Doing a little of the *Sunna* is better than striving hard in innovation."

Ibn 'Umar said, "The travelling prayer is two *ra'kats*. Whoever opposes the *Sunna* is an unbeliever."

Ubayy ibn Ka'b said, "You must follow the path of Allah and the *Sunna*. There is no slave who is on the path of Allah and the *Sunna*, remembering Allah, his eyes overflowing out of fear of his Lord, but that Allah will never punish him. There is no slave on the earth who is on the path of Allah and the *Sunna*, remembering Allah, his skin trembling out of fear of Allah, but that he is like a tree whose leaves are dry. In the same way that a tree loses its leaves when a strong wind hits it, his errors fall from him as the leaves are shaken from the tree. A minimal course in the path of Allah and the *Sunna* is better than striving hard in a path contrary to the path of Allah and the *sunna* and consenting to innovation. See that your actions – whether they are striving or

---

1. See Qur'an 4:115.
2. The *miqat* for the people of Madina on their way to *Hajj*.

minimal – are on the path of the Prophets and their *sunna*."

One of the governors of 'Umar ibn 'Abdu'l-'Aziz wrote to him about the bad conditions and the great number of thieves in his territory. Should he arrest them on mere suspicion or only with clear proof in accordance with the *Sunna*? 'Umar wrote to him, "Arrest them only with clear proof in accordance with the *Sunna*. If the truth does not put them right, Allah will not put them right."

'Ata' said that the words of Allah, **"If you quarrel over anything, then refer it back to Allah and the Messenger,"** (4:58) means that you should consult the Book of Allah and the *Sunna* of the Messenger of Allah, may Allah bless him and grant him peace, in cases of disagreement.

Ash-Shafi'i said, "The *Sunna* of the Messenger of Allah consists only in following it."

When 'Umar looked at the Black Stone, he said, "You are a stone and can neither help nor harm. If I had not seen the Messenger of Allah, may Allah bless him and grant him peace, kiss you, I would not have kissed you." Then he kissed it.

'Abdullah ibn 'Umar was seen making his she-camel turn round in a particular place and was asked why. He said,"I don't know. I once saw the Messenger of Allah doing it, so I do it."

Abu 'Uthman al-Hiri said, "Whoever gives the *Sunna* authority over himself in word and deed speaks with wisdom. Whoever gives passion authority over himself speaks by innovation."

Sahl at-Tustari said, "The bases of our school are three: following the Prophet in character and actions, eating from what is lawful, and making our intention sincere in all actions."

It has come that Allah's words **"He raises up all righteous deeds,"** (35:10) refer to following the Messenger of Allah, may Allah bless him and grant him peace.

It is related that Ahmad ibn Hanbal said, "One day I was with a group who stripped off all their clothes and went into the water. I applied the *hadith*, 'Whoever believes in Allah and the Last Day should only enter the baths with a wrapper.' I did not strip. That night I dreamt that someone said to me, 'O Ahmad, Allah has forgiven you because of your application of the *sunna* and He has made you an Imam who will be followed.' I said, 'Who are you?' He replied, 'Jibril.' "

SECTION 5
The danger of opposing his command

Opposing his command and changing his *sunna* is misguidance and innovation. It is threatened by Allah with utter bereftness and punishment.

Allah says, **"Those who oppose his command should beware of a testing trial coming to them or a painful punishment striking them,"** (24:63) and **"But if anyone splits with the Messenger after the guidance has become clear to him, and follows other than the path of the believers, We will hand him over to whatever he has turned to."** (4:114)

Abu Hurayra said that once the Messenger of Allah went to visit some graves and, while there, described his community, saying, "Some men will be driven away from my Basin as a stray camel is driven off. I will call to them, 'Come here! Come here!' It will be said, 'They made changes after you.' Then I will say, 'Get away! Get away!'"[1]

Anas related that the Prophet said, "Anyone who dislikes my *sunna* is not of me."[2]

The Prophet said, "Anyone who adds something to my commands which is not part of them is a renegade."[3]

Ibn Abi Rafi' related from his father that the Prophet said, "Do not let any of you be found reclining on his bed when he hears an injunction from me which is from among those things which I myself have commanded or forbidden so that he says, 'I do not know. We only follow what we find in the Book of Allah.'" He added a version of the *hadith* from al-Miqdam, "What the Messenger of Allah makes unlawful is like what Allah makes unlawful."[4]

Once when some writing on a shoulder-blade was brought to him, the Prophet said, "People are stupid enough to dislike what their Prophet has brought them, preferring someone else to their Prophet or another book to their book." So it was revealed, **"Is it not enough for them that We have sent down to you the Book which is recited to them?"** (29:51)[5]

The Prophet, may Allah bless him and grant him peace, said, "Those who go to extremes in speech will be destroyed."[6]

Abu Bakr as-Siddiq said, "I have not omitted doing anything that the Messenger of Allah used to do. I feared that I would deviate if I left out any of his commands."

---

1 Muslim, Malik, Abu Dawud and an-Nasa'i.
2. Muslim and al-Bukhari.
3. Ibid.
4. Abu Dawud, at-Tirmidhi and Ibn Majah.
5. Abu Dawud, ad-Darimi, Ibn Jarir and others.
6. Muslim via Ibn Mas'ud.

Chapter Two

ON THE NECESSITY OF LOVING THE PROPHET

SECTION 1
Concerning the necessity of loving him

Allah says, **"Say: 'If your fathers or your sons or your brothers or your wives or your tribe, or any wealth you have acquired, or any business you fear may slump, or any dwelling-places which please you, are dearer to you than Allah and His Messenger and fighting hard in jihad in His Way, then wait until Allah brings about His command.'"** (9:25)

This is enough encouragement, advice, proof and indication of the necessity of loving him and is sufficient to show that this duty is an immensely important obligation which is the Prophet's due. Allah censures those whose property, families and children are dearer to them than Allah and His Messenger. He threatens them by adding, "Wait until Allah brings about His command." At the end of the *ayat* He considers such people as having done wrong and informs them they are among those who are astray and not guided by Allah.

Anas reported that the Messenger of Allah said, "None of you will believe until I am more beloved to him than his children, his father and all people."[1] There is something similar from Abu Hurayra.

Anas reported that the Prophet said, "There are three things which cause anyone who takes refuge in them to experience the sweetness of belief – that Allah and His Messenger are more beloved to him than anything else; that he loves a man only for Allah; and that he dislikes the thought of reverting to disbelief as much as he would dislike being cast into the Fire."[2]

'Umar ibn al-Khattab told the Prophet, "I love you more than anything except my soul which is between my two sides." The Prophet replied, "None of you will believe until I am dearer to him than his own soul." 'Umar said, "By the One who sent down the Book on you, I love you more than my soul which is between my two sides." The Prophet said, "'Umar, now you have it!"[3]

Sahl said, "Whoever does not think that the Messenger is his master in all

---

1. Al-Bukhari, Muslim and an-Nasa'i.
2. Al-Bukhari and Muslim.
3. Al-Bukhari.

states or think that he is under the dominion of the Prophet does not taste the sweetness of his *Sunna* because the Prophet, may Allah bless him and grant him peace, said, 'None of you will believe until I am dearer to him than himself.'"

SECTION 2
On the reward for loving the Prophet

Anas said that a man came to the Prophet and asked, "When will the Last Hour come, Messenger of Allah?" "What have you prepared for it?"he asked. He replied, "I have not prepared a lot of prayer or fasting or charity for it, but I love Allah and His Messenger." The Prophet said, "You will be with the one you love."[1]

Safwan ibn Qudama said, "I did *hijra* to the Prophet and went to him and said, 'Messenger of Allah, give me your hand.' So he gave me his hand. I said, 'Messenger of Allah, I love you.' He said, 'A man is with the one he loves.'"[2] 'Abdullah ibn Mas'ud, Abu Musa al-Ash'ari and Anas related this statement from the Prophet, and Abu Dharr also has something to the same effect.

'Ali said that the Prophet took Hasan and Husayn by the hand and said, "Whoever loves me and loves these two and their father and mother will have the same degree as me on the Day of Rising."[3]

It is related that a man came to the Prophet and said, "Messenger of Allah, I love you more than my family and my possessions. I remember you and I cannot wait until I can come and look at you. I remember that I will die and you will die and I know that when you enter the Garden, you will be raised up with the Prophets. When I enter it, I will not see you." Allah then revealed, **"Whoever obeys Allah and the Messenger, will be with those whom Allah has blessed: the Prophets, the men of truth, the martyrs and the righteous. And such people are the best of company!"** (4:68) The Prophet called the man and recited the verses to him.[4]

In another *hadith* we find, "A man was with the Prophet, looking at him without turning away. The Prophet asked, "What is wrong with you?" He replied, "My father and mother be your ransom! I enjoy looking at you. On the Day of Rising, Allah will raise you up because of His high estimation of you!"[5] Allah then sent down the *ayat* mentioned above.

In the *hadith* of Anas, the Prophet said, "Whoever loves me will be with me in the Garden."[6]

---

1. Al-Bukhari.
2. At-Tirmidhi and an-Nasa'i.
3. At-Tirmidhi.
4. At-Tabarani.
5. Source unknown.
6. Al-Isfahani.

SECTION 3
On what is related from the *Salaf* and the Imams about their love for the Prophet and their yearning for him

Abu Hurayra said that the Messenger of Allah said, "Those in my community with the strongest love for me are the people who will come after me. Some of them would give their family and wealth to have seen me."[1] There is something similar from Abu Dharr.

The *hadith* of 'Umar, "I love you more than myself," has already been cited. There are similar things from other Companions.

'Amr ibn al-'As said, "There is no-one I love better than the Messenger of Allah."

'Abda bint Khalid ibn Ma'dan said, "Khalid never went to bed without remembering how he yearned for the Messenger of Allah and his Companions among the Muhajirun and Ansar, and he would name them. He said, 'They are my root and branch, and my heart longs for them. I have yearned for them a long time. My Lord, hasten my being taken to You!'"

It is related that Abu Bakr said to the Prophet, "By the One who sent you with the truth, I would be happier if Abu Talib[2] were to become Muslim than if Abu Quhayfa[3] were to. That is because the Islam of Abu Talib would delight you more." 'Umar ibn al-Khattab told al-'Abbas, "Your becoming a Muslim is dearer to me than al-Khattab becoming a Muslim because it is dearer to the Messenger of Allah."

Ibn Ishaq said that the father, brother and husband of one of the women of the Ansar were killed in the Battle of Uhud fighting for the Messenger of Allah. She asked, "What has happened to the Messenger of Allah, may Allah bless him and grant him peace?" They said, "He is as well as you would like, praise be to Allah!" She said, "Show him to me so I can look at him." When she saw him, she said, "Every affliction is as nothing now that you are safe."

'Ali ibn Abi Talib was asked, "How was your love for the Messenger of Allah?" He replied, "By Allah, we loved him more than our wealth, our sons, our fathers and our mothers, and more than cold water in a time of great thirst."

Zayd ibn Aslam said, 'Umar went out at night to observe the people and saw a lamp in a house where an old woman was teasing some wool, saying:

> "The prayer of the good be upon Muhammad,
> may the blessed bless him!

---

1. Muslim and al-Bukhari.
2. The Prophet's uncle.
3. His own father.

> I was standing in tears before dawn. If only I knew,
>   when death gives us different forms,
>   Whether the Abode will join me to my beloved!"

She meant the Prophet. 'Umar sat down in tears.

It is related that once 'Abdullah ibn 'Umar's foot went numb. He was told, "Remember the most beloved of people to you and it will go away!" He shouted, "O Muhammad!" and the feeling returned.

When Bilal was near death, his wife called out, "O sorrow!" Bilal said, "What joy! I will meet those I love, Muhammad and his party!"

It is related that a woman said to 'A'isha, "Show me the grave of the Messenger of Allah." She showed it to her and the woman wept until she died.

When the Makkans drove Zayd ibn ad-Dathima out of the Haram to kill him, Abu Sufyan ibn Harb said to him, "I ask you by Allah, Zayd, don't you wish that Muhammad were with us now to take your place so that we could cut off his head, and you were with your family?" Zayd said, "By Allah, I would not wish Muhammad to be now in a place where even a thorn could hurt him if that was the condition for my being with my family!" Abu Sufyan remarked, "I have not seen any people who love anyone the way the Companions of Muhammad love Muhammad."

Ibn 'Abbas said, "When a woman came to the Prophet (i.e. from Makka to Madina), he made her take an oath that she had not left because of her husband's wrath or desire for a new land and that she had only left out of love for Allah and His Messenger."

Ibn 'Umar stood over Ibn az-Zubayr after he had been killed and asked for forgiveness for him and said, "By Allah, according to what I know you were someone who fasted and prayed and loved Allah and His Messenger."

SECTION 4
The signs of love of the Prophet, may Allah bless him and grant him peace

Know that someone who loves a person prefers them and prefers what they like. Otherwise, he is a pretender, insincere in his love.

Someone who has true love of the Prophet, may Allah bless him and grant him peace, will manifest the following signs.

1) The first sign is that he will emulate him, apply his *Sunna*, follow his words and deeds, obey his commands and avoid his prohibitions and take on his *adab* in ease and hardship, joy and despair. Allah testifies to that, **"Say: if you love Allah, then follow me and Allah will love you."** (3:31)

2) He will prefer what the Prophet, may Allah bless him and grant him peace, has laid down as law and encouraged, over his own passions and appetites. Allah said, "**Those who were already settled in the abode, and in belief, before they came, love those who have emigrated to them and do not find in their breasts any need for what they have been given and prefer them to themselves even if they themselves are in want.**" (59:9)

3) His anger against people will only be for the sake of the pleasure of Allah. Anas ibn Malik said, "The Messenger of Allah said to me, 'My son, if you can be without any grudge in your heart against anyone in the morning and evening, be like that.' Then he added, 'My son, that is part of my *Sunna*. Whoever gives life to my *Sunna* has loved me and whoever loves me is with me in the Garden.'"[1]

Anyone who possesses this particular quality has perfect love for Allah and His Messenger. Anyone slightly lacking in it is imperfect in his love, while not entirely devoid of it. The proof of this is in what the Prophet said about the man who was given the *hadd*-punishment for drinking. A man there cursed him and the Prophet said, "Do not curse him. He loves Allah and His Messenger."[2]

4) Another of the signs of love for the Prophet is to mention him often. Whoever loves something mentions it a lot.

5) Another is great yearning to meet him. Every lover yearns for their beloved.

When the Ash'arite clan came to Madina, they chanted, "Tomorrow we will meet those we love, Muhammad and his Companions!"

6) One of its signs is that as well as mentioning him often, someone who loves him will exalt and respect him when he mentions him and display humility and abasement when he hears his name. Ishaq at-Tujibi said, "Whenever the Companions of the Prophet heard his name after he died, they were humble, their skins trembled and they wept. It was the same with many of the Followers. Some of them act like that out of love and yearning for him, others out of respect and esteem."

7) Another sign is love for those who love the Prophet and the people of his house and his Companions, both of the Muhajirun and Ansar, for his sake. Such a person will also be hostile to those who hate them and curse them. Whoever loves anyone, loves those he loves.

The Prophet said about al-Hasan and al-Husayn, "O Allah, I love them, so love them." In al-Hasan's variant, "O Allah, I love him, so love the one who loves him." He also said, "Whoever loves them loves me. Whoever loves me loves Allah. Whoever hates them hates me. Whoever hates me hates Allah."[3]

---

1. At-Tirmidhi.
2. Al-Bayhaqi.
3. Al-Bukhari.

He said, "Allah! Allah! My Companions! Do not make them targets after me! Whoever loves them loves them by loving me. Whoever hates them hates them by hating me. Whoever does something hurtful to them does something hurtful to me. Whoever does something hurtful to me does something hurtful to Allah. Whoever does something hurtful to Allah is about to be seized."[1]

He said about Fatima, "She is a part of me. Whoever hates her hates me."[2]

He said to 'A'isha about Usama ibn Zayd, "Love him for I love him."[3]

He said, "The sign of true faith is love for the Ansar and the sign of hypocrisy is hatred for them."[4]

In a *hadith* related by Ibn 'Umar we find, "Whoever loves the Arabs, loves them because he loves me. Whoever hates them hates them because he hates me." In reality, whoever loves someone loves everything he loves. This was certainly the case with the *Salaf*, even regarding permitted things and the appetites of the self.

Anas once saw the Prophet reaching for the pumpkin in a plate. He said, "I have loved pumpkin from that day."

Al-Hasan ibn 'Ali, 'Abdullah ibn 'Abbas and Ibn Ja'far came to Salma[5] and asked her to prepare some food for them which the Messenger of Allah liked. Ibn 'Umar began to wear tanned sandals dyed yellow when he saw the Prophet wearing ones like that.

8) Another sign is hatred for anyone who hates Allah and His Messenger, having enmity towards all who have enmity towards him, avoidance of all those who oppose his *Sunna* and introduce innovations into his *deen*, and finding every matter contrary to his *Shari'a* burdensome. Allah says, **"You will not find any people who believe in Allah and the Last Day having love for anyone who opposes Allah and His Messenger."** (58:22)

His Companions killed their loved ones and fought their fathers and sons to gain the pleasure of the Prophet, may Allah bless him and grant him peace. 'Abdullah ibn 'Abdullah ibn Ubayy said to him, "If you had wanted, I would have brought you his head (his father's)."

9) Another sign of it is love for the Qur'an which the Prophet brought, by which he guided and was guided, and whose character he took on so that 'A'isha said, "His character was the Qur'an." Part of love for the Qur'an is its recitation and acting by it and understanding it, and loving his *sunna* and keeping within its limits.

Sahl ibn 'Abdullah said, "The sign of the love of Allah is love of the Qur'an. The sign of love of the Qur'an is love of the Prophet. The sign of love of the

1. At-Tirmidhi.
2. Al-Bukhari.
3. At-Tirmidhi.
4. Al-Bukhari and Muslim.
5. A servant of the Prophet and *mawla* of his aunt.

Prophet is love of the *Sunna*. The sign of love of the *Sunna* is love of the Next World. The sign of love of the Next World is hatred for this world. The sign of hatred for this world is that you do not store up any of it except for provision and what you need to arrive safely in the Next World."

Ibn Mas'ud said, "No-one needs to ask himself about anything except the Qur'an. If he loves the Qur'an, he loves Allah and His Messenger."

10) One of the signs of love for the Prophet is having compassion for his community, giving them good counsel, striving for their best interests and removing what is harmful from them just as the Prophet was **"compassionate, merciful to the believers."** (9:128)

11) One of the signs of perfect love is that the one who aspires to it does without in this world and prefers poverty.

The Prophet said to Abu Sa'id al-Khudri, "Poverty for those among you who love me comes quicker than a flood from the top of the mountain to the bottom."[1]

In a *hadith* from 'Abdullah b. Mughaffal, a man said to the Prophet, "O Messenger of Allah, I love you." He said, "Take care what you say!" He said, "By Allah, I love you" three times. He said, "If you love me, then prepare for poverty quickly." There is a similar *hadith* from Abu Sa'id al-Khudri.

SECTION 5
On the meaning and reality of love for the Prophet

People disagree about what constitutes love of Allah and the Prophet. They have many things to say about it, but in reality, they are referring to different states.

Sufyan said, "Love consists of following the Messenger of Allah." It was as if he were thinking of the words of Allah, **"Say: if you love Allah, then follow me."** (3:31)

One of the scholars said, "Love of the Messenger is to believe in his victory, protect his *Sunna*, obey it and to fear being in opposition to him."

One of the scholars said, "Love is constant remembrance of the beloved."

Another said, "It is preferring the beloved."

Another said, "Love is yearning for the beloved."

One of the scholars said, "Love is the heart following the will of its master, loving what he loves and hating what he hates."

Another said, "Love is the heart's inclination to be in harmony with the beloved."

Most of these statements indicate the fruits of love rather than its reality. The reality of love is to incline to what one finds agreeable and harmonious, either:

(1) by the pleasure in its perfection – like love of beautiful forms,

---

1. At-Tirmidhi.

melodious sounds, delicious foods and drink to which one naturally inclines because they are agreeable;

(2) or by pleasure in the perfection of its noble inner qualities which is sensed by the intellect and heart – like love for the *salihun*, the *'ulama'* and people of correct behaviour whose marvellous lives and good actions have been related. Man's nature inclines to intense love for these sorts of things to the point of fanaticism. Such partisanship of one group against another and sectarianism within a nation can result in homelands being abandoned, inviolable things being dishonoured, and lives lost;

(3) or someone can love something because he finds it agreeable by reason of gaining benefit and blessing from it. The self is naturally disposed to love that which is good to it.

When you have understood this well, then examine these three causes of love in respect of the Prophet and you will find that all three things which inspire love apply to him.

The beauty of his form and outward appearance and the perfection of his character have already been mentioned, so there is no need to say any more about them.

As regards the benefit and blessing his community gain from him, we have already mentioned the qualities of Allah he possessed – his compassion for them, his mercy for them, his guiding them, his tenderness for them and his striving to save them from the Fire. He is, **"merciful, compassionate to the believers,"** (9:128) and **"a mercy to the worlds,"** (21:107) and, **"a bringer of good news, a warner and a caller to Allah by His permission."** (33:45-46) **"He recites its signs to them and purifies them and teaches them the Book and the Wisdom,"** (62:2) and **"guides them to a straight path."** (5:16)

What goodness could be worthier or of greater importance than his goodness to all the believers! What favour could be more universally beneficial and of greater use than his blessing to all the Muslims since he is their means to guidance, the one who rescues them from blind error, and the one who summons them to success and honour? He is their means to their Lord and their intercessor. He speaks up on their behalf and bears witness for them and brings them to eternal life and everlasting bliss.

So it should be clear to you that love of the Prophet must be an obligation in the *Shari'a* because of the sound traditions we have related and the nature of his overflowing goodness and universal beauty we have just mentioned.

If a man can love someone who is generous to him just once or twice in this world, as is well known to be the case, or someone who saves him from destruction or harm even once, when that damage and harm are only of a temporary nature, then the one who gives him undying bliss and protects him from the eternal punishment of *al-Jahim* should be loved more. A king is loved when his behaviour is good and a ruler is loved for his upright conduct. Someone who lives far away is loved for their knowledge or noble character. Whoever possesses all these qualities in total perfection is more entitled to be loved and more deserving of attachment.

'Ali, describing the Prophet, said, "Whoever saw him suddenly was in awe of him. Whoever mixed with him loved him." We mentioned that one of the Companions could not turn his eyes away because of his love for him.

SECTION 6
The obligation of *nasiha*[1] for the Prophet

Allah says, **"Nothing is held against the weak and sick nor against those who find nothing to spend, provided they are true to Allah and His Messenger – there is no way open against the good-doers. Allah is Ever-Forgiving, Most Merciful."** (9:92) The commentators say, "If they are true in sincere conduct towards Allah and His Messengers, they are sincere Muslims secretly and openly."

Tamim ad-Dari said that the Messenger of Allah said, "The *deen* is *nasiha* (good counsel/sincere conduct). The *deen* is *nasiha*. The *deen* is *nasiha*." They asked, "To whom, Messenger of Allah?" He said, "To Allah and His Book and His Messenger and the Imams of the Muslims and the common people."

Our Imams said, "*Nasiha* for Allah and the Imams of the muslims and their common folk is an obligation."

Imam Abu Sulayman al-Busti said, "*Nasiha* is a word used to designate the desire for what is good for the one who is its object, and it is not possible to explain it with a single word which will contain it all. Linguistically, it means sincerity (*ikhlas*) from the statement, 'I made the honey pure (*nasahtu*),' when it is clear of wax."

Abu Bakr ibn Abi Ishaq al-Khaffaf said, "*Nasiha* is doing something which contains rightness and harmony. It comes from *nisah* which is the thread with which a garment is sewn."

Nasiha to Allah consists of having sound belief in His Oneness, describing Him in the way that He deserves to be described and disconnecting Him from what cannot be attributed to Him. It is desire for what He loves and distance from what He hates and sincerity in worshipping Him.

Nasiha to His Book is belief in it, acting according to it, reciting it well, humility with it, esteem for it, understanding it and seeking *fiqh* in it and protecting it from the interpretation of the extremists and the attack of heretics.

---

1. Good counsel and sincere conduct.

Nasiha to the Messenger is confirming his prophethood and obeying him in what he commands and forbids.

Abu Sulayman and Abu Bakr said, "It is to support, help and protect him, both in life and death, and to bring his *Sunna* to life by seeking, protecting and spreading it and taking on his noble character and *adab*."

Abu Ibrahim Ishaq at-Tujibi said, "*Nasiha* to the Messenger of Allah is to confirm what he brought and to cling to his *Sunna*, spread it and urge people to it and to call to Allah, His Book and His Messenger and to the *Sunna*, and acting by it."

Ahmad ibn Muhammad said, "One of the obligations of the heart is to believe in *nasiha* for the sake of the Messenger of Allah."

Abu Bakr al-Ajurri and others said, "*Nasiha* for his sake includes two types of sincere conduct. One is *nasiha* during his lifetime and the other is *nasiha* after his death."

In his lifetime, the *nasiha* of his Companions was by helping him, protecting him, opposing his opponents, obeying him and expending their lives and property in his service as in Allah's words, **"Men who were true to their contract with Allah."** (33:23) **"They help Allah and His Messenger."** (59:8)

The *nasiha* of the Muslims for his sake after his death is by maintaining esteem, respect and great love for him, persevering in learning his *Sunna*, understanding his *Shari'a*, love for the People of his House and his Companions, avoiding things disliked in his *Sunna* and what deviates from it, hating doing that and being on guard against it, compassion for his community, seeking to learn about his character, his life and behaviour and steadfastness in acting according to it.

So from what has been said it can be seen that *nasiha* is one of the fruits of love as well as one of its signs.

Imam Abu'l-Qasim al-Qushayri related that 'Amr ibn al-Layth, one of the Kings of Khurasan and a famous hero who was known as as-Saffar,[1] was seen in a dream and was asked, "What did Allah do with you?" He replied, "He forgave me." He was asked, "Why?" He said, "One day I climbed to the peak of a mountain and looked down at my armies and their vast number pleased me. Then I wished that I could have been present with the Messenger of Allah, may Allah bless him and grant him peace, to aid and help him. Allah thanked me and forgave me because of that."

Nasiha to the Imams of the Muslims is to obey them when they command to the truth, help them, command them to the truth, remind them of it in the best way, inform them about what they have overlooked and what they do not see of the Muslims' affairs, and not to attack them nor cause trouble and dissension

---

1. Founder of the Saffarid dynasty (867-903). He was famous for fighting against the Kharijites in Sistan.

for them with people and alienate them from people.

Nasiha for the sake of the common Muslims is to guide them to their best interests, help them in the business of their *deen* and this world by word and action, warning those of them who are heedless, enlightening the ignorant, giving to those in need, veiling their faults, and repelling what will harm them and bringing what will benefit them.

Chapter Three

EXALTING HIM AND THE NECESSITY TO RESPECT AND HONOUR HIM

SECTION 1
Ayats in the Qur'an on this subject

Allah says, **"O Prophet, We have sent you bearing witness, bringing good news and giving warning so that you may all believe in Allah and His Messenger and honour him and respect him."** (48:7-8)

He says, **"O you who believe, do not put yourselves forward in front of Allah and of His Messenger... O you who believe, do not raise your voices above the voice of the Prophet."** (49:1-2)

He says, **"Do not make the Messenger's summoning of you the same as your summoning of one another."** (24:63)

So He made it an obligation to help and respect the Prophet and demanded that he be honoured and esteemed. Ibn 'Abbas said it means to honour him and al-Mubarrad that it means to respect him to the utmost. Al-Akhfash said that it means to help him. At-Tabari said that it means to assist him.[1]

In the second *ayat* above it is forbidden to speak before him. To do so was considered extremely bad behaviour according to what Ibn 'Abbas and others have said. That is preferred by Tha'lab.

Sahl ibn 'Abdullah at-Tustari said, "It means, 'Do not speak before he speaks. When he speaks, then listen to him and be silent.'" They were forbidden to go ahead and carry out a matter before he had made a decision about it or to differ about any matter – fighting or otherwise – in their *deen* unless he commanded it. They were not to precede him in this. This is what the statements of al-Hasan, Mujahid, ad-Dahhak, as-Suddi and ath-Thawri say about it.

Then Allah warns and cautions them against doing that. He says, **"Show fear of Allah. Allah is All-Hearing, All-Knowing."** (49:1) Al-Mawardi said that fear of Him means to avoid taking precedence over His Prophet.

As-Sulami said, "Fear Allah when you disregard what is due to the Prophet

---

1. The verse is also recited as *tu'azzizuhu* (honour and strengthen him) [*shadhdh* reading] rather than *tu'azziruhu* (help him).

and neglect to respect him. He hears what you say and knows what you do." Then He forbade them to raise their voices above his voice and to talk loudly to him in the way that they used to talk loudly to each other with raised voices. It is said that it means to call to each other familiarly by name.

Abu Muhammad Makki said, "It means not to speak before him and talk coarsely to him. Do not call him by name as you do each other. Respect and esteem him and call him with the noblest title you can use – like Messenger of Allah or Prophet of Allah. This is what Allah says in the other *ayat*, '**Do not make the Messenger's summoning of you the same as your summoning of one another.**'" Another scholar said that it means they should only speak to him when asking questions.

Then Allah made them fear that their actions would come to nothing if they acted in that way and cautioned them about it. It is said that the *ayat* was sent down about the delegation of the Banu Tamim. They came to the Prophet and called out to him, "O Muhammad, O Muhammad, come out to us." Allah censured them for being ignorant and described most of them as being without understanding.

It is said that the former *ayat* was sent down about a conversation between Abu Bakr and 'Umar which took place in the presence of the Prophet. It turned into a dispute and led to raised voices.[1]

It has also been said that it was revealed about Thabit ibn Qays ibn Shammash, the orator chosen by the Prophet to counter the boasting of the Banu Tamim. He was somewhat deaf and used to raise his voice. When this *ayat* was revealed, he stayed in his house, fearing that his actions were worthless. Then he went to the Prophet and said, "O Prophet of Allah, I fear that I am destroyed. Allah has forbidden us to raise our voices and I am a man with a loud voice." The Prophet said, "Thabit, are you not content to live in a praiseworthy manner and be killed as a martyr and enter the Garden?" He was killed in the Battle of Yamama.

It is related that when this *ayat* was revealed, Abu Bakr said, "By Allah, Messenger of Allah, after this I will only speak to you as one speaks to someone when telling him a secret!"

When 'Umar also spoke like someone telling a secret after that, his voice was not audible enough for the Messenger of Allah to understand so Allah revealed this about them: **"Those who lower their voices in the presence of the Messenger of Allah are people whose hearts Allah has tested for fear of Him. They will have forgiveness and a huge reward."** (49:3)

It is said that the *ayat*, **"As for those who call out to you from outside your private quarters, most of them do not use their intellects"** (49:4) was revealed

---

1. Al-Bukhari from az-Zubayr.

about some other people besides the Banu Tamim who called him by name.

Safwan ibn 'Assal related that once the Prophet was on a journey when a bedouin called to him in a loud voice, "O Muhammad! Muhammad!" He was told to lower his voice and informed that he had been forbidden to raise his voice (to the Prophet).[1]

Allah says, **"O you who believe, do not say, 'Take notice of us.'"** (2:104) One of the commentators said that this refers to something in the dialect of the *Ansar* which they were forbidden to use out of respect for the Prophet because it means, "Take notice of us and we will take notice of you." They were forbidden to say it since it means something to the effect that they will only take notice of him if he takes notice of them. It is his right to be taken notice of in any situation.

It is said that when the Jews used it in mockery of the Prophet, the Muslims were forbidden to say it to cut off the means of that happening and so as not to be like them through the use of a similar phrase. Other things have been said as well.

SECTION 2
On the esteem, respect and veneration due to him

'Amr ibn al-'As said, "There is no-one I have loved more than the Messenger of Allah, may Allah bless him and grant him peace, nor anyone I have respected more. I could never get my fill of looking at him due to my great respect for him. If I had been asked to describe him, I could not have done so because I was unable to look at him enough."

At-Tirmidhi related that Anas said. "The Messenger of Allah used to go out with his Companions from the *Muhajirun* and *Ansar* when Abu Bakr and 'Umar were with them. None of them raised their eyes to look at him except Abu Bakr and 'Umar. They would look at him and he at them. They would smile at him and he at them."

It is related that Usama ibn Sharik said, "I came to the Prophet and found his Companions sitting around him as still as if there were birds on their heads."[2] In a *hadith* describing him from Hind bint Abi Hala we find, "When he spoke, those sitting around him bowed their heads as if there were birds on top of them."

When Quraysh sent 'Urwa ibn Mas'ud to the Messenger of Allah in the year of al-Hudaybiyya,[3] he saw the unparalleled respect which his Companions displayed towards him. Whenever he did *wudu'* they ran to get his leftover

---

1. At-Tirmidhi and an-Nasa'i.
2. At-Tirmidhi.
3. 6 A.H. See p. 141, foonote 4.

wudu' water and very nearly fought over it. If he spat they took it with their hands and wiped it on their faces and bodies. If a hair of his fell they ran to get it. If he commanded them to do something, they ran to do his command. If he spoke, they lowered their voices in his presence. They did not stare at him due to their respect for him. When he returned to Quraysh, he said, "People of Quraysh! I have been to Chosroes in his kingdom, and Caesar in his kingdom and the Negus in his kingdom, but by Allah, I have not seen any king among his people treated anything like the way Muhammad is treated by his Companions."[1]

One version has, "I have never seen a king whose companions esteemed him as Muhammad is esteemed by his Companions. I have seen a people who will never abandon him."

Anas said, "I saw the Messenger of Allah when his hair was being shaved. His companions were around him and whenever a lock fell, a man picked it up."[2]

Another instance of this is when Quraysh gave 'Uthman permission to do *tawaf* of the House when the Prophet sent him as an envoy to them and he refused, saying, "I will not do it until the Messenger of Allah does."

Talha said that the Companions of the Messenger of Allah told an ignorant bedouin to ask the Prophet about what someone who had fulfilled his vow[3] was like. They were in awe of the Prophet and revered him. He asked him but he did not respond. When Talha came up, the Messenger of Allah said, "This is someone who has fulfilled his vow."[4]

Qayla said, "When I saw the Messenger of Allah sitting squatting, I trembled from fear."[5] This was due to her awe and respect for him.

Al-Mughira said, "The Companions of the Messenger of Allah would knock on his door with their fingernails."[6]

Al-Bara' ibn 'Azib said, "I wanted to ask the Messenger of Allah, may Allah bless him and grant him peace, about something but waited for years out of awe of him."[7]

SECTION 3
Respect and esteem for the Prophet after his death

It is just as necessary to have esteem and respect for the Prophet after his death as it was when he was alive. This means to show it whenever the Prophet,

---

1. Al-Bukhari.
2. Muslim.
3. Referring to the *ayat* of Qur'an, **"Among the men are those who were true to their covenant with Allah, some of them have fulfilled their vow by death and some of them are still waiting."** (33:23)
4. At-Tirmidhi.
5. Abu Dawud and at-Tirmidhi.
6. Al-Hakim and al-Bayhaqi.
7. Abu Ya'la.

his *hadith* or *sunna* are mentioned, when anyone hears his name or anything about his life or how his family and relatives behaved. It includes respect for the People of his House (*ahl al-bayt*) and his Companions.

Abu Ibrahim at-Tujibi said, "It is obligatory for every believer to be humble, fearful, show respect and be still when they mention the Prophet, may Allah bless him and grant him peace, or the Prophet is mentioned in their presence. They should be as respectful as they would have been if they had actually been in his presence taking on the *adab* which Allah taught us." That is the way our right-acting *Salaf* and past Imams behaved.

Abu Humayd said, "Abu Ja'far, the *Amir al-Mu'minin*, had a dispute with Malik in the Prophet's mosque. Malik said to him, '*Amir al-Mu'minin*, do not raise your voice in this mosque. Allah taught the people how to behave by saying, **"Do not raise your voices above the Prophet."** (49:2) He praises people with the words, **"Those who lower their voices in the presence of the Messenger of Allah."** (49:3) He censures people, saying, **"Those who call you..."** Respect for him when he is dead is the same as respect for him when he was alive.'

"Abu Ja'far was humbled by this. He asked Malik, 'Abu 'Abdullah, do you face *qibla* when you supplicate or do you face the Messenger of Allah?' He replied, 'Why would you turn your face from him when he is your means and the means of your father, Adam, to Allah on the Day of Rising? I face him and ask him to intercede and Allah will grant his intercession. Allah says, **"If, when you wronged yourselves, they had come to you."**'" (4:64)

When he was asked about Ayyub as-Sakhtiyani, Malik said, "I have not reported from anyone without Ayyub being better than him." He went on, "I went on *hajj* twice and watched him. Whenever the Messenger of Allah was mentioned, he wept until his eyes were red. When I saw him do that and the respect he had for the Prophet, I wrote down things from him."

Mus'ab ibn 'Abdullah said, "When the Prophet was mentioned, Malik would grow pale so that it distressed those with him. One day he was asked about this. He said, 'If you had seen what I have seen, you would not be surprised at what you see me do. I used to see Muhammad ibn Munkadir, the master of the Qur'an reciters. Almost every time he was asked about a *hadith*, he wept until his eyes were red. I saw Ja'far ibn Muhammad who joked and laughed a lot, but when the Prophet was mentioned in his presence, he grew pale. I never saw him relate a *hadith* of the Messenger of Allah except in a state of purity. I frequented him for a time and only saw him doing one of three things – praying, fasting or reciting Qur'an. He only spoke about what concerned him. He was one of the men of knowledge and those who fear Allah.

"'Whenever 'Abdu'r-Rahman ibn al-Qasim mentioned the Prophet, his face seemed as if the blood had drained from it and his tongue went dry out of awe of the Messenger of Allah. I used to go to 'Amir ibn 'Abdullah ibn az-Zubayr. When the Prophet was mentioned in his presence, he wept until he had no more tears to weep. I saw az-Zuhri who was one of the most easy-going and friendly of people. When the Prophet was mentioned in his presence, it was as if he did not recognise anyone and I did not recognise him. I used to come to Safwan ibn Sulayman who was one of those who were assiduous in their worship and did night prayers. When the Prophet was mentioned, he wept and did not stop weeping so that the people got up and left him.'"

It is related that when Qatada heard a *hadith* he began to sob and became very agitated.

When there were many people around Malik, he was asked, "If only you would appoint someone to whom you could dictate and then he could make the people hear." He replied, "Allah said, **'O you who believe, do not raise your voices above the voice of the Prophet.'** (49:2) The respect due to him when he is dead is the same when he was alive."

Ibn Sirin used to laugh at times but when the *hadiths* of the Prophet were mentioned in his presence he became humble. When a *hadith* of the Prophet was recited, 'Abdu'r-Rahman ibn Mahdi commanded them to be silent, saying, "Do not raise your voices above the voice of the Prophet." He interpreted the above *ayat* as meaning that people must be silent when the Prophet's *hadiths* are recited, just as if they were listening to him speaking.

SECTION 4
On the esteem of the *Salaf* for the transmission of the *hadiths* of the Messenger of Allah

'Amr ibn Maymun said, "I frequented Ibn Mas'ud for a year. I never heard him say, 'The Messenger of Allah, may Allah bless him and grant him peace,' without him keeping on saying 'the Messenger of Allah' for the whole day and his distress would increase until I saw sweat dropping from his brow. Then he would say, 'Like that, if Allah wills, or more than that, or less than that, or close to it.'"

Ibrahim ibn 'Abdullah ibn Qusaym al-Ansari, the Qadi of Madina, said, "Malik ibn Anas passed by Abu Hazim when he was teaching *hadiths* and he gave him permission to listen. He said, 'There is no place to sit and I dislike listening to a *hadith* of the Messenger of Allah, may Allah bless him and grant him peace, while standing up.'"

Malik said, "A man came to Ibn al-Musayyab while he was reclining and asked him about a *hadith*. He sat up and gave him the *hadith*. The man said to him, 'I wish you hadn't troubled yourself.' He retorted, 'I dislike giving you *hadith* from the Messenger of Allah while reclining.'"

It is related that Muhammad ibn Sirin used to laugh, but when the *hadith* of the Prophet was mentioned in his presence, he grew humble.

Abu Mus'ab said, "Malik ibn Anas would only transmit a *hadith* of the Messenger of Allah, may Allah bless him and grant him peace, while in a state of *wudu'* due to his respect for him."

Mus'ab ibn 'Abdullah said that when Malik ibn Anas taught a *hadith* from the Messenger of Allah, he did *wudu'*, got ready, put on his garment and then gave a *hadith*. He was asked about that and said, "It is a *hadith* of the Messenger of Allah, may Allah bless him and grant him peace."

Mutarrif said, "When people came to visit Malik, his slavegirl went out to them and said, 'The shaykh asks you whether you want to hear *hadiths* or have other questions.' If they had questions, he came out to them. If they had come for *hadiths*, he went and did *wudu'*, put on scent, put on new garments, a dark cloak, a turban and put the hood of his cloak on his head. A dais was set up for him. He went out in humility and kept burning aloes until he had finished teaching *hadiths* of the Messenger of Allah."

Another person said that he only sat on that dais to teach *hadiths* from the Messenger of Allah. Ibn Abi Uways said, "Malik was asked about it and he said, 'I like to show esteem for the *hadiths* of the Messenger of Allah. I will only teach them in a state of purity." He also said that Malik disliked teaching *hadiths* in the street or while he was standing up or when he was in a hurry. He said, "I like to make sure people understand the *hadiths* of the Messenger of Allah."

Dirar ibn Murra said, "They used to dislike teaching *hadiths* without being in *wudu'*." If al-A'mash wanted to teach a *hadith* when he was not in *wudu'*, he would do *tayammum*.

'Abdullah ibn al-Mubarak said, "I was with Malik when he was teaching us *hadith*. A scorpion stung him sixteen times. He changed colour and grew quite pale, but did not interrupt the *hadiths* of the Messenger of Allah. When he finished and the people had departed, I said to him, 'Abu 'Abdullah! I saw you do something extraordinary today!' He said, 'Yes, I endured it out of respect for the Messenger of Allah.'"

Ibn Mahdi said, "I walked with Malik to al-'Aqiq one day. I asked him about a *hadith* and he scolded me, saying, 'You are too good in my eyes to ask about a *hadith* of the Messenger of Allah while we are walking!'"

Qadi Jarir ibn 'Abdu'l-Hamid asked Malik about a *hadith* while he was standing up and Malik ordered that he should be arrested. He was told, "But he is a *qadi*!" He retorted, "A *qadi* should have more *adab*!"

Hisham ibn al-Ghazi asked Malik about a *hadith* while standing up and Malik struck him twenty times with a whip. Then he had pity on him and taught him twenty *hadiths*. Hisham said, "I wish that he had given me more blows and then more *hadiths*!"

'Abdullah ibn Salih said, "Malik and al-Layth only wrote down *hadith* when they were in a state of purity."

Qatada used to recommend that the *hadiths* of the Prophet only be read in a state of purity and only taught in a state of purity.

SECTION 5
Devotion to his family, descendants and wives

Part of respect for the Prophet and devotion to him is devotion to his family, his descendants and his wives, the Mothers of the Believers, as he urged and as the *Salaf* did.

Allah said, **"Allah wants to remove impurity from you, people of the House."** (33:33) He said, **"His wives are their mothers."** (33:6)

Zayd ibn Arqam related that the Messenger of Allah said, "I implore you by Allah! The People of my House!" three times. We asked Zayd who constituted the People of his House, and he said, "The family of 'Ali, the family of Ja'far,[1] the family of 'Uqayl,[2] and the family of al-'Abbas."[3]

The Prophet said, "I am leaving you something, taking hold of which will prevent you from going astray: the Book of Allah and my family, the People of my House. So take care how you follow me regarding them."[4]

The Prophet said, "Recognition of the family of Muhammad is freedom from the Fire. Love of the family of Muhammad is crossing over the *Sirat*. Friendship for the family of Muhammad is safety from the Fire."[5]

One of the *'ulama'* said, "'Recognition' in this case means recognising their place in relation to the Prophet. Recognition of that brings with it recognition of the rights and respect that are due to them because of it."

'Umar ibn Abi Salama said that **"Allah wants to remove impurity from you, People of the House,"** (33:33) was revealed in Umm Salama's house. The Prophet summoned Fatima, Hasan and Husayn and enfolded them in a garment and 'Ali was behind him. Then he said, "O Allah! These are the People of my House, so remove all impurity from them and purify them completely!"[6]

Sa'd ibn Abi Waqqas said that when the *ayat* of mutual cursing[7] was

---

1. A son of Abu Talib.
2. Another son of Abu Talib.
3. Muslim.
4. At-Tirmidhi.
5. No source given.
6. At-Tirmidhi.
7. **"And whosoever disputes with you concerning him after the knowledge that has come to you, say, 'Come, let us call our sons and your sons, our wives and your wives, our selves and your selves, then let us humbly pray and so lay the curse of Allah upon the ones who lie.'"**(3:61)

revealed, the Prophet called 'Ali, Hasan, Husayn and Fatima, and said, "O Allah! These are my family."[1]

The Prophet said about 'Ali, "Whoever has me for a master, 'Ali is his master. O Allah, befriend the one who befriends him and oppose the one who opposes him!"[2]

He also said to him, "Only a believer will love you and only a hypocrite will hate you."[3]

He said to al-'Abbas, "By the One who has my soul in His hand, belief will not enter a man's heart until he loves Allah and His Messenger. Whoever harms my uncle has harmed me. A man's uncle is like his father."[4]

He also said to al-'Abbas, "Feed 'Ali with your children, my uncle." Then he gathered them and wrapped them with his robe, saying, "This is my uncle and my father's twin and these are the people of my house, so veil them from the Fire as I am veiling them." The lintel of the door and the walls of the house said, "Amen! Amen!"[5]

He used to take the hand of Usama ibn Zayd and al-Hasan and say, "Love them, O Allah, for I love them."[6]

Abu Bakr said, "Respect Muhammad by respecting the People of his House." He also said, "By the One who has my soul in His hand, the near kin of the Messenger of Allah are dearer to me than my own kinsfolk."

The Prophet said, "Allah loves those who love Hasan."[7]

He also said, "Whoever loves these two[8] and their father and mother will be with me on the Day of Rising."

The Prophet said, "Whoever demeans Quraysh, Allah will demean him."[9]

The Prophet said, "Give preference to Quraysh and do not precede them."[10]

He said to Umm Salama, "Do not injure me by injuring 'A'isha."[11]

'Uqba ibn al-Harith said, "I saw Abu Bakr putting al-Hasan on his shoulders, saying, "By my father, he resembles the Prophet! He does not resemble 'Ali!" 'Ali was laughing.

It is related that 'Abdullah ibn Hasan ibn Husayn said, "I came to 'Umar ibn 'Abdu'l-'Aziz when I was in need of something and he said, 'If you have a need, then send for me or write to me. I am ashamed before Allah to see you at my

---

1. Muslim.
2. Ibn Hanbal.
3. Muslim.
4. At-Tirmidhi and Ibn Majah.
5. Al-Bayhaqi.
6. Al-Bukhari.
7. At-Tirmidhi.
8. Al-Hasan and al-Husayn ibn 'Ali ibn Abi Talib.
9. At-Tirmidhi.
10. Al-Bazzar.
11. Al-Bukhari.

door.'"[1]

Ash-Shab'i said, "Zayd ibn Thabit prayed in his mother's funeral prayer and then brought his mule near so he could mount it. Ibn 'Abbas came and took hold hold of the stirrup. Zayd said, 'Let go, nephew of the Messenger of Allah!' He said, 'This is the way we act with men of knowledge.' Then Zayd kissed the hand of Ibn 'Abbas. He said, 'This is the way I was commanded to act with the people of the House of the Prophet.'"[2]

Ibn 'Umar saw Muhammad ibn Usama ibn Zayd and said, "Would that he were my slave!" He was told, "That is Muhammad ibn Usama." Ibn 'Umar bowed his head and struck the earth with his hand and said, "If the Messenger of Allah had seen him, he would have loved him."

Al-Awza'i said, "The daughter of Usama ibn Zayd, the Prophet's Companion, went to see 'Umar ibn 'Abdu'l-'Aziz. A *mawla* of hers was with her holding her hand. 'Umar rose for her and walked to her and put her hands in his and then placed his hands on his garment. Then he walked some way with her, sat her in his own place and then sat down in front of her. He did not leave any request she had ungranted."

When 'Umar ibn al-Khattab allotted his son 'Abdullah three thousand and Usama ibn Zayd three thousand five hundred, 'Abdullah said to his father, "Why did you give him more than me? By Allah, he did not get to the battle ahead of me!" He said, "Because Zayd was dearer to the Messenger of Allah than your father, and Usama was dearer to him than you, so I preferred the love of the Messenger of Allah to my love."

Mu'awiya heard that Kabis ibn Rabi'a resembled the Messenger of Allah. When he came to him, he got up from his seat, met him and kissed him between the eyes and gave him al-Mirghab[3] as a fief because of his resemblance to the Messenger of Allah.

It is related that when Ja'far ibn Sulayman[4] flogged Malik ibn Anas and he was carried out unconscious, the people came in to him. He regained consciousness and said, "I testify to you that I have made my flogging a lawful act!" Later he was asked about that and said, "I am afraid of dying and meeting the Prophet with the shame that one of his family entered the Fire because of me."

It is said that the Khalif al-Mansur said that he could take retaliation on Ja'far. Malik said to him, "I seek refuge in Allah! By Allah, every time the whip left my body I made it lawful because of his kinship to the Messenger of Allah."

Abu Bakr ibn 'Ayyash said, "If Abu Bakr, 'Umar and 'Ali had come to me, I

---

1. Even though he was the Khalif, he was ashamed to have someone from the Prophet's family asking for something in public.
2. His mother was al-Nuwwar bint Malik.
3. A very valuable piece of land.
4. Abbasid governor of Madina for the Khalif, Ja'far al-Mansur; he was a descendant of al-'Abbas.

would have begun with what 'Ali needed first. Because of his kinship to the Messenger of Allah, may Allah bless him and grant him peace, I would rather fall from heaven to earth than prefer them to him."

Someone said to Ibn 'Abbas, "So-and-so has died", referring to one of the Prophet's wives. He prostrated and people asked him, "Do you prostrate at this hour?" He replied, "What sign could be greater than the departure of one of the wives of the Prophet?"[1]

Abu Bakr and 'Umar used to visit Umm Ayman, the Prophet's *mawla*. They said, "The Messenger of Allah used to visit her."

When Halima as-Sa'diyya[2] came to the Prophet, he spread out his cloak for her and took care of what she needed. When the Prophet died, she came up to Abu Bakr and 'Umar and they did the same for her.

SECTION 6
Respect for his Companions, devotion to them and recognising what is due to them

Part of respecting and obeying the Prophet, may Allah bless him and grant him peace, consists in respecting his Companions, obeying them, recognising what is due to them, following them, praising them, asking forgiveness for them, refraining from discussing their differences, showing enmity to those who are hostile towards them and shunning the misguidance of the Shi'a and the innovators and the reports of any historians or ignorant transmitters who detract from any of them. If there is something equivocal which is reported about them regarding the trials that took place between them, then adopt the best interpretation and look for the most correct way out of it since that is what they deserve. None of them should be mentioned in a bad manner nor are they to be rebuked for anything. Rather, we mention their good deeds, their virtues and their praiseworthy lives and are silent about anything else.

The Prophet said, "When my Companions are mentioned, hold back."[3]

Allah says, **"Muhammad is the Messenger of Allah, and those who are with him are hard against the unbelievers, merciful to the believers..."** (48:29) and **"The outstrippers, the first of the Muhajirun and the Ansar,"** (9:100) and **"Allah was pleased with the believers when they gave allegiance to you under the tree,"** (48:18) and **"Men who were true to their contract with Allah."** (33:23)

Hudhayfa said that the Messenger of Allah said, "Follow those after me, Abu Bakr and 'Umar."[4]

He said, "My Companions are like stars. Whichever of them you follow, you

---

1. This is a reference to the prayer that is performed during an eclipse of the sun or moon.
2. The Prophet's wet-nurse.
3. At-Tabarani.
4. At-Tirmidhi.

will be guided."[1]

Anas said that the Messenger of Allah said, "The likeness of my Companions is like salt in the food. Food is not good without it."[2]

He said, "Allah! Allah! My Companions! Do not make them targets after me! Whoever loves them loves them by my love. Whoever hates them hates them by my hatred. Whoever harms them harms me. Whoever harms me harms Allah. Whoever harms Allah is about to be seized."[3]

He said, "Do not curse my Companions. If any of you were to spend the weight of Uhud in gold, it still would not reach the measure of one of them or even one-half of it."[4]

He said, "Anyone who curses my Companions has the curse of Allah on him, and of the angels, and of all people. Allah will not accept any exchange or recompense from him."[5]

He said in the *hadith* from Jabir, "Allah chose my Companions over everything else in existence except for the Prophets and the Messengers. He chose four of them for me; Abu Bakr, 'Umar, 'Uthman and 'Ali. He made them my best Companions, and all of my Companions are good."[6]

He said, "Whoever loves 'Umar has loved me. Whoever hates 'Umar hates me."[7]

Malik ibn Anas and others said, "Whoever hates the Companions and curses them does not have any right to Muslim booty. This judgement is taken from the *ayat*, **'Those who come after them, they say, "Our Lord, forgive us and our brothers, who preceded us in belief, and do not put rancour into our hearts against those who believe."'** (59:10) He said, "Whoever is exasperated by the Companions of Muhammad is an unbeliever for Allah has said, **'He enrages the unbelievers through them.'** (48:29)

'Abdullah ibn al-Mubarak said, "There are two qualities which are the cause of salvation for whoever has them: truthfulness and love for the Companions of Muhammad."

Ayyub as-Sakhtiyani said, "Whoever loves Abu Bakr has established the *deen*. Whoever loves 'Umar has made the way clear. Whoever loves 'Uthman has been illuminated by the light of Allah. Whoever loves 'Ali has taken hold of the firm handle. Whoever praises the Companions of Muhammad is free of hypocrisy. Whoever disparages any of them is an innovator opposing the *Sunna* and the right-acting *Salaf*. It is feared that none of his actions will rise to heaven until he loves them all and his heart is sound."

---

1. Al-Bazzar.
2. Al-Bazzar.
3. Ibn Abi Hatim.
4. Muslim.
5. Ad-Daylami and Abu Nu'aym.
6. Al-Bazzar and ad-Daylami.
7. At-Tabarani.

Khalid ibn Sa'id said that the Prophet said, "O people, I am pleased with Abu Bakr, so let that be known! O people, I am pleased with 'Umar, 'Ali, 'Uthman, Talha, az-Zubayr, Sa'd, Sa'id, and 'Abdu'r-Rahman ibn 'Awf,[1] so let that be known! O people, Allah has forgiven the people of Badr and al-Hudaybiyya. O people, protect me in my Companions and my relations by marriage. Do not let any of them have cause to demand restitution from any of you for an injustice against them. A wrongful claim will not be granted tomorrow on the Day of Rising."[4]

A man said to al-Mu'afa ibn 'Imran, "Where is Mu'awiya in relation to 'Umar ibn 'Abdu'l-'Aziz?" He got angry and said, "One does not compare anyone with the Companions of the Prophet, may Allah bless him and grant him peace! Mu'awiya was his companion, his relation by marriage, his scribe, and one who was entrusted with the revelation of Allah!"

The Prophet came to a man's funeral but did not pray over him. He said, "He hated 'Uthman, so Allah hates him."[5]

The Prophet said about the Ansar, "Overlook their faults and give precedence to their good qualities."[6]

He said, "Protect me in my Companions and my relations by marriage. Anyone who protects me in them will be protected by Allah in this world and the Next. Anyone who does not protect me in them will be abandoned by Allah. Anyone abandoned by Allah is about to be seized."[7]

The Prophet said, "Whoever protects me in my Companions, I will be his guardian on the Day of Rising." He said, "Whoever protects me in my Companions will come to me at the Basin. Whoever does not protect me in my Companions will not come to me at the Basin and will only see me from a distance."[8]

Malik ibn Anas said, "This Prophet taught people the *adab* to which Allah had guided him and which made him a mercy for the worlds. He went out in the darkness of the night to al-Baqi',[9] made supplication for the people in the graves and asked forgiveness for them like someone seeing them off on a journey. Allah commanded him to do that and the Prophet commanded people to have love and friendship for them and opposition to anyone who opposes them."

It is related from Ka'b, "There is none of the Companions of Muhammad but that he will have the power of intercession on the Day of Rising." Ka'b was

---

1. These are nine of the ten Companions promised entry to the Garden by the Prophet.
4. At-Tabarani and Ibn Munda. A *mursal hadith*.
5. At-Tirmidhi.
6. Al-Bukhari and Muslim.
7. Abu Nu'aym and ad-Daylami.
8. At-Tabarani.
9. The cemetery of Madina.

asked by al-Mughira ibn Nawfal to intercede for him on the Day of Rising.

Sahl ibn 'Abdullah at-Tustari said, "Anyone who does not respect the Messenger's Companions nor esteem his commands does not believe in him."

SECTION 7
Esteem for the things and places connected with the Prophet

Part of esteem and regard for him is esteem for all the things connected to him and honour for the places in Madina, Makka or elsewhere that the Prophet touched or that are known through him.

It is related that Safiyya bint Najda said, "Abu Madhura had a lock of hair at the front of his head which touched the ground when he sat down. He was asked, 'Why don't you cut it off?' He said, 'I will not cut off something that the Messenger of Allah, may Allah bless him and grant him peace, touched with his hand.'"

Khalid ibn al-Walid had some hairs of the Prophet in his cap. In one of his battles the cap fell off and he fought for it in such a vehement manner that the Companions of the Prophet objected because of the great number of men who were killed on account of it. He said, "I did not do it for the cap itself, but because of the hair of the Prophet, may Allah bless him and grant him peace, that was in it so that I would not be stripped of its blessing and to avoid it falling into the hands of the idolaters."

Ibn 'Umar was seen to place his hand on the seat of the Prophet in the minbar and then place it on his face.

This esteem was the reason why Malik did not ride an animal in Madina. He used to say, "I am too shy before Allah to trample with an animal's hoof on the earth where the Messenger of Allah, may Allah bless him and grant him peace, is buried."

Abu 'Abdu'r-Rahman as-Sulami related that Ahmad ibn Fadluwayh, the ascetic, and a mighty archer and raider, said, "I only touch a bow with my hand when I am in a state of purity since I heard that the Prophet took a bow in his hand."

Malik gave a *fatwa* that someone who had said, "The soil of Madina is bad," should be given thirty lashes and jailed. The man had some standing in the community but Malik said, "His head should be cut off! He claims that the soil in which the Prophet, may Allah bless him and grant him peace, is buried is not good!"

The *Sahih* states that the Prophet said about Madina, "Whoever innovates something in it or gives shelter to anyone who innovates something in it has the curse of Allah, the angels and all people on him. Allah will not accept exchange or recompense from him."

It is related that Jihjah al-Ghifari took the staff of the Prophet from

'Uthman's hand and started to break it across his knee. The people shouted at him. The itch began in his knee which led to it being amputated. He died before the end of the year.[1]

The Prophet said, "Let whoever swears to a lie on my minbar take his seat in the Fire."[2]

It is related that when Abu'l-Fadl al-Jawhari came to Madina to visit and drew near its houses, he dismounted and walked weeping, reciting:

> When we saw the traces left by one who did not bequeath us
> a heart or pure intellect capable of proper recognition of his traces,
> We dismounted from our saddles to walk, out of respect for him, for
> it is clear that riders should dismount for him.

It is related that when a certain visitor looked onto the city of the Messenger of Allah, he began to recite:

> The veil is lifted from us and a moon shines out to those who look on,
> banishing all illusions.
> When our mounts reach Muhammad, it is forbidden for us
> to be found in our saddles.
> We are drawing near to the best man ever to walk on the earth,
> so we hold this ground in respect and honour.

It is related that one of the shaykhs went on *hajj* on foot and was asked why he did that. He said, "The delinquent slave coming to the home of his master mounted! If I had been able to walk on my head, I would not have walked on my feet."

One must respect the places which were the locus of revelation, those which Jibril and Mika'il visited, where the angels and the *Ruh* descended, which heard the sounds of worship and glorification, whose soil contains the body of the Master of Mankind and from which the *deen* of Allah and the *sunna* of the Messenger spread out.

One must respect the places where the *ayats* of the Qur'an were studied, the mosques in which the prayer was done, places that witnessed virtues and good deeds; the places which saw proofs and miracles; the places associated with the rites of the *deen* and the stations of the *hajj* and the stopping places[3] of the Master of the Messengers; the places where the Seal of the Prophets lived and from which prophecy gushed forth and where its waves overflowed; the places which witnessed the message and the first earth that the skin of the Prophet

---

1. The itch is a type of disease which ends up in limbs having to be amputated.
2. Malik, Abu Dawud, an-Nasa'i and Ibn Majah from Abu Hurayra.
3. i.e. 'Arafa and Muzdalifa.

touched after death. Its fragrance should be inhaled and its residences and walls should be kissed.

> O Abode of the best of the Messengers and the one by whom
>> people are guided and who was chosen to receive the *ayats*.
> For you I have intense love, passionate love,
>> and yearning which kindles the embers of my heart.
> I have a vow – if I fill my eyes with those walls
>> and the places where you walked,
> There my beturbanned grey hair will be covered with dust
>> from so much kissing.
> Had it not been for obstacles and foes, I would always visit them,
>> even if I had to be dragged by my feet.
> But I will be guided in my eagerness to greet the inhabitants
>> of those houses and rooms
> By a scent purer than effulgent musk which covers him
>> each morning and evening.
> He is endowed with pure blessings and increased in them
>> through prayers for peace and blessings on him.

Chapter Four

THE PRAYER ON THE PROPHET AND ASKING PEACE FOR HIM AND THE OBLIGATION OF DOING IT AND ITS EXCELLENCE

SECTION 1
The meaning of the prayer on the Prophet

Allah says, **"Allah and His angels pray for blessing on the Prophet."** (33:56)

Ibn 'Abbas said that the meaning of this is that Allah and His angels invoke blessings on the Prophet. It is said that Allah showers mercy on the Prophet and His angels supplicate for him.

Al-Mubarrad said, "The root of the prayer is invoking mercy. It is mercy from Allah, and from the angels it is graciousness and supplication for Allah's mercy."

It is related in the *hadith* describing the prayer of the angels for someone who sits waiting for the prayer that they say "O Allah, forgive him! O Allah, show mercy to him!"[1] This is the supplication they make.

Abu Bakr al-Qushayri said, "The prayer from Allah is mercy for anyone else other than the Prophet and for the Prophet it is distinction and more honour."

Abu'l-'Aliya said, "The prayer of Allah is His praise of the Prophet to the angels. The prayer of the angels is supplication."

The Prophet made a distinction between *salat* (prayer) and *baraka* (blessing) in the *hadith* in which he taught about making the prayer on him. This indicates that they have two separate meanings.

As for the prayer asking for peace on the Prophet which Allah has commanded His servants to do, Qadi Abu Bakr ibn Bukayr said, "This *ayat* was sent down on the Prophet and Allah commanded his Companions to ask for peace on him. Similarly, those after him were commanded to ask for peace on the Prophet when they are present at his grave and when he is mentioned."

There are three possibilities contained by the expression, *As-Salamu 'alaykum* (Peace be upon you):

1) It means safety (*salama*) for you and with you – taking the word *salam* (peace) as a verbal noun.

---

1. Al-Bukhari and Muslim from Abu Hurayra.

2) *As-Salam* means your protection, being guarded and your preservation –
in this case it is *As-Salam* as the name of Allah.

3) *As-Salam* in the meaning of *musalama* (reconciliation) and submission to
him as in the words of Allah, **"No, by your Lord, they are not believers until
they make you their judge in the disputes that break out between them, and
then find no resistance within themselves to what you decide and submit
themselves completely."** (4:65)

SECTION 2
The judgement concerning the Prayer on the Prophet

Know that, since Allah has commanded that he be blessed, the prayer on the
Prophet is a general obligation not restricted to a specific time. The Imams and
the *'ulama'* are in agreement on its obligatory nature. Abu Ja'far at-Tabari,
however, said that he thought this *ayat* only gives it the level of being *mandub*
(recommended), claiming a consensus for that. This may refer to doing it more
than once.

The obligation involved in it, the performance of which eliminates the
wrong action which would be incurred by not doing it, is to do it at least once
– as in the case of bearing witness to his prophethood. Doing it more than that
is desirable and recommended in the *sunna* of Islam.

Qadi Abu'l-Hasan ibn al-Qassar said that his companions maintained that
there is a general obligation to do it once in a lifetime while one is capable of it.

Qadi Abu Bakr ibn Bukayr said, "Allah obliges His creation to pray on His
Prophet and ask for peace on him, and he did not assign that to a specific time.
Man's obligation is to do it often and not neglect it."

Qadi Abu Muhammad ibn Nasr said, "The prayer on the Prophet is a
general obligation."

Qadi Abu 'Abdullah Muhammad ibn Sa'id said, "The position of Malik, his
companions and other people of knowledge is that the prayer on the Prophet is
a general obligation conditional on belief. It is not specific to the obligatory
prayer. Whoever blesses him once in his life has removed the obligation."

The followers of Imam ash-Shafi'i say that the obligation which Allah and
His Messenger commanded applies to the obligatory prayer. In other instances,
there is no disagreement that it is not obligatory.

The two Imams, Abu Ja'far at-Tabari and at-Tahawi, and others relate the
consensus of all the early and later *'ulama'* of the community that the prayer on
the Prophet in the *tashahhud* is not obligatory. Ash-Shafi'i is the exception,
saying that any prayer lacking the prayer on the Prophet after the last *tashahhud*
before the *salam* is invalid and also that it is not permissible to say it before this.

He had no precedent for this statement nor any observed *sunna*. He went to excess in making this statement since he opposed others before him and people like at-Tabari and al-Qushayri have censored him for that.

Abu Bakr ibn al-Mundhir said, "It is recommended that no-one pray without blessing the Messenger of Allah. However if the prayer on the Prophet, may Allah bless him and grant him peace, is omitted, then the prayer is still valid according to the school of Malik, the people of Madina, Sufyan ath-Thawri and the people of Kufa and others."

Malik and Sufyan relate that it is recommended to say it in the last *tashahhud* and that it is disliked to omit it from the final *tashahhud*. Ash-Shafi'i is the one exception, saying that if it is omitted from the prayer, the prayer must be repeated.

Ishaq ibn Ibrahim says that the prayer should be repeated if it is omitted intentionally, but not if it is due to forgetfulness.

Abu Muhammad ibn Abi Zayd related from Muhammad al-Mawwaz that the prayer on the Prophet is a duty. Abu Muhammad Yazid said, "He means that it is not one of the obligations of the prayer (but a general obligation)."

Muhammad ibn 'Abdu'l-Hakam and others, Ibn al-Qassar and 'Abdu'l-Wahhab related that Muhammad al-Mawwaz thought it was an obligation in the prayer like ash-Shafi'i.

Abu Ya'la al-'Abdi al-Maliki related that Malik's school has three opinions about it: that it is obligatory, *sunna* and recommended.

Al-Khattabi and other Shafi'ites disagreed with ash-Shafi'i. Al-Khattabi said, "It is not obligatory in the prayer. That is the statement of the *fuqaha'* with the exception of ash-Shafi'i and I do not know his precedent for it."

The proof that it is not one of the obligations of the prayer is in what the *Salaf* before ash-Shafi'i did and their agreement about it. People have criticised him for saying what he did. Ash-Shafi'i chose the *tashahhud* which the Prophet taught Ibn Mas'ud and which does not contain the prayer on the Prophet.

Similarly with Abu Hurayra, Ibn 'Abbas, Jabir, Ibn 'Umar, Abu Sa'id al-Khudri, Abu Musa al-Ash'ari and 'Abdullah ibn az-Zubayr who relate the *tashahhud* from the Prophet. They do not mention the Prophet.

Ibn 'Abbas and Jabir said, "The Prophet taught us the *tashahhud* in the same way as he taught us a *sura* of the Qur'an." Ibn 'Umar said, "Abu Bakr used to teach us the *tashahhud* on the *minbar* as children are taught at school." 'Umar ibn al-Khattab also taught it on the *minbar*.

There is a *hadith* which says, "There is no prayer for someone who does not pray on me." Ibn al-Qassar said that this means that the prayer is not complete without it or alternatively it refers to someone who has not prayed on him once in his entire lifetime. The people of *hadith* all consider the transmission of this *hadith* to be weak.

Abu Ja'far related from Ibn Mas'ud that the Prophet said, "Whoever does the prayer and does not bless me and the People of my House in it will not have his prayer accepted."

Ad-Daraqutni said, "The correct version is what Abu Ja'far Muhammad ibn al-Husayn said which is, 'If I were to offer a prayer in which I did not bless the Prophet, may Allah bless him and grant him peace, or the people of his house, I would think that it was incomplete.'"

SECTION 3
On the situations in which it is recommended to say the Prayer on the Prophet

We have already stated that it is desirable to say the prayer on the Prophet in the *tashahhud* before the supplication.

Fadala ibn 'Ubayd said that the Prophet heard a man making supplication in his prayer without blessing the Prophet. The Prophet said, "This is hasty." Then he called him and told him and the others, "When one of you prays, he should begin with praise of Allah and then pray on the Prophet and then make whatever supplication he wishes."

'Umar ibn al-Khattab stated, "Supplication and prayer are suspended between the heaven and the earth and none of it rises to Allah until you pray on the Prophet." 'Ali related something similar and added, "and on the family of Muhammad." It is related that supplication is veiled until the one making the supplication prays on the Prophet.

Ibn Mas'ud said, "When one of you wants to ask Allah for something, he should begin by praising and extolling Him as He deserves and then bless the Prophet. Then his supplication is more likely to be successful."

Jabir said that the Messenger of Allah said, "Do not make me like a rider's jug. The rider fills his jug, then puts it down and hoists up his baggage. If he needs to drink, he drinks, or if he needs to do *wudu'* he does so. If not, he pours it away. Rather put me at the beginning of the supplication, the middle and the end."[1]

Ibn 'Ata' said, "Supplication has pillars, wings, means and moments. If its pillars are acceptable, it is strong. If its wings are acceptable, it flies. If its moments are acceptable, it has success. If its means are acceptable, it wins. Its pillars are presence of the heart, compassion, humility, humbleness and the heart being suspended before Allah and cut off from reliance on means. Its wings are truthfulness and sincerity. Its moments are before dawn. Its means are the prayer on the Prophet, may Allah bless him and grant him peace."

The *hadith* says, "The supplication between the two prayers is not rejected."

Another *hadith* says, "Every supplication is veiled below heaven and when

---

1. Al-Bazzar, Abu Ya'la and al-Bayhaqi.

the prayer on me is made, then it ascends."[1]

At the end of Ibn 'Abbas' supplication which Hanash related from him, he said, "Hear my supplication! Begin with the prayer on the Prophet, may Allah bless him and grant him peace and say, "O Allah, I ask you to bless Muhammad, Your slave and Prophet and Messenger with the best of what You blessed any of Your creatures. Amen."

Among the situations when it is good to pray on the Prophet, may Allah bless him and grant him peace, are when he is mentioned, when his name is heard or written, and during the *adhan*.

The Prophet said, "Dust be upon the face of the man who does not bless me when I am mentioned in his presence."[2]

Ibn Habib disliked mentioning the Prophet when sacrificing animals. Sahnun disliked anyone saying the prayer on the Prophet when amazed and said, "The prayer on him should only be done with consideration and seeking its reward."

Asbagh related that al-Qasim said, "The two situations when only Allah is mentioned are during the sacrifice and when you sneeze. You do not say, 'Muhammad is the Messenger of Allah' after mentioning Allah. If you say, after mentioning Allah, 'May Allah bless Muhammad', it is not the same as naming him along with Allah." Ashhab said, "The prayer on the Prophet should not be made a *sunna* in it."

An-Nasa'i related from Aws ibn Aws from the Prophet the command to do much prayer on him on Friday.

One of the situations for the prayer on him is when entering a mosque. Abu Ishaq ibn Sha'ban said, "Anyone who enters the mosque should bless the Prophet and his family and ask for abundant mercy and blessings and peace on him and his family. He should say, 'O Allah, forgive me my wrong actions and open for me the doors of Your mercy.' When he leaves, he should do the same but say 'bounty' instead of 'mercy'."

'Amr ibn Dinar, speaking about the words of Allah, **"When you enter houses, then greet each other,"** (24:61) said, "If there is no-one in the house, then you say, 'Peace be upon the Prophet and the mercy of Allah and His blessing. Peace be upon us and upon the right-acting slaves of Allah. Peace be upon the people of the House and the mercy of Allah and His blessings.'" Ibn 'Abbas said that what was meant by "houses" in this instance were mosques.

An-Nakh'i said, "When there is no-one in the mosque, say 'Peace be upon the Messenger of Allah.' When there is no-one in the house, say, 'Peace be upon the people of the house, the mercy of Allah and His blessings.'"

'Alqama said, "When I enter the mosque, I say, 'Peace be upon you, O

1. At-Tirmidhi from 'Umar.
2. Muslim from Abu Hurayra.

Prophet, and the mercy of Allah and His blessings. May Allah and His angels pray on Muhammad.'" Ka'b said something similar when he entered and left but he did not include the second half.

Ibn Sha'ban used the *hadith* of Fatima, daughter of the Messenger of Allah, as a proof: "The Prophet, may Allah bless him and grant him peace, used to say it when he entered the mosque." Something similar is related by Abu Bakr ibn 'Amr ibn Hazm. He mentioned asking for peace and mercy on the Prophet with a slightly different wording.[1]

The funeral prayer is another situation in which the prayer on the Prophet is said. Abu Umama al-Ansari said that doing so is part of the *Sunna*.

One of the situations in which the community says the prayer on the Prophet and his family, and there is no objection to it, is when writing letters, after the *basmala*. This was not done in early times, but began during the government of the Banu Hashim[2] and people continued to use it in various places. Some people finish letters with it.

The Prophet said, "Whoever blesses me in a book or a letter, the angels continue to ask forgiveness for him as long as my name is on it."[3]

You should ask for peace on the Prophet in the *tashahhud* of the prayer. 'Abdullah ibn Mas'ud said that the Prophet said, "When one of you prays, let him say, 'Greetings, prayers and good things belong to Allah. Peace be upon you, O Prophet! And the mercy of Allah and His blessings.' If you say that, it will reach every right-acting slave in the heaven and the earth."[4]

This is one of the situations in which to ask for peace on him. It is *Sunna* to do it at the beginning of the *tashahhud*, although Malik said that Ibn 'Umar used to say it when he finished the *tashahhud*. In *al-Mabsut*, Malik recommended that it be said like that with the final *salam*.

Muhammad ibn Maslama said, "He meant that 'A'isha and Ibn 'Umar used to say in their *salam*, 'Peace be upon you, O Prophet, and the mercy of Allah and His blessing, and peace be upon us and the right-acting slaves of Allah. Peace be upon you.'"

The people of knowledge recommend that in his *salam* a man should intend to greet every right-acting slave in the heaven and the earth among the angels, the children of Adam and the *jinn*.

Malik said in his Collection, "It is preferred for someone following the Imam that when the Imam says the *Salam* he would say, 'Peace be upon the Prophet and the mercy of Allah and His blessings. Peace be upon us and upon the right-acting slaves of Allah. Peace be upon you.'"

---

1. As in at-Tirmidhi.
2. The 'Abbasids.
3. At-Tabarani.
4. All of the Six Books relate this.

SECTION 4
Concerning the manner of doing the prayer on the Prophet and asking for peace on him

Abu Humayd as-Sa'idi said that they said, "Messenger of Allah, how should we pray on you?" He replied, "Say, 'O Allah, bless Muhammad and his wives and his descendants as You blessed the family of Ibrahim and grant blessing to Muhammad and his wives and descendants as You granted blessing to the family of Ibrahim. You are Praiseworthy, Glorious.'"

In Malik's version from Abu Mas'ud al-Ansari, the Prophet said, "Say, 'O Allah, bless Muhammad and his family as You blessed the family of Ibrahim and grant blessing to Muhammad and the family of Muhammad as You granted blessings to the family of Ibrahim in the worlds. You are Praiseworthy, Glorious.'"

Ka'b ibn 'Ujra said that it was, "O Allah, bless Muhammad and the family of Muhammad as You blessed Ibrahim and give blessing to Muhammad and the family of Muhammad as You gave blessing to Ibrahim. You are Praiseworthy, Glorious."

'Uqba ibn 'Amr said, "O Allah, bless Muhammad, the unlettered Prophet and the family of Muhammad."

Abu Sa'id al-Khudri said that it was, "O Allah, bless Muhammad, Your slave and Your Messenger."

'Ali ibn Abi Talib said, "The Messenger of Allah counted them out on my hand, saying that Jibril had counted the prayers on his hand, saying, "This is how it was sent down from the Lord of Might." It is: O Allah, bless Muhammad and the family of Muhammad as You blessed Ibrahim and the family of Ibrahim. You are Praiseworthy, Glorious. O Allah, grant blessing to Muhammad and the family of Muhammad as You granted blessing to Ibrahim and the family of Ibrahim. You are Praiseworthy, Glorious. O Allah, show mercy to Muhammad and the family of Muhammad as You showed mercy to Ibrahim and the family of Ibrahim. You are Praiseworthy, Glorious. O Allah, show compassion to Muhammad and the family of Muhammad as You showed compassion to Ibrahim and the family of Ibrahim. You are Praiseworthy, Glorious. O Allah, grant peace to Muhammad and the family of Muhammad as You granted peace to Ibrahim and the family of Ibrahim. You are Praiseworthy, Glorious."

Abu Hurayra said that the Prophet said, "Whoever wishes to be given the fullest measure when he prays on us, the People of the House, should say, 'O Allah, bless Muhammad, the Prophet, his wives, the mothers of the believers, his descendants and the People of his House as You blessed the family of

Ibrahim. You are Praiseworthy, Glorious.'"[1]

Zayd ibn Kharija al-Ansari said, "I asked the Prophet how we should bless him and he said, 'Pray and strive in the supplication and say, "O Allah, bless Muhammad and the family of Muhammad as You blessed Ibrahim. You are Praiseworthy, Glorious."'"[2]

Salama al-Kindi said, 'Ali used to teach us the prayer on the Prophet as follows: "O Allah, the One Who spread out the flat expanses and created the heavens! Bestow Your noble prayers, Your increasing blessing and the compassion of Your tenderness upon Muhammad, Your slave and Your Messenger, the Opener of what was closed, the Seal of what came before, the one who announces the truth by the truth, the one who triumphs over the armies of falsehood as he was charged to do. He took upon himself Your command to obey You with alacrity to gain Your pleasure. He retains within him Your revelation, preserves Your guidance and carries out Your command so that people can receive Allah's blessings, kindling a brand which they can bring to their families, because of him. Hearts were guided by him after they had plunged into trials and wrong actions. He illuminated the clear signs, luminous rules and waymarks of Islam. He is Your trusty guardian, the treasurer of Your hidden knowledge, Your witness on the Day of Rising, the one You sent with Your blessings and Your Messenger by the truth as a mercy. O Allah, give him ample space in Your Eden and reward him with good multiplied many times over from Your overflowing favour, given to him without any trouble through the victory of gaining Your reward and generous gift.

"O Allah, put what he builds above what other people build and let him have a noble place of rest and hospitality. Complete his light for him and repay him from Your followers by accepted testimony and pleasing words with just words, decisive action and immense proof."

'Ali also said about the prayer on the Prophet in the *ayat*, **"Allah and His angels pray on the Prophet,"** (33:56) "At Your service and obedience, my Lord. The prayers of Allah, the Good and Merciful, the near angels, the true ones, the martyrs, the *salihun*, and anything that glorifies You, O Lord of the worlds, be upon Muhammad ibn 'Abdullah, the Seal of the Prophets, the Master of the Messengers and the Imam of the God-fearing and the Messenger of the Lord of the worlds, the witness, the bearer of good news, the one who calls people to You by Your permission, the light-giving lamp, and peace be upon him."

'Abdullah ibn Mas'ud said, "O Allah, bestow Your blessings and Your mercy on the Master of the Messengers and the Imam of the God-fearing and the Seal of the Prophets, Muhammad, Your slave and Messenger, the Imam of the Good and the Messenger of Mercy. O Allah, raise him to a praiseworthy

---

1. Abu Dawud and at-Tabarani.
2. Ad-Daylami, Abu Nu'aym, an-Nasa'i, at-Tahawi and al-Baghawi.

station which the first and the last envy. O Allah, bless Muhammad and the family of Muhammad as You blessed Ibrahim. You are Praiseworthy, Glorious. Grant blessings to Muhammad and the family of Muhammad as You granted blessing to Ibrahim and the family of Ibrahim. You are Praiseworthy, Glorious."

Al-Hasan al-Basri said, "Whoever wants to drink the fullest cup from the Basin of the Chosen-one should say, 'O Allah, bless Muhammad and the family of Muhammad and his Companions and his sons and wives and descendants and the people of his house and his relations by marriage and his *Ansar* and his Followers and those who love him and bless us along with all of them, O Most Merciful of the merciful!'"

Ibn 'Abbas used to say, "O Allah, accept the greatest intercession of Muhammad and raise him to the highest degree and grant his every request in the Next World and this as You gave that to Ibrahim and Musa."

Wuhayb ibn al-Ward used to say, "O Allah, give Muhammad the best of what he asked You for himself and give Muhammad the best of what any of Your creatures has asked You for and give Muhammad the best of all that You are asked for until the Day of Rising."

Ibn Mas'ud used to say, "When you bless the Prophet, then make the prayer on him excellent. You do not know; perhaps it will be shown to him. Say, 'O Allah, bestow Your prayers, Your mercy and Your blessing on the Master of the Messengers, the Imam of the God-fearing, the Leader of the Good and the Messenger of Mercy.'"

There are a lot of long prayers and praise of the "People of the House" which have been transmitted.

"The 'peace' as you have been taught" that Ibn Mas'ud mentioned is what he taught in the *tashahhud* when he said, "Peace be upon you, O Prophet, and the mercy of Allah and His blessing. Peace be upon us and the right-acting slaves of Allah."

In 'Ali's *tashahhud* we find, "Peace be upon the Prophet. Peace be upon the Prophets of Allah and His Messengers. Peace be upon the Messenger of Allah. Peace be upon Muhammad ibn 'Abdullah. Peace be upon us and upon the believers, men and women, those who are absent and those who are present. O Allah, forgive Muhammad and accept his intercession and forgive the People of his House and forgive me and my parents and their progeny and have mercy on them. Peace be upon us and upon the right-acting slaves of Allah. Peace be upon you, O Prophet and the mercy of Allah and His blessing."

'Ali said that supplication for the Prophet, may Allah bless him and grant him peace, is to ask for forgiveness for him. In the *hadith* about the prayer on him, also from 'Ali, is that supplication is for mercy on him. This has not come in any other known direct *hadith*.

Abu 'Umar ibn 'Abdu'l-Barr and others believed that you should not ask for mercy for the Prophet, only the prayer and blessing which are specific to him. You can ask for mercy and forgiveness for others.

Abu Muhammad ibn Abi Zayd mentioned in the prayer on the Prophet, "O Allah, show mercy to Muhammad and the family of Muhammad as You showed mercy to Ibrahim and the family of Ibrahim." This did not come in a sound *hadith*. The proof given for it is his words in the *salam*, "Peace be upon you, O Prophet, the mercy of Allah and His blessings."

SECTION 5
On the excellence of the prayer on the Prophet, asking for peace for him and supplication for him

'Abdullah ibn 'Amr said that the Messenger of Allah said, "If you hear the *mu'adhdhan*, then say what he says and bless me. Whoever blesses me once, Allah blesses him ten times. Then ask for the *wasila* for me. It is a station in the Garden which is only for one of the slaves of Allah and I hope that it will be me. Whoever asks for the *wasila*[1] for me has intercession descend on him."[2]

Anas ibn Malik related that the Prophet said, "Whoever blesses me once, Allah blesses him with ten prayers and ten wrong actions fall away from him and he is raised by ten degrees."[3] One variant adds, "and ten good actions are written for him."

Anas said that the Prophet said, "Jibril called me and said, 'Whoever prays one prayer on you, Allah prays on him ten times and raises him up by ten degrees.'"[4] In the variant of 'Abdu'r-Rahman ibn 'Awf we find, "I met Jibril who said, 'I give you the good news that Allah has said that whoever asks for peace for you, He asks for peace for him. Whoever blesses you, He blesses him.'"[5] There are similar transmissions from Abu Hurayra, Malik ibn Aws ibn al-Hadathan and 'Ubaydullah ibn Abi Talha.

Zayd ibn al-Hubab said that he heard the Prophet say, "Whoever says, 'O Allah, bless Muhammad and place him near to You on the Day of Rising,' will definitely have my intercession." Ibn Mas'ud said from the Prophet, "The nearest people to me on the Day of Rising will be those who have said the most prayers on me."[6]

Abu Hurayra said from the Prophet, "Whoever blesses me in a letter or a book, the angels continue to ask forgiveness for him as long as my name remains on that page."[7]

---

1. See section dealing with the *wasila*, p.119.
2. An-Nasa'i.
3. Al-Bayhaqi.
4. Ibn Abi Shayba.
5. Al-Hakim and al-Bayhaqi.
6. At-Tirmidhi.
7. At-Tabarani.

'Amir ibn Rabi'a said that he heard the Prophet say, "The angels will continue to bless anyone who blesses me, as long as he continues to do so, so do a lot or even a little."[1]

Ubayy ibn Ka'b said, "Once, when the first quarter of the night had gone, the Messenger of Allah got up and said, 'O people, remember Allah! The quake has come which will be followed by its sequel. Death will come with all that accompanies it.'" Ubayy asked, "Messenger of Allah, I do a lot of the prayer on you, so how much of my prayer should I devote to you?" He said, "Whatever you like." Ubayy asked, "A quarter?" and was told "Whatever you like, and if you do more it is better." He asked, "A third?" He replied, "Whatever you like, and if you do more it is better." He asked, "A half?" He replied, "Whatever you like, and if you do more it is better." he asked, "Two-thirds?" He replied, "Whatever you like, and if you do more it is better." He said, "Messenger of Allah, I will devote all my prayer to you." He said, "Then you will have enough and your wrong actions will be forgiven."[2]

Abu Talha said that he saw the Prophet more joyful than he had ever seen him before. He asked him about this and he said, "Why not, indeed, when Jibril has just left after bringing me the good news from my Lord that He has sent him to me to give me the good news that when any of my community blesses me, Allah and His angels bless them ten times for doing so?"[3]

Jabir ibn 'Abdullah said that the Prophet said, "When someone hears the call to prayer and says, 'O Allah, Lord of this perfect call and the established prayer, give Muhammad the *wasila* and excellence, and raise him up to the Praiseworthy Station which You promised him,' he will have my intercession on the Day of Rising."[4]

Sa'd ibn Abi Waqqas said, "When someone hears the *adhan* and says, 'I testify that there is no god but Allah alone with no partner and that Muhammad is His slave and Messenger, I am pleased with Allah as Lord and Muhammad as Messenger and Islam as *deen*,' he will be forgiven."[5]

Ibn Wahb related that the Prophet said, "Whoever asks for peace on me ten times, it is as if he had freed a slave."

One tradition has, "People will come to me that I only recognise by the abundance of their prayer on me."

In another *hadith* we find that the Prophet said, "The first among you to be saved from the terrors of the Day of Rising and its places will be the one who did the most prayers on me."

Abu Bakr as-Siddiq said that the prayer on the Prophet wipes out wrong

---

1. Ibn Hanbal, Ibn Majah and at-Tabarani.
2. At-Tirmidhi.
3. An-Nasa'i, Ibn Hibban and al-Bayhaqi.
4. Al-Bukhari.
5. Muslim.

actions as cold water puts out fire. Asking for peace for the Prophet is better than setting slaves free.

SECTION 6
Censure of those who do not bless the Prophet and their wrong action

Abu Hurayra said that the Messenger of Allah said, "Dust upon the face of the man who does not bless me when I am mentioned in his presence! Dust upon the face of the man who has Ramadan stripped away before he is forgiven! Dust upon the face of the man whose parents reach old age and they are not the cause of him entering the Garden!"[1]

The Prophet climbed the *minbar* and said, "Amen." Then he climbed it again and said, "Amen." Then he did it a third time. Mu'adh questioned him about this and the Prophet said, "Jibril came and said to me, 'Muhammad, whenever you are mentioned by name in front of a person and he does not bless you and then subsequently dies, he will enter the Fire. Allah will put him far away. Say "Amen."' So I said, 'Amen.' He said, 'When Ramadan comes and it is not accepted from him and he dies, it is the same. If someone has two parents – or one of them – and does not show devotion and goodness to them and then dies, it is the same.'"[2]

'Ali ibn Abi Talib said that the Prophet said, "A miser is someone who does not bless me when I am mentioned in his presence."[3]

Ja'far ibn Muhammad said that the Messenger of Allah said, "When I am mentioned in the presence of someone and he does not bless me, the path to the Garden has passed him by."[4]

Abu Hurayra said that the Prophet said, "Whenever people sit in a gathering and part without mentioning Allah and blessing the Prophet, there is confusion about what will come to them from Allah. If He wills, He will punish them. If He wills, He will forgive them."[5]

Abu Hurayra said from the Prophet, "Whoever forgets to pray on me, forgets the path to the Garden."[6]

Qatada said that the Prophet said, "Part of coarseness is for me to be mentioned in the presence of a man without him blessing me."

Jabir said that the Prophet said, "A people do not sit in a gathering and then part without saying the prayer on the Prophet but that they part on something

1. At-Tirmidhi from 'Abdu'r-Rahman or Abu Hurayra.
2. Al-Hakim.
3. At-Tirmidhi, al-Bayhaqi and an-Nasa'i.
4. Al-Bayhaqi and at-Tabarani.
5. Abu Dawud and at-Tirmidhi.
6. Al-Bayhaqi.

fouler than the smell of a corpse."[1]

Abu Sa'id said that the Prophet said, "No people sit in a gathering in which they do not bless the Prophet without grief coming upon them. When they enter the Garden, they will not see some of its reward."[2]

Abu 'Isa at-Tirmidhi related that one of the people of knowledge said, "When a man blesses the Prophet, may Allah bless him and grant him peace, once in an assembly, he is rewarded for whatever takes place in that assembly."

SECTION 7
On the Prophet's being singled out by having the Prayer on him revealed to him

Abu Hurayra said that the Messenger of Allah said, "Whenever anyone greets me with peace, Allah will return my soul to me so that I can return the greeting."[3]

Abu Bakr ibn Abi Shayba mentions that Abu Hurayra said that the Messenger of Allah said, "I will hear whoever blesses me at my grave. If someone is far away and blesses me, that is also conveyed to me."[4]

Ibn Mas'ud quotes the Prophet as saying that Allah has angels that travel round the earth to convey to him peace from his community.[5] There is a similar statement from Abu Hurayra.

Ibn 'Umar said, "Do a lot of prayer on your Prophet every *Jumu'a*. It is brought to him from you every *Jumu'a*." One version has, "None of you blesses me but that his prayer is shown to me when he finishes it."

Al-Hasan ibn 'Ali said that the Prophet said, "Bless me wherever you are. Your prayer will reach me."[6]

Ibn 'Abbas said, "There is none of the community of Muhammad who blesses him but that it reaches him."

One of them mentioned that the name of someone who blesses the Prophet is shown to the Prophet when he does it.

Al-Hasan ibn 'Ali said, "When you enter the mosque, greet the Prophet. The Messenger of Allah said, 'Do not make my house a place of 'Id and do not make your houses graves. Bless me wherever you are. Your prayer will reach me wherever you are.'"[7]

---

1. Al-Bayhaqi, at-Tayalasi and an-Nasa'i.
2. Al-Bayhaqi.
3. Ibn Hanbal, Abu Dawud and al-Bayhaqi.
4. Al-Bayhaqi.
5. Ibn Hanbal, an-Nasa'i, Ibn Hibban, al-Hakim and al-Bayhaqi.
6. Ibn Abi Shayba and at-Tabarani.
7. At-Tabarani.

Aws said that the Prophet said, "Do a lot of prayer on me at *Jumu'a*. Your prayer is shown to me."[1]

Sulayman ibn Suhaym said that he saw the Prophet in a dream and asked him, "Messenger of Allah, do you recognise the greeting of those who come to you?" He replied, "Yes, and I answer them."

Ibn Shihab said, "We heard that the Messenger of Allah said, 'Do a lot of prayer on me in the radiant night and the radiant day. It will be conveyed from you. The earth does not consume the bodies of the Prophets. There is no Muslim who blesses me but that an angel conveys it to me and names him.'"

SECTION 8
The dispute about the prayer on other than the Prophet and the other Prophets

The generality of the people of knowledge agree that it is permitted to bless people other than the Prophet.

It is related that Ibn 'Abbas said that it is not permitted to bless people other than the Prophet and that the prayer is only for the Prophets.

Sufyan ath-Thawri said that it is disliked to bless anyone except a Prophet.

I found that one of my shaykhs had written, "Malik's *madh-hab* is that it is not permitted to bless any of the Prophets except Muhammad." However, this is not known to be part of the *madh-hab*.

In *al-Mabsut*, Malik said to Yahya ibn Ishaq, "I dislike people to pray on anyone besides the Prophets. We should not exceed what we have been commanded to do."

Yahya ibn Yahya al-Laythi said, "I do not accept this statement. There is no harm in the prayer on all the Prophets or other people." For proof, he uses the *hadith* of Ibn 'Umar and the *hadith* where the Prophet taught the prayer on himself and said, "And on his wives and family." I have come across an appendix to Abu 'Imran al-Fasi in which he relates from Ibn 'Abbas the dislike of saying the prayer on anyone other than the Prophet, may Allah bless him and grant him peace. Ibn 'Abbas said, "That is what we say." It was not used previously.

'Abdu'r-Razzaq[2] related that Abu Hurayra said that the Messenger of Allah said, "Bless the Prophets of Allah and His Messengers. Allah will convey it to them as He conveys it to me."

In Arabic, "Prayer" (*salat*) means supplication and asking for mercy in general, unless a sound *hadith* or a consensus opinion restricts the meaning.

Allah says, **"He is the one who prays for blessing for you, and the angels,"**

---

1. Abu Dawud, at-Tirmidhi, an-Nasa'i and Ibn Majah.
2. A famous *hadith* scholar.

(33:43) and **"Take sadaqa from their property to purify them and cleanse them by it and pray for them,"** (9:103) and **"Those have the blessings of their Lord upon them and mercy."** (2:157)

The Prophet said, "O Allah, bless the family of Abu Wafa!"[1] When people brought their *zakat*, he said, "O Allah, bless the family of so-and-so."[2]

In the *hadith* on the prayer we find, "O Allah, bless Muhammad, his wives and descendants," another variant has, "and the family of Muhammad." It is said that this means his followers, or his community, or the People of his House. It is said that it means followers, group or tribe, or a man's children, or his people (*ahl*). It is also said that it means his family, those for whom *sadaqa* is *haram*.

Anas said, "The Prophet was asked, 'Who are the family of Muhammad?' He replied, 'Every god-fearing person.'"[3]

In the school of al-Hasan al-Basri, Muhammad himself is meant by the family of Muhammad. He used to say in his prayer on the Prophet, "O Allah, bestow Your prayers and Your blessings on the family of Muhammad," meaning himself because he did not omit the obligation which Allah had commanded. This is like when he said, "I was given one of the flutes of the family of Da'ud," i.e. one of Da'ud's flutes.[4]

In the prayer, Abu Humayd as-Sa'idi said, "O Allah, bless Muhammad, his wives and descendants."

Ibn 'Umar said that he blessed the Prophet, Abu Bakr and 'Umar. Malik mentioned this in the *Muwatta'* via Yahya al-Andalusi. The sound version is that he made supplication for Abu Bakr and 'Umar.

Ibn Wahb related that Anas ibn Malik said, "We used to supplicate for our companions in the Unseen. We would say, 'O Allah, bestow the prayers of a good person who prays at night and fasts in the day on so-and-so.'" Malik and Sufyan take the same position.

It is related that Ibn 'Abbas did not pray on anyone except the Prophets when they were mentioned since it is a mark of special esteem and respect for the Prophets, just as when Allah is mentioned, He alone has disconnection, absolute purity and exaltation unique to Him. Similarly, we know it is necessary to single out the Prophet, and all the Prophets, for the prayer and asking for peace, which is for them alone, from the command of Allah, **"Bless him and grant him peace abundantly."** (33:56)

He mentioned other people in terms of forgiveness and pleasure. Allah says, **"Say: Our Lord, forgive us and our brothers who preceded us in belief,"**

---

1. 'Alqama ibn Khalid al-Aslami.
2. Muslim and al-Bukhari.
3. At-Tabarani and ad-Daylami.
4. Al-Bukhari and Muslim.

(59:10) and **"Those who followed them with good-doing. Allah will be pleased with them."** (9:100)

Praying for peace[1] on people other than the Prophets is something which was not known in the early period as Abu 'Imran said. It was started by the Rafidites[2] and other partisans in respect of some of their Imams. They made them partners in the prayer and put them on a par with the Prophet. It is forbidden to be like such people of innovation whose claims must be opposed. The prayer on the family and wives of the Prophet is based on the principle of succession and relationship to him, not on any special quality.

The people of knowledge have said that the Prophet's prayer for someone was either supplication or as a greeting when he met someone and it does not imply esteem and respect.

They say, and Allah says, **"Do not make the calling (*du'a*) of the Messenger of Allah like your calling each other."** (24:63) Therefore it is necessary that supplication (*du'a*) for him be different than the supplication of other people for each other.

SECTION 9
Concerning the visit to the Prophet's grave, the excellence of those who visit it and how he should be greeted

Visiting his grave is part of the *Sunna* and is both excellent and desirable. Ibn 'Umar said that the Prophet said, "My intercession is assured for all who visit me."[3]

Anas ibn Malik said that the Messenger of Allah said, "Anyone who visits me in Madina for the sake of Allah is near me and I will intercede for him on the Day of Rising."[4]

He said, "Whoever visits me after my death, it is as if he visited me while I was alive."[5]

Malik disliked people saying, "We visited the grave of the Prophet, may Allah bless him and grant him peace." People have disagreed about the meaning of this statement. It is said that he disliked it because of the Prophet's saying, "Allah curses women who visit graves."[6] People relate that the Prophet then said, "I forbade you to visit the graves, but now you can visit them."[7]

---

1. i.e. saying "'*alayhi's-salam*" when he is mentioned.
2. The extreme Shi'ites who rejected 'Ali Zayn al-'Abidin when he refused to reject Abu Bakr and 'Umar.
3. Ibn Khuzayma, al-Bazzar and at-Tabarani.
4. Al-Bayhaqi and others.
5. Al-Bayhaqi.
6. Ibn Hanbal, at-Tirmidhi and Ibn Hibban from Abu Hurayra.
7. Muslim from Burayda.

The Prophet said, "Anyone who visits my grave..." and used the word "visit". It is said that this is because the visitor is considered to be better than the one visited. This has no foundation since not every visitor has this quality and so it is not a universal principle. The *hadith* concerning the People of the Garden talks about their "visit" to their Lord, so it is not forbidden to use this expression in respect of Allah.

Abu 'Imran al-Fasi said, "Malik disliked anyone saying, 'the *tawaf* of the visit', or, 'we visited the grave of the Prophet', because people normally use that for visits between themselves, and he did not like to put the Prophet on the same level as other people. He preferred a specific statement like 'We greeted the Prophet, may Allah bless him and grant him peace.'"

Moreover, it is merely recommended for people to visit each other whereas there is a strong obligation to visit the grave of the Prophet. "Obligation" here means the recommendation and encouragement to do that, not the obligation which is a legal duty.

I think the best interpretation is that Malik forbade and disliked the practice of connecting the word "grave" with the Prophet. He did not dislike people saying, "We visited the Prophet, may Allah bless him and grant him peace." This is because of the Prophet's statement, "O Allah, do not make my grave an idol to be worshipped after me. Allah was very angry with people who took the graves of their prophets as mosques." So he omitted the word "grave" in order to cut off the means and close the door to this wrong action. Allah knows best.

Ishaq ibn Ibrahim, the *faqih,* said that when someone goes on *hajj*, he should go to Madina with the intention of praying in the mosque of the Messenger of Allah, seeking the blessing of seeing his Meadow,[1] his *minbar*, his grave, the place where he sat, the places his hands touched and the places where his feet walked and the post on which he used to lean, where Jibril descended to him with the revelation, and the places connected with the Companions and the Imams of the Muslims who lived there. He should have consideration for all these things.

Ibn Abi Fudayk said that he heard someone state, "We have heard that all who stop at the Prophet's grave should recite the *ayat,* '**Allah and His angels bless the Prophet,'** (33:56) and then say, 'May Allah bless you, Muhammad.' If someone says this seventy times, an angel will call to him, 'May Allah bless you!' and all his needs will be taken care of."

Yazid ibn Abi Sa'id al-Mahri said that he went to 'Umar ibn 'Abdu'l-'Aziz and when 'Umar bade him farewell, he said, "I would like you to do something for me. When you reach Madina and see the grave of the Prophet, may Allah bless him and grant him peace, greet him for me with peace." Another said, "He used to send such greetings in his letters from Syria."

---

1. An area of the Prophet's Mosque between his tomb and the *minbar* called the *Rawda*.

One of the early Muslims said, "I saw Anas ibn Malik come to the Prophet's grave. He stopped and raised his hands so that I thought he was beginning the prayer. He greeted the Prophet and then left."

Ibn Wahb said that Malik said that when someone greets the Prophet, and makes supplication, he should stand with his face towards the grave, not towards *qibla*, draw near and greet him but not touch the grave with his hands. In *Al-Mabsut*, Malik says, "I do not think people should stand at the grave of the Prophet, may Allah bless him and grant him peace, but should greet and then depart."

Ibn Abi Mulayka said, "Anyone who wants to stand and face the Prophet should face the lamp which is in the *qibla* end of the grave at the Prophet's head."

Nafi' said, "Ibn 'Umar used to make the greeting at the grave. I saw him come to the grave a hundred times or more. He would say, 'Peace be upon the Prophet, may Allah bless him and grant him peace. Peace be upon Abu Bakr.'" Then he would leave. Ibn 'Umar was also seen to put his hand on the seat of the Prophet at the *minbar* and then place his hand on his face.

Ibn Qusayt and al-'Utbi said, "When the mosque was empty, the Companions of the Prophet used to touch the knob of the minbar which was near the grave with their right hands. Then they faced to the *qibla* and made supplication."

In the *Muwatta'* we find that Malik, according to the transmission of Yahya ibn al-Laythi, used to stand at the grave of the Prophet and would pray on the Prophet, Abu Bakr and 'Umar. According to Ibn al-Qasim and al-Qa'nabi, he made supplication for Abu Bakr and 'Umar. According to Ibn Wahb, Malik said that the greeter should say, "Peace be upon you, O Prophet, and the mercy of Allah and His blessings." In *al-Mabsut*, he greeted Abu Bakr and 'Umar.

Qadi Abu'l-Walid al-Baji said, "I think that he should supplicate for the Prophet using the term *'salat'* and use a different word for Abu Bakr and 'Umar as Ibn 'Umar indicated."

Ibn Habib said, "When you enter the Prophet's mosque, you should say, 'In the name of Allah and peace be upon the Messenger of Allah. Peace be upon us from our Lord. Allah and His angels bless Muhammad. O Allah, forgive us our wrong actions and open for us the gates of Your mercy and Your Garden and preserve us from the accursed shaytan!'

"Then you should go to the Meadow which is that part of the mosque between the grave and the minbar. Pray two *rak'ats* there in which you praise Allah before standing at the grave. Ask Him for the complete fulfillment of the intention which brought you out to visit him and for help in realising it. If your two *rak'ats* are outside the *Rawda*, that is sufficient although it is better if they are in the *Rawda*. The Prophet said, 'The area between my house and the *minbar* is one of the meadows (*rawdas*) of the Garden. My *minbar* is on one of the raised gardens of the Garden.'

"Then you stand at the grave with humility and respect, and bless him and give what praise you can. You greet Abu Bakr and 'Umar and make supplication for them and do a lot of prayer in the mosque of the Prophet night and day. Do not forget to go to the mosque of Quba' and the graves of the martyrs."

Malik said in his letter to Muhammad,[1] "The Prophet, may Allah bless him and grant him peace, should be greeted when you enter and leave (i.e. the Prophet's mosque)" Muhammad said, "When you leave the mosque, finish your time there standing at the grave. It is the same when you want to leave Madina."

Ibn Wahb relates that Fatima said that the Prophet said, "When you enter the mosque, bless the Prophet, may Allah bless him and grant him peace, and say, 'O Allah, forgive me my wrong actions and open the doors of Your mercy to me.' When you leave, bless the Prophet, may Allah bless him and grant him peace, and say, 'O Allah, forgive me my wrong actions and open the doors of Your overflowing favour to me.'"[2]

Muhammad ibn Sirin said, "When people entered the mosque, they used to say, 'May Allah and His angels bless Muhammad. Peace be upon you, O Prophet, and the mercy of Allah and His blessings. In the name of Allah we have entered and in the name of Allah we have gone out. We have relied on Allah.' They said something similar when they went out."

When the Messenger of Allah entered the mosque, he used to say, "O Allah, open the doors of Your mercy to me and make the gates of Your provision easy for me."

Abu Hurayra said, "When one of you enters the mosque, let him pray on the Prophet and say, 'Allah, open the way for me!'"

In *al-Mabsut*, Malik said, "It is not necessary for the people of Madina who enter and leave the mosque to stand at the grave. That is for strangers."

Malik also said, "There is no harm in someone who comes from a journey or leaves on a journey standing at the grave of the Prophet, may Allah bless him and grant him peace, and asking for blessing on him and making supplication for him and for Abu Bakr and 'Umar." He was told that some of the people of Madina who had neither come from a journey nor were going on a journey would do that once a day or more, sometimes once or twice on *Jumu'a* or other days, giving the greeting and making supplication for an hour. Malik said, "I have not heard this mentioned by any of the people of *fiqh* in our city. It is

---

1. One of the companions of Malik, possibly Muhammad ibn al-Hasan ash-Shaybani who was also one of the companions of Abu Hanifa.
2. In the *Sunan* Collections.

permitted to abandon it. The last people of this community are only put right by the first, and I have not heard of the first people of this community or any of the *Salaf* doing that. It is disliked except for someone who has come from or is going on a journey."

Ibn al-Qasim said, "When the people of Madina left or entered Madina, I saw that they used to come to the grave and give the greeting." He said, "That is what is considered to be the correct thing to do."

Al-Baji said, "There is a difference between the people of Madina and strangers because strangers have a specific intention for doing so whereas the Madinans live there and do not intend to go there for the sake of the grave and the greeting."

In the Book of Ahmad ibn Sa'id al-Hindi about people standing at the grave we find, "Do not cling to it and do not touch it and do not stand at it for a long time."

In the *'Utibiyya* we find, "In the mosque of the Prophet, may Allah bless him and grant him peace, begin with the prayer on the Prophet which you say before the *salam*.

"The best place for *nafila* prayers in the mosque of the Prophet is in the prayer-place of the Prophet where the post scented with *khaluq* perfume is located. In the obligatory prayer, it is best to go to the front rows. I prefer strangers to do the *nafila* prayers there rather than in their houses."

SECTION 10
The *adab* of entering the Mosque of the Prophet and its excellence, the excellence of the prayer in it and in the mosque of Makka. The Prophet's grave and *minbar*, and the excellence of living in Madina and Makka

Allah says, **"A mosque that was founded on *taqwa* from the first day is better for you to stand in."** (9:108)

It is related that the Prophet was asked, "Which mosque is that?" He replied, "My mosque."[1]

This is what was said by Ibn al-Musayyab, Zayd ibn Thabit, Ibn 'Umar and Malik ibn Anas and others, while Ibn 'Abbas said that it refers to the mosque of Quba'.

Abu Hurayra said that the Prophet said, "Mounts should only be saddled to visit three mosques: the *Masjid al-Haram*, my mosque and the *Masjid al-Aqsa*."[2]

'Abdullah ibn 'Amr ibn al-'As said that when the Prophet entered the

1. Muslim.
2. Al-Bukhari, Muslim, an-Nasa'i and Abu Dawud.

mosque, he said, "I seek refuge with Allah the Magnificent and with His noble face and timeless prayer from the accursed Shaytan."[1]

Malik said that 'Umar ibn al-Khattab heard a voice raised in the mosque and called out to the person, "Who are you?" He replied, "A man of Thaqif." He said, "If you had been from one of these two cities, I would have punished you. No-one should raise his voice in our mosques."

Muhammad ibn Maslama said, "No-one should intentionally raise his voice or do anything offensive in the mosque. He should keep himself from what is disliked." All the *'ulama'* agree that this applies to all mosques.

Qadi Isma'il said that Muhammad ibn Maslama said that in the mosque of the Prophet it is disliked for anyone to speak loudly in such a way as to distract those who are praying. This is apart from the general prohibition about raising the voice in mosques. It is disliked to raise the voice with the *talbiyya*[2] in all congregational mosques except the *Masjid al-Haram* and the Prophet's Mosque.

Abu Hurayra said that the Prophet said, "The prayer in my mosque is better than a thousand prayers in all other mosques, except the *Masjid al-Haram*."[3] People disagree about what this exception means in the same way that they disagree about the relative merits of Makka and Madina.

Malik (according to Ashhab and Ibn Nafi' and others) believes that the *hadith* saying that the prayer in the mosque of the Prophet is better than a thousand prayers in all other mosques except the *Masjid al-Haram* means that the prayer in the Prophet's mosque is better than the prayer in the *Masjid al-Haram*, but less than a thousand times better. They use as a proof for this opinion what has been related from 'Umar ibn al-Khattab when he said, "The prayer in the *Masjid al-Haram* is better than a hundred prayers in other mosques." It follows from this that the excellence of the Prophet's mosque is nine hundred prayers greater. This is based on the excellence of Madina over Makka as has been stated by 'Umar ibn al-Khattab, Malik and other people of Madina.

The people of Makka and Kufa believe in the supremacy of Makka. That is what 'Ata', Ibn Wahb and Ibn Habib among Malik's people have stated, and as-Saji related that from ash-Shafi'i. They take the exception in the previous *hadith* literally, and consider the prayer in the *Masjid al-Haram* is better. For proof they used the *hadith* of 'Abdullah ibn az-Zubayr from the Prophet, "One prayer in the *Masjid al-Haram* is better than a hundred prayers in my mosque." Qatada relates something similar.

It is also said that prayer in the *Masjid al-Haram* is a hundred thousand times

---

1. Abu Dawud.
2. The call of *"Labbayk"* (At Your service) made by the pilgrims as they set out for *hajj* and make their way to Makka.
3. Al-Bukhari and Muslim.

better than prayer in other mosques.

However, there is no dispute that the place of his grave is the best place on earth.

Qadi Abu'l-Walid al-Baji said, "The *hadith* implies the contradiction of the supremacy of the mosque of Makka over all other mosques. Its excellence in relation to Madina is not recognised by this *hadith*." At-Tahawi believed that Madina's excellence was in the obligatory prayers, while Mutarrif ibn 'Abdullah said it was in the superogatory prayers as well. He said, "Its weeks are better than other weeks, and Ramadan in Madina is better than Ramadan anywhere else."

The Prophet said, "What is between my house and my *minbar* is one of the Meadows of the Garden."[1] A similar *hadith* is related by Abu Hurayra and Abu Sa'id al-Khudri who added, "and my *minbar* is over my Basin." And in another *hadith* we find, "My *minbar* is one of the raised gardens of the Garden."

At-Tabari said that this has two meanings. One is that the word "house" means the house where he lived as it is related, "between my room and my *minbar*," and the other is that "house" refers to his grave, as is stated by Zayd ibn Aslam who said that this *hadith* should be related, "between my grave and my *minbar*." At-Tabari said, "Since his grave is in his house, both meanings come to the same thing and there is no conflict." His grave was in his room, which was his house.

Various things are said about, "My *minbar* is over my Basin." One possibility is that it actually means his *minbar* in the mosque and this is the clearest meaning. The second is that he has another *minbar* in the Next World. The third is that by his *minbar*, and being present at it, he means performing good actions which bring one to the Basin and let one drink from it.

"One of the Meadows of the Garden" can also have two meanings. One is that it assures that supplication and prayer in the *Rawda*, i.e. between the Prophet's grave and his *minbar*, merit that reward, in the same way as it is said, "The Garden is under the shadow of the sword." The second is that that area is transported by Allah and actually is in the Garden.

Ibn 'Umar and some other Companions related that the Prophet said about Madina, "No-one will be steadfast in the face of its difficulties and hardships but that I will be a witness or an intercessor for him on the Day of Rising."[2]

He said about those who left Madina, "Madina is better for them if they only knew."[3]

---

1. Al-Bukhari and Muslim.
2. Muslim.
3. Part of a long *hadith* in al-Bukhari and Muslim.

He said, "Madina is like a pair of bellows. It drives away what is impure and leaves what is pure."[1]

He said, "No-one leaves Madina out of aversion to it but that Allah gives it someone better than him."[2]

The Prophet said, "Allah will raise up whoever dies in one of the two *Harams*[3] on *hajj* or *'umra* on the Day of Rising without reckoning or punishment."[4] Another path of transmission has, "He will be raised up among the trustworthy on the Day of Rising."

Ibn 'Umar says that the Prophet said, "Whoever can die in Madina should do so for I will intercede for all who die in it."[5]

Allah says, **"The first house established for people was that at Bakka, blessed....in it is security."** (3:96)

One of the commentators says that "security" means safety from the Fire. It is said it means safety from the designs of someone who would do something if the person were outside the *Haram*. It was used as a sanctuary in the *Jahiliyya*. This is similar to His words, **"When He made the House as a place to visit for people and a sanctuary."** (2:125)

It is related that some people came to Sa'dun al-Khawlani at Monastir. They acquainted him with the fact that the Kutama (a Berber tribe) had killed a man. They had kindled a fire under him right through an entire night. It did not do anything to him and his body remained unblemished. He asked, "Had he gone on three *hajjs*?" They replied, "Yes." He said, "I was told a *hadith* that anyone who goes on *hajj* once fulfills the obligation; anyone who goes on *hajj* twice claims a debt with his Lord; and anyone who goes on *hajj* three times, Allah will make his hair and body *haram* for the Fire."

When the Messenger of Allah looked at the Ka'ba, he said, "Welcome to you! What house is greater than you or has greater inviolability than your inviolability?"[6]

He said, "No-one supplicates to Allah at the Black Corner[7] but that Allah answers it for him. It is the same beneath the water-spout."[8]

The Prophet said, "Whoever prays two *rak'ats* behind the *Maqam Ibrahim*[9] will be forgiven his past and future wrong actions and will be gathered with those who are safe on the Day of Rising."[10]

---

1. Al-Bukhari and Muslim.
2. Muslim.
3. Makka or Madina.
4. Al-Bayhaqi and ad-Daraqutni.
5. Ibn Majah, Ibn Hibban and at-Tirmidhi.
6. At-Tabarani.
7. The corner of the Ka'ba where the Black Stone is situated.
8. A drainage duct on the roof of the Ka'ba.
9. A place opposite the wall of the Ka'ba which has the door in it where the Prophet Ibrahim stood when the Ka'ba was being built.
10. Ad-Darimi.

Ibn 'Abbas said that he heard the Messenger of Allah say, "No-one supplicates for a thing in this *Multazam* of the mosque[1] but that his supplication is granted."

Ibn 'Abbas said, "I have never asked Allah for something in this *Multazam* since I heard this from the Messenger of Allah without my request being granted."

'Amr ibn Dinar said, "I have not asked Allah for anything in this *Multazam* since I heard this from Ibn 'Abbas without my request being granted."

Sufyan ath-Thawri said, "I have not asked Allah for anything in this *Multazam* since I heard it from 'Amr without my request being granted."

Al-Humaydi said, "I have not asked Allah for anything in this *Multazam* since I heard this from Sufyan without my request being granted."

Muhammad ibn Idris said, "I have not asked Allah for anything in this *Multazam* since I heard it from al-Humaydi without my request being granted."

Abu'l-Hasan ibn al-Hasan said, "I have not asked Allah for anything in this *Multazam* since I heard it from Muhammad ibn Idris without my request being granted."

Abu Usama said, "I do not remember al-Hasan ibn Rashiq transmitting this as a *hadith* but I have not asked Allah for anything in this *Multazam* since the time I heard it from him without my request being granted as far as this world is concerned. I hope that it will also be granted in the Next World."

Al-'Udhri said, "I have not asked Allah for anything in this *Multazam* since I heard it from Abu Usama without my request being granted."

Qadi Abu 'Ali said, "I have asked Allah for many things and some of them have been granted, and I hope that the rest of them will be granted out of the vastness of His bounty."

We have mentioned a few anecdotes in this section, even though they do not strictly belong to it, in order to gain the maximum benefit.

Allah gives success in following the right course by His mercy.

---

1. The wall of the Ka'ba between the door and the Black Stone.

PART THREE

On what is necessary for the Prophet and what is impossible for him, what is permitted for him and what is forbidden for him and what is valid in those human matters which can be ascribed to him

Introduction

Allah says, **"Muhammad is only a Messenger, and Messengers have passed away before him. Why, if he should die or be killed..."** (3:144) and **"The Messiah, son of Maryam, is only a Messenger. Messengers have passed away before him and his mother was a truthful woman. They used to eat food,"** (5:75) and **"We only sent Messengers before who ate food and walked in the markets,"** (25:20) and **"Say: I am a mortal like you to whom revelation has been given."** (18:10)

Muhammad and all the Prophets of mankind were sent to men. If it had not been for that, people would not have been able to have met them face-to-face, to have accepted from them and spoken with them.

Allah says, **"If We had made him an angel, We would still have made him a man."** (6:9) That is to say, if that had happened, the angel would have taken the form of a man to whom they could speak since they would not be able to face an angel and speak with it if they saw it in its true form.

Allah says, **"Say, if there had been angels on the earth walking at peace, We would have sent down upon them an angel as a Messenger from heaven."** (17:95) That is to say, it is not possible in the *sunna* of Allah to send an angel except to one who is the same as it or to one to whom Allah gives a special gift, chooses and makes strong enough to be able to face it, such as the Prophets and Messengers.

The Prophets and Messengers are intermediaries between Allah and His creation. They convey His commands and prohibitions, His warning and threat to His creatures and they acquaint them with things they did not know regarding His command, creation, majesty, power and His *Malakut*. Their outward form, bodies and structure are characterised by the qualities of men as far as non-essential matters such as illnesses, death and passing away are concerned, and they have human traits.

But their souls and inward parts have the highest possible human qualities, associated with the Highest Assembly,[1] which are similar to angelic attributes, free of any possibility of alteration or evil. Generally speaking the incapacity and weakness connected with being human cannot be associated with them. If their inward parts had been human in the same way as their outward, they would not have been able to receive revelation from the angels, see them, mix and sit with them in the way other mortals are unable to do.

If their bodies and outward parts had been marked by angelic attributes as opposed to human attributes, the mortals to whom they were sent would not have been able to speak with them as Allah has already said. Thus they have the aspect of men as far as their bodies and outward parts are concerned, and

---

1. Those brought near to the presence of Allah, or the exalted angels.

that of angels in respect of their souls and inward parts.

It is in this way that the Prophet said, "If I had taken a close friend from my community, I would have taken Abu Bakr as a friend, but it is the brotherhood of Islam. Rather your companion is the close friend of the Merciful."[1]

He said, "My eyes sleep and my heart does not sleep."[2]

He said, "I am not made the same as you but my Lord still gives me food and makes me drink."[3]

Their inward parts are disconnected from evil and free from imperfection and weakness.

This summary will certainly not be enough for all those who are concerned with this subject. Most people will require further expansion and detail and this will come in the following two chapters, with the help of Allah. He is enough for me and the best of guardians.

---

1. Al-Bukhari.
2. Ibn Sa'd.
3. Muslim and al-Bukhari.

Chapter One

CONCERNING MATTERS OF THE DEEN AND THE PROPHET'S BEING PROTECTED FROM IMPERFECTION

PREFACE

Know that unexpected events and afflictions to which a person is subject can occur to the body or senses either without intention and choice – as in the case of illness and disease – or by intention and choice. All these things can actually be categorised as actions. However, the Shaykhs have classified them into three types: belief with the heart, statement on the tongue and action by the limbs.

All men have afflictions and changes happen to them both by choice and without it in each of these categories. Although the Prophet was a man, and therefore whatever is permitted to happen to people in general could in theory happen to him, definite proofs have been established and it is agreed by consensus that such things did not happen to him and he was free of many of the afflictions which occur, with or without choice, as we will make clear to you in the exposition which follows.

SECTION 1
Concerning the belief of the Prophet's heart from the moment of his prophethood

Know that the Prophet's *tawhid*, his knowledge of Allah and the attributes of Allah, his belief in Allah, and what was revealed to him is based on the greatest possible gnosis, clear knowledge and certainty. It is free of ignorance, doubt or suspicion. The Prophet is protected in respect of these things from everything incompatible with gnosis and certainty. The Muslims have a general consensus regarding this. Clear proofs indicate that it would not be sound to impute to him anything other than the beliefs of all the Prophets.

Ibrahim's words, **"Yes, but so that my heart will be at peace,"** (2:260)[1] do

---

1. "And when Ibrahim said, 'Yes Lord, show me how You will give life to the dead,' He said, 'Why, do you not believe?' 'Yes,' he said, 'but so that my heart will be at peace.' Allah said, 'Take four birds and twist them to you and then set a part of them on every hill, then summon them, and they will come to you running.'"

not contradict this, since Ibrahim did not doubt what Allah had told him about bringing the dead to life. He wanted to put his heart at peace and to be free of any contentiousness by actually seeing the dead brought to life. He first acquired indirect knowledge of its occurrence and then subsequently he desired knowledge by direct witnessing.

A second possibility is that the Prophet Ibrahim wanted to learn about his station with his Lord and to know whether his supplication, asking his Lord for this favour, would be answered. Then Allah says, **"Do you not then believe?"** (2:260) i.e. that your station with Me and your close friendship and your being chosen are confirmed.

A third possibility is that he is asking for increase in certainty and peace of mind, even though he did not doubt in the first instance. Knowledge, and speculative knowledges in particular, can vary in strength, and, whereas it is impossible for doubt to occur where necessary knowledges are concerned, it is permitted in speculative ones. He wanted to move from speculation and report to actually witnessing it, to rise from the knowledge of certainty to the vision of certainty. A report is not the same as eye-witnessing. This is why Sahl ibn 'Abdullah at-Tustari said, "He asked for the cover to be lifted from his eyes so that he could be increased in his firm state by the light of certainty."

A fourth possibility is that he used, as an argument against the idolaters, the fact that their Lord brings to life and makes die. He sought this favour from his Lord in order to confirm his argument by eye-witnessing.

A fifth possibility, as someone said, is that Ibrahim is making a request using *adab* and that what is really implied is: "Give me the power to bring the dead to life, implying: so that my heart will be at rest from this desire."

A sixth possibility is that he saw in himself doubt and what could be doubted, but he was answered and he was increased in nearness.

Our Prophet said, "We are more likely to doubt than Ibrahim." The Prophet's statement negates the possibility of any doubt on Ibrahim's part. It eliminates any negative thoughts that the Companions might have had about Ibrahim, i.e. the meaning is: "We are certain of the Rising and that Allah will bring the dead to life. If Ibrahim had doubted, we would have been more likely to doubt than him." The Prophet said this, either by way of *adab*, or because the Prophet meant by 'we' his community who were, of course, subject to doubt, or by way of humility and compassion if the story of Ibrahim is taken to apply to the experience of his state or to his increase in certainty.

If, in this context, you ask about the meaning of Allah's words, **"If you are in doubt about what We have sent down to you, ask those who recite the Book before you,"** (10:94) then beware! May Allah make your heart firm! Beware of letting anything that certain commentators have mentioned from Ibn 'Abbas or anyone else cause you to think anything which suggests doubt on the part of the Prophet concerning what was revealed to him, even if his doing so would be part of humanness. That is not permissible for him at all.

Ibn 'Abbas said that the Prophet did not doubt nor question. Something similar comes from Ibn Jubayr and al-Hasan al-Basri. Qatada said that the Prophet said, "I do not doubt and do not question."

There is also some disagreement about what the *ayat* means. It is said that what is meant is, "O Muhammad, say to the doubters, 'If you are in doubt.'" Some commentators have said that the other parts of the *sura* indicate this interpretation. Allah says, **"Say: O people, if you are in doubt about my deen."** (10:104) It is said that here the Arabs and people other than the Prophet are meant in the same way that in Allah's words, **"If you associate, your actions will fail,"** (39:65) the Prophet is being addressed, but the import is intended for others. This is similar to, **"Do not be in doubt about what these men worship."** (11:109) There are many other similar instances.

Bakr ibn al-'Ala' said, "Don't you see that Allah says, **'Do not be among those who deny the signs of Allah.'** (10:95) It is the Prophet who is being denied in what he is calling to, so how can he be among those who deny Him? This shows that someone else is meant. It is like Allah's words, **'The Merciful, ask one who is informed about Him.'** (25:59) The one being commanded here is not the Prophet. The Prophet, rather, is the one who is informed and questioned. He is not the asker. Such doubt is what led to some other people besides the Prophet being commanded to ask those who recite the Book regarding what Allah has related about the history of past nations – but not, however, about what the Prophet called to regarding *tawhid* and the *Shari'a*. This is like His words, **'Ask about those We sent of Our Messengers before you.'** (43:45) The idolaters are meant while the words are directed to the Prophet."

It is also said that this *ayat* means: "Ask Us about those We sent before you."

Then Allah continues with the question, **"Have We appointed apart from the Merciful any deities to be worshipped?"** (43:45) in order to negate that suggestion.

It is said that the Prophet, may Allah bless him and grant him peace, was commanded to ask the other prophets this question during the Night Journey. His certainty was too strong to need to ask the question. It is related that he said, "I do not ask, I have enough." Ibn Zayd related that.

It is said that this *ayat* means: "Ask the nations to whom We sent Prophets, if their Prophets had come to them without *tawhid*." This is what Mujahid, as-Suddi, ad-Dahhak and Qatada said it meant.

The sum of this is that the Prophet is informing us about what the Messengers were sent with. Allah did not give permission to anyone to worship other-than-Him. This refutes the Arab idolaters when they said, **"We worship** them to come near Allah in proximity," (39:3) referring to the idols.

A similar use of language is used in the Qur'an when Allah says, **"Those who were given the Book know that it was sent down from your Lord with the truth, so on no account be among the doubters,"** (6:114) i.e. concerning their knowledge that you are indeed the Messenger of Allah even if they do not affirm that. That does not mean that the Prophet was entertaining doubts about what was mentioned at the beginning of the *ayat*. It is like what has already been mentioned, i.e. "O Muhammad, say to those who doubt, 'Do not be among the doubters.'"

This is shown by His words at the beginning of the *ayat*, **"Should I seek some other judge than Allah?"** (6:114) in which the Prophet is clearly addressing others.

It is said that this *ayat* (10:94) is in fact an affirmation as in His words, **"Did you say to people: 'Take me and my mother as gods apart from Allah?'"** (5:116) Allah knows very well that 'Isa, peace be upon him, did not say that.

It is said that the meaning of the *ayat* is: "You are not in doubt, so ask and you will be increased in your peace of mind and will have greater knowledge and certainty."

It is said that the meaning is: "If you are in doubt about what We have honoured and preferred you with, then ask them about your description in the previous books and the extent of your virtues recorded in them."

It is related from Abu 'Ubayda at-Tamimi that the meaning is: if you have misgivings from other people regarding the revelation.

You may also ask about the meaning of His words, **"Until when the Messengers despaired and thought that they had been deceived (regarding Allah's promise of victory)..."** (12:110) using the reading *kudhibu*. We say that the correct meaning is what 'A'isha said.[1] We seek refuge with Allah from the Messengers thinking such a thing about their Lord. It means, according to most commentators, that when the Messengers despaired, they thought that those of their followers who had been promised victory had rejected them.

It is said by Ibn 'Abbas, an-Nakh'i, Ibn Jubayr and others that the word "thought" in the *ayat* refers to the followers and the communities of the Prophets and Messengers, not the Prophets and Messengers themselves. That meaning is relayed by Mujahid, who reads it as *kadhabu* (they lied). But do not

---

1. It is related about 'A'isha in al-Bukhari that 'Urwa ibn az-Zubayr asked her about this *ayat* and whether it should be read *kudhibu* (deceived) or *kudhdhibu* (called liars). She said that it was *kudhdhibu* (called liars). He said, "Indeed! They had been certain about that and then thought that they had been deceived." She said, "I seek refuge with Allah! The Messengers would never think that of their Lord!" He said to her, "So what is this *ayat* about?" She said, "It refers to the followers of the Messengers who believed and trusted in their Lord and then endured long affliction. Help was deferred until the Messengers despaired of those of their people who called them liars and the Messengers thought that their followers had been called liars. Then Allah's help came."

preoccupy yourself with a rare commentary which does not befit the station of the *'ulama'*, let alone the Prophets.

It is like what is related in the *hadiths* and *sira* about what happened at the beginning of the revelation when the Prophet said to Khadija, "I am afraid for myself." It does not mean that he doubted what Allah had brought him after he had seen the angel. It means that he feared that his strength might not be enough to bear the encounter with the angel with the result that his heart might burst and he would die.

He said this, according to what is in the *Sahih*, either after he met the angel or before he met him when Allah was informing him of his prophethood by means of the first extraordinary experiences which happened to him when the stones and trees greeted him and prophetic dreams and good news began. As has been related in one of the paths of transmission, the first thing to happen to him was a dream. Then he was shown a similar thing in the waking state. That was to make it easier for him, so that prophethood would not come suddenly and directly upon him making his human frame unable to bear it on its first appearance.

In the *Sahih* we find from 'A'isha that she said, "The first intimation that the Messenger of Allah had of revelation was true dreams." She said, "Then he was made to love retreat until the Truth came to him when he was in the Cave of Hira'."

Ibn 'Abbas said that the Prophet remained in Makka for fifteen years hearing a voice and then seeing a light and nothing else for seven years. Then he received revelation for eight years.

Ibn Ishaq related that one of the *Salaf* said that the Prophet mentioned his experience in the cave of Hira' and said, "He came to me when I was asleep and said, 'Recite!' I said, 'What shall I recite?'"

There is a similar *hadith* from 'A'isha which states that Jibril seized him and recited the *sura* to him, **"Recite in the name of your Lord."** (96:1) Then he said, "He left me and I woke up and it was as if something had been taken from my heart. Now nothing was more hateful to me than a poet or someone possessed. I said, 'Quraysh will never say this of me! I shall go to the top of a mountain and throw myself off and kill myself.' While I was intending to do that, I heard a voice calling from heaven saying, 'O Muhammad, you are the Messenger of Allah and I am Jibril.' I looked up and there was Jibril in the form of a man."

It is clear from this that what the Prophet said and what he intended to do occurred before he met Jibril and before Allah had informed him of his prophethood, his being made known and being chosen for the message.

This is similar to the *hadith* from 'Amr ibn Shurahbil in which the Prophet, may Allah bless him and grant him peace, is reported as saying to Khadija, "Since I have been in retreat, I have heard a voice and I fear, by Allah, that this is due to some foolishness on my part."[1]

---

1. Al-Bayhaqi.

Hammad ibn Salama said that the Prophet said, "I hear a voice and see a light and I fear that there is some madness in me."[1]

According to this, if it is true that he said "the most hateful thing to me is a poet or one possessed" or phrases which imply doubt in the truth of what he saw, all of that was at the beginning of his affair before the angel met him and informed him from Allah that he was His Messenger. But how can it be so, when some of these things have not come by sound paths of transmission?

As for after Allah had informed him and after he had met the angel, doubt is not valid in that case for it is not permissible for him to doubt what he received. Ibn Ishaq related that the Messenger of Allah used to have a talisman against the evil eye before the revelation descended on him. After the Qur'an had descended on him and he was afflicted with something of the evil eye, Khadija asked him, "Shall I send someone to you to make a talisman for you?" He replied, "No, not now."

There is also the *hadith* where Khadija experimented regarding the matter of Jibril by uncovering her head. She did that to confirm the soundness of the prophethood of the Messenger of Allah and of what the angel brought and to remove her own doubts, not for the sake of the Prophet, and so that she would be informed about his state.

It has come in the *hadith* of 'Abdullah ibn Muhammad ibn Yahya ibn 'Urwa from Hisham ibn 'Urwa from his father from 'A'isha that Waraqa commanded Khadija to test the matter in that way. In the *hadith* of Isma'il ibn Abi Hakim, Khadija said to the Messenger of Allah, "Son of my uncle, will you tell me when your companion comes to you?" He replied, "Yes." When Jibril came, he told her. She said to him, "Sit by my side." At the end of the *hadith*, she said, "It is not a shaytan. It is an angel, son of my uncle, so be firm and re-joice." She believed him. This indicates that she sought to verify it for herself by what she did and to demonstrate her belief. It was not done for the sake of the Prophet.

Ma'mar ibn Rashid al-Yamani spoke about the gap in the revelation. We have heard that the Prophet was so sad that he went out at times to throw himself off a mountain. Ma'mar did not give an *isnad* or mention the line of transmission for what he said. It could only possibly be applied to the Prophet at the very beginning of his affair or because of the denial of his message by those to whom he conveyed it. It is as Allah says, **"Perhaps you will consume yourself with grief over them if they do not believe in these words."** (18:6)

This interpretation is confirmed by the *hadith* which Sharik ibn 'Abdullah an-Nakh'i related from 'Abdullah ibn Muhammad ibn 'Aqil from Jabir ibn 'Abdullah. When the idolaters gathered in the Dar an-Nadwa[2] to discuss the Prophet and they agreed that they should say that he was a sorcerer, that was

---

1. At-Tabarani.
2. A house in Makka where the Quraysh used to meet to discuss matters and make decisions.

difficult for him to bear and he wrapped himself in his garment, enshrouding himself in it. Jibril came to him and said, **"O enwrapped!"** and, **"O enshrouded!"** (73 and 74)

Or he might have feared that the gap was due in some way to himself and thus feared that it was a punishment from his Lord. No rejection of this possibility has come which would cause it to be objected to. There is something similar in the case of the flight of Yunus, when he feared that his people would call him a liar regarding the punishment with which he had threatened them. Allah says about Yunus, **"He thought that We would have no power over him,"** (21:87) meaning: We would not constrict him. Makki said that he desired the mercy of Allah and hoped that He would not make it difficult for him when he left. It was said that he had the good opinion of his Lord that He would not exact punishment from him. It is said that it means: "We will give others power over him." It is said that it means: "We will punish him for his anger and departure."

'Abdu'r-Rahman ibn Zayd said that it means: "Did he think that We would not have power over him? It is not fitting to think that a Prophet would be ignorant of one of his Lord's attributes. It is the same when He says, **'When he went out in anger.'"** (21:87)

The sound position is that he was angry with his people because of their disbelief as Ibn 'Abbas, ad-Dahhak and others stated. His anger was not directed at his Lord since anger at Allah amounts to opposition to him. Opposition to Allah is disbelief. It is not proper for the believers, so how could it be proper for the Prophets?

It is said that he was afraid his people would call him a liar or kill him. It is also said that he was angry at one of the kings when he commanded his people to revert to a matter which Allah had commanded on the tongue of a previous Prophet. Yunus said to him, "Do you think that another has better standing with Him than me?" But the king was determined to do it so he left in anger because of that.

It is related from Ibn 'Abbas that Yunus' mission and prophethood took place after the fish had cast him out. For proof he took the *ayat,* **"We cast him into the wilderness and he was sick and We made a tree of gourds grow over him and We sent him to a hundred thousand or more."** (37:147) He also used as a proof Allah's words, **"Do not be like the man of the fish,"** (68:48) which He follows with, **"His Lord chose him and made him one of the righteous,"** (68:50) therefore indicating this story happened before he became a Prophet.

If you were to ask about the meaning of the Prophet's words, "My heart becomes rusted over so that I ask forgiveness of Allah a hundred times every day,"[1] and as he said elsewhere, "more than seventy times a day," beware lest

---

1. Muslim.

you should think that this rusting over implies whispering or doubt coming into his heart. According to Abu 'Ubayd, the meaning of rust in this sense is what covers the hearts. Its root is the layers of cloud that cover the sky. Another said that the rust is something which covers the hearts but not completely, like fine mist in the air which does not stop the light of the sun from coming through.

Similarly, it is not to be understood from this *hadith* that his heart was covered a hundred times, or more than seventy times, a day since the expression used in most of the transmissions does not necessarily mean that. The number refers to the prayer for forgiveness not to the rusting over. The term "rusting over" may indicate heedlessness of the heart, lapses of the self or forgetting the constant remembrance and contemplation of Allah. This was forced on the Prophet by his having to contend with men, community politics, family preoccupations, meeting both friends and enemies, the needs of the self, and the burdensome responsibility of carrying out the Message and bearing the Trust. In all of this, he was obeying his Lord and worshipping his Creator.

However, because the Prophet, may Allah bless him and grant him peace, is the highest of creation with Allah, the most elevated in degree, the most complete in gnosis, and his state is purity of heart, freedom from anxiety, isolation with his Lord and turning to Him with all of himself, and because this, his station with Allah, is the higher of his two states, the Prophet was able to see when he was absent from this exalted state and preoccupied with other things. He saw this as a falling away from his sublime state and high station and therefore asked Allah to forgive him. This is the most fitting interpretation of the *hadith* and the best known one.

Many people have inclined to this interpretation, skirting it without completely encompassing all its implications. We have approached its hidden meanings and unveiled it for those who seek benefit from it. It is based on the fact that lapses, inattention and forgetfulness in things other than the path of conveying the Message are permissible for the Prophet as we will show.

A group of the masters of hearts and shaykhs of *tasawwuf* believed that the Prophet was altogether free of this and too sublime for any forgetfulness or lapses, so that for them the *hadith* refers to the business of this community which worried and saddened him due to his concern for his people and his great compassion for them. He therefore asked for forgiveness for them. They said that the "rusting over" of his heart could in this instance be the *sakina* covering it as indicated by Allah's words, **"Allah sent down His sakina on him."** (9:40)

His asking forgiveness is to display his slavehood and need. Ibn 'Ata' said,

"His asking forgiveness is to inform his community that they must ask for forgiveness." Someone else said that it was to tell them to be continually cautious and not to rely solely on trust.

It is possible that this "rusting over" is a state of fear and awe which covered his heart and caused him to ask forgiveness out of thankfulness to Allah and clinging to his slavehood as he indicated when he said, "Should I not be a thankful slave?"

Relating to these last possibilities some variants of this *hadith* have, "My heart is covered more than seventy times a day so I ask forgiveness of Allah."

You might ask the meaning of Allah's words to Muhammad, **"If Allah wished, He would have gathered them all to guidance. Do not then be among the ignorant."** (6:75) and the words of Allah to Nuh, **"Do not ask for what you do not have any knowledge of. I warn you so that you will not be one of the ignorant."** (11:46)

Know that you should not pay any attention to the statement of those who say that the *ayat* regarding the Prophet means: "Do not be among those who are in ignorance. If Allah had willed, He would have gathered them to guidance."

And that the *ayat* regarding Nuh when the Prophet says, "Do not be among those who are ignorant that the promise is true when he said, **'Your promise is true,'**" means, "Do not be among those who are ignorant that Allah's promise is true." If this were the case it would imply ignorance of one of Allah's qualities, and that is a quality which the Prophets are not permitted to have. What is meant here is a warning that they should not take on the hallmarks of the ignorant in their affairs. It is as if Allah were saying, "I warn you."

There is no proof in any *ayat* that the Prophets have any quality which they are forbidden to have. But how can that be true, you ask, when the *ayat* regarding Nuh says, **"Do not ask about what you do not have knowledge of."** (11:46) It is better to apply that *ayat* to what comes after it than to what comes before it because such asking needs permission (*idhn*). It was permitted to ask about it at the beginning, but then Allah forbade Nuh to ask about what was concealed and hidden from him in the Unseen regarding why his son had to be destroyed. Then Allah perfected His blessing on Nuh by informing him why that was the case when He said, **"He is not one of your family. It is not a right action."**

Similarly our Prophet was commanded in another *ayat* to cling to patience in the face of his people's opposition and not to be so distressed by it that he approached the state of the ignorant in the intensity of his grief. Abu Bakr ibn Furak related this interpretation. It is said that the speech is to the community of Muhammad and means that they should not be among the ignorant. Abu

Muhammad Makki said, "There are many *ayats* like this in the Qur'an."

This clearly shows that the Prophets must necessarily be protected from ignorance after the commencement of their prophethood. If you were to say that if their protection from this defect is confirmed and it is not permissible for them to have any such thing, then what is the meaning of Allah's threat to our Prophet when he did what he did and was cautioned about it? The answer is that it is the same as when Allah says, **"It has been revealed to you and to those before you, 'If you associate others with Allah, your actions will come to nothing and you will be among the losers,'"** (39:65) and **"Do not call on what will neither help you nor harm you apart from Allah. If you do that, you will be among the wrong-doers."** (10:106) Allah also says, **"Then We would make you taste the double of life and the double of death, and you would have found none to help you against Us,"** (17:75) and **"We would have seized him by the right hand,"** (69:45) and **"If you obey most of those in the earth, they will misguide you from the way of Allah. They only follow supposition, conjecturing."** (6:116) Allah says, **"Or do they say, 'He has forged a lie against Allah'?** *Had Allah willed, He would have sealed your heart,* **and Allah eradicates the false and verifies the truth by His words. He has knowledge of the thoughts in the breasts,"** (42:24) and **"O Messenger, convey that which has been sent down to you from your Lord.** *If you do not do it, you have not conveyed His message.* **Allah will protect you from men. Allah does not guide the people who disbelieve,"** (5:67) and **"Fear Allah and do not obey the unbelievers and hypocrites."** (33:1)

Know, may Allah grant you and us success, that it is not valid or permissible for the Prophet not to convey the message or to oppose his Lord's command. The Prophet cannot associate anything with Allah nor say things about Him which should not be said nor forge lies against Him nor misguide anyone. His heart is not sealed, and he does not obey the unbelievers. However, Allah made his affair easy by clarifying what he conveyed to his opponents. If the Prophet had not conveyed it in this way, it would be as if he had not conveyed it at all. He was comforted and his heart strengthened when Allah said, **"Allah will protect you from people."** (5:67)

This is the same as when Allah said to Musa and Harun, **"Do not fear,"** (20:46) to strengthen their insight in conveying and making manifest the *deen* of Allah and to remove fear of the enemy which would weaken them.

As for His words, **"If he had made up any sayings and ascribed them to Us, We would have seized him by force,"** (69:44-45) and **"Then We would have made you taste double punishment in life,"** (17:75) it means that this would be the repayment of someone who did that and it would have been his repayment if he had been one of those who had done it – but of course he did not do it.

In the same vein Allah says, **"If you obey many who are in the earth, they**

will misguide you from the way of Allah." (6:106) Who is being referred to here is other than him as in His words, **"If you obey those who reject,"** (3:149) and, **"If Allah had willed, He would have sealed your heart,"** (42:24) and, **"If you associate, your actions will fail,"** (39:65) and similar *ayats*. The one who is meant in these *ayats* is someone other than the Prophet and it is the state of the person who associates that is being talked about. That is not permissible for the Prophet, peace be upon him.

Allah says, **"Fear Allah and do not obey the unbelievers."** (33:65) It does not say that he did obey them. Allah was forbidding him to do what they wanted and commanding him to do what He wanted as in His words, **"Do not drive away those who call on their Lord."** (6:52) The Prophet did not drive them away and he was not one of the wrongdoers.

SECTION 2
The protection of the Prophets from defects before prophethood

People disagree about whether the Prophets were protected from defects and that sort of thing before they were Prophets. The correct position is that, even before they were Prophets, they were protected from ignorance about Allah and His attributes and from any doubt concerning these things.

The traditions and reports from the Prophets support each other regarding the fact that they did not have any imperfection in this respect from the time they were born and that they grew up with *tawhid* and belief. The lights of gnosis and subtle breezes of happiness from the Unseen rose up in them naturally as we have noted in Part One of this book. None of the traditionists transmitted that anyone who was chosen and made a Prophet was ever known to have been subject to disbelief or idol-worship before he was a Prophet. The documentation of this matter is all based on actual transmission.

Some people have concluded that some hearts are naturally averse to someone who is like this. The Quraysh attacked our Prophet with all their fabrications and the unbelievers insulted the previous Prophets in any way they could and invented things which Allah has reported or authorities have transmitted. In all of this we nowhere find any reproach directed at any Prophet by the unbelievers for rejecting their gods after having believed in them or chiding him for leaving what he had previously joined them in doing.

If this had been the case, they would have censured their Prophet for denying what he had worshipped before. That would have been more decisive as an argument than criticising him for ordering them to leave their gods and what their fathers were worshipping before.

That none of them did that is a proof that they could not find any way to do so since if the Prophets had done such things, it would have been transmitted.

They would not have been silent about it, just as they were not silent about the change of *qibla*. They said, **"What has turned them from their *qibla* which they used to face."** (2:142)

Qadi al-Qushayri found a proof of the Prophets being free of this in the words of Allah Almighty, **"When We took a contract from the Prophets and you, and from Nuh, and Ibrahim, and Moses, and Jesus son of Mary. We took a solemn compact from them,"** (33:7) and **"When Allah took the contract of the Prophets: 'Now that We have given you a share of the Book and Wisdom, and then a Messenger comes to you confirming what is with you, you must have iman in him and help him.'"** (3:80)

He maintained that Allah purified the Prophet, may Allah bless him and grant him peace, in this contract. It is extremely unlikely that a contract would be taken from him before he was created. Allah took this compact from all the other Prophets to believe in the Prophet and help him many aeons before his physical birth. The Prophet being subject to idol-worship or any other wrong actions is therefore only deemed permissible by a heretic. This is what al-Qushayri means. How could such a thing be when Jibril had come to him and split open his heart when he was young, brought out a spot from it and said, "This is the portion of Shaytan in you."[1] Then he washed his heart and filled it with wisdom and belief as traditions have demonstrated.

There is no confusion concerning what Ibrahim said about the sun, the moon and the stars when he said, "This is my Lord." It is said that this happened when he was a child and began to look and seek for proof before the age of obligation. Most intelligent scholars and commentators believe that he said what he said to rebuke and inform his people. It is also said that it is a question eliciting negation, and so in fact it means: "How could this be my Lord?!"

Az-Zajjaj said, "This is my Lord," means according to what his people used to say, in the same way as Allah says, **"Where are My partners?"** (28:74) i.e. according to the idolaters' claims. This indicates that Ibrahim did not worship any of the things he mentioned and never associated anything at all with Allah.

Allah says, **"When he said to his father and his people, 'What do you worship?'"** (26:71) Then He continues, **"Have you considered what you worship, you and your fathers, the elders? They are an enemy to me except for the Lord of the worlds."** (26:75-77)

Allah says of Ibrahim, **"When he came to his Lord with a sound heart,"** (37:84) i.e. free of idol-worship, and He mentions the words of Ibrahim, **"Turn me and my sons away from serving idols."** (14:35)

One might also question the meaning of the words of Ibrahim, **"'If my Lord does not help me, I will be among the misguided people.'"** (6:77)

It is said that it means: "If he does not confirm me with His help, I will be

---

1. From Anas in Muslim.

like you in your misguidance and false worship." It reflects his cautiousness and concern. In any case, he was protected from misguidance from before the beginning of time.

One might also ask the meaning of His words, **"Those who rejected said to their Messengers: 'We will drive you out of your land or you will return to our religion,'"** (14:13) and then later the Messengers' words, **"We would be forging lies against Allah if we were to return to your religion after Allah has saved us from it."** (7:89) Do not let the expression, "return" cause you any doubts, thinking that it means that there is any notion of their going back to the religion of their people. When this word is used in Arabic it does not necessarily mean something reverting to its original state. Thus it says in the *hadith* about the people of *Jahannam*, "They return to darkness," although they were not in darkness in the first place. It is like what the poet[1] said:

> Such noble qualities! Not two bowlfuls of milk
> mingled with water which later returns to urine.

If you were to ask the meaning of His words, **"He found you misguided and guided you,"** (93:7) the answer is that this is not the kind of misguidance which implies disbelief. At-Tabari said that it refers to misguidance from the prophethood to which He guided him. As-Suddi and others said that He found him among the people of misguidance, protected him from it and guided him to belief and right guidance.

It is said that he was misguided from his *shari'a*, i.e. you did not know it. Misguidance in this case means bewilderment. This is why the Prophet retreated to the Cave of Hira to seek what would enable him to turn to his Lord and give him a *shari'a* and then Allah guided him to Islam as al-Qushayri has said.

It is said that it means: "You did not recognise the truth, so He guided you to it." This is what Allah means when He says, **"He taught you what you did not know,"** (4:113) according to 'Ali ibn 'Isa ar-Rumani.

Ibn 'Abbas said that he did not have the kind of misguidance which constitutes an act of rebellion. It is said that it means that Allah made the matter clear to him by clear proofs. It is said that He found him misguided between Makka and Madina and guided him to Madina. It is said that He found him and guided the misguided by him.

Ja'far ibn Muhammad said, "Allah found him misguided from the love He had borne for him since before time began," i.e. the Prophet did not recognise it, and then Allah gave him recognition of it.

Al-Hasan ibn 'Ali recited it as, "One misguided found you and was guided by you."

---

1. Umayya ibn Abi as-Salt.

Ibn 'Ata' said, "'**He found you misguided**' means longing for Allah's recognition." The "misguided" can mean the lover as is indicated by Allah's words describing Ya'qub, "**You are in your old misguidance**," (12:95) i.e. your old love. They definitely were not referring to the *deen*. If they had said that about a Prophet of Allah, they would have been unbelievers. That is like when He says, "**We see you are in clear misguidance**," (12:30) i.e. clearly in love.

Al-Junayd said that it means that Allah found him bewildered regarding the exact meaning of what had been sent down to him, so He guided him to it, saying, "**We sent down the remembrance to you**." (16:44) It is said it means that Allah found him when no-one else recognised his prophethood and then He helped him and guided the fortunate by him.

I do not know of any commentator who has said that it means that he was misguided from belief.

The same thing occurs in the story of Musa when he says, "**I did it then, being one of the misguided**,"[1] (26:20) meaning, according to Ibn 'Arafa, one of those in error who do something unintentionally.

Abu Mansur al-Azhari said that it means among the forgetful as when Allah says, "**He found you misguided and guided you**," (93:7) meaning forgetful as in the words of Allah, "**If one of them becomes misguided...**" (2:282)

If you ask for the meaning of His words, "**You did not know what the Book was, or belief**," (42:52) as-Samarqandi said that this refers to the time before the revelation when the Prophet did not know how to recite the Qur'an or how to call creation to belief.

Qadi Abu Bakr al-Baqillani said that it does not mean the belief which is obligatory. He went on to say that the Prophet, may Allah bless him and grant him peace, always believed in Allah's oneness but then the obligations were sent down which he did not previously know and by which he was increased in belief. This is the best meaning.

If you were to ask what His words, "**Before that you were one of the heedless**," (12:3) mean then know that this does not mean the same as, "**Those who are heedless of Our signs**." (10:7) Abu 'Abdullah al-Harawi related that it means heedless of the story of Yusuf since he only learned it by relation.

It is like what 'Uthman ibn Abi Shayba related from Jabir that the Prophet used to be present with the idolaters at their religious assemblies. He heard two angels behind him and one said to the other, "Go and stand behind him." The other replied, "How can I stand behind when he is told to touch the idols?" So he did not attend with them ever again.

Ahmad ibn Hanbal disliked this *hadith* and said that it is fabricated. Ad-Daraqutni said its *isnad* is weak. The *hadith* is generally disliked and there is no disagreement about the weakness of its *isnad*. One does not use it.

---

1. A reference to when, as a young man, Musa had accidentally killed another man in Egypt.

What is known about the Prophet, may Allah bless him and grant him peace, is different from this according to the people of knowledge. He said, "Idols were made hateful to me."

Umm Ayman related that once the Prophet's uncle and his family told him to attend one of their festivals and they were intent on his going in spite of his hatred for it. He went with them and returned in terror. He said, "Whenever I drew near an idol, someone tall and white appeared to me, shouting, 'Get back! Do not touch it!'" He did not attend any of their festivals after that.[1]

There is what is related about him in the story of Bahira[2] who asked him to make an oath by al-Lat and al-'Uzza when he met him in Syria on a journey with his uncle, Abu Talib, when he was a child. Bahira had seen some of the signs of prophethood in him and was testing him by asking this. The Prophet said to him, "Do not ask me by these two. By Allah, nothing is more hateful to me than the two of them." Bahira said to him, "By Allah, I was only testing you when I asked you by them." He said, "Ask what you like."

It is known from his *sira* that Allah gave the Prophet, may Allah bless him and grant him peace, success before his prophethood in opposing the idolaters in their stopping at Muzdalifa during the *Hajj*. He used to stop at 'Arafa because it was the stopping place of Ibrahim.

SECTION 3
The Prophet's knowledge of the affairs of this world

The commission of the Prophets regarding *tawhid*, belief and revelation and their protection in such matters has already been made clear. As for what their hearts were bound to beyond the scope of these matters, it is generally agreed that they were filled with knowledge and certainty. They encompassed gnosis and knowledge of the matters of the *deen* and this world which cannot be surpassed. Whoever reads the reports, studies the *hadith* and reflects on them, will discover this to be true. We have already made it clear in respect of our Prophet in Chapter Four of the First Part of this book. The Prophets were, however, not all equal in their states of gnosis.

As for things connected to this world, it is not a precondition that the Prophets be protected from a lack of knowledge about them or from believing them to be different from how they actually are. This does not constitute a blemish in them since their chief concern is the Next World and information about it, and the business of the *Shari'a* and its laws. The affairs of this world are quite different to that.

This is in contrast to the people of this world – **"They know the outward form**

---

1. In Ibn Sa'd from Ibn 'Abbas from Umm Ayman.
2. A Christian hermit who lived by the caravan route to Syria.

of this world while they are heedless of the Next." (30:7) – as we will make clear in this chapter, Allah willing. However, it must not be said that the Prophets do not know anything of those affairs of this world, lack of knowledge about which would constitute a heedlessness and stupidity of which they are free.

Indeed, they were sent to the people of this world to be followed both in their policies and in their guidance. They look to the best interests of their people both in respect of the *deen* and this world. This would not be compatible with a total absence of knowledge of the affairs of this world. The states and lives of the Prophets concerning this matter are well-known and they are famous for the way they dealt with this world.

As for any matters concerned specifically with the details of the *deen*, the only sound position is that the Prophet, may Allah bless him and grant him peace, knew everything about them and it is not permissible for him to be ignorant about any of them at all because all of them came to him directly by revelation from Allah. It is not possible to have any doubts about him concerning this – as we have already shown – so how can any ignorance be possible for him? He either obtained certain knowledge directly or he achieved it by his own *ijtihad* if it was a matter about which no revelation had been sent down. This is according to the statement which says that *ijtihad* regarding such things is allowable for him based on the *hadith* transmitted from Umm Salama in which the Prophet said, "I will decide between you by my own opinion concerning that for which no revelation has been given." Reliable men have related this as sound.

An instance of it, according to some people, is the story of the captives of Badr and the permission for those left behind (from the expedition to Tabuk). Furthermore, all he held to be correct as a result of his *ijtihad* was definitely sound and true. This is the truth and no attention should be paid to anyone who contradicts it and says that it is permissible for him to err in his *ijtihad*.

This has nothing to do with the opinion which considers that the people of *ijtihad* are rightly guided even when they make an error, an opinion which is true and correct with us, nor with the statement that the truth lies only on one side when a question is decided. The Prophet is protected from any error at all in *ijtihad* where matters of the *Shari'a* are concerned. This is because the statement about the error of the people of *ijtihad* came after the *Shari'a* had been confirmed. The opinion of the Prophet and his *ijtihad* was concerning that for which no revelation had come, so nothing had previously been prescribed for it.

This is regarding those things that the Prophet had a particular concern about. As for those matters of the *Shari'a* about which he had no specific concern, he initially knew nothing of them except what Allah had taught him and he became completely established in knowledge of them, either by revelation from Allah or by permission to prescribe and judge by what Allah had shown him. Regarding many such things, he had to wait for revelation.

When the Prophet died, he knew everything about the *Shari'a* and its sciences were firm and exact with him without any room for doubt, hesitation or ignorance. In short, it is not permissible for the Prophet to have been ignorant of any of the details of the *Shari'a* to which he was commanded to summon people since it would not have been correct for him to call to something he did not know.

As for his knowledge of the hidden realms of the heavens and the earth and Allah's creation, and his elaborating about His beautiful names, His greatest signs, the matters of the Next World, the preconditions of the Final Hour, the states of the happy and the wretched, the knowledge of what was and what would be, and what he only knew by revelation, he was, as has already been made clear, protected regarding these things, untouched by doubt or query in his knowledge of them. He had absolute certainty regarding them. However, it is not necessary for him to have knowledge of every single detail concerning them, even though the knowledge he did have concerning them was more than most men possess. It is as the Prophet said, "I only know what my Lord has taught me,"[1] and "There has not occurred to the heart of man..."[2]

There is the statement, **"No soul knows what comfort is hidden in store for it as a recompense for what they were doing."** (32:17)

Musa said to al-Khidr, **"Shall I follow you so you can teach me some of what you know as right guidance?"** (18:66)

The Prophet, may Allah bless him and grant him peace, said, "I ask you by every name with which You have named Yourself, those I know of them and those I do not know. The Unseen is with You."[3]

Allah says, **"Above every-one with knowledge is a knower."** (12:76)

Zayd ibn Aslam and others said about this *ayat*, "Until the knowledge ends up with Allah."

This is is not hidden since the things He knows are not contained by anything and they have no end.

This is what can be said about the Prophet's belief in *tawhid* and *Shari'a*, gnoses and matters of this world.

SECTION 4
Protection from Shaytan

Know that the community agree that the Prophet was protected from Shaytan and defended against him. Shaytan did not inflict any form of injury

---

1. Al-Bayhaqi.
2. *Hadith qudsi* in Muslim and al-Bukhari.
3. Ad-Daylami from Anas.

on the Prophet's body nor interpose his whisperings into the Prophet's thoughts.

'Abdullah ibn Mas'ud said that the Messenger of Allah said, "Everyone of you is given a companion from the *jinn* and a companion from the angels." They asked, "You as well, Messenger of Allah?" He said, "Me as well, but Allah has helped me against him and he has given up."[1]

Mansur added, "He only commands me to good."[2] 'A'isha relates something similar saying, "I am safe from him."[3] Some people prefer the reading "I am safe from him." The reading "he has given up" (*aslama*) means that the *jinn* companion moved from the state of disbelief to Islam and so would only command to the good like the angel. This is the literal meaning of the *hadith*.

If this was what happened to his intimate *shaytan* and associate, the one who is given power over the children of Adam, how could it be any different for a *shaytan* who was far from him and could not keep his company nor bear to be near the Prophet?

Traditions in other places have come about the *shaytans* pitting themselves against the Prophet out of a desire to extinguish his light, kill him and distract him since they despaired of leading him astray. They failed completely like the one who accosted him while he was praying. The Prophet seized him and took him prisoner.

In the *Sahih* Collections, Abu Hurayra said that the Prophet, may Allah bless him and grant him peace, said, "Shaytan appeared to me in the form of a cat[4] and attacked me in order to break my prayer, so Allah gave me power over him. I repelled him, grabbing him by the throat. I wanted to shackle him to a pillar so that you could look at him in the morning, but I remembered the words of my Lord to my brother Sulayman, **'Lord, forgive me and give me a kingdom that no-one after me should have. You are the Giving.'**" (38:35)[5] Allah drove him away a loser.

In the *hadith* of Abu'd-Darda', the Prophet said, "The enemy of Allah, Iblis, came to me brandishing a brand of fire in my face." The Prophet was doing the prayer and he sought refuge with Allah and cursed Shaytan. He said, "Then I wanted to seize him so he could be shackled and in the morning the children of Madina could play with him."[6]

A similar thing is mentioned in the *hadith* of the Night Journey. An *'ifrit* came at the Prophet with a fiery torch. Jibril told the Prophet how to seek refuge from Shaytan as is mentioned in the *Muwatta'*. When Shaytan was unable to

---

1. Muslim.
2. Ibid.
3. Reading *aslamu* instead of *aslama*.
4. The "form of a cat" is an addition to what is in the *Sahih* and comes from 'Abdu'r-Razzaq ibn Hammam.
5. Part of Allah's special gift to Sulayman was that he had power to command the *jinn*.
6. Al-Bayhaqi.

harm him by direct contact, he sought the means through the Prophet's enemies – as in the case of Quraysh trying to kill the Prophet when *Shaytan* took on the form of an old man from Najd to instigate it. In the Battle of Badr, he took on the form of Suraqa ibn Malik. This is referred to by the words of Allah, **"When Shaytan made their actions look good to them and said, 'Today no-one will overcome you.'"** (8:48) Another time he was warned about Shaytan at the time of the Oath of 'Aqaba.[1] In all of this Allah protected the Prophet from Shaytan and guarded him from his harm and evil.

The Prophet, may Allah bless him and grant him peace, said, "'Isa was protected from his touch. Shaytan came to thrust his hand on his hip when was born, attacking the veil."[2]

When the Prophet was given a medicine in his illness and was told, "We feared that you had pleurisy," he said, "Pleurisy is from Shaytan and Allah has not given him any power over me."[3]

If it is asked what His words, **"If a provocation (*nazgh*) from Shaytan provokes you, seek refuge with Allah,"** (7:200) mean, one of the commentators has said that it refers to His words, **"and turn away from the ignorant."** (7:199) Then He says, **"If he provokes you,"** i.e. anger provokes you to turn away from them, then seek refuge in Allah.

It is said that *nazgh* (provocation, incitement) here means corruption as in the words of Allah, **"After Shaytan set me and my brothers at variance (*nazagha*)."** (12:100) It is said that "provokes you" means to incite and entice you. "*Nazgh*" is the worst kind of whispering.

Allah commanded him to seek refuge from Shaytan when anger moved him against his enemies or Shaytan wanted to goad him against them since evil thoughts, which are the subtlest form of whispering, could not reach the Prophet, may Allah bless him and grant him peace. He was protected from them and this is the cause of his complete inviolability and why Shaytan had no mastery or power over the Prophet even though he often opposed him. Other things have also been said about this *ayat*.

It is also not possible for Shaytan to have taken on the form of an angel to confuse the Prophet, either at the beginning of his prophethood or after it. The fact that this can be relied on is a proof of the miraculous nature of the revelation. The Prophet, may Allah bless him and grant him peace, did not doubt that what the messenger brought from Allah was true – either by reason

---

1. When some people who had come to Madina pledged their allegiance to the Prophet. When they had all taken the oath, Shaytan shouted from the top of 'Aqaba, "People of the stations of Mina, do you want this reprobate and the apostates with him? They have come to make war on you!" The Prophet said, "This is Izb (small one) of the Hill, the son of Azyab. Do you hear, enemy of Allah, I swear to make an end of you!"
2. Muslim and al-Bukhari from Abu Hurayra. The "veil" either means the placenta or a special veil with which Allah veiled 'Isa.
3. *Al-Muwatta'.*

of a necessary knowledge which Allah created specially for him or by reason of indisputable evidence which made it clear. **"The Words of your Lord are perfect in truthfulness and justice. No-one can change His Words."** (6:115) If you ask what the words of Allah, **"We did not send any Messenger or Prophet before you without Shaytan insinuating something into his recitation (*tamanna*)[1] while he was reciting,"** (22:52) mean, then know that people say various things about what it means – some are simple and some are more complicated, some are good and some are bad.

The most appropriate thing that is said, and what the commentators agree about is that "*tamanna*" here means recitation. Shaytan either tries to distract the reciter by inducing thoughts and reminders of this world so that illusion and forgetfulness enter into what he recites or he makes those who hear it misunderstand it by mishearing or misinterpreting the words. Allah eliminates that "fancying", cancelling it out so that any confusion is cleared up and the accuracy of His signs is ensured. This *ayat* will be discussed in a fuller fashion than this, Allah willing.

As-Samarqandi speaks of the objections that are raised against those who maintain that Shaytan overpowered the angel of Sulayman. Claims of this kind are not valid. We will discuss Sulayman's story later in order to clarify it. There are also those who say that the body referred to in the story was the child who was born to him.[2]

Abu Muhammad Makki said concerning the story of the Prophet Ayyub when he said, **"Shaytan has afflicted me with exhaustion and suffering"** (38:41) that no-one is permitted to interpret it as meaning that Shaytan was the one who made him ill and damaged his body. It only happened by the action of Allah and by His command in order to test him and be the means of rewarding him. Makki said regarding this, "It is said that Shaytan's affliction or 'touching' was what he whispered to his family."

If you were to ask the meaning of what Allah says about Yusha' (Joshua), **"Only Shaytan made me forget it"**, (18:63) His words about Yusuf, **"Shaytan made him forget to mention him to his Lord,"** (12:42) the words of the Prophet when he overslept the prayer on the Day of the Valley, "This valley has Shaytan in it," and what Musa said when he struck the man, **"This is from the action of Shaytan,"** (28:15) know that these words can apply in all these situations because the Arabs have the linguistic habit of describing everything ugly in a person or action as Shaytan or the action of Shaytan. It is as Allah said, **"Its spathes are like the heads of *shaytans*."** (37:65) The Prophet said, "Fight him, for he is a *shaytan*,"[3] in reference to someone who passes in front of a person who is praying.

---

1. *Tamanna* is usually translated as "fancying" although here we see that it means recitation.
2. See Qur'an 38:34.
3. Muslim and al-Bukhari.

Apart from this, the statement regarding what Yusha' said does not in any case need to be answered since it is not confirmed that Yusha' was a Prophet at the time. Allah says, **"When Musa said to his servant."** (18:60) It is related that Yusha' became a Prophet after the death of Musa or shortly before his death. Musa said that to him before he was a Prophet, as the Qur'an makes clear.

The incident involving Yusuf also took place before he became a Prophet. The commentators say there are two interpretations of Allah's words, **"Shaytan made him forget it."** (12: 42) One is that Shaytan made one of Yusuf's companions in the jail forget to mention Yusuf's case to his lord. He forgot to mention the situation of Yusuf to the King, and such things come from *Shaytan*.

None of this entails Shaytan having any power over either Yusuf or Yusha' to *whisper* to them or provoke them. The incidents occurred through their thoughts being occupied by other things and this is what caused them to forget what they forgot.

As for the Prophet's words, "This valley has Shaytan in it," it does not say that Shaytan had any power over him or whispered to him as he made clear when he continued, "Shaytan came to Bilal and continued to lull him as a child is lulled to sleep."[1]

In that valley Shaytan had power over Bilal who was entrusted with watching for dawn. This is if we take the words of the Prophet, may Allah bless him and grant him peace: "This valley has Shaytan in it" to mean that that was the reason why he slept past the prayer. We could, however, make it the reason why he left the valley and did not pray in it. This is what is indicated by the *hadith* of Zayd ibn Aslam. There is no room for conjecture and contention in this whole matter due to its clarity and lack of obscurity.

SECTION 5
The truthfulness of the Prophet in all states

Clear proofs confirm the miracle of the truthfulness of the Prophet's words. The community agrees that he was protected in what he conveyed and could not say anything contrary to the message, whether by intention, forgetfulness or error.

Intentional opposition to the message is disproved by the proof of the established miracle – which is Allah's word. The Prophet spoke the truth in everything he said according to the consensus of the people of the *deen*.

The *Shari'a* rejects the possibility that opposition to the message could occur through error according to Abu Ishaq al-Isfara'ini and whoever follows him. That view is arrived at only by following the consensus. According to Qadi Abu Bakr al-Baqillani and those who agree with him, the Prophet's protection from it is not a direct consequence of the Qur'anic miracle itself, because they

---

1. Malik and al-Bayhaqi from Zayd ibn Aslam.

disagree about what the proof of the miracle actually entails. We will not discuss this at length. Let us rely on the consensus of the Muslims.

It is not possible for the Prophet to contradict any of the *Shari'a* that he conveyed and communicated from his Lord or any of what was revealed to him by Allah as revelation, either intentionally or unintentionally, whether in a state of pleasure or anger, or in health or sickness.

'Abdullah ibn 'Amr asked, "Messenger of Allah, shall I write down all that I hear from you?" He replied, "Yes." He said, "Both when you are pleased and angry?" The Prophet replied, "Yes, I only ever speak the truth whatever my state."[1]

So the Qur'anic miracle establishes his truthfulness and supports the fact that he only speaks the truth and only conveys the Truth from Allah. The miracle is evident from Allah's words to him, "You have spoken the truth in everything you have conveyed from Me." And the Prophet himself said, "I am the Messenger of Allah to you. I will convey to you everything I have been sent with and make clear to you what has been revealed to you." And Allah says, **"Nor does he speak from whim. It is only a Revelation revealed"** (53:3-4); **"The Messenger has brought you the truth from your Lord"** (4:170); **"Whatever the Messenger gives you you should accept and whatever He forbids you you should forgo."** (59:7) It is not valid for there to be any reports which contradict anything he reported in any way at all.

If error or forgetfulness had been possible for the Prophet, he would not have been different from other people and the Truth would have been mixed up with falsehood.

The miracle of the Qur'an contains a general confirmation of his truthfulness. The Prophet is therefore necessarily free from all these deficiencies by both proof and consensus, as has been stated by Abu Ishaq al-Isfara'ini.

SECTION 6
Refutation of certain suspicions

In this section we will deal with certain questions posed by calumniators.

One of them is what is related about the Prophet's recitation of the *sura* entitled "The Star" (53). It is said that he recited, **"Have you really considered al-Lat and al-'Uzza and Manat, the third, the other one?"** (53:19) and then added, "Those are the high-soaring cranes whose intercession is hoped for."[2] When the Prophet finished the *sura*, he prostrated, and the Muslims prostrated and so did the unbelievers since they had heard him praise their gods.

One of the transmissions says that Shaytan cast it on the Prophet's tongue

---

1. Ibn Hanbal, Abu Dawud and al-Hakim.
2. Transmitted by Ibn Jarir, Ibn al-Mundhir and Abu Hatim with a broken *isnad* from Sa'id ibn Jubayr.

while he was hoping for something to be sent down on him to bring his people nearer. Another version says he was hoping that nothing would be sent down on him which would alienate them.

This story goes on to say that Jibril then came to him and the Prophet recited the *sura* to him. When he reached these words, Jibril said to him, "I did not bring you these." The Prophet, may Allah bless him and grant him peace, was distressed because of this and Allah Almighty sent down the following *ayat* to console him, **"We did not send any Messenger or Prophet before you without Shaytan insinuating something into his recitation while he was reciting. But Allah revokes whatever Shaytan insinuates and then Allah confirms His Signs – Allah is All-Knowing, All-Wise"** (22:52) and **"They were really near to inveigling you from some of what We have revealed to you hoping you would invent something against Us. Then they would have taken you as their intimate."** (17:73)

Know that we have two approaches for discussing the problems posed by this *hadith*. One approach considers its source to be weak and the other considers it sound.

As for the first approach, it is enough for you to know that this *hadith* is not related by any of the people of sound *hadith* [1] nor does anyone reliable relate it with a sound direct *isnad*. It is only commentators and historians who are fascinated by strange things, be they sound or faulty, that are fond of this kind of thing. Qadi Bakr ibn al-'Ala' al-Maliki spoke the truth when he said that people were put to the test by some sectarians and commentators, and the heretics continued to adhere to the story in spite of the weakness of its transmission, the disarray of the various versions of it, the gap in its *isnad* and the discrepancy in its words. One variant says that it took place during the prayer while another says that it was sent down on him while he was summoning the people. Another says that he said it happened while he was sleepy and yet another says that his self spoke to him and made him forgetful. Another variant says that Shaytan said it on his tongue and when the Prophet, may Allah bless him and grant him peace, recited it to Jibril, he said, "This is not how I recited it to you." Another says that Shaytan told them that the Prophet had recited it and when the Prophet heard that, he said, "By Allah, it was not sent down like that."

None of the commentators who relate this story [2] nor the Followers [3] gave it an *isnad* or traced it back to one of the Companions. Most of its paths of transmission are weak. The *marfu' hadith* containing it from Shu'ba from Abu Bishr from Sa'id ibn Jubayr from Ibn 'Abbas, says, "I imagine (showing the doubtfulness of it) that the Prophet was in Makka."

---

1. i.e. the authors of the Six Books.
2. Like Ibn Jarir, Abu Hatim and Ibn al-Mundhir.
3. Such as az-Zuhri and Qatada.

Abu Bakr al-Bazzar says that this *hadith* is not known with a direct connected *isnad* except from Shu'ba and he was unsure about it.[1]

As for the implications, it has already been clearly shown, proof has been established and the community is in agreement that the Prophet was protected and free from things like this, both from any desire for something like this to be revealed to him, in which there is praise for other gods than Allah – which is disbelief – and also from Shaytan being able to overcome him and make the Qur'an obscure to him in such a way as to make him put in it what is not actually part of it. It is not conceivable that the Prophet could believe that something which was not part of the Qur'an was part of it so that Jibril would have to inform him of it. All of this is impossible for the Prophet. It is impossible for the Prophet to have said this from himself intentionally. That would amount to either disbelief or forgetfulness and he is protected from both these things.

It has been confirmed both by proofs and by consensus that the Prophet is protected from any disbelief coming into his heart or onto his tongue, either intentionally or through forgetfulness, or that what the Angel cast into him should resemble anything that Shaytan can cast, or that Shaytan should have a way to get to him, or for him to forge lies against Allah intentionally, or through forgetfulness regarding something that had not been revealed to him.

Allah says, **"If he had made up any sayings and ascribed them to Us, We would have seized him by force,..."** (69:44-45) and He says, **"Then We would have let you taste a double punishment in life and double in death. You would not have found any helper against Us."** (17:75)

The second point to be made is the general impossibility of this story. If these words had been as they are related, it would have been incongruous, contradictory, mixing praise and censure, and feeble. That would not have been hidden from the Prophet and the Muslims and leaders of the idolaters who were with him. It is not concealed from the most insignificant person who reflects on it, so how could it have been hidden from people who had great knowledge and were thoroughly versed in the science of eloquent, sound Arabic?

The third point is that it is known that the habit of the hypocrites and the idolaters, those who were weak of heart and the ignorant Muslims was to bridle at the first opportunity. His enemies would use the slightest excuse to cause confusion about the Prophet and abuse the Muslims. They gloated over them time after time. Those with a sickness in their hearts who had professed Islam abandoned it at the least doubt. However, in spite of this, no-one related anything about this story other than the weak version that has already been mentioned. If the story had actually been true, Quraysh would definitely have used it to attack the Muslims, and the Jews would have used it as a proof

---

1. There is a lengthy discussion on the weakness of its *isnad* which is omitted.

against the Muslims as in the haughtiness they used regarding the relation of the Night Journey which led to the apostasy of some of the Muslims who were weak. The same thing also happened in relation to the circumstances of the Treaty of Hudaybiyya.[1]

There would have been no temptation or trial greater than this affliction if it had really occurred. There would have been nothing which the enemy would have used to provoke dissension more than such an event if it had been possible to do so, but not a single word of it is related, neither from the recalcitrant nor from any Muslim. This shows that the whole story is false and not to be accepted, and there is no doubt that one of the *shaytans* of men or *jinn* foisted this *hadith* onto one of the heedless people of *hadith* in order to cause confusion among weak Muslims.

The fourth point is that the people who transmitted this story maintained that Allah's words, **"They were really near to inveigling you from some of what We have revealed to you hoping you would invent something against Us. Then they would have taken you as their intimate"** (17:73) were sent down about it. These two *ayats* in fact refute the tradition they have related because Allah says that they only very nearly beguiled to make him forget. If it had not been that He had made him firm, he would have relied on them.

The contents of this *ayat* and what is understood from it is that Allah protected him from forging a lie and made him firm so that he did not rely on them at all, let alone a lot. They relate in their weak traditions that, in addition to the reliance and the forging, the Prophet added praise of their gods and that he said, "I have forged against Allah and said what He did not say." This is contrary to what is to be understood from the *ayat* and would make the *hadith* weak, even if it had been sound. This is similar to what He says in another *ayat*, **"Were it not for Allah's favour to you and His mercy, a group of them would almost have managed to mislead you. But they mislead no-one but themselves and do not harm you at all."** (4:113)

It is related from Ibn 'Abbas, "All the things about which the Qur'an says 'almost' or 'nearly' did not occur."

Allah says, **"The brightness of His lightning almost blinds the sight."** (24:43) It does not in fact do so. **"I nearly conceal it,"** (20:15) means He did not do so.

Qadi al-Qushayri said that when the Prophet passed by their gods, Quraysh and Thaqif tried to make him look at them and promised him that they would believe in him if he did. He did not and would not do it. Ibn al-Anbari said that the Messenger did not go near them nor rely on them. Other *tafsirs* on the meaning of this *ayat* have mentioned what we have mentioned regarding what

---

1. Some people were upset by this treaty because they thought it put the Muslims in a weak position.

Allah said about His Messenger being protected which shows that this matter is without basis.

All that remains to be learned from the *ayat* is that Allah strengthened His Messenger by protecting him and making him firm regarding what the unbelievers were about to do when they wanted to beguile him. What is meant by that is that the Prophet was protected and free from it. This is what should be understood from the *ayat*.

The second approach is based on considering the *hadith* to be sound. In which case, the Imams of the Muslims have different responses to that, of varying strengths.

One from Qatada and Muqatal is that the Prophet was dozing when reciting this *sura* and these words flowed on his tongue as if he were asleep. This would not be not valid for the Prophet in any of his states nor would Allah have created that on his tongue nor could Shaytan overcome him either while asleep or awake because the Prophet was completely protected.

Al-Kalbi said that the Prophet was speaking to himself when Shaytan said that on his tongue. In Ibn Shihab's version from Abu Bakr ibn 'Abdu'r-Rahman, he said that he forgot and when told about it said that it was from Shaytan. All of these things are impossible for the Prophet in any state. Shaytan has no power to make him say things.

It is said that perhaps the Prophet, may Allah bless him and grant him peace, said it, while he was reciting, by way of rebuke for the unbelievers in the same way that Ibrahim said, **"This is my Lord,"** (6:76) according to one of the interpretations and as Ibrahim also said, **"Rather the greatest of them did this."** (21:63) After a silence and then a clarification of the words, he returned to his recitation. This is possible if the separation was clear and the context indicated what was meant. In this case what he said was not part of what is recited. This is one of the things that Qadi Abu Bakr has mentioned. There is no argument against this interpretation in what is related about him being in the prayer. It is not impossible that the words occurred before the prayer.

That which appears to be true in Qadi Abu Bakr's opinion, and that of others among precise people who hold the same opinion, regarding the interpretation of this *hadith*, if indeed it is sound, is that the Prophet was reciting the Qur'an slowly as his Lord had commanded him to, making the *ayats* distinct and precise in his recitation as has been reliably related about his practice. It was possible that Shaytan was lurking nearby and during the silence slipped in different words which were attuned to the voice of the Prophet, so that the unbelievers present thought that the Prophet had said them and so publicised them. As far as the Muslim is concerned, this does not impair the preservation of the *sura*, which occurred before that incident, as Allah revealed. They were certain about the Prophet's censure of idols.

Musa ibn 'Uqba related something similar in his book *The Raids,* saying that the Muslims did not hear these words. Shaytan cast them into the ears of the idolaters and into their hearts. What is related about the Prophet's sorrow was because of the publicity given to the incident and the uncertainty which made it a cause for trial.

Allah says, **"We did not send any Messenger or Prophet before you without Shaytan insinuating something into his recitation while he was reciting..."** (22:52) *"Tamanna"* here means recitation. Allah Almighty also says, **"They know nothing of the Book except wishful thinking,"** (2:78) i.e. from its recitation. He further says, **"Allah revokes whatever Shaytan insinuates,"** (22:52) meaning, take it away and remove all doubt concerning it and make the *ayat* clear.

It has been said that the *ayat* means that a state of forgetfulness came over the Prophet when he was reciting and then he became conscious of it and returned from it. This is roughly what al-Kalbi was indicating about the *ayat,* when he said that he was speaking to himself, taking "when he was fancying" to mean "was speaking to himself." Something similar to this is related in the transmission of Abu Bakr ibn 'Abdu'r-Rahman.

This forgetfulness in the recitation is valid only if it in no way alters the meaning, changes the phrases or adds something that is not part of the Qur'an. It might constitute omitting an *ayat* or a word of it. However, the Prophet never remained in this state of forgetfulness. He was conscious of it and reminded of it immediately as we will mention when discussing what sorts of forgetfulness are permitted for him and what are not.

Part of what is known regarding the interpretation of this incident is that Mujahid related this story of the "high-soaring cranes." If we consider the story to be valid, then we must say that it is not impossible that this was part of the Qur'an. According to this version, what is meant by the high-soaring cranes and their intercession being hoped for is that they are angels. Al-Kalbi says that they are angels. The unbelievers used to believe that the idols and the angels were the daughters of Allah. This is refuted in this *sura* by the words of Allah Almighty, **"Do you have males and He females?"** (53:21) By this Allah denies their assertion. It is correct to hope for intercession from the angels. When the idolaters interpreted it as referring to their gods, Shaytan made it ambiguous to them, decked it out to them in their hearts and cast that impression into them. Then Allah Almighty abrogated what Shaytan cast and made His *ayat* clear and cancelled the recitation of the two phrases which Shaytan had been able to make unclear, in the same way that many other parts of the Qur'an were abrogated and their recitation cancelled.

There is a wisdom in Allah's sending it down and there is a wisdom in its abrogation. **"He misguides many by it and guides many by it. But He only** misguides the degenerate," (2:26) and **"so that He can make what Shaytan insinuates a trial for those with sickness in their hearts and for those whose hearts are hard – the wrongdoers are across a deep divide – and so that those who have been given knowledge will know it is the truth from your Lord and believe in it and their hearts will be humbled to Him."** (22:53-54)

Another explanation is that when the Prophet recited this *sura* and reached the mention of al-Lat, al-'Uzza and Manat, the third, the other, the unbelievers feared he would bring something that censured them and they preceded him in praising them with these words. They then mixed them in with the recitation of the Prophet and publicised it as was their custom.

They said, **"Do not listen to this Qur'an. and talk about it. Drown it out so that perhaps you may gain the upper hand."** (41:26) This action was ascribed to Shaytan since he provoked them to do it. They announced the interpolated passage and publicised it saying that the Prophet had said it. He was distressed about it because they had lied and they had forged lies against him. Allah consoled him when He said, **"We did not send before you..."** (22:52) He made clear for the people the truth from the false and the Qur'an was preserved and its *ayats* were made exact. He repudiated what the enemy had made obscure and Allah ensured this by His words, **"It is We who have sent down the Reminder and We will preserve it."** (15:9)

*   *   *

Another thing brought up by people desiring to make trouble is the story of Yunus when he threatened his people with punishment from their Lord. When they turned in repentance, the punishment was removed from them. He said, "I will never return to them as a liar," and left in anger.

Know that none of the reports related about this subject say that the Prophet Yunus actually said to them, "Allah will destroy you." What is said is that he called for their destruction. A supplication is not the same as a report which must be truthful. He said to them, "May the punishment come to you in the morning at such-and-such a time." Then Allah removed the punishment from them and prevented it from reaching them. Allah says about it, **"...except the people of Yunus. When they believed We removed from them the punishment of disgrace in the life of this world."** (10:98) It is related in tradition by Ibn Mas'ud that Yunus saw signs and visions of the punishment. Sa'id ibn Jubayr said that the punishment was covering them as a cloth covers the grave.

People might ask about the meaning of what is related about 'Abdullah ibn Abi Sarh and the fact that he used to be one of the scribes of the Messenger of Allah, and then became an apostate and idolater and went over to Quraysh telling them that he used to change what Muhammad said whenever he wanted. He said, "He used to dictate to me, 'Mighty, Wise' and I would say, 'Or Knowing, Wise,' and he would say, 'Yes, that is correct.'" In another *hadith* the Prophet said to him, "Knowing, Wise." He asked, "Shall I write 'Hearing, Seeing'?" The Prophet said, "Write whatever you like."

In the *Sahih*, Anas said that a Christian used to write for the Prophet after he had become Muslim. Then he apostatised and used to say, "Muhammad only knows what I wrote for him."

Know that stories like this do not occasion any doubt in the believer's heart since they originate from someone who became an apostate and rejected Allah. We do not accept the traditions of the doubtful Muslim. How could we then accept them from an unbeliever who is capable of forging lies against Allah and His Messenger that are even more horrendous than this?

The wonder is that people with sound intellects can occupy themselves with stories like this when they come from unbelieving enemies of Allah who hate the *deen* and forge lies against Allah and His Messenger.

It did not come from any of the Muslims nor did any of the Companions mention that they had witnessed what this man falsely said against the Prophet of Allah. **"Those who do not believe in Allah's Signs are merely inventing lies. It is they who are the liars."** (16:105)

What is mentioned in the *hadith* of Anas and the story itself do not contain anything that indicates that Anas actually saw it. Perhaps he related something he had heard. Al-Bazzar considers the *hadith* to be faulty and related from Thabit who is not followed. Humayd related it from Anas, and it may be that Humayd heard it from Thabit. This is why the compilers of the *Sahih* collections do not relate the *hadith* from either Humayd or Thabit. The sound *hadith* is that of 'Abdullah ibn 'Aziz ibn Rafi' from Anas which the people of the *Sahih* relate. We mentioned it above and it does not contain any statement from direct experience. Its only source is a Christian apostate.

Even if the *hadith* had been sound, no aspersion is cast by it nor any doubt about the Prophet regarding what was revealed to him. It is not possible for him to forget or err in it or change what had been conveyed to him. It does not constitute an attack on the composition of the Qur'an or on its being from Allah since there is nothing in the *hadith* beyond the fact that the scribe said to the Prophet, "Knowing, Wise," or that he wrote it and then that the Prophet said to him. "It is like that." His tongue or heart went ahead to one or two of the words that had been sent down on the Messenger before he manifested it. The dictation of the Messenger indicates that. It must have occurred due to the strength of the linguistic ability of the scribe, his knowledge of Arabic, and the excellence of his mind and intelligence. It is the same thing that happens when someone knowledgeable listens to verse and hastens to rhyme it, or listening to the beginning of a beautiful speech goes ahead to complete it. That does not happen with all speech as it did not happen, in this case, in every *sura* or *ayat*.

It is the same as when the Prophet, may Allah bless him and grant him peace, said, "Both of them are correct." This can refer to two ways of reciting or two different readings of the *ayats,* both of which were sent down on the Prophet. He dictated one of them and the scribe, due to his intelligence and knowledge of language, added the other and then mentioned it to the Prophet who told him that it was correct. Then Allah made exact what He made exact and abrogated what He abrogated. This is found concerning parts of some *ayats* as for instance when He says, **"If You punish them, they are Your slaves. If You forgive them, You are the Mighty, the All-Wise."** (4:18) This is what most people recite. However there is a group who recite, **"You are the Ever-Forgiving, the All-Merciful."** This is not part of the recognised Qur'an.

It is the same with certain words which have come with two variations in other places. Most people recite both variations and both are confirmed in the copy of the Qur'an. An example is the *ayat,* **"Look at the bones and how We will give them life (*nunshiruha*),"** where we also find, **"make them move (*nunshizuha*)."** (2:259) This does not occasion any doubt nor necessitate error on the part of nor doubt about the Prophet.

It is said that this could have referred to occasions when the scribes wrote from the Prophet, may Allah bless him and grant him peace, for people in respect of what was other than the Qur'an. When the scribe did that he described Allah and named Him however he liked.

SECTION 7
His state in reports concerning this world

What we have mentioned so far has been concerned with the transmission of the revelation. As for reports which are not part of revelation nor a source of legal judgement nor news of the Next World and which concern matters of this world and its states, it is necessary to believe that the Prophet did not give a report about anything which is contrary to the Giver of Knowledge – either intentionally or through forgetfulness or in error. He was protected from that in pleasure and anger, in gravity and jest, and in health and illness. The proof of this is that the *Salaf* agree and there is consensus about it.

We know that the obligation and custom of the Companions was to accept all of the Prophet's states and confirm all the reports about him and everything that occurred. They did not hesitate or vacillate regarding any of it. They did not seek to justify his states and whether or not he was forgetful.

When 'Umar expelled Ibn Abi'l-Huqayq from Khaybar, Ibn Abi'l-Huqayq argued with him, using as a pretext the fact that the Messenger of Allah said that the Jews could remain there. 'Umar argued against him quoting the words of the Prophet, "How will it be when you are expelled from Khaybar?" The Jew said, "That was just a little jest from Abu'l-Qasim." 'Umar told him, "You lie, enemy of Allah."[1]

Also none of the reports, traditions, biographies and character studies of the Prophet, which investigate the smallest details, relate that he was ever corrected for an error in any word that he uttered or that any suspicion was ever voiced about anything the Prophet reported. If such a thing had occurred, it would have been handed down in the same way as the story which is told about him concerning the fecundation of dates and his retraction of what he had indicated to the Ansar.[2] That was a matter of opinion and not a prophetic report.

There were also other matters which do not form part of this category. Like when he said, "By Allah, I do not make an oath about anything and then see something better than it, without doing the second thing and then expiating my oath."[3] Or when he said, "You come to me with quarrels and it may be that one of you will have a better argument than the other so I might grant him some of his brother's right. In that case he cuts a piece of the Fire for himself."[4] He also said, "Take water, Zubayr, until the water reaches wall height."[5] We will clarify this and similar things later.

Also, if anyone is known to lie in any report so that his report is somewhat divergent (from the generally accepted version) in any respect whatsoever, all his reports are to be doubted, his *hadiths* are considered suspicious and his statements are not given credence. This is why the people of *hadith* and the *'ulama'* abandon all the *hadith* which come from someone known to have prejudice, neglectfulness, bad memory and frequent error even though he may otherwise be a reliable person.

Furthermore, if the Prophet were to lie intentionally regarding matters of this world, that would amount to an act of rebellion. Lying a lot is a serious wrong action by consensus, and the station of prophethood is far removed from anything of this nature. A single instance of it is regarded as ugly and repugnant and would make the perpetrator shameful and subject to contempt.

As for things which are not as bad as this, is it possible for minor instances of this type of thing to take place in the case of a Prophet? There is some disagreement about this.

The correct position is to disconnect prophethood from all such things, great or small, whether deliberate or inadvertent, since the very foundation of

---

1. Al-Bukhari.
2. In Muslim from Talha and Anas.
3. Muslim and al-Bukhari from Abu Musa al-Ash'ari.
4. Muslim and al-Bukhari from Umm Salama.
5. In the Six Collections. Az-Zubayr had a dispute with one of the Ansar about some irrigation water which passed through az-Zubayr's land first. The Prophet gave a judgement to which the Ansari objected, saying, "He is your cousin." The Prophet's face went red and then he said this.

prophethood involves the Prophet in question conveying, informing, clarifying and attesting to the truth of the message he has been given. To allow anything of this kind in respect of the Prophet would detract from that. Anything which occasions doubt would be incompatible with the miraculous nature of prophethood.

We can definitely state that verbal discrepancy is not permitted for the Prophets in any case, either intentionally or unintentionally. Nor are we indulgent with anyone who is not extremely careful about saying that it is permitted for the Prophets to be subject to a state of forgetfulness regarding even things that are not directly connected with their message. Furthermore, it is not permitted for them to have lied before they were Prophets nor for them to have been known for that in their worldly affairs and situations because that would detract from them and make them liable to be doubted and it would make people's hearts averse to confirming them later.

Look at what happened in the time of the Prophet, may Allah bless him and grant him peace, between Quraysh and other nations. The people they visited asked the envoys from Quraysh about the Prophet's truthfulness and what they knew about him in that respect. They admitted that he was known for being truthful. Transmissions agree that the Prophet was protected from lying both before and after prophethood. We have mentioned some of the traditions concerning this in Chapter Two at the beginning of the book. They will clarify the truthfulness of what we have indicated to you.

SECTION 8
Refutation of certain objections

You might ask the meaning of what the Prophet said in the *hadith* concerning forgetfulness related by the *faqih* Abu Ishaq Ibrahim ibn Ja'far in which Abu Hurayra said that the Messenger of Allah performed the 'Asr prayer and then gave the *salam* after only two *rak'ats* upon which Dhu'l-Yadyan got up and said, "Messenger of Allah, has the prayer been shortened or have you forgotten?" The Messenger of Allah said, "It was not one or the other of those things."[1] Dhu'l-Yadyan said, "It must have been one of them, Messenger of Allah." Know that the *'ulama'* have answers to that, some of which are fair and some of which are somewhat arbitrary and haphazard.

My position is that the matter can only be based on either a position which allows a Prophet to have doubt and error regarding things which are not actually part of the message – and this explanation is one which we consider to be false – in which case this *hadith* and others like it pose no problem. Or, according to the position of those who say oversight and forgetfulness are

---

1. In one version it says, "The prayer is not shortened nor have I forgotten."

impossible for the Prophet, the whole event took place in order to institute a *sunna*. That being the case, in which case the Prophet spoke the truth in what he said because he did not forget and the prayer was not shortened. According to this opinion, his action was deliberate and took this form in order to show anyone who did the same what the *sunna* is in such circumstances. This is a very commendable opinion which we will mention in its proper place.

As for the impossibility of oversight on his part where speech is concerned and the permissibility of oversight by him where no speech is concerned, there are various answers concerning this matter.

One answer is that the Prophet was speaking about what he thought was the case and what he was aware of. As for his denial that he shortened the prayer, it would be true and verifiable both inwardly and outwardly. As for his forgetting, the Prophet reported about what he believed to be the case and thought that he had not forgotten. It was as if the statement referred to what he thought, even if he did not express it in that way. This is also true.

The second possibility is that, "I did not forget it" refers to the *salam*, i.e. I gave the *salam* but overlooked the number of *rak'ats*. That is possible, but improbable.

A third position, and the most improbable of all, is that held by those who make the Prophet's words, "It was not one or the other of those things," mean that it was not both shortening and forgetfulness that were involved, but only one of them. However the phrase cannot really be understood in this way. He meant that neither was the prayer shortened nor did he forget.

This is what I have seen our Imams say. All the positions are possible, although the second is improbable and the third is arbitrary and inaccurate. What I say and what appears to me to be the closest of all these positions to the truth is that "I did not forget" is a negation, meaning: "It is very bad for anyone to say, 'I forgot such-and-such an *ayat*.' The truth is he was made to forget." And indeed in one of the versions, he said, "I did not forget, but I was made to forget."

When Dhu'l-Yadayn asked him, "Has the prayer been shortened or have you forgotten?" the Prophet denied that it was shortened and that he had forgotten by himself or that anything of that nature could occur. He was made to forget so that someone else would question him. He then realised that he had been made to forget and that the reason for it was so that a *sunna* should be established. All he said was true. The reality of the situation was that he was made to forget.

Another position is what I found in the words of one of the Shaykhs. He said that the Prophet used to become distracted (*sahw*) in his prayer but did not forget (*nisyan*). He was occasionally distracted from the movements of the prayer by concentration on the contents of the prayer. This was not due to heedlessness and would not contradict his words,"It was not shortened and I did not forget."

In my opinion, the Prophet's words were directed at one of the two kinds of forgetfulness. He meant that he did not give the *salam* after only two *rak'ats* in order not to complete the prayer. Rather, he forgot but his forgetfulness was not of his own making. The proof of that are his words, "I do not forget but am made to forget. I make a *sunna*." May Allah give success to the correct one.

As for the stories in the text of the Qur'an containing the words of Ibrahim in which he tells three lies, two being **"I am sick,"** (37:89) and **"Rather the greatest of them did this,"** (21:63) and the third contained in the *hadith* when he said to the king about his wife, "She is my sister," know that all these are not lies, intentional or otherwise. They fall under the category of equivocation which is not the same as lying.

As for Allah's words quoting Ibrahim, **"I am sick,"** al-Hasan al-Basri and others have said it means "I become sick" as every creature is subject to illness. This is the excuse he made to his people for not going out to the festival with them. It is said that it means "I am ill, as death has been decreed for me," or "I am sick at heart because of what I have seen of your rejection and obstinacy." It is said that he used to get a fever when a certain star rose in the sky. When he saw it, he excused himself as was his custom. None of these things constitute a lie. In each case he was telling the truth.

It is also said that he was alluding to the weakness of his persuasiveness with them and his weakness in being unable to make clear to them the truth of their position regarding the stars with which they were occupied so much. All these instances took place with this in mind. He worked out his argument against them while he was weak. He himself had no doubts and his belief was not weak. It was his argument that was weak and the evidence for it, as we find in the expression, "A sick (feeble) argument." This was until Allah inspired him with his proof and sound argument against them by the stars, the moon and the sun whose text Allah has given.[1]

As for his words, **"The greatest of them did this,"** (21:63) he made it conditional. It is as if he were saying: "If it can speak, it did this." This was to censure his people. This is the truth about this matter and there is no disagreement about it.

As for his statement, "My sister," it is made clear in the *hadith*. He said, "You are my sister in Islam," and that is the truth for Allah says, **"The believers are brothers."** (49:10)

If you say that the Prophet called them lies when he said, "Ibrahim only told three lies" which can be found in the *hadith* concerning intercession,[2] that means

---

1. See Qur'an 6:75-79.
2. Al-Bukhari and Muslim from Abu Hurayra.

that he spoke words whose outward form was that of lying. Inwardly these words are true although their outward meaning was understood differently from their inward meaning, so that Ibrahim was apprehensive about being punished for them.

As for the *hadith* about when the Prophet wanted to go on a raid and pretended that he was going to another place, there is no dispute about that either. He concealed his intention so that the enemy would not be put on guard and did so by asking about another place and asking for reports about it and alluding to it. He did not say, "Prepare for such-and-such a raid," or "We will head for such-and-such a place."

You might ask about the meaning of Musa's words when he was asked, "Which person has the most knowledge," and he replied, "I know most," and then Allah censured him for that because he did not attribute his knowledge to Him, saying, "Rather a slave of Ours at the junction of the two seas knows more than you," citing this as a tradition in which Allah Almighty has reported he was not like that (i.e. he was not being truthful). Know that in one of the versions of this *hadith*, Ibn 'Abbas said that Musa was asked, "Do you know anyone with more knowledge than you?" In this case, his answer about his own knowledge is true beyond dispute or doubt.

In the other version, what he said refers to his belief and opinion as if he had explicitly stated his superiority in knowledge because his state of prophethood and being chosen demanded it. This gives information about his belief and is true without dispute. By "I know more" he meant what the obligations of prophethood demand regarding the sciences of *tawhid*, the *Shari'a* and the politics of the community. Al-Khidr knew more than he did about other matters which no-one can know unless he has been taught by Allah concerning some of the sciences of the Unseen. Musa knew more in general and al-Khidr knew more in particular by what he had been taught. This is indicated by His words, **"We had also given him knowledge direct from Us."** (18:65)

According to the *'ulama'*, Allah censured Musa in this case, and objected to what he said because he did not relate his knowledge to Allah as the angels did when they said, **"We have no knowledge except what You have taught us,"** (2:31) or it was because He was not pleased with Musa's words in terms of the *Shari'a*. Allah knows best, but that was in case those who had not reached his perfection of self-purification and high rank in the community, might be tempted to imitate him in what he said. They would be destroyed by that self-praise and it would involve in their case pride, arrogance and gross presumption. Even if the Prophets, peace be upon them, are free of these vices, others are subject to them except those who are protected by Allah. Protecting oneself is better for the self, so that is what should be practised.

This is why the Prophet said, preserving himself from the same thing happening in his case, and this is part of the knowledge he was given, "I am the Master of the children of Adam, and it is no boast." This *hadith* is one of the arguments used by those who maintain that al-Khidr was a Prophet since he said, "I know more than Musa," and the *wali* cannot have more knowledge than a Prophet whereas the Prophets vary in knowledge.

Al-Khidr says in the Qur'an, **"I did not do it of my own volition."** (18:82) He indicated that what he did came through revelation. Those who say that he was not a Prophet say that it is possible that his action was based on the command of another Prophet. This is weak because we do not know that there was another Prophet at the time of Musa except his brother Harun. None of the people of traditions have related anything which can be relied on regarding this.

If we consider "I know more than you" not to be a general statement, but a particular one concerning a specific case, there is no need to affirm that al-Khidr was a Prophet. That is why one of the shaykhs said that Musa knew more than al-Khidr regarding what he took from Allah and that al-Khidr knew more regarding the knowledge that had been given to him than Musa did. Another said that Musa went to al-Khidr for instruction in *adab*, not to be taught knowledge.

SECTION 9
The Prophets' protection from outrageous and grave wrong actions

As for actions of the limbs (including saying things with the tongue other than the kind of reports which have been discussed) and belief in the heart regarding matters other than *tawhid*, whose sciences have already been mentioned, the Muslims agree that the Prophets were protected from outrageous actions and grave wrong actions. There is a consensus on this and the school of Qadi Abu Bakr al-Baqillani have taken this position. Others say that it is forbidden by logical proof for them to do such things as well as by consensus. Most take the latter position and Abu Ishaq al-Isfara'ini has chosen it.

Similarly there is no disagreement that the Prophets are protected from concealing the message and from being incapable of conveying it because all of this is under the protection of the prophetic miracle itself. There is a consensus about all these things.

Most people say that the Prophets were protected from this by Allah and that they were protected in their decisions and efforts – with the exception of Husayn an-Najjar who said that they have no capacity whatsoever to commit acts of rebellion against Allah.

As regards minor wrong actions, some of the *Salaf* and other people like at-

Tabari and other *fuqaha'*, *hadith* scholars and theologians (*mutakallimun*) say that it is permissible for the Prophets to commit them. We will present their arguments regarding this matter. Others have believed that we should suspend judgement since, while the intellect cannot consider their committing such minor wrong actions to be impossible, there is no decisive statement about either point of view in the *Shari'a*. Other *fuqaha'* and theologians believe that the Prophets were protected from minor wrong actions just as they were protected from the major ones. These *fuqaha'* have said that people disagree about minor wrong actions and the difference between them and major ones.

Ibn 'Abbas and others said that anything that amounts to rebellion against Allah is a major wrong action, but some are called minor in relation to the more serious ones. Opposition to the Creator in any matter at all constitutes a major wrong action.

Qadi Abu Muhammad 'Abdu'l-Wahhab said that it is not possible to say that there is a minor wrong action in acts of rebellion against Allah, except in as far as one is pardoned for certain of them for having avoided major wrong actions. In spite of that, they do not have a different judgement from that of major wrong actions. If a person does not repent and turn away from them, nothing will wipe them out. Overlooking them is up to Allah. That is also the position of Qadi Abu Bakr al-Baqillani, some of the Ash'arite Imams and most of the Imams of the *fuqaha'*.

Some of the Imams have said it follows from both statements without disagreement that the Prophets are protected from repeating minor wrong actions since that would become a major wrong action, and they are protected from any small wrong action which could lead to a lack of modesty or which would cause a decline in manly virtue or which would incur contempt and baseness. This is also part of what, by consensus, the prophets are protected from, because this sort of thing lessens a man's station and detracts from the one who does it and makes people's hearts averse to him. The Prophets are free of that.

Connected to this are those things that are permissible (*mubah*) but would lead to things like the forbidden by bringing the Prophet out of the "permissible" into the forbidden.[1] Some of them believed that the Prophets are protected from intentionally doing anything disliked.

As a proof of the Prophets' protection from minor wrong actions, one of the Imams used as an argument the fact that that their actions are imitated and their actions and *sira* are followed absolutely. Most of the Maliki, Shafi'i, and Hanafi *fuqaha'* do not demand specific evidence and some of them hold their protection from minor wrong actions to be absolute, although they disagree about how the judgement is reached. Ibn Khuwayz Mindad and Abu'l-Faraj al-Laythi have

---

1. The legal principle called *sadd adh-dhara'i* used by Imam Malik.

related that Malik said it is obligatory to hold to that opinion, as has also been stated by al-Abhari, Ibn al-Qassar and most of our companions,[1] the people of Iraq,[2] and the Shafi'ites, Ibn Surayj, al-Istakhari and Ibn Khayran. Most of the Shafi'ites say that it is only recommended to believe that.

One group believe that minor wrong actions are permissible (*mubah*) for the Prophets. Some of them limit following the Prophets to matters of the *deen* and those actions by which nearness to Allah is known to be intended. Another says that the permissible in the Prophet's actions is not limited. He says that if minor wrong actions had been permitted for the Prophets, it would not be possible to follow them in their actions since the intention of each of their actions was not necessarily made distinct. It would not be possible to know whether an individual action would bring about nearness, whether it was permissible, forbidden or an act of rebellion. It is not valid for a man to be commanded to obey the command when it might be an act of rebellion, especially in the case of those who prefer to follow action rather than words if there is a dispute between the two.

We add as further evidence the fact that both those who allow minor wrong actions and those who forbid them for our Prophet, may Allah bless him and grant him peace, agree that he did not persist in anything objectionable in either word or deed and that when the Prophet saw something and was silent about it, it indicated that it is permitted. How would it be possible for him to behave like that in respect of the actions of others if it was permissible for he himself to do what was disliked? According to this approach, the Prophet was definitely protected from doing what was disliked since something forbidden or recommended which was done as a direct result of imitating what the Prophet did would be incompatible with being rebuked for doing it and with the prohibition against doing what is disliked.

It is also known that the Companions were in the habit of imitating the actions of the Prophet, whatever they were and in every way, just as they obeyed whatever he said. They threw away their signet-rings when he threw his away. They discarded their sandals when he discarded his. They used as a proof for facing Jerusalem when going to the lavatory the fact that Ibn 'Umar saw him doing so. Others found a proof for other actions both in the category of worship and general custom by saying, "I saw the Messenger of Allah, may Allah bless him and grant him peace, do it."

He himself said, "Have I not informed you that I kiss while I am fasting?" And for a proof, 'A'isha said, "The Messenger of Allah and I used to do it," (referring to kissing not invalidating the fast). The Messenger of Allah was angry with the Companion who was reported to have said, "Allah has allowed

1. i.e. the Maliki '*ulama*'.
2. i.e. the Hanafis.

His Messenger what He will," (meaning that the Prophet could do things which other people were not allowed to do). He said, "I am the one among you with the greatest fear of Allah and I have the greatest knowledge of the limits He has imposed." There are numerous traditions regarding this.

However, it is known that in general the Companions followed and imitated his actions absolutely. If opposition to him regarding any of his actions were permitted, it would not be proper. The Companions' minute investigation into finding out what the Prophet did is evident, and the Prophet censured the man for making him an exceptional case.

As for permissible things, the Prophets are permitted to do them since there is no reproach for doing such things. Their livelihoods are just like those of other people and they have the authority to engage in seeking them. However, because of the high station they have been given, the lights of gnosis to which their breasts have been expanded, and the concentration on Allah and the Next World for which they have been chosen, they only take from the permissible things those that are absolutely necessary since they have fear of Allah regarding their journey through this world, their keeping their *deen* correct, and what they need in this world. Everything they take by way of permissible things is connected to obedience and becomes an act bringing about nearness to Allah as we made clear at the beginning of the book in the section on the qualities of our Prophet, may Allah bless him and grant him peace.

The immense favour of Allah to His Prophet, may Allah bless him and grant him peace, and to all the Prophets should be clear to you since He has made all their actions acts of nearness and obedience, far from any possibility of opposition or trace of rebellion.

SECTION 10
The Prophets' protection from acts of rebellion before they were Prophets

There is disagreement about whether the Prophets, peace be upon them, were protected from acts of rebellion before they became Prophets. Some people deny this possibility and others allow it. The sound position, Allah willing, is that they were free of every fault and were protected from anything which might occasion doubt. How much more so when it is a matter of prohibited things. However, acts of rebellion and prohibited things only exist after a *shari'a* has been actually established.

People disagree about the state of the Prophet before he was given revelation and whether or not he followed a previous *shari'a*. The majority say that he did not follow anything. According to this, acts of rebellion did not in fact exist nor could they be considered in respect of him since the rules of a *shari'a* are connected to commands and prohibitions and the establishment of that *shari'a*. The proofs presented by those who make this statement vary.

The Sword of the *Sunna* and model for all sects of the community, Qadi Abu Bakr al-Baqillani believed that the path of knowledge lies in transmission and in original reports received by means of oral transmission. His argument is that, if it had been the case that the Prophet was following a previous *shari'a*, that fact would have been transmitted and it would have been impossible for it to have been concealed since the Prophet was someone whose affair was important and whose life was necessarily the subject of great scrutiny as has been vaunted by the people of the *Shari'a*. They do not use this as a proof and nothing of its kind has been handed down. One group believe that it is logically forbidden for the reason that it is highly unlikely for someone to be followed who was known to be a follower. Their reasoning is based on considering things to be logically either correct or incorrect and this is not a proper method.[1]

Qadi Abu Bakr states that it is more proper to depend on transmission. Others, like Abu'l-Mu'ali have said that one must reserve judgement where this matter is concerned and not give an absolute judgement about it since neither of the two points of view are logically impossible nor is the path of transmission clear on behalf of either of them.

A third group said that the Prophet, may Allah bless him and grant him peace, used to act by the *Shari'a* of a Prophet before him, and then they disagreed about whether or not to specify that *Shari'a*. Some of them did not specify it and some of them ventured to do so. They vary about whose *Shari'a* it was. Some say Nuh, some Ibrahim, some Musa, some 'Isa.

The clearest position lies in what Qadi Abu Bakr affirmed. The most unlikely position is that of those who specify the *Shari'a* since if that had been the case, it would have been transmitted as we have said and it would not be concealed from us. They have no proof in the fact that 'Isa was the most recent of the prophets thus making his *Shari'a* binding for those after him since it is not confirmed that 'Isa's call was universal. The sound position is that no Prophet had a universal call except for our Prophet, may Allah bless him and grant him peace.

Allah's words, **"Follow the religion of Ibrahim, a man of pure natural belief"** (16:123) do not constitute a proof for those of that opinion nor do His words, **"He has laid down the same deen for you as He enjoined on Nuh."** (42:13) The general precept of this *ayat* implies his following them in *tawhid*.

The same thing applies when He says, **"Those are the ones Allah has guided, so be guided by their guidance."** (6:90) Among them Allah named those who were not actually Messengers and who did not have their own *Shari'a*, such as Yusuf, the son of Ya'qub, according to the opinion of those who

---

1. This was the position of the Mu'tazilites.

say that Yusuf was not a Messenger. Allah named a group of them in this last *ayat*, all of whom have their different laws which cannot be combined. He indicated that what is meant is that they all agree on *tawhid* and the worship of Allah.

SECTION 11
Oversight and Forgetfulness in Actions

What we have been talking about are those actions of opposition which are intentional and are called rebellion and fall within the realm of personal responsibility. As for unintentional actions, like oversight and forgetfulness regarding the obligations of the *Shari'a*, when the *Shari'a* confirms that nothing has been said about these actions and no punishment has been prescribed for them, the state of the Prophets regarding such matters is that there is no punishment for them and such actions are not acts of rebellion, just as they are not for their communities.

There are two types of oversight and forgetfulness. One is that which has been conveyed and confirmed by the *Shari'a*, connected to judgments, and has reached the community by action and in which the Prophet is followed. The other type concerns things which were particular to him alone.

As for the first type, there is a group of *'ulama'* who consider it to be oversight in speech. We have already mentioned that there is general agreement that this is impossible for the Prophet and he is protected from it occurring, either deliberately or unintentionally. Similarly, the *'ulama'* say that actions which the Prophet did in this context do not have any element of contrariness in them, whether done intentionally or unintentionally, because actions have the same meaning and result as words. If such things were to happen to the Prophets, it would occasion doubt and provoke people to attack them. The *'ulama'* sought excuses to account for the *hadiths* containing examples of oversight by various methods which we will mention.

Abu Ishaq inclined to this position. Most of the *fuqaha'* and theologians have believed that some discrepancy in the case of actions of conveying the *deen* and rules of the *Shari'a*, either by simple oversight or without any deliberate intention, is allowed for him as is confirmed by the *hadiths* regarding forgetfulness in the prayer.

They make a distinction between actions and words as far as conveying the *deen* is concerned, because the miracle of prophethood is based on truthfulness in speech, and thus the opposite of truthfulness would be incompatible with the miracle of prophethood. But as for oversight in actions, this is not incompatible with the miracle and does not detract from prophethood. Errors in action and inattention of the heart are among the characteristics of the human being and as the Prophet, may Allah bless him and grant him peace, said, "I am a man. I forget as you forget. When I forget, remind me."[1] Indeed, the state of forgetfulness and oversight here in respect of the Prophet constitutes a means of gaining knowledge and positive confirmation of the *Shari'a* as the Prophet, may Allah bless him and grant him peace, stated, "I forget or am made to forget in order to make a *sunna*."[1] It is also related, "I do not forget, but am made to forget in order to make a *sunna*."

This state in fact enhances his conveying of the message and completes the blessing for him. It is far from being a quality of imperfection or target of attack.

Those who do say that oversight is permitted add a precondition that the Messengers cannot remain in oversight or error. Rather, the Messengers recognise it for what it is and take note of it immediately according to some – which is the sound position – or before they actually complete the action according to others. As for the actions of the Prophet which did not involve conveying the *deen* or clarifying its rules or which were peculiar to him alone in his *deen* and his own heart's remembrance or what he did not do with the intention of being followed in it, most of the *'ulama'* agree that oversight and error is permitted for him in these things as well as lapses of concentration and inattention of his heart. That is in respect of what he had to endure from other creatures, community politics, family business and dealing with his enemies. It is not something that was repeated and happened only rarely.

As the Prophet, may Allah bless him and grant him peace, himself said, "My heart becomes rusted over, so I seek forgiveness of Allah." There is nothing in this which diminishes his rank and is incompatible with the prophetic miracle.

There is a group of Sufis and the people of the science of the hearts and spiritual stations who believe that oversight, forgetfulness, inattention and lapses are forbidden for the Prophet altogether. They have various schools of thought regarding the *hadiths* concerning this matter which we will mention in due course.

SECTION 12
Discussion of the above-mentioned *hadith* on the Prophet's oversight

In the earlier sections, we have mentioned the kinds of oversight which were permitted and forbidden to him. We consider it impossible with regard to his spoken reports and where words concerning the *deen* are concerned, and we permit its occurrence in actions connected with the *deen* but only in the circumstances which we presented.

There are three sound *hadiths* which are related about oversight on the part

---

1. Al-Bukhari and Muslim from Ibn Mas'ud.
2. *Al-Muwatta'*.

of the Prophet in the prayer. The first is the *hadith* of Dhu'l-Yadayn about his giving the *salam* after two *rak'ats*. The second is the *hadith* of Ibn Buhayna about his standing up after two *rak'ats*. The third is the *hadith* of Ibn Mas'ud which states that the Prophet prayed the Dhuhr prayer with five *rak'ats*. All these are the result of oversight in action.

Allah's wisdom in them is that by them a *sunna* was created since conveying by means of action is more sublime than conveying by means of speech. It is conditional on the fact that he did not continue in oversight, but was made aware of it in order for him to remove any confusion and manifest the benefit in it.

Forgetfulness and oversight in respect of the Prophet are not incompatible with the prophetic miracle and do not detract from confirmation of it. The Prophet said, "I am a man. I forget as you forget. When I forget, remind me." He also said, "May Allah show mercy to so-and-so who reminded me of such-and-such an *ayat* I was omitting [or forgetting]." He said, "Truly I forget (*la'nsi*) or am made to forget in order to create a *sunna*."

It is said that some transmitters were unsure about the wording and related it as, "I do not forget, (*lâ ansi*) but am made to forget..." Ibn Nafi' and 'Isa ibn Dinar believe it is not a negative statement, but is an oath.[1]

Qadi Abu'l-Walid al-Baji said that what these two scholars said is possible when it is taken to mean that he forgets while he is awake and is made to forget when he is asleep;[2] or that he forgets as is the normal pattern for man by being distracted from a thing and by oversight; or he is made to forget while he is wrapped in concentration. So he ascribed one of the two forms of forgetfulness to himself since he shares in what causes it, and denied that he had the other kind of forgetfulness since he was made to forget.

One group among the people who understand the meaning of the *hadiths* and from among the theologians believe that the import of the *hadith* is that the Prophet used to suffer from oversight (*sahw*) in the prayer but not forgetfulness (*nisyan*) because forgetfulness involves distraction, heedlessness and disorder. They said that the Prophet is free of forgetfulness and that oversight means being preoccupied by something else. The Prophet used to suffer from oversight in his prayer and to be distracted from the movements of the prayer by the inward content of the prayer, not by inattentiveness, as he said, "I do not forget."

One group believe that any kind of forgetfulness was forbidden for him. They maintain that his oversight was intentional and deliberate in order to create a *sunna*. This opinion is desirable, but self-contradictory. There is not

1. This is a discussion referring to the Arabic particle *la* which can bear different meanings – here either the energetic (truly) or the negative.
2. The author says that this is most unlikely because the Prophet said, "My eyes sleep, but my heart does not sleep."

much benefit in this interpretation because how can it be possible to overlook something deliberately in any situation? They have no proof for their statement that he was commanded to deliberately adopt forgetfulness to create a *sunna* because he said, "I forget or am made to forget." One of these two is affirmative and negates the contradictory idea of deliberateness, and he also said, "I am a man like you. I forget as you forget."

One of the great Imams, Abu'l-Muzaffir al-Isfara'ini, inclined to this interpretation. Others have not approved of it and nor do I. Neither group have any evidence in the words of the Prophet, "I do not forget but am made to forget," since that does not negate the principle of forgetfulness at all. It negates the word forget (*nisyan*) in the expression and shows dislike of its use.

It is as the Prophet said, "It is very bad for anyone to say, 'I forgot such-and-such an *ayat*.' Rather he was made to forget." He was not inattentive or lacking concern for the prayer in his heart. He was distracted from the prayer by the prayer, part of it making him forget another part, in the same way that he left the prayer on the Day of the Trench until its time had passed when he was occupied with being on guard against the enemy. He was distracted by one act of obedience from another act of obedience.

It is said[1] that four prayers were left on the Day of the Ditch: *Dhuhr, 'Asr, Maghrib* and *'Isha'*.[2] Those who believe that it is permitted to delay the prayer because of fear have used that as a proof since it was not possible to perform the prayer until a time of security. This is the position of the school of Syria. The sound version is that the principle of the Fear Prayer came later and abrogates it.

If you asked what could be said about the Prophet, may Allah bless him and grant him peace, sleeping past the prayer on the Day of the Valley[3] when he said on another occasion, "My eyes sleep and my heart does not sleep," the *'ulama'* have various answers regarding that.

One of them is that what is meant is the state of his heart when his eyes are asleep as a general rule. Other meanings are rare, and what is other than one's normal habit is rare. The words of the Prophet in the *hadith*, "Allah took our souls," make this interpretation sound and Bilal said about the incident, "I have never encountered such a sleep."

However, things like this happened in order that Allah might affirm a particular principle and provide a basis for a *sunna* and so that he could manifest the *Shari'a*. It was as the Prophet said on another occasion, "Had Allah so wished, we would have woken up. But He wanted it to be an example for those after you."

---

1. By Ibn Mas'ud as related by at-Tirmidhi and an-Nasa'i.
2. The sound version according to Muslim and al-Bukhari is that it was *'Asr*. The *Muwatta'* says that it was *Dhuhr* and *'Asr*.
3. On the Makka road in the valley of Tabuk.

The second answer is that sleep did not overwhelm his heart to such an extent that he would incur the state of minor impurity. It is related that he was guarded and protected. He slept until he could be heard snoring and then prayed without doing *wudu'*.

The *hadith* of Ibn 'Abbas mentioned that he did *wudu'* when he got up from sleep when he had slept with his wife. It is not possible to use it as a proof of his having to do *wudu'* because of sleep alone since it might have been on account of touching his wife or for some other minor impurity. How could it be when the other *hadith* itself says, "He slept until I heard him snoring." When it was time to pray, he prayed without doing *wudu'*.

It is said that his heart did not sleep because he was given revelation while asleep. The story of the Valley only referred to the sleep of his eyes preventing him from seeing the sun. It had nothing to do with the action of the heart. The Prophet said, "Allah took our souls. If He had wished, He would have returned them to us at another time."

If it is said that if it was not his habit to sleep deeply, he would not have said to Bilal, "Watch for morning for us," the answer is that it was part of the Prophet's habit to pray in the darkness before *Subh* and to watch for the beginning of the dawn. This could not be said about someone whose eye is asleep since dawn is something which is perceived by the physical senses. In this instance, he charged Bilal to watch and inform him of the beginning of dawn. It would be the same if he had been prevented from watching for dawn by something other than sleep.

If it is asked what the Prophet's prohibition means in the statement, "I forgot," when the Prophet also said, "I forget as you forget. When I forget, then remind me," and when he also said, "He reminded me of such-and-such an *ayat* which I had forgotten," you should know that there is no contradiction in these phrases.

As for the prohibition about saying, "I forgot such-and-such an *ayat*," it is possible that it was one which was abrogated in the Qur'an, i.e. it did not entail inattention. Allah compelled him to forget it in order to wipe out what He wished and to confirm what He wished. He was reminded of whatever oversight or inattention there was in it and it is correct to say "I forgot" in respect of it.

It has been said that the Prophet meant this as a recommendation to ascribe that action to its Creator. The other interpretation is based on the fact that it is permissible for the slave to acquire the action for himself. He was permitted to omit the *ayats* he omitted after he had conveyed what he was commanded to convey and had transmitted it to people. Then he asked to be reminded about it by his community or by his own self – except for anything that Allah had decreed should be abrogated and wiped out from the hearts and not remembered at all. It is possible that the Prophet forgot in this manner on one occasion, and it is possible that he was made to forget something before he conveyed it in a way that would neither change the revelation's composition, confuse its judgements nor cause any gaps in it. Then he was reminded of what he had forgotten. It is impossible for his forgetfulness to last because Allah has promised to preserve His Book and He took charge of making sure it was conveyed in its completeness.

SECTION 13
The Refutation of those who say that small wrong actions are permissible for the Prophet and an examination of their arguments

The *fuqaha'*, the people of *hadith* and the theologians who follow them who say that it is permissible for the Prophets to commit minor wrong actions take the literal meaning of many things in the Qur'an and *hadith* as a proof for their position. If they were to hold to the literal meaning, it would lead them in many instances to allowing major wrong actions, to the breaking of the consensus and to saying things that are not appropriate for a Muslim to say.

This is all the more the case when what they use as proofs are things whose meaning is disputed, and whose possible meanings are contradictory and about which the *Salaf* said different things.

Because there is no consensus about this, and what is used to demonstrate it is a matter of dispute, and proofs exist to indicate the error of their words and the soundness of other positions, it is in fact obligatory to abandon that position for what is known to be sound.

We will look at some of these things, Allah willing. They include Allah's words to the Prophet, **"So that Allah may forgive you your earlier errors and any later ones"** (48:2); **"Ask forgiveness for your wrongdoing and for the men and women who believe"** (47:19); **"We removed your load from you which weighed down your back"** (94:4); **"Allah pardon you! Why did you excuse them ...?"** (9:43); **"Were it not for a decree which had already preceded from Allah, a terrible punishment would have afflicted you on account of what you took"** (8:68); and **"He frowned and turned away because the blind man came to him."** (80:2-3)

There are also some statements that Allah makes when relating the stories of other prophets such as **"Adam disobeyed his Lord and became misled"** (20:121) and **"Then when He granted them a healthy, upright child, they made what He had given them co-partner with Him."** (7:19) He says that Adam said, **"Our Lord, we have wronged ourselves."** (7:23) Allah says that Yunus said, **"Glory be to You, I have been among the wrongdoers."** (21:87)

Allah mentions the story of Da'ud and says, **"Da'ud realised that We had put him to the test. So he begged forgiveness from his Lord and fell down prone, prostrating, and repented. So We forgave him for that and he has nearness to Us and a good Homecoming."** (38:24) Allah says about Yusuf, **"She wanted him and he would have wanted her."** (12:24) He also relates the story about Yusuf's brothers. He says about Musa, **"So Musa hit him, dealing him a fatal blow. He said, 'This is part of Shaytan's handiwork.'"** (28:15)

There is also what the Prophet said in his supplication, "O Allah, forgive me my past and future wrong actions, what I conceal and what I make known,"[1] and he made other similar supplications. The Prophet said, "My heart becomes rusted over, so I seek forgiveness of Allah." In Abu Hurayra's version, "I seek forgiveness of Allah and I turn to Him in repentance more than seventy times a day."

Allah quotes Nuh saying, **"If You do not forgive me and have mercy on me."** (11:47) Allah said to Nuh, **"Do not address Me concerning the wrongdoers. They shall be drowned."** (11:37) He quotes Ibrahim saying, **"He who I sincerely hope will forgive my mistakes on the Day of Reckoning."** (26:82) He quotes Musa saying, **"I have turned to You in repentance."** (7:143) He says, **"We tested Sulayman."** (38:34) There are other such instances.

As for using His words, **"So that Allah may forgive you your earlier errors and any later ones,"** as a proof, the commentators disagree about what it means. It is said that what is meant is before and after prophethood. It is said that what is meant is those of the Prophet's wrong actions which had occurred or had not occurred. Allah told the Prophet he was forgiven for them. It could mean forgiveness for what was before prophethood and protection after it. Ahmad ibn Nasir stated that. It is said that it refers to his community. It is said that it means from forgetfulness, inattention and faulty interpretation. At-Tabari said that and al-Qushayri preferred it. It is said that "past" refers to what Adam did and "future" means the wrong actions of his community. As-Samarqandi and as-Sulami have related that interpretation from Ibn 'Ata'.

It is like the interpretation of His words, **"Ask forgiveness for your wrongdoing and for the men and women who believe."** (47:19) Makki said that when the Prophet was addressed here, it was his community that was intended.

It is said that when the Prophet was commanded to say, **"I have no idea what will be done with me or you. I follow only what has been revealed to me. I am only a clear warner,"** (46:9) the unbelievers gloated about this, so Allah revealed, **"...so that Allah may forgive you your earlier errors and any later ones."** (48:2)

Ibn 'Abbas pointed out that the fate of the believers is mentioned in the *ayat* which follows it.[2] The intent of *the ayat* is that the believer is forgiven without

---

1. Al-Bukhari and Muslim.
2. Which ends **"so that He might admit the believing men and women into gardens..."**

being punished for any wrong action even if it existed.

One of them said that forgiveness here means being free of faults.

As for His words, **"We removed from you your burden which weighed down your back,"** it is said that it means his previous wrong actions from before his prophethood as has been stated by 'Abdu'r-Rahman ibn Zayd and al-Hasan al-Basri and implied by Qatada.

It is said that it means he was preserved from wrong action before prophethood and protected against it. If that had not been the case, his back would have been weighed down. As-Samarqandi related something to that effect.

It is said that what is meant by it is that what weighed down his back was the burden of the message until he conveyed it. Al-Mawardi and as-Sulami have related that.

Makki said that it means that Allah removed the burden of the *Jahiliyya* from him.

It is said that it means the weight of the concern of his secret, his bewilderment and his seeking out his *Shari'a* until Allah gave it to him. Al-Qushayri has related something to that effect.

It is said that it means that Allah lightened his burden for him by preserving what he asked to be preserved.

"Weighed down your back," means that it was about to be weighed down, so the meaning of the *ayat* for those who make it refer to the time before prophethood is that it relates to the Prophet's concern for the matters which he did before he was a Prophet and which were forbidden to him after he became a Prophet. He thought of them as burdens which weighed him down and was apprehensive because of them.

It could be that the word **"remove"** means Allah's protecting him from wrong actions which would have weighed down his back if they had existed. Or else it is from the weight of the message. Or else it is from what weighed on him and occupied his heart concerning what he had done in the *Jahiliyya*. Or the burden is removed by the fact that Allah told him that He had preserved His revelation as the Prophet had requested.

With regard to the *ayat*, **"Allah pardon you! Why did you excuse them until it was clear to you which of them were telling the truth and until you knew the liars?"** (9:43) the Prophet had had no command about this matter from Allah before the prohibition so it cannot be counted as rebellion and Allah did not consider it an act of rebellion.

Niftawayh said, "Allah kept him far from this! He was given a choice regarding the two matters." The scholars have said that he could do what he liked concerning things about which he had not received revelation.[1] Allah

---

1. i.e. by the use of *ijtihad*.

says, **"Give permission to any of them you please."** (24:62) When he gave them permission, Allah informed him that he did not know about their secret thoughts. If he had not given them permission, they would have remained behind in any case.[1] There is no objection to him regarding what he did.

The word "pardon" (*'afa*) in this *ayat* does not mean "forgive". It bears the same meaning as when the Prophet said, "Allah has pardoned (exempted) you from paying *zakat* on horses and slaves." In other words it was not obligatory for them and therefore not binding on them.[2]

Al-Qushayri said, "Pardon (*afw*) is not only used in Arabic for pardoning a wrong action." He said that the meaning of *'afa* in **"Allah pardon you"** is that He did not consider it a wrong action for him. Ad-Da'udi said that it is said that this was to honour him, whilst Makki said that it is an invocation similar to expressions like "May Allah make you right" and "May He exalt you," and As-Samarqandi has related that it means "Allah has guarded you."

As for Allah's words regarding the captives of Badr, **"It is not fitting for a Prophet to take captives until he has let much blood in the land. You desire the goods of this world whereas Allah desires the Next World. Allah is Almighty, All-Wise,"** (8:67) they do not necessitate a wrong action on the part of the Prophet. The *ayat* contains clarification about something that was particular to him and demonstrates the way he was preferred above the other Prophets. He himself said, "No Prophet before me was given this," and also, "Booty was made lawful to me and it was not made lawful for any Prophet before me."

If it is asked what then is the meaning of the words, **"You desire the goods of this world,"** (8:67) it is said that it is addressed to those among the community in Madina who desired that and whose goal was solely the goods of this world and to amass great quantities of them. Allah does not mean the Prophet, may Allah bless him and grant him peace, or the great among his Companions. It is related from ad-Dahhak that this was revealed when the idolaters were defeated in the Battle of Badr and the people were busy stripping the dead and gathering the booty from the slain so that 'Umar feared the enemy would fall on them.

Allah says, **"Were it not for a decree which had already preceded from Allah, a terrible punishment would have afflicted you on account of what you took."** (8:68) The commentators disagree about the meaning of this *ayat*. It is said that it means if it had not been that Allah only punishes people after a prohibition has come down.[3] He would have punished them. This also negates

---

1. It is related that there were some people who said, "Ask the Messenger of Allah for permission. If he gives you permission, then sit down. If he does not give you permission, then sit down anyway." "Sitting down" here means to refuse to go out on the expedition.
2. Abu Dawud, at-Tirmidhi and an-Nasa'i from 'Ali.
3. Quoted by at-Tabari from Muhammad ibn 'Ali ibn al-Husayn ibn 'Ali ibn Abi Talib.

the idea that what happened with the captives was an act of rebellion.

It is also said that it means if it had not been for their belief in the Qur'an, which is the Book that ensures pardon, they would have been punished for taking the booty.[1]

It is said that it means that, if it had not been that you believed in the Qur'an and were therefore among those for whom booty is lawful, you would have been punished as those who exceed the limits are always punished. It is said that it means that, if it had not already been written on the Preserved Tablet that booty was lawful for you, you would have been punished for it. All of this negates the possibility of wrong action and rebellion because the one who does what is lawful for him is not a rebel.

Allah says, **"So make full use of any booty you have taken which is lawful and good; and fear Allah. Allah is Ever-Forgiving, Most Merciful."** (8:69)

It is said that the Prophet was given a choice regarding this matter. 'Ali relates that Jibril came to the Prophet on the Day of Badr and said, "Let your Companions choose what to do about the captives. If they like, they can kill them. If they like, they can take ransom for them, but if they do, in the coming year a like number of them will be slain." They said, "We will take the ransom, and let some of us be killed."

This is a proof of the soundness of what we have said. They only did what they had permission to do although some of them inclined to the weaker of the two options instead of killing them which would have been better. They were punished for that and the weakness of the choice they made and the correctness of the other choice was made clear to them. However, none of them were rebels nor were they committing a wrong action.

At-Tabari indicated something similar and said, "If a punishment had descended from heaven, only 'Umar would have been safe from it," indicating that this was due to his correct opinion and the opinion of those who took the same position by exalting the *deen*, the victory of its word and the obliteration of the enemy. If this action had incurred a punishment, 'Umar would have been saved from it. 'Umar was mentioned because he was the first to say that they should be killed. However, Allah did not decree punishment for them because He wanted to make lawful for them what had already happened.

Al-Da'udi said that this report is not confirmed, and even if it had been confirmed, it is not permissible to hold that the Prophet gave a judgement about something about which there was no text or proof and when no command had been given to him about it. Allah cleared him of that.

Qadi Bakr ibn al-'Ala' said that in this *ayat* Allah told His Prophet that his interpretation was in harmony with what had been predestined for him in making booty and ransom lawful. In the raid of 'Abdullah ibn Jahsh in which

---

1. Ibn 'Atiyya in his *Tafsir*.

Ibn al-Hadrami was killed, the Muslims offered al-Hakam ibn Kaydan and his companion for ransom and Allah did not censure them for doing that. That was more than a year before Badr.

All of this indicates that the action of the Prophet regarding the captives was based on interpretation and insight and precedent. Allah did not censure him for what he did with them. Allah knows best, but Allah meant the immense import of the whole affair of Badr, and the great number of captives taken, to show His blessing and confirm His favour to them by informing them about what He had written in the Preserved Tablet making that lawful for them. It was not censure, objection nor considered to be a wrong action. This is what was meant.

*   *   *   *

As for the story connected with the *ayat*, **"He frowned and turned away,"** (80:1) it does not assert the existence of any wrong action on the part of the Prophet. Allah informed him that the person to whom he was devoting his attention was one of those who would not be purified. If the state of the two men had been unveiled to him, then it would have been better to have turned to the blind man.[1]

What caused the Prophet to be occupied with that unbeliever was an act of obedience to Allah. He was conveying His message and extending friendship for the sake of Allah as He had prescribed. It was not an act of rebellion or opposition. What Allah did, in saying what He said to him, was to inform him about the comparative state of the two men and the weakness of the unbeliever. He indicated that he should turn from him as He said, **"But it is not up to you whether or not he is purified."** (80:7)

It is also said that by **"he frowned and turned away"** Allah was referring to the action of the unbeliever who was with the Prophet as Abu Tammam has related.

*   *   *   *

As for the story of Adam when Allah says, **"The two of them ate from it..."** (20:121) after He had said, **"But do not approach this tree and so become wrong-doers,"** (2:35) **"Did I not forbid you this tree,"** (7:22) and the clear

---

1. 'Abdullah ibn Umm Maktum.

statement that it was rebellion, **"Adam disobeyed his Lord and became misled,"** (20:121) it is said that it means he made a mistake. Allah told us about his excuse when He said, **"We made a contract with Adam before, but he forgot. We did not find that he had a firm resolve."** (20:115)

'Abdu'r-Rahman ibn Zayd said that he forgot Iblis' enmity to him and the contract which Allah had made with him when He said, **"Here is an enemy for you and your wife."** (20:117) It is also said that he forgot because of what Iblis showed them.

Ibn 'Abbas said that man (*insan*) is called "man" because he made a contract and then forgot about it (*nasiya*). It is said that Adam did not intend opposition by eating from the tree wrongly, but that he and Hawwa' were deceived by Iblis' oath to them, **"I am one of those who give you good advice,"** (7:21) imagining that no-one would swear by Allah and then break their oath. Adam's excuse is related in various traditions.

Ibn Jubayr related that Iblis swore to them by Allah until he beguiled them because the believer can be deceived. It is said that Adam forgot and did not intend to oppose Him and so Allah said, **"We did not find that he had a firm resolve,"** i.e. intention for opposition. Most commentators agree that resolution means determination and steadfastness.

It is said that when he ate from the tree, it resulted in drunkenness and this caused weakness because Allah described the wine of the Garden as not causing intoxication. When Adam forgot, it was not an act of rebellion. The same thing happens if one is confused and errs since it is agreed that someone who forgets and overlooks falls outside the jurisdiction of responsibility.

Shaykh Abu Bakr ibn Furak and others have said that it is possible that this occurred before Adam became a Prophet. Their proof is in His words, **"Adam disobeyed his Lord and became misled. But then his Lord selected him and turned to him and guided him."** (20:122) Allah mentions election and guidance after rebellion.

It is said that he ate from the tree because of the way he interpreted Allah's prohibition. He did not know that it was that tree which he was forbidden because he interpreted Allah's prohibition as referring to a particular tree, not to an entire species of tree. This is why it is said that his repentance was for the fact that he abandoned caution, not for an act of rebellion.

It is also said that he interpreted Allah's prohibition to him as not forbidding him in a way that made it unlawful.

It is said that in any case, Allah says, **"Adam disobeyed his Lord and became misled"** and then says, **"He turned to him and guided him."**

It is mentioned in the *hadith* of intercession that Adam said of his wrong action, "I was forbidden to eat from the tree, and so I rebelled." The answer to this and other things will come at the end of this section, Allah willing.

*   *   *

As for the story of Yunus, some of it has already been discussed earlier. There is no mention of wrong action in Yunus' story. The Qur'an says of him, **"He ran away"** and **"He went out in anger."** It is said that Allah took revenge on him because he left his people and fled from the punishment. It is said that when he promised them punishment and then Allah pardoned them, he said, "By Allah, I will never face them as a liar." It is said that they used to kill people who lied, and he feared that. It is said that he was too weak to bear the burden of the message.

It has already been stated that he did not lie to them. None of this contains any mention of rebellion. Allah says, **"He ran away to the laden ship."** (37:140) Some commentators say that this happened because he separated himself from his people.[1]

As for his statement, **"I was one of the unjust,"** injustice (*dhulm*) means to put something in other than its proper place. According to some of them, that is his admission of his wrong action. As for his leaving his people without the permission of his Lord or because of his weakness regarding what he was made to bear or his calling for punishment against his people, Nuh called for the destruction of his people and was not punished.

Al-Wasiti said, "He was disconnecting his Lord from injustice and ascribing the action to himself, acknowledging it as his just deserts. His statement is like that of Adam and Hawwa', **'Our Lord, we have wronged ourselves,'** (7:23) since they were the cause of their being in a place other than where they had first been put. They themselves were responsible for their expulsion from the Garden and their descent to the earth."

*   *   *

As for the story of the Prophet Da'ud,[2] one only has recourse to what the traditionists have written about him which has been taken from the People of the Book who have altered and changed things. Allah does not give a text for any of it and it has not come down to us in any sound *hadith*.

What Allah says about the matter is contained in His words, **"Da'ud realised that We had put him to the test. So he begged forgiveness from his Lord and fell down prone, prostrating, and repented. So We forgave him for that and he has nearness to Us and a good Homecoming."** (38:24-25). In it, Allah says that he was "repentant". The meaning of Allah's testing of him, is to

---

1. The position of al-Mubarrad.
2. What is referred to is the story of the wife of Uriah.

331

try him. According to Qatada, repentant here means obedient, and this is the better interpretation.

Ibn 'Abbas and Ibn Mas'ud said that Da'ud only told the man to leave his wife with him so that he would be able to see that she was provided for. Allah censured him for that, warned him and objected to his preoccupation with this world. This cannot be relied on. It is said that he proposed to her when another man had already proposed to her. It is said that in his heart he wanted her husband to be killed.

As-Samarqandi said that his wrong action for which he asked forgiveness was his statement to one of the protagonists,[1] **"He has wronged you,"** so that he considered him wronged merely by the statement of his adversary. It is said that he was fearful, thinking of the trial that had been opened up in front of him, of his kingdom and this world.

Ahmad ibn Nasr, Abu Tammam and other careful scholars believe that what these traditions ascribe to Da'ud should be refuted.

Ad-Da'udi has said that there is no confirmed report about the story of Da'ud and Uriah (Uriya') and that it is not permissible to suppose that a Prophet would want to kill another Muslim.

It is said that the two adversaries who argued before him really were arguing about a ewe, taking the *ayat* literally.

*　　　　　*　　　　　*

As for the story of Yusuf and his brothers,[2] there is no fault in Yusuf regarding anything that happened. There is no confirmation that the brothers were Prophets so that one would need to discuss their actions, although the Tribes and their number are mentioned in the Qur'an together with the Prophets. The commentators have said that all that means is that there are Prophets among the descendants of the Tribes.

It is said that they were young when they did what they did to Yusuf. That is why they did not recognise Yusuf's station when they were together with him. This is why they said, **"Why not send him out with us tomorrow so he can enjoy himself and play about?"** (12:12) If they had actually been Prophets, they would never have done such a thing. Allah knows best.

As for the statement, **"She wanted him and he would have wanted her had he not seen the Clear Proof of his Lord,"** (12:24) according to the position of most of the *fuqaha'* and people of *hadith*, the soul's desire is not punishable and does not amount to a wrong action. The Prophet said from his Lord,[3] "When

---

1. Two angels in the form of men who brought an argument before him about the man with only a single sheep having his sheep added to the man with many sheep. See Qur'an 38:23-24.
2. See Qur'an 12.
3. In a *hadith qudsi* which is related in Muslim.

My slave desires something and does not do it, a good action is written for him." There is no act of rebellion in the mere fact of his desire. The *fuqaha'* and theologians say that "desire" is when the soul is prepared to do something. The soul is forgiven for the desires and thoughts it is not prepared to act on. This is the truth, and Allah willing, Yusuf's desire was of this kind.

He said, **"I do not say my self was free from blame,"** (12:53) meaning "I cannot declare that it was free of this desire." Or he may have said that out of humility and admission of the soul's opposition even though he was purified and innocent. Abu Hatim related from Abu 'Ubayda that desire did not enter Yusuf. The words take the form of a conditional clause, i.e. she desired him and if it had not been for that fact that he saw the angel of his Lord, he would have desired her.

Allah said about the woman, **"I tried to seduce him, but he resisted me,"** (12:32) and **"That happened so We might avert from him all evil and lust,"** (12:24) and **"She barred the doors and said, 'Come over here.' He said, 'Allah is my refuge! He is My Lord and has been good to me with where I live.'"** (12:23) It is said that the words "**my Lord**" refers to Allah and it is also said that they refer to the king.

It is said "**He would have wanted her**" means wanted to restrain and admonish her. It is said that it means he grieved her by refusing her. It is said that it means to look at her. It is said that it means he desired to beat her and repel her. It is said that in any case all this happened before he was a Prophet.

One of the scholars has mentioned that the women continued to incline towards Yusuf with lust until Allah made him a Prophet and cast the majesty of prophethood on him. Then his majesty distracted all who saw him from his beauty.

*   *   *

As for the report about Musa and the man he killed, Allah says that the man was one of Musa's enemies. It is said that he was a Copt who followed the religion of Pharaoh. The Qur'an indicates that all this took place before Musa was a Prophet. Qatada said that he struck him with his staff without intending to kill him, so there was no act of rebellion involved. He said, **"This is part of Shaytan's handiwork,"** (28:15) and, **"I have wronged myself, so forgive me."** (28:15) According to Ibn Jurayh, he said that because he did not have leave to kill until commanded to do so.

An-Naqqash said that he did not kill the man intentionally, but struck him a blow to put a stop to his injustice. He said that it is said that this occurred before he was a Prophet as is indicated by Allah's words, **"We tested you with many trials,"** (20:40) i.e. tested you with affliction after affliction. It is said that this refers to what happened to him with Pharaoh, and it is said that it refers to his being thrown in the ark into the Nile and other things. It is said that it means He made him completely pure, as Ibn Jubayr and Mujahid have stated, because in Arabic this word is used to mean the purification of silver in the fire. The root of "*fitna*" is to test and display what is hidden, although it is used in the *Shari'a* to mean a temptation leading to something disliked.

Similarly it is related in sound *hadith*[1] that the Angel of Death came to Musa and Musa smote the angel in the eye, knocking it out. This *hadith* does not contain anything that suggests that Musa acted excessively or did something he should not have done since the business was an outward matter which was permitted. Musa was defending himself from someone who had come to kill him. The angel had taken on human form, and so it was not possible for Musa to know that it was the Angel of Death. Therefore he defended himself strenuously and this resulted in the form which the Angel of Death had taken on as a test from Allah, losing an eye. When the angel came to him later and told him that he was Allah's messenger to him, Musa submitted.

Both modern and early scholars have said various things about this *hadith* and I believe the best interpretation to be that of Shaykh Imam Abu 'Abdullah al-Mazari. Ibn 'A'isha and others used to interpret the description of his blow to the eye-socket and his knocking the eye out of it as a turn of phrase.

*   *   *

As for the story of Sulayman and what the commentators have related about his wrong action and Allah's statement, **"We tested (*fatanna*) Sulayman,"** (38:34) it means to put him to the test. He was afflicted, as the Prophet related,[1] as follows: "At night, he went around to a hundred wives (or ninety-nine) on a horse which he used for striving in the way of Allah. His friend said to him, 'Say, "If Allah wills."' He did not say it and only one of his wives became pregnant and she gave birth to half a child." The Prophet said, "By the One in whose hand my soul is, if he had said, 'If Allah wills,' they would have striven in the way of Allah."

The people of meanings say that "half" means the dead body which was cast on his chair when it was shown to him and that was his punishment and test. It is said that the child died and was cast dead on his chair. It is said that his wrong action was avarice and desire. It is said that he did not say, 'If Allah wills,' when he was overwhelmed and overcome by desire.

It is said that his punishment was that his kingdom was stripped away and his wrong action was that he was tempted to judge unjustly in favour of one of

---

1. Muslim and al-Bukhari from Abu Hurayra.
2. In Muslim and al-Bukhari and elsewhere.

his favourite wife's relations. It is said that he was punished for a wrong action into which one of his wives tempted him.

What the historians transmit about Shaytan taking on the form of Sulayman, overcoming his kingdom, and governing his community with unjust rule is not true because the *shaytans* do not have this power and the Prophets were protected from things of this nature.

If the question is put: "Why did Sulayman not say, 'If Allah wills' in this story?" there are various answers. One is what is related in the sound *hadith* to the effect that he simply forgot to say it. That was so that the will of Allah would be carried out. The second is that he did not hear his companion and was distracted from him.

Sulayman said, **"Give me a kingdom the like of which will never be granted to anyone after me."** (38:35) Sulayman did not do this out of jealousy or desire for this world. His goal, according to the commentators, was that no-one would have the power Sulayman was given in the same manner that Shaytan seized that power when it was stripped from Sulayman in the period of his affliction. This is according to those who take that position.

It is said that he wanted it to be a sign of excellence and a special gift from Allah to him by which he would be singled out as other Prophets and Messengers of Allah were singled out with special signs from Him.

It is said that it was in order that it be a proof and evidence of his prophethood in the same way that making iron soft was for his father, bringing the dead to life was for 'Isa, and like the special gift of intercession to Muhammad.

*   *   *

As for the story of Nuh,[1] it justifies what he did in that he asked about his son, relying on the literal meaning of Allah's words when He said, **"and your family"** in the *ayat*, **"So when Our command came and the oven boiled over, We said, 'Load into it a pair of every species, *and your family* – except for those against whom the Word was preordained – and all those who believe. But those who believed with him were only a few."** (11:40) He followed the natural implications of the expression and wanted to know what was hidden from him in it. He did not doubt Allah's promise. Allah made it clear to him that his son was not one of his family whom He had promised to save since he was an unbeliever and his actions were not righteous. He informed Nuh that his son would be drowned with those who had acted unrighteously. He forbade Nuh to speak to Him about the unrighteous. Nuh was censured for his interpretation

---

1. This refers to the incident, talked of in the Qur'an, when Nuh tried to save his unbelieving son and said to Allah, **"O my Lord, my son is of my family, and Your promise is true."** (11:45)

and became apprehensive because he had been audacious towards his Lord by asking Him what he had not been given permission to ask for.

According to an-Naqqash, Nuh did not know about the disbelief of his son. Other things have been said about the *ayat*, but none of them entail Nuh committing an act of rebellion, except for the first interpretation we mentioned in which he ventured to intercede on behalf of someone for whom he had not been given permission, even though there was no prohibition against him doing it.

*   *   *

It is related in the *Sahih* collections[1] that our Prophet was once stung by an ant and then burned a whole colony of ants. Allah revealed to him, "An ant stings you and then you burn one of the communities who glorify Allah?!" The *hadith* does not say that what he did was an act of rebellion, but that he did what he thought was correct and right by killing a number of the species who had done him this injury and prevented him from enjoying something that Allah had permitted. What happened was that the Prophet alighted in the shade of a tree and when the ant stung him, he turned his mount away from it, fearing a repetition of the injury.

In what Allah revealed to him, there is nothing that entails an act of rebellion. Allah recommended that he bear it with steadfastness and abandon revenge. It is as Allah says, **"If you are patient, it is better to be patient,"** (16:126) since he did what he did because the ant had injured him merely by behaving in accordance with its intrinsic nature. He sought to avenge himself and prevent the harm which had come to him from the ants there. Nowhere was there a command which forbade him doing so which, if there had been, would have made his action an act of rebellion against Allah.

If one asks about the meaning of the Prophet's words, "There is no-one who was not touched by wrong action – or very nearly so – except Yahya son of Zakariyya,"[2] the answer is in what we have already stated concerning the wrong actions of the Prophets which occurred without intention and arose from oversight and inattention.

SECTION 14
The state of the Prophets in their fear and asking forgiveness

It may be that you are led to question that the Prophets are protected from committing wrong actions and acts of rebellion, as is maintained by the various

---

2. From Abu Hurayra.
2. Ibn Hanbal from Ibn 'Abbas, *marfu'*.

opinions of the scholars, by asking what Allah means when He says, **"Adam disobeyed his Lord and became misled,"** (20:121) and other such things which can be found in the Qur'an and sound *hadith* about the Prophets admitting to wrong actions and their repentance and asking forgiveness, and their weeping and apprehension for what they had done, wondering by this whether people become apprehensive, repent and ask forgiveness for nothing. You should know that the degree of the Prophets in stature, sublimity, and their knowledge of Allah and of His *sunna* with His slaves, and of the extent of His authority and of the force of His power is part of what leads the Prophets to fear Him and be apprehensive about being punished for things which others are not punished for and which people have neither been forbidden from nor commanded to do in their affairs. However, they are taken to task on account of these things and censured because of them and put on their guard about being punished for them. Even though they do them as a result of interpretation, oversight or increase in the permitted matters of this world, they are fearful and apprehensive about them. They are wrong actions only in relation to their high position, and acts of rebellion only in the relation to the perfection of their obedience. They are not like other people's wrong actions and acts of rebellion.

The word for wrong action (*dhanb*) is derived from the lowest and basest of things. *Dhanab*, is the tail of a thing, i.e. the end of it. The "tails" (*adhnab*) among people are the basest ones among them. These things we are talking about in relation to the prophets are the lowest of their actions and the worst of their states because they are purified and their inward and outward parts filled with sound action, excellent words, overt and hidden remembrance of Allah and fear and esteem of Him, secretly and openly.

Other people are soiled by major wrong actions, ugly things and deviations. These "failings" of the Prophet are like good actions for other people as in the saying, "The good actions of the righteous are the evil actions of those who are brought near," i.e. they see them as evils in relation to their high state. Similarly "rebellion" consists of abandonment and opposition. According to the expression, however, there is still opposition and abandonment in oversight or interpretation.

Allah says of Adam, **"He became misled,"** i.e. he was ignorant that the tree was the one which had been forbidden to him. The "error" is ignorance. It is said that he made a mistake in seeking immortality when he ate, and his expectations were disappointed.

Yusuf was criticised for saying to one of his companions in prison, **"'Mention me when you are with your lord' (i.e. Pharaoh). But Shaytan made him forget to remind his Lord (i.e. Allah), and so he remained in prison for several years."** (12:43) It is said that the meaning is that Yusuf was made to forget to remember Allah. It is also said that his companion was made to forget to mention him to his master the king. The Prophet said, "If it had not been for these words of Yusuf, he would not have remained in prison as long as he did."[1]

Ibn Dinar said that when Yusuf said this, he was told, "You have taken other-than-Me as a guardian so I will lengthen the term of your imprisonment." He said, "My Lord, the extent of my affliction made my heart forget."

One scholar said that the Prophets were punished for the slightest thing because of their position with Allah, while these things are ignored in the case of all other creatures since other people lack concern about them because of the extent of their bad behaviour. Those who argue that the Prophets are protected from all wrong actions say what we say, namely that the Prophets are taken to task for oversight and forgetfulness while others are not punished for it. They have a higher station, so their state in such matters is more reprehensible than the state of others.

However, you should know that the kind of punishment referred to here is not punishment as it is defined for others. We say that the Prophets are punished for their lapses in this world so that it will increase their degree. They are tested in this way so that their awareness of it will be a means for the raising of their degree as in the words of Allah, **"But then his Lord selected him and turned to him and guided him."** (20:122)

Allah says to Da'ud, **"We forgave him for that."** (38:25) After Musa says, **"I turn in repentance to You,"** Allah says to Musa **"I have chosen you over all mankind."** (7:143, 144)

After Allah mentions the trial of Sulayman and his repentance, He says, **"So We subjected the wind to him to blow at his command, softly, wherever he directed. And the shaytans, every builder and diver, and others of them, yoked together in chains. 'This is Our gift: so bestow it or withhold it without reckoning.' He will have nearness to Us and a good Homecoming."** (38:36-40)

One of the theologians said that the errors of the Prophets are outwardly errors, while in reality they are marks of honour and acts that bring nearness. This is like what we have already stated. Other people learn from the mistakes of the Prophets and those who do not have their degree take note of their punishment for what they did and are increased in awareness and caution and concern for taking account of their actions, so as to remain thankful for blessings and steadfast in afflictions by seeing what happened to the people of this high, protected level. This is why Salih al-Murri said that the case of Da'ud has been mentioned as a means of expansion for those who turn in repentance.

Ibn 'Ata' said that Allah does not state anywhere in the story of Dhu'n-Nun (lit. Man of the Fish, i.e. Yunus) that he was imperfect. The story was mentioned in order to increase our Prophet's desire for steadfastness.

Some people say that since minor wrong actions are forgiven by the

---

1. Related by Ibn Jarir and at-Tabarani from Ibn 'Abbas.

avoidance of major wrong actions and since there is no dispute about the Prophets being protected from major wrong actions, their minor wrong actions must be forgiven in this way (i.e. by their avoidance of major wrong actions). What then do these people say is the meaning of the Prophets' punishment for minor wrong actions, their fear and their repentance if these actions would have been automatically forgiven if they had existed? They give our answer about their being punished for the actions of oversight and interpretation.

It is said that the Prophet's abundance of asking forgiveness and his repentance comes from clinging to humility, slavehood and admission of imperfection, out of thanks to Allah for His blessing. He said when he was given security from being punished for his former and latter wrong actions, "Should I not be a thankful slave?" He also said, "I am the one among you with the most fear of Allah and I know the most about fearful awareness."[1]

Al-Harith ibn Asad al-Muhasibi said, "The fear experienced by the angels and the Prophets is the fear which comes from esteem of Allah and devotion to the worship of Allah because they are safe from punishment." It is said that they had this fear so that they would be followed in it and their communities would make a *sunna* of them. The Prophet said, "If you knew what I know, you would laugh little and weep much."[2]

There is also another subtle meaning in their repentance and asking forgiveness which one of the *'ulama'* has indicated. That is seeking the love of Allah.

Allah says, **"Allah loves those who turn back from wrongdoing and He loves those who purify themselves."** (2:222) The Messengers and the Prophets began again to ask for forgiveness, repent, regret and return in every case to seek the love of Allah. Asking forgiveness means turning to Allah.

Allah says to His Prophet having forgiven him his past and future wrong actions, **"Allah turned to the Prophet, and the Muhajirun and the Ansar."** (9:117) Allah says, **"Glorify your Lord's praise and ask His forgiveness. He is the Ever-Turning."** (110:3)

SECTION 15
The benefit of the sections investigating the Prophet's protection from wrong action

The truth should by now be clear to you that the Prophet was protected from being ignorant of Allah and His attributes in any way. Logically and by consensus, the Prophet was protected before prophethood from being in any

---

1. Al-Bukhari.
2. Ibn Hanbal, Muslim, al-Bukhari, at-Tirmidhi, an-Nasa'i and Ibn Majah from Anas. Al-Hakim has it from Abu Dharr. Others have it from Abu'd-Darda'.

state at all which was incompatible with knowledge, and he was protected after it according to oral reports and transmission. It is absolutely impossible both logically and by the *Shari'a* itself, that the Prophet should have been ignorant of anything concerning the *Shari'a* he confirmed or concerning the revelation he conveyed from his Lord.

The Prophet was also protected from telling lies and making contradictory statements either intentionally or unintentionally from the time Allah made him a Prophet and sent him as a Messenger. Such things are impossible for him according to the *Shari'a*, by consensus, by examination and by proof. He was also absolutely free of those things before he was a Prophet.

He was free of major wrong actions by consensus and from minor ones, as we have made clear, and from lasting oversight and inattention, and from continuing in error and forgetfulness regarding what he prescribed in the *Shari'a* for the Community. He was protected in all his states – pleasure and anger, gravity and jest.

You must hold onto this fact like a miser guards his gold and value these sections as they should be valued and know their great benefit and importance. The one who is ignorant of what is necessary for the Prophet or what is impossible for him and who does not know the rules governing these matters is not safe from believing some things to be different from the way they really are. So he might ascribe things to the Prophet that must not be ascribed to him. Thus he could be destroyed by his ignorance and fall into the chasm of the lowest level of the Fire, his false opinion and his believing what is not permitted for him to believe having brought him to the Abode of Ruin. That is why the Prophet protected the two men who saw him at night in the mosque with Safiyya by saying, "It is Safiyya." Then he added, "Shaytan runs through the son of Adam as blood flows through him and I feared that something might be cast into your hearts which could cause you to be destroyed."[1]

This is one of the benefits of what we have discussed in these sections. Because of his ignorance, it may be that an ignorant man might not know what the matter really is. When he hears something doubtful he might think that discussing it is one of the means to gain knowledge when it would be far better to be silent. It should be clear to you that this is connected to the benefit which we have just mentioned.

The second benefit concerns what is necessary for the foundations of *fiqh* and what minor questions of *fiqh* are also based on. By it one is freed from most of the controversies arising from the disagreement of the *fuqaha'* concerning a number of questions. It concerns judgements based on what the Prophet said and did which is a vast subject and one of the major sources of *fiqh*. Such judgements have as their fundamental premise the fact that the Prophet was

1. Muslim and al-Bukhari from Safiyya.

truthful in his reports and in what he conveyed. Oversight is not possible in respect of what he said and the Prophet was protected from deliberate opposition to Allah in all his actions. As scholars disagree about the occurrence of minor wrong actions, so they also disagree about copying his actions. This matter is fully dealt with in the books of the science of the fundamental principles of *fiqh* so we will not go into it in depth.

The third benefit is for the judge and the *mufti* concerning what it is necessary for them to know in respect of anyone who ascribes any of these things to the Prophet and describes the Prophet as having them. If someone does not recognise what is permitted and what is forbidden for the Prophet, and what there is either consensus or dispute about, how can he decide on a *fatwa* regarding such matters? Without this knowledge how can he know whether what a person says is imperfect or praiseworthy? He is either in danger of unjustly shedding the blood of a Muslim which is *haram* or of overlooking the Prophet's right and thus violating respect for the Prophet.

In the same way, the masters of legal methodology (*usul*), the Imams of the *'ulama'* and the precise scholars have disagreed about whether the angels are protected from wrong action and it is this matter which we will address in the following section.

SECTION 16
On the protection of the angels from wrong action

The Muslims agree that the judgement concerning the Messengers among the angels is the same as that for the Prophets and that they are protected from the same things that the Prophets are protected from. The angels are like the Prophets with their communities in respect of the duties they have with regard to conveying revelation to the Prophets.

The *'ulama'* disagree about angels other than the Messengers among them. One group believes that all of them are protected from acts of rebellion and they use as a proof Allah's words, **"They do not disobey Allah in what He orders them and carry out what they are ordered to do"** (66:6); **"There is not one of us who does not have a known station. We are those drawn up in ranks. We are those who glorify"** (37: 165-166); **"Those in His presence do not consider themselves too great to worship Him and do not grow tired of it. They glorify Him by night and day, without ever flagging"** (21: 19-20); **"Those who are with your Lord do not consider themselves too great to worship Him"** (7:206); **"Noble, virtuous"** (80:16); and **"No-one may touch it except the purified,"** (56:79) and similar reports.

Another group believe that these are special qualities restricted to the angels who are Messengers and those among them who are brought near to Allah.

They take as a proof things which the people of reports and commentaries mention which we will mention later, clarifying their position if Allah wills.

The correct position is that all of them are protected and their high rank is free from anything that might lower their rank and station from the sublimity of their high degree. One of our shaykhs indicated that there is no need for any *faqih* to involve himself in discussing their protection. I say that any discussion concerning this matter must be based on what has been said regarding the protection of Prophets in respect of the benefits which we have mentioned – except for the benefit of words and actions which must be omitted in this instance.

Something that those who do not consider it necessary for all angels to be protected use as a proof, is what is said in the traditions and commentaries regarding the story of Harut and Marut[1] and what 'Ali and Ibn 'Abbas related about them and their temptation. You should know that these reports do not relate anything, either weak or sound, from the Messenger of Allah himself and there is nothing which is taken by analogy. The commentators disagree about the meaning of what the Qur'an says about them.

What one of them stated was rejected by many of the *Salaf* as we will show. These reports are taken from the books of the Jews and from their fabrications. What Allah told us about at the beginning of the passage concerned their forging lies like that against Sulayman and their declaring him to be an unbeliever. That story contains an immense atrocity. We will deal with that by removing the cover from these ambiguities, Allah willing.

Scholars disagree about whether Harut and Marut were angels or men and whether they are meant as "two angels." Is the recitation truly "two angels (*malakayn*)"[2] or is it "two kings (*malikayn*)"?[3]

Are Allah's words **"What was sent down"** or are they **"It was not sent down** (*ma unzila*)"? Is **"They do not teach anyone"**[4] negative or affirmative?

Most of the commentators believe that Allah tested people by the two angels who instructed them in magic, making it clear that the use[5] of magic amounts to disbelief. Whoever learns it disbelieves and whoever leaves it believes.[6]

Allah quotes them as saying, **"We are merely a trial and temptation, so do not disbelieve."** (2:102) They taught magic to people with a warning, i.e. they told those who came to learn it, "Do not do it. It parts a man and his wife. Do not suppose that it is good. It is magic, so do not disbelieve."

According to this interpretation, what the two angels did was an act of

---

1. See Qur'an 2:102.
2. As is found in the Seven Readings of the Qur'an.
3. As found in a rare reading from al-Hasan al-Basri and others.
4. This could also be taken to be "What they teach to anyone."
5. One text has "the knowledge".
6. This is the position of Malik and Ibn Hanbal. Ash-Shafi'i considers it to be a major wrong action.

obedience and they acted as Allah had commanded them. It was not rebellion. It was a trial for others.

Ibn Wahb has related that Khalid ibn Abi 'Imran mentioned Harut and Marut as teaching magic. Ibn Wahb added, "We absolve them of this." One of the scholars recited the verse as meaning, **"It was not sent down on the two angels."** (2:102) Khalid took this position and he possessed both esteem and knowledge. He absolved them even from teaching the magic which other scholars said that they had permission to teach provided that they made it clear that it was disbelief and a test and trial from Allah. How is it possible to do anything other than absolve them from all major wrong actions, acts of rebellion and the disbelief mentioned in these traditions? Khalid, as well as Ibn 'Abbas, said that the verse is a negative statement.

Makki said that the implication of the words, **"Sulayman did not disbelieve,"** means that he did not disbelieve by believing the magic which the *shaytans* fabricated against him and which the Jews followed and he said that the two angels were Jibril and Mika'il.

The Jews allege that the two angels did that, just as they also claim that Sulayman used magic. Allah calls them liars: **"But the *shaytans* disbelieved and taught people magic, and what had been sent down on the two angels/kings at Bablyon, Harut and Marut."** (2:102) It is said that they were two men who disbelieved. As-Sakan said that Harut and Marut were two infidels from the people of Babel. He must have recited "What was sent down on the two kings" by this interpretation. 'Abdu'r-Rahman ibn Abza said that the two kings were Da'ud and Sulayman. As-Samarqandi said that they were two kings from the tribe of Isra'il whom Allah transformed. The recitation as *"malikayn* (two kings)", however, is rare.

The interpretation of the *ayat* according to the evaluation of Abu Muhammad Makki is good. It absolves the angels and removes impurity from them and considers them absolutely pure. Allah described them as being purified and **"Noble, virtuous."** (80:16) **"They do not disobey Allah in what He orders them and carry out what they are ordered to do."** (66:6)

Another thing that is brought up by people is the story of Iblis being a leader of the angels and one of the guardians of the Garden; however, Allah made him an exception among the angels when He said, **"They prostrated except for Iblis."** (2:24)

This is also a subject of disagreement. Most deny that he was an angel and say that he was *Abu'l-Jinn* (father of the *jinn*) as Adam was *Abu'l-Ins* (the father of men). That is what al-Hasan, Qatada and Ibn Zayd said. Shihr ibn Hawshab said that he was one of the *jinn* whom the angels threw to earth when the *jinn* became corrupt. Making an exception outside the general category being referred to is common and allowed in the Arabic language.

Allah says, **They have no real knowledge of it, just conjecture."** (4:157)

Another thing related in the traditions[1] is that some of the angels rebelled against Allah and were burned. They were commanded to prostrate to Adam and refused, so they were burned. Sound traditions refute this, so it is not to be given any consideration. Allah knows best.

1. Ibn Jarir from Ibn 'Abbas and Ibn Abi Hatim from Yahya ibn Kathir.

Chapter Two

THE STATES OF THE PROPHET IN RESPECT OF THIS WORLD AND WHAT NON-ESSENTIAL HUMAN QUALITIES HE COULD HAVE

SECTION 1
The states of the Prophets in relation to human conditions

We have already stated that our Prophet and all the Prophets and Messengers were men. His body and outward parts were mortal and subject to the accidents, changes, pains, illnesses and death to which all men are subject. None of this involves imperfection because something can only be imperfect in comparison with something more perfect and complete of its own type. Allah has decreed that all the people of this world will live and die in it and then come out of it. He has created all men in the domain of vicissitudes.

Therefore the Prophet became ill, suffered complaints, and was afflicted by heat and bitter cold. He was touched by hunger and thirst, anger and displeasure. He felt fatigue and experienced weakness and old age. He fell and was scratched. The unbelievers inflicted a head injury on him and broke his tooth. He drank poison and was bewitched. He treated himself and was cupped and had talismans and amulets. When his term was fulfilled, he died and met the Highest Friend and was rescued from the abode of test and affliction.

These are characteristics of humanness which cannot be avoided. Other Prophets suffered even greater afflictions than he did. They were killed, thrown into the fire and sawn in half. Allah made their affliction the cause of the death of some of them at certain times and He protected others of them as He later protected our Prophet from people.

Even though our Lord did not protect our Prophet from the hand of Ibn Qami'a in the Battle of Uhud nor veil him from the eyes of his enemies when the people of Ta'if cursed him, he was veiled from the eyes of Quraysh when he went to Mount Thawr, and the sword of Ghawrath, the stone of Abu Jahl and Suraqa's horse were held back from him. Although Allah did not protect the Prophet from the magic of Labid ibn al-A'sam, He did protect him from the greater poison of the Jewess.[1]

---

1. When a woman of Khaybar gave him and some of the Companions a poisoned sheep to eat.

345

Allah's Prophets were both tested and guarded in that manner. That is part of Allah's perfect wisdom and it makes clear their honour in these situations, makes their affair clear and completes His word among them. Their humanity is confirmed by their trial, and any possibility of confusion regarding them is removed from weak people so they will not become misled by the miracles which appear at their hands as the Christians were misled about 'Isa the son of Maryam. The Prophets' afflictions are actually a solace for their communities and increase their reward with their Lord, and perfect them in the eyes of the One who is good to them.

Some scrupulous scholars say that these events and changes which are mentioned are specific to their human bodies which are mortal. They are what is endured by all the children of Adam because they are the same species.

Inwardly, the Prophets are generally free of these human attributes, and connected to the Highest Assembly and the angels, so that they can take from them and receive revelation from them. The Prophet said, "My eyes sleep but my heart does not sleep." He said, "I am not like you in my form. My Lord gives me food and drink at night."[1] He also said, "I do not forget, but I am made to forget so that He can make a *sunna* by what I do."

He said that his secret, his inward and his soul are different from his body and outward form and that none of the events which affect his outward form – weakness, hunger, sleepnessness and sleep – affect his inward. This is not the case with other men.

When other men sleep, their bodies and hearts are overwhelmed by sleep. The Prophet was present with his heart in sleep the same as when he was awake to the extent that it is reported in tradition that he was protected from minor impurity in sleep since his heart was awake.

Similarly when other people are hungry, their bodies grow weak and listless and they become totally useless. The Prophet said, "I am not like you in my form. My Lord gives me food and drink at night."

Similarly, I say that in all these states of fatigue, sickness, sorcery and hunger, nothing affected his inward nor did they overflow onto his tongue or limbs in a way that was not fitting for him as happens to other men, a subject which we will begin to clarify later.

SECTION 2
His state in relation to sorcery

If you were to say that sound reports have come that the Prophet was bewitched, such as 'A'isha's words, "The Messenger of Allah, may Allah bless

---

1. Al-Bukhari.

him and grant him peace, was bewitched until it seemed to him that he had done something when he had not done it,"[1] and another variant which says, "Until it seemed to him that he had come to his wives when he had not come to them," asking the question that since those who have been bewitched have this confused state, what was the Prophet's state in respect of this and how could such a thing happen to him when he was protected, know that this *hadith* is sound and people agree on it. Only heretics attack it, make use of it due to their feeblemindness, and complicate things in order to occasion doubts regarding the *Shari'a.*

Allah has freed the *Shari'a* and the Prophet from any ambiguity whatsoever. Sorcery is a type of illness and it arises from permissible causes which are just the same as any other type of illness to which he was subject and which did not detract from his prophethood.

As for the report that it used to seem to him that he had done something when he had not done it, none of that concerns conveying the Message or laying down the *Shari'a* or detracts from his truthfulness since the established proof and the consensus agree that he was protected from that.

What we are talking about concerns what was allowed to happen to him regarding things of this world. He was not sent because of these things and was not preferred for their sake. He was exposed to them like all men. It is impossible for him to imagine that he had not done something when he had actually done it.

This is explained in the variant *hadith*, "until it seemed to him that he had come to his wives, but he had not come to them." Sufyan said concerning this, "This was the strongest effect of the magic." No contradictory statement has been reported to the effect that he had done it. It was only thoughts and imagination. It is said that what is meant by the *hadith* is that he used to imagine he had done something which he had not done. To imagine something is not to believe it to be true. So it does not affect his belief being exact and his words sound.

These are the answers which I have found among our Imams concerning this *hadith*. Every aspect of them is satisfactory.

However, a more sublime interpretation has appeared to me concerning the *hadith*, which is yet further from the attacks of the misguided, and is taken from the *hadith* itself. 'Abdu'r-Razzaq related this *hadith* from Ibn al-Musayyab and 'Urwa ibn az-Zubayr, quoting them as saying, "A Jew of the Banu Zurayq put a spell on the Messenger of Allah, may Allah bless him and grant him peace, and placed the charm in a well until the Messenger of Allah nearly doubted his sight. Then Allah showed him what the Jew had done and the Prophet had the charm taken out of the well." Something similar is related from al-Waqidi,

---

1. Al-Bukhari.

'Abdu'r-Rahman ibn Ka'b and 'Umar ibn al-Hakam.

It is mentioned from 'Ata' al-Khurasani from Yahya ibn Ya'mar that the Messenger of Allah was kept from 'A'isha for a year. Then while the Prophet was asleep, two angels came to him. One of them sat at his foot and the other at his feet, and they had a discussion about what had happened to him. 'Abdu'r-Razzaq said that he was kept from 'A'isha for a whole year until he doubted his own sight. Muhammad ibn Sa'd related from Ibn 'Abbas, "The Messenger of Allah, may Allah bless him and grant him peace, was ill and kept from his wives, food and drink. Two angels came to him..."[1]

It should be clear to you from these variants that the magic had power over his outward limbs, not over his heart, belief and intellect. It affected his sight and kept him from sexual intercourse with his wives and from eating. It weakened his body and made him ill. That is what was meant by, "It seemed to him that he had come to his wives although he had not come to them," i.e. it appeared to him from his activity and previous habit that he had the strength to come to them. When he came near them, the magic spell struck him and he could not come to them as happens when someone is under a spell and is hindered. Perhaps it was like Sufyan indicated when he said, "This was the strongest effect of the magic." 'A'isha said in the other variants that it seemed to him that he had done something when he had not done it. This is the sort of thing that disturbed his sight as the *hadith* mentions. He thought that he saw one of his wives or someone else do something, but it was not as he imagined due to what afflicted his sight and weakened his eye. None of that affected his discrimination.

Since this is the case, nothing that was mentioned about the magic attack on him and its effect occasions doubt, and heretics cannot find a way to cause dissension among people by making use of it.

SECTION 3
The Prophet's states with respect to worldly matters

We will examine the Prophet's worldly states with respect to his beliefs, reports and actions.

As for worldly beliefs, one aspect of his state in this regard is that it was possible for him to believe something concerning the matters of this world based on one interpretation when the opposite was true, or to be subject to doubt or supposition regarding them. These matters are not the same as matters of the *Shari'a*.

Rafi' ibn Khadij said that the Messenger of Allah came to Madina while they

---

1. Al-Bayhaqi with a weak *isnad*.

were pollinating the dates and asked, "What are you doing?" They told him and he said, "Perhaps it would be better not to do it." So they left it and there were less dates. They mentioned that to him and he said, "I am a man. If I command you to do something in your *deen*, then do it. If I tell you something from opinion, I am but a man."[1] Anas added, "You know better the affairs of your world." Another variant has, "I had an opinion, so do not blame me for having an opinion."

In the *hadith* from Ibn 'Abbas we find, "I am a man. What I tell you from Allah is true. In what I say from myself, I am but a man. I can err and I can be right." This is what he said about himself regarding his opinions about the affairs of this world. That is not the case with any words which came from him or his *ijtihad* when laying down the *Shari'a* or making a *sunna*.

This matter is also illustrated by what Ibn Ishaq has related about the time the Prophet dismounted near the waters of Badr. Al-Hubab ibn al-Mundhir said to him, "Is this a place where Allah has made you dismount so we cannot go forward or is it simply a question of opinion, military tactics and strategy." He said, "It is opinion, military tactics and strategy." Al-Hubab said, "Then this is not the place to dismount. Continue until we come nearer the water, towards the enemy. We can alight there and then we can fill up the wells beyond it. We will drink and they will not drink." The Prophet said, "You have indicated the correct course of action," and did what al-Hubab had suggested.

Allah said to the Prophet, **"Consult with them in the affair."** (3:159) The Prophet wanted to placate one of his enemies with a third of the dates of Madina. He took counsel with the Ansar and, after hearing their opinion, changed his mind. Fallibility of this kind which pertains to any such worldly matters which do not involve the science of the *deen*, its beliefs or teachings are permitted to him since none of this implies imperfection or demotion. They are ordinary things capable of being known by anyone who attempts to learn and occupy himself with them. The heart of the Prophet, however, was filled with gnosis of Allah's lordship. He was full of the sciences of the *Shari'a*. His mind was directed towards the best interests of his community in this world and the *deen*.

But such fallibility only happened in respect of certain matters. The rare case is allowed and in things which concern observing this world and its fruits, not in doing such things often, followed by stupidity and inattention.

Many transmissions have come from the Prophet showing a deep knowledge of the matters of this world and understanding of the fine points concerning the best interests of his people and the politics of the different groups of his followers which was a miracle among men. This has already been discussed in the chapter of this book devoted to his miracles.

---

1. Muslim from Talha.

SECTION 4
The Prophet's judgements

As for what the Prophet thought concerning his human capacity to judge, the recognition of the true from the false, and the science of distinguishing the beneficial from the corrupt, this is similar to the previous topic.

Umm Salama reported that the Prophet said, "I am a man and you bring your quarrels to me. Perhaps one of you might know how to argue more eloquently than the other, and so I would decide in his favour according to what I hear. Whoever is given a judgement which contains any of his brother's right should not take any of it or a piece of the Fire will be cut out for him."[1] The transmission of az-Zuhri from 'Urwa reads: "Perhaps one of you might be more eloquent than the other and so I would suppose that he was speaking the truth and give judgement in his favour."

His judgements were based on the apparent evidence and what the prevailing opinion demanded through the testimony of witnesses, swearing on oath, looking for the most likely interpretation, and recognising a hawk from a handsaw while knowing what the wisdom of Allah demands concerning these things.

If Allah had so willed, He would have acquainted the Prophet with the secrets of His slaves and the hidden consciences of his community and then he would have judged between them by pure certainty and knowledge without any need for confession, clear proof, oath or probability. However, since Allah has commanded his community to follow the Prophet and imitate his actions, states, decisions and life, and since this knowledge, had it existed, would have been part of his special knowledge by which Allah preferred him, his community would not have had any way of following him in this respect nor of establishing a proof, through the precedent of one of his cases in his *Shari'a*, because they would not know what he had been shown in that case which caused him to reach the judgement he reached. It would have been by a hidden element of Allah's teaching to him by which he was able to see into their secrets. The community as a whole would not have access to it.

Allah made the Prophet's judgement proceed according to what was clear and apparent, in which he and other men are equal, so as to enable his community to imitate him completely both in respect of particular judgements and also as regards arriving at a judgement. The community have taken his *Sunna* from this outward knowledge and certainty since clarification

---

1. Muslim and al-Bukhari.

by action is more sublime than that by verbal reports due to the comparative nature of verbal expressions and their openness to different interpretations. Reaching judgement by outward actions has a more subtle clarification, is clearer in judgement and has greater benefit for the needs of disputes and quarrels. It was also in order to enable the community to be guided by all the judgements he made and so that verification of what has been related from him would be made possible and the rule of his *shari'a* could be established. Hidden within these judgements is some of the knowledge of the Unseen which the Knower of the Unseen has kept back. **"He is Knower of the Unseen, and does not divulge His Unseen to anyone – except a Messenger with whom He is well pleased."** (72:26) He teaches him what He wills of it and keeps to Himself what He wills. None of this detracts from his prophethood nor does it lessen his protection.

SECTION 5
The Prophet's reports relating to this world

As for what the Prophet said about this world through his reports about his states and the states of others and what he said he would do or did, we have already stated that resistance to Allah regarding these things is impossible for him in every case and in any respect, whether intentionally or by oversight, in health or illness, pleasure or anger. The Prophet was protected from that. This applies to the contents of straightforward reports in which what was said could be either true or false.

As for non-explicit statements whose outward meaning may appear to be different from their inward, he is permitted to say such things as that in the context of the affairs of this world, especially when the welfare of others is intended. This includes things like concealing the target of raids so that the enemy would not be put on guard.

Another aspect of this is what has been related about the jokes he told to amuse his community and make the hearts of the believers cheerful in his company and consolidate their love and their joy. For instance he said, "I will let you ride on the child of the she-camel." He said to the woman who asked him about her husband, "Is he the one who has white in his eyes?" All of this was true because every camel is the child of a she-camel and every man has white in his eye. The Prophet said, "I make jokes but I only speak the truth." This has all come in reports.

As for the area concerning reports which take the form of command or prohibition in connection with the matters of this world, it is not fitting for him nor indeed permitted for him to command anyone to do something or forbid anyone from doing something when he was doing the opposite. The Prophet said, "It is not for a Prophet to deceive the eyes."[1] So how could he deceive people's hearts?

If you asked what Allah means in the story of Zayd ibn Haritha by His words, **"When you said to him whom Allah has blessed and you yourself have greatly bountyed, 'Keep your wife to yourself and show fear of Allah,' while concealing something in yourself which Allah wished to bring to light, you were fearing people when it is more right to fear Allah. When Zayd divorced her We married her to you so that there should be no restriction for the believers regarding the wives of their adopted sons when they have divorced them. Allah's command is always carried out,"** (33:37) know without doubt that the Prophet, may Allah bless him and grant him peace, is innocent of the apparent meaning and he ordered Zayd to keep his wife when Zayd wanted to divorce her as a group of the commentators have mentioned.

The soundest version concerning this matter is in what the commentators have related from 'Ali ibn Husayn. Allah knew better than His Prophet that Zaynab bint Jahsh would be one of his wives. When Zayd complained about her to the Prophet, he told him, "Keep your wife and fear Allah." He hid in himself what Allah had intimated to him about his marriage to her but Allah brought it into the open by bringing her marriage to an end through Zayd's divorcing her.

'Amr ibn Fa'id said that az-Zuhri said that Jibril came to the Prophet to tell him that Allah would make him marry Zaynab bint Jahsh. That was what he concealed in himself. The commentators verify this by Allah's saying, **"Allah's command is always carried out,"** i.e. you must marry her. This makes it clear that the only thing Allah revealed about the matter was that he was going to marry her. He indicated that what the Prophet concealed was part of what Allah had intimated to him.

Allah continues in this story, **"There is no restriction on the Prophet regarding anything Allah allots to him."** (33:37) He indicates that the Prophet was in no way at fault in the matter. At-Tabari said that Allah would not say His Prophet had acted wrongly by doing something He had made lawful for Messengers before him.

Allah then continues, **"This was Allah's pattern with those who passed away before,"** (33:38) i.e. among the Prophets regarding what He had made lawful for them.

If it had been the way it is related in the *hadith* of Qatada, where it talks of what happened in the heart of the Prophet when he admired Zaynab and wanted Zayd to divorce her, there would have been a great fault in it and which would not befit him. That would rather have been the action of someone who

---

1. Al-Hakim, an-Nasa'i and Abu Dawud

extends his eyes to what has been forbidden to him of the fruits of the life of this world.[1] Doing this would have been manifesting in respect of Zayd that same blameworthy envy referred to in the *ayat* alluded to above, which is not pleasing to Allah and to which no godfearing person is prone. How then could that be the case with the master of the Prophets?

Al-Qushayri stated that saying such a thing is a great audacity on the part of the one who says it and a lack of recognition of what is due to the Prophet and of his supreme excellence. How could it be said that he saw her and admired her when she was his cousin and he had been seeing her since the time when she was born. Women did not veil themselves from him and he himself had married her to Zayd.

Allah made Zayd divorce Zaynab and marry the Prophet to remove the barrier set up by ties of adoption and invalidating its customs. He says, **"Muhammad is not the father of any of your men."** (33:40) And He says, **"So that there should be no restriction for the believers regarding the wives of their adopted sons."** (33:37)

Abu'l-Layth as-Samarqandi said that if people ask what is the benefit in the Prophet commanding Zayd to keep Zaynab when Allah had informed him that she was to be his wife, it is that the Prophet forbade Zayd to divorce his wife because of the disharmony between Zayd and her while concealing in himself what Allah had informed him about it. When Zayd divorced her, he feared that people would say he was marrying his son's wife, so Allah commanded him to marry her to make what he was doing lawful for his community as Allah said, **"So that there should be no restriction for the believers regarding the wives of their adopted sons."** (33:37)

It is said that the Prophet's command to Zayd to keep Zaynab was to restrain the appetite which comes to the self from its desire. If we allow this, it must be that he saw her and suddenly thought her beautiful. Things like this are unobjectionable since it is the nature of the Banu Adam[1] to find beauty beautiful. The sudden glance is forgiven. Then he restrained himself from her and told Zayd to keep her.

Abu Bakr ibn Furak said that the Prophet was free of hypocrisy and manifesting the opposite of what was inside him. Allah freed him of that when He said, **"There is no restriction on the Prophet regarding anything Allah allots to him."** (33:38) Whoever thinks that about the Prophet has lied.

He said that the timidity (*khashya*) referred to here does not mean fear itself (*khawf*). It means to be modest or shy, i.e. he was shy before them because they would say, "He has married his son's wife." The Prophet's fear of people was because of the lies spread by the hypocrites and Jews when they made

---

1. See Qur'an 20:131.
2. The sons of Adam, i.e. mankind.

controversies for the Muslims by saying, "He has married his son's wife" after he had forbidden them to marry the wives of their sons. Allah censured him for this and freed him from paying any attention to them concerning what He had made lawful for him as He censured him for his deference to his wives' pleasure in *Sura at-Tahrim* when He said, **"Why do you make forbidden what Allah has made lawful for you?"** (66:1)

This is the same as when Allah says to him, **"Fearing people when it is more right to fear Allah."** (33:37)

Al-Hasan ibn 'Ali and 'A'isha related, "If the Messenger of Allah, may Allah bless him and grant him peace, had concealed anything, he would have concealed this *ayat* since it contains blame of him and uncovers what he had concealed."

SECTION 6
The *hadith* of the Prophet's will

People might ask, taking into consideration the truth that the Prophet's protection as far as his words are concerned is confirmed in all his states and it is not sound for there to be any contradiction or confusion in them whether they are by intention or inadvertant, in health or sickness, in seriousness or in jest, pleasure or anger, about the meaning of the following *hadith* regarding his will.[1]

Ibn 'Abbas said, "When the Messenger of Allah, may Allah bless him and grant him peace, was near death, some men were in the room and the Prophet said to them, 'Come, I will write a document for you so that you will not be misguided after it.' One of them ['Umar] said, 'The Messenger of Allah, may Allah bless him and grant him peace, is overcome by pain.'" One variant has, "Come to me and I will write a letter for you so that you will never be misguided after me." They disagreed and said, "What is wrong with him? Is he delirious?" They asked him about it and then he said, "Leave me, I am better as I am."

One of the variants says, "The Prophet is delirious (*yahjuru*)." One variant has, "*hajara*". It is also related as "*A hujru?*" and "*A hujra?*"[2]

'Umar said, "The Prophet is in great pain and we have the Book of Allah which is enough for us." There was a lot of argument and the Prophet said, "Get away from me."

One version said that the People of the House disagreed and argued and some said, "Go near so that the Messenger of Allah can write a document for you." Others said what 'Umar said.

---

1. In Muslim and al-Bukhari.
2. Various readings of the verb.

The Imams said concerning this *hadith* that the Prophets were not protected from illnesses and the resulting great pain, unconsciousness and other physical effects. They are protected in the course of any illness from any words which might detract from their miracle or lead to the disruption of their *shari'as* through delirium or disturbance.

On this basis, those who transmit the verb in the *hadith* as *hajara*, meaning "he is delirious" are not correct. When someone is delirious, one says, "*Hajara hujran*", and when someone speaks in an unseemly manner, one says, "*Ahjara hujran*." *Ahjara* is transitive of *hajara*. The soundest and most fitting reading of the *hadith* is "Is he not delirious?" with the sense of negation on the part of the one who thought that he should not write a document.

This is how it is in the *Sahih* collection of al-Bukhari and in the transmission of all the transmitters of the version of the *hadith* from az-Zuhri. It is also in the version of the *hadith* from Muhammad ibn Salam from Sufyan ibn 'Uyayna, and al-Usayli has it like that in his edition of al-Bukhari and it is like that elsewhere. It is also related like that from Muslim in the version of the *hadith* from Sufyan and others.

The variant of *hajara* (he is delirious) can be taken as having the interrogative particle (*a*) elided, so it really is "*a hajara* (Is he delirious?)."

Or it could be taken to express the astonishment and bewilderment at the gravity of the Prophet's condition and the severity of his pain, a state which caused the people to be in disagreement about the command to write something down, all of which might cause the speaker to be unsure of what was said. It could be read as *hujra* (unclear speech) due to the intensity of pain. It was not because the relater believed that the Prophet was allowed to speak irrationally.

Compassion could have moved them to guard him, although Allah said, **"Allah will protect you from the people."** (5:67)

One version has "*a hujran*? (is it delirious talk?)", which is the transmission of Abu Ishaq al-Mustamli in the *Sahih* in the version of the *hadith* from Ibn Jubayr from Ibn 'Abbas in the transmission of Qutayba. This could refer to the disputants, i.e. "Have you come with your disputes to the Messenger of Allah, may Allah bless him and grant him peace, so there is *hujr* and objectionable words in his presence?" *Hujr* means unseemly words.

The *'ulama'* disagree about the meaning of this *hadith*: How could the Companions dispute after he had commanded them to bring him something to write on? One of the *'ulama'* has said that the obligatory nature of the commands of the Prophet were understood in this context to only be either recommended or allowed. Perhaps the context of his words was such that they understood it not to be a direct order. Rather it was a matter which was left to their choice. Some of them did not understand that and said, "Ask him about it." When they disagreed, he withdrew from it since it was not a firm order and since they agreed with the opinion 'Umar had expressed.

The *'ulama'* say that 'Umar might have forbidden them to obey him due to his compassion for the Prophet because it would be a burden on him to dictate the letter and would have caused him hardship. He said, "The Prophet, may Allah bless him and grant him peace, is in very great pain."

It is said that 'Umar feared that he would write down commands that they would be unable to carry out and then they would be forced into wrong action through opposition. He thought that the most compassionate thing for the community regarding these matters would be the use of *ijtihad*, judgement arrived at through investigation, and seeking the correct solution, for the one who is right in his *ijtihad* is rewarded and the one who errs is also rewarded.

'Umar knew that the *Shari'a* was confirmed and the *deen* established and that Allah had said, **"Today I have perfected your deen for you,"** (5:3) and the Prophet had said, "I am leaving you the Book of Allah and my family." 'Umar said, "The Book of Allah is enough for us," to refute those who were arguing with him and not to refute the Prophet's command.

It is said that 'Umar feared that the hypocrites and those who had sickness in their hearts would make use of it to cause trouble since the document would be written in seclusion which would enable them to invent false statements about it – as did the Rafidites and others.

It is said that the Prophet offered to write something down for the purpose of counsel and advice. Did they agree on that or differ? When they differed, he left it.

Another group have said that the *hadith* means that the Prophet was answering something he had been asked with regard to this document. He did not initiate the command to write something down, but some of his companions had asked him for it and he was replying to their request. Others objected to that for reasons that we have already mentioned.

A proof is in a similar story where al-'Abbas said to 'Ali, "Come along with us to the Messenger of Allah, may Allah bless him and grant him peace. If there is any command for us, we will know it." 'Ali disliked that and said, "By Allah, I will not do it."

Another proof is found in the words of the Prophet, "Leave me. I am better as I am," i.e. the situation I am in now is better than giving the command. I leave you with the Book of Allah if you leave what you have asked me for.

It is mentioned that what was sought was for him to write down who would be khalif after him and that he specify who it should be.

SECTION 7
Study of other *hadiths*

People might ask about the import of the *hadith* narrated by Abu Hurayra in which he stated he heard the Messenger of Allah say, "O Allah! I am a man who becomes angry as men become angry. I have taken a contract with You that You will not break. Whenever I injure, curse or flog a believer, make it an expiation for him and an act of drawing near which will bring him near to You on the Day of Rising."[1] One variant has, "Who does not deserve it," and in another version we find, "Whenever I curse, inveigh against, or flog a Muslim, make it purification, a prayer and mercy for him."

How could it be correct for the Prophet to curse someone who did not deserve to be cursed or revile someone who did not deserve to be reviled or flog someone who did not deserve to be flogged or do other such things out of anger when he was protected from anything of that kind?

By the wisdom which has already been mentioned, the Prophet judged that people should be flogged or chastened by his curse or vilification according to the demands of their outward state. Then because of his compassion for his community, and his mercy and kindness for the believers by which Allah described him, and his being on guard lest Allah should accept his invocation against anyone he cursed, the Prophet asked Him to make his curse and his action a mercy for that person. That is what he meant by "who does not deserve it." It was not that the Prophet was moved by anger and provoked by displeasure causing him to do something like this to a Muslim who did not deserve it.

This is the correct meaning. It is not understood from his words, "I am angry as men are angry" that anger moved him to do something that should not be done. It is possible that what is meant is that anger for Allah moved him to punish someone by his curse or vilification when what they had done was something that could be tolerated and could be pardoned or something about which he was given the choice between punishment and pardon. It is possible that it came as compassion and to teach his community fear and as a caution for those who exceed the limits of Allah.

It is possible that what is related here about the Prophet's curse and his invocations against other people in other situations refers to what he said without deliberate intention, being rather Arab usage and not meant to be responded to, such as when he said, "May your right hand be dusty," and "May Allah not fill your belly," and "May she scratch and wound her face (i.e. she is annoying)," and other things.

---

1. Muslim.

It is related in his biography in more than one place that the Prophet did not use bad language. Anas said, "He did not vilify nor use bad language nor curse. He used to say to one of us whom he was censuring, 'What is wrong with him? May his brow be dusty!'"[1] So the *hadith* can be given this connotation. Then the Prophet was apprehensive that what he had said might be carried out and answered, so he asked his Lord, as he said in the *hadith*, to make his statement a purification, mercy and an act bringing about nearness.

This was compassion and kindness for whoever he had cursed so that there would not be any fear about the curse of the Prophet and so that the fact of having been cursed by him would not lead a person to despair.

It could also be a request from him to his Lord for someone he had flogged or cursed justly and correctly, asking Him to make it an act of expiation for that person for what he had done and to efface what he had committed. His punishment in this world would then be the cause of his pardon and forgiveness. It has come in another *hadith*, "Whoever does something and is punished for it in this world, it is an expiation for him."[2]

People might ask about the meaning of the *hadith* of az-Zubayr and the statement of the Prophet to him when he was arguing with an Ansari about the stream, "Take water, Zubayr, until the water reaches ankle-depth." The Ansari said to him, "Is he your nephew then, Messenger of Allah?" The face of the Messenger of Allah, may the blessings of Allah be upon him, changed colour and he said, "Take water, Zubayr, until it reaches wall-height."

The answer is that the Prophet can be clearly absolved from doing anything which a Muslim might have reason to find doubtful in respect of this story. The Prophet first recommended that az-Zubayr restrict himself to a portion of his just rights by following a middle way in order to be conciliatory. When the other man was not pleased with that and insisted and said what should not be said, then the Prophet gave az-Zubayr his full right.

This is why al-Bukhari dealt with this *hadith* in the chapter concerning when the Imam counsels conciliation and peace and the one judged against refuses the judgement. He mentioned at the end of the *hadith*, "So the Messenger of Allah gave az-Zubayr his full right."

The Muslims use this *hadith* as a basis for judgement in such cases. The Prophet, may Allah bless him and grant him peace, is followed in all that he did whether he was in a state of anger or pleasure. Although a judge is forbidden to give a decision when he is angry, the Prophet is the same in either anger or pleasure since he was protected in his anger. The Prophet's anger was for Allah, not for himself, as we know from a sound *hadith*.

The same thing applies to the *hadith* about his giving 'Ukasha retaliation

---

1. Al-Bukhari.
2. Muslim and al-Bukhari from 'Ubada ibn as-Samit.

against himself when the action was not intentional or provoked by anger. 'Ukasha told him, "You hit me with the stick and I do not know whether it was intentional or whether you meant to hit the camel." The Prophet said, "Seek refuge with Allah, 'Ukasha, from thinking that the Messenger of Allah would do that to you intentionally."

A similar case can be found in another *hadith* when the Prophet offered a Bedouin retaliation. The man said, "I have forgiven you." The Prophet had struck him with a whip since he kept hanging on the rein of his she-camel. The Prophet told him to stop and said, "You will get what you deserve." The man refused, so after the third time he struck him. What the Prophet did in this case was to correct someone who did not stop when he was told to. It was a matter of *adab*. But he was apprehensive, since the man had a right in the matter, until he had received his pardon.

As for the *hadith* of Sawad ibn 'Amr, "I came to the Prophet, may Allah bless him and grant him peace, when I had some *khaluq* perfume on (a yellow dye with a scent). He cried out, '*Warz! Warz!* Get back! Get back!' He pushed me in the stomach with a stick he was holding and hurt me. I cried out, 'Retaliation, Messenger of Allah!' and he uncovered his stomach for me."

The Prophet, may Allah bless him and grant him peace, struck him because he saw something objectionable on him. Perhaps he did not mean to hit him with the stick except to make him take note. When there was pain from it which he had not intended, he sought to absolve himself from it in the way that we have already mentioned.

SECTION 8
The Prophet's actions in this world

We have already said that the judgement on the Prophet's actions in this world is that they are protected from rebellion and falling into the category of disliked actions. The possibility of oversight and error on his part exists in the way that we have mentioned but it in no way detracts from his prophethood. The cases of its occurence are rare since most of his actions are exact and correct.

Most or all of his actions were acts of worship and acts of drawing near as we have made clear, since the Prophet, may Allah's blessings be upon him, only acted in this world for his needs to the extent that was necessary to fulfill the essentials, to keep his back straight, and to give benefit to his body which was engaged in worshipping his Lord, establishing his *Shari'a* and managing his community. Such actions as took place between him and people were acts of kindness which he did or excellent words which he said or bringing someone who was astray back to the right path or compelling someone obstinate or treating someone who was envious, and all of these things are connected to his sound actions and included within the duties of his acts of worship.

The Prophet adapted his actions in this world according to the situation and arranged things accordingly. He rode a donkey on short journeys and a camel on long journeys. He rode a mule in battles as a sign of firmness. He would exercise horses and get them ready for the day of danger and when the alarm was raised. It was the same with his clothes. All his states were according to the best interests of his community and himself.

Similarly, he would do a worldly action to help his community, as an act of good policy or from dislike of the opposite of that action. If he became aware of a course of action that might possibly be better, he would abandon the first action for what was better unless he thought that his first action was the better of the two. He acted thus in matters of the *deen* when he had a choice between two things – as he did when he left Madina and set out for Uhud although he thought Madina should be fortified. He did not kill the hypocrites although he knew exactly who they were because he did not want people to say, "Muhammad kills his Companions," as has come in *hadith*.[1]

He did not build the Ka'ba on the foundations established by Ibrahim because he wanted to preserve the hearts of Quraysh and respect them regarding its alteration. He was alert to the fact that their hearts would be averse to change and saw that it might provoke their earlier enmity to the *deen* and its people. He told 'A'isha, "If it had not been that your people had only recently ceased to be unbelievers, I would have completed the House on the foundations of Ibrahim."[2]

The Prophet would do an action and then abandon it if there was a better action than it, like moving from the closest waters of Badr at hand to those nearest to the enemy.

Similarly as he said, "If I had known at the beginning of my affair what I knew at the end of it, I would not have driven the sacrificial animals."[3]

The Prophet was cheerful to unbelievers and his enemies hoping to win them over and he was patient with the ignorant and rash. He said, "The worst people are those whose harm people fear because of their evil."[4] He gave them gifts in order to make them love his *shari'a* and the *deen* of his Lord.

He did the servant's chores at home. In gatherings he sat in such a way that none of his limits protruded. It seemed as if there were birds on the heads of those sitting with him. [i.e. because they were so still.] He conversed with his

---

1. Al-Bukhari.
2. Muslim and al-Bukhari.
3. In the chapter on the '*Hajj* of Farewell' in Muslim and al-Bukhari.
4. Muslim and al-Bukhari from 'A'isha.

Companions about the topics they brought up themselves and admired what they admired and laughed at what they laughed at. His joy and justice encompassed everyone. Anger did not provoke him nor did he curtail what someone was due nor conceal things from his Companions. He said, "It is not proper for a Prophet to deceive the eyes."[1]

You might ask about the time that the Prophet said to 'A'isha regarding someone who had come to see him, "A bad son of a tribe," and then when that man came to see him, the Prophet spoke gently to him and laughed with him. When the man left, 'A'isha asked him about that and the Prophet said, "The worst people are those whom people fear because of their evil." How could he say what he said outwardly and then show the opposite of what he felt?

The answer is that the Prophet behaved that way with such men to court their friendship, employing these tactics in order to make their belief firm and to bring them into Islam by it. He saw that people were responsive to this and that treating them like that would attract them to Islam. Things like this move from being defined as affability for the sake of this world to policy of the *deen*. He tried to win their friendship with the vast wealth which Allah Almighty gave him, so why not with soft words? Safwan said, "He gave to me when he was the most hateful of people to me. He kept giving to me until he became the most beloved of people to me."

The statement "a bad son of his tribe" is not slander. It is a statement about what he knew about the person to someone who did not know about him so that they would be on their guard about that person's state and be careful of him and not trust him completely, especially when he was someone who was obeyed and followed. It is necessary to do this to avoid harm. It is not slander. It is permitted and necessary at certain times, as is the custom of the people of *hadith* when they declare certain transmitters, and some of those who attest to the reliability of witnesses, to be unsound.

If it is asked what is the meaning of the problem raised by the *hadith* of Barira about what the Prophet said to 'A'isha when she told him that the owners of Barira refused to sell her unless they could have the *wala'* (i.e. be her heirs), the Prophet told her, "Buy her and grant the precondition of the *wala'*." She did so. Then he made a speech and said, "What is wrong with people who make preconditions which are not in the Book of Allah? Every precondition which is not in the Book of Allah is void."[2] The Prophet had told her to grant them the precondition and they sold Barira based on that. If it had not been for that, and Allah knows best, they would not have sold her to 'A'isha, as they did not sell her until they had made the precondition. But then the Prophet voided the precondition although he had made deceit and trickery *haram*.

---

1. Muslim and al-Bukhari and others.
2. Muslim and al-Bukhari.

Know that the Prophet is innocent of what occurs to the ignorant mind about this. Because the Prophet is free from that, the people of knowledge dislike this addition to his words, "Grant them the precondition in the *wala'*," since it is not in most transmissions of the *hadith*. Even if it is, it can still mean "against them."

Allah says, **"The curse will be upon them,"** (13:25) and, **"If you do evil, it is against yourselves."** (17:7) Based on this, the Prophet said that 'A'isha should grant them the precondition for the *wala'*. The Prophet then stood up and warned about what they had done by earlier imposing the precondition of the *wala'*.

A second possibility is that his words, "Grant them the precondition of the *wala'*," are not a command, but rather conciliation and information that this precondition of theirs would not benefit them after the Prophet had made it clear to them that the *wala'* belongs to the one who frees the slave. It was as if he were saying, "Give the precondition or do not give the precondition, it does not matter either way."

The third possibility is that the reason "Grant them the *wala'* as a precondition," was said, was to show them the judgement in such cases and make the *sunna* about it clear to them, i.e. that the *wala'* belongs to the one who sets free. Then after this, the Prophet stood up to make that clear and to rebuke their opposition to what he had already said.

It may be asked what is the meaning of what Yusuf did to his brother when he put the goblet in his saddlebag and then seized him for stealing it, and what happened to his brothers in that story when he said, "You are thieves," when they had not stolen.

Know that the *ayat* indicates that what Yusuf did was by the command of Allah from His words, **"In that way We devised a cunning scheme for Yusuf. He could not have held his brother according to the statutes of the King – except that Allah willed it."** (12:76) If that was the case, there is no objection to what he did. What was in it was what was in it. Moreover, Yusuf informed his brother, **"I am your brother. Do not be distressed."** (12:69) What happened after this was with his brother's agreement and desire and the certainty that it would end well for him and that evil and harm would be removed from him by that.

As for Allah's mentioning the calling out of, **"Caravan! You are thieves!"** (12:70) Yusuf did not say that, so there is no need for any reply to remove the suspicion. It might well be, giving a favourable interpretation of what was said, that the speaker, whoever he was, based his accusation on the outward appearance of the situation.

It is said that that was said because of what the brothers had previously done to Yusuf and their selling him.

Other things have been said as well. We should not say that the Prophets said such things when it is by no means certain that they really did say them and we have to seek to absolve them from such words. It is not necessary to apologise for the errors of others.

SECTION 9
The wisdom contained in the illnesses and afflictions of the Prophets

You might ask what could be the wisdom contained in the illnesses by which Muhammad and the other Prophets were affected and the severity of their suffering and the purpose of the afflictions with which Allah tested them – as in the cases of Ayyub, Ya'qub, Danyal, Yahya, Zakariyya, 'Isa, Ibrahim, Yusuf and others, when they were the best of His creation and those He loved most and His pure friends. Know that all of Allah's actions are just and all His words are true. **"No-one can change His Words."** (6:115) Allah tests His slaves in order that, as He has said to them, **"We might observe how you would act,"** (10:14) and, **"to test which of you is best in action,"** (67:2) and, **"so that Allah will know those who believe,"** (3:140) and, **"Allah knowing those among you who had struggled and knowing the steadfast,"** (3:142) and, **"We will test you until We know the true fighters among you and those who are steadfast and test what is reported of you."** (47:31)

Allah put the Prophets to the test by means of various types of affliction in order to increase their position and elevate their rank. Afflictions were the cause which elicited the states of steadfastness, pleasure, thankfulness, submission, reliance, entrusting, supplication and entreaty and confirmed the Prophets' insight into mercy towards people who were tested and compassion for those who were suffering affliction. Their affliction was a reminder and warning for others so that people would emulate the Prophets in affliction and find solace in the trials which befell them and imitate them in steadfastness. Affliction erased any small mistakes into which they slipped and their acts of heedlessness so that they would meet Allah purified and cleansed and thereby their wage would be more complete and their reward more abundant.

Mus'ab ibn Sa'd said that his father, Sa'd ibn Abi Waqqas, said that he asked the Messenger of Allah, "Which people have the greatest affliction?" He answered, "The Prophets, and then the best of men (*al-amthal*). The best of men are those who are tested in accordance with their adherence to the *deen*. Affliction continues to afflict the worshipper until it leaves him walking on the earth free of error."[1]

It is as Allah has said, **"How many a Prophet has fought, and many thousands with him. They did not give up in the face of what assailed them**

---

1. At-Tirmidhi.

in the Way of Allah, nor did they weaken nor did they yield. Allah loves the steadfast..." (3:146)

Abu Hurayra reported that the Prophet, may Allah bless him and grant him peace, said, "The affliction of a believer continues in respect of himself, his children and his property until he meets Allah free of all wrong action."[1]

From the transmission of Anas, the Prophet said, "When Allah desires good for one of His slaves, He brings the punishment forward to him in this world. When Allah desires evil for a man, He keeps his wrong action back for him until He brings it on the Day of Rising."[2]

In another *hadith* we find, "When Allah loves a slave, He tests him in order to hear his supplication."[3]

As-Samarqandi related, "All those who are honoured by Allah suffer more affliction so that their excellence will be clear and their reward will be inevitable."

It is related that Luqman said, "My son, gold and silver are tested by fire and the believer is tested by affliction."

It is related that Ya'qub was afflicted through Yusuf because once, while he was praying, he had turned to the sleeping Yusuf out of love.[4]

It is said that one day the Prophet Ya'qub was with his son Yusuf eating a roasted calf. They were both laughing. They had an orphan neighbour who smelled the aroma and desired the meat. He wept and his grandmother wept because he was weeping. There was a wall between them so Ya'qub and his son were not aware of them. Therefore Ya'qub was punished for the orphan's weeping by his grief for Yusuf until his eyes became liquid and went blind out of grief. When he learned about the neighbour, for the rest of his life he commanded a caller to call out on his roof, "Are there any to break their fast? Let them eat with the family of Ya'qub." Yusuf was punished by the affliction which Allah has related about him.

Al-Layth related that the reason for Ayyub's affliction was that he went with the people of his village to see their king, and they spoke to the king about his injustice. The villagers were all plain-spoken towards the king except Ayyub. He was polite towards him because he feared for his crops, so Allah punished him with his affliction.

The affliction of Sulayman was for the incident we have already mentioned when he intended to give judgement on behalf of his wife's relatives, or for an act of rebellion which occurred in his house which he did not know about.

This was what lay behind the intense illness and pain suffered by the Prophet. 'A'isha said, "I have never seen anyone in greater pain than that which

---

1. At-Tirmidhi.
2. Ibid.
3. Ad-Daylami from Abu Hurayra.
4. Al-Qurtubi in his *tafsir* without an *isnad*.

the Messenger of Allah suffered."[1]

'Abdullah ibn Mas'ud said, "I saw the Prophet suffering an intense fever in the course of his illness. I said, 'You have a very high fever.' He said, 'Yes, I have a fever as great as that of two of you.' I said, 'That is because you have the reward twice over!' He said, 'Yes, that is the case.'"[2]

Abu Sa'id al-Khudri reported that a man placed his hand on the Prophet, may Allah bless and grant him peace, and said, "By Allah, I cannot place my hand on you because of the intensity of your fever!" The Prophet said, "I am one of the company of Prophets. The affliction is doubled for us. A Prophet can be tested by lice until it kills him. A Prophet can be tested by poverty. They rejoice in affliction as they rejoice in ease."[3]

Anas ibn Malik reported that the Messenger of Allah said, "Immense reward comes with immense affliction. When Allah loves a people, He tests them. Whoever is pleased will experience Allah's pleasure. Whoever is angry will experience Allah's anger."[4]

The commentators say that His words, **"Anyone who does evil will be repaid for it,"** (4:123) mean that the Muslim will be repaid for his misfortunes in this world, so it will be an expiation for him.[5] This is also related from 'A'isha, Ubayy and Mujahid.

Abu Hurayra reported that the Prophet said, "When Allah desires good for someone, he gives him affliction."[6]

In 'A'isha's version we find, "There is no misfortune which strikes a Muslim but that Allah gives him expiation for it, even the thorn which pricks him."[7]

The Prophet said in the variant of Abu Sa'id, "No fatigue, pain, anxiety, sorrow, injury or grief strikes the believer, even to the extent of a thorn that pricks him, but that by it Allah expiates his errors for him."

The *hadith* from 'Abdullah ibn Mas'ud goes, "There is no Muslim who is afflicted by harm but that Allah removes his errors from him as the leaves fall from the trees."[8]

Another wisdom which Allah placed in illnesses and pain in respect of the bodies of the Prophets, and their intensity at the time of their deaths, was that this would weaken the power of their selves so that it would be easy for their spirits to come out when they were taken. The death struggle and the intensity of its throes were made lighter for them by their previous illness and the

---

1. Muslim and al-Bukhari.
2. Ibid.
3. Ibn Majah and al-Hakim.
4. At-Tirmidhi.
5. This explanation is related from Abu Bakr as-Siddiq.
6. Al-Bukhari.
7. Al-Bukhari and Muslim.
8. Ibid.

weakness of their bodies and souls from that, as opposed to being seized by sudden death, as can be seen by the intensity and gentleness of different states of death, and the comparative difficulty and ease with which they occur.

The Prophet said, "The believers are like tender plants in the fields. The wind blows them here and there."[1]

In Abu Hurayra's version we find, "When the wind comes to them, it makes them bend. When it is still, they are upright. That is how it is with the believer. He bends with affliction. The unbeliever is like the sturdy cedar which stands straight until Allah makes it snap."[2]

It means that the believer is stricken and suffers affliction and illness but he is pleased with how he is used by the decrees of Allah, obeying them, yielding to them with pleasure and lack of wrath, as the tender plants of the fields obey and submit to the wind, and bend when the winds blow. Then Allah removes the winds of affliction from the believer and makes him straight and healthy as the tender plants of the fields are straight when the air is still. The believer returns to gratitude towards His Lord and recognition of the blessing He has shown him by removing the affliction. He waits for mercy and reward to come to him. When this is the case, the final illness is not hard for him and its throes and agony are not intense for him because he has accustomed himself by means of earlier pains and he recognises the reward which it contains. He has adjusted himself to misfortune, fragility and weakness by the continuation of illness or its intensity.

The unbeliever is different. He is well in most states and strong and healthy in his body, like the sturdy cedar, until Allah desires to destroy him and snaps him immediately while he is unaware and takes him suddenly without kindness or compassion. His death is a more intense grief for him and enduring its throes is a more intense pain and punishment in spite of his strength and healthy body. The punishment of the Next World is more intense. It is like uprooting the cedar. It is as Allah says, **"Then We seized them suddenly when they were not expecting it."** (7:95)

That is the way of Allah with His enemies as we find in His words, **"We seized each one of them for his wrong action. Against some We sent a sudden squall of stones; some of them were seized by the Great Blast..."** (29:40) He brought death to all of them suddenly while they were in a state of insolence and heedlessness and He brought it to them suddenly in the morning without their being able to prepare for it. This is why it is mentioned that the *Salaf* disliked sudden death, as Ibrahim ibn Yazid an-Nakha'i said, "They disliked seizure which is like someone being seized by sorrow, i.e. anger, meaning sudden death."

A third wisdom contained in illness is that it is a harbinger of death. The

---

1. Al-Bukhari and Muslim from Ka'b ibn Malik and Jarir.
2. Muslim.

366

intensity of the fear of the advent of death is reduced according to the intensity of the illness. The one afflicted prepares and knows that if it is contracted for him he will meet his Lord. He turns from this world with its great misfortune and his heart is connected to the Next World. He withdraws from all those things whose consequences he fears – whether from Allah or people. He gives people their due and looks to see what bequests he needs to give to those he is leaving behind or what matters he is under contractual obligation to fulfill.

Our Prophet was forgiven his past and future actions, but in his illness he sought to clear himself of anyone to whom he owed money or a physical right. He offered retaliation against himself and his property and offered people reprisal against him as has come in al-Fadl ibn 'Abbas' *hadith* and the *hadith* concerning the delegations. He advised men and *jinn* after him to hold to the Book of Allah and to his family, and that the Ansar were his repository (of secrets). He called for a paper on which to write a document so that his community would never be misguided after him, either regarding definite instructions about the khalifate – or Allah knows best what he meant. Then he thought better of it.

That is how it is with the lives of the believing slaves of Allah and the godfearing *awliya'*.[1] The unbelievers are generally denied this advantage. Allah gives them enjoyment in order to increase their wrong actions and leads them on little by little from where they do not know. Allah says, **"What are they waiting for but one Great Blast to seize them while they are quibbling? They will not be able to make a will or return to their families."** (36:49-50)

That is why the Prophet said about a man who had died suddenly, "Glory be to Allah! As if there was anger against him! The one who is deprived of making a will is truly deprived!" He said, "Sudden death is a rest for the believers and a seizure of grief for the unbeliever or deviant."[2]

That is because death usually comes to the believer when he is prepared for it, waiting for its arrival, and so it is easy for him however it comes and leads to his rest from the toil and harm of this world. It is as the Prophet said, "Resting and given rest from it."[3]

Death comes to unbelievers and deviators suddenly without preparation or any previous warning. It comes to them suddenly, so it stupefies them and they cannot return and are not waiting. Death is the most intense thing for man and separation from this world is the most horrid and hateful thing to befall him.

The Prophet indicated this when he said, "Whoever wants to meet Allah, Allah wants to meet him. Whoever hates to meet Allah, Allah hates to meet him."[4]

---

1. The "friends" of Allah. See Glossary.
2. *Sahih hadith* from 'A'isha in Ibn Hanbal.
3. Muslim and al-Bukhari from Abu Qatada.
4. Muslim and al-Bukhari from 'Ubada ibn as-Samit.

PART FOUR

**The judgements concerning those who think
the Prophet imperfect or curse him**

Introduction

The rights of the Prophet and the devotion, respect, esteem and honour that are owed to him are made clear in the Book and the *Sunna* and the consensus of the community. In His Book, Allah has made it *haram* to harm him. The community agree that anyone among the Muslims who disparages him or curses him is to be killed.

Allah says, **"Those who harm Allah and His Messenger, Allah has cursed them in this world and the Next World. He has prepared a humiliating punishment for them,"** (33:57) and **"Those who harm the Messenger of Allah have a painful punishment,"** (9:61) and **"It is not for you to hurt the Messenger of Allah and you should not ever marry his wives after him. That is something terrible with Allah."** (33:53)

Allah says, prohibiting the use of equivocal expressions in respect of the Prophet, **"O you believe, do not say 'Observe us' but 'regard us' and listen."** (2:104) This is because the Jews used to say, "Observe us, Muhammad," i.e. listen to us and hear us. They were using an equivocal expression, intending to make fun, so Allah forbade the believers to be like them and cut off the means to doing so by prohibiting the believers from using that expression so that the unbelievers and hypocrites would not be given an opportunity to insult and mock the Prophet.

It is said that it was censured because it was a common expression among the Jews which had the meaning, "Listen, you did not hear." It is also said that it was censured because, for the Ansar, it contained lack of manners and lack of respect and esteem because in the Ansari dialect it meant, "Look at us, and we will look at you." They were forbidden to say it since it meant that they would only look at him when he looked at them. The Prophet, may Allah bless him and grant him peace, must be observed whatever the case.

Similarly he forbade the use of his *kunya* saying, "Name yourselves with my name, but do not use my *kunya*." This was to protect himself and guard himself from harm since he had once answered a man who called out, "Abu'l-Qasim!" and the man said, "I did not mean you. I was calling him."[1]

After this it was forbidden to use his *kunya* as a name so he would not be annoyed by answering a call addressed not to him but to someone else. The hypocrites and mockers made this a means of annoying and belittling him. They would call him, and then when he turned, they would say, "We meant this one," pointing to someone else. Their intention was to inconvenience him and belittle him as is the custom of mockers and the insolent. The Prophet was protected from their harm in every way. The meticulous *'ulama'* restrict this

---

1. Al-Bukhari and Muslim.

prohibition to the time he was alive and allow the Prophet's *kunya* to be used after his death since the cause of harm is no longer there.

People have taken different positions regarding this *hadith*. This is not the place to discuss it, and what we have mentioned below is the position most people adhere to and the correct one, Allah willing. It is based on esteem and respect for him, and is a recommendation, not a prohibition.

This is why he forbade the use of his name since Allah had forbidden that he be called by his name when He said, **"Do not make your calling the Messenger among you like your calling each other."** (24:63) Therefore the Muslims called him "Messenger of Allah", "Prophet of Allah" and some of them called him by his *kunya*, "Abu'l-Qasim", in certain instances.

Anas related from the Prophet something that indicates that it is disliked to call people by his name since it could cause disrespect, "You call your sons Muhammad and then you curse them."[1]

Abu Ja'far at-Tabari related that 'Umar wrote to the people of Kufa, "Do not call anyone by the name of the Prophet." Muhammad ibn Sa'd related that he observed a man called Muhammad while another man was cursing him and saying to him, "May Allah do such a thing to you, Muhammad!" 'Umar said to his nephew, Muhammad ibn Zayd ibn al-Khattab, "I do not think that Muhammad, may Allah bless him and grant him peace, should be cursed on account of you. By Allah, you will not be called Muhammad as long as I am alive." He called him 'Abdu'r-Rahman. By doing this, he wanted to forbid people being called with the names of Prophets out of the desire to honour them, so he changed their names and said, "Do not name yourselves with the names of the Prophets," and he did not say anything further on it.

The correct position is that using the Prophet's name and *kunya* is permitted after the death of the Prophet by the proof of the agreement of the Companions about it. Some of them named their sons Muhammad and gave them the *kunya*, Abu'l-Qasim.

It is related that the Prophet gave 'Ali permission to do so and the Prophet also said that his name would be the name of the Mahdi and his *kunya*.

The Prophet used his name for Muhammad ibn Talha, Muhammad ibn 'Amr ibn Hazm, Muhammad ibn Thabit and others. He said, "It will not harm any of you to have one, two or three Muhammads in the house."

1. Al-Hakim, al-Bazzar and Abu Ya'la.

Chapter One

CLARIFICATION ABOUT CURSING THE PROPHET OR SAYING THAT HE IS IMPERFECT BY ALLUSION OR CLEAR STATEMENT

SECTION 1
The Judgement of the *Shari'a* regarding someone who curses or disparages the Prophet

Know that all who curse Muhammad, may Allah bless him and grant him peace, or blame him or attribute imperfection to him in his person, his lineage, his *deen* or any of his qualities, or alludes to that or its like by any means whatsoever, whether in the form of a curse or contempt or belittling him or detracting from him or finding fault with him or maligning him, the judgement regarding such a person is the same as the judgement against anyone who curses him. He is killed as we shall make clear. This judgement extends to anything which amounts to a curse or disparagement. We have no hesitation concerning this matter, be it a clear statement or allusion.

The same applies to anyone who curses him, invokes against him, desires to harm him, ascribes to him what does not befit his position or jokes about his mighty affair with foolish talk, satire, disliked words or lies, or reviles him because of any affliction or trial which happened to him or disparages him, because of any of the permissible and well-known human events which happened to him. All of this is the consensus of the *'ulama'* and the *imams* of *fatwa* from the time of the Companions until today.

Abu Bakr ibn al-Mundhir said that the bulk of the people of knowledge agree that whoever curses the Prophet is killed. These include Malik ibn Anas, al-Layth, Ahmad ibn Hanbal and Ishaq ibn Rahawayh, and it is the position of the Shafi'i school. Qadi Abu'l-Fadl said that it is based on the statement of Abu Bakr as-Siddiq. His repentance is not accepted. Something similar was stated by Abu Hanifa and his people, ath-Thawri and the people of Kufa and al-Awza'i about the Muslims. However, they said that it constitutes apostasy.

At-Tabari related something similar from Abu Hanifa and his companions about anyone who disparages the Prophet, proclaims himself quit of him or calls him a liar.

Sahnun said about those who curse the Prophet, "This is apostasy in exactly the same way as heresy (*zandaqa*) is. Therefore there is some dispute about whether such a person should be called to repent (as a Muslim) or whether he is an unbeliever. Is he to be killed by a *hadd*-punishment (as a Muslim) or for disbelief?" We will make this clear in Chapter Two. We do not know of any dispute among the *'ulama'* of the community and the *Salaf* regarding the permissibility of shedding his blood.

Several people have mentioned that the consensus is that he is to be killed and considered an unbeliever. One of the Dhahirites, Abu Muhammad ibn Ahmad al-Farisi, however, indicated that there is some disagreement about whether to consider someone who belittles the Prophet as an unbeliever. The best-known position has already been stated.

Muhammad ibn Sahnun said that the *'ulama'* agree that anyone who reviles the Prophet and disparages him is an unbeliever and the threat of Allah's punishment is on him. The community's judgement on him is that he be killed. Anyone who has any doubts about such a person's disbelief and punishment is also an unbeliever. For a proof of this, Ibrahim ibn Husayn ibn Khalid, the *faqih*, uses the instance of Khalid ibn al-Walid killing Malik ibn Nuwayra for referring to the Prophet as "your companion."[1]

Abu Sulayman al-Khattabi said, "I do not know of any Muslim who disagrees about the necessity of killing such a person if he is a Muslim."

Ibn al-Qasim reports from Malik in the book of Ibn Sahnun, the *Mabsut*, and the *'Utibiyya* and Ibn Mutarrif relates the same from Malik in the book of Ibn Habib, "Any Muslim who curses the Prophet is killed without being asked to repent."

Ibn al-Qasim said in the *'Utibiyya*, "Anyone who curses him, reviles him, finds fault with him or disparages him is killed. The community say that he should be killed just like the dualist. Allah made it obligatory to respect the Prophet and be dutiful to him."

In the *Mabsut* from 'Uthman ibn Kinana we find, "Any Muslim who reviles the Prophet is killed or crucified without being asked to repent. The Imam can choose between crucifying him or killing him." In the variant of Abu'l-Mus'ab and Ibn Abi Uways, they heard Malik say, "Anyone who curses the Messenger of Allah, may Allah bless him and grant him peace, reviles him, finds fault with him or disparages him is killed, be he Muslim or unbeliever, without being asked to repent."

Asbagh said, "He is killed in every case, whether he conceals it or makes it public, without being asked to repent because his repentance is not recognised." 'Abdullah ibn 'Abdu'l-Hakam said that and at-Tabari related something similar from Malik.

Ibn Wahb related that Malik said, "Anyone who says that the Prophet's

---

1. This took place durings the *Ridda* war. Malik ibn Nuwayra was one of those who refused to pay *zakat*.

cloak (or button) was dirty, thereby intending to find fault with him, should be killed."

One of our *'ulama'* says that people agree that anyone who curses any of the Prophets using the expression "Woe to him" or anything disliked is to be killed without being asked to repent.

Abu'l-Hasan al-Qabisi gave a *fatwa* that a man who called the Prophet "the porter, the orphan of Abu Talib" should be killed.

Abu Muhammad ibn Abi Zayd gave a *fatwa* to kill a man who was listening to some people discussing what the Prophet looked like. When a man with an ugly face and beard walked by, he said to them, "You want to know what he looked like? He looked like this passer-by in physique and beard." Abu Muhammad said, "His repentance is not accepted. He lied, may Allah curse him. That could not come out of a heart with sound belief."

Ahmad ibn Abi Sulayman, the companion of Sahnun, said, "Anyone who says that the Prophet was black should be killed."

He was told about a man to whom someone said, "No, by the right of the Messenger of Allah," and he replied, "Allah did such a thing to the Messenger of Allah," mentioning some ugly words. People said to him, "What are you saying, enemy of Allah?" Then he said some even harsher things and added, "I wish for a scorpion for the Messenger of Allah." When someone asked him for a *fatwa* about this man, Ibn Abi Sulayman said, "Testify against him and I will be your partner," i.e. in killing him and getting the reward.

Habib ibn ar-Rabi' said that is because trying to explain away the literal expression is not accepted because it is clear contempt and lack of respect for the Messenger of Allah. His blood is permitted.

Abu 'Abdullah ibn 'Attab gave a *fatwa* about a tax-collector who said to a man, "Pay and complain to the Prophet. If I ask or am ignorant, the Prophet was ignorant and asked," to the effect that he be killed.

The *fuqaha'* of Andalusia gave a *fatwa* that Ibn Hatim, the scholar of Toledo, be killed and crucified because there was testimony that he made light of what is due to the Prophet. In the course of a debate, he called him "the orphan" and "the in-law of the lion (i.e. 'Ali)," and claimed that his doing-without (*zuhd*) was not intentional. He alleged that if he had been able to have good things, he would have eaten them. He said other similar things.

The *fuqaha'* of the Qayrawan[1] and the companions of Sahnun gave a *fatwa* for the killing of Ibrahim al-Ghazari, a poet and master of many sciences. He was one of those who attended the assembly of Qadi Abu'l-'Abbas ibn Talib for debate. He was accused of objectionable things like mocking Allah, His Prophets and our Prophet. Qadi Yahya ibn 'Umar and other *fuqaha'* summoned him and commanded that he be killed and crucified. He was stabbed and

---

1. The great mosque and early centre of Islamic learning located south of Tunis.

crucified upside down. Then he was brought down and burned. One of the historians related that when the post to which he was tied was lifted up, the body turned around away from *qibla*. It was a sign to all and the people said, "Allah is greater!" Then a dog came and licked his blood. Yahya ibn 'Umar said, "The Messenger of Allah, may Allah bless him and grant him peace, spoke the truth," and he mentioned a *hadith* in which the Prophet said, "A dog will not lick a Muslim's blood."[1]

Qadi Abu 'Abdullah ibn al-Murabit said, "Whoever says that the Prophet was defeated is asked to repent. If he repents, it is all right. If not, he is killed because it detracts from the Prophet. Such a disparaging remark could not be said about the Prophet by anyone with understanding of his affair and certainty about his inviolability."

Habib ibn Rabi' al-Qarawi said that the school of Malik and his companions is that anyone who says anything disparaging about the Prophet is killed without being asked to repent.

Ibn 'Attab said that the Book and *Sunna* require that someone who intends to even slightly harm or disparage the Prophet, either by allusion or clear statement, must be killed.

Anything like this which is something that the *'ulama'* consider to be a curse or disparagement necessitates that the one who says it be killed. Neither the early or later people disagree about that, but they disagree about the basis for killing him as we have indicated. We will make this clear later.

This is also my position regarding the judgment of anyone who belittles him or insults him about having been a shepherd, oversight, forgetfulness, sorcery, any wound he received, the defeat of one of his armies, injury by an enemy, the intensity of his illness or his being attracted to his wives. The judgement of all this is that the one who intends to disparage him by it is killed. The position of the *'ulama'* is as we have already stated and it will be proved by what follows.

SECTION 2
The proof of the necessity of killing anyone who curses the Prophet or finds fault with him

The Qur'an says that Allah curses the one who harms the Prophet in this world and He connected harm of Himself to harm of the Prophet. There is no dispute that anyone who curses Allah is killed and that his curse demands that he be categorised as an unbeliever. The judgement of the unbeliever is that he is killed.

---

1. The source of this *hadith* is not known.

Allah says, **"Those who harm Allah and His Messenger, Allah has cursed them in this world and in the Next, and has prepared for them a humiliating punishment."** (33:57) He said something similar about those who kill the believers. Part of the curse on them in this world is that they are killed. Allah says, **"Cursed they will be. Wherever they are found, they are seized and all slain."** (33: 61) He mentions the punishment of those who fight, **"That is humiliation in this world for them."** (5:45) "Killing" (*qatl*) can have the meaning of "curse".[1] Allah says, **"May the conjecturers be killed!"** (51:11) and **"May Allah fight them! How they are perverted!"** (9:30) i.e. may Allah curse them.

This is because there is a difference between their harming Allah and His Messenger and harming the believers. Injuring the believers, short of murder, incurs beating and exemplary punishment. The judgement against those who harm Allah and His Prophet is more severe – the death penalty.

Allah says, **"No, by your Lord, they will not believe until they have you judge between them in what they disagree about."** (4:65) He removes the badge of belief from those who find an impediment in themselves against accepting the Prophet's judgement and do not submit to him. Anyone who disparages him is opposing his judgement.

Allah says, **"O you who believe, do not raise your voices above the voice of the Prophet and be not loud in your speech to him as you are loud to one another lest your actions fail."** (49:3) Such an action only comes about through disbelief and the unbeliever is killed.

Allah says, **"When they come to you, they greet you with a greeting which Allah never greeted you with."** Then He says, **"Jahannam is enough for them, an evil homecoming."** (58:9)

Allah says, **"Among them are some who insult the Prophet and say that he is only an ear,"** (9:61) and, **"Those who harm the Messenger of Allah have a painful punishment."** (9:61)

Allah says, **"If you ask them, they will say, 'We were only plunging and playing.' Say, 'What, were you then mocking Allah, His signs and His Messenger? Make no excuses. You have disbelieved after your belief.'"** (9:67-68) The commentators say, **"You have disbelieved"** refers to what they have said about the Messenger of Allah.

We have already mentioned the consensus. As for the traditions, al-Husayn ibn 'Ali related from his father that the Messenger of Allah said in respect of this matter, "Whoever curses a Prophet, kill him. Whoever curses my Companions, beat him."[2]

In a sound *hadith* the Prophet commanded that Ka'b ibn al-Ashraf be

---

1. "*Qâtalahu Allah*" (May Allah kill him) or "*qutila*" (May he be killed) are curses.
2. At-Tabarani and ad-Daraqutni.

killed. He asked, "Who will deal with Ka'b ibn al-Ashraf? He has harmed Allah and His Messenger." He sent someone to assassinate him without calling him to Islam, in distinction to other idol-worshippers. The cause of that lay in his causing harm to the Prophet. That indicates that the Prophet had him killed for something other than idol-worship. It was for causing harm. Abu Rafi,' who used to harm the Messenger of Allah and work against him, was also killed.

Similarly on the Day of the Conquest, he ordered the killing of Ibn Khatal and his two slavegirls who used to sing his curses on the Prophet.

In another *hadith* about a man who used to curse the Prophet, the Prophet said, "Who will save me from my enemy?" Khalid said, "I will," so the Prophet sent him out and he killed him.

Similarly the Prophet commanded that a group of unbelievers who used to injure and curse him, like an-Nadr ibn al-Harith and 'Uqba ibn Abi Mu'ayt, be killed. He promised that a group of them would be killed before and after the conquest. They were all killed except for those who hurried to become Muslim before they were overpowered. Al-Bazzar related from Ibn 'Abbas that 'Uqba ibn Abi Mu'ayt cried out, "O company of Quraysh, why is it that I alone among you am to be killed without war?" The Prophet said, "For your disbelief and your forging lies against the Messenger of Allah."

'Abdu'r-Razzaq mentioned that a man cursed the Prophet, causing the Prophet to say, "Who will save me from my enemy?" Az-Zubayr said, "I will." He sent az-Zubayr and he killed him.

It is related that a woman used to curse the Prophet and he said, "Who will save me from my enemy?" Khalid ibn al-Walid went out and killed her.

It is related that a man forged lies against the Prophet and he sent 'Ali and az-Zubayr to kill him.

Ibn Qani' related that a man came to the Prophet and said, "Messenger of Allah, I heard my father say something ugly about you, so I killed him," and that did not distress the Prophet.

Al-Mujahir ibn Abi Umayya, the Amir of Yemen, reported to Abu Bakr that a woman there in the time of the *Ridda*[1] chanted curses against the Prophet, so he cut off her hand and pulled out her front teeth. When Abu Bakr heard that, he said to him, "If you had not done what you already did, I would have commanded you to kill her because the *hadd* regarding the Prophet is not like the *hadd* regarding others."

Ibn 'Abbas said that a woman from Khatma[2] satirised the Prophet and the Prophet said, "Who will deal with her for me?" A man from her people said, "I will, Messenger of Allah." The man got up and went and killed her. He told the

1. See Glossary.
2. A tribe allied to the Aws. She was 'Usma' bint Marwan.

Prophet who said, "Two goats will not lock horns over her."[1]

Ibn 'Abbas said that a blind man had an *umm walad* who used to curse the Prophet. He scolded her and restrained her, but she would not be restrained. That night she began to attack and revile the Prophet, so he killed her. He told the Prophet about that and he said he had shed her blood with impunity.[2]

In the *hadith* of Abu Barza as-Aslami it says, "One day I was sitting with Abu Bakr as-Siddiq and he became angry at one of the Muslim men." Qadi Isma'il and other Imams said that the man had cursed Abu Bakr. An-Nasa'i related it as, "I came to Abu Bakr and a man had been rude and answered him back. I said, 'Khalif of Allah, let me strike off his head!' He said, 'Sit down. That is not for anyone except the Messenger of Allah, may Allah bless him and grant him peace.'"

Qadi Abu Muhammad ibn Nasr said, "No-one disagreed with him." So the Imams take this as a proof that anyone who does anything that might anger, harm or curse the Prophet in any way should be killed.

There is also the letter of 'Umar ibn 'Abdu'l-'Aziz to his governor in Kufa. He had asked his advice about killing a man who had cursed 'Umar. 'Umar wrote back to him, "It is not lawful to kill a Muslim for cursing anyone except the Messenger of Allah. Whoever curses him, his blood is lawful."

Harun ar-Rashid asked Malik about a man who had reviled the Prophet and he mentioned to him that the *fuqaha'* of Iraq had given a *fatwa* that he be flogged. Malik became angry and said, "Amir al-Mu'minin! There is no continuation for a community after it curses its Prophet! Whoever curses the Companions of the Prophet is to be flogged."

I do not know which of those Iraqi *fuqaha'* gave Harun ar-Rashid that *fatwa*. We have already mentioned that the school of the people of Iraq[3] is that he be killed. Perhaps they were among those who were not known for knowledge or those whose *fatwas* were unreliable or idiosyncratic, or it is possible that what the man said was not taken to be a curse and there was a dispute as to whether or not it was a curse or he had retracted it and repented of it. None of these things were mentioned to Malik at all. However, the consensus is that anyone who curses him is to be killed as we have already stated.

That he is to be killed can be deduced by reflection and consideration. Anyone who curses or disparages the Prophet has shown clear symptoms of the sickness of his heart and proof of his real convictions and belief. That is why most of the *'ulama'* judge him to be an apostate. This is what is transmitted by the people of Syria from Malik, al-Awza'i, ath-Thawri, Abu Hanifa and the people of Kufa.

---

1. An expression meaning there will be no disagreement about the matter.
2. Abu Dawud, al-Hakim and al-Bayhaqi.
3. i.e. the Hanafis.

The other position is that it is not a proof of disbelief, and so the person in question is killed by the *hadd*-punishment but he is not adjudged to be an unbeliever unless he persists in his words, not denying them nor refraining from them. To be judged an unbeliever, his statement must either be a clear statement of disbelief, like calling the Prophet a liar, or originate from mocking words and censure. His open avowal of what he said and lack of repentance for it is an indication that he finds it lawful and this constitutes disbelief, so there is no disagreement that he is an unbeliever. Allah says about people like this, **"They swear by Allah that they did not speak. They said the words of disbelief. They disbelieved after their Islam."** (9:76)

The commentators said that this refers to the statement, "If what is said by Muhammad is true,[1] we are worse than monkeys."

It is said that it refers to what one of them[2] said, "Our likeness with respect to that of Muhammad is only as the words of the one who says, 'Feed your dog and it will devour you.' When we return to Madina, the mighty will drive out the weaker."

It is said that even if the one who says this conceals it, the same judgement applies to him as to the heretic and he is killed because he has changed his *deen*. The Prophet said, "Strike off the heads of all who change their *deen*."

Because upholding the Prophet's honour is an obligation owed by his entire community and anyone who curses a free man of his community is given a *hadd*-punishment, the punishment of someone who curses the Prophet is that he is to be is killed because of the immensity of the worth of the Prophet and his elevation over others.

SECTION 3
The reasons why the Prophet pardoned some of those who harmed him

It might be asked why the Prophet did not kill the Jew who said to him, "Death be upon you" when this is a curse,[3] and why he did not kill the other man[4] who said in this respect, "This is a dividing out by which the face of Allah is not intended." When he annoyed the Prophet by saying that, the Prophet said, "Musa was harmed by worse than this,"[5] and was patient. And why he did not kill the hypocrites who used to harm him often.

Know that at the beginning of Islam the Prophet used to court people's

---

1. About the conquest of the fortresses of Syria. This was spoken by al-Jallas ibn Suwayd who later repented of what he had said.
2. 'Abdullah ibn Ubayy, known as the leader of the hypocrites in Madina.
3. Al-Bukhari and elsewhere.
4. Dhu'l-Khusawsira.
5. Al-Bukhari.

friendship and he made their hearts incline to him. He made them love belief and adorned it in their hearts and he treated them gently to encourage them. He said to his Companions, "You are sent to make things easy. You were not sent to scare people away." He said, "Make things easy and do not make them hard. Soothe and do not scare away."[1]

He said, "Let it not be said that Muhammad killed his Companions."[2] The Prophet cajoled the hypocrites and unbelievers, was cheerful in their company and lenient to them and endured their harm. He was patient when they were coarse. But it is not permitted for us to be patient with them in such cases. Allah says, **"You will continue to come upon some act of treachery on their part, except for a few of them, so pardon them and overlook."** (5:15) Allah says, **"Repel the bad with something better and, if there is enmity between you and someone else, he will be like a close friend."** (41:35) That was because people at the beginning of Islam needed to be brought close. People are unanimous about that.

Once Islam was firmly established and Allah had given it victory over all other *deens*, any such detractor that the Muslims had power over and whose affair was well-known was put to death. A case in point is that of Ibn Khatal and others whom the Prophet said should be should killed on the Day of the Conquest and those among the Jews and others whom it was possible to kill by assassination. There were others who were captured but rectified their behaviour before they came into the Prophet's company and joined the group of those who manifested belief in him. Among such people who had harmed him were Ka'b ibn al-Ashraf,[3] Abu Rafi',[4] an-Nadr ibn al-Harith[5] and 'Uqba ibn Abi Mu'ayt.

The same applied to another group who could have been killed with impunity like Ka'b ibn Zuhayr[6] and Ibn az-Zaba'ra[7] and others who harmed the Prophet but then surrendered and met him as Muslims.

The inward parts of the hypocrites were veiled and the Prophet judged according to the outward. Most of these things were uttered by them in secret and among people of their own sort. Then they swore by Allah that they had not said them and uttered words of belief.

In spite of this, the Prophet desired to make them return to Islam. The Prophet was patient with their faults and their coarseness as all the Resolute

---

1. Ibn Hanbal, al-Bukhari and Muslim, and an-Nasa'i from Anas.
2. To 'Umar in the story of Ubayy ibn Salul.
3. A Jewish enemy who was assassinated.
4. A Jew from Khaybar.
5. Captured at Badr and put to death.
6. A poet who later wrote a famous poem for the Prophet.
7. Another poet who became Muslim when Makka was conquered.

Prophets[1] were patient until many of these people returned both inwardly and outwardly to Islam and were as sincere in secret as they appeared openly. Then Allah helped many of them and some of them established the *deen* as wazirs, helpers, defenders and Ansar as the traditions attest.

Because of this, some of our Imams have questioned whether their statements[2] were confirmed enough with the Prophet to raise a complaint. A single person who did not have the rank of testimony might have transmitted them – such as a child, a slave or a woman. Taking life is only permitted when there are two just witnesses. This can be applied to the affair of the Jews' greeting.[3] They twisted it with their tongues and did not make it clear.

Don't you see how attention was drawn to this matter by A'isha? If the Jew had clearly enunciated it, she would not have been the only person to recognise it. That is why the Prophet informed his Companions about what the Jews were doing and the lack of sincerity in their greeting and the deceit it contained through the twisting of their tongues and how they were really attacking the *deen*. He said, "When a Jew greets one of you, he says, 'Death be upon you,' so say 'and upon you'."

Similarly, one of our companions in Baghdad[4] said, "The Prophet did not kill the hypocrites in spite of what he knew about them. It has not been related that a clear proof was established regarding their hypocrisy. That is why the Prophet left them alone. Furthermore, the matter was secret and inward while their outward was Islam and belief and they were among the people of the *dhimma* and treaty and proximity. People were also new to Islam and could not distinguish the bad from the good. It is known that some of the Arabs who are mentioned as being suspected of hypocrisy are among the group of believers and the Companions of the Messenger and the helpers of the *deen* according to outward judgement of them. If the Prophet had killed them for their hypocrisy when it had not emerged from them because he knew what they concealed in themselves, those who were hostile would have found something to go on about, fugitives would have been suspicious and the impetuous would have spread lies. More than one person would have been alarmed and feared the company of the Prophet and coming into Islam. The claimant would have made false claims and the wrong-acting enemy would have thought that he was killed out of enmity and desire for revenge." Malik ibn Anas also said something to this effect.

That is why the Prophet said, "Let it not be said that Muhammad killed his

1. The Resolute Prophets are said to be five: Nuh, Ibrahim, Musa, 'Isa and Muhammad, or those mentioned in *Suras* 7 and 26 who are Nuh, Hud, Salih, Sulayman, Lut and Nuh, or the eighteen Prophets mentioned in *Sura* 6, or all the Messengers except for Ayyub.
2. When the Jews said, "Death be upon you."
3. i.e. only one person reported what the Jews had said.
4. Perhaps Qadi 'Abdu'l-Wahhab al-Baghdadi al-Maliki.

Companions." The Prophet said, "Those are the ones whom Allah has forbidden me to kill." This is not the same as applying the outward judgments to the Companions – such as the *hadd*-punishments for fornication, killing and similar things when the crimes were evident and people in general knew about them.

Muhammad ibn al-Mawwaz said, "If the hypocrites had openly shown their hypocrisy, then the Prophet would have killed them."

Qadi Abu'l-Hasan ibn al-Qassar and Qatada spoke regarding the commentary of Allah's words, **"If the munafiqun and those with sickness in their hearts and the rumour-mongers in Madina do not desist, We will set you onto them. Then they will only be your neighbours for a very short time. They are an accursed people. Wherever they are found they should be seized and mercilessly put to death. This is Allah's pattern..."** (33:60-62) and said that it means when they openly display hypocrisy.

Muhammad ibn Maslama related in the *Mabsut* from Zayd ibn Aslam that Allah's words, **"O Prophet, strive against the unbelievers and the hypocrites and be harsh to them,"** (9:75) abrogates what came before it.

One of our shaykhs said that perhaps the words of the bedouin who said, "This is a dividing out by which the face of Allah is not intended," and "Be just!" were not understood by the Prophet as an attack or suspicion. He saw them as an error of opinion regarding the matters of this world and as striving for the best interests of people. He did not think anything of them and saw them as belonging to the kind of harm which should be forgiven and endured. That is why he did not punish him.

Something similar is said about the Jews for saying, "Death be upon you." There was no clear curse in it nor supplication except for death which all men must meet. It was said that what they meant was, "May you dislike your religion," "death" meaning boredom and disgust. This is a supplication for the *deen* to become boring which is not a clear curse. Therefore al-Bukhari has a section called, "The Chapter on when the *dhimma* or other people curse the Prophet by allusion." One scholar has said that the allusion is not a curse, but rather to cause harm. We have already stated that cursing and harm are the same in respect to him.

Qadi Abu Muhammad ibn Nasr deals with this *hadith*[1] by quoting some of what has already been mentioned. It is not mentioned in this *hadith* whether this Jew was one of the people of the *dhimma* and those subject to treaty or from those with whom the Muslims were at war. Things established by proof are not abandoned in favour of mere probability. The most suitable and evident reasons for the Prophet not punishing him was the intention to seek friendship

---

1. About what the Jew said.

and trying to bring such people around to the *deen* – perhaps they would believe. That is why al-Bukhari puts the *hadith* of "The Sharing-out and the *Khawarij*" under the title "Chapter: Whoever gave up fighting the *Khawarij* in order to create friendship and so that people might not harbour an aversion to him."

The Prophet forebore what the Jews had done when he was bewitched and poisoned, which is more terrible than being cursed, until Allah helped him and gave him permission to kill those Jews who had acted against him and to drive them out of their fortresses and to cast terror into their hearts. He prescribed emigration for those of them he wished, removed them from their houses and demolished their homes at their own hands and the hands of the believers. He openly cursed them and said, "Brothers of pigs and monkeys." He said that the swords of the Muslims could be used against them[1] and removed them from their neighbourhood and caused their land, homes and property to be inherited by others[2] so that the word of Allah would be uppermost and the word of those who rejected underneath.

People might say that it has come in the sound *hadith* [3] from 'A'isha that the Prophet never took revenge on his own behalf for anything that happened to him unless the respect of Allah was violated, then he took revenge for the sake of Allah. Know that this does not necessarily mean that he did not take revenge against those who cursed him or harmed him or called him a liar. These actions contravene some of the inviolable things of Allah and so the Prophet took revenge for them. What he did not take revenge for was those things which were connected to bad behaviour in word or action toward himself or his property which were not intended to harm him, but were merely part of the natural coarse and ignorant disposition of the bedouins or the insolent nature of man in general, such as the bedouin pulling his cloak until it made a mark on his neck or the man raising his voice in his presence or the bedouin arguing about the Prophet buying his horse to which Khuzayma testified. Another example was when two of his wives supported one another against him and other such things which it is best to overlook.

One of our *'ulama'* has said that it is *haram* to harm the Prophet by any action, even if it is an allowable (*mubah*) action. In respect of men other than the Prophet, permitted actions are allowed, even if they harm someone. A proof is found in the general statement, **"Those who harm Allah and His Messenger, Allah has cursed them in this world and the Next."** (33:58)

In the *hadith* about Fatima, the Prophet said, "She is part of me. What harms her harms me. I do not make *haram* what Allah has made *halal*, but the daughter

---

1. The Banu Qurayza.
2. The Banu'n-Nadir.
3. In al-Bukhari and elsewhere.

of the Messenger of Allah and the daughter of the enemy of Allah[1] can never be together with the same man."[2]

Another example of his forbearance might have been something said by an unbeliever to harm him at a time when the Prophet still hoped that he would later become Muslim, such as when he forgave the Jew who had bewitched him, the bedouin who wanted to kill him and the Jewess who poisoned him – although it is also said that he killed her.

He forgave this sort of harm to himself from the People of the Book and the hypocrites, desiring to bring about their friendship and that of others as we have already confirmed. Success is by Allah.

SECTION 4
The judgment regarding someone who maligns the Prophet without deliberation or really believing what he has said

We have already discussed killing the person who, with intent, curses the Prophet, belittles him or slights him in any way. The judgement in this case is clear.

The second case concerns when it is necessary to clarify what someone has said. This applies to someone who speaks about the Prophet without intending to curse or belittle him and not believing his words to be true, but who nonetheless speaks about the Prophet using words of disbelief which curse him, revile him or call him a liar or ascribe to him something that is not permitted or deny one of his necessary attributes, all of which constitutes disparagement in respect of him. For instance, he might ascribe a major wrong action to the Prophet, or say that he had failed to convey the message or had fallen short in a judgement between people or he might lower his rank, the honour of his lineage, the extent of his knowledge or his asceticism, or deny a famous matter reported from him which has come by many paths of transmission with the intention of refuting the report, or say something insolent and ugly or of a cursing nature in respect of him. However, the state of this individual indicates that he does not mean to censure the Prophet nor to curse him but that ignorance, discontent, drunkenness, carelessness, arrogance or hasty speech has led him to say what he has said.

The judgement in this case is the same judgement as that applied to the first individual. Such a person is killed without hesitation since no-one is excused for disbelief by ignorance or by claiming a slip of the tongue or by any of the things which we have mentioned if his intellect is basically sound. The only exception is when someone is forced to do it while his heart is at rest in belief.

1. Referring to Juwayriyya, the daughter of Abu Jahl, who had been offered in marriage to 'Ali.
2. Al-Bukhari.

This was the *fatwa* given by the people of Andalusia against Ibn Hatim when he denied the asceticism of the Messenger of Allah and his family.

Muhammad ibn Sahnun said that someone in the hands of the enemy who curses the Prophet is killed unless it is known that he was forced to become Christian or was compelled to say that against his will. Abu Muhammad ibn Abi Zayd said that one cannot claim the excuse of a slip of the tongue in the cases of this kind.

Abu'l-Hasan al-Qabisi gave a *fatwa* that someone who reviles the Prophet while he is drunk should be killed because it is assumed that the drunkard believes that and does it when he is not drunk. Furthermore, the *hadd*-punishments for slander, murder and all the *hudud* are not removed by drunkenness because the person brought the state of drunkenness on himself. This is because someone who drinks wine knowing that it will confuse his intellect and cause him to do disliked things is the same as someone who intends doing the things that this will inevitably bring about. It is on this basis that we make divorce, emancipation, retaliation and the *hadd*-punishments binding on the drunkard.

This judgement is not refuted by the *hadith* in which Hamza said to the Prophet, "Are you other than the slave of my father?"[1]

The Prophet knew that Hamza was drunk and turned away because at that time wine had not yet been forbidden. Thus there was no wrong action in the offences ensuing from it. The judgement was that what ensued from it was pardoned as is the case with what ensues from sleep or drinking a trustworthy remedy.

SECTION 5
Is the one who says such things an unbeliever or an apostate?

The third case concerns whether, when someone intentionally calls the Prophet a liar in what he said or brought or denies and rejects his prophethood or his message and its existence or disbelieves in it, he has, by saying this, moved to a different *deen*.

The consensus is that this person is an unbeliever and must be killed. Then one looks to see whether what he said constitutes a clear statement, in which case the judgement is the same as that for apostasy. There is strong disagreement about whether he is asked to repent or not.

According to another position, his repentance would not in any case prevent his execution because of what is due to the Prophet, if he in fact disparaged him in his lies.

---

1. Muslim and al-Bukhari from 'Ali.

If he conceals what he said, he is judged as a heretic (*zindiq*). Repentance does not prevent his being executed according to the Malikis as we will clarify. Abu Hanifa and his companions said that it is lawful to kill anyone who declares himself free of Muhammad or calls him a liar. He is an apostate unless he retracts that.

Ibn al-Qasim said that if a Muslim says that Muhammad is not a Prophet or was not sent or that the Qur'an was not revealed to him, he is killed for being a liar. Any Muslim who disbelieves in the Messenger of Allah has the status of an apostate. It is the same with someone who openly declares that he denies the Prophet. He is like an apostate and is called upon to repent. Ibn al-Qasim said something similar about anyone who calls himself a Prophet and says that he has received revelation.

Sahnun and Ibn al-Qasim said that it is the same whether he makes that claim secretly or openly. Asbagh said that he is the same as an apostate because he has rejected the Book of Allah by forging lies against Allah.

Ashab said that any Jew who calls himself a Prophet, claims that he has been sent to people or says that there is a Prophet after our Prophet is asked to repent if he openly declares that. If he repents, he is left. If not, he is killed. This is because he rejects the Prophet who said, "There is no Prophet after me." Therefore he forges lies against Allah in making his claim to the messengership and prophethood.

Muhammad ibn Sahnun said, "Anyone who doubts a single letter which Muhammad, may Allah bless him and grant him peace, brought, is a denying unbeliever."

He said that the judgement against anyone who rejects the Prophet is that he is killed.

Ahmad ibn Sulayman, Sahnun's companion, said that whoever says that the Prophet was black is killed. The Prophet was not black.

Abu 'Uthman al-Haddad said something similar and said that if someone said that the Prophet died before his beard began to grow or that he was in Tahart (Morocco) and not Tihama, he is killed because this constitutes denial.

Habib ibn ar-Rabi' said that it is disbelief to alter his description and its details. The one who does that openly is an unbeliever. He is asked to repent. The one who conceals it is a heretic and is killed without being asked to repent.

SECTION 6
The judgement regarding words that could be construed to be a curse

The fourth case is when someone makes a general statement which is doubtful and might refer to the Prophet or to someone else, or there is uncertainty regarding what was meant by it and whether it is free of what is disliked or evil. In this instance there is some hesitation and the opinion of the *mujtahids* varies. Those who follow the *mujtahids* hesitate to make a definite statement since anyone who is executed must be executed by a clear proof and those allowed to live are allowed to live by a clear proof.

Some of these people prefer to uphold the inviolability of the Prophet and protect his honour, and so they venture to execute those who fall into this category. Some people exalt the inviolability of taking life and avert the *hadd* from this person because of doubt as to the meaning of his statement.

Our Imams disagree about a man who becomes angry with another man to whom he owes money so that he says to him, "Bless Muhammad, may Allah bless him and grant him peace!" Then the one seeking repayment says to him, "May Allah not bless the one who blesses him!"

Sahnun was asked, "Is not this man the same as someone who reviles the Prophet? Or who reviles the angels who bless him?" He said that it was not taken like that since it arose from his anger and he did not specify whom he was vilifying.

Abu Ishaq al-Barqi and Asbagh ibn al-Faraj said that such a man is not killed because he has reviled other people. This is similar to what Sahnun said because he did not make anger mitigation for the vilification of the Prophet. The position he took was because he did not consider the words definite and there was no context there to indicate direct vilification of the Prophet nor vilification of the angels. The context indicated that what was meant were people in general. The man had said to him, "Bless the Prophet." His words and his curse were applied to the man who was blessing the Prophet at that moment and his curse was the result of the other man telling him to bless the Prophet when he was angry. This is what Sahnun meant and it, however, is based on understanding the reasoning of the one who said it. Al-Harith ibn Miskin the Qadi and others believed that the man should be killed for something like this.

Abu'l-Hasan al-Qabisi reserved judgement about killing a man who said, "Every owner of a hotel is a cuckold, even if he were a sent Prophet." He ordered that the man be bound in chains and confined until he could come up with a clear proof derived from the content of his words and his intention and whether he really intended by that hotel-keepers of his own time. It is well known that there could not be any sent Prophet among them, so the matter would become less severe if that were what he intended. The Qadi, however, said that the literal sense of what he had said applies to everyone with a hotel, modern or ancient, and that there may have been Prophets and Messengers among the ancients who earned money by keeping a hotel.

He said that it is not valid to spill a Muslim's blood except when the matter is clear. Anything which is the result of interpretation must be closely examined. This is what he meant.

Abu Muhammad ibn Abi Zayd spoke about those who said, "May Allah curse the Arabs," "May Allah curse the Banu Isra'il," and, "May Allah curse the Banu Adam," and said that they did not mean the Prophets, but the unjust among them. He can be disciplined for that at the discretion of the Sultan. Similarly he gave a *fatwa* about someone who said, "May Allah curse the one who made intoxicants *haram*," saying that the man did not know who had made them *haram*.

Ibn Abi Zayd also spoke about someone who had cursed the *hadith*, "No selling by a city dweller to a bedouin," and cursed what had brought it and excused him for his ignorance and lack of knowledge of the *sunan*, but said that such a man was to be strongly disciplined. That was because he did not intend to curse Allah or the Prophet. He was cursing the people who had forbidden it on the basis of the *fatwas* of Sahnun and his companions.

The same applies to insolent people who say to each other in insults things like "son of a thousand pigs" or "son of a thousand dogs." There is no doubt that among that number of his ancestors there are bound to be a number of Prophets. It may even reach Adam, so one must restrain him and make it clear that the speaker was ignorant and discipline him. If it is known that he intended to curse the Prophets among his forebears, then he is executed.

A statement regarding things of this nature is treated in a much stricter fashion in the case of someone saying to a Hashimite,[1] "May Allah curse the Banu Hashim," and then saying, "I only meant the unjust among them." Or if he says something ugly about his ancestors to one of the descendants of the Prophet knowing that he is one of the descendants of the Prophet. There is nothing in either of the two statements to suggest that he singled out certain ancestors and removed the Prophet from those he cursed.

I saw that Abu Musa 'Isa ibn Manas said about someone who said to another man, "May Allah curse you up until Adam!" that he is executed if he sticks to it.

Our shaykhs disagreed about someone who testified to something against someone else and then said to him, "Do you doubt me?" and the other replied, "The Prophets were doubted, so why not you?" Our Shaykh, Abu Ishaq ibn Ja'far, says that he is executed because of the ugliness of the expression. Qadi Abu Muhammad ibn Mansur hesitated to condemn him to death due to the lack of definiteness. He took it as a report about those among the unbelievers who doubted. The Qadi of Cordoba, Abu 'Abdullah ibn al-Hajj, gave a similar *fatwa*. Qadi Abu Muhammad had the man bound and put him in prison for a long time. He later took an oath from him rejecting what had been testified

---

1. A member of the clan of the Prophet.

against him since there was weakness in some of the testimony against him. Then he released him.

I saw our Shaykh, Qadi Abu 'Abdullah ibn 'Isa, when he was a judge and a man was brought to him who had spoken insolently to a man named Muhammad, going over to a dog, kicking it and saying, "Get up, Muhammad!" The man disliked that and some people testified against the man who had said it. He commanded that he be jailed and investigated him to see whether he kept the company of anyone whose *deen* was suspect. When he did not find anything to confirm doubt in his belief, he had him flogged and then released him.

SECTION 7
The judgement on someone who describes himself with one of the attributes of the Prophets

The fifth case is when the speaker does not intend to disparage the Prophet nor mention a fault nor curse him. However, he appropriates some of the Prophet's attributes or cites one of his states which were allowed for him alone in this world, likening himself or someone else to him. Or he might mention an unfortunate occurrence which happened to the Prophet or a mishap connected to him, not saying it by way of consolation and verification but rather with the intention of promoting himself or someone else or to liken him to the Prophet or out of lack of respect for the Prophet or meaning what he says as a joke.

An example of this is someone who says, "If something is said about me, it was also said about the Prophet," or, "If I am called a liar, the Prophets were called liars," or, "I am safe from the tongues of people while the Prophet of Allah and His Messengers were not safe from them," or, "I am patient as those of resolution were patient," or, "like the patience of Ayyub," or, "The Prophet of Allah was patient and endured his enemy and was forbearing in much the same way as I am." It is like the words of al-Mutanabbi:

> I am in a community to which Allah has brought a stranger,
> like Salih in Thamud.

And similar things are found in the poems of arrogant men who indulge themselves and speak carelessly like al-Ma'arri:

> You were Musa to whom the daughter of Shu'ayb came,
> although you are no pauper.

There is something terrible at the end of the poem which contains contempt and belittlement of the Prophet and preference for the state of someone else.

> If it had not been that revelation was cut off after Muhammad,
> we would have said that Muhammad is a stand-in for his father.
> He is like him in excellence even though Jibril
> did not bring him a message.

The first half of the second verse contains something terrible since it makes someone similar in excellence to the Prophet, may Allah bless him and grant him peace.

There are two possible ways that this kind of insidiousnesss shows itself. One is that this "excellence" lowers the Prophet and the other is in order to remove excellence from him. The latter is more terrible.

We find a similar thing in another poem:

> When his banners are raised, they are set in motion
> between the wings of Jibril.

Another of the people of this time[1] said:

> He fled from eternity and sought protection with us.
> Allah made Ridwan's heart patient.

Another example is what Hassan al-Masisi, an Andalusian poet, said about Muhammad ibn 'Abbad, known as al-Mu'tamid, and his wazir, Abu Bakr ibn Zaydun:

> It is as if Abu Bakr were Abu Bakr ar-Rida and
> Hassan was Hassan and you are Muhammad.

There are many more examples like this.

We have a lot of evidence of things of this nature but we are extremely loathe to relate them and thus publicise them. People are loose in speech, indulging themselves by entering through this narrow door and attaching no importance to the gravity it entails. They do not realise what a terrible wrong action lies in it. They speak about what they do not know, **"and you reckon it to be a light thing, while it is a mighty thing with Allah."** (24:16)

This is especially the case with the poets. The worst of them regarding clear

---

1. i.e. the time of the author, Qadi 'Iyad.

statements and free speech were Ibn Hani' al-Andalusi and Ibn Sulayman al-Ma'arri. Many of their words reach the limit of scorn, disparagement and even clear disbelief.

We have given the answer to this. Now we intend to discuss this subject through the examples we have given. All of this, even if it does not contain a curse or relate to disparagement of the angels and Prophets (and I do not mean the two wretched verses of al-Ma'arri nor the intention of the speaker to belittle and show contempt), nevertheless contains no respect for prophethood nor esteem for the message nor regard for the chosen ones nor consideration for the honour that is due them. Such people make another person similar to the Prophet regarding the honour in which they are held or regarding a blemish which they mean to make light of, or make a resemblance in connection with the delight of his company, or extol a quality to beautify someone's words by means of the one whose importance Allah has exalted and whose worth He has honoured and whose respect and obedience He has made binding. Allah forbade that the Prophet be spoken to loudly or that a voice be raised in his presence. This right is defended by execution, discipline, imprisonment or strong reprimand depending on the enormity of what the person has said, the ugliness of what he has uttered, whether this sort of thing is a habit with him or a rare occurrence, the context of his words, and his regret for what he has done.

The early people objected to this sort of thing. Harun ar-Rashid rebuked the poet Abu Nuwas for saying,

> If the magic of Pharaoh remains in you,
> the staff of Musa is in a wealthy hand.

Ar-Rashid said to him, "Son of a stinking uncircumcised woman! You are mocking the staff of Musa!" He commanded that he be removed from his army that very night. Al-Qutaybi mentioned that the part of this poem for which Abu Nuwas was censured and charged with disbelief were his words about Muhammad al-Amin[1] when he likened him to the Prophet by saying:

> The two Ahmads compete in similarity. They are alike in
> character and formed like a piece of a single shoelace.

They also objected to his words:

> How can hope not be with you
> when the Messenger of Allah is among your party?

---

1. Al-Harun ar-Rashid's son.

Because of the right of the Messenger and the obligation to esteem him, his position is too lofty for anyone to be related to it.

The judgement regarding things like this are as we have already detailed in the *fatwas* about this subject. The *fatwas* of the Imam of our school, Malik ibn Anas, and his companions have already been presented.

There are incidents from the transmission of Ibn Abi Maryam about a man who rebuked another man for poverty. He retorted, "Do you rebuke me for poverty when the Prophet, may Allah bless him and grant him peace, herded sheep?" Malik said, "He has alluded to the Prophet, may Allah bless him and grant him peace, outside its proper place and I think that he should be disciplined." He added, "When people of wrong action are censured, they should not say that the Prophets before them erred."

'Umar ibn 'Abdu'l-'Aziz said to a man, "Search out a scribe for us whose father was an Arab." One of his scribes said, "But the Prophet's father was an unbeliever." He said, "You dare make this comparison!" He dismissed him, saying, "You will never write for me again."

Sahnun disliked people saying the prayer on the Prophet on account of astonishment, unless it was out of regard and proper consideration because of the respect and esteem for him which Allah has commanded.

Al-Qabisi was asked about a man who said to an ugly man, "Like the face of Nakir!" and to a frowning man, "Like the face of angry Malik!" He asked, "What did he mean by that? Nakir is one of the questioners of the grave, and they are angels. What did he mean? Is it terror which filled him when he saw him because of his face or was he simply averse to look at him because of his ugly appearance? If this is the case, it is terrible because it is a way of belittlement and humiliation, so there is a more severe punishment."

There is no clear statement here which might be construed as cursing an angel. The curse falls on the one addressed. There is exemplary punishment by flogging and imprisonment for the insolence involved. He said, "As for mentioning Malik, the Guardian of the Fire, the one who mentioned him in connection with his dislike of the other man frowning was being coarse unless the man who frowned possessed power and hence the first man was alarmed by his frown. In that case the speaker compared him to Malik to censure the one who frowned for what he did and for holding to, in spite of injustice, the attribute of Malik, the angel who obeys his Lord in his action. It is as if he were saying, 'By Allah! He has the anger of Malik!' For this reason his punishment is lighter." However he should not allude to this sort of thing. If he was praising the frowner for his frown and used the quality of Malik to express his praise, that is even worse, and he should be severely punished. There is, however, no censure in this statement against the angel. If he had intended to blame the angel, then he should have been put to death.

Abu'l-Hasan al-Qabisi also said that a young man known as Khayr said something to a man and the man said to him, "Shut up, you are illiterate." The youth retorted, "Wasn't the Prophet, may Allah bless him and grant him peace, illiterate?" He was denounced for that and the people called him an unbeliever. The young man became fearful about what he had said and showed regret. Abu'l-Hasan said, "It is an error to say that he is an unbeliever. But he made a mistake in quoting this quality of the Prophet as an argument. If he asks for forgiveness, repents, admits it and takes refuge in Allah, he will be left alone because what he said did not reach the limit of killing, and as for discipline, the one who voluntarily repents must be spared it."

There was a case where one of the *qadis* of Andalusia asked for a *fatwa* from our Shaykh, Abu Muhammad ibn Mansur,[1] about a man who was demeaned for something by another man and he said to him, "You mean to say that I am imperfect? Well, I am a mortal and all mortals are touched by imperfection, even the Prophet, may Allah bless him and grant him peace." He gave a *fatwa* that the man should be jailed for a long time and painfully punished since he did not intend to curse. One of the Andalusian *fuqaha'* gave a *fatwa* that the man should be killed.

SECTION 8
The judgement regarding someone who quotes such words from someone else

The sixth case is when the speaker quotes something of this nature from someone else. In this case, one looks at the form his story takes and the context of his words. The judgement about it varies accordingly. It can be seen as belonging to one of four categories: obligatory, recommended, disliked or forbidden.

If he reports it by way of testimony and to give information about the speaker, to rebuke him and make known what he has said, out of aversion to it and in order to make other people dislike it and to make the testimony of the one who said it unreliable, it must be taken heed of and the one who does this is praised.

This is the case if he quotes it in a book or in an assembly in order to refute the perpetrator and criticize him and in order to carry out his legal obligation regarding the matter. Sometimes it is obligatory for him and sometimes only recommended depending on the state of the one who is relaying what was said and the state of the one from whom it is relayed.

If the person who made the original statement is among those from whom

---

1. The chief *qadi* there at that time.

knowledge is taken, or who transmit *hadiths* or give judgement or testimony or *fatwas* on people's rights, it is obligatory for the one who heard the derogatory statement to repeat what he heard from him and to make people averse to him and to testify against him according to what he has said. Any Muslim Imam who comes to hear what was said must make the man's disbelief and the corruption of his words clear in order to cut off his harm from the Muslims and establish the due of the Master of the Messengers.

This is the case particularly if the man in question is one of those who admonish the masses or teach children. If this is something his heart contains, he is not safe from casting it into their hearts. In such cases, the obligation to deal with him is confirmed by the right of the Prophet and the right of the *Shari'a*. If the speaker is not someone of this standing, then it is still a specific obligation to establish the due of the Prophet and to protect his honour and help him against harm, whether he is alive or dead. This is a duty for every believer. If someone makes the truth clear, and the case against the detractor is definite and evident, then no-one else is obliged to testify but it is still recommended for many people to give testimony against such a person and to help in warning against him. The *Salaf* agreed that the state of anyone whose reliability in giving *hadith* is suspect is to be made clear, so it must be even more binding with someone of this nature.

Abu Muhammad ibn Abi Zayd was asked whether a witness who has heard something of this nature said in respect of Allah should give testimony. He said that if it is expected that judgement will be effected through his testimony, then the witness should testify. That is what should happen if it is known that the judge does not think that execution would ensue as a result of his testimony. The speaker should be asked to repent and should be disciplined. The witness then gives testimony and must do so.

As for being allowed to relate these words for any intention other than in these two instances, I do not think that it should be included in this subject at all. One does not amuse oneself at the expense of the honour of the Messenger of Allah, may Allah bless him and grant him peace, or soil one's mouth by saying bad things about him to anyone, either mentioning or quoting someone else's words without an intention for something allowed in the *Shari'a*.

As for the previous aims, they vary between the obligatory and the recommended. Allah relays the statements of those who forged lies against Him and against His Messengers in His Book in order to reject their words and warn about their disbelief, to threaten them, and refute them by what He has revealed in His perfect Book.

Similarly, examples of this are found in the sound *hadith* of the Prophet.

The *Salaf* and later Imams of guidance agreed that it was permissible to use stories about disbelief and heretics in their books and assemblies to make them clear to people and to refute that sort of thing. Although it has been reported that Ahmad ibn Hanbal objected to al-Harith ibn Asad al-Muhasibi doing this,[1] Ahmad ibn Hanbal himself did something similar when he refuted the *Jahmiyya*[2] and those who said that the Qur'an was created.[3] It is permitted to relate this sort of thing.

It is, however, forbidden to relate things that curse the Prophet or show contempt for his position, in tales, night talk, titbits, stories of the people and their good and bad words, the jests of the brazen and the anecdotes of foolish people. All this kind of thing is forbidden. Some of them are more strongly forbidden than others. Some of them incur punishment.

If someone says something unintentionally without realising the weight of his words or something he would not normally say or words which are not offensive in themselves and he does not approve of them or find them correct, he is restrained from it and forbidden to repeat what he has said. If he is put right by some disciplinary action, that is commendable. If what he says is offensive in itself, then the action taken should be more severe.

It is related that a man asked Malik about someone who had said that the Qur'an was created. Malik said about the questioner, "He is an unbeliever, so kill him." The man said, "But I related it from someone else." Malik said, "We heard it from you." Malik did this as a means of restriction and accusation of error. The proof is that he did not actually carry out the execution.

If a relater in this kind of instance is suspected of being the real author of what he says while ascribing it to someone else or it is his habit to do this, or it appears that he admires the statement he is conveying, or he is enthusiastic about such things and makes light of them, or he memorizes things like this and seeks them out, or he relates poems satirizing the Prophet and cursing him, then the judgment of this person is the same as that of someone who actually curses himself. He is punished for what he said and the fact that he ascribes it to someone else does not help him. He is killed immediately and dispatched to his appointed place in Hell.

Abu 'Ubayd al-Qasim ibn Salam said about someone who had memorized half of a line in which the Prophet was satirized, "It constitutes disbelief."

One of those who wrote on the subject of consensus mentioned that the consensus of the Muslims was to forbid the transmission of anything in which the Prophet was satirized or to write or read such things. They should be left where they are found without being touched. May Allah have mercy on our god-fearing *Salaf* who guarded their *deen*! They excluded this sort of thing from

---

1. In what he said about the Mu'tazilites in his *Kitab ar-Ri'aya*.
2. A sect originating in Khorasan who followed Jahm ibn Safwan. He said that the Garden and the Fire were not eternal and that belief was gnosis, not affirmation. He also believed in total predestination and that man was totally compelled in all he did with no choice whatsoever.
3. Or that man creates his actions, which is the position of the Mu'tazilites and the *Qadariyya*.

the *hadiths* about the raids and from the *sira* and left out its transmission except for a few things which were not too offensive which they mentioned in order to show the revenge of Allah on those who said them and how those who forged lies against the Prophet were punished for their wrong action.

Abu 'Ubayd al-Qasim ibn Salam was careful regarding the satirical poems of the Arabs he quoted in his books. He alluded to the name of any person satirized by a metric equivalent of his name to keep his *deen* innocent and to preserve himself from being a partner, in what was said, in criticising anyone by his quotation or its publication. How much more should this be the case with someone who attacks the honour of the Master of Men, may Allah bless him and grant him peace?

SECTION 9
The states of the Prophet which can be mentioned for the sake of instruction

The seventh case is when someone mentions what is permitted for the Prophet, or disagrees about what is permitted for him, regarding those ordinary human matters that happened to him. He might associate them with the Prophet or mention the severity of things by which he was tested and which he endured in the way of Allah – the harshness of his enemies, their injuring him, knowledge of his beginning, his life and the suffering he met in his time, and what he did for his livelihood. All these things have come by way of transmission and through study and through knowing what is sound in respect of the inviolability of the Prophets and what is permitted for them.

This is different from the six previous cases since there is no fault, imperfection, contempt, or belittlement involved in it for the speaker either by way of expression or intention. However, discussion about these things must only take place among the people of knowledge or intelligent students of the *deen* who understand what is intended and realise its benefits. Others should avoid it if they do not have sufficient understanding or it is feared that it might become a trial for them.

Because of what the story contains, one of the *Salaf* disliked teaching women *Sura Yusuf* (12) due to the weakness of their understanding and their lack of intellect and perception.

The Prophet said, speaking about having been hired to herd sheep at the beginning of his state, "There is no Prophet who has not herded sheep."[1] Allah informed us about the same thing regarding Musa. If this is mentioned in the proper way there is no fault in it. However, it is different if someone intends

---

1. Muslim and al-Bukhari from Jabir.

fault and contempt by it. It was the custom of the Arabs to do that. Indeed, there is far-reaching wisdom in that for the Prophets. Allah raised them by degrees in His esteem and trained them by their herding sheep so that they would be able to manage their communities both by reason of the honour which they had already been shown before-time and the knowledge they had gained by their experience.

Similarly, Allah mentions the fact that the Prophet was an orphan and poor in order to show His favour to him and to demonstrate how He honoured him. There is no objection to someone mentioning this if his intention is to learn about the Prophet's situation and beginnings and to marvel at Allah's gift to him and His great favour to him. Indeed, it contains a proof of his prophethood and the soundness of his call since Allah gradually gave him victory over the leaders of the Arabs and all those of their nobles who opposed him and his importance grew until he had conquered them and taken over their reins of power and captured the property of many other communities. Allah gave him victory, supported him with His own help and through the help of the believers, bringing their hearts together, and He helped him by means of designated angels.

If he had been the son of a king or someone with a long-standing following, many ignorant people would have supposed that to have been the cause of his victory and what caused him to be elevated. This is why Heraclius questioned Abu Sufyan about him and asked, "Was there a king among his forebears?" and then said, "If there had been a king among his forefathers, we would have said that he was a man who was seeking his fathers' kingdom."

His being an orphan was part of the way he was described, and one of the signs mentioned, in the previous books and reports of previous communities. That is how he is mentioned in the book of Armiya[1] and how he was described by Ibn Abi Yazin to 'Abdu'l-Muttalib and by the monk Bahira to Abu Talib.

The same applies to his being described by Allah as being illiterate. That is praise in his case, and a virtue and the basis of his miracle since his greatest miracle was the Qur'an. It is connected to the knowledges and insights which the Prophet was given and by which he was preferred. This has already been covered in Part One. When something like this comes from a man who could not read or write, did not study and was not taught, it provokes amazement and profound consideration. This is a miracle for a mortal man and there is no imperfection in it since the goal of reading and writing is to gain knowledge. Literacy is a tool for this and a means of gaining understanding, not an end in itself. If the fruit and goal of something is obtained without them, there is no need for the means and cause.

---

1. Probably Jeremiah.

Illiteracy is a fault in others because it indicates ignorance and is a sign of stupidity. Glory be to the One who made the Prophet's affair different from other people's and placed his honour in something that for others is a fault, and his life in what would have meant death for others. He had his heart split open and what was inside of it removed, and that was the perfection of his life, the extreme strength of his self and the firmness of his heart. For other people, it would have resulted in their destruction and death. It is the same with much of what is related concerning him and his life – about his making do with little of this world, his clothes, food, transport, his humility and employing himself in his business and serving in his house, his doing without and turning away from this world. Both the trivial and important things of this world were the same for him since its affairs pass away swiftly and its states are overturned.

All of these things are among his virtues and good qualities and part of his nobility. Whoever mentions them as virtues or with that intention has a good purpose. Whoever quotes these things in other than their proper context has a bad purpose which is connected to what we have been talking about in the previous sections.

The same applies to traditions which people quote about the Prophet or any of the other Prophets in which there is some outward ambiguity which might be construed as referring to matters not befitting them. Such traditions need to be properly explained. What they refer to is unclear. People should only relate sound *hadiths* concerning them and quote only what is firmly known.

May Allah have mercy on Malik! He disliked teaching any *hadiths* which might lend themselves to doubt or whose meaning was obscure. He said, "What prompts people to teach this sort of *hadith*?" He was told, "Ibn 'Ajlan related them." He retorted, "He is not one of the *fuqaha'*, and I wish that people would make him agree to leave these *hadiths* and help him to quote the good ones. Most of them do not lead to any positive action."

It is related that a group of the *Salaf*, or rather all of them, disliked discussion about anything that did not lead to action.

The Prophet brought this *deen* to an Arab people who understood the speech of the Arabs in its proper context and usage. They knew its figurative expressions, metaphors, rhetoric and terseness. It was not obscure for them. Then foreigners got hold of it and illiterates delved into it. They scarcely understood what the Arabs meant at all except in the case of clear texts and statements. They could not grasp what was alluded to when it was concise, revelatory, rhetorical or indirect. Therefore they disagreed about how to interpret it and applied it literally or differed widely concerning its meaning.

As for any *hadiths* which are not sound, they must not be mentioned at all, either in respect of Allah or in respect of the Prophets. The meaning of such *hadiths* should not be discussed at all. The correct thing to do is to discard them and not be occupied with them. The only reason to mention them is merely in order to inform people that they are weak in text and weak in *isnad*.

The Shaykhs objected to Abu Bakr ibn Furak concerning himself with obscure words in weak, fabricated *hadiths* which are without foundation or which were transmitted from the people of the Book who mixed truth with falsehood. It would have been enough for him to discard them and make it clear that they were weak. That removes any necessity of discussing them since the goal in speaking about an obscurity is to remove doubt regarding it and to pluck it out by the roots. Discarding them removes doubt and heals the soul.

SECTION 10
The necessary *adab* when mentioning reports about the Prophet

When someone speaks, either in the course of study or when teaching, about what is permitted for the Prophet and what is not permitted regarding his states he must, as we mentioned in the previous section, show esteem and respect for him. He must be careful about what he says and not be careless. The signs of *adab* should be apparent on him when he mentions the Prophet. If he mentions the hardships the Prophet endured, he should show apprehension and grief, and antipathy towards his enemies, and wish that he could have protected the Prophet, may Allah bless him and grant him peace, from it if he had been able to and to have helped him if it had been possible.

When he begins to discuss the subject of inviolability and speaks about his words and actions, he must be careful to use good expressions and have *adab* in what he says as much as possible. He should avoid anything repugnant in it and ugly terms – such as "ignorance", "lying" or "rebellion".

When he speaks about difficult things, he should say, "Is it not possible that there was a discrepancy in the words or that something had been reported differently from the way it happened by oversight or error?" He should avoid the expression "lying" altogether. When he speaks regarding knowledge, he should say things like, "Is it not possible that he only knew what he was taught? Is it not permitted for him not to have had knowledge of certain things until they were revealed to him?" He should not use "ignorance" since that word is ugly and repugnant. When speaking of actions, he should say, "Is opposition permitted for him in repect of certain commands and prohibitions and by the occurrence of some wrong actions?" These are better words and show better *adab* than,"Is it permitted that he rebel or do a wrong action, or a certain type of rebellion?"

This is part of respect for the Prophet, may Allah bless him and grant him peace, and the esteem and consideration which are his by right. I saw one of the *'ulama'* who did not protect the Prophet in this way and displayed ugliness regarding him. I did not find his expressions correct, and found that one of the tyrants attributed false reports to him which he had not, in fact, said, all because he had ceased to be careful in the way he expressed himself. This *'alim* was denounced for his scornfulness and the tyrant was declared an unbeliever.

Since things like this are considered ordinary good manners and are employed by people in their daily society and speech, it is still more necessary to employ them in respect of the Prophet, may Allah bless him and grant him peace, and it is more important to hold closely to them in his case. The excellence of the phrase used can make a thing good or ugly. The formulation of the phrase and its refinement is what exalts or abases a particular matter.

This is why the Prophet said, "There is magic in eloquence."[1] If someone quotes something in order to reject it and be clear of it, there is no harm in stating the term and being explicit, like saying, "Lying is not permitted for him at all, nor doing a major wrong action in any way nor tyranny in judgement in any case." But in spite of this, he must show esteem, respect and consideration when the Prophet is mentioned. Intense states were seen in the *Salaf* when he was simply mentioned as we have already noted in Part Two.

Some of them even held to this when they recited the *ayats* of the Qur'an. In it, Allah relates the words of His enemies and those who rejected His signs and forged lies against Him. So they lowered their voices in those places out of esteem for their Lord, exaltation of Him and apprehension about being like those who rejected Him.

---

1. Malik, Ibn Hanbal, al-Bukhari, Abu Dawud and at-Tirmidhi from Ibn 'Umar.

Chapter Two

THE JUDGEMENT AGAINST SOMEONE WHO CURSES THE PROPHET,
REVILES HIM, DISPARAGES HIM OR HARMS HIM, AND
HOW SOMEONE WHO DOES THIS SHOULD BE PUNISHED;
ABOUT CALLING ON HIM TO REPENT AND THE
STATUS OF HIS INHERITANCE

SECTION 1
The statements and opinions on the judgement of
someone who curses or disparages the Prophet

We have already stated what constitutes cursing and harming the Prophet, and we have mentioned the consensus of the *'ulama'* that anyone who says or does that should be killed. The Imam can choose between simply killing him or crucifying him, according to the judgements we have mentioned and whose proofs we have confirmed.

Know then that the best known position in the school of Malik and his companions and the statement of the *Salaf* and most of the Maliki *ulama'* is that such a person is killed as a *hadd*-punishment and not for disbelief, if he shows repentance for what he has done. This is why their opinion is that his repentance is not accepted, nor does his apology and seeking to save himself spare him as we have stated before. According to this statement, his judgement is the same as that of the *zindiq* and someone who conceals his disbelief.

According to this position, it makes no difference if he repents when he is in custody when testimony as to what he has said has been presented or if he himself comes in repentance, because it is an obligatory *hadd* which is not removed by repentance just as is the case with any other *hadd*.

Shaykh Abu'l-Hasan al-Qabisi says, "When a person's curse is proven and then he repents of what he has done and shows his repentance, he is killed for the curse as a *hadd*-punishment." Abu Muhammad ibn Abi Zayd said something similar. However, his repentance is of profit to him with Allah.

Ibn Sahnun says that when a heretic reviles the Prophet and then repents of having done it, his repentance does not prevent him being executed.

They have also disagreed about a *zindiq* who comes in repentance. Qadi Abu'l-Hassan ibn al-Qassar relates two statements about that:

1) Some of the Shaykhs say that he is killed on account of his confession because he could have veiled himself. It is feared that he might be confessing out of fear that it will be brought out against him and that is why he has made haste to repent.

2) Some of them say that his repentance is accepted because the proof of its soundness is the fact that he has confessed to it, so it is as if we have come upon his inward. It is the opposite with someone who is forced by clear evidence to admit his guilt. This is the position of Asbagh.

The question regarding someone who curses the Prophet is more serious. There is no way to conjecture any dispute such as we find in the previous case because it involves a right connected to the Prophet, may Allah bless him and grant him peace, and to his community because of him. Repentance cannot remove it at all just as is the case with other human rights (*huquq*).

If a *zindiq* repents after he is in custody, his repentance is not accepted according to Malik, Al-Layth ibn Sa'd, Ishaq ibn Rahawayh and Ahmad ibn Hanbal. According to Ash-Shafi'i, it is accepted. There is disagreement about what Abu Hanifa and Abu Yusuf said. Ibn al-Mundhir related from 'Ali ibn Abi Talib that he is asked to repent.

Muhammad ibn Sahnun said, "A Muslim does not escape execution by repentance when he has cursed the Prophet because he did not change from his *deen* to another *deen*. He did something which entails the *hadd*-punishment of execution. Unlike the *zindiq*, there is no pardon for it because he did not move outwardly from one *deen* to another."

As a proof for not taking his repentance into consideration, Qadi Abu Muhammad ibn Nasr said that the difference between someone who curses the Prophet and someone who curses Allah, according to the famous statement about being asked to repent, is due to the fact that the Prophet, may Allah bless him and grant him peace, was a human being and humans are a species to which blemish can be attached except for the one whom Allah has honoured with prophethood. The Creator is absolutely free of all faults. He is not in a category that can be connected to blemish.

Cursing the Prophet is not like apostasy for which repentance is accepted because apostasy is only connected to the apostate and does not involve a right due to another man. Therefore the apostate's repentance is accepted. When someone curses the Prophet, that is connected to a human right. It is like an apostate who murders or slanders someone while he is an apostate. His repentance does not remove the punishment for murder or slander. When the repentance of the apostate is accepted, his crimes are not removed – fornication, theft, or anything else. The one who curses the Prophet is not killed for his disbelief. He is killed in order to preserve esteem for the Prophet and to free him of any blemish. The punishment for what such a person has done is not averted by repentance.

Qadi Abu Muhammad means – and Allah knows best – that this is due to the fact that his curse is not part of a statement entailing disbelief, but has the meaning of contempt and scorn, or that the stigma of disbelief is removed from a person outwardly because of his repentance and his manifestation of his regret, and Allah knows best what is inside him. However the judgement for the curse remains the same.

Abu 'Imran al-Qabisi said that whoever curses the Prophet and then leaves Islam is killed and not asked to repent because the curse violates one of the rights due to people for which the apostate is still responsible. The statement of these shaykhs is based on the position that someone who does this is killed for a *hadd*, and not for disbelief. This requires some elaboration.

As for the transmission of Al-Walid ibn Muslim from Malik and those whom we have mentioned who agree on it and the people of knowledge who take the same position, they clearly state that cursing the Prophet amounts to apostasy. They said that the perpetrator is asked to repent of it, and if he repents, he is severely punished. If he refuses, he is killed. In this approach, he incurs the judgement of the apostate absolutely.

The first position is better known and clearer as we have already stated. We will enlarge on this a little. Those who do not think that it is apostasy demand execution on the basis of it being a *hadd*. We say that there are two possibilities: either he denies the testimony against him or he renounces what he did and shows repentance for it. We kill him for the *hadd* when disbelief is confirmed against him in respect of the Prophet, may Allah bless him and grant him peace, and his demeaning what Allah has exalted in respect of the due of the Prophet. We make his judgement regarding inheritance and other things that of the *zindiq* since it was known from him and he either denied it or repented.

People might ask how it can be affirmed on the one hand that he is an unbeliever and have disbelief proven against him and then on the other hand not judge him according to its judgements by asking him to repent with the consequences that that entails.

We say that, even if we confirm the judgement of being an unbeliever against him which entails execution, we still do not make it absolute because of his affirmation of *tawhid* and prophethood, his denial of the testimony against him or his claim that it was a mistake on his part and rebellion. The application of certain judgments of disbelief on certain individuals is not impossible, even if particular aspects of it are not confirmed in their case – such as being killed for abandoning the prayer. If it is known that he cursed in the belief that it was permissible for him to do so, there is no doubt that that makes him an unbeliever. It is the same if he curses the Prophet to himself. He is an unbeliever if he calls the Prophet a liar, rejects him or anything of that nature. This is something about which there is no doubt and which incurs execution.

If he repents of it, we do not accept his repentance and we kill him after he has repented. His execution in this case is for a *hadd* because of what he has said and for his earlier disbelief. After this, his affair is in the hands of Allah who is aware of the soundness of his renunciation and knows his secret thoughts.

Someone who does not show repentance and admits to the testimony against him and persists in it is an unbeliever by his words and by his considering it lawful to attack the honour of Allah and the honour of His Prophet, may Allah bless him and grant him peace. He is killed as an unbeliever without dispute.

According to these details, you can make use of the statements of the *'ulama'*. Minimize their differences regarding the way they reach their proof for the judgement, and assess their disagreement regarding inheritance in this case and other things in the proper measure and their aims will become clear for you if Allah wills.

SECTION 2
The judgement on an apostate if he repents

If we were to discuss when it is sound to be asked to repent, the differences regarding this follow the same ruling as the differences about the repentance of an apostate, since they are the same. The *Salaf* disagreed about whether that was obligatory or not, its proper form, and the period of time allowed for it.

Most of the people of knowledge believe that an apostate should be asked to repent. Ibn al-Qassar related that it is a consensus from the Companions that the statement of 'Umar is correct in asking someone to repent and none of them objected to it. That was the position of 'Uthman, 'Ali, and Ibn Mas'ud. 'Ata' ibn Abi Rabah, an-Nakh'i, ath-Thawri, Malik and his companions, al-Awza'i, ash-Shafi'i, Ahmad ibn Hanbal, Ishaq ibn Rahawayh and the people of opinion[1] said the same.

Tawus, 'Ubaydullah ibn 'Umayr and al-Hasan al-Basri in one of two transmissions from him, said that such a person should not be asked to repent. That was the position of 'Abdu'l-'Aziz ibn Abi Salama al-Majishun which he quoted from Mu'adh ibn Jabal although Sahnun said that it did not come from Mu'adh. At-Tahawi related it from Abu Yusuf, and it is the position of the Dhahirites.[2]

The Dhahirites said that his repentance helps him with Allah, but does not

---

1. According to an-Nawawi, this refers to the Shafi'is and Hanafis among the people of Khorasan.
2 The Dhahirite *madh-hab* of Da'ud and Ibn Hazm, now extinct.

save him from execution because the Prophet said, "Whoever changes his *deen*, kill him."[1]

It is related from 'Ata' that if he is someone who was born a Muslim, he is not asked to repent. The one who has become a Muslim is asked to repent.

Most of the *'ulama'* say that the male and female apostate are the same in this respect. It is related from 'Ali that the female apostate is not killed, but enslaved. 'Ata' and Qatada also said that. It is related from Ibn 'Abbas, "Women are not killed for apostasy."[2] Abu Hanifa said that. Malik, however, said, "Free and slave, man and woman are the same concerning that."

As for the time allowed for repentance, the majority position, which is related from 'Umar ibn al-Khattab, is that such a person is given time to repent for a period of three days during which time he is kept in prison.

Although there is some disagreement about this, it is one of the two positions of ash-Shafi'i.[3] Ahmad ibn Hanbal and Ishaq ibn Rahawayh also adopted it and Malik approves it, saying such a precaution is better, but this is not the position of everyone. Shaykh Abu Muhammad ibn Abi Zayd said that Malik meant delaying punishment for three days.

Malik also said that he accepted the statement of 'Umar regarding the apostate being imprisoned for three days and the chance to repent being offered to him each day. If he repents, he is all right. Otherwise he is killed. Abu'l-Hasan ibn al-Qassar said that there are two versions from Malik about delaying for three days and whether it is obligatory or recommended.

The people of opinion approve of asking him to repent and delaying his execution. It is related that Abu Bakr as-Siddiq asked a woman to repent and she did not, so he killed her.

Ash-Shafi'i said that an apostate is asked to repent once. If he does not repent then he is killed. Al-Muzani approved of that. Az-Zuhri said that he is called to Islam three times. If he refuses, he is killed.

It is related from 'Ali that he is given two months to repent. An-Nakh'i said that he is given time to repent without a time limit – ath-Thawri also took this position – as long as his repentance is hoped for. Ibn al-Qassar related from Abu Hanifa that he is asked to repent three times in three days or three weeks, once each day or week.

The Book of Muhammad from Ibn al-Qasim says that the apostate is called to Islam three times. If he refuses, his head is cut off. There is disagreement about whether he is threatened or one is harsh to him during the time he is being asked to repent so that he will repent or whether that is not the case.

Malik said, "I do not know anything about making him go hungry or thirsty

---

1. Muslim and al-Bukhari from Ibn 'Abbas.
2. Following the *hadith* which forbids killing women.
3. The other position is that he is asked to repent immediately and is executed if he does not.

while he is being asked to repent. He should be given food which will not harm him."

Asbagh said that on the days when he is asked to repent, he is made to fear execution and Islam is offered to him. In the book of Abu'l-Hasan at-Tabithi, it says that he should be warned on those days and reminded of the Garden and made to fear the Fire.

Asbagh said that it does not matter where he is imprisoned, whether with other people or alone, so long as one is sure of where he is. His property is made a *waqf* if it is feared that he will ruin it for the Muslims, and he is given food and drink from it. Similarly, he should continually be asked to repent, no matter how often he reverts and apostasises. The Messenger asked Nabhan, who became an apostate, to repent four or five times.

Ibn Wahb related Malik's position as being that the apostate is continually asked to repent, no matter how often he reverts. That is the position of ash-Shafi'i and Ahmad ibn Hanbal, and Ibn al-Qasim also said it. Ishaq ibn Rahawayh said that he is killed the fourth time.

The people of opinion said that if he does not repent the fourth time, he is killed without being asked to repent. If he repents, he is beaten painfully and is not released from prison until he shows the humility of repentance.

Ibn al-Mundhir said that we do not know anyone who obliges disciplinary measures for the apostate when he returns to Islam. This is based on the school of Malik, ash-Shafi'i and Abu Hanifa.

SECTION 3
The Judgment on the apostate whose apostasy is not established

What we have been talking about is the judgement regarding the one for whom apostasy is established by confession or irrefutable witnesses. As for the one against whom the testimony is incomplete – as when only one person or a group of people testify against him – or his statement is established, but its import is unclear and not explicit, if he repents, his repentance is accepted according to one statement.[1]

This removes execution from him, but the Imam must use his *ijtihad* about what to do with him according to how well known his state is, the strength or weakness of the testimony against him, the number of those who heard him, whether his *deen* is suspect and whether he is known for insolence and brazenness.

Whoever has a strong case against him is severely punished by close confinement in prison and should be tightly bound in chains to the extent

---

1. Related from Malik via al-Walid ibn Muslim.

which he can bear as long as he is not prevented from standing up to fulfill his needs nor prevented from performing the prayer. That is the judgement regarding someone who should be killed, but whose execution is prevented through the existence of some doubt. A close watch is kept on him because of the doubt and difficulty of his affair. The intensity of his punishment varies according to the circumstances. Al-Walid related from Malik from al-Awza'i that it is still apostasy. If he repents, he is punished. In *al-'Utibiyya* and *The Book of Muhammad*, it mentions, on the transmission of Ashab, that Malik said that if the apostate repents, he is not punished. Sahnun also said this.

Abu 'Abdullah ibn 'Attab gave a *fatwa* about someone who cursed the Prophet when two witnesses testified against him but only one of them was *'adl* (a reliable witness) – that he should be painfully punished and imprisoned for a long time until his repentance was clear.

Al-Qabisi said something of the general import that, if someone's case requires that he be executed but some element of doubt intervenes to make the sentence uncertain, he must not be released from prison and he should be imprisoned for a long time, even the longest possible time, and whatever chains he can bear are put on him.

In the event of a doubtful case, al-Qabisi said that he should be heavily chained and confined to prison until it is clear what should be done with him.

Al-Qabisi said concerning another similar case, "Blood should only be spilled if the matter is clear. Disciplining with the whip, imprisonment and severe punishment should be imposed on the insolent.

If only two witnesses testify against him and it is established that they are hostile or unreliable, thus removing the accusation from him, and no-one else says anything against him, his case is lighter and the judgement against him is dropped. It is as if there had been no testimony against him unless someone acceptable offers testimony. If the two witnesses are from people with whom he has a feud, they are ineligible because of their hostility. However, even if the judgement is not carried out against him on the basis of their testimony, the suspicion they are speaking the truth still remains. The judge has to make his own investigations to see whether he should be punished.

Allah is the master of right guidance.

SECTION 4
The judgement regarding *dhimmis* regarding this matter

As for a *dhimmi*, who, by making a clear curse or a curse by allusion, makes light of the Prophet's worth or describes him in any way other than the way by which he would normally reject him in his *deen*, there is no disagreement about him being killed unless he becomes Muslim, because he has not been given protection (*dhimma*) or a treaty in order to allow him to do this.

Most of the *'ulama'* say this, except for Abu Hanifa, ath-Thawri and their followers among the people of Kufa. They said that he is not killed because his *shirk* is a much worse offence. He is disciplined and flogged.

One of our shaykhs took the following words of Allah as a proof that he should be killed, **"If they break their oaths after their contract and attack your deen, then fight the leaders of unbelief; they have no sacred oaths. Perhaps they will give over."** (9:12) For proof, he used the fact that the Prophet killed Ibn al-Ashraf and people like him. No treaty has been made with them nor have they been given protection in order to allow them to do this. It is not permitted for us to allow them to behave in this way.

When they do what neither the treaty nor their *dhimma* status allows them, then they violate their *dhimma* status and fall into the category of unbelievers and people with whom the Muslims are at war. So they are killed for their disbelief. Furthermore, *dhimma* status does not remove any other of the *hudud* of Islam from them, such as cutting off the hand for theft or executing someone for a murder committed by one of them, even if that is permissible by their own *deen*.

It is the same when they curse the Prophet, may Allah bless him and grant him peace. They are killed for it. Our companions have mentioned obvious things which entail dispute which, when mentioned by a *dhimmi* in the manner by which he would normally reject the Prophet in his *deen*, must be investigated, according to what Ibn al-Qasim and Ibn Sahnun say.

Abu'l-Mus'ab talked about a dispute among his companions in Madina. They disagreed about what happens when a *dhimmi* curses the Prophet and then becomes a Muslim. Some said that his Islam removes his execution because Islam wipes out what was before before it, which is in contradistinction to a Muslim who curses him and then repents. That is because we know that inwardly the unbeliever is angry towards the Prophet and disparages him in his heart. But we prevent him from displaying that openly. If he does display it openly, it is only further opposition to the authority over him and breaking the treaty. When he converts from his first religion to Islam, what occurred before he became Muslim falls away. Allah says, **"Say to those who reject: if you leave off, then what you did before will be forgiven you."** (8:40)

The case of a Muslim is different since we had supposed his inward to be the same as his outward and that is different from what he now displays. After his return to Islam we do not agree with nor trust his inward since his secret has appeared. The judgement that was established against him remains and none of it is removed from him.

Others say that when a *dhimmi* becomes Muslim, it does not prevent his execution because the right owed to the Prophet demands it. He violated the Prophet's honour, and his intention was to connect imperfection and blemish to the Prophet. His becoming Muslim does not prevent execution for that, just as the rights of Muslims against him for any murder and slander that he did before be became a Muslim would be binding on him. Since we do not accept the repentance of a Muslim, it is more fitting that we should not accept the repentance of an unbeliever.

Malik in the *Book of Ibn Habib* and *Al-Mabsut*, Ibn al-Qasim, Ibn al-Majishun, Ibn 'Abdu'l-Hakam and Asbagh have said that the *dhimmi* who curses our Prophet or one of the Prophets, peace be upon them, is executed unless he becomes a Muslim.

Ibn al-Qasim stated the same in *Al-'Utibiyya*. It is also stated by Muhammad ibn al-Mawwaz and Ibn Sahnun. Sahnun and Asbagh said that he is not told to become Muslim nor not to become Muslim. If he becomes Muslim, that is his repentance.

In *The Book of Muhammad*, the companions of Malik have told us that he said that whoever curses the Messenger of Allah or any other Prophet, be he Muslim or unbeliever, is killed without being asked to repent.

It has been related to us that Malik said, "unless the unbeliever becomes a Muslim." Ibn Wahb related from Ibn 'Umar that a monk made a verbal attack on the Prophet, may Allah bless him and grant him peace. Ibn 'Umar asked, "Why didn't you kill him?"

'Isa related that Ibn al-Qasim talked about a *dhimmi* who says, "Muhammad was not sent to us. He was sent to you. Our Prophet is Musa," or 'Isa and similar things. He said that there is nothing against him because Allah has confirmed them in this sort of thing.

As for the *dhimmi* who curses the Prophet, says that he is not a Prophet, was not sent by Allah or the Qur'an was not sent down upon him or that it is something he made up, he is killed.

Ibn al-Qasim said, "When the Christian says, 'Our religion is better than yours. Your religion is a donkey's religion,' and similar ugly words, or hears the *mu'adhdhin* say, 'I testify that Muhammad is the Messenger of Allah,' and says something detrimental, he receives a painful punishment and a long imprisonment."

If he reviles our Prophet with something known to be a form of vilification, he is killed unless he becomes a Muslim. Malik said that more than once, and he never mentioned that if he does become Muslim, he is asked to repent. Ibn al-Qasim said, "In my opinion, his words can be taken to mean if he becomes a Muslim of his own accord."

Ibn Sahnun said in the matter of Sulayman ibn Salim al-Yahudi (the Jew) who said to the *mu'adhdhin*, "You lie when you testify," that he should be punished painfully and imprisoned for a long time.

In *An-Nawadir* [1] from the version of Sahnun from Malik we find that any Jew or Christian who reviles the Prophet in other than the normal way by which the Jews and Christians reject him is beheaded unless he becomes a Muslim.

Muhammad ibn Sahnun said that, if it is asked why is he killed for cursing the Prophet, may Allah bless him and grant him peace, when part of his religion is to curse him and call him a liar, the answer is that we did not make the treaty with him to let him do that nor to kill us nor to take our property. If he kills one of us, we kill him, even if something in his religion makes it lawful. That is the case when he openly curses our Prophet, may Allah bless him and grant him peace.

Sahnun said that, if doing so were allowed, it would be like people with whom the Muslims were at war paying the *jizya*-tax to us on condition that they could curse the Prophet. There is no-one who disagrees with the judgement that this would not be allowed. Similarly the terms of a treaty do not apply to anyone who curses the Prophet. If one of them does that, his blood becomes lawful for us. Just as being a Muslim does not protect someone who curses the Prophet from being killed, nor does *dhimma* status.

However, what Ibn Sahnun has mentioned about his own and his father's position is different from what Ibn al-Qasim says about what lightens the punishment for those who say such things when what they say is part of their normal state of disbelief. It must be taken into consideration that what Sahnun said is different from what is related about this matter from the people of Madina.

Abu'l-Mus'ab said, "A Christian was brought to me who said, 'By the One who chose 'Isa over Muhammad'. There was a dispute about him before me. So I beat him until I killed him, or he lived for a day and a night. I commanded someone to drag him by the feet and throw him onto a dungheap and the dogs ate him."

Abu'l-Mus'ab was asked about a Christian who said, "'Isa created Muhammad," and he said that he should be killed.

Ibn al-Qasim said that Malik was asked about a Christian in Egypt against whom there was testimony that he had said, "Poor Muhammad, he tells you that he is in the Garden! It does not help him because the dogs will eat his legs!" They asked whether they should kill him so that people would be saved from him. Malik said that he thought that he should be beheaded. He said, "I almost did not say anything about it and then I thought that I could not remain silent."

---

1. A book by Ibn Abi Zayd, author of the *Risala*.

Ibn Kinana said in *Al-Mabsut* that any Jew or Christian who reviles the Prophet can be burned by the Imam. If he likes, he can kill him and then burn his body. If he likes, he can burn him alive when he is so bold as to curse him.[1]

Someone had written to Malik from Egypt and Ibn Kinana mentioned the case that Ibn al-Qasim cited above. He said that Malik commanded him to write that he should be killed and his head should be struck off. Ibn Kinana wrote that and then said, "Abu 'Abdullah,[2] I will also write, 'He should be burned with fire.' He said, 'He deserves that and what he did merits it.' So I wrote it with my own hand in his presence and he did not object to it or censure me. The paper was dispatched like that. The man was killed and burned."

'Ubaydullah ibn Yahya al-Laythi and Ibn Lubaba and a group of our Andalusian comrades of the past gave a *fatwa* to kill a Christian woman who openly denied Allah and that 'Isa was Allah's Prophet and rejected Muhammad as a Prophet, but stated that if she wanted to become a Muslim they should accept that and it would remove the sentence of execution.

More than one of the later ones, including al-Qabisi, Ibn al-Katib, and Abu'l-Qasim ibn al-Jallab said that whoever curses Allah and His Messenger, be he a Muslim or unbeliever, is killed without being asked to repent.

Qadi Abu Muhammad ibn Nasr related that there are two versions transmitted about whether a *dhimmi* who curses and then becomes a Muslim is saved from execution because of becoming Muslim.

Ibn Sahnun said that the *hadd* of slander and similar things are human rights. They do not fall away from the *dhimmi* when he becomes a Muslim. The *hudud* concerning transgressions against Allah leave him because of his Islam but not the *hadd* involving slander against a human being, neither a Prophet nor anyone else.

When the *dhimmi* slanders the Prophet and then becomes Muslim, he still receives the *hadd* for slander. But you must investigate to discover what is obliged against him – is it the *hadd* of slander of the Prophet which necessitates execution due to the immense inviolability of the Prophet, may Allah bless him and grant him peace, over others, or is execution prevented because of his Islam so that he is given the *hadd* punishment of eighty lashes? Reflect on it.

---

1. This is the school of Malik and other *'ulama'*. Ash-Shafi'i says that burning is not permissible except in the case of retaliation based on the *hadith*, "Whoever burns, We will burn him..." Malik bases his position on the fact that 'Ali did this and that the Prophet said about a certain apostate, "If you find him, burn him." Abu Hanifa maintained that this had been abrogated.
2. Malik.

SECTION 5
Regarding the inheritance of someone who is killed for cursing the Prophet, and whether one washes him and says the funeral prayer over him

The *'ulama'* disagree about the inheritance of someone who is executed for cursing the Prophet. Sahnun believed that his property devolves on the Muslim community since, before he reviled the Prophet, may Allah bless him and grant him peace, his disbelief resembled that of the *zindiq*.

Asbagh said that his inheritance goes to his Muslim heirs if what he said was in private. If he openly declared it and made it public, his inheritance goes to the Muslim community. He is killed in either case without being asked to repent.

Abu'l-Hasan al-Qabisi said that if he is killed while denying the testimony against him, the judgement on his inheritance goes according to his avowal, i.e. he is considered a Muslim and the inheritance is for his heirs. Killing is the *hadd* which is confirmed for him. It does not affect the inheritance.

The same pertains if he admits the curse and shows remorse. He is killed since that is the *hadd*. The judgement regarding inheritance and all other judgements about him are those that apply to any Muslim.

If he admits the curse and persists in it and refuses to repent, he is killed as an unbeliever and his inheritance goes to the Muslim community. He is not washed nor prayed over nor shrouded. His private parts are covered and he is buried as unbelievers are buried.

Shaykh Abu'l-Hasan al-Qabisi said that the case of someone who openly states his curse and persists in it is clear and without dispute because he is an apostate and unbeliever who does not repent and does not renounce his unbelief. The inheritance is dealt with in the way that Asbagh has said. The book of Ibn Sahnun deals similarly with the *zindiq* who persists in his words. Something similar was stated by Ibn al-Qasim in *Al-'Utibiyya*.

In the book of Ibn Habib, a group of Malik's companions speak about someone who openly proclaims his disbelief. Ibn al-Qasim is mentioned as saying that, according to judgement, he is an apostate and that his Muslim heirs do not inherit from him nor do the people of the religion to which he has apostatised. Neither his bequests nor his emancipation of slaves is permitted. Asbagh said that he is killed for that and dies in the state of apostasy.

Abu Muhammad ibn Abi Zayd said that there is disagreement about the inheritance of the *zindiq* who publicly makes repentance when repentance is not accepted from him. As for the *zindiq* who persists in what he says, there is no dispute that he is not inherited from.

Abu Muhammad said one prays over someone who curses Allah and then dies when there was judged to be no clear proof against him or the proof was deemed unacceptable.

Asbagh related from Ibn al-Qasim in the book of Ibn Habib that if it is proved that someone has rejected the Messenger of Allah, may Allah bless him and grant him peace, or if he publicly adopts a religion by which he leaves Islam, his inheritance goes to the Muslim community.

Rabi'a ibn Abi 'Abdu'r-Rahman, ash-Shafi'i, Abu Thawr and Ibn Abi Layla all say the same as Malik: the inheritance of the apostate goes to the Muslim community, his heirs do not inherit from him.

Malik differs in that from Ahmad ibn Hanbal, 'Ali ibn Abi Talib, Ibn Mas'ud, Ibn al-Musayyab, al-Hasan, ash-Sha'bi, 'Umar ibn 'Abdu'l-'Aziz, al-Hakim, al-Awza'i, al-Layth, Ishaq and Abu Hanifa who all said that his Muslim heirs do inherit from him.

It is said that this refers to everything he possessed before he became an apostate. Anything he gained while an apostate is for the Muslim community.

Abu'l-Hasan al-Qabisi goes into some detail in his answer to this question and what he says is clear and good. It is based on the opinion of Asbagh and differs from the statement of Sahnun. The difference is based on two statements of Malik about the inheritance of the *zindiq*. Once Malik gave the judgement that the Muslim heirs of a *zindiq* should inherit from him when clear proof of his state had been established against him but he denied it, or he admitted it and showed repentance. Asbagh, Muhammad ibn Maslama and more than one of Malik's companions said that this was because he is demonstrating his Islam by his denial or his repentance. His judgement is the same as the judgement of the hypocrites who had a treaty with the Messenger of Allah, may Allah bless him and grant him peace.

Ibn Nafi' related from Malik in *Al-'Utibiyya* and *The Book of Muhammad* that the *zindiq's* inheritance is for the community of Muslims because his property follows his blood, i.e. they have a right over his property as they have over his life.

A group of Malik's companions also said that, including Ashhab, al-Mughira, 'Abdu'l-Malik ibn al-Majishun, Muhammad ibn Maslama and Sahnun. Ibn al-Qasim said in *Al-'Utibiyya* that if a *zindiq* admits the testimony against him and repents, he is killed and he does not leave any inheritance. If he persists in his denial until he dies or is killed, he leaves normal inheritance.

Malik said that it is the same with everyone who conceals disbelief. They inherit from each other with the normal inheritance of Muslims.

Abu'l-Qasim ibn al-Katib was asked whether, in the case of a Christian who curses the Prophet, may Allah bless him and grant him peace, and is killed, the people of his religion inherit from him or whether the Muslims do. He said that the Muslims inherit. This is not based on the grounds of inheritance because there is no inheritance between the people of two different religions,[1] but is based on it being part of their booty since the Christian broke his treaty. This is the meaning of his statement in short.

---

1. As related in sound *hadith*.

Chapter Three

CONCERNING THE JUDGEMENT ON ANYONE WHO CURSES ALLAH, HIS ANGELS, HIS PROPHETS, HIS BOOKS AND THE FAMILY OF THE PROPHET AND HIS COMPANIONS

SECTION 1
The judgement on someone who curses Allah and the judgement regarding asking him to repent

There is no disagreement that any Muslim who curses Allah is an unbeliever whose blood is *halal*. There is disagreement about whether he is asked to repent.

Ibn al-Qasim said in *al-Mabsut* and it is mentioned in the book of Ibn Sahnun, and Muhammad ibn al-Mawwaz related from Malik in the book of Ishaq ibn Yahya: "Any Muslim who curses Allah is killed without being asked to repent unless he forges lies against Allah by apostasy to another religion which he adopts and openly displays. In that case he is asked to repent. If he does not openly display his apostasy, he is not asked to repent."

In *Al-Mabsut*, Mutarrif ibn 'Abdullah and 'Abdu'l-Malik ibn Habib said something similar. Al-Makhzumi, Muhammad ibn Maslama and Ibn Abi Hazim said that a Muslim is not killed for cursing until he has been asked to repent which is also the position of ash-Shafi'i. It is the same with the Jews and the Christians. If they repent, their repentance is accepted from them. If they do not repent, then they are killed. They must be asked to repent. All this is the same as apostasy. That is also what Qadi Abu Muhammad ibn Nasr has related from the Maliki school.

Abu Muhammad ibn Abi Zayd gave a *fatwa* about what was related regarding a man who was cursing a man but cursed Allah at the same time. The man said, "I meant to curse Shaytan but my tongue slipped." Ibn Abi Zayd said, "He is killed for his outward display of disbelief and his excuse is not accepted. As for what is between him and Allah, it is pardoned."

The *fuqaha'* of Cordoba disagreed about Harun ibn Habib, the brother of 'Abdu'l-Malik, the *faqih*. He was very miserable and discontent and there was testimony presented against him. Part of it was that when he had recovered from an illness, he said, "In this illness I have met with what I would not have deserved had I killed Abu Bakr and 'Umar." Ibrahim ibn Husayn ibn Khalid[1] gave a *fatwa* that he should be killed because his words implied that Allah was unjust and had wronged him. Such an allusion is like an explicit statement. The man's brother, 'Abdu'l-Malik ibn Habib, Ibrahim ibn Husayn ibn 'Asim and Sa'id ibn Sulayman, the Qadi, judged that he should not be executed; however he was to be given a heavy sentence of imprisonment and a harsh punishment because of the possible implication of his words and his turning to complaint.

The people who say that someone who curses Allah should be asked to repent are in fact saying that what he did is disbelief and pure apostasy and has no right in it connected to other than Allah. They make it exactly like disbelief without Allah having been cursed and like changing openly to another religion than Islam.

The reason for not asking the Muslim who curses Allah to repent is because he did what he did after openly displaying his Islam, before the Muslims suspected him, and when the Muslims thought that his tongue would only express what he believed, since no-one indulges himself in this sort of thing. Therefore his judgement is that of the *zindiq* and his repentance is not accepted. If he changes religion and utters the curse as an apostate, this removes the noose of Islam from his neck as opposed to the first man who held to Islam. The judgement of such a man is that of the apostate. He is asked to repent according to the well-known statement of the schools of most of the *'ulama'*.

This is the position of Malik and his companions as we have already made clear and about which we mentioned the disagreements in its proper section.

SECTION 2
The judgement about ascribing to Allah something that does not befit Him through *ijtihad* and error

There is also the case of someone who ascribes to Allah what does not befit Him, not in the form of a curse, apostasy or with the intention of disbelief but by interpretation, individual *ijtihad* and error. This can lead to sectarianism and innovation by connecting Allah to things, or one of His attributes to a physical limb, or negating an attribute of perfection, and it was the cause of disagreement among the *Salaf* and those who came later. Does one place the one who has said such a thing and his creed in the category of disbelief?[2] The statement of Malik and his companions varies concerning this matter, but they do not disagree about killing people who do this if they actually form a separate sect. They are asked to repent. If they repent, it is all right. If not, they are killed.

---

1. A Maliki *faqih* in Cordoba.
2. The position of al-Ash'ari is that the people of sects are not unbelievers. This is the general position of most of the Hanafi and Shafi'i *fuqaha'*.

They disagree about an individual who does this. Most of the statements of Malik and his Companions say that one does not call such individuals unbelievers or kill them. There can be severe punishment and long imprisonment until they renounce what they have said and their repentance is clear, as 'Umar did with Sabigh ibn Sharik.[1]

This is what Muhammad ibn al-Mawwaz and 'Abdu'l-Malik ibn al-Majishun said about the *Khawarij* and what Sahnun said about all the people of sects. The statement of Malik in the *Muwatta'* explains it when he related what 'Umar ibn 'Abdu'l-'Aziz and his grandfather, Marwan ibn al-Hakam, and his uncle, 'Abdu'l-Malik ibn Marwan,[2] had said about the *Qadiriyya*,[3] "They are asked to repent. If they repent, it is all right. If not, they should be killed."

'Isa ibn Ibrahim al-Ghafiqi said that Ibn al-Qasim said that the different sects, the *Ibadiyya* [4] and *Qadariyya* and those like them among the people of innovation and those who distort the interpretation of the Book of Allah and differ from the consensus of the community are asked to repent whether they make that public or conceal it. If they repent it is all right. If not, they are killed but their inheritance still goes to their heirs.

Ibn al-Qasim also said something like that in *The Book of Muhammad* about the *Qadariyya* and others: "Asking them to repent is to say them, 'Abandon your position.'" Something similar is said in *al-Mabsut* about the *Ibadiyya*, the *Qadariyya* and other people of innovation. He said that they are Muslims, but should be killed for their evil opinion.

This is what 'Umar ibn 'Abdu'l-'Aziz did. Ibn al-Qasim said that whoever says that Allah did not speak directly to Musa is asked to repent. If he repents, it is all right. If not, he is killed.

Ibn Habib and some of our companions consider them and those like them among the *Khawarij*, the *Qadariyya* and the *Murji'ites*[5] to be unbelievers. Something like this is also related from Sahnun about someone who said that Allah does not have the attribute of speech. Anyone who says such a thing is an unbeliever.

The position transmitted from Malik varies. The people of Syria, Abu Mushir al-Ghassani and Marwan ibn Muhammad at-Tatiri said that such people are unbelievers.

---

1. Someone who constantly studied the ambiguous (*mutashabihat*) and equivocal parts of the Qur'an. 'Umar ordered that he be beaten and forbade people to sit in his gathering.
2. All Umayyad khalifs.
3. A group who denied the Decree.
4. A sect of *Khawarij* who claimed that whoever opposed them was an unbeliever.
5. A group who believed that rebellion against Allah is not harmful when one believes, and obedience is not useful if one disbelieves. They are declared to be unbelievers because they reject what has been transmitted by the community about the *deen*.

Malik was consulted about the marriage of a *Qadiri*. He said, "Do not marry him. Allah says, **'A believing slave is better than an idol-worshipper.'**" (2:222)

It is also related from Malik, "All the people of sects are unbelievers." He said that whoever describes part of Allah's essence and then points to a part of his own body – hand, hearing or sight – then that amounts to a definite statement on his part because he has made Allah like himself.

He said about someone who said that the Qur'an is created, "He is an unbeliever, so kill him." He said in the version of Ibn Nafi', "He should be flogged and painfully beaten and imprisoned until he repents." In the version of Bishr ibn Bakr at-Tinnisi we find, "He is killed and his repentance is not accepted."

Qadi Abu 'Abdullah al-Bartakani and Qadi Abu 'Abdullah Sahl at-Tustari among the Imams of Iraq[1] said that the answer regarding such people varies. Any of them who calls for support and summons people is killed. Based on this difference, the position also varies about having to re-do a prayer performed behind such people.

Ibn al-Mundhir related from ash-Shafi'i that the *Qadiri* is not asked to repent. Most of the statements of the *Salaf* consider them unbelievers. Among those who said so were al-Layth ibn Sa'd, Sufyan ibn 'Uyayna and Ibn Lahi'a. That ascription is related from them about a man who said that the Qur'an was created. Ibn al-Mubarak, 'Uthman ibn al-Hakam al-Awdi, Wukay' ibn al-Jarrah, Hafs ibn Ghiyath, Abu Ishaq al-Fazari, Hushaym ibn Bishr and 'Ali ibn 'Asim said that as well.

This has also been the statement of most of the people of *hadith*, the *fuqaha'* and the *mutakallimun* regarding the *Khawarij*, the *Qadariyya*, the people of misguiding sects and the people of innovated interpretation. It was also the position of Ahmad ibn Hanbal. It was also applied to the *Waqifa*.[2]

Among those from whom the latter statement, about not calling them unbelievers, is related are 'Ali ibn Abi Talib, Ibn 'Umar, and al-Hasan al-Basri. It is the opinion of a certain group of the *fuqaha'*, thinkers and the *mutakallimun*.

They use as a proof the fact that the Companions and the Followers inherited from the people of Harura[3] including those who were known to be *Qadariyya* among those who had died. They were buried in Muslim graves as Muslims and the rules of Islam were applied to them.

Isma'il, the Qadi, said that Malik said that the *Qadariyya* and other people of innovation are asked to repent. If they repent, they are left alone. If not, they are killed because it is part of making corruption in the land. He said that the opinion of Imam Malik was that anyone who makes war should be killed. If he

---

1. i.e. the Malikis in Iraq.
2. Those who refrain from making any judgement.
3. A Kharijite city in Iraq.

is not killed, he will kill. The corruption caused by those making war is to property and people's best interests in this world, although it also enters the *deen* by its affecting the *hajj* and *jihad*. The most terrible aspect of the corruption of the people of innovation is toward the *deen*, even if it does affect matters of this world by the agitation they engender among the Muslims.

SECTION 3
Verification of the statement about considering faulty interpreters to be unbelievers

We have already mentioned the position of the *Salaf* in considering the people of innovation and sects which have originated through false interpretation to be unbelievers when they make a statement which would lead in the natural course of things to disbelief, even if they stop there and do not actually say what they are leading up to. The *fuqaha'* and the *mutakallimun* vary regarding this matter according to their differences.

Some of them think that it is correct to consider as an unbeliever anyone whom most of the *Salaf* said was an unbeliever. Some of them have rejected this and did not think that these people should be expelled from the body of believers. That is the statement of most of the *fuqaha'* and *mutakallimun*. They said that although the people referred to are deviants, rebels, misguided, we inherit from them as from any other Muslims and they are judged as Muslims.

This is why Sahnun said that someone who prays behind them does not have to repeat the prayer. He said that all the companions of Malik have stated this, such as al-Mughira, Ibn Kinana and Ashhab. He said that this is because such a person is a Muslim and his wrong action does not take him out of Islam.

Others were unsure about it and they hesitated to say either that such a person was an unbeliever or the opposite of it. Malik made two different statements concerning it. They hesitate about whether to repeat a prayer performed behind them.

Qadi Abu Bakr al-Baqillani, the Imam of the people of verification of the truth, believed something like this. He said that it is a difficult abstruse matter since these people do not clearly articulate disbelief. They utter a statement which leads to it. The Qadi's statement in respect of the question is uncertain, reflecting the uncertainty of what his Imam, Malik ibn Anas, said. In one place he said that those who do consider them unbelievers by interpretation do not consider it lawful (*halal*) to marry them, eat meat they have slaughtered nor to say the funeral prayer over their dead. They disagree about the status of their inheritance, following the difference regarding the apostate's inheritance. He also said, "We also allow them to bequeath to their Muslim heirs, but they do not inherit from the Muslims." By and large he inclined to not calling them unbelievers in the end.

Similarly, what his Shaykh, Abu'l-Hasan al-Ash'ari, says about it is unclear. By and large, he does not say that such people are unbelievers. Disbelief is in one single quality which is denial of the existence of the Creator. He once said, "Whoever believes that Allah is a physical body, the Messiah, or any other such idea he might have picked up somewhere, does not recognise Him, and is an unbeliever."

Abu'l-Mu'ali showed a similar approach in his answers to Abu Muhammad 'Abdu'l-Haqq when he asked him about this matter. He made the excuse that any decision about it was difficult because placing an unbeliever within the religion or expelling a Muslim from it was something terrible in the *deen*.

Others among the meticulous scholars have said that one must be cautious about calling the people of interpretation unbelievers. There is a danger of making the blood of those who pray and affirm Allah's unity lawful. The error which leaves a thousand unbelievers untouched is lighter than the error of taking the life of a single Muslim.

The Prophet said, "When they say it (the *shahada*), their blood and property is protected from me except for a right, and their reckoning rests with Allah."[1]

Protection is absolute when the *shahada* has been declared and has not been denied. Protection only falls away by something decisive, and there is no decisive statement in the *Shari'a* about this nor any clear analogy. The expressions in the *hadith* on the subject are open to interpretation. What they clearly do contain is that the *Qadariyya* are unbelievers since the Prophet said, "They have no share in Islam." The Prophet also called the *Rafidites* associators and cursed them. Similarly someone who calls the *Khawarij* and other such sectarians unbelievers finds in this *hadith* a proof for his calling them so.

Others have replied that phrases like these have come in the *hadith* about people who are not unbelievers in order to show extreme disapproval. Their position amounts to hidden disbelief rather than clear disbelief and hidden *shirk* rather than clear *shirk*.

Similar statements[2] are related about showing off, disobeying parents and husbands, lying and other acts of rebellion. So the *hadith* has two possible interpretations, and it is only taken as being decisive when there is a clear proof.

The Prophet called the *Khawarij* "the worst of people". This is the quality of the unbelievers.[3] He said, "An evil tribe under the sky. Blessing for the one who kills them or the one whom they kill."[4]

1. Al-Bukhari.
2. Such as, "They have no share in Islam," etc.
3. See Qur'an 98:6.
4 'Ali killed them at Nihrawan.

He said, "When you find them, kill them as you would kill any enemy."[1] The apparent meaning of this statement is that they are unbelievers, especially when they are likened to an enemy. Those who think that they should be called unbelievers use this as a proof.

People who take the other position say that they are killed since they came out against the Muslims and attacked them as the *hadith* itself indicates, "They fight the people of Islam." In this case, killing them is a *hadd* and not on account of their disbelief. Killing and its lawfulness is linked to the consideration of aggression, not to the state of the one killed. Not everyone given a death sentence is judged to be an unbeliever. Compare that to what Khalid said in the *hadith*, "Let me strike off his head, Messenger of Allah." He replied, "Perhaps he prays."[2]

Then they use as a proof the Prophet's words, "They recite the Qur'an and it does not pass their throats,"[3] when he informed them that belief does not enter their hearts.

It is like that when the Prophet said, "They pass through the *deen* as an arrow passes through game. They will not return to the *deen* until the arrow returns to the bowstring." The Prophet continued, "The arrow went too fast to be smeared by dung and blood," indicating that the person concerned had no connection to Islam at all.[4]

The others answered that the meaning of, "It does not pass their throats," is that they do not understand its meaning in their hearts, nor are their breasts expanded to it nor do their limbs act by it.

They use as a counter-argument his words about the notch of the arrow. This necessitates doubt in his case.

They take the words of Abu Sa'id al-Khudri concerning this *hadith* as a proof, "I heard the Messenger of Allah, may Allah bless him and grant him peace, say, 'He goes out in (*fi*) this community' and he did not say 'from (*min*) this community'." Abu Sa'id was precise in his transmission and exact in his choice of words.

Other people have countered this position by pointing out that the expression "*fi*" is not necessarily an explicit statement that they are not part of the community as opposed to the expression "*min*" which indicates a separation. So they are part of the community.

However, this *hadith* is related from Abu Dharr, 'Ali, Abu Umama and others as being, "He goes out from (*min*) my community" and "will be from (*min*) my community." The meanings of these prepositions are shared. There is

---

1. Muslim and al-Bukhari from Abu Sa'id al-Khudri.
2. Ibid.
3. Al-Bukhari. This *hadith* is related about the *Khawarij*.
4. Muslim and al-Bukhari.

no statement which expels them from the community by "*fi*" nor includes them in the community by "*min*". Abu Sa'id did well in making what he reported clear. This is part of what indicates the vast capacity of the Companions' understanding, their precision in expressing the meanings which they extracted from phrases, formulating them and protecting them in the transmission.

There are many confused and foolish statements about this matter among the schools of thought recognised by the people of the *sunna* and among other factions. The best of them is what Jahm[1] and Muhammad ibn Shabib[2] said, "Disbelief in Allah is ignorance of Him. No-one is an unbeliever for anything other than that."

Abu'l-Hudhayl said: "Every interpreter whose interpretation makes Allah like His creation, attacks His actions or denies His words is an unbeliever. Whoever confirms the existence of anything existing from before endless time which is not said to be Allah is an unbeliever."

One of the *mutakallimun* said, "If the interpreter is someone who has fundamental knowledge of the basis of the matter and his false interpretation deals with one of the attributes of Allah, then such a person is an unbeliever. If his interpretation is not in this area, then he is deviant. If he is someone who has no grasp of the basis of the matter, then he is in error and is not an unbeliever."

'Ubaydullah ibn al-Hasan al-'Anbari believed that the statements of the *mujtahids* regarding the roots of the *deen* should be considered correct when they refer to those areas which are open to interpretation. The various groups among the community differ regarding this matter. When all but one agree about the truth in the roots of the *deen* concerning something, the one who errs in it is a wrong-doer, a deviator and a rebel. The dispute is about whether to consider him an unbeliever or not. Qadi Abu Bakr al-Baqillani relates something similar to what 'Ubaydullah said from Da'ud al-Isbahani.[3] He said some people related from Da'ud and al-'Anbari that they said that about all those who have knowledge of Allah – glory be to Him! – among the people of our religion or from other religions who are trying as hard as they can to seek the truth.

Al-Jahiz and Thumama[4] said something similar – that Allah has no proof against many of the common people, women, idiots and those who blindly follow among the Jews and Christians and others since they do not have a natural disposition which is capable of drawing conclusions from proof. Al-Ghazzali stated something close to this in the *Kitab at-Tafriqa*.

Anyone who says such things about the disbelief of someone who does not

---

1. Ibn Safwan, a *Mu'tazili*.
2. Another *Mu'tazili*.
3. Founder of the Dhahirite school.
4. Both *Mu'tazilites*.

consider any of the Christians and Jews or any who leave the *deen* of the Muslims unbelievers, or hesitates to call them unbelievers, or doubts it, is himself an unbeliever according to the consensus.

Qadi Abu Bakr al-Baqillani said this is because Allah and the Messenger tell us, and the consensus agrees, that they are unbelievers. Whoever hesitates concerning that has denied the text and report or doubts it. Rejection of it and its denial only occur from an unbeliever.

SECTION 4
Clarification of which statements amount to disbelief, what one hesitates about or is disputed and what does not amount to disbelief

Know that substantiation of this section and the removal of doubt must be referred to the *Shari'a*. The intellect does not have a free hand in it.

The clear judgement regarding this is that disbelief consists of every statement which explicitly denies Allah's lordship or oneness, or constitutes the worship of other-than-Allah or associates something else with Allah. Among those who do this are the *Dahriyya*,[1] all factions of the people of dualism, the *Daisaniyya*,[2] the Manichaeans and those like them among the Sabians,[3] Christians and Magians,[4] and those who associate others with Allah by worshipping idols, angels, devils, the sun, the stars, fire or anything other than Allah among the idol-worshippers of the Arabs and the people of India, China, Sudan and elsewhere who do not consult a divine book.

The judgement of disbelief is the same in respect of the Qarmatians,[5] the people who believe in incarnation, those who believe in transmigration of souls among the *Batiniyya*,[6] the *Tayyara*[7] among the *Rafidites*, the *Bayaniyya*,[8] and the *Ghurbaniyya*.[9]

It is the same with those who admit the divinity of Allah and His oneness, but believe that He is neither Living nor Timeless, but that He is temporal or has a form or claim that He has a son, a consort or a parent or that He was begotten from something or came into existence from it or that eternal things other-than-Him were with Him before time or that there was someone who

1. Atheists who attribute events to time like the evolutionists.
2. A sect of Zoroastrians who believe in a creator of good and a creator of evil, and living light and the dead darkness.
3. Meaning those who worship the angels or the stars.
4. Fire-worshippers.
5. Carmathians, a group of dualist Isma'ilis.
6. Esotericists who say that the Qur'an is not to be taken literally.
7. An extreme Shi'ite group.
8. Who say that the spirit of Allah was incarnate in 'Ali.
9. An extreme Shi'ite group who say that the message was meant for 'Ali.

fashioned the earth other than Him or there is something other than Him that manages it. All of these conjectures constitute disbelief according to the consensus of the Muslims. This also applies to the statements of various philosophers, astrologers and naturalists.

It is the same with someone who claims to sit with Allah, ascend to Him and speak directly to Him or that He is incarnate in any individual as is stated by some of the false Sufis, esotericists, Christians, and Qarmatians. Similarly, we are certain of the disbelief of anyone who says that the world is eternal and that it will go on forever, or entertains doubts which are based on the positions of some of the philosophers and *Dahriyya*, or says that there is transmigration of souls and that they move forever through different individuals and are punished and receive bliss in them according to their purity or their corruption.

It is the same with anyone who admits Allah's divinity and oneness, but denies prophethood in general or the prophethood of our Prophet, may Allah bless him and grant him peace, in particular, or that of any of the Prophets about whom Allah has given information, after that person has knowledge of it – he is an unbeliever without a doubt. This applies to the Hindus, most of the Jews and the Arians among the Christians, the *Ghurbaniyya* from the *Rafidites* who claim that Jibril was sent to 'Ali, the atheists, the Qarmatians, the Isma'ilis and the *'Anbariyya* among the *Rafidites*, while some of these groups also have aspects of disbelief in common with the earlier groups.

The same applies to those who believe in Allah's oneness, the truth of prophethood and the prophethood of our Prophet, may Allah bless him and grant him peace, but say that the Prophets can lie regarding what they brought. Whether or not he claims there is benefit in that, he is still an unbeliever according to the consensus. This is the case with the false philosophers, some of the esotericists, the *Rafidites,* the extreme Sufis and the people of *Ibaha*.[1]

These people claim that the outward parts of the *Shari'a* and most of the reports the Messengers have brought about what was and what will be among the matters of the Next World, the Gathering and the Rising, and the Garden and the Fire are not as they are stated and how they are normally understood from the words. According to them these reports are used to address creatures with their best interests in view since it is not possible to explain the reality of these things to them because of the limitations of human understanding. Thus the words of these people invalidate the *Shari'a*, make the commands and prohibitions void, deny the Messengers and create doubts about what they brought. It is the same with someone who attributes deliberate lies to our Prophet regarding what he conveyed and reported about, or doubts his

---

1. Those who permit the *haram*.

truthfulness, or curses him, or says that he did not convey the message or scorns him or any of the Prophets or shows contempt for them and harms them. He is an unbeliever by consensus.

Similarly, we consider to be unbelievers those who have the belief of some of the ancients that every type of animal had a warner and a Prophet – the monkeys, the pigs, riding beasts, worms, etc. They take as a proof the words of Allah, **"Every community has a warner which has passed away in it."** (35:25) That would lead to describing the Prophets of these species together with their blameworthy qualities. Such a statement contains contempt for the lofty rank of prophethood. There is consensus among the Muslims that this is not the case and that the one who says it should be denied.

Similarly we consider to be unbelievers those who acknowledge the sound basis of what has preceded and the prophethood of our Prophet, but say that he was black, or died before he grew a beard, or was not in Makka and the Hijaz, or was not a Qurayshi. This is because they describe him with other than his known attributes and that amounts to denying and rejecting him. Considered as unbelievers also are people who claim that anyone else was a Prophet along with our Prophet or after him, such as the *'Isawiyya* [1] among the Jews who say that Muhammad's message was specifically for the Arabs, and the *Khurramiyya* who say that there is a continuing succession of Messengers, and like most of the Rafidites who say that 'Ali shared in the message with the Prophet, may Allah bless him and grant him peace, and every Imam among such people who is put on the same par as Muhammad in respect of the proof and prophethood, like the *Bazi'iyya* and the *Bayaniyya* [2] who say that Bazi', Bayan ibn Isma'il al-Hindi and their likes were Prophets, or who claims prophethood for himself or allows the status of prophethood to be acquired and its rank reached by purity of heart – like the philosophers and the extreme Sufis.

This also applies to those of them who claim that they have received revelation even if they do not lay claim to prophethood, or claim that they ascend to heaven, enter the Garden, eat from its fruits, and embrace its Houris. All of these people are unbelievers who deny the Prophet because the Prophet said that he was the Seal of the Prophets and there would be no Prophet after him. He reported from Allah that he was the Seal of the Prophets and that he was sent to all men. The community are united in agreement that this statement is taken literally and that what is to be understood from it is what is meant literally and not an intepretation or abstraction. There is no doubt that all those sects who make false claims are unbelievers absolutely, by consensus and report.

---

1. From 'Isa ibn Ishaq al-Yahudi who claimed to be a Prophet and lived in the time of the Khalif, Marwan al-Himar. He had a large Jewish following.
2. Extreme Rafidite sects.

Similarly there is a consensus about the disbelief of anyone who contradicts the text of the Book or a single *hadith* whose transmission is agreed upon and certain, and it is agreed that this is to be taken literally. For instance, the *Khawarij* are considered to be unbelievers because they invalidate maternal kinship. That is why also we consider to be unbelievers those who do not think that those who have adopted a religion other than Islam are unbelievers, or who hesitate about them or are unsure or consider their position valid. Even if he displays his Islam while doing so, believes in Islam and believes that every position except Islam is invalid, he is still an unbeliever since he has manifested the opposite of that.

Similarly, we absolutely declare the disbelief of everyone who makes a statement that results in the misguidance of the community, and all who declare the Companions to be unbelievers – for instance, what the *Kumayliyya*[1] among the *Rafidites* say about all of the community after the Prophet being unbelievers since they did not advance 'Ali, and they further declare that 'Ali was an unbeliever since he did not advance himself and seek the advancement he was due. These people have disbelieved in various ways because they have completely invalidated the *Shari'a* since they destroy the transmission of it and the Qur'an by claiming that they have been transmitted by unbelievers. This – and Allah knows best – is what Malik indicated by one of his two statements about killing anyone who declared that the Companions were unbelievers. Then they have disbelieved in another way because they have cursed the Prophet, may Allah bless him and grant him peace, by what they say and by their claim that he gave a contract to 'Ali, knowing that he would disbelieve after him. The curse of Allah be upon them! May Allah bless His Messenger and His family!

Similarly, we consider people to be unbelievers by their doing any action which the Muslims agree can only issue from an unbeliever, even if the one who does it clearly states that he is a Muslim in spite of doing that action – such as prostrating before idols, the sun, the moon, the cross or fire, and frequenting churches and synagogues with their people, wearing their clothes by putting on the *zunnar* belt,[2] or having a monk's tonsure.

Similarly the Muslims agree about the disbelief of anyone who makes it lawful to murder, drink wine or fornicate, which Allah has made *haram*, after he knows that Allah has made it *haram* – like the people of *Ibaha* among the Qarmatians and some of the extreme Sufis.

---

1. Extreme *Rafidites* who believed in transmigration, incarnation and that prophethood was a light which passed from one man to another and that it was the right of 'Ali. They say that the Companions all became unbelievers when they offered allegiance to Abu Bakr, 'Ali along with them.

2. Worn to show that the wearer is not a Muslim.

We also declare absolutely the disbelief of whoever denies and rejects one of the pillars of the *Shari'a* and what is definitely known by multiple transmission to be one of the actions of the Messenger on which there is a complete consensus – like someone who rejects the obligatory nature of the five prayers and the number of their *rak'ats* and prostrations. Such a man might say, "Allah made the prayer a general obligation on us. As for its being five or with these particular attributes and conditions, I do not know that for certain since no clear text has come in the Qur'an. The report about it from the Messenger, may Allah bless him and grant him peace, is only a single report."

Similarly, people agree about the disbelief of those among the *Khawarij* who say that the prayer only takes place at the beginning and end of the day.

The *Batiniyya* are unbelievers by what they say about the obligatory prayers being the names of men whose government has been commanded and the foul things and *haram* things being names of men they have been commanded to reject.

One of the false Sufis said that when the soul has been purified by worship and long striving a point is reached where the self has been eliminated and everything is permitted to it and the contract of the *Shari'a* is removed from it.

Similarly, anyone who rejects Makka, the House, the *Masjid al-Haram* as being the site for the *hajj* or the description of the *hajj*, or says, "The *hajj* is obligatory in the Qur'an as is taking a *qibla*, but as for it being this customary form and its taking place in Makka, the House and the *Masjid al-Haram*, I do not know whether this is the case or not. Perhaps those who transmitted that the Prophet, may Allah bless him and grant him peace, explained it as such made a mistake and misconstrued it," are unbelievers. There is no doubt that such a person and those like him are unbelievers if they are people thought to possess knowledge of the matter and have mixed with the Muslims and kept their company for a long time.

If he is a new Muslim, then he is told, "Your proper course is to ask the Muslims about these things which you do not yet know. You will not find any dispute among any of them without exception, right back to the contemporaries of the Messenger of Allah that these matters are as you have been told and that the place of pilgrimage is Makka and that the house which is found there is the Ka'ba and that it is the *qibla* to which the Messenger of Allah and the Muslims have prayed and to which they go on *hajj*. This is what the Prophet did and the Muslims have done. The description of the prayers mentioned are those which the Prophet did. He explained what Allah meant by the prayers and made their limits clear. So you have knowledge as they had knowledge. Do not doubt this from now on."

Anyone who doubts these things and denies them after he has looked into them and kept the company of Muslims is an unbeliever by agreement. He has no excuse by claiming that he does not know and he is not considered to be telling the truth. His outward conceals his unbelief since it is not possible that he does not know this. Furthermore when he allows the community from first to last to have been in illusion and error regarding what they have transmitted about these things and what they agree to be the statement of the Messenger and his action and the commentary of what Allah means by them, he thereby casts doubt on the entire *Shari'a,* since they are the ones who have transmitted both it and the Qur'an. Such a statement would completely unravel the rope of the *deen.* Whoever says such a thing is an unbeliever.

It is the same with anyone who denies the Qur'an, or a single letter of it, or alters any of it, or adds to it – as was done by the *Batiniyya* and the Isma'ilis – or claims that it is not a proof of prophethood for the Prophet or that it does not contain either proof or miracle. That is like the statement of Hisham al-Fuwati[1] and Ma'mar as-Saymari[2] that the Qur'an does not give evidence of Allah and that there is no proof of prophethood in it for His Messenger, and it does not indicate either reward or punishment or judgement. They must be considered unbelievers because of that statement.

Similarly, we declare both these men to be unbelievers because they deny every single miracle of the Prophet, may Allah bless him and grant him peace, standing as a proof for him, or the creation of the heavens and the earth being a proof of Allah. That is because that is contrary to the consensus and multiple transmissions from the Prophet which use these things as a proof, as well as contradicting the clear statements of the Qur'an to that effect.

Similarly, anyone who denies anything which is in the Qur'an after he knows that it is part of the Qur'an in the copies of the Qur'an that the Muslims possess, and is not ignorant of it nor a new Muslim, is an unbeliever. For proof of his denial, such a man uses either the fact that he does not consider its transmission to be sound and he has no knowledge of it, or he maintains its transmitter to be someone doubtful. We declare him to be an unbeliever by the two previously mentioned criteria, because he denies the Qur'an and he denies the Prophet, may Allah bless him and grant him peace although he does so by veiled allusion. It is the same with anyone who denies the Garden, the Fire, the Rising, the Reckoning or Resurrection. He is an unbeliever by consensus because of the clear reference to these things in the Qur'an and by the consensus of the community about the soundness of their transmission by many paths.

Similarly unbelief applies to anyone who acknowledges their existence, but says that what is meant by the Garden, the Fire, the Gathering, the Rising and the Reward and Punishment are meanings which are not to be taken

1. A Qadari.
2. Leader of a sect.

literally, saying that they are spiritual pleasures and inner meanings, as is said by the Christians, philosophers, esotericists and some of the false Sufis. They claim that the Rising means death or simply passing away, the collapse of the form of the spheres of the heavens, and the dissolution of the world, as has been stated by some of the philosophers. Similarly, we absolutely declare the disbelief of the extreme *Rafidites* when they claim that the Imams are better than the Prophets.

As for someone who rejects what is known by multiple transmission concerning historical accounts, biographies, and geographical descriptions but whose rejection does not lead to the invalidation of the *Shari'a* nor lead to the denial of a pillar of the *deen*, such as denying the raid of Tabuk or Mu'ta, or the existence of Abu Bakr and 'Umar, the murder of 'Uthman or the khalifate of 'Ali, which are known by necessary transmission, then when this denial does not contain denial of the *Shari'a*, there is no way to call such a person an unbeliever by his rejection of any of these things or his denial of having any knowledge of them, since in this there is nothing more than stupidity. An example of this is when Hisham al-Fuwati and 'Abbad as-Saymari denied that the Battle of the Camel and the war of 'Ali against those who opposed him took place.

As for someone who declares these and other such things open to doubt in order to create suspicion about the transmitters and to make the Muslims doubt them, we declare without reservation that he is an unbeliever by that since it would lead to invalidation of the *Shari'a*.

As for the one who rejects the consensus[1] itself when that consensus has not come by way of transmission by multiple paths from the Prophet who gave us the *Shari'a*, most of the *mutakallimun*, some of the *fuqaha'* and speculators in this area say that whoever disagrees with a sound consensus, which satisfies the preconditions of consensus generally agreed upon, is an unbeliever. Their proof lies in the words of Allah, **"Whoever makes a breach with the Prophet after guidance has been made clear to him and follows a path other than that of the believers, him We shall turn over to what he has turned to and We shall roast him in Jahannam, an evil home-coming,"** (4:115) and the Prophet's words, "Whoever disagrees with the community by the length of a hand has cast off the rope of Islam from his neck."[2] They quote the consensus that anyone who disagrees with the consensus is an unbeliever.

Others hold that one stops short of absolutely declaring the disbelief of those

---

1. *Ijma'*: it really means resolution (*'azm*) as when it says in the Qur'an, **"When they agreed on their matter."** (12:102) Then it came to mean the agreement of the *mujtahidin* of this community after the time of the Prophet. Al-Baghawi says that there are two types of consensus: general, which is like the consensus of the community about the prayer and the number of *rak'ats*, and particular, like saying that a person who rejects other such things is an unbeliever unless it is through ignorance.
2. Abu Dawud in the *Sunan*.

who disagree with a consensus which is based on the transmission of the *'ulama'*.

Others believed that there should be hesitatation about considering someone who disagrees with the consensus to be an unbeliever when it is a matter of opinion – like considering an-Nizzam[1] to be an unbeliever for disputing the consensus because what he said was contrary to the consensus of the *Salaf* in the manner of their argumentation.

*   *   *

Qadi Abu Bakr al-Baqillani said that he considered disbelief in Allah to be ignorance of His existence and belief in Allah to be knowledge of His existence. No-one should be made an unbeliever by a statement or an opinion unless that amounts to ignorance of Allah. If someone rebels by a word or an action against a clear statement of Allah and His Messenger or against the consensus of the Muslims, such behaviour only exists from an unbeliever. If someone furnishes justification for such behaviour, he has disbelieved. It is not because of his word or action, but because of the disbelief which it implies.

According to Qadi Abu Bakr disbelief in Allah only occurs in one of three ways. One of them is ignorance of Allah. The second is doing an action or making a statement which Allah and His Messenger have said, or all the Muslims are agreed, only issues from an unbeliever – such as prostrating to idols, going to churches, and adopting the *zunnar*-belt of the Christians and attending their festivals along with them. The third is when their statement or action is incompatible with knowledge of Allah.

He said that even if these last two are not actually ignorance of Allah, they are a sign that the one who does them is an unbeliever stripped of belief.

As for someone who denies one of Allah's essential attributes or rejects it, reflect on what that means. It is as if he were saying, "Allah is not knowing, nor powerful, nor does He have will or speech," or similar things about the attributes of perfection which are necessary for Allah.[2] Our Imams have firmly stated by consensus that anyone who denies Him one of these attributes and strips Him of it is an unbeliever.

That is the basis of Sahnun calling someone who said, "Allah does not have speech,"[3] an unbeliever. He does not call the people of interpretation unbelievers as we have already stated.

Regarding someone who is ignorant of one of these attributes, the *'ulama'*

---

1. A poet and Mu'tazili *mutakallim* who died in 231.
2. The attributes of perfection are existence, self-sufficiency, power, will, knowledge, life, hearing, sight, speech.
3. i.e. one of the attributes of perfection.

disagree. Some of them consider this disbelief. That is related from Abu Ja'far at-Tabari and others. Abu'l-Hasan al-Ash'ari also said it once.

A group of them, including al-Ash'ari, considered that this does not remove the name of believer from him. Al-Ash'ari said that is because he does not believe absolutely that his position is correct. He supposes that, by it, he is within the *deen* and the *Shari'a*. These people used the *hadith* of the black woman as a proof. The Prophet only asked her about *tawhid* and nothing else. They said that if most people were to be questioned about the attributes and tested, there would only be a few who would actually know them.

There is a *hadith* which mentions a man saying, "If Allah has power (*qadara*) over me..." (One variant adds, "Perhaps I will mislead Allah.") The Prophet said, "May Allah forgive him."

One of the *'ulama'* explained this *hadith* making various points. Part of what he said is that "*qadara*"(to have power) could have the meaning of "*qaddara*"(to decree). The man was not doubting Allah's power to give him life, but only the Raising from the dead itself which is only known through the *Shari'a*. Perhaps the *Shari'a* had not yet brought them an absolute statement regarding it so that doubt about it would automatically entail disbelief. Intellects are allowed free scope in things which are not actually defined by the *Shari'a*. Or else "*qadara*" might mean to constrict and it is what he has done to himself in his contempt for himself and his anger at his own rebellion against Allah. It is said that he said what he said without fully understanding his words or controlling his expression, being overcome by fear and terror which took away his intellect, and therefore he was not punished for it. It is said that this was during the time of the gap [in the revelation],[1] and a time when pure *tawhid* alone was sufficient.

It is said that this expression was one of the stylistic devices of the Arabs whose form is not explicit and whose meaning must be defined. It is called "the knowing pretending to be ignorant" and there are other examples of it in their language. It is like Allah's words, **"Perhaps he will remember or fear,"** (20:45) and **"Either we or you are upon right guidance or in clear misguidance."** (34:25)

There is also the case of someone who affirms the active attribute and denies the passive, saying, "I say that Allah is Knowing but without knowledge, Speaking but without speech," and similar things about all the attributes. This is the case with the school of the Mu'tazilites. If someone defends the conclusion to which this statement inevitably leads, he is an unbeliever because, by denying knowledge, he in fact denies the attribute of the Knower since only one with knowledge is described as knowing. It is as if in his opinion he has

---

1. A time near the beginning of the Revelation when a considerable time elapsed without any of the Qur'an being revealed.

clearly stated the conclusion to which his statement leads. The same applies to all the factions of the people of interpretation among the anthropomorphists, the *Qadariyya* and others. Whoever does not punish them for the conclusion reached from their statement nor take them to task for what their position leads to does not think that they are unbelievers.

Such a person says that because by stopping short of actual denial of the active attribute (i.e. that Allah is Knowing), they in effect say, "We do not say that He is not Knowing, and we do not deny the final statement which you claim for us. Both you and we believe that it is disbelief. We say that our statement does not lead to that position according to our premises." For these two reasons, there is disagreement about the disbelief of the people of interpretation.

When you understand this, the cause of the disagreement of the people concerning this matter will become clear to you. The correct position is not to call them unbelievers and to avoid any absolute statement to the effect that they are outside the *deen* and to allow the judgements of Islam to proceed with them as regards retaliation, inheritance, marriage, blood money, the prayer over them, burying them in the graves of the Muslims and all Muslim transactions. However, one should be harsh towards them by subjecting them to severe punishment, firm restraint and ostracism until they revert from their innovation. This is the way the First Generation behaved towards such people.

Those who made these statements about *Qadar* and developed the opinions of the *Khawarij* and the *Mu'tazila* were alive in the time of the Companions and the generation after them. Neither the Companions nor the *Tabi'un* denied them a grave nor cut off the inheritance of any of them. However they did ostracize them and discipline them through beating, exile, and execution, according to their states, because they were deviators, misguided, rebels and people of great wrong action according to the precise scholars and the people of the *Sunna*. However, they did not say that they were unbelievers – as opposed to those who express a different position. May Allah give success to the correct position.

Qadi Abu Bakr al-Baqillani said: "As for the questions of the Threat and the Promise,[1] the Vision,[2] the creation of actions,[3] the everlastingness of non-essential matters[4] and the auto-generation of things,[5] and other fine points like

1. A fundamental *Mu'tazilite* doctrine that Allah must carry out a promise or a threat He makes.
2. The *Mu'tazilites* say that Allah will not be seen in the Next World.
3. The *Mu'tazilite* doctrine that man creates his own actions.
4. Al-Ash'ari says that non-essential matters like colour do not last forever, but many people of the *Sunna* disagree with him.
5. In which the Mu'tazilites and philosophers believe – like knowledge being generated by a proof and being acquired on account of that proof.

these, the prohibition on declaring those who hold such positions to be unbelievers is clear, since ignorance concerning any of these things cannot be considered ignorance of Allah. Nor do the Muslims agree about the disbelief of the one who is ignorant of any of these things."

This clarifies the judgment on any Muslim who curses Allah.

SECTION 5
The judgement on a *dhimmi* who curses Allah

As for *dhimmis*, it is related from 'Abdullah ibn 'Umar that a certain *dhimmi* attacked the honour of Allah beyond what his religion allowed and used as a proof. Ibn 'Umar drew his sword against him and went after him and the man fled.

Malik in *The Book of Ibn Habib* and *al-Mabsut*, and Ibn al-Qasim in *al-Mabsut* and *The Book of Muhammad*, and Ibn Sahnun all say, "Any Jew or Christian who reviles Allah in any way other than what constitutes part of their belief is killed without being asked to repent." Ibn al-Qasim added, "unless he becomes a Muslim." He said in *al-Mabsut*, "voluntarily."

Asbagh said, "This is because the way in which they disbelieve is part of their religion. They have been given a treaty based on that – i.e. their claim that Allah has a female consort, a partner and a son. But as for other lies and vilification, they were not given a treaty for them, so such things break their treaty."

Ibn al-Qasim said in *The Book of Muhammad*, "Anyone among other religions who reviles Allah in any other way than the way He is mentioned in his Book is killed unless he becomes Muslim."

Al-Makhzumi in *Al-Mabsut*, Muhammad ibn Maslama and Ibn Abi Hazim said, "He is not killed until he has been asked to repent, be he Muslim or unbeliever. If he repents, he is all right. If not, he is killed."

Mutarrif and 'Abdu'l-Malik said something similar to what Malik said. Abu Muhammad ibn Abi Zayd said that whoever curses Allah in any way other than that by which he normally disbelieves is killed unless he becomes a Muslim.

We have already mentioned the statement of Ibn al-Jallab. We have also mentioned the statement of 'Ubaydullah, Ibn Lubaba and other shaykhs of the people of Andalusia about the Christian woman and their *fatwa* and consensus to kill her because she cursed – in accordance with the way which she normally disbelieved – Allah and the Prophet.[1] This accords with other statements about

---

1. See above p. 412.

any *dhimmis* who curse the Prophet because of the way in which they disbelieve in him.

There is no difference in the way they are treated between whether they curse Allah or curse His Prophet because they are given the treaty provided that they do not manifest anything of their disbelief and that they do not subject us to listening to anything of that kind. If they do so, that breaks their treaty.

The *'ulama'* disagree about a *dhimmi* who is also a *zindiq* from his own *deen*. Malik, Mutarrif, Ibn 'Abdu'l-Hakam and Asbagh said that he is not killed because he goes from disbelief to disbelief.

'Abdu'l-Malik ibn al-Majishun said that he is killed because he has adopted a religion which has been confirmed for no-one and for which *jizya*-tax is not taken.

Ibn Habib said, "I do not know anyone who says anything else."

SECTION 6
The judgement on anyone who claims divinity or utters falsehoods and lies about Allah

As for someone who forges lies against Allah by laying claim to divinity or messengership, or denies that Allah is his Creator or his Lord or says, "I have no Lord," or speaks nonsense along these lines while he is drunk or in a fit of madness, there is no dispute that anyone who says such things or claims them while his intellect is sound is an unbeliever as we have already stated. However, his repentance is accepted, as is generally understood, and his regret helps him and saves him from execution so he should express it. However, he is not safe from severe punishment.

The chastisement is not lightened for him so that people like him will be deterred from uttering such things and he will be prevented from repeating his disbelief or his ignorance. If he repeats such things, it will be known that he has made light of his retraction, and that is a proof of the evil of his heart and the falseness of his repentance. In that case he becomes like the *zindiq* who inwardly does not believe. We do not accept further retraction.

The judgement is the same whether a man is drunk or sober, but in the case of a madman or imbecile, such people do not know what they are saying in their state of dementia and total absence of discrimination, so no attention is paid to what they say. If they say anything of this kind when able to discriminate, even if they do not have full possession of their intellect and are not considered responsible, they are punished for it so that they will refrain from doing it again, in the same way that such people are disciplined for any reprehensible actions they do. They continue to be disciplined until they stop doing it just as an animal is trained to curb bad character until it becomes docile.

'Ali ibn Abi Talib burned someone who laid claim to divinity.

'Abdu'l-Malik ibn Marwan executed al-Harith al-Mutanabbi and crucified him. More than one of the khalifs and kings did that to people who made such claims. The *'ulama'* of their time agreed that they had acted correctly. Anyone who disagrees that the claims of such people consitutes disbelief is himself an unbeliever.

In the days of the 'Abbasid khalif, al-Muqtadir, the *fuqaha'* of Baghdad among the Malikis and the Qadi of the Qadis, Abu 'Umar al-Maliki, agreed to kill al-Hallaj and crucify him for his laying claim to divinity and incarnation and his words, "I am the Truth," even though he outwardly kept to the Shari'a. They did not accept his repentance.

That is also how they judged Ibn Abi'l-Faraqid[1] who made a similar claim to that of al-Hallaj later on in the time of the Khalif, ar-Radi billah. The Qadi of the Qadis of Baghdad at that time was Abu'l-Husayn ibn Abi 'Umar al-Maliki.

Ibn 'Abdu'l-Hakam said in *al-Mabsut*, "Anyone who claims to be a Prophet is killed."

Abu Hanifa and his companions said, "Whoever denies that Allah is his Creator or his Lord or says, 'I do not have a Lord' is an apostate."

Ibn al-Qasim said in *The Book of Ibn Habib* and Muhammad said in *al-'Utibiyya* that someone who claims to be a Prophet is asked to repent, whether he says it secretly or makes it public. He is like an apostate. Sahnun and others also said that. Ashhab said it regarding a Jew who claimed to be a Prophet and claimed that he was a Messenger to the Muslims. If someone makes that claim public, he is asked to repent. If he repents, he is all right. Otherwise, he should be killed.

Abu Muhammad ibn Abi Zayd said that anyone who curses his Creator and claims that his tongue slipped and that he meant to curse *Shaytan* is killed for his disbelief and his excuse is not accepted. This is based on the other statement that repentance is not accepted from someone who does this.

Abu'l-Hasan al-Qabisi said about the drunk who says, "I am Allah, I am Allah," that if he repents, he is disciplined. If he reverts again to saying such things, he is dealt with as a *zindiq* because this is the disbelief of those who mock.

SECTION 7
The judgment on the one who unintentionally counters the majesty of his Lord by disreputable words and foolish expressions

There is also the case of someone who utters disreputable or foolish words

---

1. He was well-known in Baghdad. He claimed to be divine and said that he could bring the dead to life. The Khalif ar-Radi billah ordered that he be arrested so he fled. After he was captured, he was judged to be an unbeliever and was executed in 322.

not caring what he says so that what he says makes light of the greatness and majesty of his Lord, or who, by making examples endows certain things with attributes by which Allah alone is exalted, or appropriates words to describe a creature which are only proper to describe his Creator, without having any deliberate intention of disbelief or of making light of Allah or deliberate godlessness.

If he repeats such things and is known for them, that indicates that he is someone who mocks his *deen*, makes light of the sanctity of his Lord and is ignorant of the incommensurate nature of His might and greatness. This constitutes disbelief without a doubt. It is the same if what he says indicates scorn and disparagement of his Lord.

Some of the *fuqaha'* of Cordoba, Ibn Habib and Asbagh ibn Khalid, gave a *fatwa* that a man known as Ibn Akhi 'Ajab[1] should be killed. He had gone out one day and got caught in the rain. He said, "The leather-piercer has begun to sprinkle water from his leather-skins." Certain *fuqaha'*, Abu Zayd, the author of *ath-Thamaniyya*, 'Abdu'l-'A'la ibn Wahb and Aban ibn 'Isa hesitated about spilling his blood. They thought that it was idle talk for which discipline would be sufficient. The Qadi at that time, Musa ibn Ziyad, gave a *fatwa* to the latter effect.

Ibn Habib said, "His blood is on my neck. Shall the Lord we worship be reviled and we not help Him! We should then be bad slaves who did not serve Him!" He wept, left the assembly and went to the Amir, 'Abdu'r-Rahman ibn al-Hakam al-Umawi. 'Ajab, the man's paternal aunt, was one of the Amir's favourites. Ibn Habib informed the Amir about the disagreement of the *fuqaha'* and the Amir granted leave for the position of Ibn Habib and his companion to be followed and commanded that Ibn Akhi 'Ajab be killed. He was killed and crucified in the presence of the two *faqihs*. The Qadi was dismissed because he was suspected of sycophancy in this case, and the Amir rebuked and reviled the *fuqaha'*.

As for a single slight fault which issues from someone or a lapse which is an exception to the rule and contains neither disparagement or contempt, he is punished for it and disciplined according to what it demands, how terrible its meaning is, and the state of the one who said it. Both its cause and context are examined.

Ibn al-Qasim was asked about a man who called another man by his name and he answered him, "At Your service, O Allah, at Your service." He said that if he is ignorant or said it out of stupidity, there is nothing against him, meaning that he is not killed for it. The ignorant is restrained and taught, and the idiot is disciplined. If he said it with the intention of putting the man in the position of his Lord, he has disbelieved. This is the import of what he said.

---

1. The nephew of 'Ajab, the favourite wife of 'Abdu'r-Rahman al-Umawi, the Amir of Cordoba.

Many foolish and suspect poets have been extravagant in this context and made light of the perfection of Allah's holiness. They have done things which we refuse to mention in our book and on our tongue. If it had not been that we intended to give the conclusions concerning the cases which we have already related, we would not even have mentioned any of the things we have found hard to mention which have been related in these sections.

Then there is what ignorant people and captious tongues have uttered in this respect – like the statement of one of the Arabs:

> Lord of the slaves, what is wrong between us and You! You used to
>   give us rain, so this is not seemly on Your part.
> Send down rain on us without disdain.

Other such words have been uttered by the ignorant and by those who have not been put right by the straightening of the discipline of the *Shari'a* and correct knowledge about this matter. Such things seldom come from any except an ignorant man who must be taught and restrained. Harshness should be shown to him so that he will not repeat such things like it again.

Abu Sulayman al-Khattabi said that words such as these are irresponsible. Allah is far removed from such things.

'Awn ibn 'Abdullah said, "Each of you should exalt his Lord and not mention His name in passing conversation lest he says things such as, 'May Allah disgrace the dog and do such-and-such to him.'"

Part of what we have learned from our shaykhs is that the name of Allah should be only rarely mentioned unless it is in connection to obedience to Him. He used to say to people, "May you be repaid with good!" and he did not say, "May Allah repay you with good," out of respect for the name of Allah lest it be demeaned by use in other than an act intended to bring about nearness to Him.

A reliable source related to us that Imam Abu Bakr ash-Shashi used to censure the thelogians from plunging into a lot of discussion about Him and mentioning His attributes. This was due to his respect for the name of Allah. He said: "Those people use 'Allah', the Mighty, the Majestic, like a handkerchief."

Things said in this area fall into the same category as things said by someone who curses the Prophet, may Allah bless him and grant him peace, in the aspects which we have detailed. Allah is the One who gives success.

SECTION 8
The judgement on the one who curses the Prophets in general and the angels

The judgement on anyone who curses the Prophets of Allah in general and His angels, mocks them, calls them liars regarding what they have brought, or rejects them and denies them, is the same as the judgement about cursing our Prophet, may Allah bless him and grant him peace, which we have already mentioned.

Allah says, **"Those who reject Allah and His Messenger and desire to make division between Allah and His Messengers, and say, 'We believe in some and reject some,' desiring to take a way between this and that, those are truly the unbelievers, and We have prepared a humiliating punishment for the unbelievers,"** (4:150) and **"Say: 'We believe in Allah and what was sent down to us and what was sent down to Ibrahim, a man of pure faith, he was no idolator.' Say: 'We believe in Allah and in that which has been sent down on us and sent down on Ibrahim, Isma'il, Ishaq and Ya'qub and the Tribes, and that which was given to Musa and 'Isa and the Prophets, of their Lord. We make no division between any of them.'"** (2:137) And Allah says, **"All believe in Allah and His angels and His books and His Messengers. We do not distinguish between any of His Messengers."** (2:286)

Malik, as recorded in *The Book of Ibn Habib*, Muhammad ibn 'Abdu's-Salam, Ibn al-Qasim, Ibn al-Majishun, Ibn 'Abdu'l-Hakam, Asbagh and Sahnun all said that anyone who reviles one or all of the Prophets or disparages any of them is killed and not asked to repent.

Any *dhimmi* who curses them is also killed unless he becomes Muslim. Sahnun related from Ibn al-Qasim, "Any Jew or Christian who curses the Prophets in any way other than that by which he normally disbelieves is beheaded unless he becomes Muslim."

The dispute about this has already been presented. The Qadi of Cordoba, Sa'id ibn Sulayman, said in one of his answers, "Anyone who curses Allah and His angels is killed." Sahnun said, "Anyone who reviles one of the angels must be killed."

In *An-Nawadir*, Ibn Abi Zayd quotes Malik as saying about someone who said, "Jibril erred with the revelation. The Prophet was really 'Ali ibn Abi Talib," "He is asked to repent. If he repents, he is all right. Otherwise he is killed." Sahnun said something similar.

Another example of this was what was said by the *Ghurabiyya* among the *Rafidites.* They were called that because they said that the Prophet, may Allah bless him and grant him peace, was so much like 'Ali that they were like one crow (*ghurab*) is to another.

Abu Hanifa and his companions have as their basic position that anyone who calls one of the Prophets a liar, disparages one of them or declares himself free of any of them is an apostate.

Abu'l-Hasan al-Qabisi said about a man who said about another, "As if it were the face of angry Malik,"[1] that if it is known that he intended to censure the angel, he is killed.

All of this is about those who speak about the angels and the Prophets, whether about specific ones we know to be one of the angels or Prophets because there is mention of them in Allah's Book, or ones we know about by multiple transmission and they are known and agreed upon by absolute consensus – like Jibril, Mika'il, Malik, the Guardians of the Garden and of *Jahannam*, the *Zabbaniyya*,[2] the Bearers of the Throne who are mentioned in the Qur'an as being among the angels, and those among the Prophets who are named in the Qur'an, or like 'Azra'il, Israfil, Ridwan, the guardians, and Munkar and Nakir among the angels whose identity is agreed upon and accepted.

As for those whose reports are not specifically confirmed and about whom no consensus exists that they are among the angels or the prophets – like Harut and Marut among the angels, al-Khidr, Luqman, Dhu'l-Qarnayn, Maryam, Asiya (wife of Pharaoh), Khalid ibn Sinan (who is mentioned as being the Prophet of the people of ar-Rass) and Zoroaster whose prophethood is claimed by the Magians and historians, there is no judgement against someone who curses them or rejects them in the manner of the judgements we have been talking about since it is not established that the same respect is necessary for them. However, those who disparage and harm them should be stopped from doing so, and they should be disciplined according to the status of the one he spoke against, especially if that involves someone whose truthfulness and excellence is well-known, even if his prophethood is not confirmed.

As for rejecting the fact that any of these were Prophets or saying they were not angels, if the one who says it is one of the people of knowledge, there is no objection because the *'ulama'* disagree about it. If he is one of the common people, he should be restrained from plunging into things like this. If he does it again, he is disciplined since he should not discuss such things.

The *Salaf* disliked people of knowledge speaking about this sort of thing which does not contain anything that can be acted upon. So how much more should this apply to the common people.

---

1. The angel in charge of the inhabitants of the Fire.
2. The angels who thrust the unbelievers into the Fire.

SECTION 9
Judgement in relation to the Qur'an

Know that anyone who treats the Qur'an or a copy of the Qur'an or any part of it flippantly, or curses it or denies it, even to the extent of a letter or an *ayat* of it, or calls any or all of it a lie or calls anything that it clearly states, or any of its judgements or reports, a lie or affirms anything it denies or denies anything it affirms with full knowledge of that or doubts any of it, he is an unbeliever by the consensus of the people of knowledge.

Allah said, **"It is a mighty book. The false does not come to it from before it nor after it. A sending down from One Wise, Praiseworthy."** (41:42-43)

Abu Hurayra said that the Prophet, may Allah bless him and grant him peace, said, "Doubt (*shakk*) concerning the Qur'an is disbelief."

Ibn 'Abbas said that the Prophet said, "If any Muslim denies any *ayat* of the Book of Allah, it is lawful to strike off his head."

It is the same with someone who denies the Torah, the Injil or any of the revealed books of Allah or rejects them, curses them, reviles them or mocks them. He is an unbeliever.

The Muslims agree that the Qur'an which is recited in all the areas of the earth, the recognised copy which the Muslims possess and what it gathers between its covers from the beginning of **"Praise be to Allah, the Lord of the worlds,"** (1:1) to the end of **"Say: I seek refuge with the Lord of men,"** (114:1) is the word of Allah and His revelation which was sent down on His Prophet Muhammad, may Allah bless him and grant him peace, and that all that is in it is true. Whoever intentionally disparages a letter of it, changes it for another letter in its place or adds a letter to it which the copy of the Qur'an does not contain, there is consensus on the matter and it is agreed that it is not part of the Qur'an and if he does it intentionally, he is an unbeliever.

This is why it was the opinion of Malik that anyone who curses 'A'isha, may Allah be pleased with her, accusing her of having lied should be killed because he has opposed the Qur'an. Whoever opposes the Qur'an is killed, i.e. because he has denied what it contains.

Ibn al-Qasim said, "Anyone who says that Allah did not speak directly to Musa is killed." 'Abdu'r-Rahman ibn Mahdi took that position.

Muhammad ibn Sahnun said about someone who said that the two *suras* asking for refuge (113 and 114) are not part of the Book of Allah that he should be beheaded unless he repented. It is said that it was the same for anyone who denied a single letter of it. He said, "That is what is done if a witness testifies that someone has said, 'Allah did not speak directly to Musa,' or if someone testifies that he has said, 'Allah did not take Ibrahim as a close friend,' because both statements amount to calling the Prophet, may Allah bless him and grant him peace, a liar."

Abu 'Uthman al-Haddad said, "All who profess *tawhid* agree that the rejection of a single letter of the revelation is disbelief."

When Abu'l-'Aliyya listened to a man reciting with him, he did not say to him, "It is not as you have recited." He said, "As for myself, I recite it as such-and-such." Ibrahim an-Nakh'i heard about that and said, "I think that he had heard that anyone who rejects a letter of it has rejected all of it."[1]

'Abdullah ibn Mas'ud said that whoever rejects an *ayat* of Qur'an has rejected all of it. Asbagh ibn al-Faraj said that whoever denies any part of the Qur'an has denied all of it. Whoever denies it has rejected it. Whoever rejects it has rejected Allah.

Al-Qabisi was asked about a man who quarrelled with a Jew who swore to him on the Torah. The man retorted, "Allah curse the Torah!" A witness testified against him regarding that, and then someone else testified that he had asked the man about the matter and he had said, "I cursed the Torah of the Jews." Abu'l-Hasan said that a single witness did not necessitate execution. The second witness connected the matter to a quality which allowed for interpretation since the man might think that the Jews did not hold to anything from Allah by reason of the fact that they had changed and altered it. If two witnesses had agreed that he had cursed the genuine Torah alone, then the case would have been different.

The *fuqaha'* of Baghdad agreed to ask Ibn Shunbudh al-Muqri' who, along with Ibn Mujahid, was one of the presiding Imams of the reciters then, to repent for his recitation and his recitation of odd letters which were not in the recognised version of the Qur'an. They resolved that he should cease doing that and formally repent of what he had done in a document in which he testified against himself regarding that in the assembly of the Wazir, Abu 'Ali ibn Muqla, in 323 AH. Among those who gave a *fatwa* concerning that was Abu Bakr al-Abhari.

Abu Muhammad ibn Abi Zayd gave a *fatwa* to discipline someone who said to a child, "May Allah curse your teacher and what he has taught you." He said, "I meant bad manners, and I did not mean the Qur'an." Abu Muhammad said, "As for anyone who curses the copy of the Qur'an, he should be killed."

SECTION 10
The judgement on the one who curses the People of the House, the Prophet's wives and his Companions

Cursing the people of the Prophet's house, his wives and his Companions, and disparaging them is *haram*, and the one who does it is cursed.

'Abdullah ibn Mughaffal said that the Messenger of Allah said, "Allah,

---

1. i.e. he was concerned that the alternative reading was a correct reading.

Allah, my Companions! Do not make them a target after me. Whoever loves them, it is by my love that he loves them. Whoever hates them, incurs my hate by doing so. Whoever harms them has harmed me. Whoever harms me has harmed Allah. Whoever harms Allah is about to be seized."[1]

The Messenger of Allah, may Allah bless him and grant him peace, said, "Do not curse my Companions. Whoever curses them, the curse of Allah and the angels and all people is on him. Allah will not accept any recompense or counterweight from him."

The Prophet said, "Do not curse my Companions. A people will come at the end of time who will curse my Companions. Do not join them and do not join with them and do not marry with them and do not sit in their assemblies. If they are ill, do not visit them."

The Prophet said, "Whoever curses my Companions, beat him."

The Prophet, may Allah bless him and grant him peace, reported that cursing and harming them harmed him. It is *haram* to harm the Prophet, may Allah bless him and grant him peace.

He said, "Do not harm me concerning 'A'isha." He said about Fatima, "She is part of me. What harms her harms me."

The *'ulama'* disagree about this. The best known position is that adopted by the school of Malik that there is *ijtihad* and painful discipline for that. Malik said, "Whoever reviles the Prophet, may Allah bless him and grant him peace, is killed. Whoever reviles his Companions should be disciplined."

He also said, "Whoever reviles any of the Companions of the Prophet – Abu Bakr, 'Umar, 'Uthman, Mu'awiya or 'Amr ibn al-'As – is killed if he says that they were subject to misguidance or disbelief. If he reviles them in another way as people curse each other, he is given a severe punishment."

Ibn Habib said, "Those Shi'ites who go to extremes in hating 'Uthman and declare themselves free of him are given strong discipline. Whoever adds to that hatred towards Abu Bakr and 'Umar, the punishment for him is more intense, and his beating is repeated and he is imprisoned for a long time until he dies. Only someone who curses the Prophet is to be sentenced to death."

Sahnun said, "Whoever rejects one of the Companions of the Prophet – 'Ali, 'Uthman or others – is painfully punished."

Abu Muhammad ibn Abi Zayd related from Sahnun about someone who said that Abu Bakr, 'Umar, 'Uthman and 'Ali were misguided and unbelievers that he should be killed. Whoever curses other Companions in the same such way is given a severe punishment.

It is related from Malik that anyone who curses Abu Bakr is flogged whereas anyone who curses 'A'isha is killed. He was asked, "Why?" He said, "Whoever attacks her has opposed the Qur'an."

---

1. Sound *hadith* in al-Tirmidhi.

Ibn Sha'ban related this from Malik because Allah has said, **"Allah wishes that you should never repeat the like of it again if you are believers,"** (24:18) whoever does repeat the like of it has disbelieved.

Abu'l-Hasan as-Saqli related that Qadi Abu Bakr ibn at-Tayyib said that whenever Allah mentions in the Qur'an what the idol-worshippers ascribe to Him, He glorifies Himself, as in His words, **"They said: The Merciful has taken a son. Glory be to Him!"** (2:118) and many other *ayats*. For instance, Allah says, referring to what the hypocrites ascribed to 'A'isha, **"Why, when you heard it, did you not say: It is not for us to speak about this. Glory be to You!"** (2:17) He glorified Himself in declaring her innocence from evil as He glorified Himself in declaring Himself free of evil. This corroborates the statement of Malik about killing those who curse 'A'isha.

The meaning of this – and Allah knows best – is because He considered people cursing 'A'isha a terrible thing as He considered people cursing Himself terrible. Cursing her is equivalent to cursing His Prophet, may Allah bless him and grant him peace, and He associates the cursing of His Prophet and harming him with harm of Himself. The judgement on the one who harms Him is that he is killed as it is with the one who harms His Prophet, as we have already stated.

A man reviled 'A'isha in Kufa. He was brought before Musa ibn 'Isa al-'Abbasi who asked, "Who brought this man here?" Ibn Abi Ya'la said, "I did." He said, "Flog him eighty times and shave his head," and he was turned over to the barbers.

It is related that 'Umar ibn al-Khattab threatened to cut out the tongue of 'Ubaydullah ibn 'Umar when he was told about how 'Ubaydullah had reviled al-Miqdad ibn al-Aswad. He said, "Let me cut out his tongue so that he will never again revile any of the Companions of the Prophet, may Allah bless him and grant him peace."

Abu Dharr al-Hawari related that a bedouin who had satirised the Ansar was brought before 'Umar ibn al-Khattab. He said, "If he had not been a Companion, I would have prevented him from troubling you any longer."

Malik said, "Anyone who disparages any of the Companions of the Prophet, may Allah bless him and grant him peace, does not have a right to any booty. Allah divided the booty into three classes. Allah says, '**For the poor and the Muhajirun,**' (59:9) and He says, '**Those who made their dwelling this abode and those in belief before them.**' (59:10) Those are the Ansar. Then He says, '**Those who come after them say, "Our Lord, forgive us and our brothers who went ahead of us with belief."**' (59:11) Therefore anyone who disparages them has no right to the booty of the Muslims."

In the book of Ibn Sha'ban it says, "If someone says that one of the Companions is the son of a whore, and his mother was a Muslim, he is given the *hadd*-punishment for slander, according to some of our companions, twice over. One *hadd* on account of the Companion in question and another *hadd* for his mother. I do not consider it the same when someone slanders the Companions as a whole in a single statement because in this case a particular person was specified." This is based on the Prophet's words, may Allah bless him and grant him peace, "Whoever curses my Companions, flog him."

It further says that anyone who slanders the mother of one of the Companions who was an unbeliever is given the *hadd* for slander because he has cursed that Companion. If any of the descendants of this Companion are alive, they carry out the necessary punishment on the offender. Otherwise it is up to the Imam to approve of any Muslim who agrees to carry it out.

This is not the same as the rights of people other than the Companions, due to the respect the Companions have by virtue of their keeping company with the Prophet, may Allah bless him and grant him peace. If the Imam hears that someone has said something slanderous about a Companion and there is testimony against him, he must carry out the punishment.

There are two positions regarding someone who curses one of the wives of the Prophet, may Allah bless him and grant him peace, other than 'A'isha. One position is that he is killed because he has cursed the Prophet, may Allah bless him and grant him peace, by cursing his wife. The other is that she is considered to be like the other Companions. He is flogged with the *hadd* for slander. Ibn Sha'ban takes the first position.

Abu Mus'ab related from Malik that someone who curses someone who is connected to the House of the Prophet is given a painful beating and imprisoned for a long time until his repentance is clear because he has made light of what is due to the Messenger, may Allah bless him and grant him peace.

Abu'l-Mutarrif ash-Sha'bi, the *faqih* of Malaga, gave a *fatwa* against a man who had objected to someone asking that a certain woman swear by the night. The man had said," Even if she had been the daughter of Abu Bakr as-Siddiq, she would only have been asked to swear by the day." Someone described as being a *faqih* thought that the man's statement was proper. Abu'l-Mutarrif said, "Mentioning the daughter of Abu Bakr in such a manner requires that he be beaten severely and given a lengthy imprisonment."

The *faqih* who thought that the man's statement was proper was someone who deserved the name of *fisq* (deviation) rather than the name of *fiqh*. He was confronted about this matter and reprimanded, and neither his *fatwa* nor his testimony were accepted. It was a further injury and hateful to Allah.

Abu 'Imran spoke about a man who said, "Even if Abu Bakr as-Siddiq had testified against me..." He said, "If he means that his testimony in the matter in question is something for which the testimony of a single witness is not accepted, there is nothing against him." If he meant something else, he is beaten to the point of death. This punishment was mentioned in one version.

*   *   *   *   *

Here ends what we have formulated. The goal to which we aspired has been accomplished. The precondition we laid down for each division has been fulfilled as far as is necessary to satisfy the seeker. Each chapter provides a path to its goal and purpose.

I have related anecdotes in it which are both rare and unusual. I sipped from waterholes of realisation which have not been attained before in most books. I have set it down without any excess. If I had found sufficient words written previously about this matter or a useful model for it in another book, that would have been enough to quench my thirst.

To Allah we owe great humility and a great debt of gratitude for what we have received from Him for His sake and we seek pardon for any ostentation or hypocrisy which might have crept into it. His gift comes to us through His bountiful generosity and His pardon reaches us by virtue of the nobility of His Chosen One and the guardian of His revelation.

We passed sleepless nights investigating the virtues of His Messenger and we concentrated our thoughts on discovering his special qualities, hoping to protect ourselves from the burning Fire by protecting his noble honour. May He place us among those who are not driven away when the one who alters the *deen* is driven away from the Basin of the Prophet! May He make them a means for us, and for those who are concerned with imitating them and acquiring them, to enable us to obtain a treasure which we will find on the day when every self finds the good it has done brought present. By this work we hope to gain His pleasure and full reward. May He single us out for the elect company of our Prophet and His community and gather us among the first squadron and the people of the right gate among the people of his intercession!

We praise Allah for what He has guided us to of the totality of the Prophet and for the way He has inspired us and opened our inner eye to perceive and understand the realities of what we have set down. We seek refuge with Him from making supplication with a supplication which is not heard, from knowledge which does not benefit and from action which does not elevate. He is the Generous One. Those who place their hopes in Him are not disappointed. Those He disappoints do not have any to help them. He does not turn away the supplication of those who aspire nor does He let the action of the corrupt prosper.

He is enough for us and the best Guardian. May His blessing be upon our master and Prophet Muhammad, the seal of the Prophets, and on his family and all his Companions and grant them peace abundantly. Praise be to Allah, the Lord of the worlds.

Glossary of Arabic Words

adab – correct behaviour inward and outward.

adhan – the call to prayer.

'adl – a person of good reputation whose testimony is acceptable in court.

'alim – a man of knowledge. In this context a man learned in Islam.

Amir al-Mu'minin – The Commander of the Believers, a title of respect given to the Khalif.

Ansar – lit. Helpers, the people of Madina, who welcomed and aided the Messenger of Allah, may Allah bless him and grant him peace. See also *Muhajirun*.

'Asr – afternoon, and in particular the obligatory afternoon prayer.

awliya' – plural of *wali*. See *wali*.

awqiya – a measure of weight, about an ounce.

ayat – lit. a sign, a verse of the Qur'an.

Badr – a place near to the Red Sea coast about 95 miles to the south of Madina where, in 2 AH in the first battle fought by the newly established Muslim community, the 300 Muslims led by the Messenger of Allah, may Allah bless him and grant him peace, overwhelmingly defeated 1000 Makkan idol-worshippers.

baraka – a blessing, any good which is bestowed by Allah, and especially that which increases; a subtle beneficent spiritual energy which can flow through things and people or places.

Basmala – the expression, "In the name of Allah, the Merciful, the Compassionate."

Buraq – the mount on which the Prophet made his Night Journey.

Dajjal – the false Messiah whose appearance marks the imminent end of the world.

deen – the life-transaction, lit. the debt of exchange between two parties, in this usage between the Creator and the created. Allah says in the Qur'an, "Surely the *deen* with Allah is Islam." (3:19)

Dhahirites – a school of *fiqh* which derived its judgements from the literal (*dhahir*) text of the Qur'an and Sunna. Also called the Da'udi school after its founder, Da'ud ibn Khalaf.

dhikr – lit. remembrance, mention. In a general sense all *'ibada* (see below) is *dhikr*. In common usage it has come to mean invocation of Allah by repetition of His names or particular formulae.

dhimma – obligation or contract, in particular a treaty of protection for non-Muslims living in Muslim territory.

dhimmi – a non-Muslim living under the protection of Muslim rule.

du'a' – making supplication to Allah.

Fajr – dawn, first light, and in particular the post-dawn *sunna* prayer.

faqih, pl. **fuqaha' –** a man learned in knowledge of *fiqh* (see below) who by virtue of his knowledge can give a legal judgement (*fatwa*).

Fatiha – "The Opening", the opening *sura* of the Qur'an.

fatwa – an authoritative legal opinion or judgement made by a *faqih* (see above).

fiqh – science of the application of the *Shari'a* (see below).

fitna, pl. **fitan –** a trial or affliction whereby one is tried or proved, a temptation, civil war and strife, faction and slaughter.

fitra – the first nature, the natural, primal condition of mankind in harmony with nature.

fuqaha' – see *faqih*.

Furqan – "The Discrimination", a name of the Qur'an.

gharib – a category of *hadith* denoting rarity.

hadd, pl. **hudud –** lit. the limits, Allah's boundary limits for the *halal* and the *haram*. The *hadd* punishments are the specific fixed penalties laid down by Shari'a for specified crimes.

hadith, pl. **ahadith** (*hadiths*) – reported speech, particularly of the Prophet Muhammad, may Allah bless him and grant him peace.

hadith qudsi – Those words of Allah on the tongue of his Prophet, may Allah bless him and grant him peace, which are not part of the Revelation of the Qur'an.

hajj – the yearly pilgrimage to Makka.

halal – permitted by the *Shari'a*.

hamam – a public bath.

haram – forbidden by the *Shari'a*; also an inviolable place or object.

hasan – lit. good, a category of *hadith*, which is reliable, but whose *isnad* is not perfect.

hays – dates mixed with butter, sometimes with *sawiq* added.

Hijr – the semi-circular unroofed enclosure at one side of the Ka'ba, whose low wall outlines the shape of the original Ka'ba built by the Prophet Ibrahim, peace be upon him.

hijra – emigration in the way of Allah. Islam takes its dating from the Hijra of the Prophet, may Allah bless him and grant him peace, to Madina.

himma – aspiration, ambition, purpose, desire.

Hira' – a mountain two miles north of Makka where, in a cave, the Prophet used to go into retreat before the revelation came to him.

Homage of ar-Ridwan – which the Muslims took to avenge 'Uthman when they thought that Quraysh had murdered him at al-Hudaybiyya. See footnote p. 139.

'ibada – act of worship.

'ifrit – a powerful type of *jinn*.

ihram – the conditions of clothing and behaviour adopted by someone on *hajj* or *'umra*.

ihsan – being absolutely sincere to Allah in oneself.

ijma' – lit. consensus, a legal term used in the *Shari'a* to denote a position not specifically drawn from the Qur'an or the *sunna*, but on which the *mujtahids* of the Muslims are generally agreed.

ijtihad – lit. to struggle – to exercise personal judgement in legal matters when there is no known precedent.

ikhlas – sincerity.

Imam – the one who leads the prayer, an eminent scholar.

Iman – belief.

Injil – the original Gospel.

'Isha' – evening, and in particular *'Isha'* prayer, the obligatory night prayer.

'isma – preservation of the Prophets from wrong action.

isnad – the chain of transmission of a *hadith*.

Jabarut – the world of divine power.

Jahannam – a name for Hell.

Jahiliyya – the Time of Ignorance, before the coming of Islam.

Jahim – the fire of Hell.

Jibril – the archangel Gabriel who brought the revelation to the Prophet.

jihad – struggle, especially warfare to establish Islam.

jinn – unseen beings created of smokeless fire who co-habit the earth together with mankind.

jizya – a protection tax imposed on non-Muslims under the protection of Muslim rule.

Jumu'a – the day of gathering, Friday, and particularly the *Jumu'a* prayer.

Ka'ba – the cube-shaped building at the centre of the Masjid al-Haram in Makka. Also known as the House of Allah.

Kalam – the science of investigating religious belief.

Kalim – the Prophet Musa, to whom Allah spoke.

karama, pl. **karamat –** miraculous gifts and favours which Allah gives to His friends (*awliya'*).

Kawthar – it is said that it is a river in the Garden, abundant blessing, intercession, the Prophet's Basin, etc. See Part I, Chapter 1 , Section 10.

khaluq – a kind of yellowy perfume.

Kharijites, *pl.* **Khawarij –** a sect who believed that committing major wrong actions turns a Muslim into a unbeliever.

kunya – a respectful and affectionate way of calling people as the 'Father of so-and-so' or the 'Mother of so-and-so'.

madh-hab – a school of *fiqh* (see above). There are four main Sunni *madh-habs*: Hanifi, Maliki, Shafi'i and Hanbali. There were also *madhhabs* which are no longer in existence – the Awza'i, Dhahiri, that of Sufyan ath-Thawri and the Jaririyya (the *madh-hab* of at-Tabari).

Maghrib – the time of sunset, lit. the west. In particular, the Maghrib prayer which is just after sundown.

Malakut – the angelic world.

Maqam Ibrahim – The place where Ibrahim stood which marks the place of prayer following *tawaf* of the Ka'ba.

marfu' hadith – a tradition from a Companion containing words attributed to the Prophet but whose *isnad* does not trace back to the Prophet.

Masjid al-Aqsa – the "Furthest Mosque" in Jerusalem.

Masjid al-Haram – the "Protected Mosque", the name of the mosque built around the Ka'ba in the *Haram* at Makka.

Mathani – said to be the first long *suras* , or the *Fatiha* and various other things, see Part I, Chapter 1, Section 10.

matn – the text of a *hadith*.

mawla, pl. **mawali** – a person with whom a tie of *wala'* (see below) has been established by manumission. It usually refers to the freed slave, but it can also mean the former master.

mawquf – a category of tradition which only refers to the sayings or doings of the Companions.

Mika'il – the archangel Michael.

minbar – steps on which the Imam stands to deliver the *khutba* on the day of *Jumu'a*.

miqat – one of the designated places for entering into *ihram* for *'umra* or *hajj*.

Mi'raj – the ascent of the Prophet to heaven in the Night Journey.

mu'adhdhin – the one who gives the *adhan*, the call to prayer.

mubah – permitted actions for which there is neither punishment nor reward.

mudd – a measure of volume, approximating to a double-handed scoop.

Muhajirun – Companions of the Messenger of Allah, may Allah bless him and grant him peace, who accepted Islam outside Madina and made *hijra* (see above) to Madina, particularly those who came with him from Makka.

muhsin - someone who possesses the quality of *ihsan*.

mu'jiza – a evidentiary miracle given to a Prophet to prove his prophethood.

mujtahid – someone who is qualified to use *ijtihad*, i.e. make independent decisions in judgements.

al-Multazam – the area between the Black Stone and the door of the Ka'ba, where it is recommended to make *du'a'* (see above).

mursal – *hadith* from a Follower (*Tabi'i*) when it is not known from which Companion he got it.

Mutakallimun – those who study the science of *kalam* (see above).

nafila – a voluntary act of *'ibada* (see above).

nasiha – good advice, sincere conduct.

qadi – a judge.

qibla – the direction faced in prayer, which is towards the Ka'ba in Makka.

rak'a – a unit of prayer (*salat*), a complete series of standing, bowing, prostrations and sittings.

Rafidites – a group of the Shi'a, known for rejecting Abu Bakr and 'Umar as well as 'Uthman.

rajaz – a type of poetry which has a special meter.

Rawda – the part of the Prophet's mosque between his grave and the minbar.

Ridda – apostasy or defection of the Arab tribes after the death of the Prophet.

riwaya – a reading or transmission of the Qur'an or another text.

ruh – the spirit which gives life; the angel Jibril.

sa' – a measure of volume equal to four *mudds*.

sadaqa – giving in the way of Allah.

Sahih – sound, usually in reference to *hadith*. The two most reliable collections of hadith by al-Bukhari and Muslim are both called *Sahih*.

sakina – the presence of Allah sometimes made clear by a sign, also the feeling of peace of mind and security.

Salaf – the 'early years', used generally to describe the early generations of the Muslims, particularly the Companions of the Messenger of Allah, may Allah bless him and grant him peace.

salam – see taslim.

salat – translated in the text as prayer. The ritual prayer of the Muslims.

salih, pl. **salihun** – a spiritually developed man.

sawiq – a mush made of wheat or barley.

shadhdh – one of the rarer readings of the Qur'an; they are authentic, but only have consensus and not multiple transmission.

shahada – lit. to witness, to bear witness that there is no god but Allah and that Muhammad is the Messenger of Allah.

Shari'a – lit. a road. It is the legal modality of a people based on the revelation of their Prophet. The last *Shari'a* in history is that of Islam. It abrogates all previous *shar'ias*.

Shaytan, pl. **shayatin** – a devil, particularly Iblis (Satan).

shirk – the unforgiveable wrong action of worshipping something other than Allah or associating something with Him.

sira – biography of the Prophet.

Sirat – the narrow bridge which must be crossed to enter the Garden.

siwak – toothstick from the 'araq tree. It is a *sunna* to use it.

Subh – morning, particularly the *Subh* obligatory prayer, prayed between first light (*Fajr*) and the onset of sunrise.

Suffa – a veranda attached to the Prophet's mosque in Madina where poor Muslims used to sleep.

Sunan – Collections of *hadith*.

sunna pl. **sunan** – lit. a form, the customary practice of a person or group of people. It has come to refer almost exclusively to the practice of the Messenger of Allah, Muhammad, may Allah bless him and grant him peace, but also comprises the customs of the First Generation of Muslims in Madina.

sura – a large unit of Qur'an linked by thematic content, composed of *ayats* (see above). There are 114 *suras* in the Qur'an.

tafsir – commentary on the Qur'an.

tahaddi – the challenge issued to people to bring something like the Qur'an.

talbiya – the calling of *'labbayk'*, 'At your service,' on the *hajj*.

tasawwuf – Sufism.

tashahhud – lit. to make *shahada* (witnessing). In the context of the prayer it is a formula which includes the *shahada*. It is said in the final sitting position of each two *rak'a* (see above) cycle.

taslim – giving the greeting, "Peace be upon you" (*as-Salamu 'alaykum*). Prayer ends with a *taslim*.

tawaf – circling the Ka'ba, *tawaf* is done in sets of seven circuits.

tawhid – the doctrine of Divine Unity.

'ulama' – pl. of **'alim**. See above.

Umm al-Mu'minin – lit. Mother of the Believers, an honorary title given to the wives of the Prophet, may Allah bless him and grant him peace.

Umm al-Qur'an – lit. the Mother of the Qur'an, the opening *sura* of the Qur'an, *al-Fatiha*. Also said to be its source in the Unseen.

umm walad – a slavegirl who has born her master a child. She cannot be sold and becomes free when her master dies.

'umra – the lesser pilgrimage. It can be peformed at any time of the year.

Al-'Utbiyya – a book attributed to Muhammad ibn Ahmad ibn 'Abdu'l-'Aziz ibn 'Utba al-Umawi al-Qurtubi, the faqih, one of the leading Imams of Andalusia.

wahy – revelation.

wala' – the tie of clientage, established between a freed slave and the person who frees him, whereby the freed slave becomes integrated into the family of that person.

wali – guardian, person who has responsibility for another person, used particularly for the person who 'gives' a woman in marriage. Also someone who is a "friend" of Allah, thus possessing the quality of *wilaya*.

wasila – something which makes something else take place. The High Place with Allah reserved for the Prophet on the Last Day.

wasq, pl. **awsaq** – a measure of volume equal to sixty *sa's* (see above).

wilaya – friendship, in particular with Allah.

wudu' – ritual washing to be pure for the prayer.

Zabur – the Psalms of Da'ud.

zakat – a wealth tax. It is one of the *arkan* (indispensable pillars) of Islam.

Zamzam – the well in the *Haram* of Makka.

zindiq – a term used to describe a heretic whose teaching is a danger to the community. The term is derived from the pre-Islamic Persian Sasanid code.

zunnar – a special belt worn by non-Muslims.

Glossary of *hadith* collections referred to in the text

The Six *Sahih* Collections are
> The *Sahih* of al-Bukhari
> The *Sahih* of Muslim
> The *Sunan* of Ibn Majah
> The *Sunan* of Abu Da'ud
> The *Jami'* of at-Tirmidhi
> The *Sunan* of an-Nasa'i

The main *Musnad* collection is that of Ibn Hanbal.
Other collections mentioned include:
> Abu Nu'aym, *Dala'il*
> Abu Ya'la. *Musnad*
> Abu'sh-Shaykh
> al- Baghawi, *Masabih as-Sunna*, English trans.
> al-Bayhaqi, *Kitab as-Sunan al-Kubra, Dala'il*
> al-Bazzar
> ad-Daraqutni, *Sunan*
> ad-Darimi, *Sunan*
> ad-Daylami, *Musnad al-Firdaws*
> al-Hakim, *al-Mustadrak*
> Ibn Abi 'Umar al-'Adani, *Musnad*
> Ibn Abi Dunya, *Kitab al-'Izza*
> Ibn Abi Hatim, *Tafsir*
> Ibn Abi Shayba, *Al-Musannaf? fi'l-Ahadith wa'l-Athar*
> Ibn 'Adi, *al-Kamil*
> Ibn 'Asakir, *Ta'rikh*
> Ibn Hajar al-'Asqalani, *Tadhhib at-Tadhhib*
> Ibn Hibban al-Busti, *Sahih*
> Ibn Ishaq, *Sirat Rasul Allah*, English trans. by Guillaume
> Ibn Jarir, *Tafsir*
> Ibn al-Jawzi, *Kitab al-Wafa'*
> Ibn Khuzayma, *Sahihq*
> Ibn Lal, *Makarim al-Akhlaq*
> Ibn Mardawayh, *Tafsir*
> Ibn Munda, *al-Ma'rifa*
> Ibn Sa'd, *Tabaqat*
> Malik ibn Anas, *al-Muwatta'*
> ash-Shafi'i, *al-Umm*
> as-Suyuti, *Jam' al-jawami'*
> at-Tabarani
> at-Tabari
> at-Tahawi, *Muskil al-Athar*

457

Glossary of the People Mentioned in the Text

al-'Abbas ibn 'Abdu'l-Muttalib: the uncle of the Prophet. He was born two years before the Prophet. He was in charge of the provision of pilgrims in the *Jahiliyya*. He was present at the Pledge of 'Aqaba with the Ansar before he was Muslim. He was forced to attend Badr with the idol-worshippers. He ransomed himself and returned to Makka. He emigrated before the Conquest of Makka and was present at it. He remained firm with the Prophet in the Battle of Hunayn and died in Madina in 32 AH.

'Abbas ibn Mirdas as-Sulami: from Egypt, one of those who had made wine forbidden to himself in the *Jahiliyya*. He became a sincere Muslim. His mother was al-Khansa', the famous poetess. He died in the khalifate of 'Umar around 18 AH.

'Abbas ibn Suhayl ibn Sa'd as-Sa'idi: the authors of the *Sunan* transmit from him. He lived to be over 90 and died around 114 AH.

'Abd b. Humayd: Imam and Hafiz who died in 249 AH.

'Abda bint Khalid ibn Ma'dan: she related from her father and Ibn Hibban mentioned her as reliable.

'Abdullah ibn 'Abbas: ibn 'Abdu'l-Muttalib al-Hashimi, Abu'l-'Abbas, the son of the uncle of the Prophet. He was born when the Banu Hashim were in the ravine three years before the *hijra*. He is called the "sage of the Arabs". He went on expeditions in North Africa with 'Abdullah ibn 'Amr ibn al-'As in 27 AH. He was tall with reddish fair skin and was of heavy build. The Prophet made supplication for him, rubbed his head and spat into his mouth and said, "O Allah, give him understanding in the *deen* and the knowledge of interpretation." 'Ata' said, "I have never seen an assembly nobler than that of Ibn 'Abbas, with more *fiqh* and greater fear. The people of *fiqh*, Qur'an and poetry each took their portion from him. He died in 68 AH in at-Ta'if.

'Abdullah ibn Abi Awfa: he and his father were Companions. He was present at the battles with the Messenger of Allah. The Prophet made a supplication for him when he brought his *sadaqa* to him. He said, "O Allah, bless the family of Abu Awfa."

'Abdullah ibn Ubayy al-Khazraji: he had hoped to be the ruler of the Ansar in Madina before the *hijra* of the Prophet. However the Islam of the Ansar brought him much booty and so he became Muslim openly. He had some of the *Jahiliyya* in him and love of leadership. He was the leader of the hypocrites and died in the Prophet's lifetime.

'Abdullah ibn Abi Sarh: the Companion, the scribe of the Prophet. He became Muslim on the day Makka was conquered and emigrated and then apostatised and became

Muslim again and remained a strong Muslim. He was given an appointment in 'Uthman's khalifate. When 'Uthman was killed, 'Abdullah retired from people and devoted himself to his *'ibada.* He asked Allah to let him die after the prayer, and he died after the *taslim* of the *Subh* prayer.

'Abdullah ibn 'Amr ibn al-'As: the Companion. There were twelve years between him and his father. His mother was Rayta bint Munabbih. The Prophet used to say, "Excellent are the people of the House, 'Abdullah, 'Abdullah's father and 'Abdullah's mother." He became Muslim before his father. He did a lot of *'ibada* and transmitted a lot from the Prophet so that it was said that he transmitted more than Abu Hurayra. However, he lived in Egypt and few people came to see him there. Abu Hurayra lived in Madina and people came there from all directions. He died in Palestine when he was 73.

'Abdullah ibn al-Hamsa' al-'Amiri: the Companion. It is said that he is 'Abdullah ibn Abi'l-Jud'a' at-Tamimi or al-Kinani.

'Abdullah ibn al-Harith: az-Zubayri, lived in Egypt, and was the last of the Companions to die there in a town called Suft. That was in 85 AH.

'Abdullah ibn Jahsh: the son of the Prophet's aunt, Umayma bint 'Abdu'l-Muttalib. One of those who made *hijra* twice. He was called al-Mujda' (mutilated) because he was killed at Uhud or it is said that his nose and ears were cut off.

'Abdullah ibn Mas'ud: He went on *hijra* twice and was present at Badr and the later battles. He clung to the Prophet and carried his sandals. He was the first to recite the Qur'an openly in Makka. He died in Madina in 32 AH.

'Abdullah ibn al-Mubarak: one the scholars and Imams. His mother was from Khwarizm and his father was Turkish. He was a man who knew *hadith, fiqh,* literature, grammar, language, poetry, and who was eloquent, ascetic, scrupulous, and fair, a man who spent the night in prayer and *'ibada,* went on *hajj* and military expeditions, a man of courage and chivalry. He wrote many books and died in 181 AH.

'Abdullah ibn Mughaffal: a Companion from Muzayna and one of those who were at the Tree for the Homage of Ridwan. Al-Hasan al-Basri and others related from him. He died in Basra in 66 AH. Al-Hasan said, "No-one more noble than him ever settled in Basra."

'Abdullah ibn Qurt: the Companion, amir over Hims under Mu'awiya. The authors of the *Sunan* and Ibn Hanbal and others transmit from him. He was killed in Byzantine territory in 56 AH.

'Abdullah ibn Rawaha: ibn Tha'laba al-Ansari, the poet of the Prophet and his third general after Zayd ibn Haritha and Ja'far ibn Abi Talib in the expedition to Mu'ta where he was killed after his two companions were killed. In the Prophet's lifetime, he attended all the battles except the Conquest of Makka because he was already dead. He died in 8 AH.

'Abdullah ibn Salam: He became Muslim in the time of the Prophet after the Prophet came to Madina. He was a rabbi and Torah scholar, and knew the Qur'an. The Prophet testified that he would go to the Garden. In the *Jahiliiyya*, his name was Husayn but the Prophet called him 'Abdullah. He died in 43 AH.

'Abdullah ibn ash-Shankhir: ibn 'Awf, the Companion. The compilers of the Six Collections transmit from him.

'Abdullah ibn 'Umar ibn al-Khattab: born three years after the Prophet's mission. He did *hijra* when he was ten. The Prophet refused to let him take part in Badr or Uhud, but he was allowed to take part in the Ditch. He died in 73 AH.

'Abdullah ibn Unays: one of the Ansar. He was present at the Battle of Uhud.

'Abdullah ibn Zayd: ibn Tha'laba al-Khazraji al-Ansari. He died in 32 AH when he was 64 and 'Uthman prayed over him.

'Abdullah ibn Ziba'ra: a brave poet from Quraysh and one of the hardest people against the Prophet. Nothing is heard of him after he became Muslim.

'Abdullah ibn az-Zubayr: He was the first child born to the Muslims after the *hijra*. His birth was a defeat for the Jews because they had announced that they had put a spell on the Muslims and they would not bear any children. He proclaimed himself Khalif after the death of Mu'awiya in 64 AH and al-Hajjaj laid siege to him at the Ka'ba where he was killed in 73 AH.

'Abdu'l-Malik ibn Majishun: see Ibn Majishun.

'Abdu'l-Malik ibn Marwan: one of the kings of the Marwanid Umayyads who was born in 26 AH and died in 86 AH.

'Abdu'r-Rahman ibn Abi 'Amra: the compilers of the Six Books transmit from him with the exception of ad-Daraqutni. He is reliable.

'Abdu'r-Rahman ibn Abi Bakr as-Siddiq: a Companion son of a Companion. His name in the *Jahiliyya* had been 'Abdu'l-Ka'ba and the Prophet gave him the name 'Abdu'r-Rahman. He was one of the bravest of Quraysh and among their first marksmen and also an excellent poet. He died before allegiance was offered to Yazid in Makka in 53 AH.

'Abdu'r-Rahman ibn 'Awf: One of the ten promised the Garden and one of the six companions in the council to elect the Khalif. He became Muslim early on before the house of al-Arqam was used. He emigrated twice and was present at Badr and all the battles. He became very wealthy in Madina and was known for his generosity. He was tall and fair with a bit of reddishness and a handsome face. He died in 31 AH and is buried in al-Baqi'.

'Abdu'r-Rahman ibn Mahdi: see Ibn Mahdi.

'Abdu'r-Rahman ibn Zayd ibn Aslam al-Madani: he related from his father and Ibn al-Munkadir. Asbagh, Qutayba and Hisham related from him and thought him weak. He wrote a *tafsir*. The authors of the *Sunan* transmit from him. He died in 182 AH.

'Abdu'r-Rahman ibn Zayd ibn al-Khattab: al-Qurashi al-'Adawi, his mother was Lubaba the daughter of Abu Lubaba al-Ansariyya. He was born in 5 or 6 AH. He married Fatima the daughter of 'Umar, and she bore him 'Abdullah. Yazid made him amir of Makka.

'Abdu'r-Razzaq ibn Hammam: author of books and considered to be reliable. The Six transmitted from him. He died in 211 AH.

Abu 'Ali Husayn ibn Muhammad: *qadi* and *hadith* scholar of the people of Zaragosa. He travelled extensively in the east between 481 and 490 AH. He became Qadi of Almeria in spite of his objections. He was martyred in a raid.

Abu'l-'Aliya: see Rafi' ibn Mahran.

Abu 'Amra Bashir ibn 'Amr al-Ansari: a Companion who was at Badr. He was killed at Siffin on the side of 'Ali.

Abu Awfa 'Alqama ibn Khalid al-Aslami: the Companion, the last of the Companions to die in Kufa in 87 AH. His son was also a Companion and was present with his father at the Pledge of Ridwan.

Abu Ayyub al-Ansari, Khalid ibn Zayd: one of the Banu'n-Najjar. He was present at 'Aqaba, Badr, Uhud, the Ditch and all the battles. He was brave, god-fearing and steadfast. When Yazid ibn Mu'awiya raided Constantinople in Mu'awiya's khalifate, Abu Ayyub went along. He attended the battles, fell ill and was buried at the base of the fortifications of Constantinople in 52 AH.

Abu Bakr as-Siddiq: 'Abdullah ibn 'Uthman, the khalif of the Messenger of Allah, born either two years or six years after the Year of the Elephant. He was the best of the Companions. He fought the apostates and defeated them and established the pillars of Islam after the Prophet's death. He died in 13 AH when he was 63 and was buried beside the Messenger of Allah.

Abu Bakr al-Hudhali: one of the elegant men of literature with excellent poetry, a student of Muhammad ibn 'Umar, known as Ibn al-Qutiyya.

Abu Bakr ibn 'Abdu'r-Rahman al-Makhzumi al-Qurayshi: a Follower and one of the seven *fuqaha'* of Madina according to some. One of the martyrs of Quraysh who was called *ar-Rahib* (the monk) because of his asceticism. He died in 94 AH.

Abu Bakr ibn 'Amr ibn Hazm: Muhammad, *qadi* and amir of Madina. Born two years before the Prophet's death and the Prophet named him Muhammad. It is said that he was born in Najran in 10 AH when his father was in charge of it for the Prophet and from whom he received a letter telling him to name him Muhammad. He died in 126 AH and the Six transmit from him.

Abu Bakr ibn 'Ayyash ibn Salim al-Asadi: the reciter, one of the scholars. They disagree about his name and say eleven different things. He died in 293 AH when he was 96. Al-Bukhari and the Four transmit from him.

Abu Bakr ibn Bukayr al-Qurayshi: at-Tamimi al-Maliki al-Baghdadi: the reliable *faqih* who wrote excellent books, including the *Ahkam al-Qur'an*. He was Iraqi.

Abu Bakr ibn Furak, Muhammad ibn al-Hasan: A great scholar in *fiqh*, grammar, the roots and *kalam*, and a very scrupulous one. He was tested in the *deen* and had debates which led to his dismissal and he died of poison on his way back from Ghazna in 46 AH. He was buried in Nishapur and people visit his grave. He was a Shafi'i.

Abu Bakr ibn Sabiq: excellent scholar of the Maliki school.

Abu Bakr Muhammad: see Ibn Dasa.

Abu Bakr Muhammad ibn Tahir: a scrupulous scholar who died around 330 AH.

Abu Bakra Mani' ibn al-Harith ath-Thaqafi: he withdrew at the Battle of the Camel. He used to say that he was *mawla* of the Prophet. He was called Abu Bakra because he descended from the walls of at-Ta'if by a winch (*bakra*) when he was prevented from leaving.

Abu Barza al-Aslami: a Companion. He became Muslim early on and went to the battles with the Prophet. He died in Basra in 64 AH.

Abu'd-Darda': 'Umaymir, an Ansari from Khazraj who became Muslim after Badr. He died in 32 AH. The Six and Ibn Hanbal transmit from him, and his virtues are famous.

Abu Dharr: Jundub ibn Junada. The Prophet said about him, "The sky has not covered and the earth has not carried anyone more truthful than Abu Dharr." He also said, "May Allah have mercy on Abu Dharr! He lives alone and will die alone and will be gathered alone." He died in ar-Rabadha in 31 AH.

Abu Faraj: 'Umar ibn Muhammad al-Laythi al-Maliki, the author of *al-Hawi* on Maliki *fiqh*. He died in 330 or 331 AH.

Abu Habba al-Badri: 'Amir ibn 'Abdu 'Amr. Al-Waqidi mentioned that he was present at Siffin with 'Ali.

Abu'l-Hamra': There were two Companions with this name. One of them was the *mawla* of the Messenger of Allah. His name was Hilal ibn al-Harith. The other was Ibn Zufr who was at Hims.

Abu Hanifa: founder of the Hanafi school, one of the four Imams, the *faqih* and *mujtahid*. He grew up in Kufa and al-Mansur asked him to be Qadi. He refused and al-Mansur imprisoned him and beat him until he died. He was one of the best in logic and had noble character. He died in 150 AH.

Abu'l-Hasan al-Qabisi: Born in 324 AH. He was blind and his books are very sound and accurate. "Qabisi" is from Gabès (a city in North Africa). He was not from there, but was known by his uncle there. He died in 403 AH in Qayrawan.

Abu Hudhayfa al-Arhabi: Maslama ibn Suhayb al-Kufi. He related from Hudhayfa, Ibn Mas'ud, 'Ali and 'A'isha. Ibn Hibban mentioned that he was reliable.

Abu Humayd as-Sa'idi: 'Abdu'r-Rahman ibn 'Amr ibn Sa'd al-Khazraji of Madina, a Companion. The Six and Ibn Hanbal related from him. He died in the 60s AH.

Abu Hurayra: 'Abdu'r-Rahman ibn Sakhr. It is said that the Prophet gave him that *kunya* because he saw him carrying a cat in his sleeve. He became Muslim in the year of Khaybar and was present there. He clung to the assembly of the Prophet and was steadfast and ascetic. He is considered to be one of the Companions with the greatest memory. Things are related from him which are not related from others. It says in al-Bukhari that he said, "No-one remembered more than me except for 'Abdullah ibn 'Amr ibn al-'As. He wrote them down, but I did not." The Prophet made a supplication for him to remember and after that he never forgot anything he heard. He died in Madina.

Abu Ishaq: 'Amr ibn 'Abdullah, a great Follower and one of the scholars of *hadith*. He took from a number of Companions and Followers. He fasted and prayed a lot and went on expeditions. The compilers of the Six Books transmit from him. He died in 127 AH.

Abu Ishaq az-Zajjaj: Imam of Arabic and *tafsir* and the student of al-Mubarrad and the Shaykh of Abu 'Ali al-Farisi. He was a glass-maker (*zajjaj*). He died in 311 AH.

Abu Jahl: the enemy of Allah and one of those who did great injury to the Prophet. He was killed at Badr by Mu'awwidh and Mu'adh, sons of 'Afra'.

Abu Jahm ibn Hudhayfa: he is 'Amir or 'Ubayd: he became Muslim when Makka was conquered and kept the company of the Prophet. He was important in Quraysh. He died in Mu'awiya's time. There was severity in him and his sons. He helped in rebuilding the Ka'ba with Ibn az-Zubayr and remarked that he had worked on the Ka'ba twice – once in the *Jahiliyya* and once in Islam.

Abu'l-Jawza': Aws ibn 'Abdullah al-Basri. He related the *hadith* of the conquests. He related from 'A'isha, Safwan ibn 'Assal and others. He is reliable and the Six transmitted from him. He was killed in 83 AH.

Abu Juhayfa: His name was Wahb ibn 'Abdullah. The Prophet died when he was an adolescent. Ibn Hanbal relates from him. He died in 72 AH.

Abu Kabsha: a man who left the old *deen* of the *Jahiliyya* and began to worship Sirius. They likened the Messenger to him or to his foster father who had a daughter called Kabsha.

Abu Lahab: the uncle of the Prophet whose name was 'Abdu'l-'Uzza. He was called Abu Lahab (father of flame) because of his complexion and he is mentioned by it in the Qur'an to indicate that he belongs to *Jahannam*. He died after Badr.

Abu'l-Layth as-Samarqandi: from the city of Samarqand in Transoxiana. A lofty Imam known as the Imam of Guidance. He is Mudar ibn Muhammad the Hanafi *faqih*, famous for lofty books like the *Tafsir, an-Nawazil,* and *Tanbih al-Ghafilin wa'l-Bustan.* He died in 373 AH.

Abu Madhura: the *mu'adhdhan* of the Messenger of Allah in Makka. He did not continue giving the *adhan* after the Prophet died. A Companion who died in 59 or 60 AH. Muslim, Ibn Hanbal and the authors of the *Sunan* transmit from him.

Abu Mas'ud 'Uqba ibn 'Amr al-Ansari: a Companion who was at the Second Pledge of 'Aqaba, He lived at Badr and died in Madina in 40 AH in Mu'awiya's time. He was appointed over Kufa by 'Ali when he went to Siffin.

Abu Muhammad al-Usayli: 'Abdullah ibn Ibrahim ibn 'Umar al-Umawi, scholar of *hadith* and *fiqh* from the people of Asila in the Maghrib. He travelled in search of knowledge and returned to Andalusia at the end of the reign of al-Mustansir. He died in Cordoba in 392 AH.

Abu Muhammad ibn 'Abdu'l-Mu'min: one of the the shaykhs of Ibn 'Abdu'l-Barr. He was an honest merchant who met the great *'ulama'*. He was very precise and accurate as adh-Dhahabi says in *Mizan al-I'tidal.*

Abu Muhammad ibn Abi Talib: see Abu Talib al-Makki.

Abu Muhammad ibn Abi Zayd: author of the *Risala*, a Maliki Imam.

Abu Muhammad ibn Nasr, 'Abdu'l-Wahhab ibn Nasr: the Maliki *qadi*. He was a poet, *faqih* and a man of letters with many books in every area. At the end of his life, he travelled to Egypt and became wealthy. He died in 421 AH.

Abu Musa al-Ash'ari: famous Companion whose name was 'Amir ibn Qays. He died in Makka or Kufa in 44 or 52 AH.

Abu Mus'ab Ahmad ibn Abi Bakr az-Zuhri: qadi and scholar of Madina. He listened to Malik and his party and others related from him. He is reliable.

Abu Qatada: see al-Harith ibn Rib'a.

Abu Quhafa: the father of Abu Bakr, 'Uthman ibn 'Amir ibn 'Amr. He became Muslim on the day Makka was conquered and became a good Muslim. He died after Abu Bakr in 14 AH.

Abu Rafi': the client of the Messenger of Allah. His name was Ibrahim, or Aslam or Thabit.

Abu Rimtha at-Taymi: Rifa'a ibn Yathri. He related from the Prophet and Iyad and Thabit related from him. The three authors of the *Sunan* related from him and Ibn Khuzayma, Ibn Hibban and al-Hakam consider his *hadiths* to be sound.

Abu Sa'id al-Khudri: Sa'id ibn Malik ibn Sinan, a Companion of high rank, famous among the *fuqaha'* of the Companions and one of the Companions of the Tree who died in Madina and was buried in al-Baqi' in 64 AH. Many *hadiths* are related from him.

Abu Salama: ibn 'Abdu'r-Rahman ibn 'Awf, a Follower: one of the Seven *fuqaha'* of Madina.

Abu Salih Dhakwan az-Zayyat: the *mawla* of Juwayriya bint al-Ahmas al-Ghatafani. One of the most reliable of people. He has many *hadiths* and is firm in respect of the *hadith* of Abu Hurayra. He died in 101 AH.

Abu Sufyan ibn al-Harith: ibn 'Abdi'l-Muttalib, the uncle of the Prophet and his milk brother through Halima as-Sa'diya. His name was al-Mughira. It is also said that his name was Abu Sufyan and his brother was al-Mughira. He resembled the Prophet.

Abu Sufyan Sakhr: He became Muslim when Makka was conquered and was present with the Prophet at the Battle of Hunayn. He gave a lot of his wealth. He was the shaykh of Makka and their leader and the leader of Quraysh after Abu Jahl. He died in 31 AH and was buried in al-Baqi'.

Abu Talha: Zayd ibn Sahl al-Ansari al-Khazraj, one of the best of the Companions and the husband of Umm Sulaym. He was shooting in front of the Prophet at Uhud. He died in 50 AH.

Abu Talib: the uncle of the Prophet who was a helper and father to the Prophet, but did not become a believer. He died in 10 AH.

Abu Talib al-Makki: Abu Muhammad ibn Abi Talib, Shaykh of the Sufis and people of the *Sunna*. He was from Qayrawan and from there moved to Andalusia and lived in Cordoba. He had extensive knowledge of *tafsir* and other sciences. He wrote a large *tafsir* and the *Qut al-Qulub*. He died in Cordoba in 437 AH and was buried there.

Abu Thawr: Malik ibn Nimt al-Hamdani, "Dhu'l-Mis'ar", came to the Prophet on his return from Tabuk with many of his Muslim people in the delegation of Hamdan. During 'Umar's khalifate, he emigrated to Syria with 4000 slaves whom he set free.

Abu't-Tufayl: 'Amir ibn Wathila al-Kinani, a companion who was a poet. He was born at the beginning of the *hijra* and died in 110. He was the last of the Companions to die.

Abu Umama: al-Bahili and as-Sahmi. He is Sadi ibn 'Ajlan. The Six transmit from him. He was one of the last of the Companions in Hims. He died in 81 AH.

Abu Umama al-Ansari: Sa'd ibn Sahl, born in the time of the Prophet who named him and blessed him. He died in 100 AH and the Six transmit from him.

Abu 'Umar at-Talamanki: the Imam, reciter and *hafiz*. He is Ahmad ibn 'Abdullah, the scholar of Cordoba who was born in 340 AH. Ibn Hazm, Ibn 'Abdu'l-Barr and other Imams related from him. He was a leader in the science of recitations (*qira'at*) who had great concern for *hadith* and was an Imam in the *Sunna*. He died in 429 AH.

Abu 'Uthman al-Hiri: Sa'id ibn Isma'il, the Sufi Shaykh in Nishapur. He died in 298 AH. He was one of the great men of asceticism and Sufi Shaykhs. He was the companion of Abu Hafs an-Nisapuri.

Abu'l-Waddak: Jibr ibn Nawf al-Bistami al-Kufi, the Follower. Considered reliable by Ibn Ma'in and Ibn Hibban.

Abu Walid Hisham ibn Ahmad: an Imam of Cordoba, ascetic and a *hadith* scholar, known as Ibn al-'Awwad, a shaykh well-versed in grammar and Arabic language and considered very precise and accurate by his student, Qadi 'Iyad.

Ahmad ibn Hanbal: Abu 'Abdullah, born in Baghdad in 164 AH and grew up there. He was devoted to the *sunna* so that he became its Imam in his time. He learned *fiqh* from ash-Shafi'i. Founder of the Hanbali *madhhab*. He died in 241 AH.

Ahmad ibn Salih Abu Ja'far at-Tabari al-Misri: reliable. He listened to Ibn 'Uyayna. Al-Bukhari and others related from him. He had comprehensive knowledge and the authors of the *Sunan* transmitted from him. He died in 248 AH.

al-Ahnaf ibn Qays at-Tamimi: a master of Tamim, one of the great, astute, eloquent, brave, conquering men who was a model of forbearance. He was born in Basra and lived in the time of the Prophet but did not meet him. When he was angry, a hundred thousand men would be angry for him without knowing why he was angry. He died in 72 AH.

'A'idh ibn 'Amr ibn Hila al-Muzani: Abu Hubayra. He was one of those who offered allegiance under the Tree. He lived in Basra and died in the emirate of Ibn Ziyad.

'A'isha bint Abi Bakr: *Umm al-Mu'minin.* Married the Prophet when she was nine. She related 2210 *hadiths* from the Prophet. She died in Madina and was buried in al-Baqi' in 58 AH.

al-Ajurri: Muhammad ibn al-Husayn, the Shafi'i *faqih* and *hadith* scholar. Born in Baghdad and then moved to Makka. He died in 360 AH.

al-Akhnas: ibn Shurayq. He is Ubayy ibn Shurayq ath-Thaqafi. He is called al-Akhnas (pug-nosed) because he went back with the Banu Zuhra at Badr and became Muslim. He was present at Hunayn and died in the beginning of 'Umar's khalifate.

'Ali ibn Abi Talib: the first person to become Muslim. He was born ten years before the Prophet was sent. He was brought up by the Prophet and did not leave him. He went on all his expeditions except for Tabuk when the Prophet left him behind. He married Fatima, the Prophet's daughter. He was killed in 40 AH.

'Ali ibn al-Hakam al-Bannani al-Basri: he related from Anas and Abu 'Uthman al-Hindi and a group including Nafi'. Al-Bukhari and the Four transmitted from him. He died in 131 AH.

'Ali ibn al-Husayn ibn 'Ali ibn Abi Talib: called Zayn al-'Abidin: one of those taken as a model in forbearance and scrupulousness. He secretly gave to a hundred houses in Madina. He died in 94 AH.

'Ali ibn 'Isa: Abu'l-Husayn, an Imam in grammar, language, *tafsir*, and *kalam*. He wrote a great *tafsir*, and was the student of Ibn Darid. He was born in Baghdad in 296 AH but his family came from Samarra. He died in 384 AH.

'Alqama ibn Khalid ibn al-Harith al-Aslam, Abu Wafa: a Companion. The last Companion to die in Kufa in 87 AH. His son was also a Companion and was present with him at Ridwan.

'Alqama ibn Qays an-Nakh'i, Abu Shibl: the Follower. He was the *faqih* of Iraq who was like Ibn Mas'ud in his guidance, character and virtue. He was born in the lifetime of the Prophet and died in Kufa in 62 AH.

al-A'mash: Abu Muhammad Sulayman ibn Mahran al-A'mash, a famous Follower whose family came from Rayy. He was a scholar in the Qur'an, *hadith* and shares of inheritance. He was a leader in useful knowledge and sound action. He was very poor and needy. He grew up in Kufa and died there in 148 AH.

Amina bint Wahb: The mother of the Prophet. He was her only child. She died when he was six.

al-'Amiri: from the Banu 'Amir who came as a delegation to the Prophet. His name was 'Atiyya or Qibt ibn 'Amir. He died at the end of the 80s AH.

'Amir ibn Rabi'a ibn Ka'b: the famous Companion who became Muslim early on and emigrated and was at Badr. He died on the night that 'Uthman was murdered.

'Amir ibn at-Tufayl ibn Malik: from the Banu 'Amir ibn Sa'sa'a, the knight of his people. One of the poets and leaders of his people in the *Jahiliyya*. He is Abu 'Ali. He was born and grew up in Najd. He participated in many battles and was an old man when Islam came. He went to the Prophet in Madina after Makka had been conquered intending to assassinate him but did not dare. The Prophet invited him to Islam and 'Amir made it a precondition that he give him half of Madina's fruits and put him in command after the Prophet. He refused so he went home resentful. He died en route before he reached his people. He had only one eye, having lost the other in a battle and died childless. He was the nephew of Labid the Poet.

'Ammar ibn Abi 'Ammar: the *mawla* of the Banu Hadhim, Abu 'Amr al-Makki, a Follower considered to be reliable by Abu Dawud and Ibn Hibban and others. He died while Khalid ibn 'Abdullah was governor of Iraq.

'Ammar ibn Yasir al-Kinani: Abu'l-Yaqazan, a Companion and one of the brave men of judgement. He is one of the first to become Muslim and openly state it. He emigrated to Madina and was present at Badr, Uhud, the Ditch and the Pledge of Ridwan. The Prophet called him "*at-tayyib al-mutayyib* (the pleasant and good)". He was the first to build a mosque in Islam. 'Umar put him in charge of Kufa and he remained there for a time until dismissed. He was present at the Battle of the Camel and Siffin with 'Ali, being killed in Siffin at the age of 93.

'Amr ibn al-'As: one of the "four clever men" of the Arabs. The others were Mu'awiya, al-Mughira and Ziyad. He was a great military general and died on the night of the *'Id al-Fitr* in 43 AH.

'Amr ibn 'Awf al-Muzani: a Companion who became Muslim early on and was present at the battles. He died in the time of Mu'awiya.

'Amr ibn Dinar: Abu Muhammad, client of Qays al-Misri, d. 126 AH.

'Amr ibn al-Harith: Ibn Abi'd-Darir, the brother of Juwayriyya, the wife of the Prophet. A Companion.

'Amr ibn Maymun: the Follower. He lived at the time of the Prophet but did not meet him. He was reliable and died in 74 AH.

'Amr ibn as-Sa'ib: one of the most excellent of the Followers and reliable men. He related from Usama ibn Zayd and many related from him. Abu Dawud transmits from him.

'Amr ibn Umayya ibn Khuwaylid: the Companion whom the Messenger of Allah entrusted to despatch his affairs. He took his letter to the Negus who replied to it. He and his wife, Umm Habiba, became Muslim after Uhud. He was present at Bi'r Ma'una and died in Madina during Mu'awiya's khalifate.

Anas ibn Malik al-Ansari al-Khazraji: the Companion, he served the Prophet when he was eight or ten years old and stayed with him for twenty years. 2206 *hadith* are related from him. The Prophet made a supplication that he would have blessing in his property, children and life and would have forgiveness. He was one of the wealthiest of people. When he died, he had about 120 children. He had a garden which had a crop twice a year. He lived so long he was weary of life. He died in 93 AH when he was 100 years old. He is buried near Basra.

'Antara: the son of Mu'awiya ibn Shaddad al-Qays, one of the Arab champions and famous men of eloquence. He composed one of the *mu'allaqat* poems (which were hung in the Ka'ba because of their excellence). He died an unbeliever in the *Jahiliyya*.

Arbad ibn Qays: the brother of Labid ibn Rabi'a by his mother. Labid was a Companion and Arbad was a poet as well. Allah sent a lightning-bolt which consumed him. He disbelieved in Allah. About him Allah revealed, *"He sends thunderbolts and strikes with them whomever He wills while they dispute about Allah who is Strong in subtly attaining His end."* (13:13)

Asbagh ibn Faraj: the *mawla* of 'Umar ibn 'Abdu'l-'Aziz. He was a *faqih* of Egypt who related from Ibn Wahb, ad-Da'udi and others. Al-Bukhari and others related from him. Ibn Ma'in said, "He had the greatest knowledge of the opinion of Malik – he was truthful, scholarly and scrupulous." He died in 225 AH.

al-Ash'ari, Abu'l-Hasan 'Ali ibn Isma'il: he was a Mu'tazilite, later to leave them. He became an unrivalled great scholar, the Imam of the People of the *Sunna* and author of famous books. He died in 324 AH.

al-Ash'ath: ibn Qays: he came to the Prophet with his people and apostatised after his death and was brought to Abu Bakr. He became Muslim again and then went out with Sa'd to Iraq. He lived in Kufa until he died in 40 AH.

Ashhab ibn 'Abdu'l-'Aziz ibn Da'ud al-Qaysi al-Misri: the *faqih*. He relates from al-Layth, Malik and others, and Sahnun related from him. He died eighteen days after ash-Shafi'i at the age of 64.

Asma' bint Abi Bakr: 'A'isha's sister and daughter of Abu Bakr as-Siddiq, the mother of 'Abdullah ibn az-Zubayr. She had fluent Arabic, and was quick-witted. The story of her behaviour with al-Hajjaj after the death of her son is famous. She lived to be 100 and died in 73 AH.

Asma' bint 'Umaysh: a Companion who was important. She became Muslim before the Prophet entered the house of al-Arqam. She was the wife of Ja'far ibn Abi Talib and then of Abu Bakr and then 'Ali. She died in about 40 AH.

al-Asma'i: 'Abdu'l-Malik ibn Qurayb ibn Asma', Imam of Basra in language, grammar and literature and rarities. He was born in Basra in 123 and died there in 210 AH.

al-Aswad ibn Yazid ibn Qays an-Nakh'i: one of the great Followers, known for his transmission from Ibn Mas'ud and famous for his *fiqh*, memory, asceticism and great *'ibada*. He was the scholar of Kufa in his time. He died in 75 AH.

'Ata' ibn Yasar: Abu Muhammad al-Madani, one of the great Followers. He died in 94 or 103 AH.

'Atiyya as-Sa'di: from the tribe of Banu Sa'd. He came with his father to the Prophet.

'Awf b. Malik: 'Abdu'r-Rahman al-Ashja'i, the excellent Companion. He lived in Syria and died in the time of 'Abdu'l-Malik in 73 AH.

'Awn ibn 'Abdullah: *faqih* and ascetic. It is said that he transmitted *mursal* from the Companions. He was not a Follower. He is reliable and died in about 160 AH.

al-Awza'i: Imam and founder of the *madhhab* followed by the people of the Maghrib before they became Maliki. He lived in Syria until he died as a *murabit* in the port of Beirut.

Ayman al-Habashi al-Makki: his mother was Umm Ayman, the nurse of the Prophet and his *mawla*, the brother of Usama ibn Ziyad by his mother. Martyred at Hunayn.

Ayyub as-Sakhtiyani: Imam Abu Bakr al-Basri the Follower, Master of the *fuqaha'* and *hadith* scholars. Malik, ath-Thawri and others related from him. The Six transmit from him. He died in 131 AH.

Bakr ibn al-'Ala': the Maliki qadi, one of the sons of 'Imran ibn al-Husayn. He died in 334 AH.

Al-Baji, Abu'l-Walid: a great Maliki scholar and Imam. Author of important books.

Baqi ibn Mukhallid, Imam Abu 'Abdu'r-Rahman al-Qurtubi: a *mujtahid* who did not imitate anyone and whose supplication was answered. It is said that he recited the entire Qur'an every night in thirteen *rak'ats*. He went on seventy expeditions. He was born in 201 and died in 276 AH.

al-Baqillani: Muhammad ibn at-Tayyib, Imam of the people of the *Sunna*, d. 403 AH. He is not Abu Bakr ibn al-'Arabi.

al-Bara' ibn 'Azib: al-Ansari al-Awsi, he was present at Uhud and went on fifteen expeditions with the Prophet and went on eighteen journeys with him. He died in Kufa in 72 AH.

Baraka bint Yasar: the client of Abu Sufyan ibn Harb. A *muhajira*. She was serving Umm Habiba when the Prophet married her. It is said that she accidentally drank the Prophet's urine from a flask under his bed.

Barira bint Safwan: the client of 'A'isha. They disagree about whether she was a Copt or Abyssinian. She is the one with whom 'Abdu'l-Malik ibn Marwan sat and to whom she said, "'Abdu'l-Malik! I see qualities in you. You are suited to undertake command. But if you do so, then beware of blood."

al-Bazzar: Abu Bakr Ahmad ibn 'Amr, a *hafiz* and *hadith* scholar from the people of Basra. He compiled two *Musnads*, a large one called *al-Bahr az-Zakhir* and a small one. He died in Ramla in 292 AH.

Bilal ibn Abi Rabah: the first Abyssinian to come to Islam. He became Muslim while he was a slave of Umayya who tortured him. Abu Bakr bought him and set him free. He became the *mu'adhdhan* of the Prophet. He died in Syria.

Bilal ibn al-Harith al-Muzani: the Companion. He came to the Prophet with the delegation of Muzayna and settled outside of Madina. He died in 60 AH when he was 80.

al-Bukhari: Abu 'Abdullah Muhammad ibn Isma'il, travelled in search of knowledge to all the men of *hadith* of the cities. He started to frequent the company of the shaykhs when he was 11. He said that he produced the *Sahih* from the cream of 6000 *hadiths*, and did not write down any *hadith* in it until he had prayed two *rak'ats*. He was born in 194 and died in 256 AH.

Burayda ibn al-Hasib: Abu 'Abdullah, a Companion who became Muslim before Badr when the Prophet was making his *hijra*. He went on ten expeditions with the

Prophet and he was present at al-Hudaybiyya. He died in Marv in Khorasan on an expedition in the time of Mu'awiya or Yazid in 63 AH.

ad-Dahhak ibn Muzahim: the Companion. He related from Abu Hurayra, Ibn 'Abbas and other Companions. The authors of the *Sunan* and others transmitted from him. He died in 105 AH.

ad-Daraqutni: 'Ali ibn 'Umar, from Dar al-Qutn, a part of Baghdad. He was an Imam unrivalled in his age. He had knowledge of traditions and weaknesses and the names of the men and their states in justice, truthfulness and knowledge of the schools of the *fuqaha'*. He was born in 306 and died in 385 AH.

ad-Da'udi: Ahmad ibn Nasr, the commentator on al-Bukhari. He died in Tlemcen in 440 AH.

Dihya al-Kalbi: the son of Ibn Khalifa, the famous Companion. He died in the khalifate of Mu'awiya. He was one of the most beautiful of people and that is why Jibril took on his form.

Dhu'n-Nun al-Misri: the ascetic and gnostic of Allah, Abu'l-Fayd Thawban ibn Ibrahim, a man of knowledge and virtue. Died in 245 AH.

Dimad ibn Tha'laba al-Azdi: a true friend of the Prophet before he was sent. He came to Makka and became Muslim at the beginning of Islam. He was intelligent, a perfumer and maker of talismans.

ad-Dulabi: Abu Bishr Muhammad ibn Ahmad al-Ansari ar-Razi: the *hadith* scholar and author of various works. The great ones related from him – like at-Tabarani and Abu Hatim. He died between Makka and Madina in 113 AH.

Fadala ibn 'Ubayd ibn Faqid al-Ansari al-Awsi: Abu Muhammad, a Companion. Mu'awiya appointed him *qadi* of Damascus. He was present at Uhud and al-Hudaybiyya. He died in 153 AH. Ibn Hanbal and others transmit from him.

al-Fadl ibn 'Abbas al-Hashimi: a courageous Companion and notable man. He was oldest of al-'Abbas' children. He stood firm at Hunayn. He rode on the same camel behind the Prophet on the Hajj of Farewell. After the Prophet's death, he went on *jihad* to Syria and was martyred at the Battle of Ajdadayn in Palestine. It is also said that he died of the plague.

al-Farra': Imam Abu Zakariya Yahya ibn Ziyad. He was one of the most intelligent of the Kufans and the one with the most knowledge of the arts of literature and *tafsir*. Az-Zamakhshari relied on him. He died in 207 AH on the Makkan road when he was 63.

Fatima bint 'Abdullah: 'Uthman was her son. He was Abu 'Abdullah ibn Bashir ath-Thaqafi, a great Companion and fighters. He was appointed *qadi* of Kufa and related that his mother saw the birth of the Prophet.

Fatima az-Zahra', daughter of the Prophet. She and Maryam bint 'Imran are the best of the women of the world. She married the Prophet's nephew, 'Ali. She was the only daughter of the Prophet to survive him. She died in 11 AH, six months after the Prophet's death when she was 30 or less.

Ghaylan ibn Salama ath-Thaqafi: became Muslim after the conquest of Ta'if. He was a poet. He died at the end of the khalifate of 'Umar.

Hafs ibn 'Ubaydullah ibn Anas: Ibn Hibban mentioned that he is reliable. Abu Hatim says that it is only established that he heard *hadith* from his grandfather.

Hafsa bint 'Umar al-Khattab: One of the wives of the Prophet. She was married to Hisn ibn Hudhayfa before she married the Prophet. He was present at Badr and then died in Madina. She died in Madina in 41 AH.

al-Hajjaj ibn Yusuf ibn al-Hakam: Abu Muhammad, a clever and bloodthirsty general and orator. He was born and grew up in Ta'if in the Hijaz and then moved to Syria where he attached himself to Rawh ibn Zanba', the deputy of 'Abdu'l-Malik ibn Marwan. He was one of his *Shurta* (police) and then he continued to be successful until 'Abdu'l-Malik put him in charge of the army. He ordered him to kill 'Abdullah ibn az-Zubayr and put him in command for twenty years. He founded the city of Wasit. All the historians agree that he was bloodthirsty. He died in Wasit. Water flowed over his grave and destroyed it.

al-Hakam ibn Abi'l-'As: He is Abu Marwan and the uncle of 'Uthman. He was one of those who became Muslim at the Conquest of Makka. The Prophet sent him and his son Marwan out to Ta'if and 'Uthman brought him back when he learned that he had repented. He died in 'Uthman's khalifate.

Hakim b. Hizam: a nephew of Khadija, the wife of the Prophet. He lived for 120 years, half of it in Islam. He was the only person to be born inside the Ka'ba. He died in 60 AH in Madina.

Halima bint 'Abdullah as-Sa'diya: the Prophet's wet-nurse. Her husband was al-Harith ibn 'Abdu'l-'Uzza. She and her husband and children became Muslim.

Hammad: Shu'ba, Malik and others related from him. He is a truthful man but one who was considered prone to error. He does not have the force of Malik. Muslim and the Four transmitted from him. He died in 199 AH.

Hammam ibn Yahya al-'Awdhi: a reliable Imam from whom the Six transmitted. He died in 163 AH.

Hamza ibn 'Abdu'l-Muttalib: of Quraysh, the uncle of the Prophet and one of his valiant leaders in the *Jahiliyya* and Islam. He was born and grew up in Makka. He was one of the proudest and most obstinate of Quraysh. When Islam appeared, he wavered about accepting it and then he learned that Abu Jahl had been contemptuous towards the Prophet, he went to Abu Jahl and hit him and proclaimed himself a Muslim. Hamza emigrated with the Prophet to Madina and was present at Badr and other battles, Al-Masa'ini said that he was he was the first to hold the banner of the Messenger of Allah. Hamza's emblem in times of war was an ostrich feather which he put on his chest. At Badr, he fought with two swords and performed great deeds. He was killed at Uhud and the Muslims buried him in Madina.

Hanash ibn 'Abdullah: the Follower, one of those who entered Andalusia at the beginning of Islam there. He relates from 'Ali, ibn 'Abbas and others.

Hanzala ibn Abi 'Amir ibn Sayfi known as al-Ghasil. In the *Jahiliyya* his father, 'Amr, was called *ar-Rahib* (the monk). He talked of the mission and the Hanifiyya *deen*. When the Prophet was sent, 'Amr visited him alone and left Madina. He was present with Quraysh at the Battle of Uhud and returned to Makka with them. Then he left for Byzantium and died there in 9 AH. His son Hanzala became a Muslim and was a good Muslim. He was martyred at Uhud. He is called al-Ghasil (the washed) because the angels washed him when he was martyred as he was in *janaba*. He was killed by Abu Sufyan ibn Harb.

Hanzala ibn Hidhaym ibn Hanifa at-Tamimi: he, his father and grandfather were Companions.

al-Harbi: Ibrahim ibn Ishaq, from Baghdad. Died in 107 AH.

al-Harith ibn 'Abdu'l-'Uzza: the husband of Halima as-Sa'diya. He became Muslim and was a good Muslim.

al-Harith ibn Asad al-Muhasibi: He was called al-Muhasibi because he frequently called himself to account (*muhasiba*) and because of his asceticism. He was an excellent scholar, held in high esteem among the people of his time in both outward and inward knowledge, and wrote many books. His father died leaving him a great deal of wealth, but he refused to take any of it because his father had been a Qadiri. He died in 243 AH.

al-Harith ibn Miskin: a famous Umayyad *faqih*, the *mawla* of Marwan. He studied with Ibn 'Uyayna, Ibn Wahb and Ibn al-Qasim. Abu Dawud, an-Nasa'i and others related from him. He lived to about 90 AH. He was reliable in *hadith* and a Maliki *faqih*. During the *Mihna*, the Khalif al-Ma'mun brought him to Baghdad but refused to respond to the question of the creation of the Qur'an. He remained in prison until al-Mutawakkil took office and then he was released and returned to Egypt. Al-Mutawwakil made him *qadi* of Egypt.

al-Harith ibn Rib'i: Abu Qatada, a Companion from the Ansar, the horseman of the Prophet. Ibn Hanbal and the authors of the Six transmit from him. He died in 54 AH.

al-Harith ibn Simma: he was present at Badr. He was martyred with those whom the Prophet sent with 'Amir ibn Malik on the day of the well of Ma'una where they were treacherously killed.

Haritha ibn Wahb al-Khuza'i: the brother of 'Ubaydullah ibn 'Umar by the same mother. He related from the Prophet and Hafsa and others. He has four *hadith* in the two *Sahih* volumes.

al-Hasan al-Basri: One of the most splendid Followers in asceticism, knowledge and showing the truth. He went for thirty years without laughing. He met many Companions and transmitted many *hadiths*. His mother served Umm Salama, the wife of the Prophet. He died in Basra in 116 AH when he was 88.

al-Hasan ibn 'Ali ibn Abi Talib: the grandson of the Prophet, the *Amir al-Mu'minin*. He was born in 3 AH. He died in Madina in 50 AH and is buried in al-Baqi'.

Hassan ibn Thabit al-Khazraji al-Ansari: Abu'l-Walid, the poet of the Prophet. He lived sixty years in the *Jahiliyya* and sixty in Islam. He praised the Prophet and defended the honour of Islam with his tongue and eloquence. He died in Madina in 54 AH.

Hatib ibn Abi Balta'a al-Lakhmi: a Companion who attended all the battles with the Messenger of Allah. He was a good archer and had extensive trade as a merchant. The Prophet sent him with Kinana to the Muqawqis, the master of Alexandria. He died in Madina. He was one of the knights and poets of Quraysh in the *Jahiliyya*.

Hatim at-Ta'i: famous for his generosity. He lived in the *Jahiliyya* shortly before the Prophet was sent. His son 'Adi became Muslim and was one of the great Companions.

Hudhayfa ibn al-Yaman: Born in Madina. He and his father became Muslim and were present at Badr where the idol-worshippers made for them. They were present at Uhud where his father was martyred. He was present at the Ditch and later battles. 'Umar appointed him over al-Mada'in where he remained until he died in 36 AH.

Humayd: the client of Talha al-Khuza'i. He is reliable. The Six Imams transmitted from him although he inserts some things. He died while he was standing in the prayer in 142 AH.

al-Husayn ibn Muhammad, famous *hafiz* with useful books. He died in 498 AH.

Huyayy ibn Akhtab: a Jew of the Banu'n-Nadr and one of their leaders, the father of Safiyya, the wife of the Prophet, a great opponent of Islam. He did great harm to the Muslims and was captured on the Day of Qurayza and killed.

Ibn 'Abbas: see 'Abdullah ibn 'Abbas.

Ibn 'Abdi'l-Barr an-Numayri, Abu 'Umar, *hafiz* of the Maghrib and Shaykh al-Islam, author of *al-Isti'ab*, He was born in 368 and died in 463 AH.

Ibn Abi Hala: Hind ibn Abi Hala, the son of Khadija, Umm al-Mu'minin, by her first husband, Abu Hala. He was the foster son of the Prophet and looked at him as much as he wished. He is known as Hind the Describer because the Companions were too much in awe of the Prophet to look at him for long. He was killed in the Battle of the Camel on 'Ali's side.

Ibn Abi Layla: Muhammad ibn 'Abdu'r-Rahman al-Ansari, the famous *faqih* who had a recitation (*qira'a*). Hamza, one of the five reciters, studied with him. He has the greatest *fiqh* and knowledge of the people of his time. He had the rank of *mujtahid*.

Ibn Akhtab: two brothers, Huyayy and Abu Yasir, who died unbelievers. Huyayy was the father of Safiyya, the Prophet's wife.

Ibn 'Ata': Abu 'Abdullah Muhammad, the shaykh of his time, died in 399 AH.

Ibn Dasa: Abu Bakr Muhammad, known as Ibn Dasa, one of the shaykhs of *hadith*, famous as one of those who related the *Sunan* of Abu Dawud. Abu Nu'aym al-Isbahani related it from him with an *ijaza*.

Ibn Fuhayra: 'Amir, the *mawla* of Abu Bakr. Abu Bakr bought him from at-Tufayl of Azd and set him free. He became Muslim. He tended the sheep of Abu Bakr and brought the Prophet and him food in the Cave and then made *hijra* with them. He was at Badr and Uhud and was killed at B'ir Ma'una. His body was not found among the dead and it was said that the angels had buried him.

Ibn Furak: see Abu Bakr ibn Furak.

Ibn Habib: 'Abdu'l-Malik as-Sulami, one of the children of 'Abbas ibn Mirdas the Companion. He is a *faqih* and grammarian, doctor and scholar of *hadith* and *tafsir*, but he did not have full criticism of *hadith*. He died in 288 or 289 AH.

Ibn al-Hanafiyya: Abu 'Abdullah Muhammad, son of 'Ali ibn Abi Talib. Al-Hanafiyya was his mother. A great Imam and Muslim and al-Bukhari and others transmitted from him. One of the great Followers. Died in Madina in 80 AH.

Ibn Hanbal: see Ahmad ibn Hanbal.

Ibn Ishaq: Muhammad. A great scholar. He has rare *hadith* which are sometimes disacknowledged because of his vast memory. He wrote the Maghazi. He died in 151 AH.

Ibn al-Jallab, Abu'l-Qasim: known by his *kunya*. He was the companion of Qadi Abu Bakr al-Abhuri. He wrote books and died in 378 AH.

Ibn Jubayr: see Sa'id ibn Jubayr.

Ibn Jurayj: 'Abdu'l-Malik, called Abu'l-Walid, a reliable Imam, the first to write works in Islam. He died in 150 AH.

Ibn Khalawayh: Muhammad, grammarian, linguist, and literist in Baghdad and then moved to Syria. Studied with Ibn al-Anbari and as-Sayrafi. Wrote excellent books and good poetry. He died in Aleppo in 370 AH.

Ibn al-Madini: 'Ali ibn 'Abdullah, Abu Hasan. The Imam of the people of *hadith* in his time. An-Nasa'i says that it is as if Allah only created him for this business. He died in 234 AH when he was 73.

Ibn Mahdi, 'Abdu'r-Rahman al-Basri, known as al-Lu'lu'i, one of the *hadith* scholars. Ibn al-Madini said, "Ibn Mahdi is the person with the greatest knowledge of *hadith*." Az-Zuhri said, "I never saw a book in his hand," i.e. he knew his *hadith* by heart. Ibn Hanbal and the Six transmitted from him. He died in 196 AH.

Ibn al-Majishun: 'Abdu'l-Malik ibn Majishun. The *faqih* and companion of Malik. He died in 214 or 212 AH. The Six transmitted from him. His name was actually Maymun or Ya'qub.

Ibn Mujahid: Ahmad ibn Musa at-Tamimi: the chief of the reciters, and the first to compile the recitations. He was born in 245 AH.

Ibn al-Mundhir: Abu Bakr: Imam Abu Bakr Muhammad ibn Ibrahim an-Nisapuri, a reliable scholar and Imam of his age. He died in Makka in 309 or 310 AH.

Ibn al-Munkadir: he is Muhammad ibn al-Munkadir at-Taymi who had *hadith* from his father and from 'A'isha and Abu Hurayra. The authors of the Six transmit from him.

Ibn al-Muqaffa': 'Abdullah, one of the Imams of the Book, the first to translate the books of logic from Persian. He was born in Iraq as a Zoroastrian and became Muslim through 'Isa ibn 'Ali, the uncle of as-Saffah. He was suspected of dualism and executed in Basra by its amir, Sufyan al-Muhallabi in 142 AH.

Ibn Qani': 'Abdu'l-Baqi ibn Qani' al-Umawi al-Baghdadi, the author of the *Dictionary of the Companions*. He died in 351 AH. He related *hadith* in this book and at-Tabarani relates from him.

Ibn Qasim: Abu'l-'Atiqi 'Abdu'r-Rahman who had both knowledge and asceticism. An Imam and *faqih*. He kept the company of Malik for twenty years and went to him twelve times, and spent a thousand dinars each time. Al-Bukhari, Abu Dawud and an-Nasa'i transmit from him. He is reliable. He died in Egypt in 191 AH.

Ibn Qassar: Abu'l-Hasan 'Ali ibn 'Umar, a reliable *faqih* and *qadi* who has a book on the differences. He is a Maliki Imam. He died in 398 AH.

Ibn Rahawayh: see Ishaq ibn Rahawayh.

Ibn Sa'd: see Muhammad ibn Sa'd.

Ibn Sha'ban: Abu Ishaq al-Misri al-Maliki, or Muhammad Qasim al-Misri. He died in 155 AH. Ibn Hazim says he is weak.

Ibn Shanbudh: Abu'l-Hasan Muhammad ibn Ahmad, one of the scholars of recitation in the same generation as Ibn Mujahid who was his rival. He was an eminent scholar in spite of his carelessness. Scholars objected to some of his recitations.

Ibn Shihab: Muhammad ibn Muslim az-Zuhri. A *faqih* and *hadith* scholar, one of the most knowledgeable of the Followers. He saw ten of the Companions. 'Umar ibn 'Abdu'l-'Aziz wrote to all regions, "You must have Ibn Shihab. You will not find anyone with more knowledge of the past *sunna* than him." He died in 124 AH.

Ibn Sirin: Muhammad ibn Sirin al-Basri al-Ansari by *wala'*. The Imam of his time in the sciences of the *deen* in Basra, a Follower who is reliable in *fiqh* and who relates *hadith* and is related from by the Six Imams. He was known for his scrupulousness and dream interpretation. He died in 110 AH.

Ibn Suriya: 'Abdullah ibn Suriya al-A'war. One of the Jewish rabbis in Madina. He is the one who covered up the *ayat* of stoning with his hand. They disagree about whether he became Muslim or died an unbeliever.

Ibn 'Umar: see 'Abdullah ibn 'Umar.

Ibn 'Uyayna: see Sufyan ibn 'Uyayna.

Ibn Wahb: Abu Muhammad 'Abdullah ibn Wahb al-Fihri al-Misri, one of the scholars in *hadith*. He was asked to be *qadi* but was averse and cut himself off until he died in 196 AH. He learned his *fiqh* with Malik and related from him and others. He wrote down the *Muwatta'*.

Ibn az-Zubayr: see 'Abdullah ibn az-Zubayr.

Ibn Zahr: 'Abdullah ibn Zahr al-Ifriqi, the authors of the *Sunan* relate from him and al-Bukhari transmits from him.

Ibrahim ibn Muhammad ibn Ibrahim: Abu Ishaq al-Isfara'ini, scholar of *fiqh* and the sources. He was called Ruknu'd-din. He grew up in Isfara'in and then went to Nisapur. He built a great madrasa there and taught in it. Then he travelled to Khorasan and certain regions of Iraq. He was famous and reliable in the transmission of *hadith*. He had debates with the Mu'tazilites in Nisapur. He died in Isfara'in in 418 AH.

Ibrahim ibn Yazid: an-Nakh'i, Abu 'Imran, one of the great Followers in correctness, truthfulness, transmission and memory of *hadith*. The *faqih* of Iraq. He was an Imam and *mujtahid* who had a *madh-hab*. He died in 96 AH.

Al-'Ida' ibn Khalid: he became Muslim when Makka was conquered and was a good Muslim.

Ihban ibn Aws al-Aslami: the Companion who settled in Kufa and died in the khalifate of Mu'awiya.

'Ikrima ibn 'Abdullah: the client of Ibn 'Abbas, a Follower, one of the *fuqaha'* of Madina and its Followers. He is one of the Imams who is followed in *tafsir* and *hadith*. He died in 107 AH.

'Imran ibn Husayn al-Khuza'i, called Abu 'Ubayd: he became Muslim at Khaybar and went on many expeditions. He carried the banner of Khuza'a. He was one of the best Companions and one of their *fuqaha'*. He died in 52 AH.

al-'Irbad ibn Sariyya as-Sulami: a famous Companion who was one of the people of the Suffa. He is one of those about whom it was revealed, "*...neither against those who, when they came to you, for you to mount them, and you said, 'I do not find anything on which to mount you,' turned away with their eyes overflowing with tears.*" (9:92) He became Muslim early on and died in 75 AH.

al-Isfara'ini: see Ibrahim ibn Muhammad.

Ishaq ibn 'Abdullah ibn Abi Talha al-Ansari: the Six *Sahih* Collections transmit from him, and he transmitted from his father and others. He was a Follower, an authority and reliable. He died in 132 AH.

Ishaq ibn Rahawayh at-Tamimi: called Abu Ya'qub al-Maruz, the scholar of Khorasan in his time and the Amir al-Mu'minin in *hadith*. He revived the *sunna* in the east. He travelled throughout the lands to gather *hadith*. Whenever he heard anything he remembered it and did not forget it. Ibn Hanbal, al-Bukhari, Muslim, at-Tirmidhi, an-Nasa'i and others took from him. He lived in Nisapur and died there in 238 AH.

Isma'il ibn Ishaq al-Azdi al-Basri: the *qadi* and scholar in all areas of knowledge and in literature. He knew the book of Sibuwayh well and so was claimed to be one of al-Mubarrad's people. He died suddenly in Baghdad in 282 AH.

Jabir ibn 'Abdullah: the Companion. He was born in Abyssinia when his parents emigrated there. He was generous and eloquent. He was present at all the battles except Badr. The Prophet asked forgiveness for him twenty-five times when he paid his father's debt. He related 1500 *hadiths*. He was the last of the Companions to die in Madina ca. 80 AH.

Jarir ibn 'Abdullah al-Bajali: the master of his people, came to the Prophet in 10 AH. He was very handsome so that 'Umar described him as being the "Yusuf of this community". He had great influence in the victory of Qadisiyya. Then he lived in Kufa. He died in 51 AH.

Jubayr ibn Muhammad ibn Mut'im: related from his father and grandfather. Abu Dawud transmits one *hadith* from him. Ibn Hibban mentioned him as reliable.

Jubayr ibn Mut'im: a Companion who became Muslim after Hudaybiyya. His sons Muhammad and Rafi' related from him and Ibn al-Musayyab related from him. He was a serious master. The Six Imams and Ibn Hanbal transmit from him. He died in 59 AH.

al-Jubba'i: Abu 'Ali Muhammad ibn 'Abdu'l-Wahhab, one of the early Imams of the Mu'tazilites who was very proficient in the science of *kalam*. Al-Ash'ari studied with him for a period of forty years and then reversed his position and became the Imam of the people of the *Sunna*. He had excellent debates with him. Al-Jubba'i died in 303 AH.

Jabir ibn Samura: Abu 'Abdullah, the nephew of Sa'd ibn Abi Waqqas. He died in Kufa in 72 AH.

Ja'far ibn Abi Talib al-Hashimi: one of the bravest Companions, known as "Ja'far at-Tayyar". He was the brother of 'Ali and was ten years older than him. He was one of the first people to become Muslim. He was at the Battle of Mu'ta in 8 AH and martyred there with seventy wounds in his body.

Ja'far ibn Muhammad as-Sadiq ibn 'Ali ibn al-Husayn ibn 'Ali ibn Abi Talib: He was born in 80 AH. He is one of the most eminent men and scholars of the People of the House. He died in 184 AH and was buried in al-Baqi' in the same grave with his father, grandfather and uncle.

Ja'far ibn Sulayman ibn 'Ali ibn 'Abdullah ibn 'Abbas: the cousin of Abu Ja'far al-Mansur for whom he was the governor of Madina.

Jami' ibn Shaddad: Abu Damra al-Asadi al-Muharibi al-Kufi, Abu Dawud and an-Nasa'i transmit from him. He was considered reliable and died in 118 AH.

al-Junayd: Abu'l-Qasim ibn Muhammad: shaykh of his time and unique of his age. His family originated from Nihawand and he grew up in Iraq. His *fiqh* was taken from ath-Thawri and Sufyan. He took his *tariqa* from as-Sirri as-Saqati and al-Muhasibi. He died in 297 AH. He was one of the Shafi'i *fuqaha'* and is buried in Baghdad.

al-Juwayni: Abu'l-Mu'ali: Imam of the Two Harams, 'Abdu'l-Malik ibn 'Abdullah, the Imam of the Arabs and non-Arabs, unique in his time, the possessor of virtues and author of excellent books. He was the shaykh of al-Ghazzali and died in 478 AH.

Ka'b al-Ahbar: also known by his proper name, Ka'b ibn Mati'. He was alive in the time of the Prophet, but did not see him. He became Muslim in the khalifate of Abu Bakr and kept the company of 'Umar. A lot is related from him and the Companions related from him. He lived in the Yemen and then in Hims after he became Muslim, and he died there in 'Uthman's khalifate in 32 AH.

Ka'b ibn Malik: a famous poet who was at 'Aqaba and gave his allegiance there. He missed Badr but was at Uhud and the later battles. He stayed behind from the expedition to Tabuk and was one of the three who repented and were turned to. He died in Syria during Mu'awiya's khalifate.

Ka'b ibn 'Ujra: Abu Muhammad, a Companion who was present at the Pledge of Ridwan and died in 51 or 52 AH. The Six and others transmit from him.

Ka'b ibn Zuhayr al-Muzani: he and his brother Bujayr were excellent poets and his brother became Muslim before him. After his brother became Muslim, Ka'b wrote a poem insulting the Prophet and his brother wrote him a letter saying that the enemies of the Messenger of Allah were as good as slain. Ka'b became distressed and went in repentance to the Prophet and recited a poem addressed to the Prophet which begins, "Su'ad is gone," and then the Prophet gave him his cloak.

al-Kalbi, Abu'n-Nasr Muhammad ibn as-Sa'ib: genealogist, commentator, transmitter and historian. Most say that he is not reliable.

Kathir ibn Zayd al-Aslami: the *mawla* of the Banu Sahm. He has many *hadiths*, although there is some weakness and looseness in his *hadiths*. He died at the end of the khalifate of Abu Ja'far around 158 AH.

Khadija bint Khuwaylid: the first wife of the Prophet who endured many of the burdens of the call with the Prophet at the beginning of his message. The best of his wives because of all that she endured up until she died after the Muslims had been beseiged in the ravine of the Banu Hashim before the *hijra*.

Khalid ibn 'Abdu'l-'Uzza al-Khuza'i: Abu Khannas, he was a Companion. Ibn Mas'ud related from him. He was the nephew of Khadija. He emigrated to Abyssinia the second time and died en route.

Khalid ibn Ma'dan: a Syrian Follower who related from Ibn 'Umar, Thawban and Mu'awiya. One of the great Followers and one of their leading men of *zuhd*. He met seventy Companions. The Six *Sahih* Collections transmit from him. He used to say 40,000 *tasbihs* every day. He died in 104 AH.

Khalid ibn Sa'id ibn al-'As ibn Umayya: a Companion. He was the third, fourth or fifth to become Muslim. There is no *hadith* from him in the Six Books, but others like at-Tabarani relate from him.

Khalid ibn al-Walid: the Sword of Allah. He was one of the nobles of Quraysh in the *Jahiliyya* and was with the idol-worshippers in the wars against Islam until the *'umra* of al-Hudaybiyya. He became Muslim before Makka was conquered. Abu Bakr sent him to fight the apostates and then to Iraq and then to Syria. He made him commander of the commanders there. When 'Umar became khalif, he dismissed Khalid and appointed Abu 'Ubayda ibn al-Jarrah in his place. He died in

Hims. He was an eloquent speaker and resembled 'Umar in his character and description.

Kharija ibn Zayd: al-Ansari al-Madani the Follower. One of the seven *fuqaha'* of Madina. Died in 99 AH.

al-Khattabi: Abu Sulayman Hamd, a leader in all branches of knowledge, especially *hadith*, *fiqh* and literature. He was a Shafi'i and wrote excellent books, including *Ma'alam as-Sunan*, *Gharib al-Hadith*, *Explanation of the Beautiful Names of Allah* and others. He was an excellent poet and died in Bust in 308 AH.

Khawla bint Qays al-Ansariya an-Najjariya: a Companion, married to Hamza ibn 'Abdu'l-Muttalib, the Prophet's uncle.

Khubayb ibn Yasaf: one of the Ansar. He is also known as Abu Yasaf or Isaf. He did not become Muslim until the Prophet had left for Badr. He became Muslim and joined him and was present at Badr.

Khuraym ibn Fatik: he was present at Badr and died in Raqqa in the time of Mu'awiya. Ibn 'Asakir related from him.

al-Kisa'i: Abu'l-Hasan 'Ali ibn Hamza, one of the seven reciters, the Imam of grammar, language and recitations. He lived to the age of 70 and was given the title of al-Kisa'i by his shaykh Hamza because he wore the *kisa'* (a kind of garment). He died in 183 AH in Rayy.

Kurayb ibn Abi Muslim: a *mawla* of the Banu Hashim, a Follower considered to be reliable. He died in Madina in 98 AH.

Labid: a man from the Banu Zurayq, a subtribe of the Ansar. He was either a Jew or a hypocrite.

al-Layth ibn Sa'd ibn 'Abdu'r-Rahman al-Fihri al-Misri: the excellent *faqih* about whom it was said, "He had more *fiqh* than Malik but his companions wasted him." He was a Follower of the Followers and died in 175 AH. Malik said that he was one of the people of knowledge.

Lubana bint al-Harith ibn Harb: called Umm al-Fadl after her daughter, al-Fadl. She was married to al-'Abbas, the uncle of the Prophet. One of the nobles of Quraysh. It is said that she was the first woman to become Muslim after Khadija.

Luqman ibn 'Anqa': said to be the nephew of the Prophet Da'ud and it was from him that he took his wisdom. They disagree about whether he was a Prophet or a *wali*. Most have the opinion that he was a *wali* going by the *hadith* related from Ibn 'Umar from the Prophet, "Luqman was not a Prophet, but he was a servant who reflected much and who had excellent certainty. He loved Allah and Allah loved him and gave him wisdom."

al-Makhzumi: al-Mughira ibn 'Abdu'r-Rahman al-Makhzumi, the *faqih* of Madina after Malik. Born 124 AH and died in 188 AH.

Makki: See Abu Talib al-Makki.

Malik ibn Anas: born in Madina in 95 AH, the famous Imam of Madina in *fiqh* and *hadith*. One of the four Imams. It is enough that ash-Shafi'i was one of his pupils. He had great knowledge and *deen*. He died in Madina in 189 AH.

Malik ibn Aws ibn al-Hadhathan: from the tribe of Hawazin, he lived in both the *Jahiliyya* and Islam. The Six Collections transmit from him. There is disagreement about whether he was a Companion who saw the Prophet and related *hadith* directly from him, or a Follower with *mursal hadith*. It is probable he was a Follower. He died in 92 AH.

Malik ibn Sa'sa'a al-Khazraji al-Mazini: al-Bukhari, Muslim, at-Tirmidhi, an-Nasa'i and Ibn Hanbal transmit from him. There is only the *hadith* of the *Isra'* (Night Journey) related from him in the books. An-Nawawi said that he related five *hadith* from the Prophet and al-Bukhari and Muslim agree on the one mentioned, which is the best *hadith* concerning the *Isra'*.

Malik ibn Sinan: the father of Abu Sa'id al-Khudri. He was one of the great Companions. At Uhud, he drank the Prophet's blood and the Prophet said,"Whoever has my blood touch his will not mix with wrong action." He was killed as a martyr in that battle.

Malik ibn Yukhamir: Saksaki al-Himsi: said to have been a Companion, but more likely a Follower. He related from Mu'adh ibn Jabal, 'Abdu'r-Rahman ibn 'Awf and others. He died in 70 AH.

Ma'mar ibn Rashid: the scholar of the Yemen. He related from az-Zuhri and others and many related from him. The Six Collections transmit from him. He died in 153 AH in the Yemen.

Marwan ibn al-Hakam: the Umayyad Khalif who was born in 2 AH. He did not transmit anything. His reign lasted nine months and some days. He died in Ramadan in 65 AH.

Masruq ibn Ajda' al-Hamdani: one of the scholars. He learned *fatwa* from Shurayh. The Six *Sahih* Collections transmit from him. He is called Masruq (stolen) because he was stolen as a child and then found. He died in 63 AH.

al-Mawardi, 'Ali ibn Habib the Qadi: he has splendid books on *tafsir*, Shafi'i *fiqh* and the *usul* and *hadith* like *al-Hawi* and *al-Ahkam as-Sultaniyya*. He died in 450 AH when he was 86.

al-Miqdad ibn 'Amr al-Bahrani: famous as al-Aswad because he was a grave-digger. He was a famous Companion and a great hero. He was one of the first seven people to become Muslim and the first to fight on a horse in the way of Allah. He was present at Badr and other battles and lived in Madina. He died in 'Uthman's khalifate and was buried in Madina.

al-Miqdam ibn Ma'dikarib al-Kindi: Abu Salih, a Companion who settled in Hims and the authors of the *Sunan* transmit from him as did Ibn Hanbal. He was one of those who came to the Prophet from Kinda. He died in Syria in 87 AH when he was 71.

Mu'adh ibn Jabal: al-Khazraji al-Ansari: a leading authority of the science of the *halal* and the *haram*. He had a very clear white face, shining teeth and dark eyes. He was present at the Battle of Badr when he was 11. The Prophet appointed him governor over Yemen. He was the best of the young men of Madina in forbearance, modesty and generosity, handsomeness. He died of the great plague in 17 AH.

Mu'arrid ibn Mu'ayqib: al-Yamami, he died in the time of 'Ali.

Mu'awiya ibn Abi Sufyan: a Companion son of a Companion, the *Amir al-Mu'minin*. He died in 60 AH. He possessed the wrapper and the cloak of the Prophet and some of his hair and nails, He was shrouded in this cloak and wrapper and the hair and nails were placed in his mouth and nose according to his will.

Mu'awiya ibn Thawr: he came to the Prophet in a delegation when he was an old man with his son Bishr. The Prophet made supplication for him and rubbed his head and gave him ten goats. It is related that the Prophet taught Mu'awiya and his son *Yasin*, the *Fatiha* and the last two *suras*.

Mu'awwidh ibn 'Afra': an Ansar. He and his brother killed the enemy of Allah, Abu Jahl. He was martyred at the Battle of Badr.

al-Mubarrad: Abu'l-'Abbas Muhammad ibn Yazid, the master of grammar and Arabic in Basra. He studied with Abu 'Amr al-Jurmi and Abu 'Uthman al-Mazini. He wrote many books, the most famous of which is *al-Kamil*. Born in 210 and died in 285 AH.

al-Mughira ibn Nawfal ibn al-Harith: the Companion. He was born in Makka before the *hijra* and was one of the helpers of 'Ali. He was a *qadi* in 'Uthman's khalifate.

al-Mughira ibn Shu'ba: he became Muslim before the *'umra* of al-Hudaybiyya and was present there and at the Pledge of Ridwan. He was one of the most astute of the Arabs. He died in 50 AH.

al-Muhajir ibn Abi Umayya: his name had been al-Walid and the Prophet disliked it and named him al-Muhajir because al-Walid was the name of a tyrant of Egypt. He was the brother of Umm Salama, the Prophet's wife. The Prophet sent him to the Yemen to al-Harith ibn 'Abdu'l-Kilal al-Himyari and put him in charge of *zakat*. In the *Ridda*, Abu Bakr sent him to fight the apostates in the Yemen and he won victories and great renown in the Yemen.

al-Muhallab ibn Qubala: said to be the one who came to the Messenger of Allah with a scrotal hernia, although it is also said that that was al-Muhallab ibn Yazid.

Muhammad ibn 'Abdu'l-Hakam: Abu 'Abdullah al-Misri, the companion of ash-Shafi'i. In his time, there was no-one who had greater knowledge of what the Companions and the Followers had said. He was born in 182 AH and died in 268 or 269 AH. An-Nasa'i transmits from him. He transmitted from Ibn Wahb and others.

Muhammad ibn 'Ali Zayd al-'Abidin ibn al-Husayn ibn 'Ali: Abu Ja'far al-Baqir, he was very devout and did a lot of *'ibada*. He was born in Madina and died in al-Hamima and was buried in Madina in 114 AH.

Muhammad ibn Jubayr ibn Mut'im: a Follower from Madina, reliable, but with few *hadith*. He died in the khalifate of Sulayman ibn 'Abdu'l-Malik.

Muhammad ibn Ka'b al-Qurazi: Abu Hamza, one of the allies of al-Aws. He lived in Kufa and then Madina, a Follower. He related from many Companions. He was one of the best of the people of Madina in knowledge and *fiqh*. He died in 108 AH.

Muhammad ibn Maslama al-Ansari: Abu 'Abdu'r-Rahman al-Madani, the ally of the Banu 'Abdu'l-Ashhal. He was born twenty-two years before the Prophet's mission. He was a Companion and was present at Badr. He died in Madina in 43 AH.

Muhammad ibn al-Mawwaz: Imam Muhammad ibn Ibrahim, one of the excellent Maliki Imams who is reliable. He was from Alexandria. He died in one of the Syrian fortresses where he was hiding, fleeing from civil strife. He died in 281 AH.

Muhammad ibn Sa'd: the great reliable Imam, the *mawla* of the Banu Hashim, author of the *Tabaqat*, He died in 204 AH.

Muhammad ibn as-Sa'ib al-Kalbi, Abu Nasr: Qur'an commentator, *hadith* scholar and genealogist. At-Tirmidhi transmits from him. He was from the tribe of Kalb and died in 184 AH.

Muhammad ibn Uhayha al-Awsi: Ibn 'Abdu'l-Barr counts him as a Companion but Ibn Hajar is not sure.

Muhammad ibn Usama ibn Zayd ibn Haritha: Zayd **was** the *mawla* of the Messenger of Allah and he related from his father. He died in the khalifate of al-Walid ibn 'Abdu'l-Malik.

Muhammad ibn Ziyad: Abu'l-Harith al-Madani, a Follower. The authors of the Six Collections transmit from him. Ibn Hanbal, Ibn Ma'in, at-Tirmidhi, an-Nasa'i, Ibn al-Junayd and Ibn Hibban consider him reliable.

al-Muhasibi: see al-Harith ibn Asad al-Muhasibi.

Mujahid: Abu Muhammad ibn Jibr, one of the great Followers. The authors of the *Sunan* and others transmit from him. *Hadith* scholars consider him reliable as adh-Dhahabi has mentioned. He was born in the khalifate of 'Umar in 21 AH and died in Makka in 102 AH while in sajda.

al-Mukhtar ibn 'Ubayd ath-Thaqafi: His father became Muslim in the Prophet's lifetime but did not see him so is not considered to be a Companion. This man claimed that Jibril came to him. He began to praise Ibn az-Zubayr and Muhammad ibn al-Hanafiyya, and gained power in Kufa. He was a partisan for the Shi'a. Many people joined him and he tried to undertake to avenge al-Husayn and killed many of those who had killed him. He was very influential and gave prophetic utterances, claiming that he received revelation and had a chair which resembled the Ark of the Banu Isra'il. He was misguided and misguided others. He persisted in that until he was killed by Mus'ab ibn az-Zubayr.

al-Mundhir ibn Malik al-'Abdi an-Niffari: he related from Ibn 'Abbas and others. The authors of the *Sunan* transmit from him. He was eloquent and reliable. He died in 109 AH.

Musa ibn Isma'il: one of the *hadith* scholars from whom al-Bukhari and Abu Dawud relate. 'Abbas ad-Dawri said, "We wrote 35,000 *hadith* from him. He is reliable and firm. The authors of the Six Collections transmit from him. He died in 223 AH.

Mus'ab ibn 'Umayr ibn Hashim al-Qurashi: a brave Companion, one of the first people to become Muslim. He became Muslim in Makka and concealed it. When he told his family, they locked him up. He fled with those who emigrated to Madina. He was the first to gather for the *Jum'a* in Madina. He was known as "the Reciter". It was through him that Usayd ibn Hudayr and Sa'd ibn Mu'adh became Muslim. He was present at Badr and carried the banner at Uhud and was martyred. In Makka, he was a young man with youth, beauty and blessing. When he displayed his Islam, he became ascetic. He was called "Mus'ab the Good." It is said that it was about him and his companions that the *ayat* was revealed, "*Among the believers are men who were true to their covenant with Allah.*"

Musaylima ibn Tamama al-Hanafi: born and raised in Yamama and came in delegation to the Prophet. During the lifetime of the Prophet, he proclaimed himself a Prophet and wrote a letter saying, "From Musaylima the Messenger of Allah to Muhammad the Messenger of Allah." The Prophet replied, "To Musaylima the Liar." That was at the end of 10 AH. He was killed by Khalid ibn al-Walid in the *Ridda* wars in the khalifate of Abu Bakr in 12 AH.

Muslim: Abu'l-Husayn Muslim ibn al-Hajjaj, one of the Imams. He came to Baghdad more than once and gave *hadith* there. He composed his *Sahih* from 3000 *hadith*, and it is said to be the soundest book of *hadith*. Born in 206 AH and died in 261 AH.

Muslim ibn Abi 'Imran al-Azdi al-Kufi: he related from 'Ata', Mujahid, Sa'id ibn Jubayr and others. Ibn Hanbal, Abu Hatim, an-Nasa'i and others said that he is reliable.

al-Mustawrid ibn Shaddad al-Qurashi: he settled in Kufa. He and his father were Companions. He was present at the conquest of Egypt. He died in Alexandria in 45 AH.

Mutarrif ibn 'Abdullah, Abu Mus'ab: the *mawla* of Maymuna al-Hilaliyya. He was the nephew of Malik ibn Anas. He died in 220 AH.

al-Muttalib ibn Abi Wada'a al-Qurashi: he was the same age as the Prophet. He was captured at the Battle of Badr and the Prophet said, "He has a son Kays who is a wealthy merchant," indicating he would ransom his father and that was indeed the case.

al-Muzani: Abu Ibrahim ibn Isma'il. Ash-Shafi'i said about him, "If he had debated with Shaytan, he would have defeated him." He died in 264 AH.

Nafi': the *mawla* of 'Abdullah ibn 'Umar who bought him from the booty of Khorasan. The teacher of the Shaykh al-Islam Malik. He is a famous reliable Imam and Follower. The *Sunan* transmit from him. He died in Madina in 117 AH.

an-Nadr ibn al-Harith: someone who was very hostile to the Prophet. He was captured at Badr and the Prophet ordered 'Ali to kill him.

an-Nakh'i: see Ibrahim ibn Yazid.

an-Naqqash: Abu Bakr Muhammad ibn al-Hasan, reciter and commentator. He related from Abu Muslim al-Kajji and his generation. He became the shaykh of the reciters of the variants in his time although he had some weaknesses.

an-Nasa'i: Abu 'Abdu'r-Rahman ibn Shu'ayb, born in 225 AH. He studied with the great Imams and scholars and went to those who were mentioned as having knowledge in his time. He was a Shafi'i and wrote on the rites of *Hajj* according to the Shafi'ites. His scrupulousness led to his being killed. He compiled one of the Six *Sahih* Collections of *hadith*. He died in Makka in 303 AH and is buried there.

Niftawayh: title of Abu 'Abdullah Ibrahim ibn Muhammad, born in 244 and died in 323 AH.

an-Nu'man ibn Bashir: the Khazraji Ansari Companion who was at the Battle of Badr. He was the first to offer his allegiance to Abu Bakr although very young and was with Khalid ibn al-Walid when he left Yamama in 64 AH. An-Nu'man was the first child born after the *hijra*. He was born four months after it. Mu'awiya appointed him governor over Hims and Kufa.

an-Nu'man ibn Muqarrin al-Muzani: Abu 'Amr, one of the Companions present at the conquest of Makka. He was the banner bearer of Muzayna on that day. He settled in Basra and then moved to Kufa. He fought al-Hamdani and defeated him. 'Umar sent him to attack Isfahan and he conquered it. Then he went to Nihawand where he was martyred in 21 AH. When 'Umar heard of his death, he entered the mosque and announced his death to the people from the minbar. Then he put his hand on his head, weeping.

an-Nuwwar bint Malik ibn Mu'awiya al-Ansariyya: she transmitted from the Prophet. She was married to Thabit ibn Qays and then 'Umara. Her son was Zayd ibn Thabit.

Qatada ibn Di'ama: Abu'l-Khattab as-Sadusi, related from 'Abdullah ibn Sirjis, Anas and many people. He died in 117 AH.

Qatada ibn an-Nu'man al-Awsi: the brother of Abu Sa'id al-Khudri from the same mother. He is Abu 'Amr al-Ansari. He was present at the Battle of Badr and Abu Sa'id al-Khudri, his son 'Umar ibn Qatada, Mahmud ibn Labid and others related from him. He lived to be 65.

Qatan ibn Haritha al-'Ulaymi: a Companion who came to the Prophet and asked him to pray for him and his people for rain.

Qayla bint Makhrama: Hanafiyya and Duhaybiyya related from her.

Qays ibn Sa'd: The captain of the *Shurta* (guard) for the Prophet. He was tall and well-built and a good officer with intelligence and cleverness. He died in Madina at the end of Mu'awiya's khalifate.

Qays ibn Zayd al-Judhami: also known as Qays al-Agharr. It is related that he came to the Prophet and he made him leader over his village and wiped his head and made supplication for him. His son Na'il was in charge of of Judham in Syria.

al-Qushayri: Abu'l-Qasim 'Abdu'l-Karim, the shaykh of Khorasan in his time in asceticism and knowledge of the *deen*. He was based at Nisapur and died there in 465 AH. He has various books, the most famous of which is the *Risala al-Qushayriya* about *tasawwuf* and the biographies of the Sufis, and the *Lata'if al-Isharat* on *tafsir*.

Qadi al-Qushayri: 'Abdu'r-Rahman, the son of Imam Abu'l-Qasim 'Abdu'l-Karim, died in 514 AH in Nisapur.

al-Qutaybi: 'Abdullah ibn Muslim ad-Dinawari al-Baghdadi: the famous Imam, he takes his name by his relationship to his grandfather, Qutayba. He died in 276 AH and wrote many books.

Quzman: the *mawla* of one of the Ansar. He was brave, but a hypocrite. He fought fiercely so that the Companions admired him, but it was not for Allah. Allah acquainted the Messenger of Allah with his state.

ar-Rabi' ibn Anas: Abu Hatim al-Bakri al-Basri, the Follower. He lived in Khorasan. A truthful man who related from Anas, but had some weaknesses in his transmissions. He died in 139 AH.

ar-Rabi' ibn Khuthaym: he related from Ibn Mas'ud and Abu Ayyub and many people related from him. He was reliable. Ibn Mas'ud said to him, "If the Prophet had seen you, he would have loved you." The authors of the Six Collections transmit from him. He died in 67 AH.

Rafi' ibn Mahran: Abu'l-'Aliy: a Follower. He became Muslim in the khalifate of Abu Bakr. Muslim and al-Bukhari transmit from him. He wrote a *tafsir* and died in 90 AH.

ar-Razi: Muhammad ibn 'Umar, Imam of *tafsir* who was unique in his time in judgement and transmission and basic sciences. He is a Qurashi from Tabaristan, born in Rayy.

Rukana: ibn 'Abdu Yazid: a Companion. He became Muslim when Makka was conquered. He was famous for his strength in wrestling and no-one could throw him. The Prophet wrestled with him and threw him. He died in Madina in Mu'awiya's khalifate in 42 AH.

as-Sabbagh: Abu Nasr, a great Imam who was the leader of the Shafi'ites in his time. He was very godfearing and scrupulous. He died in 477 AH.

Sa'd ibn Abi Waqqas: one of the Ten promised the Garden and the last of them to die. He was the first to shoot an arrow in the way of Allah. He was one of the six people of the Council after 'Umar's death. He died at al-'Aqiq and was carried to Madina and prayed over in the mosque. He died in 55 AH.

Safina: the *mawla* of the Messenger of Allah. His name was Ruman and the Prophet named him Safina because on one of his journeys, the Prophet saw him carrying his baggage and said, "You are a ship (*safina*)." He was one of his servants. Muslim and other authors of the *Sunan* transmit from him.

Safiyya bint Najda: the wife of Abu Mahdhura. Ayyub ibn Thabit related from her and she related from her husband.

Safwan ibn Qudama: from Tamim. Both he and his son, 'Abdu'r-Rahman, were Companions although it is said that his son was a Follower.

Safwan ibn Sulaym: an Imam and Follower. The authors of the *Sunan* related from him. He died in 132 AH.

Safwan ibn Umayya ibn Khalaf al-Jumahi. Abu Wahb. A Companion. He was very eloquent. He was one of the nobles of Quraysh in the *Jahiliyya* and Islam. He became Muslim on the Day of the Conquest of Makka and was present at Hunayn and Ta'if. When the Prophet gave him an enormous gift, he said, "By Allah, only a Prophet would be content to give such a gift," and became Muslim. The authors of the Six Collections transmit from him. He was at Yarmuk. He died in Mu'awiya's khalifate in Makka in 42 AH. He has twenty-three *hadith* in Muslim and al-Bukhari.

Sahl ibn 'Abdullah ibn Yunus at-Tustari: famous man of right action, unique in knowledge and scrupulousness. A Sufi shaykh and ascetic. He had famous miracles (*karamat*) and kept the company of Dhu'n-Nun al-Misri in Makka. He was born in 200 AH in Tustar and died in Basra in 273 AH.

Sahl ibn Sa'd as-Sa'idi, one of the famous companions. It is said that his name was Huzn (sadness) and the Prophet changed it. Az-Zuhri said the Prophet died when Sahl was 15. He was the last of the Companions to die in Madina. He died in 91 AH.

Sahnun: Abu Sa'id 'Abdu's-Salam, the Maliki *faqih* and *qadi* of North Africa. He met Malik but did not take from him. He wrote the *Mudawanna* on Maliki *fiqh* and more from Malik than anyone else. He died in 240 AH.

as-Sa'ib ibn Yazid: a Companion. He was born in the beginning of the first year of the *hijra*. He was with his father when the Prophet went on the Hajj of Farewell. 'Umar put him in charge of the market of Madina. He was one of the last of the Companions to die there. He has twenty-two *hadith* in the *Sahih* volumes.

Sa'id ibn Abi Karb: or Kurayb. A Follower whom Abu Zur'a considers to be reliable and whom Ibn Hibban says is unknown.

Sa'id ibn al-Musayyab: Imam of the Followers and their master. He had both *fiqh* and *hadith* and *'ibada* and scrupulousness. It is related that he prayed the *Subh* prayer with the *wudu'* from *'Isha'* for fifty years. He said, "I have not missed the first *takbir* nor looked at the back of a man's neck in the prayer for fifty years." He was born in the last two years of the khalifate of 'Umar. He died in Madina in 91 AH.

Sa'id ibn Jubayr: one of the Followers and one of the scholars and transmitters of *hadith*. He related from Ibn 'Abbas and others and the authors of the *Sunan* related from them. Al-Hajjaj killed him unjustly in 95 AH.

Sa'id ibn Mina' al-Makki: Abu'l-Walid, the *mawla* of al-Bukhtari ibn Abi Dhibab. He is reliable according to Ibn Hibban, Abu Hatim and an-Nasa'i.

Sa'id ibn Zayd ibn 'Amr: a Companion, and one of ten promised the Garden. He was present at all the battles except for Badr. He was one of those of judgement and courage. He died in Madina in 51 AH.

Salama ibn al-Akwa': one of the Companions who offered allegiance under the Tree. He went on seven expeditions with the Prophet, including al-Hudaybiyya, Khaybar and Hunayn. He was a brave warrior. He is one of those who made the expedition into North Africa in 'Uthman's reign. He has seventy-seven *hadith* attributed to him and died in Madina.

Salim ibn Abi'l-Ja'd al-Ashja'i al-Kufi: one of the great Followers and reliable ones. He related from Ibn 'Abbas and others. He died in 100 AH.

Salma, the servant girl of the Prophet. It is said that she was the *mawla* of Safiyya, the Prophet's aunt. She was the wife of Abu Rafi', and was the *mawla* of Fatima. She is the one who told Hamza that Abu Jahl had cursed the Prophet so Hamza got angry and went and cracked Abu Jahl's head open. This led to him becoming Muslim.

Salman al-Farisi: Abu 'Abdullah, the *mawla* of the Prophet and lofty Companion. He was from Isfahan and did not leave the Prophet after he was set free. He called himself "Salman al-Islam". He had been one of the men of knowledge among the Companions and one of their men of asceticism. He had read the books of the Persians, the Greeks and the Jews. While travelling to the land of the Arabs, he met a caravan of the Banu Kalb who enslaved him and sold him to a man from Qurayza. Salman heard about Islam and went to Quba' to hear what the Prophet said and became Muslim. The Muslims helped him buy his freedom. He gave the Prophet the idea of digging the ditch. The Prophet said, "Salman is one of us, the People of the House." An-Nawawi says that they agree that he lived to a great age and died in al-Mada'in and was buried there in 35 or 36 AH. The Messenger of Allah said of him, "The Garden yearns for him."

as-Samarqandi, Abu'l-Layth: see Abu'l-Layth.

Samura ibn Jundub: a Companion who was courageous and a leader. He grew up in Madina and settled in Basra and was its governor in the time of Ziyad and after him. He died in Kufa in 60 AH.

Sawad ibn 'Amr: an Ansar and Companion. He is not Sawad ibn Ghaziyya.

ash-Sha'bi: 'Amir ibn Sharahil, a Follower famous for his intelligence. He was the companion of 'Abdu'l-Malik. He was one of the reliable men of *hadith* and died in Kufa in 103 AH.

Shaddad ibn Aws: a Companion who settled in Jerusalem and died in Syria in 58 AH.

ash-Shafi'i: Abu 'Abdullah Muhammad ibn Idris, the scholar of Makka. Born in Ghazza in 150 AH and grew up in Makka. He knew the Qur'an by heart when he was seven. He knew grammar, poetry and language. He memorised the *Muwatta'* in a single night. He gave *fatwas* when he was 15. He travelled to Yemen and then Baghdad and then lived in Egypt. He is the founder of one of the four *madhhabs*. He died in 204 AH.

Sharik ibn Abi Namr: the truthful, reliable Follower, Qadi of Madina. He died in 40 AH.

Shayba ibn 'Uthman ibn Abi Talha: famous Companion. He was the servant of the Ka'ba and had its keys. He became Muslim when Makka was conquered or at Hunayn. He died in 59 AH. Al-Bukhari, Ibn Hanbal and Abu Dawud transmit from him.

ash-Shayma': Judama, the daughter or sister of Halima as-Sa'diyya. She became Muslim as did her father, al-Harith, when he came to Makka.

as-Simintari: he is Abkar ibn 'Atiq ibn 'Ali, one of the men of worship and ascetic people of Jazira and an excellent man who wrote books on sciences and knowledges.

as-Suddi: Isma'il ibn 'Abdu'r-Rahman, famous *hadith* scholar about whom there is some disagreement. Some say he is reliable and others that he lies. He was a Follower from Kufa. He died in 127 AH. Sudd is a place in Madina.

Sufyan ath-Thawri: the scholar of his age in asceticism and *hadith*. The Six Imams transmitted from him. He died in 161 AH.

Sufyan ibn 'Uyayna: one of the scholars and Imams from whom the compilers of the Six *Sahih* Collections transmit. He was one of the Followers of the Followers. He met eighty-six of them. He lived in Makka. He was born in 107 AH and died in 198 AH.

Sufyan ibn Wukay': *hafiz* and Imam. At-Tirmidhi and ad-Daraqutni and others transmit from him. He died in 247 AH.

Suhayl ibn 'Amr: Abu Yazid al-Qurashi, one of the orators of Quraysh. He became Muslim on the day Makka was conquered and was martyred at Yarmuk. It is also said that he died in Syria in 18 AH. Al-Waqidi says that he died in 19 AH in the plague. He used to make speeches urging the idol-worshippers to kill the Prophet. When he was captured at Badr, 'Umar said, "An eloquent man, Messenger of Allah! Let me pull out his two lower front teeth and he will never again speak against you." The Prophet refused.

as-Sulami, Abu 'Abdu'r-Rahman: a shaykh of the Sufis and author of a book on their history, ranks and *tafsir*. He was born in 330 and died in 412 AH.

Sulayman ibn al-Ash'ath: also known as Abu Dawud as-Sijistani, one of the shaykhs of Ibn Hanbal. His virtues are well-known. He was born in 202 and died in 275 AH in Basra.

Suraqa ibn Malik: a Companion. He became Muslim at Ta'if after Makka had been conquered. He died in 24 AH. He was a poet.

Surayj ibn Yunus: One of the Imams of *hadith* in Baghdad. Muslim, al-Baghawi and Abu Hatim transmitted from him. He died in 235 AH.

at-Tabari: Muhammad ibn Jarir Abu Ja'far, one of the scholars and author of famous books. He was from Tabaristan. He did a lot of *tawaf* and *'ibada*. He was born in 224 and died in 310 AH.

at-Tahawi: Ahmad ibn Muhammad ibn Maslama al-Azdi later al-Misri al-Hanafi. The Imam of *hadith* of great value with the *kunya* of Abu Ja'far. He was a Shafi'i and then became a Hanafi. He has excellent books. He was born in 239 and died in 321 AH.

Talha ibn 'Ubaydullah at-Taymi: Abu Muhamma, the Companion, one of the ten promised the Garden and the first to unsheathe his sword in the cause of Islam. He was the cousin of the Prophet and became Muslim when he was twelve. He was present at Uhud and other battles. At Uhud, he used his own body to shield the Prophet and was shot by an arrow in his hand so that his fingers were paralysed.

He carried the Messenger of Allah on his back so he could climb a boulder. He was killed at the Battle of the Camel in 36 AH.

Tamim ad-Dari: the son of Hani' ibn Habib with the *kunya* of Abu Ruqayya. Tamim became Muslim in 9 AH and settled in Madina and then moved to Syria after 'Uthman's murder. He was from the People of the Book who knew their books and had read in them that the Messenger of Allah would be sent. He came to the Prophet and believed in him. He was given a grant of land in Jerusalem.

Tariq ibn 'Abdullah al-Muharibi: he settled in Kufa. An-Nasa'i transmits from him.

Tawus: Imam 'Abdu'r-Rahman ibn Kaysan al-Yamani, he was called Tawus (Peacock) because he was the Peacock of the Qur'an reciters. He was Persian. He was the leader of the Followers in being a proof of knowledge. He was a man of action and asceticism. The authors of the *Sunan* and others transmit from him. He died in Makka and was buried in 106 AH. He went on *hajj* forty times and prayed *Subh* with the *wudu'* from *'Isha'* of the previous night for forty years.

Thabit al-Bunani: the Six Collections transmit from him. He was the leader of the men of knowledge and worship in his time. He died in 127 AH.

Thabit ibn Qays ibn Malik: an Ansari Khazraji. He was the *khatib* of the Ansar and had a loud voice. The Messenger of Allah testified that he was one of the people of the Garden. He died in the Battle of Yamama in 12 AH in Abu Bakr's khalifate.

Tha'laba: Ahmad ibn Yahya ibn Zayd. He was known as the Imam of the Kufans in grammar and language. He transmitted poetry and was a *hadith* relater known for his memory and good diction. He was reliable and a proof. He was born in Baghdad and died there in 291 AH.

Thawban: the *mawla* of the Messenger of Allah, a famous companion. The Prophet bought him and then set him free. He served the Prophet until he died and then moved to ar-Ramla and then Hims and died there in 54 AH.

at-Tufayl ibn Abi Ka'b al-Ansari al-Khazraji: born in the time of the Prophet. Ibn Sa'd and Ibn Hibban consider him reliable.

at-Tufayl ibn 'Amr al-Azdi: He was called "Dhu'n-Nur". He was one of the great Companions and one of the "Companions of Light" who are six: Usayd ibn Hudayr, 'Abbad ibn Bishr, Hamza ibn 'Amr al-Aslami, Qatada ibn an-Nu'man, al-Hasan ibn 'Ali and at-Tufayl. He was killed in the Battle of Yamama in 12 AH.

Thuwayba: a slave-girl set free by Abu Lahab. She became Muslim and died in Makka after the *hijra*.

Tihfa: an-Nahdi from Nahd, a Yemeni tribe. He was their orator when they came to the Prophet in 9 AH.

at-Tirmidhi: Muhammad ibn 'Ali, he is not the author of the *Sunan*. He related from his father and many people related from him when he came to Nisapur in 285 AH. He lived to be about 80. People attacked his beliefs because of something he said in one of his books.

at-Tirmidhi, Abu 'Isa ibn Muhammad ibn 'Isa, he was born in 209 AH and is one of the great scholars. He was proficient in *fiqh* and had many books on the science of *hadith*. His book *as-Sahih* is one of the best and most useful books. It is said, "Whoever has this book in his house, it is as if he had a prophet speaking." He died in Tirmidh in 279 AH.

at-Tujibi, Abu Ibrahim Ishaq: *hadith* scholar. He died in 352 AH.

'Ubaydullah ibn 'Abdullah ibn 'Utba al-Hudhali, the *mufti* of Madina and one of the "Seven *Fuqaha'* of Madina", one of the scholars of the Followers. He was the teacher of 'Umar ibn 'Abdu'l-'Aziz. He was a reliable man, a good poet, a *faqih* with many *hadiths* and knowledge of poetry. He went blind. He died in Madina in 98 AH.

'Ubaydullah ibn Talha al-Ansari: he is Anas' brother by his mother. He was a Follower. He died in the time of al-Walid and the Prophet named him.

Ubayy ibn Ka'b: al-Ansari al-Bukhari. Master of the Qur'an reciters. He was one of those at 'Aqaba the second time. He was present at Badr and all the battles. 'Umar called him "the master of the Muslims". The Imams transmit his *hadith* in their *Sahih* collections. He was the first to write for the Prophet. He died in 19 or 32 AH in 'Uthman's khalifate.

Ubayy ibn Khalaf: one of those who harmed the Prophet in Makka. He is the one who stirred up 'Uqba until he spat in the Prophet's face. The Prophet killed him in battle, confirming the saying, "The most wretched of people is the one who kills a prophet or is killed by a prophet."

'Ukasha ibn Mihsan al-Asadi: from the Banu Ghanm, a Companion. He was present at all the battles and he is the one about whom the Prophet said, "'Ukasha has beaten you to it." He was killed in the War of *Ridda* in Najd.

Ukaydir ibn 'Abdu'l-Malik: a king of Kinda. They disagree whether or not he became Muslim and was a Companion. Some say that he died a Christian.

Umama: the daughter of Abu'l-'As and Zaynab, the Prophet's daughter. The Prophet was very fond of her. 'Ali married her after Fatima's death. Then she married al-Mughira ibn Nawfal and died while still married to him.

'Umar ibn 'Abdu'l-'Aziz ibn Wuhayb: the client of Zayd ibn Thabit. Abu Dawud transmits from him in the *Marasil*. Adh-Dhahabi says he is unknown.

'Umar ibn 'Abdu'l-'Aziz ibn Marwan al-Umawi al-Qurashi: his mother was Layla bint 'Asim ibn 'Umar ibn al-Khattab. He was a Follower and a great Imam. People say he was the sixth of the khalifs. He related from 'Abdullah ibn Ja'far, Anas, Ibn al-Musayyab and others. The Six Collections transmit from them. He died in 101 AH when he was 40. He was Khalif for two years and five months and some days. His virtues are famous.

'Umar ibn Abi Salama al-Makhzumi: a Companion and related by suckling to the Prophet through Thuwayba, the *mawla* of his uncle, Abu Lahab. His mother was Umm Salama, the Prophet's wife. He was born in Abyssinia in 8 AH or earlier. He was appointed over Bahrayn in the time of 'Ali and was at the Battle of the Camel with him. He died in Madina in 83 AH in the khalifate of 'Abdu'l-Malik ibn Marwan.

'Umar ibn al-Khattab: the *Amir al-Mu'minin*. The Prophet called him Abu Hafs and gave him the name al-Faruq when he became Muslim at the house of al-Arqam. He was born thirteen years after the Prophet in Makka. He herded sheep for his father and later became a merchant. His voice carried weight among his people and he was known for his strength and severity. He became Muslim in the sixth year of the Prophet's mission when he was 26. He was one of the strongest defenders of Islam. He became Khalif after Abu Bakr in 13 AH. He was assassinated by Abu Lu'lu'a in 23 AH when he was 63. His khalifate had lasted ten years and six months.

'Umar ibn Shu'ayb: a famous Companion. The four authors of the *Sunan* transmit from him. He died in 118 AH and is buried in Ta'if.

Umayma bint Subah: the mother of Abu Hurayra. Sometimes her name is said to be Maymuna. Abu Hurayra was keen for her to become Muslim.

'Umayr ibn Sa'd al-Awsi al-Ansari: a Companion and ascetic. He took part in the conquest of Syria and 'Umar appointed him over Hims. He stayed there a year and then was recalled to Madina. He came and then 'Umar ordered him to return and he refused. He died in 'Umar's time, although it is said that he lived until the time of Mu'awiya. 'Umar said, "I wish I had men like 'Umayr ibn Sa'd to help me with the affairs of the Muslims."

'Umayr ibn Wahb ibn Khalaf: Abu Umayya, a Companion, known for bravery. He was slow to accept Islam. He was at Badr with the idol-worshippers and the Muslims captured his son. He returned to Makka. Safwan ibn Umayya took him aside in the *Hijr* and said, "I will discharge your debt and take care of your family as long they live and I will give you such-and-such if you go to Muhammad and kill him." 'Umayr agreed and went to Madina and came into the mosque with his sword looking for Muhammad. The Prophet said, "What brought you?" He replied, "I came to ransom my son." He asked, "Why are you armed?" He said, "I forgot I was wearing it." He said, "What did Safwan ibn Umayya allot you in the *Hijr*?" He denied it and the Prophet told him what he had done. He was amazed and became Muslim. He returned to Makka and announced his Islam and then emigrated to Madina. He was present with the Muslims at Uhud and later battles.

Umayya ibn Khalaf ibn Wahb: one of the chiefs of Quraysh in the *Jahiliyya*. He lived to the time of Islam and was captured at Badr by 'Abdu'r-Rahman ibn 'Awf. Bilal saw him and called to the people to kill him which they did.

Umm Ayman: Baraka bint Muhsin, the client of the Messenger of Allah and his Abyssinian nurse who had been freed by his father. She and her son Ayman became Muslim and then she married Zayd ibn Haritha. She died five months after the Prophet's death.

Umm Habiba bint Abi Sufyan: wife of the Prophet. Her name was Ramla. She was one of the first to become Muslim. She died in 44 AH.

Umm Hani': the daughter of Abu Talib and sister of 'Ali, a very worthy Companion. She became Muslim when Makka was conquered. The Prophet proposed to her and she excused herself saying that she was a woman with children. The Six Collections relate from her. She lived until after 'Ali's time.

Umm Ma'bad: 'Atika bint Khalid. The Prophet enjoyed her hospitality on his *hijra*. She was from the tribe of Khuza'a. A Companion.

Umm Salama: the most intelligent of the Prophet's wives. Her name was Hind, and is sometimes said to have been Ramla. She had been married to Abu Salama. She was the last of the Prophet's wives to die during the rule of Yazid.

Umm Sulaym bint Milhat al-Ansariya: mother of Anas ibn Malik, the Prophet's servant. Her name was Ramla or ar-Ramda'. She married Malik ibn an-Nadr in the *Jahiliyya* and bore Anas in the *Jahiliyya*. She became Muslim with the first Ansar to become Muslim. Malik was angry and left for Syria and then died there. After him she married Abu Talha. She took a dagger to Hunayn with which to pierce the belly of any of the idol-worshippers who got near the Prophet. She offered her son Anas to serve the Prophet when he was ten.

Unays al-Ashhali: one of the Ansar who was a Companion of the Prophet. Shahr ibn Hawshab related from him.

Unays ibn Junada ibn Sufyan al-Ghiffari: the older brother of Abu Dharr. He was a poet.

'Uqayl ibn Abi Talib: the brother of 'Ali and Ja'far and the oldest. He was Abu Yazid. He delayed becoming Muslim until the conquest of Makka and emigrated at the beginning of 8 AH. He had been captured at Badr and was ransomed by his uncle, al-'Abbas. He knew the lineages of Quraysh and their history. He was a man of counsel. He died at the beginning of Yazid's khalifate or in Mu'awiya's khalifate.

al-'Uqayli: Imam Abu Ja'far Muhammad ibn 'Amr, the author of the *Kitab ad-Du'afa'*. He is reliable and died in 322 AH.

'Uqba ibn 'Amr: see Abu Mas'ud.

'Uqba ibn 'Amir al-Juhani, the Companion. He related a great deal from the Prophet. He was a reciter and knew about the shares of inheritance and *fiqh*. He was eloquent, a poet and a writer and was one of those who compiled the Qur'an. He died in 58 AH.

'Uqba ibn al-Harith: of Quraysh. He became Muslim on the day Makka was conquered. He died in the khalifate of Ibn az-Zubayr.

'Urwa ibn Abi'l-Ja'd: al-Bariqi or al-Azdi. Sometimes it is said "ibn al-Ja'd." He was a famous Companion. The Six Collections and Ibn Hanbal transmit from him. 'Umar appointed him Qadi of Kufa.

'Urwa ibn az-Zubayr ibn al-'Awwam, a reliable Follower with many *hadiths*. A reliable man of knowledge and *taqwa*. Born in the last six years of 'Uthman's khalifate and died in 94 AH.

Usama ibn Sharik ath-Tha'labi: a Companion from whom the four *Sunan* relate.

Usama ibn Zayd ibn Haritha, Abu Muhammad: his mother was Umm Ayman, the wet-nurse of the Prophet. He was born in Islam and the Prophet died when Usama was 20. The Prophet had put him in command of a large army, but died before he left and Abu Bakr carried out the Prophet's order. 'Umar honoured and respected him. He withdrew from the civil strife after 'Uthman's death and later settled in Madina, dying there in 54 AH at the end of Mu'awiya's khalifate.

'Utba ibn Farqad: Abu 'Abdullah, the Companion. He was present at Khaybar. He built a house and mosque in Mosul. His son, 'Amr, is considered to be one of the *awliya'*. 'Utba lived in Kufa and was made governor of Mosul.

'Utba ibn Rabi'a ibn 'Abdu Shams, the father of Hind, who was the mother of Mu'awiya. The one who killed 'Ubayda ibn al-Harith at Badr as an unbeliever.

'Uthman ibn 'Affan ibn Abi'l-'As: from Quraysh, the *Amir al-Mu'minin* and Dhu'n-Nurayn. He was the third of the Rightly-Guided Khalifs and one of the ten promised the Garden. He was born in Makka and became Muslim early on. He was very generous and very modest. He completed the compilation of the Qur'an and many conquests were carried out in his time. He was murdered unjustly on the morning of the *'Id al-Ad-ha* while reading the Qur'an in his house in Madina in 35 AH.

'Uthman ibn Hunayf: the brother of 'Abbad and Sahl, the sons of Wahb. He was a Companion and transmitted *hadith*. He was put in charge of the Sawad region of Iraq and Basra and lived until the time of Mu'awiya.

Uways ibn 'Amir al-Qarni: he is said to be the best of the Followers by the testimony of the Prophet. He lived in the time of the Prophet but did not see him since he was looking after his mother. He died at Siffin in 37 AH on 'Ali's side.

Wa'il ibn Hijr: al-Kindi: the Prophet gave the good news of him before he came, then he came and became Muslim. The Prophet welcomed him, brought him close and spread out his cloak for him and made him sit on it and prayed for blessing for him. He appointed him over the Qayls of Hadramawt. He was one of the kings of Himyar. He died in 49 AH.

Wa'ila ibn al-Asqa': al-Laythi, he became Muslim before Tabuk and took part in the expedition. He was one of the people of the Suffa and served the Messenger of Allah for three years. He died in 83 AH when he was 105.

Wahb ibn Munabbih: al-Anbari al-Yamani, Abu 'Abdullah, a famous Follower who listened to some of the Companions and related from them. It is agreed that he is reliable. The Six transmit from him. He died in 114 AH.

al-Walid ibn al-Mughira al-Makhzumi: the Qurashi leader who was the father of Khalid ibn al-Walid. He died an unbeliever.

al-Walid ibn Muslim, Abu'l-'Abbas ad-Dimishqi: the *mawla* of the Umayyads, the scholar of the people of Syria. He was born in 140 AH and died in 194 or 195 AH.

al-Walid ibn 'Ubada ibn as-Samit: he was born in the lifetime of the Prophet and died in the khalifate of 'Abdu'l-Malik ibn Marwan. He is reliable, but has few *hadith*. Al-Bukhari, Muslim, at-Tirmidhi, and Ibn Majah transmit from him and he related from his father.

al-Waqidi: was *qadi* in Baghdad from al-Ma'mun. He related many *hadith* from Malik and ash-Shafi'i and others relate from him. It is confirmed that he is weak. He died in 211 AH.

Waraqa ibn Nawfal: one of the most intelligent and knowledgeable men of his time, a famous poet. He became a Jew and then a Christian and was monkish. He believed in the prophethood of Muhammad, but did not live to the time of the Message. Most call him a Companion. The Prophet gave him a place in the Garden in a dream.

al-Wasiti: Abu Bakr ibn Musa, Imam and gnostic of Allah, and one of al-Junayd's companions. He was one of the most esteemed scholars and Sufis. He was from the city of Wasita. He died in 32 AH.

Wukay' ibn al-Jarrah: Abu Sha'ban, a firm *hafiz* and *hadith* scholar of Iraq in his time. He refused the qadiship of Kufa out of scrupulousness when ar-Rashid wanted to appoint him to it. He died in 197 AH.

Yahya ibn Adam: Abu Zakariyya, one of the scholars from whom the Six Collections transmit. He is considered reliable. He died in 203 AH.

Yahya ibn al-Hakam al-Jubba'i known as al-Ghazzal: an Andalusian poet known for the sharpness of his thought, the correctness of his opinion, the excellence of his answers and his position concerning every subject. He died in 250 AH.

Yahya ibn Yahya al-Laythi: Andalusian scholar. Related the *Muwatta'* from Malik.

Ya'la ibn Sayyaba (or Murra): his father was Murra and his mother Sayyaba. He was a Companion

Yazid al-Faqir: a reliable Imam. He is Yazid ibn Suhayb. He was called the poor (*faqir*) because he had an affliction in his spine (*faqar*) about which he used to complain. Abu Hanifa related from him as did the authors of the Six Collections and a reliable group of scholars.

Yunus ibn Bukayr, Abu Bakr ash-Shaybani, a reliable Imam. He is said to be truthful. He died in 199 AH.

Yunus ibn Yazid al-Ayli al-Qurashi: he related from az-Zuhri and Nafi'. He died in 159 AH.

az-Zajjaj: Abu Ishaq Ibrahim ibn Muhammad, Shaykh of Arabic, Imam in literature, author of excellent books. His *tafsir* is famous and he was precise in the *deen*. He died in Baghdad in 306 AH when he was eighty.

Zayd ibn Arqam ibn Qays al-Khazraji: he was too young for Uhud and was present at the Ditch. He went on ten expeditions with the Prophet. He died in Kufa in 66 AH.

Zayd ibn Aslam: the *faqih*, and client of 'Umar. He was reliable and his *hadith* was sound. He related from Ibn 'Umar and Jabir. The authors of the Six transmit from him. He died in 136 AH.

Zayd ibn ad-Dathinna: a Companion who was captured with Khubayb and sold to the Makkans who killed him.

Zayd ibn Haritha: a Companion who was kidnapped as a child in the *Jahiliyya* and Khadija bought him and gave him to the Prophet when he married her. Before Islam, the Prophet adopted him and set him free and married him to his cousin. People continued to call him,"Zayd ibn Muhammad" until the *ayat* was revealed to call people by their fathers' names. He was one of the first Companions to become Muslim. Whenever the Prophet sent him on an expedition, he put him in charge of it. He loved him and advanced him and made him commander on the expedition of Mu'ta in which he was martyred.

Zayd ibn al-Hubab: Abu'l-Husayb al-Khurasani, He died in 203 AH. He was neither a Companion nor a Follower.

Zayd ibn Sa'na: one of the Jewish rabbis who became Muslim in the Prophet's time, being the greatest of them in wealth and knowledge. He was a Companion and a good Muslim and attended the battles. He died when the Prophet returned from Tabuk.

Zayd ibn Suhan: the brother of Sa'sa'a. It is said that he visited the Prophet and it is also said that he was a Follower. He was a man of asceticism and *'ibada* and is said to have been a man of many virtues. He is considered by adh-Dhahabi to have been a Companion. *Suhan* means dry.

Zayd ibn Thabit ibn Qays: Ansar and famous Companion, scribe of the revelation and leader of judgement, *fatwa*, recitation, and shares of inheritance in Madina. He died in 45 AH.

Zaynab: the oldest of the Prophet's daughters. She married Abu'l-'As ibn ar-Rabi' who was one of the idol-worshippers captured at Badr. The Prophet set him free. He became Muslim in 7 AH and was returned to a state of marriage with Zaynab. She died in the Prophet's lifetime in 8 AH.

Zaynab bint Jahsh al-Asadiyya: the wife of the Prophet. She had first been married to Zayd ibn Haritha. He divorced her and then the Prophet married her. Her name was Barra and he named her Zaynab. She died in 20 AH.

Zaynab bint Khuzayma: wife of the Prophet, called the "Mother of the Poor."

Zaynab bint Umm Salama: the daughter of the Prophet's wife, Umm Salama. Her father was Hudhayfa known as *Zad ar-Rakib*. Zaynab was the stepdaughter of the Prophet and the sister of Ibn az-Zubayr by milk. She was married to 'Abdullah ibn Zamqa and bore him children. She was one of the most intelligent and one of those with the greatest *fiqh* in her time. Zaynab was born in Abyssinia and her mother brought her back with her. Her name had been Barra and the Prophet changed it to Zaynab.

Ziyad ibn 'Abdullah al-Basri an-Numayri: some say he is reliable and some weak.

az-Zuhri: see Abu Mus'ab Ahmad ibn Abi Bakr az-Zuhri.

Synopsis of the Section Contents

PART ONE

CHAPTER ONE

Section 1: Concerning praise of him and his numerous excellent qualities:
A Messenger has come to you from among yourselves – the wisdom in the Messenger being from among yourselves – clarification of the word, "yourselves" – the creature is connected to his Creator by means of the Messengers – *We only sent you as a mercy to the worlds* – the breezes of his mercy touch every creature – Jibril, the strong and trusty, became one of the trusty by his mercy – The Messenger is one of the lights of guidance and blessing – expanding the breast – removing the burden – exalting his fame – *Obey Allah and the Messenger* – the principle of tenderness between Creator and creature – what the scholars have said about using the same pronoun for the Creator and the creature – the different commentaries on the meaning of *as-Sirat al-Mustaqim* – *the firmest handle* – the blessing of Allah – he has come with the truth.

Section 2: Allah's describing him as a witness, and the praise and honour entailed by that:
A witness – a bringer of good news – a warner – a caller – a luminous lamp – his description in the Torah – transmissions from the Torah describing him – his mercy to the believers – the excellence of his community derives from his worth – on his testifying to his community's truthfulness – a sure footing for the believers.

Section 3: Concerning Allah's kindness and gentleness to him:
Allah pardon you! – kindness before chiding – the Prophet was given a choice and was not chided – instruction in proper behaviour (*adab*) by the Qur'an – chiding before a fault has occurred is one of the signs of love – they did not doubt his truthfulness, but they doubted what he brought – denial – being addressed by a praiseworthy quality is higher than being addressed by name.

Section 4: Concerning Allah's swearing by his immense worth:
Swearing by his life – Allah did not swear by the life of anyone else – Yasin – Taha – he alone has the oath about being a Messenger – his matery – Makka's nobility because of him – Allah made it secure because he was in it – the meanings of the separated letters – *Qaf* – the Star – Dawn.

Section 5: Concerning Allah's oath to confirm his place with Him:
The Forenoon – the reason for its revelation – the aspects of how he is esteemed in this *sura* – the oath – the clarification of his position with Allah – the end is better – the pleasing gift – his bringing his community out of the Fire – numerous blessings – being an orphan – declaring blessing – *the Star when it plunges* – the meanings of *the Star* – his virtues in this *sura* – indirect allusion – the purity of his

pure in life and pure in death" – the one who drank his blood – the one who drank his urine – he was born circumcised – no-one ever saw his private parts – he was protected.

Section 4: His great intellect, eloquence and the acuteness of his faculties:

He was the most intelligent of people – people's intellects are like a grain of sand compared to him – he could see both in front of him and behind him – he could see in the dark – he could see angels and jinn – his vision of the Negus, Jeruslaem and the Ka'ba – his vision of Musa – throwing down Rukana – throwing down Abu Rukana – his swift gait – his laugh was a smile.

Section 5: His eloquence and sound Arabic:

His eloquence – he addressed every group with their dialect – his words to Dhu'l-Mish'ar al-Hamdani and other amirs of Hadramawt – his letter to Hamdhan – his words to Nahd – his letter to Wa'il ibn Hujr – the *hadith* of 'Atiyya as-Sa'di – the *hadith* of al-'Amiri – his normal speech – examples of his eloquence and comprehensive statements – he had both the purity of the desert and eloquence of the city – the divine support of revelation – Umm Ma'bad's words about his speech.

Section 6: The nobility of his lineage, the honour of his birthplace and the place where he was brought up:

The best of Banu Hashim – Makka and its nobility – the best generation was that of the Prophet – he had the best person and the best family – he was the best of the best – his light descended to earth – none of his ancestors was accused of fornication.

Section 7: His state regarding the necessary actions of daily life:

What is excellent when it is little – eating a lot indicates greed – eating a little indicates contentment – a lot of sleep indicates feebleness – evidence of that – take a little of both – the belly is the worst container to fill – a lot of sleep comes from a lot of food and drink – whoever sleeps a lot loses a lot – he did not fill his stomach – he did not ask for food – the *hadith* of Barira – reclining – his sleeping little – sleeping on the right side.

Section 8: His marriage and things connected to it:

Marriage indicates perfection and health – logically and in the *Shari'a* – forbidding celibacy – marriage does not detract from asceticism – the ascetics among the Companions had many wives – the Prophet Yahya – the celibacy of 'Isa – answers to that – an extra virtue – a lot of wives did not distract him from worshipping his Lord, indeed it increased his worship – his love for women and scent was for the Next World, not this world – preferred over people by four – rank – the harm of rank – his place in the hearts before he became a Prophet – the awe felt by people who saw him.

Section 9: Things connected to money and goods:

The common people respect the wealthy – wealth in itself is not a virtue but can be used for something praiseworthy – wealth with avarice and miserliness is not having it – the miser is the treasurer of someone else's property – what the Prophet was given of the wealth of the earth – he did not keep a single dirham – his rest by spending – asceticism in maintenance, clothes and dwelling – boasting by clothes is not a quality of honour – clean clothes.

Section 10: His praiseworthy qualities:

The qualities which intelligent people agree are praiseworthy – the *Shari'a's* praise of them – good character – his character was the Qur'an – he was sent to perfect noble character – his qualities were not acquired – good character is a natural part of the disposition of the Prophets – the character of Yahya – 'Isa - Sulayman – Musa and Pharaoh – Ibrahim – Ishaq – Yusuf – the Prophet's hatred of idols, poetry and the deeds of the *Jahiliyya* from the time he was a child – is character innate or acquired?

Section 11: His intellect:

Intellect – the branches of intellect – his knowledges – an unlettered prophet – his knowledge was commensurate with his intellect.

Section 12: His Forbearance, long-suffering and pardon:

The difference between these expressions – forbearance – long-suffering – patience – pardon – injury only increased him in patience – he was the furthest of people from wrong action – he was not sent to curse – the supplication of Nuh – the Prophet pardoning people and his supplication for them – why he was compassionate to them – Ghawrath ibn al-Harith and his attempt to assassinate the Prophet – the best of people – his pardoning the Jewess who wanted to kill him – his patience with the hypocrites – his patience with people's coarseness – he never helped himself – his forbearance when someone wanted to kill him – one of his signs was that his forbearance overcame his wrath – extreme ignorance only increased him in forbearance – his position with Quraysh when he had power over them – his position with Abu Sufyan when he was in his power.

Section 13: His generosity and liberality:

The difference between the meanings of generosity and liberality – generosity – liberality – he never said "No" to anything he was asked – he was the most generous of people and even more generous in Ramadan – he gave the gift of someone who does not fear poverty – he did not store up anything for the next day.

Section 14: His courage and bravery:

Definition of courage – bravery – his courage at Hunayn – he was found in dangerous situations – he was the first to respond to an alarm – he was the first to strike in the attack – he killed Ubayy ibn Khalaf at Uhud – evil is a person who is killed by a Prophet.

Section 15: His modesty and lowering the glance:

Definition of modesty – lowering the glance – instances.

Section 16: His good companionship, good manners and good nature:

'Ali's description of him – his cheerfulness – Ibn Abi Hala's description – he accepted gifts, however small – Anas, his servant, describes his master – his concern for people's worries – the noblest of people – he smiled the most – the servants of Madina brought their water to him for blessing.

Section 17: His compassion and mercy:

Allah gave him two of His names – his gift effaces wrath – the coarse Arabs are like the stray camel made tame with wisdom – his clear heart towards his Companions – his compassion to his community – his mercy – his compassion to the unbelievers and desire for their children to believe – his counselling people to be kind.

Section 22: On the Prophet's supplication being answered:

His supplication for people – blessing in progeny – the blessing for the property of 'Abdu'r-Rahman ibn 'Awf – his supplication for Mu'awiya – the answer of the supplication for Sa'd – supplication for 'Umar – his supplication for rain – supplication for Abu Qatada – supplication for an-Nabigha – supplication for Ibn 'Abbas – supplication for 'Abdullah ibn Ja'far – supplication for al-Miqdad – supplication for 'Urwa – supplication for the mother of Abu Hurayra – supplication for 'Ali – supplication for Fatima – supplication for at-Tufayl – supplication against Mudar and then for them – supplication against Chosroes – supplication against a youth – supplication against the man eating with his left hand – supplication against 'Utba – supplication against those who injured him – supplication against al-Hakam – supplication against Muhallim.

Section 23: On his *karamat* and *barakat* and things beings transformed for him when he touched them:

The horse of Abu Talha – the liveliness of the horse of Ju'ayl – a slow donkey – the blessing of his hairs in the cap of Khalid – using his shirt for healing – the staff of the Prophet – the well of Quba' – the well of Anas – the water of Nu'man – al-Hasan and al-Husayn sucking his tongue – the skin of Malik's mother – planting trees for Salman – a drink of *sawiq* – a palm bough giving light – 'Ukasha's sword was a stick – a sword from a palm stick – the sheep of Umm Ma'bad – the sheep of Anas – water changes to milk and butter – the blessing of 'Umayr ibn Sa'd – 'Utba's scent – the blaze of 'A'idh – al-Agharr – the blessing of Hanzala's head – the beauty of Zaynab – healing the mad – the day of Hunayn – Abu Hurayra complains of forgetfulness.

Section 24: The Prophet's knowledge of the unseen and future events.

Section 25: Allah's protecting the Prophet from people and his being enough against those who injured him:

"Go, my Lord has protected me" – the bearer of firewood – she could not see him – during the *hijra* – the story of Suraqa – the herdsman forgot – Abu Jahl and the stone – his vision removed – treachery of the Banu Qurayza – the treachery of Huyayy – Abu Jahl and the ditch of fire – a fiery flame.

Section 26: His knowledges and sciences.

Section 27: Reports of the Prophet's dealings with the angels and *jinn*:

In the form of a man – in the form of Dihya – seeing the *jinn* – the tune of the *jinn* – Khalid advances on al-'Uzza and kills a black woman – he captures Shaytan.

Section 28: Reports about his attributes and the signs of his messengership.

Section 29: What is related about his birth.

Section 30: Conclusion and Appendix:

The miracles of our Prophet are more evident than the miracles of earlier Prophets – the great number of his miracles and the miracles of the Qur'an – style and composition – reports about the knowledges of the unseen – clear miracles and magic in the time of Musa – medicine in the time of 'Isa – eternal miracles do not cease – school of the Sarfa – the worship of the Banu Isra'il.

PART TWO

CHAPTER ONE

Section 1: The obligation to believe in him:
Belief is only completed by it – belief is the confirmation of the heart and affirmation by the tongue – man has not been given access to the inner secrets of people – the confirmation of the heart without the tongue – testimony.

Section 2: The obligation to obey Him:
Obeying him is part of belief – obeying the Messenger – "Whoever obeys me will enter the Garden" – the likeness of the Prophet.

Section 3: The obligation to follow Him and obey his *Sunna:*
The reason for the revelation of *"Say: if you love Allah follow me."* – love is obedience – "Whoever is pleased with what I say is pleased with the Qur'an."

Section 4: What is related from the *Salaf* and the Imams about following his *Sunna,* taking his guidance and the *Sira:*
"We do as we saw him doing" – clinging to the *sunna* is salvation – the people of the *sunna* have the greatest knowledge of the Book of Allah – what 'Umar said to the Black Stone – following the Prophet – eating the *halal* – sincere intention – forgiveness for applying the *sunna.*

Section 5: The danger of opposing his command.

CHAPTER TWO

Section 1: Concerning the necessity of loving him:
Love and its extent – the pleasure of love – what 'Umar said.

Section 2: On the reward for loving the Prophet:
The wisdom of the Prophet in answering a question with another question – a man is with the one he loves – a picture of the love of the Companions.

Section 3: What is related from the *Salaf* and the Imans about their love for the Prophet and their yearning for him:
Those with the strongest love for him – 'Umar's love – the love of 'Amr ibn al-'As – an illustration of love – the love of Abu Bakr – "Every affliction now is nothing" – 'Ali's love – a love of an old woman and 'Umar's tears – Bilal's love – a woman who died for love – Zayd ibn ad-Dathima.

Section 4: On the signs of love for the Prophet:
Emulation – preferring what the Allah has laid down – loving Allah and His Messenger – remembrance – yearning to meet him – respect for him when he is mentioned – the state of the Companions when he was mentioned – what the beloved loves is also loved – his love for the Companions – his love for Fatima – his love of Usama – love for the Ansar – love of the Qur'an – asceticism is one of the signs of love for him – love and affliction.

Section 5: On the meaning and reality of love for the Prophet:
Love is following – love is constant remembrance – altruism – yearning – humility of the heart – inclination of the heart.

Section 6: The obligation of *nasiha* to the Prophet:
The meaning of *nasiha* – *nasiha* for Allah – *nasiha* for His Messenger – another meaning – his counsel when he was alive – his counsel after his death – *nasiha* for the Muslim Imams – nasiha for the common Muslims.

CHAPTER THREE

Section 1: *Ayats* in the Qur'an on this subject:
To honour him – the adab of speech and listening – the adab of calling – the one about whom that was sent down – "Observe us".

Section 2: On the esteem, respect and veneration due to him:
The Companions' esteem for him – sitting as if there were birds on their heads – taking his *wudu'* water.

Section 3: Respect and esteem for the Prophet after his death:
Respect for him after his death is like respect for him alive – Abu Ja'far al-Mansur and Malik – the state of Ayyub as-Sakhtiyani when he was mentioned – his weeping – going pale – being in a state of purity – humility – *adab* of reading *hadith*.

Section 4: On the esteem of the *Salaf* for the transmission of the *hadiths* of the Messenger of Allah:
The scrupulousness of 'Abdullah ibn Mas'ud – dislike of taking the *hadith* standing up – dislike of taking *hadith* lying down – being in *wudu'* – the state of Malik when giving *hadith* – the scorpion and Malik – other incidents.

Section 5: Devotion to his family, descendants and wives:
The People of his house – 'Ali – 'Abbas – Zayd and al-Hasan – al-Hasan and al-Husayn – Malik and Ja'far ibn Sulayman.

Section 6: Respect for his Companions, devotion to them and recognising what is due to them:
Good interpretation – being silent about other things – they are like the stars – they are like salt in the food – "Whoever loves them loves them by my love" – being free of hypocrisy – none are like them – preserve me in the Companions – the intercession of the Companions.

Section 7: Esteem for the things and places connected to the Prophet:
Not cutting off a lock of hair touched by the Prophet – Khalid's cap – Ibn 'Umar and the minbar – Malik did not ride in Madina – the excellence of Madina – the Prophet's staff – walking in Madina – the virtues of Madina.

CHAPTER FOUR

Section 1: The meaning of the prayer on the Prophet:
Baraka – asking for mercy and supplication – the meaning of *salam*.

Section 2: The judgement about the prayer on the Prophet:
General obligation – obligation to do it once – an obligation in the prayer.

Section 3: On the situations in which it is recommended to say the prayer on the Prophet:
Tashahhud – in the supplication – in the beginning, middle and end of the supplication – the pillars of supplication – the wings of supplication – times of

PART THREE

CHAPTER ONE

the weakness of this *hadith* – the import of this *hadith* – the Prophet was not ignorant of any of Allah's attributes – angry with his people, not his Lord – the event before prophethood – rust – asking forgiveness.

Section 2: The protection of the Prophets from defects before prophethood:
The Prophets grew up with tawhid and belief – removing the portion of Shaytan – Ibrahim and the stars.

Section 3: The Prophet's knowledge of the affairs of this world:
Not ignorant of any of the details of the Shari'a.

Section 4: Protection from Shaytan:
Protection in body and thought – Shaytan coming against him – *nazgh* – Yusha' and Musa – the Valley.

Section 5: The truthfulness of the Prophet in all states.

Section 6: Refutation of certain suspicions:
The "High Cranes" – weakness of the *hadith* – the Prophet's protection from disbelief intentionally or unintentionally – Shaytan imitating the voice of the Prophet – Yunus and his people – the scribe of the Messenger – other doubtful things – a Christian who used to write and then apostatised – the transmission of a suspect Muslim is not accepted let alone an apostate – forgeries and lies.

Section 7: His state in connection with reports concerning this world:
Quraysh acknowleged his truthfulness before he was a Prophet.

Section 8: Refutation of certain objections:
Forgetfulness in the prayer – deliberate to make a sunna – he did not forget and spoke the truth – oversight is preoccupation – forgetfulness is inattention – distracted from the prayer by what the prayer contained – what is said about Ibrahim – indirect expression – "I am sick" – the Prophet's pretending in his raids – Musa coming to al-Khidr for instruction.

Section 9: The Prophets' protection from outrageous and grave wrong actions:
Consensus – logic and consensus – minor wrong actions – protection from both major and minor wrong actions – what the Ash'arites and others said – their state in permissible things – they only took what they needed.

Section 10: The Prophets' protection from acts of rebellion before they were Prophets:
The position of Qadi Abu Bakr – in relation to the rest of the Prophets.

Section 11: Oversight and forgetfulness in respect of actions.

Section 12: Discussion of the hadiths on the Prophet's oversight:
Oversight is impossible in reports – Dhu'l-Yadayn – the *hadith* of Ibn Buhayna – the *hadith* of Ibn Mas'ud – the wisdom and conditions of oversight.

Section 13: The refutation of those who say that small wrong actions are permissible for the Prophet and an examination of their arguments:
Refutation of the one who allows them to have minor wrong actions – their evidence in the difference of the commentators regarding what it means – the meaning of *"your past and future wrong actions"* – the meaning of forgiveness – *"burden which weighed down your back"* – "Why did you give them permission?" – the people of knowledge do not consider it to be censure – he was given a choice

PART FOUR

CHAPTER TWO

Section 1: The statements and opinions on the judgement of someone who curses or disparages the Prophet:

If he repents he is killed by the *hadd* not for disbelief according to Malik and most scholars – a right which is not removed by repentance – apostasy.

Section 2: The judgement on the apostate if he repents:

The apostate is asked to repent – his repentance benefits him with Allah – does not avert execution if he cursed the Prophet.

Section 3: The judgment on the apostate whose apostasy is not established.

Section 4: The judgement on the *Dhimmi* regarding this matter.

Section 5: Regarding the inheritance of someone who is killed for cursing the Prophet, and whether one washes him and says the funeral prayer over him.

CHAPTER THREE

Section 1: The judgement on someone who curses Allah and the judgement regarding asking him to repent.

Section 2: The judgement about ascribing to Allah something that does not befit Him through *ijtihad* and error:

There is no disagreement that they are to be executed if they form a sect – those who are doubtful – those who say the Qur'an is created – the Qadiri is not asked to repent.

Section 3: Verification of the statement about considering faulty interpreters to be unbelievers:

Disbelief consists of being ignorant of the existence of Allah.

Section 4: Clarification of which statements amount to disbelief, what one hesitates about or is disputed and what does not amount to disbelief:

The intellect has no scope in it.

Section 5: The judgement on the *dhimmi* who curses Allah.

Section 6: The judgement on anyone who claims divinity or utters falsehoods and lies about Allah:

Drunkenness is no excuse.

Section 7: The judgment on the one who unintentionally counters the Majesty of his Lord by disreputable words and foolish expressions.

Section 8: The judgement on the one who curses the Prophets in general and the angels.

Section 9: Judgement in relation to the Qur'an.

Section 10: The Judgement on the one who curses the People of the House, the Prophet's wives and the Companions, may Allah bless him and them and grant them peace. Amin.

Biographical Note on the Author of the Shifa'

His full name was Abu'l-Fadl 'Iyad ibn Musa ibn 'Iyad ibn 'Imrun ibn Musa ibn Muhammad ibn 'Abdullah ibn Musa ibn 'Iyad al-Yahsubi, the famous Imam. He was born in Ceuta in the month of Sha'ban, 496 AH and lived there although his family originated from Andalusia.

According to his son, Muhammad, his ancestors originated in Andalusia and then moved to the city of Fes, staying in the Qarawiyyin at some point. 'Imrun moved to Ceuta after having lived in Fes.

Qadi 'Iyad was the Imam of his time in *hadith* and its sciences. He was a scholar of *tafsir* and its sciences, a *faqih* in *usul*, a scholar in grammar, language and Arabic speech, as well as in the battles and lineages of the Arabs. He had insight into judgements and had the legal competence to write contracts. He preserved and knew the Maliki *madhhab*. He was an excellent poet, familiar with literature and an eloquent orator. He was steadfast, forbearing and a good companion. He was generous and gave a lot of *sadaqa*. He was constant in action and tenacious in the truth.

He travelled to Andalusia in 509 in search of knowledge. In Cordoba he studied with Qadi Abu 'Abdullah Muhammad ibn 'Ali ibn Hamdin and Abu'l-Husayn ibn Siraj, Abu Muhammad ibn 'Attab and others. He received an *ijaza* from Abu 'Ali al-Ghassani. In the east, he studied with Qadi Abu 'Ali Husayn ibn Muhammad as-Sadafi and others. He was very keen to meet the shaykhs and learn from them. He was taught by Abu 'Abdullah al-Mazini. He wrote to him to ask for an *ijaza*. Abu Bakr at-Tartushi gave him an *ijaza*. One of his shaykhs was Qadi Abu'l-Walid ibn Rushd. The author of *as-Sila al-Bashkuwaliyya*, who may have had it from Abu Zayd, said that he had a hundred shaykhs, some of whom he merely listened to and some of whom gave him an *ijaza*.

His son, Muhammad, mentioned Ahmad ibn Baqi, Ahmad ibn Muhammad ibn Muhammad ibn Makhul, Abu't-Tahir Ahmad ibn Muhammad as-Salafi, al-Hasan ibn Muhammad ibn Bakra, Qadi Abu Bakr ibn al-'Arabi, al-Hasan ibn 'Ali ibn Tarif, Khalad ibn Ibrahim ibn an-Nahhas, Muhamamd ibn Ahmad ibn al-Hajj al-Qurtubi, 'Abdullah ibn Muhammad al-Khashani and others. It would take too long to list them all.

The author the *Sila* said that he compiled many *hadith* and had great interest in the science of *hadith* and was intent on gathering and learning them. He was one of the people of proficiency in knowledge and understanding.

When he returned from Andalusia, the people of Ceuta held him in great esteem for his discourses on the *Mudawwana* when he was about thirty years old. Then he was asked to give legal advice and then appointed *qadi* of his city. He remained in this post for a long time and his conduct as *qadi* was universally praised. Then he was transferred to the *qadiship* of Granada in 531, but did not remain there very long and became *qadi* of Ceuta once again. The author of the *Sila* says that he went to Granada and the people there learned some of what he knew.

When the Muwahhids were victorious, he travelled to Sila to meet their Amir and stayed until the affairs of the Muwahhids became unsettled in 543. After this Qadi 'Iyad's situation became untenable and he went to live in Marrakesh, an exile from his home, finally dying and being buried there.

He wrote many excellent books including *Kamal al-Mu'allim*, a commentary on the *Sahih* of Muslim, and the *Shifa'*, which is a most extraordinary book. No-one disputes the fact that it is totally unique nor denies him the honour of being the first to compose such a book. Everyone relies on it and writes about it usefulness and encourages others to read and study it. Copies of it have spread east and west. He also wrote the *Kitab Mashariq al-Anwar* (The Rising of Lights), on the explanation of the *gharib hadith* in the *Muwatta'*, Muslim and al-Bukhari. He determines the proper vowelization of phrases, elucidates doubtful passages and misspellings and verifies the names of the transmitters. If this book had been written in gold or weighed against jewels, it would not cover its worth.

He wrote the *Kitab at-Tanbihat al-Mustanbita* (Discovered Admonitions) on the *Mudawwana* in which he put all the unusual phrases as they should be properly vowelled and he formulated its questions. He wrote the *Kitab Tartib al-Madaraik wa Taqrib al-Masalik* on Imam Malik ibn Anas and the notable men of the Maliki *madhhab*.

He compiled the *Kitab al-I'lam bi-hudud qawa'id al-Islam* (Signs on the limits of the Rules of Islam), the *Kitab al-Ilma' fi dabt ar-Riwaya wa Taqyid as-Sama'* (Indication of the accurate determination of the *riwaya* and the recording of oral tradition), the *Kitab Bughya ar-Ra'id lima tadammanahu hadith Umm Zar'* (The Benefits contained in the *hadith* of Umm Zar'), the *Kitab al-Ghanima* on his shaykhs, the *Kitab al-Mu'jam* on the Shaykhs of Ibn Sakra, the *Kitab Nazm al-Burhan 'ala hujja jazm al-Adhan* (The Order of the Proof of the soundness of shortening the *Adhan*), and the *Kitab Masa'ila al-Ahl al-Mashrut baynahum at-Tazawur* (Book of Questions).

Some of his books remained unfinished. Among them are: *al-Maqasid al-Hisan fima yalzam al-Insan* (The Excellent Goals of what a man must do), *Kitab al-'Uyun as-Sitta fi akhbar Sabta* (The Six Sources in the Reports of Ceuta), *Kitab Ghaniya al-Katib wa'l-bughya at-Talib fi as-Sudur at-Tarassul* (The Wealth of the Writer and the Desire of the Seeker), *Kitab al-Ajwuba al-Muhabbira 'ala'l-as'ila al-mutakhayyira* (Answers to Selected Questions), *Kitab Ajwiba al-Qurtubiyyin* (Answers to the Cordobans), *Kitab Ajwiba 'amma nazala fi ayyam quda'ihi min nawazil al-ahkam fi safar, Kitab Sirr as-Sara fi adab al-quda'* (His answers on what occurred in the days he was *qadi*), and the Book of his speeches. He only delivered speeches which he himself had written. He also wrote a lot of poetry.

He died in Marrakesh in the month of Jumada al-Akhira or Ramadan in 544 AH. It is said that he was poisoned by a Jew. He was buried at the Gate of Ilan inside the city. His surname, "Yahsubi", comes from Yahsub ibn Malik, the tribe of Himyar in Yemen.

Taken from the *Dibaj adh-Dhahab* by Ibn Farhun.